Credo

Jaroslav Pelikan

Credo

Historical and Theological Guide

to Creeds and Confessions of Faith

in the Christian Tradition

Yale University Press   New Haven and London

Designed by Sonia Shannon
Set in Sabon type by Tseng Information Systems, Durham, North Carolina
Printed in the United States of America.

Library of Congress Cataloging-in-Publication Data
Creeds & confessions of faith in the Christian tradition / edited by
Jaroslav Pelikan and Valerie Hotchkiss.
p.   cm.
Includes bibliographical references and indexes.
Contents: v. 1. Rules of faith in the early church. Eastern Orthodox affirmations
of faith. Medieval Western statements of faith — v. 2. Creeds and confessions of
the Reformation era — v. 3. Statements of faith in modern Christianity —
v. [4]. Credo / Jaroslav Pelikan.
ISBN 0-300-09391-8 (set) (cloth : alk. paper)
ISBN 0-300-09388-8 (v. [4]) (cloth : alk. paper)
1. Creeds. 2. Creeds—History and criticism. I. Title: Creeds and confessions
of faith in the Christian tradition. II. Pelikan, Jaroslav Jan, 1923-
III. Hotchkiss, Valerie R., 1960– IV. Pelikan, Jaroslav Jan, 1923– Credo.
BT990.C64 2003
238—dc21
2003043067

A catalogue record for this book is available from the British Library.

The paper in this book meets the guidelines for permanence and durability
of the Committee on Production Guidelines for Book Longevity
of the Council on Library Resources.

10 9 8 7 6 5 4 3 2 1

Contents

Preface

Credo is intended to serve two distinct but not, I trust, incompatible purposes, as is evident even from its design and appearance. In its format and binding it is identical with the volumes of texts making up *Creeds and Confessions of Faith in the Christian Tradition*, edited by Valerie R. Hotchkiss and myself, for which it is intended to be a general historical introduction, making it possible for those volumes to economize on space by limiting themselves in their headnotes to the specific historical material needed for each document. At the same time, *Credo* is not numbered consecutively with those volumes, because it is also intended to be a freestanding monograph and reference work in its own right, even a textbook, also for readers who do not have the volumes of the set. For that reason, references to creeds and confessions are by article and section rather than by volume and page in our edition, so that those who have access to other editions, printed or electronic, in the original or in a translation, can easily find their way around. In the Abbreviations for Creeds and Confessions in the front matter of this volume, therefore, the locations of the texts are indicated first by the volume and pages for our edition, and, if possible, by the volume and pages of some other edition, in the original language or in translation. Although it seemed appropriate in the several parts of *Creeds and Confessions of Faith* to employ varying formats for the titles of creeds and confessions—in Part Five, for example, where the confessions come from the era defined by denominationalism, the name of the sponsoring church appears first, then the title of the confession and the date—I have, for the sake of consistency, made the format as uniform as possible here in *Credo,* both in the body of the book and in the Abbreviations at the front. Because neither the thousands of pages of the printed version of *Creeds and Confessions of Faith in the Christian Tradition* nor its CD-ROM supplement can come close to including all the existing texts, I have felt free in this companion volume to draw some citations and quotations also from creeds and confessions that we have not been able to reproduce in the set; in such a case, the passage can be located in an edition that is listed for that text in the front matter under Editions, Collections, and Reference Works.

On a more personal note: I am continuing in this work the lifelong scholarly research into the history of confessions that began with my Ph.D. dissertation at the University of Chicago in 1946 on *The [First] Bohemian Confession* of 1535 and that has continued since then with several publications on other creeds and confessions. I should also add that both this companion volume *Credo* (especially its last five chapters) and the five parts of *Creeds and Confessions of Faith in the Christian Tradition* have been a natural progression from the five volumes of my magnum opus, *The Christian Tradition: A History of the Development of Doctrine,* which the University of Chicago Press published between 1971 and 1989; the subjects of the five chapters and of the five parts correspond to those of the five volumes. To avoid repetition, especially of its massive documentation of primary sources and its extensive bibliographies of secondary works, I have felt free here to make continuing cross-references to it. Because that work cut across the historical periods by which scholars of Christian history usually identify themselves, and because it was able to do so only by narrowing its line of vision from the entire history of Christianity to "what the church of Jesus Christ believes, teaches, and confesses on the basis of the word of God," as its opening sentence defined, the decades of research in the primary sources on which it was based had necessarily brought me into close contact with most (though not quite all) of the creeds and confessions of faith that are now collected in the volumes of *Creeds and Confessions of Faith,* where the emphasis is primarily on the creeds and confessions as such rather than, as it was in *The Christian Tradition,* on their doctrines. My definition of the territory I intended to explore in my history of doctrine had been based on a cartography that prompted many colleagues and students during the years of its composition to urge that I was uniquely positioned to undertake next a new collection that would replace Philip Schaff's *Creeds of Christendom,* which first appeared in 1877 and has been in continual use ever since.

As a rule, biblical quotations are from the Revised Standard Version (RSV), which is therefore not usually identified. Sometimes they are from the New Revised Standard Version (NRSV); and occasionally (for example, to retain the distinction, lost in modern English, between the second person singular pronouns "thou/thee," even as applied to human persons, and the second person plural personal pronouns "ye/you"), they are from the Authorized ("King James") Version (AV). For the sake of consistency and comparability in the numbering of the Book of Psalms, in which the Greek Septuagint and the Latin Vulgate deviate from the Hebrew and therefore from the translations that followed the Hebrew, the Hebrew system of numbering has been employed throughout. But for biblical quotations that are cited from creeds and confessions, the version of the Bible quoted here is the version quoted there, or the translation into some other language there has in turn been translated into English here, regardless of whether that translation agrees with the original Hebrew or Greek of the biblical passage. Also for the sake of consistency, the spelling of proper names here in *Credo* as well as throughout *Creeds and Confessions of Faith in the Christian Tradition* has been conformed to that of the third edition of *The Oxford Dictionary of the Christian Church* (ODCC), with a few minor exceptions such as Hus (not "Huss"), the Council of Basel (not "Basle"), and *The Smalcald Articles* (not "Schmalkaldic").

To be as fair as possible in a field where the virtue of fairness is often very difficult to achieve (and sometimes rather hard to find), I have striven in the nomenclature of Christian communions, confessions, and churches to identify them as they identify themselves, and yet to be reader-friendly. A significant part of the problem lies, to put it typographically, in capitalization. Every Christian creed or confession claims to be *orthodox,* after its fashion; every Christian church wants to define itself as *catholic, evangelical,* and *reformed,* at least in some sense; every Christian believer strives to be a *disciple of Christ,* howsoever "the cost of discipleship" may be understood. But when these terms are capitalized, they become denominational and confessional labels and are most often used by their adherents without a qualifying term. In the present context, however, such qualifying compounds as *Roman* Catholic and *Eastern* Orthodox have often seemed to be necessary. The nomenclature for Anglicanism presents special complications in a book about creeds and confessions: whatever may be the right way to speak about Anglican polity or Anglican liturgy, the Anglican *confession,* which was during the Reformation and technically still is

The Thirty-Nine Articles of the Church of England, is a Protestant confession that belongs to the Reformed family of confessions. I have reflected that ambivalence by sometimes distinguishing "Anglican" from "Protestant" and sometimes ignoring the distinction.

    In a work that spans so many centuries and so many cultures, I have drawn on works written in many languages, as I have listed them in the Bibliography and in "Editions, Collections, and Reference Works." But as much as possible, I cite these other sources, too, secondary as well as primary, in available English translations, on the assumption that scholars who are able to handle the original language can readily locate a passage on the basis of such a reference whereas readers who have only English cannot negotiate their way on the basis of a reference to a work in another language. In quoting these earlier English translations of creeds, confessions, and other sources, I have felt free to modernize spelling, punctuation, and capitalization, without calling attention to the changes each time. For the transliteration of postclassical Greek, including proper names, book titles, and technical terms, I have, despite the shifts in pronunciation, applied the system prescribed for classical Greek by my standard guide in this and all such matters, *The Chicago Manual of Style* (14th ed.), but with these exceptions, which are recommended by the *ALA-LC Romanization Tables* of the Library of Congress: I use the English "y" for the Greek "υ" except in diphthongs, where I use "u"; and I use "ch" rather than "kh" for the Greek "χ." For the Cyrillic alphabet, I have continued my longstanding practice of adapting the system prescribed by the *Slavic and East European Journal,* because its use of diacritical marks and of other correspondences (for example, "ch" not "kh" for the Cyrillic "х" and therefore "č" not "ch" for the Cyrillic "ч," and also, of course, "Ja" not "Ya" for the Cyrillic "Я") makes possible an easy and consistent movement between those Slavic languages that use the Cyrillic alphabet and those that use the Roman alphabet.

    In writing *Credo,* more than with my many other books and multivolume editorial projects over more than fifty years, I have had ample reason to learn again just how much even a scholar who has followed Adolf von Harnack's injunction to "be a bit of a monk and get off to a very early start" actually depends on the aid and counsel of others. Above all, Valerie R. Hotchkiss, the associate editor of *Creeds and Confessions of Faith in the Christian Tradition,* combines an editor's discernment with a scholar's learning, a techie's skill, and a librarian's prowess, without all of which neither the set of volumes nor this book could ever have been completed. During the several years that I have devoted to the writing of the volume, and to the simultaneous editing of *Creeds and Confessions of Faith in the Christian Tradition,* I have had the opportunity to present material from it to audiences in several countries and from many confessional (and nonconfessional, or even anticonfessional) backgrounds; as always, I have benefited greatly from their questions and criticisms, as well as from the comments of various scholarly readers, whether known or anonymous. Among the many other colleagues and former students whose advice at various stages has helped me have been (in alphabetical order): Gerald H. Anderson, C. J. Dyck, Brian A. Gerrish, Susan Billington Harper, Patrick Henry, E. Ann Matter, James J. O'Donnell, Lamin O. Sanneh, Barbara von Schlegell, Philip Shen, Bishop Kallistos Ware, Robert L. Wilken, and Charles Willard. Special gratitude, which is repeated and expanded in the "Acknowledgments" for *Creeds and Confessions of Faith in the Christian Tradition,* must go to the institutional sponsors of the entire project and of this book (this time in chronological order): Yale University and its several libraries; Yale University Press, for its encouragement and expertise; the Lilly Endowment, with its generous and visionary support; Boston College, which, by appointing me as the first incumbent of its Joseph Chair, enabled me to design the structure of *Credo;* the Annenberg School for Communication of the University of Pennsylvania, under whose auspices I wrote the bulk of it; and the Library of Congress, whose matchless bibliographical and technical resources were daily available to me during the year I spent as its first Kluge Scholar.

At the 125th anniversary of the publication of Philip Schaff's *Creeds of Christendom*

Abbreviations for Creeds and Confessions

All citations of councils and synods—unless accompanied by "act" (= *Acts*), "can" (= *Canons*), "decr" (= *Decrees*), or some other abbreviation —refer specifically to their creedal or doctrinal formulations.

Abbreviation	Title and Date	Location
Abst Prin	*Abstract of Principles for Southern Baptist Seminary,* 1858	**3:316–20;** McBeth 1990, 304–15
Ad tuendam	*Ad tuendam fidem of Pope John Paul II,* 1998	**3:871–76**
Adv	*The Fundamental Beliefs of the Seventh-Day Adventist Church,* 1872	**3:359–64**
Afr Orth	*Doctrine of the African Orthodox Church,* 1921	**3:435–36**
A-L	*Anglican-Lutheran Pullach Report,* 1972	*Gr Agr* II 14–34
Alex	*The Creed of Alexander of Alexandria,* c. 321–24	**1:79–81;** Hahn, 15; *NPNF*-II 3:39–40
Am Bap	*The Statement of Faith of the American Baptist Association,* 1905	Lumpkin, 378–79
Ang Cat	*The Anglican Catechism,* 1549/1662	**2:364–71;** Schaff, 3:517–22
Ans	*The Evangelical Counsel of Ansbach* [*Ansbacher Evangelischer Ratschlag*], 1524	Schmidt-Schornbaum, 183–322
Ant 325	*The First Synod of Antioch,* 325	**1:84–86**

Abbreviation	Title and Date	Location
Ant 341	*The Second [Dedication] Synod of Antioch,* 341	**1:87–89**; Hahn, 153–56; NPNF–II 4:461
Ap	*The Apostles' Creed*	**1:667–69**; *BLK* 21–25; Cochrane, 303–4; Fabbri, 3; Gerrish, 56; Kolb-Wengert, 21–22; Leith, 24–25; Tappert, 18; *Triglotta* 2:30–31; Schaff, 2:45–55
Ap Const	*The Apostolic Constitutions,* c. 350–80	Hahn, 9–10, 129; Schaff, 2:39
Apol Aug	*The Apology of the Augsburg Confession,* 1531	CD-ROM; *BLK* 139–404; Fabbri, 58–328; Kolb-Wengert, 109–294; Tappert, 100–285; *Triglotta* 2:97–451
Ar	*The Creeds of Arius and Euzoius,* c. 320 and 327	**1:75–78**; Hahn, 186–87; Schaff, 2:28–29
Arist	*The Creed of Aristides of Athens,* 2d c.	**1:51–52**
Arm Ev	*Armenian Evangelical Churches,* 1846	**3:261–63**
Arn	*The Arnoldshain Theses,* 1957	**3:558–61**
Assem	*The Statement of Fundamental Truths of the Assemblies of God,* 1914	**3:426–31**
Ath	*The Athanasian Creed* [*Quicunque vult*]	**1:673–77**; *BLK* 28–30; Denzinger, 75–76; Fabbri, 6–8; Gerrish, 62–64; Hahn, 150; Kelly 1964, 17–20; Kolb-Wengert, 23–25; Schaff, 2:66–71; Tappert, 19–21; *Triglotta* 2:30–35

Abbreviation	Title and Date	Location
Aub	*The Auburn Declaration,* 1837	**3:250–55;** Schaff, 3:777–80
Aug	*The Augsburg Confession*	**2:49–118;** *BLK* 31–137; Fabbri, 11–57; Gerrish, 87–125; Kolb-Wengert, 30–105; Leith, 63–107; Noll, 81–121; Schaff, 3:3–73; Tappert, 23–96; *Triglotta* 2:37–95
Ger	*German,* 1530	
Lat	*Latin,* 1530	
Var	*Variata,* 1540	Reu, 2:398–411
Balamand	*Uniatism, Method of Union of the Past, and the Present Search for Full Communion:* Joint International Commission for Theological Dialogue Between the Catholic and Orthodox Church, Balamand, Lebanon, 1993	**3:848–51;** *Gr Agr II* 680–85
Bap Assoc	*The Doctrinal Statement of the North American Baptist Association,* 1950	Lumpkin, 377–81
Bap Aus	*Doctrinal Basis of the Baptist Union of Victoria, Australia,* 1888	Lumpkin, 416–20
Bap Conf	*The Statement of Beliefs of the North American Baptist Conference,* 1982	**3:808–12**
Bap Gr Br	*The Statement of the Baptist Union of Great Britain and Ireland,* 1888	Lumpkin, 344–46
Bap NZ	*The Doctrinal Basis of the New Zealand Baptist Union,* 1882	Lumpkin, 416

Abbreviation	Title and Date	Location
Barm	*The Barmen Declaration [Theologische Erklärung zur gegenwärtigen Lage der Deutschen Evangelischen Kirche]*, 1934	**3:504–8**; Cochrane, 332–36; Leith, 517–22; Niesel, 333–37
Bas Bek	*The First Confession of Basel [Baseler Bekenntnis]*, 1534	**2:272–79**; Augusti, 103–9; Böckel, 108–14; Cochrane, 89–96; Fabbri, 630–37; Niemeyer, 78–104
Bat	*The Confession of Faith of the Protestant Christian Batak Church (H. K. B. P.)*, 1951	**3:543–55**; Anderson, 213–38; Leith, 555–66
BCP	*The Book of Common Prayer*, 1549, 1552, 1662, 1928, 1979	Blunt
BEC	*The Profession of Faith of the Salvadoran Basic Ecclesial Communities*, 1984	**3:844–45**
Belg	*The Belgic Confession*, 1561/1619	**2:405–26**; Augusti, 170–98; Bakhuizen van den Brink, 50–141; Böckel, 477–507; Cochrane, 185–219; Fabbri, 701–33; Niemeyer, 360–89; Niesel, 119–36; Schaff, 3:383–436
BEM	*Baptism, Eucharist, and Ministry* ["The Lima Text" of Faith and Order], 1982	**3:813–40**; *Gr Agr* 465–503

Abbreviation	Title and Date	Location
Bern	*The Ten Theses of Bern,* 1528	**2:215–17;** Böckel, 35–39; Cochrane, 45–50; Fabbri, 621–22; Leith, 129–30; Niemeyer, 14–15; Schaff, 3:208–10
Boh I	*The [First] Bohemian Confession,* 1535	**1:796–833;** Augusti, 273–326; Böckel, 777–827; Niemeyer, 771–818; Pelikan, 80–149
Boh II	*The [Second] Bohemian Confession,* 1575	CD-ROM; Böckel, 827–49; Niemeyer, 819–51; Reu, 2:424–33
Bonn I	*The Fourteen Theses of the Old Catholic Union Conference at Bonn with Greeks and Anglicans,* 1874	**3:365–67;** Schaff, 2:545–51
Bonn II	*The Old Catholic Agreement at Bonn on the Filioque Controversy,* 1875	Schaff, 2:552–54
Boston	*The Declaration of the Boston National Council,* 1865	Walker, 562–64
Brngr 1059	*The First Confession of Berengar,* 1059	**1:728–29;** Denzinger, 690
Brngr 1079	*The Second Confession of Berengar,* 1079	**1:728–29;** Denzinger, 700
Br St Luth	*The Brief Statement of the Doctrinal Position of the Evangelical Lutheran Synod of Missouri, Ohio, and Other States,* 1932	**3:487–503;** *Doct Dec* 42–57
Camb Dec	*The Cambridge Declaration of the Alliance of Confessing Evangelicals,* 1996	**3:861–66**

Abbreviation	Title and Date	Location
Camb Plat	*The Cambridge Platform,* 1648	**3:63–91;** Leith, 385–99; Walker, 194–237
Chal	*The Council of Chalcedon,* 451	**1:172–81;** *COD-DEC* 75–103; Denzinger, 300–303; Fabbri, 5; Gerrish, 65; Hahn, 146–47; Karmirēs, 1:173–76; Leith, 34–36; Mansi, 7:107–18; Michalcescu, 3–4; *NPNF*–II 14:243–95; Schaff, 2:62–65
Chile	*The Creed of the Evangelical Presbyterian Church of Chile,* 1983	**3:841–43**
Chin Man	*The Christian Manifesto of the Three-Self Patriotic Movement: "Directions of Endeavor for Chinese Christianity in the Construction of New China,"* 1950	**3:537–39;** Anderson, 249–50
Chin Un	*The Bond of Union of the Church of Christ in China,* 1927	**3:483–84;** Anderson, 249
Chr Dec	*Common Christological Declaration Between the Catholic Church and the Assyrian Church of the East,* 1994	**3:852–55;** *Gr Agr II* 711–12
Chr Sci	*Tenets of the Mother Church of Christ, Scientist,* 1879/1892/1906	**3:370–71**
CNI	*The Church of North India/Pakistan, Plan of Church Union: The Doctrines of the Church,* 1965	**3:700–702**

Abbreviation	Title and Date	Location
Cologne	The [Mennonite] Concept of Cologne, 1591	2:749-54
Com Cr	The "Commission" Creed of the Congregational Church, 1883/1913	3:372-74; Walker, 577-82
Com Dec	Common Declaration of Pope John Paul II and [Armenian] Catholicos Karekin I, 1996	3:867-70; Gr Agr II 707-8
Confut	The Confutation of the Augsburg Confession, 1530	Reu, 2:348-83
Cons rep	The Reaffirmed Consensus of the Truly Lutheran Faith [Consensus repetitus fidei vere lutheranae], 1655	Henke
Const	The Council of Constance, 1414-18	COD-DEC 403-51; Denzinger, 1151-1279
CP I	The First Council of Constantinople, 381	1:160-63; COD-DEC 21-35; Denzinger, 151; Karmirēs, 1:130-31; Michalcescu, 2; NPNF-II 14:162-90
CP II	The Second Council of Constantinople, 553	1:183-215; COD-DEC 105-22; Denzinger, 421-38; Hahn, 148; Karmirēs, 1:185-97; Leith, 45-50; Mansi, 9:367-90; Michalcescu, 5-7; NPNF-II 14:297-323
CP III	The Third Council of Constantinople, 680-81	1:216-29; COD-DEC 123-30; Denzinger, 550-59; Hahn, 149; Karmirēs, 1:221-24; Leith, 50-53; Mansi, 11:631-40; Michalcescu, 7-9; NPNF-II 14:344-46; Schaff, 2:72-73

Abbreviation	Title and Date	Location
CP 360	The Creed of the Synod of Constantinople of 360	Hahn, 167
CP 879–80	The Synod of Constantinople of 879–80	Karmirēs, 1:268–71
CP 1054	The Edict of Michael Cerularius and of the Synod of Constantinople of 1054	**1:309–17;** Karmirēs, 1:343–48; Mansi, 19:812–21; PG 151:679–82; Will, 155–68
CP 1341	The Synod of Constantinople of 1341	**1:318–33;** Karmirēs, 1:354–66; PG 151:679–82
CP 1347	The Synod of Constantinople of 1347	Karmirēs, 1:366–74
CP 1351	The Synod of Constantinople of 1351	**1:334–74;** Karmirēs, 1:374–407; PG 151:717–68
CP 1691	The Synod of Constantinople of 1691	Karmirēs, 2:779–83; Mansi, 37:463–72
CP 1838	The Synod of Constantinople of 1838	Karmirēs, 2:894–902; Mansi, 40:269–76
Craig	Craig's Catechism, 1581	Torrance, 97–165
Crg Sh Cat	Craig's Short Catechism, 1592	Torrance, 243–54
CSI 1929	The Scheme of Union of the Church of South India, 1929/1942	Schaff, 3:951
CSI 1947	The Constitution of the Church of South India, 1947	**3:517–24;** Anderson, 228–34
Cumb Pres	The Confession of the Cumberland Presbyterian Church, 1814/1883	**3:223–41;** Schaff, 3:771–76
Cum occas	Cum occasione of Pope Innocent X, 1653	**3:101–3;** Denzinger, 2001–7
Cyp	The Creed of Cyprian of Carthage, 250	Hahn, 12; Schaff, 2:20

Abbreviation	Title and Date	Location
Cyr Jer	*The Baptismal Creed of Jerusalem*, c. 350	**1:94–95**; Denzinger, 41; Hahn, 124; Schaff, 2:31–32
Czen	*The Hungarian Confession [Confessio Czengerina]*, 1570	Augusti, 241–53; Niemeyer, 539–50
Dec Addr	Thomas Campbell, *Declaration and Address*, 1809: "Propositions"	**3:219–22**
Def Plat	*The Definite Platform* (Lutheran), 1855	**3:291–315**
Denck	*Hans Denck's Confession Before the Council of Nuremberg*, 1525	**2:665–72**; Bauman, 51–53
Dêr Bal	*The Dêr Balyzeh Papyrus*, c. 200–350	**1:66–67**; Denzinger, 2; Kelly, 89; Leith, 19
Design	*Christian Church (Disciples of Christ): The Design for the Christian Church*, 1968	**3:726–29**
Dict Pap	*The Dictatus Papae of Pope Gregory VII*, 1075	**1:730–32**
Did	*The Didache*, c. 60–150	**1:41–42**
Dordrecht	*The Mennonite Confession of Faith of Dordrecht*, 1632	**2:768–87**; Fabbri, 922–37; Gerrish, 218–34; Leith, 292–308; Loewen, 63–70; Lumpkin, 66–78
Dort	*The Canons of the Synod of Dort*, 1618–19	**2:569–600**; Augusti, 198–240; Bakhuizen van den Brink, 218–81; Böckel, 508–43; Bray, 455–78; Fabbri, 885–921; Niemeyer, 690–728; Schaff, 3:550–97

Abbreviation	Title and Date	Location
Dosith	*The Confession of Dositheus and of the Synod of Jerusalem,* 1672	**1:613–35;** Karmirēs, 2:746–73; Gerrish, 310–41; Kimmel, 1:425–88; Leith, 485–517; Mansi, 34:1723–62; Michalcescu, 123–82; Robertson; Schaff, 2:401–44
Ecth	*The Ecthesis of Emperor Heraclius,* 638	**1:150–54;** *BZ* 69:21–23; Mansi, 10:991–98
Edict	*The Edict of Emperor Justinian on the True Faith,* 551	**1:122–49;** Schwartz, 73–110; Wesche, 163–98
18 Diss	*Eighteen Dissertations Concerning the Entire Christian Life and of What It Consists, by Balthasar Hubmaier,* 1524	Lumpkin, 19–21
Eng Dec	*The Declaration of the Congregational Union of England and Wales,* 1833	Schaff, 3:730–34; Walker, 542–52
Ep Apost	*The Epistula Apostolorum,* c. 150	**1:53–54;** Denzinger, 1; Leith, 17
Eph 431	*The Council of Ephesus,* 431	**1:164–71;** *COD-DEC* 37–74; Denzinger, 250–68; Karmirēs, 1:138–56; Michalcescu, 2–3; *NPNF*-II 14:191–242
Form Un	*The Formula of Union,* 433	**1:168–71;** *COD-DEC* 69–70; Denzinger, 271–73
Epiph	*The Creeds of Epiphanius,* 373/374	**1:100–101;** Denzinger, 42–45; Hahn, 125–26; *NPNF*-II 14:164–65; Schaff, 2:32–38

Abbreviation	Title and Date	Location
Ess	*Friends General Conference, Belief,* 1900	**3:399–401**
Eun	*The Confession of Eunomius to the Emperor,* 383	**1:105–9**; Hahn, 190
Eus	*The Creed of Eusebius of Caesarea,* 325	**1:82–83**; Denzinger, 40; Hahn, 188; Leith, 27–28; *NPNF*-II 4:74; Schaff, 2:29–30
Ev All	*The Nine Articles of the Evangelical Alliance,* 1846	**3:259–60**; Schaff, 3:827–28
Fac	*The Creed of Facundus of Hermiane,* 6th c.	Hahn, 51
F&O Ban	*Commission on Faith and Order of the World Council of Churches at Bangalore: A Common Statement of Our Faith,* 1978	**3:782–85**
F&O Edin	*Faith and Order Conference at Edinburgh: The Grace of Our Lord Jesus Christ; The Affirmation of Union,* 1937	**3:511–16**; Leith, 569–74
F&O Laus	*Faith and Order Conference at Lausanne: The Call to Unity,* 1927	**3:471–82**
Fid cath	*On the Catholic Faith* [*De fide catholica*], by Boethius, c. 517–22	**1:699–706**; *LCL* 74:52–71
Fid rat	*A Reckoning of the Faith* [*Fidei ratio*], by Ulrich Zwingli, 1530	**2:249–71**; Böckel, 40–61; Niemeyer, 16–35
Flor	The Council of Basel-Ferrara-Florence-Rome	**1:751–65**; *COD-DEC* 523–91; Denzinger, 1300–1308
Arm	*The Bull of Union with the Armenians,* 1439	

Abbreviation	Title and Date	Location
Un	*The Decree of Union with the East*, 1439	
Form Conc Epit	*The Formula of Concord The Epitome*, 1577	**2:166–203;** *BLK* 735–1102; Fabbri, 367–600; Kolb-Wengert, 486–660; Schaff, 3:93–180; Tappert, 464–636; *Triglotta* 2:774–1103
Sol Dec	*The Solid Declaration*, 1577	CD-ROM
42 Art	*The Forty-Two Articles of the Church of England*, 1553	Bray, 284–311; Niemeyer, 592–600
Free Meth	*Articles of Religion of the Free Methodist Church*, 1866	3:335–40
Free-Will Bap	*The Confession of the Free-Will Baptists*, 1834/1868/1948	Lumpkin, 367–76; Schaff, 3:749–56
Fréjus	*The Synod of Fréjus*, 796/797	**1:725–27;** Denzinger, 616–19
Friends I	*A Confession of Faith Containing XXIII Articles*, 1673	**3:136–48**
Friends II	*Theses Theologicae of Robert Barclay* [*The Confession of the Society of Friends, Commonly Called Quakers*], 1675	Schaff, 3:789–98
Gall	*The French Confession* [*Confessio Gallica*], 1559/1571	**2:372–86;** Augusti, 110–25; Böckel, 459–74; Cochrane, 137–58; Fabbri, 663–76; Gerrish, 150–63; Niemeyer, 311–39; Niesel, 65–79; Schaff, 3:356–82

Abbreviation	Title and Date	Location
Geloof	*The Doctrine of the True Mennonites or Baptists [De Geloofsleere der Waare Mennoniten of Dopgezinden] by Cornelis Ris*, 1766/1895/1902	**3:155–200**; Loewen, 85–103
Gen Bap	*General Baptists: The Faith and Practice of Thirty Congregations Gathered According to the Primitive Pattern*, 1651	**3:92–100**; Lumpkin, 171–88
Gennad	*The Confession of Faith of Gennadius II*, 1455–56	**1:385–91**; Karmirēs, 1:432–36; Michalcescu, 11–21; *PG* 160:333–52
Genv Cat	*The Geneva Catechism*, 1541/1542	**2:320–63**; Augusti, 460–531; Böckel, 127–72; Niemeyer, 123–90; Niesel, 1–41; Torrance, 3–65
Genv Con	*The Geneva Confession*, 1536	**2:311–19**; Cochrane, 117–26; Fabbri, 654–62; Noll, 123–32
Ghana	*Ghana Church Union Committee: The Faith of the Church*, 1965	**3:703–8**
Greg I	*The Creed of Pope Gregory I*, d. 604	Hahn, 231
Greg Palam	*The Confession of the Orthodox Faith by Gregory Palamas*, 1351	**1:375–78**; Karmirēs, 1:407–10; Michalcescu, 11–21; *PG* 160:333–52
Greg Thaum	*The Creed of Gregory Thaumaturgus* (c. 213–c. 270)	**1:70–71**; Hahn, 185; Schaff, 2:24–25
Heid	*The Heidelberg Catechism*, 1563	**2:427–57**; Augusti, 532–77; Bakhuizen van den Brink, 144–217; Böckel,

Abbreviation	Title and Date	Location
		395–424; Cochrane, 305–31; Fabbri, 734–69; Niemeyer, 390–461; Niesel, 136–218; Noll, 133–64; Schaff, 3:307–55
Helv I	*The First Helvetic Confession* [*The Second Basel Confession*], 1536	**2:280–91**; Augusti, 94–102; Böckel, 115–26; Cochrane, 97–111; Fabbri, 638–51; Niemeyer, 105–23; Schaff, 3:211–31
Helv II	*The Second Helvetic Confession*, 1566	**2:458–525**; Augusti, 3–93; Böckel, 281–347; Cochrane, 220–301; Fabbri, 770–862; Leith, 131–92; Niemeyer, 462–536; Niesel, 219–75; Schaff, 3:233–306, 831–909
Hipp	*The Creeds of Hippolytus*, c. 170–236	**1:60–61**; Denzinger, 10; Hahn, 6; Leith, 23
Hond	*The Credo* from *The Mass of the Marginalized People*, Honduras, 1980	**3:795–97**; Link, 45
Horm	*The Confession of Hormisdas* [*Libellus fidei*], 515	Denzinger, 363–65
Hub Chr Cat	*The Christian Catechism of Balthasar Hubmaier*, 1526	**2:673–93**
Ign	*The Creeds of Ignatius of Antioch*, c. 107	**1:39–40**; *ANF* 1:69–70; Hahn, 1; Leith, 16–17; Schaff, 2:11–12
Ild	*The Confession of Ildefonsus of Toledo*, 7th c.	Denzinger, 23; Hahn, 55

Abbreviation	Title and Date	Location
Ineff	Ineffabilis Deus of Pope Pius IX, 1854	3:289–90; Denzinger, 2800–2804; Leith, 442–46; Schaff, 2:211–12
Iren	The Creeds of Irenaeus of Lyons, c. 180–c. 200	1:48–50; ANF 1:330–31; Hahn, 5; Leith, 20–21; Schaff, 2:12–16
Irish	The Irish Articles of Religion, 1615	2:551–68; Bray, 437–52; Fabbri, 865–84; Schaff, 3:526–44
Jer II 1	The Reply of Ecumenical Patriarch Jeremias II to the Augsburg Confession, 1576	1:392–474; Karmirēs, 1:443–503; Mastrantonis, 30–105
Jer II 2–3	The Second and Third Replies to the Lutherans of Patriarch Jeremias II of Constantinople, 1579, 1581	CD-ROM; Karmirēs, 2:435–89; Mastrantonis, 151–214, 288–307
Just	The Creeds of Justin Martyr, 155	1:45–47; Hahn, 3; Leith, 18
Korea	The Theological Declaration by Christian Ministers in the Republic of Korea, 1973	3:742–43; Anderson, 241–45
Lam	Lamentabili of Pope Pius X, 1907	3:402–8; Denzinger, 3401–66
Lamb Art	The Lambeth Articles, 1595	2:545–46; Bray, 399–400; Fabbri, 863–64; Schaff, 3:523–25
Lamb Quad	The Lambeth Quadrilateral [The Chicago/Lambeth Quadrilateral], 1886/1888	3:375–76; Fabbri, 1032–34
Lat 649	The Lateran Synod of 649	1:709–14; Denzinger, 500–522
Lat 1215	The Fourth Lateran Council of 1215: The Lateran Creed	1:739–42; COD-DEC 227–71; Denzinger, 800–820; Leith, 56–59

Abbreviation	Title and Date	Location
Laus Art	The Lausanne Articles, 1536	2:292–95; Cochrane, 113–16; Fabbri, 652–53
Laus Cov	The Lausanne Covenant, 1974	3:753–60
LDS	The Articles of Faith of the Church of Jesus Christ of Latter-Day Saints (Mormons), 1842	3:256–58
Leuen	The Leuenberg Agreement [Konkordie reformatorischer Kirchen in Europa], 1973	3:744–52; ER 25:355–59; Rusch-Martensen 1989, 144–54
Lit Chrys	The Divine Liturgy According to Saint John Chrysostom	1:269–95; Brightman, 353–99; Holy Cross 1–40; Kallis, 44–195; Karmirēs, 1:289–315; Kokkinakis, 86–143; Michalcescu, 277–98; OCA 29–87
Loll	The Twelve Conclusions of the Lollards, 1395	1:784–90
London I	The [First] London Confession of the Particular Baptists, 1644	3:47–62; Lumpkin, 144–71
London II	The Assembly or Second London Confession, 1677/1678	Lumpkin, 235–95
Lucar	The Eastern Confession of the Christian Faith by Cyril Lucar, 1629 (1633)	1:549–58; Bradow 1960, 190–204; Karmirēs, 2:565–70; Kimmel, 1:24–44; Michalcescu, 262–76
LuRC 4	Lutheran–Roman Catholic Conversation 4: All Under One Christ, 1980	Gr Agr 241–46

Abbreviation	Title and Date	Location
LuRC Just	Lutheran–Roman Catholic Joint Declaration on the Doctrine of Justification, 1999	3:877–88
Luth Lg Cat	The Large Catechism of Martin Luther, 1529	CD-ROM; BLK 543–733; Kolb-Wengert, 379–480; Tappert, 358–461; Triglotta 2:565–773
Luth Sm Cat	The Small Catechism of Martin Luther, 1529	2:29–48; BLK 499–541; Kolb-Wengert, 347–75; Leith, 107–26; Noll, 59–80; Schaff, 3:74–92; Tappert, 338–56; Triglotta 2:531–63
Lyons	The Second Council of Lyons, 1274	1:743–44; COD-DEC 314; Denzinger, 850–61
Madag	The Statement of Faith of the Church of Jesus Christ in Madagascar, 1958/1968	3:562–65
Marburg	The Marburg Articles, 1529	2:791–95; Reu, 2:44–47
Mark Eph	The Confession of Faith of Mark of Ephesus, 1439	1:379–84; Karmirēs, 1:422–25; PG 160:115–204
Masai	The Masai Creed, c. 1960	3:568–69; Donovan, 200; Marthaler, 417
Menn Con	The Mennonite Confession of Faith, 1963	3:674–85
Meros	The Faith in Detail [Kata meros pistis], 6th c.?	Caspari, 18–21
Meth Art	The Methodist Articles of Religion, 1784/1804	3:201–7; Leith, 353–60; Schaff, 3:807–13
Meth Braz	The Social Creed of the Methodist Church of Brazil, 1971	3:732–35

Abbreviation	Title and Date	Location
Meth Kor	*The Doctrinal Statement of the Korean Methodist Church,* 1930	**3:485–86;** Anderson, 241
Metr Crit	*The Confession of Metrophanes Critopoulos,* 1625	**1:475–548;** Karmirēs, 2:498–561; Michalcescu, 183–252
Mogila	*The Orthodox Confession of the Catholic and Apostolic Eastern Church by Peter Mogila,* 1638/1642	**1:559–612;** Karmirēs, 2:593–686; Kimmel, 1:56–203; Malvy-Viller, 1–124; Michalcescu, 22–122; Overbeck, 6–162; Schaff, 2:275–400
Morav	*The Easter Litany of the Moravian Church,* 1749	**3:149–54;** Schaff, 3:799–806
Morav Am	*Moravian Church in America: The Ground of the Unity,* 1995	**3:856–60**
Munif	*Munificentissimus Deus of Pope Pius XII,* 1950	**3:534–36;** Denzinger, 3900–3904; Leith, 457–66; Schaff, 2:211–12
N	*The Creed of Nicaea,* 325	**1:156–59;** *COD-DEC* 5; Denzinger, 125–26; Hahn, 142; Gerrish, 59; Karmirēs, 1:122–23; Leith, 29–31; Mansi, 2:665–68; *NPNF*–II 14:3
Naz	*Articles of Faith of the Church of the Nazarene,* 1908	**3:409–14**
N-CP	*The Niceno-Constantinopolitan Creed [“The Nicene Creed”],* 381	**1:160–63;** *COD-DEC* 24; Denzinger, 150; Gerrish, 59–60; Hahn, 144; Karmirēs, 1:130–31; Leith, 31–33; Mansi, 3:565–66; *NPNF*–II 14:163; Schaff, 2:57–58

Abbreviation	Title and Date	Location
Occ	*The Western [Occidental] Recension*	**1:670–72;** *BLK* 26–27; Cochrane, 303; Denzinger, 150; Fabbri, 4; Kolb-Wengert, 22–23; Schaff, 2:58–59; Tappert, 18–19; *Triglotta* 2:30–31
New Hamp	*The New Hampshire [Baptist] Confession, 1833/1853*	**3:242–49;** Leith, 334–39; Lumpkin, 360–77; Schaff, 3:742–48
Nic I	*The First Council of Nicaea, 325*	**1:156–59;** *COD-DEC* 1–19; Michalcescu, 1; *NPNF*-II 14:1–56; Schaff, 2:60–61
Nic II	*The Second Council of Nicaea, 787*	**1:230–41;** *COD-DEC* 133–38; Denzinger, 600–615; Karmirēs, 1:238–50; Leith, 53–56; Mansi, 13:373–80; Michalcescu, 10; *NPNF*-II 14:521–87
No Afr	*North African Creeds*	**1:110–12, 683–84**
Novat	*The Creeds of Novatian, c. 240–50*	**1:68–69;** Hahn, 11; Schaff, 2:21
Oberlin	*The Declaration of the Oberlin National Council, 1871*	Walker, 570–76
Orange	*The Synod of Orange, 529*	**1:692–98;** Denzinger, 370–97; Hahn, 174; Leith, 37–45
Origen	*The Creed of Origen, c. 222–30*	**1:62–65;** Hahn, 8; Schaff, 2:21–23
Pasc	*Pascendi dominici gregis of Pope Pius X, 1907*	Denzinger, 3475–3500
Patr	*The Profession of Faith of Patrick, 5th c.*	**1:690–91**
Petr Ab	*The Confession of Faith of Peter Abelard, 1139–42*	**1:735–38;** Gilson 1960, 107–8

Abbreviation	Title and Date	Location
Philad	The Philadelphia Baptist Confession, 1688/1689/1742	Lumpkin, 348–53; Schaff, 3:738–41
Philip Ind	The Declaration of the Faith and Articles of Religion of the Philippine Independent Church, 1947	3:525–31; Anderson, 255–60
Philip UCC	The Statement of Faith of the United Church of Christ in the Philippines, 1986/1992	3:846–47
Phot	The Encyclical Letter of Photius, 866	1:296–308; Karmirēs, 1:321–30; PG 102:721–41
Pol Br	The Catechesis and Confession of Faith of the Polish Brethren, 1574	2:709–44
Pol Nat Ch	The Confession of Faith of the Polish National Catholic Church, 1912/1914	3:423–25
Polyc	The Creed of Polycarp of Smyrna, c. 150	1:43–44
Prague	The Four Articles of Prague, 1420	1:791–95
Pres So Afr	The Declaration of Faith of the Presbyterian Church in South Africa, 1979/1981	3:793–94; Vischer, 27–28
Pres USA	Confession of the United Presbyterian Church in the United States, 1967	3:714–25
R	The Roman Symbol, 2d c.	1:681–82; Gerrish, 55
Rac	The Racovian Catechism, 1605	Rees
RCA	Reformed Church in America: Our Song of Hope, 1978	3:786–92

Abbreviation	Title and Date	Location
Ref All	North American Area Council of the World Alliance of Reformed Churches: The Statement of Faith, 1965	3:712–13
Ref Ep	The Declaration of Principles of the Reformed Episcopal Church in America, 1873/1875	Schaff, 3:814–26
Remon	The Remonstrance or Arminian Articles, 1610	2:547–50; Bakhuizen van den Brink, 282–87; Böckel, 544–640; Schaff, 3:545–49
Resp Non-Jur	The Responses of Eastern Orthodox Patriarchs to the Non-Jurors, 1718/1723	Karmirēs, 2:788–820; Mansi, 37:395–472
Resp Pius IX	The Response of Eastern Orthodox Patriarchs to Pope Pius IX, 1848	3:264–88; Karmirēs, 2:905–25; Mansi, 40:377–418
Richmond	The Richmond Declaration of Faith of the Friends Yearly Meeting, 1887	3:377–92
Ries	The [Mennonite] Short Confession of Faith of Hans de Ries, 1610	2:755–67; Dyck, 11–19
Rom Syn	The Creed of the Synod of Rome, 680	1:722–24; Denzinger, 546–48
Russ Cat	The Christian Catechism of the Orthodox Catholic Greco-Russian Church, 1839	Schaff, 2:445–542
Sacr ant	Sacrorum antistitum [Anti-Modernist Oath] of Pope Pius X, 1910	3:419–22; Denzinger, 3537–50
Salv Arm	Religious Doctrines of the Salvation Army, 1878	3:368–69

Abbreviation	Title and Date	Location
Sard	The Western Creed of Sardica, 343	1:90–93; Hahn, 157; NPNF–II 3:71–72
Sav	The Savoy Declaration of Faith and Order, 1658	3:104–35; Schaff, 3:707–29; Walker, 354–408
Sax	The Saxon Confession, 1551	Schaff, 3:181–89
Sax Vis	The Saxon Visitation Articles, 1592	Fabbri, 611–20; Schaff, 3:181–89
Schleit	The Schleitheim Confession, 1527	2:694–703; Leith, 281–92; Lumpkin, 22–31; Noll, 47–58
Scot I	The [First] Scots Confession, 1560	2:387–404; Augusti, 143–69; Böckel, 643–61; Cochrane, 159–84; Fabbri, 677–700; Niemeyer, 340–56; Niesel, 79–117; Schaff, 3:437–79
Scot II	The King's Confession [The Second Scots Confession], 1581	2:541–44; Böckel, 661–63; Niemeyer, 357–59; Schaff, 3:480–85
Send	The Consensus of Sandomierz [Consensus Sendomiriensis], 1570	Augusti, 254–64; Niemeyer, 553–61
Sens	The Decrees of the Synod of Sens Against Abelard, 1140/1141	1:733–34; Denzinger, 721–39
17 Art	The Seventeen Articles for the Use of Visitors in Saxony, 1527/1528	LW 40:263–320
Shema	The Shema of Dt 6.4–9, 11.13–21, Nm 15.37–41	1:29–31
Sheng Kung	The Sheng Kung Hui Pastoral Letter of the Anglican Bishops of China, 1950	3:540–42

Abbreviation	Title and Date	Location
Shkr	*The Concise Statement of the Principles of the [Shaker] Only True Church*, 1790	3:208–13
Sirm 357	*The Second ["Blasphemy"] Synod of Sirmium*, 357	Hahn, 161; *NPNF*-II 9:6–7
Sirm 359	*The Creed of the Fourth Synod of Sirmium*, 359, and *The Creed of Constantinople*, 360	**1:96–99**; Hahn, 165; *NPNF*-II 4:454
67 Art	*The Sixty-Seven Articles of Ulrich Zwingli*, 1523	**2:207–14**; Böckel, 3–9; Cochrane 33–44; Fabbri, 603–10; Niemeyer, 3–13; Noll, 37–46; Schaff, 3:197–207
Smal Art	*The Smalcald Articles* and *The Treatise on the Power and Primacy of the Pope*, 1537	**2:119–65**; *BLK* 405–68; Fabbri, 329–66; Kolb-Wengert, 297–328; Tappert, 288–318; *Triglotta* 2:453–529
Smyr	Confession of the Presbyters of Smyrna Against Noetus, c. 180–200	**1:58–59**
So Bap	*The Faith and Message of the Southern Baptist Convention*, 1925	**3:437–44**; Lumpkin, 390–400
Soc Ch	*The Social Creed of the Churches*, 1908/1912/1933	**3:417–18**
Socin	*Confession of Faith of Laelius Socinus [Lelio Sozini]*, 1555	**2:704–8**
Soc Meth	*The Social Creed of Methodism*, 1908	**3:415–16**; *Meth Doct & Disc*, 479–81
Sri Lanka	*The Scheme of Church Union in Ceylon: Faith and Order*, 1963	**3:686–99**

Abbreviation	Title and Date	Location
Swed Bap	*The Confession of Faith of the Swedish Baptists*, 1861	**3:321–23**; Lumpkin, 407–10
Syl	*The Syllabus of Errors of Pope Pius IX*, 1864	**3:324–34**; Denzinger, 2901–80; *Dublin Review* (1865), 513–29; Schaff, 2:213–33
10 Art	*The Ten Articles*, 1536	**2:296–310**; Bray, 162–74
Tert	*The Creeds of Tertullian*, c. 203–10	**1:55–57**; *ANF* 3:598; Hahn, 7, 44; Leith, 21–22; Schaff, 2:16–20
Test Dom	*The Testamentum Domini*, 4th–5th c.	Denzinger, 61
Tetrapol	*The Tetrapolitan Confession*, 1530	**2:218–48**; Augusti, 327–68; Böckel, 363–94; Cochrane, 51–88; Niemeyer, 740–70
Thdr Mops	*The Creed of Theodore of Mopsuestia*, c. 350–428	Denzinger, 51
39 Art	*The Thirty-Nine Articles of the Church of England*, 1571	**2:526–40**; Augusti, 126–42; Böckel, 664–79; Bray, 285–311; Fabbri, 1017–31; Gerrish, 185–99; Leith, 266–81; Niemeyer, 601–11; Noll, 211–27; Schaff, 3:487–516
Am	*The American Revision*, 1801	
Thorn	*The Colloquy of Thorn* [*Collegium charitativum*], 1645	Augusti, 411–42; Niemeyer, 669–89
Tig	*The Zurich Consensus* [*Consensus Tigurinus*], 1549	**2:802–15**; Böckel, 173–81; Niemeyer, 191–217
Togo	*The Evangelical Church of Togo: Our Faith*, 1971	**3:736–37**

Abbreviation	Title and Date	Location
Tol I	*The First Synod of Toledo, 400/447*	**1:685–89;** Denzinger, 188–208; Hahn, 168
Tol III	*The Third Synod of Toledo: The Profession of Faith of Recared, 589*	**1:707–8;** Denzinger, 470; Hahn, 176
Tol XI	*The Eleventh Synod of Toledo, 675*	**1:715–21;** Denzinger, 525–41; Hahn, 182
Tome	*The Tome of Pope Leo I, 449*	**1:113–21;** *COD-DEC* 77–82; Denzinger, 290–95; *NPNF*-II 14:254–58
Toraja	*Confession of the Church of Toraja, 1981*	**3:798–807;** Vischer, 48–58
Trans	*The Transylvanian Confession of Faith, 1579*	**2:745–48;** Williams, 1131–33
Trent	*The Council of Trent, 1545–63*	**2:819–71;** *COD-DEC* 657–799; Denzinger, 1500–1835; Gerrish, 259–92; Leith, 399–439; Noll, 165–205; Schaff, 2:77–206
Trid Prof	*The Tridentine Profession of Faith, 1564*	**2:872–74;** Denzinger, 1862–70; Leith, 439–42; Noll, 207–10; Schaff, 2:207–10
True Con	*A True Confession of the English Separatists (Brownists), 1596*	**3:31–46;** Lumpkin, 79–97; Walker, 41–74
UCC	*The Statement of Faith of the United Church of Christ, 1959/1981*	**3:566–67**
Ulph	*The Confession of Ulphilas, 383*	**1:102–4;** Hahn, 198
Unam	*Unam Sanctam of Pope Boniface VIII, 1302*	**1:745–47;** Denzinger, 870–75
Un Ch Can: Crd	*New Creed of the United Church of Canada, 1968/1980/1994*	**3:730–31**

Abbreviation	Title and Date	Location
Un Ch Can: Union	*The Basis of Union of the United Church of Canada,* 1925	**3:445–52;** Schaff, 3:935–38
Un Ch Japan	*United Church of Christ in Japan: The Confession of Faith,* 1954	**3:556–57;** Anderson, 253–54
Un Pres	*The Confessional Statement of the United Presbyterian Church of North America,* 1925	**3:453–70**
Un Ref Ch	*United Reformed Church (The Reformed Association of the Church of Christ in Britain): The Basis of Union,* 1972/ 1981/1997/2000	**3:738–41;** Moss, 281–82
Utrecht	*The Old Catholic Declaration of Utrecht,* 1889	**3:393–96**
Vald	*The Profession of Faith of Valdes,* 1180	**1:769–73**
Vat I	*The First Vatican Council,* 1869–70	**3:341–58;** *COD-DEC* 811–16; Denzinger, 3000–3075; Leith, 447–57; Schaff, 2:234–71
Vat II	*The Second Vatican Council,* 1962–65	**3:570–673;** *COD-DEC* 817–1135; Denzinger, 4001–345
Vienne	*The Council of Vienne: Decree on the Foundation of the Catholic Faith,* 1311–12	**1:748–50;** *COD-DEC* 360–61; Denzinger, 900–904
Wald	*The Confession of the Waldenses,* 1655	**1:774–80;** Fabbri, 991–1016; Schaff, 3:757–70
Wash	*The Washington Profession of the Unitarian General Convention,* 1935	**3:509–10;** Robinson 1970, 160

Abbreviation	Title and Date	Location
WCC	*The Doctrinal Basis of the World Council of Churches*, 1948/1961	**3:532–33;** Leith, 574–77
West	*The Westminster Confession of Faith*, 1647	**2:601–49;** Bray, 487–520; Fabbri, 938–88; Leith, 192–230; Schaff, 3:600–673
Am	*The American Revision, 1729*	
West Sh Cat	*The Westminster Shorter Catechism*, 1648	**2:650–62;** Schaff, 3:674–703
Winch	*The Winchester [Universalist] Profession, 1803*	**3:217–18**
Witness	*Statement of Faith of the Jehovah's Witnesses*, 1918	**3:432–34**
Witt Art	*The Wittenberg Articles, 1536*	CD-ROM; Bray, 119–61
Witt Conc	*The Wittenberg Concord, 1536*	**2:796–801**
Wrt	*The Württemberg Confession*, 1552	Reu, 2:418–24
Wyclif	*John Wycliffe: A Confession on the Eucharist, 1382*	**1:781–83**
Zambia	*The Constitution of the United Church of Zambia, 1965/1984*	**3:709–11**

act	acts
anath	anathema
art	article
can	canon
ch	chapter
con	conclusion
decr	decree

def	definition
ecth	ecthesis
ep	epistle
int	introduction
par	paragraph
pr	preface
q	question
st	stanza
ttl	title

Editions, Collections, and Reference Works

ABD	*The Anchor Bible Dictionary.* Edited by David Noel Freedman. 6 vols. New York: Doubleday, 1992.
ACW	*Ancient Christian Writers.* Edited by Johannes Quasten et al. 58 vols. to date. Westminster, Md.: Newman Press, 1946– .
Anderson	Anderson, Gerald H., ed. *Asian Voices in Christian Theology.* Maryknoll, N.Y.: Orbis Books, 1976.
ANF	*The Ante-Nicene Fathers.* Alexander Roberts and James Donaldson, editors. Reprint ed. 10 vols. Grand Rapids, Mich.: William B. Eerdmans, 1950, etc.
Augusti	Augusti, Johann Christian Wilhelm, ed. *Corpus Librorum Symbolicorum qui in Ecclesia Reformatorum auctoritatem publicam obtinuerunt.* Elberfeld: Bueschler, 1827.
Bakhuizen van den Brink	Bakhuizen van den Brink, J. N. *De Nederlandse Belijdenisgeschriften.* Amsterdam: Bolland, 1976.
Bauer-Arndt-Gingrich	Bauer, Walter. *A Greek-English Lexicon of the New Testament and Other Early Christian Literature.* Translated and adapted by William F. Arndt and F. Wilbur Gingrich. 2d ed. Chicago: University of Chicago Press, 1979.
Bauman	Bauman, Clarence, ed. *The Spiritual Legacy of Hans Denck.* Leiden: E. J. Brill, 1991.
Beck	Beck, Hans-Georg. *Kirche und theologische Literatur im byzantinischen Reich.* Munich: C. H. Beck'sche Verlagsbuchhandlung, 1959.
Blaise-Chirat	Blaise, Albert, and Henri Chirat. *Dictionnaire latin-français des auteurs chrétiens.* Strasbourg: Le Latin Chrétien.

Blass-   Blass, Friedrich, and Albert Debrunner. *A Greek*
  Debrunner   *Grammar of the New Testament and Other Early*
               Christian Literature. Edited and translated by
               Robert W. Funk. Chicago: University of Chicago
               Press, 1961.

BLK   *Die Bekenntnisschriften der evangelisch-lutherischen*
               Kirche. 11th ed. Göttingen: Vandenhoeck und
               Ruprecht, 1992.

Blunt   Blunt, John Henry, ed. *The Annotated Book of*
               Common Prayer, Being an Historical, Ritual, and
               Theological Commentary on the Devotional System
               of the Church of England. Rev. ed. New York: E. P.
               Dutton, 1903.

Böckel   Böckel, Ernst Gottfried Adolf, ed. *Die*
               Bekenntniszschriften der evangelisch-reformirten
               Kirche. Leipzig: F. A. Brockaus, 1847.

Bray   Bray, Gerald Lewis, ed. *Documents of the English*
               Reformation. Minneapolis, Minn.: Fortress Press,
               1994.

Brightman   Brightman, Frank Edward, ed. *Liturgies Eastern and*
               Western. Oxford: Clarendon Press, 1896.

Caspari   Caspari, Carl Paul, ed. *Alte und neue Quellen zur*
               Geschichte des Taufsymbols und der Glaubensregel.
               Christiania: Mallingische Buchdruckerei, 1879.

Chr Trad   *The Christian Tradition: A History of the Development*
               of Doctrine. By Jaroslav Pelikan. 5 vols. Chicago:
               University of Chicago Press, 1971–89.

Cochrane   Cochrane, Arthur C., ed. *Reformed Confessions of the*
               Sixteenth Century. Philadelphia: Westminster Press,
               1966.

COD   *Conciliorum Oecumenicorum Decreta*. Edited by
               Joseph Alberigo et al. 3d ed. Bologna: Istituto per
               le scienze religiose, 1973. (Pagination identical with
               that of *DEC*.)

CWS   *The Classics of Western Spirituality*. Edited by John
               Farina. 104 vols. to date. New York: Paulist Press,
               1978–.

Day   Day, Peter D., ed. *The Liturgical Dictionary of Eastern Christianity*. Collegeville, Minn.: Liturgical Press, 1993.

DEC   *Decrees of the Ecumenical Councils*. Edited by Norman P. Tanner et al. 2 vols. Washington, D.C.: Georgetown University Press, 1990. (Pagination identical with that of *COD*.)

DEM   *Dictionary of the Ecumenical Movement*. Edited by Nicholas Lossky, José Míguez Bonino, John Pobec, Tom Stransky, Geoffrey Wainwright, and Pauline Webb. Grand Rapids, Mich.: William B. Eerdmans, 1991.

Denzinger   Denzinger, Heinrich, ed. *Enchiridion symbolorum definitionum et declarationum de rebus fidei et morum*. [1854.] 37th ed. Edited by Peter Hünermann. Freiburg: Herder, 1991. (Cited by paragraph numbers.)

Doct Dec   *Doctrinal Declarations of the Lutheran Churches*. Saint Louis, Mo.: Concordia Publishing House, 1957.

Donovan   Donovan, Vincent J. *Christianity Rediscovered*. 2d ed. Maryknoll, N.Y.: Orbis Books, 1982.

Dossetti   Dossetti, Giuseppe Luigi, ed. *Il simbolo di Nicea e di Costantinopoli: Edizione critica*. Rome: Herder, 1967.

DTC   *Dictionnaire de théologie catholique*. Edited by Alfred Vacant, Emile Mangenot, and Emile Amann (15 vols., 1903–50); and "Tables Générales," edited by B. Loth and A. Michel (3 vols., 1951–72). Paris: Libraire Letouzey et Ané.

EC   *The Encyclopedia of Christianity*. Edited by Erwin Fahlbusch, Jan Milič Lochman, John Mbiti, Jaroslav Pelikan, and Lukas Vischer. Translated by Geoffrey W. Bromiley. Foreword by Jaroslav Pelikan. Grand Rapids, Mich.: William B. Eerdmans, 1999–.

Fabbri   Fabbri, Romeo, ed. *Confessioni di fede delle chiese cristiane*. Bologna: Edizioni Dehoniane, 1996.

Fabricius   Fabricius, Cajus, ed. *Corpus Confessionum: Die Bekenntnisse der Christenheit*. Berlin: Wilde Gruyter, 1928–43.

Gass   Gass, Wilhelm. *Symbolik der griechischen Kirche*. Berlin: Reimer, 1872.

Gerrish   Gerrish, Brian A., ed. *The Faith of Christendom: A Source Book of Creeds and Confessions*. New York: World Publishing, 1963.

Gr Agr   *Growth in Agreement: Reports and Agreed Statements of Ecumenical Conversations on a World Level*. Edited by Harding Meyer and Lukas Vischer. Geneva: World Council of Churches; New York: Paulist Press, 1984.

Gr Agr II   *Growth in Agreement II: Reports and Agreed Statements of Ecumenical Conversations on a World Level, 1982–1988*. Edited by Jeffrey Gros, Harding Meyer, and William G. Rusch. Geneva: World Council of Churches; Grand Rapids, Mich.: William B. Eerdmans, 2000.

Hahn   Hahn, August. *Bibliothek der Symbole und Glaubensregeln der Alten Kirche*. 3d ed. Edited by G. Ludwig Hahn. Foreword by Adolf Harnack. [1897.] Reprint ed. Hildesheim: Georg Olms Verlagsbuchhandlung, 1962. (Cited by document numbers.)

Hefele-Leclercq   Hefele, Karl Joseph, and Henri Leclercq. *Histoire des conciles d'après les documents originaux*. 11 vols. Paris: Letouzey et Ané, 1907–52.

Henke   Henke, Ernst Ludwig Theodor, ed. *Theologorum Saxonicorum consensus repetitus fidei vere Lutheranae*. Marburg: Typis Elwerti Academicis, 1846.

Holy Cross   *Hē Theia Leitourgia: The Divine Liturgy*. Brookline, Mass.: Holy Cross Orthodox Press, 1985.

Horst   Horst, Irvin B., ed. and tr. *Mennonite Confession of Faith Adopted April 21st, 1632, at Dordrecht, The Netherlands*. Lancaster, Pa.: Lancaster Mennonite Historical Society, 1988.

Kallis   Kallis, Anastasios, ed. *Liturgie: Die Göttliche*
                 Liturgie der Orthodoxen Kirche Deutsch-Griechisch-
                 Kirchenslawisch. Mainz: Matthias-Grünewald-
                 Verlag, 1989.

Karmirēs   Karmirēs, Ioannēs. *Ta dogmatika kai symbolika*
                 mnēmeia tēs orthodoxou katholikēs ekklēsias [The
                 dogmatic and symbolic monuments of the Orthodox
                 Catholic Church]. 2 vols. 2d ed. Graz: Akademische
                 Druck- und Verlagsanstalt, 1968. (Cited by page
                 numbers of this edition.)

Kelly   Kelly, John Norman Davidson. *Early Christian*
                 Creeds. 3d ed. London: Longman Group, 1972.

Kimmel   Kimmel, Ernst Julius, ed. *Libri symbolici ecclesiae*
                 orientalis. *Appendix* edited by H. J. C. Weissenborn.
                 Jena: Apud Carolum Hochhausenium, 1843–50.

Kokkinakis   Kokkinakis, Athenagoras, ed. and tr. *The Liturgy of*
                 the Orthodox Church. London: Mowbrays, 1979.

Kolb-Wengert   Kolb, Robert, and Timothy J. Wengert, eds. *The*
                 Book of Concord: The Confessions of the Evangelical
                 Lutheran Church. Minneapolis, Minn.: Fortress
                 Press, 2000.

Lacoste   Lacoste, Jean-Yves, ed. *Dictionnaire critique de*
                 théologie. Paris: Presses Universitaires de France,
                 1998.

Lampe   Lampe, Geoffrey W. H., ed. *A Patristic Greek*
                 Lexicon. Oxford: Clarendon Press, 1961.

LCL   *Loeb Classical Library*. Cambridge, Mass.: Harvard
                 University Press.

Leith   Leith, John H., ed. *Creeds of the Churches: A Reader*
                 in Christian Doctrine from the Bible to the Present.
                 Garden City, N.Y.: Doubleday, 1963.

Loewen   Loewen, Howard John, ed. *One Lord, One Church,*
                 One Hope, and One God: Mennonite Confessions of
                 Faith. Elkhart, Ind.: Institute of Mennonite Studies,
                 1985.

LTK   *Lexikon für Theologie und Kirche*. 2d ed. Edited by
                 Josef Höfer and Karl Rahner. 10 vols. and index.
                 Freiburg: Herder, 1957–67.

Lumpkin	Lumpkin, William L., ed. *Baptist Confessions of Faith*. Rev. ed. Valley Forge, Pa.: Judson Press, 1969.
LW	*Luther's Works*. American edition. Edited by Jaroslav Pelikan and Helmut T. Lehmann. 55 vols. Saint Louis, Mo.: Concordia Publishing House; Philadelphia: Muhlenberg Press [Fortress Press], 1955–.
McGlothlin	McGlothlin, William Joseph, ed. *Baptist Confessions of Faith*. Philadelphia: American Baptist Publication Society, 1911.
Malvy-Viller	Malvy, Antoine, and Marcel Viller, eds. *La confession orthodoxe de Pierre Moghila*. Rome: Orientalia Christiana Analecta, 1927.
Mansi	Mansi, Giovanni Domenico, ed. *Sacrorum conciliorum nova et amplissima collectio*. 31 vols. Florence: Antonio Zatta, 1759–98.
Marthaler	Marthaler, Berard L. *The Creed*. Mystic, Conn.: Twenty-Third Publications, 1987.
Mastrantonis	Mastrantonis, George, ed. *Augsburg and Constantinople: The Correspondence Between the Tübingen Theologians and Patriarch Jeremiah II of Constantinople on the Augsburg Confession*. Brookline, Mass.: Holy Cross Orthodox Press, 1982.
Meth Doct & Disc	*The Doctrines and Discipline of the Methodist Episcopal Church*. New York: Eaton and Mains, 1908.
Michalcescu	Michalcescu, Jon, ed. *Thēsauros tēs Orthodoxias: Die Bekenntnisse und die wichtigsten Glaubenszeugnisse der griechisch-orientalischen Kirche*. Introduction by Albert Hauck. Leipzig: J. C. Hinrichs, 1904.
Müller	Müller, E. F. Karl. *Die Bekenntnisschriften der reformierten Kirche in authentischen Texten mit geschichtlicher Einleitung und Register*. Leipzig: A. Deichert, 1903.
Niemeyer	Niemeyer, Hermann Agathon, ed. *Collectio Confessionum in Ecclesiis Reformatis Publicatarum*. Leipzig: Julius Klinkhardt, 1840.

Niesel   Niesel, Wilhelm, ed. *Bekenntnisschriften und Kirchen-*
                      ordnungen der nach Gottes Wort reformierten Kirche.
                      Munich: Christian Kaiser Verlag, [1938].

Noll   Noll, Mark A., ed. *Confessions and Catechisms of*
                      the Reformation. Grand Rapids, Mich.: Baker Book
                      House, 1991.

NPNF   *A Select Library of the Nicene and Post-Nicene*
                      Fathers of the Christian Church. First and Second
                      Series. Reprint ed. 22 vols. Grand Rapids, Mich.:
                      William B. Eerdmans, 1956.

OCA   *The Divine Liturgy According to St. John Chrysostom,*
                      with Appendices. The Orthodox Church in America.
                      2d ed. South Canaan, Pa.: St. Tikhon's Seminary
                      Press, 1977.

ODCC   *The Oxford Dictionary of the Christian Church.* 3d
                      ed. Edited by F. L. Cross and E. A. Livingstone.
                      Oxford: Oxford University Press, 1997.

OED   *A New [Oxford] English Dictionary on Historical*
                      Principles. Edited by J. A. H. Murray, H. Bradley,
                      W. A. Craigie, and C. T. Onions. 12 vols. and 4 vols.
                      of Supplement. Oxford: Oxford University Press,
                      1884–1933.

Overbeck   Overbeck, J. J., ed. *The Orthodox Confession of*
                      the Catholic and Apostolic Eastern Church from the
                      Version of Peter Mogila. London: Thomas Baker,
                      1898.

Pelikan   Pelikan, Jaroslav. "Luther and the *Confessio*
                      Bohemica." Ph.D. diss., University of Chicago, 1946.

PG   *Patrologia Graeca.* Edited by Jacques-Paul Migne.
                      162 vols. Paris: Lutetiae Parisiorum, 1857–66.

PL   *Patrologia Latina.* Edited by Jacques-Paul Migne.
                      221 vols. Paris: Lutetiae Parisiorum, 1844–64.

Prav Slov   *Polnyj pravoslavný bogoslovský enciklopedičeský slovar'*
                      [Complete encyclopedic dictionary of Orthodox
                      theology]. 1913. Reprint ed. London: Variorum
                      Reprints, 1971.

PRE   *Realencyklopädie für protestantische Theologie und*
                       Kirche. Edited by Johann Jakob Herzog and Albert
                       Hauck. 3d ed. 21 vols. and index. Leipzig: J. C.
                       Hinrichs'sche Buchhandlung, 1896–1909.

Quasten   Quasten, Johannes, et al. *Patrology.* 4 vols. Westmin-
                       ster, Md.: Newman Press and Christian Classics,
                       1951–86.

Raby   Raby, F. J. E., ed. *The Oxford Book of Medieval Latin*
                       Verse. Oxford: Clarendon Press, 1959.

Rahner-   Rahner, Karl, and Herbert Vorgrimler. *Theological*
   Vorgrimler   *Dictionary.* Edited by Cornelius Ernst. Translated by
                       Richard Strachan. New York: Herder and Herder,
                       1965.

Rees   Rees, Thomas, tr. *The Racovian Catechism, with*
                       Notes and Illustrations. London: Longman, Hurst,
                       Rees, Orme, and Brown, 1818.

Reu   Reu, J. Michael, ed. *The Augsburg Confession: A*
                       Collection of Sources with an Historical Introduction.
                       2 vols. Chicago: Wartburg Publishing House, 1930.

Robertson   Robertson, J. N. W. B., ed. and tr. *The Acts and*
                       Decrees of the Synod of Jerusalem, Sometimes Called
                       the Council of Bethlehem, Holden under Dositheus,
                       Patriarch of Jerusalem in 1672. London: Thomas
                       Baker, 1899.

Schaff   Schaff, Philip, ed. *Bibliotheca Symbolica Ecclesiae*
                       Universalis: The Creeds of Christendom. 3 vols.
                       New York: Harper and Brothers, 1877. 6th ed., by
                       David S. Schaff. Reprint ed. Grand Rapids, Mich.:
                       Baker Book House, 1990.

Schmidt-   Schmidt, Wilhelm Ferdinand, and Karl Schornbaum,
   Schornbaum   eds. *Die fränkischen Bekenntnisse: Eine Vorstufe der*
                       Augsburgischen Konfession. Munich: Christian Kaiser
                       Verlag, 1930.

Schwartz   Schwartz, Eduard, ed. *Drei dogmatische Schriften*
                       Iustinians. Munich: Bayerische Akademie der
                       Wissenschaften, 1939.

Sophocles   Sophocles, Evangelinus Apostolides, ed. *Greek Lexicon of the Roman and Byzantine Periods (From B.C. 146 to A.D. 1100)*. Boston: Little, Brown, 1870.

Tappert   Tappert, Theodore G., Jaroslav Pelikan, Robert H. Fischer, and Arthur Carl Piepkorn, ed. and tr. *The Book of Concord: The Confessions of the Evangelical Lutheran Church*. Philadelphia: Muhlenberg Press, 1959.

Torrance   Torrance, Thomas F., ed. *The School of Faith: The Catechisms of the Reformed Church*. New York: Harper and Brothers, 1959.

Triglotta   *Concordia Triglotta*. Edited by G. Friedrich Bente. 2 vols. in 1. Saint Louis, Mo.: Concordia Publishing House, 1921.

Underhill   Underhill, Edward Bean, ed. *Confessions of Faith and Other Public Documents Illustrative of the History of the Baptist Churches of England in the Seventeenth Century*. London: Hanserd Knollys Society, 1854.

Walker   Walker, Williston, ed. *The Creeds and Platforms of Congregationalism*. [1893.] Reprint ed. Introduction by Douglas Horton. Boston: Pilgrim Press, 1960.

Wesche   Wesche, Kenneth Paul, ed. and tr. *On the Person of Christ: The Christology of Emperor Justinian*. Crestwood, N.Y.: Saint Vladimir's Seminary Press, 1991.

Will   Will, Cornelius, ed. *Acta et scripta quae de controversiis ecclesiae Graecae et Latinae saeculo undecimo composita extant*. [1861.] Reprint ed. Frankfurt: Minerva, 1963.

Williams   Williams, George Huntston. *The Radical Reformation*. 3d ed. Kirksville, Mo.: Sixteenth Century Journal Publishers, 1992.

I

Definition of Creed
and Confession

Every Sunday all over the world, millions and millions of
Christians recite or sing (or, at any rate, hear) one or another creed, and most of them have had a creed spoken
over them, or by them, at their baptism. Therefore we
all know what a creed is—as long as no one asks us to
define it (as Augustine once said about time).[1] But used with *creed* or
confession, the verb *define* [Latin *definire,* Greek *horizein*] or the noun
definition [*horos* in Greek] is, in the first instance, a technical term for
the process of legislating what the church is required to believe, teach,
and confess;[2] *ho horos tēs pisteōs* is even translated in a standard lexicon of Byzantine Greek as "the confession (rule) of faith, the creed."[3]
The Third Council of Constantinople in 680–81, which was the sixth
of the ecumenical councils, spoke of itself as "defining in unison [*sym-
phōnōs horizousa*],"[4] and Pope Pius XII in 1950 announced the bodily
assumption of the Virgin Mary as a teaching that "we pronounce, declare, and define [*pronuntiamus, declaramus et definimus*]."[5] Councils
and popes also use the term to refer to promulgations by their predecessors, as when the third ecumenical council, the Council of Ephesus
in 431, spoke of the creed "which was defined [*horistheisan*] by the holy
fathers who were gathered together in the Holy Spirit at Nicaea" at
the first ecumenical council, in 325.[6] In that technical sense, definition

1. Augustine *Confessions* 11.13.17 (*NPNF*–I 1:168).
2. Lampe, 973–75; Blaise-Chirat, 247. See also chapter 7.3 below, "Creeds and
Confessions as Instruments of Concord."
3. Sophocles, 819.
4. *CP III.*
5. *Munif* 44; see also, for example, *Unam* 8.
6. *Eph 431.*

presupposes at least two necessary conditions: the definability of the doctrine being propounded, that is, its verification by Scripture and/or tradition;[7] and the competency of the defining authority to issue a binding statement of faith and doctrine.[8] This technical use and meaning of "the *definition* of creed and confession" plays a continuing role in this historical introduction as well as throughout the texts collected in the volumes of *Creeds and Confessions of Faith in the Christian Tradition*, sometimes in their titles.[9]

But the chief purpose of speaking about the *definition* of creed and confession in the introduction to this volume, which is in turn intended to serve as an introduction both to the study of Christian creeds and confessions as such and, more specifically, to an entire collection entitled *Creeds and Confessions of Faith in the Christian Tradition*, is the more elementary one of trying to identify with some precision just what a *creed* or a *confession* is and just what its language means.[10] Although there is a considerable overlapping between these two terms, also in the usage of the churches and in the nomenclature of the texts appearing in *Creeds and Confessions of Faith in the Christian Tradition*, the word *creed* is defined by *Merriam-Webster's Collegiate Dictionary* as "a brief authoritative formula of religious belief," and the word *confession* as "a formal statement of religious beliefs"; as far as possible, that distinction is observed here. In fact, however, a Christian creed or confession of faith, like the Christian church to which it belongs and the Christian tradition of which it is a primary expression (though by no means the sole expression), is easier to describe than it is to define. Therefore what has been said of the term *church*, that "it is impossible to start with a formal definition" because this must follow from a consideration of ecclesiology rather than precede it,[11] would apply as well to *creed* and *confession of faith*, which could best be defined only a posteriori, after creeds and confessions of faith from twenty centuries have been examined.

7. *Chr Trad* 5:247–52; O'Gara 1988.
8. *Chr Trad* 4:50.
9. For example, *Chal*.
10. Mananzan 1974 raises these questions in the context of linguistic philosophy.
11. Florovsky 1972–89, 1:57.

Nevertheless, to start with a "working definition" or at any rate a "working description" as distinct from such a "formal definition," the formulations of several standard theological reference works —two of them Roman Catholic, two Eastern Orthodox, two Anglican, and two Protestant—may be helpful:

> **Creed, Confession of Faith:** In theological usage this term does not primarily mean the act of confessing the faith but a series of propositions in which the magisterium and Tradition have sought to provide a more or less complete formulation of the content of faith. This is also called a profession of faith or *symbolum*.[12]

> **Confessions of Faith:** Verbal confessions of faith can take on multiple forms, but there is one form that is privileged in certain formularies, called "symbols of faith" or "credo," . . . which present the three "articles of faith" concerning, respectively, the Father, the Son, and the Holy Spirit.[13]

> The creed is an exposition, in few but precise words, of that doctrine which all Christians are bound to believe.[14]

> **Symbol, Symbol of Faith:** Because of the Western custom of designating the confessions of faith as "symbols," the word "symbol" came into use in application to what in the Greek East was called "the teaching of the faith."[15]

> **Creed:** A creed is a concise, formal, and authorized statement of important points of Christian doctrine.[16]

> For hundreds of years Christians have been accustomed to understand by the word *creed* a fixed

12. Rahner-Vorgrimler, 111.
13. Lacoste, 248.
14. *Russ Cat* 66.
15. *Prav Slov* 2:2056–59.
16. *ODCC* 430.

formula summarizing the essential articles of their religion and enjoying the sanction of ecclesiastical authority. . . . an official, textually determined confession of
faith.[17]

Creeds of Christendom: Historically considered,
creeds are convenient summaries arising out of definite
religious situations, designed to meet urgent contemporary needs, and serving as tests of orthodoxy. Therefore they are inadequate in new crises and unable to
secure uniformity of belief.[18]

Confession of Faith: In confession, the Christian community gives its expression to God's saving action and
fellowship with Christ. . . . Through confession, faith
in Jesus Christ takes a binding communal form, even
as it includes personal confession.[19]

As these various definitions indicate, two of the earliest technical terms employed by Christian writers to identify such creeds and
confessions of faith were "symbol [Greek *symbolon*, Latin *symbolum*]"
and "rule of faith [Greek *kanōn tēs pisteōs*, Latin *regula fidei*]," both of
which are still part of the Eastern Orthodox and the Roman Catholic
theological vocabularies. Nevertheless, to avoid the kind of misunderstanding that inevitably resulted when Johann Adam Möhler's pioneer-
ing *Symbolik*[20] was translated into English in 1843 under the title *Sym-
bolism*, it is usually preferable to render the Greek word *symbolon* or
the Latin word *symbolum* with the English word *creed* rather than with
symbol. As for the term "rule of faith," the confessions of the Protestant
Reformation, because of the debates over the relation between the authority of Scripture and the authority of church and tradition, tended
to restrict the term in the precise sense to Scripture.[21] But even there,

---

17. Kelly, 6–7.
18. Ferm 1945, 208 (Conrad Henry Moehlman).
19. *EC* 1:632 (Hans G. Ulrich).
20. Möhler [1832] 1958.
21. *Form Conc Epit* pr 1; *West* 1.2; see chapter 5.4 below, "Confessional Rules of
Biblical Hermeneutics," and Syndogmaticon 1.4.

the rise of the requirement of confessional subscription within Protestantism significantly modified this exclusivism of the principle of *sola Scriptura*.[22]

22. See chapter 9.4 below, "Confessional Subscription as Legal Compliance."

CHAPTER ONE

Continuity and Change in Creeds and Confessions

THE OVERWHELMING IMPRESSION that any new reader will carry away from reviewing any of the collections of creedal and confessional texts from various historical periods listed above under "Editions, Collections, and Reference Works," or the volumes of *Creeds and Confessions of Faith in the Christian Tradition,* must surely be their sheer repetitiveness. Above all the creeds from the period of the early church, and then once again, though this time at much greater length, the confessions from the age of the Protestant Reformation, do seem to be making the same points over and over and over again, often in the same esoteric and archaic terminology, citing the same biblical passages as proof texts, and pronouncing the same condemnations upon the same old heresies (or upon each other's new heresies)—and all with the same sense of total self-confidence and utter rectitude. Not only are they constantly making tacit or overt cross-references to one another, in substantiation or in refutation as the case may be. But the differences between them, which came out of theological controversy and which went on to spawn still further theological controversy (and then, of course, to generate still further creeds and confessions, seemingly ad infinitum), must at least sometimes seem to any modern reader to be so minute as well as so marginal that only a specialist in historical theology would be able to tell the various confessional positions apart or, for that matter, would even be interested enough to care to do so. That impression is no less forceful even when such a reader happens to be a serious Christian believer, who cares deeply about the integrity of Christian faith and teaching.

Such repetitiveness is, of course, no accident. It is intended to condemn those who "rashly seek for novelties and expositions of another faith,"[1] and above all to document—even actually to celebrate— the continuity of these creeds and confessions of faith not only with the other orthodox creeds and confessions that have preceded them but above all with what is cherished as the authentic apostolic tradition. In the opening words of his *Ecclesiastical History,* Eusebius of Caesarea, the first historian of the church and himself the source for an important creed (preserved by Athanasius),[2] calls this tradition "the successions from the holy apostles [*tas tōn hierōn apostolōn diadochas*]."[3] As the use of Eusebius by later confessions suggests,[4] this phrase probably refers in the first instance to the linear succession of the bishops of the church through their predecessors all the way back to the original twelve apostles, for which he himself provides some of the most important historical documentation, specifically for the diocese of Rome and the diocese of Alexandria.[5] But his interest throughout the *Ecclesiastical History* is not only in these lists of bishops but also in the interrelations between the two concerns that a later chapter of this book, following ecumenical precedent, calls "faith" and "order," the apostolic teaching of the church and the apostolic structure of the church.[6] For as the bishops who stand in the legitimate apostolic succession, according to Eusebius, are charged with responsibility for preserving and defending the true and apostolic faith of the church, so also the apostolic order of the church serves as a sign of the integrity of its faith and doctrine.[7] Thus Eusebius's *Ecclesiastical History* is setting forth in narrative form an understanding of the relation between faith and order that was widely held throughout the early centuries of the church.[8] Throughout the ensuing centuries, moreover, that understanding of continuity and change goes on characterizing the orthodox and catholic view of the relation between the changeless gospel and the creed. It is articulated

1. *Lat 649* anath 20.
2. *Eus.*
3. Eusebius *Ecclesiastical History* 1.1.1 (*NPNF*-II 1:81).
4. *Dosith* decr 10.
5. Eusebius *Ecclesiastical History* 4.1, 4.21 (*NPNF*-II 1:175, 198–99).
6. See chapter 4 below, "Faith and Order."
7. Eynde 1933, 180, 213.
8. See Campenhausen 1969.

epigrammatically by Charles Williams, speaking about the Council of Nicaea in 325: "The nature of the Church had not changed, and only fools suppose that it had. . . . It had become a creed, and it remained a Gospel," so that in later centuries of Christian history, he continues, "the Gospels may have been neglected but the Creed never failed."[9]

1.1. Continuity versus Change in the Decrees of the Ecumenical Councils

Underlying the creedal and conciliar definition of orthodoxy from the beginning have been three shared presuppositions: first, that there is a straight line, of the kind Williams describes, from the Gospels to the creed; consequently, second, that the true doctrine being confessed by the councils and creeds of the church is identical with what the New Testament calls "the faith which was once for all delivered to the saints";[10] and therefore, third, that continuity with that faith is the essence of orthodoxy, and discontinuity with it the essence of heresy.[11] On the basis of those presuppositions, the affirmation of creedal continuity and the repudiation of creedal novelty dominate the decrees of each of the seven councils of the ancient church that are recognized by both East and West as "ecumenical" and authoritative:[12]

Nicaea I (325).[13] Already in the issuance of the first creed or statement of faith ever officially adopted to be binding on the universal church rather than merely on a local or a regional church, the creed promulgated at the first ecumenical council, the Council of Nicaea in 325, under the watchful eye of the recently converted Emperor Constantine I, the accompanying warnings and canons make it clear that "the catholic and apostolic church anathematizes" any and all those so-called Christians who presume to deviate from this creed or who take it upon themselves to alter it.[14] Going even beyond his predecessor Constantine in backing the authority of *The Creed of Nicaea* with the police power of the Roman empire, Emperor Theodosius I in an

9. C. Williams [1939] 1956, 49, 88.
10. Jude 3.
11. See the discussion in Person 1978, and Syndogmaticon 1.5.
12. Bogolepov 1963; Huizing and Walf 1983.
13. Hefele-Leclercq, 1–I:335–632.
14. *N* anath.

edict issued on 27 February 380 equated that creed of the year 325 with the very "faith which we believe to have been communicated by the apostle Peter to the Romans and maintained in its traditional form to the present day."[15] Thereby he was ascribing to Nicene orthodoxy a massive and unbroken continuity of catholic and apostolic tradition, which went back three centuries to the authority of the prince of the apostles, Simon Peter, and through him to Christ himself,[16] and which was intended to be preserved unchanged for as many more centuries into the future as the world and the church militant might stand. Moreover, Emperor Theodosius forbade any change or deviation from this apostolic and Nicene faith, at pain of both temporal and eternal punishment.[17]

   Constantinople I (381).[18] The bishops (all of them from the East) who met at Constantinople for the second ecumenical council in 381, the year following this edict of Emperor Theodosius, warned no less solemnly in their first canon against changing or tampering with *The Creed of Nicaea:* "The profession of faith of the holy fathers who gathered in Nicaea in Bithynia is not to be abrogated, but is to remain in force [*Mē atheteisthai tēn pistin tōn hagiōn paterōn . . . alla menein ekeinēn kyrian*]."[19] But the First Council of Constantinople in 381 did not simply repeat the text of the creed that the Council of Nicaea had decreed in 325.[20] Rather, in response to the new problematics of the theological situation a half-century after Nicaea, it promulgated its own "new" creed, beginning "We believe in one God the Father allpowerful, maker of heaven and earth, and of all things both seen and unseen"; among other new clauses, this creed contained a greatly amplified confession about the Holy Spirit, and therefore a more comprehensive statement of the doctrine of the Trinity than that of Nicaea had been.[21] In scholarly usage this "new creed" is now usually labeled *The Niceno-Constantinopolitan Creed,* which is the title being followed

15. *Theodosian Code* 16.1.2.
16. Mt 16.18–19.
17. See chapter 8.2 below, "Civil Law on Adherence to Creeds."
18. Hefele-Leclercq, 2–I:1–48.
19. *CP I* can 1.
20. Lehmann and Pannenberg 1982.
21. *N-CP* 8–12.

here; the title was not contemporary to its composition but is the invention of modern studies in creedal history.[22] It might suggest, as was once supposed, that this was a simple revision and expansion by the Council of Constantinople of *The Creed of Nicaea* from 325; but there is reason to believe that it was actually an existing baptismal creed or that it was based upon one.[23] But with the important substitution (or, if it was originally a baptismal creed, the restoration), in the usage of both the East and the West, of the singular "I believe [*Pisteuō, Credo*]" for the council's original plural "We believe [*Pisteuomen*]," as well as of singulars for plurals in later verbs, and of course with the far graver substitution in the West of the formula "from the Father and the Son [*ex Patre Filioque*]" for the council's original wording, "from the Father [*ek patros*]" in speaking about the procession of the Holy Spirit,[24] it is this creed of the second ecumenical council that is usually identified as *The Nicene Creed.* Such is the title it bears not only in the service books of millions of worshipers who belong to the several major denominations that use it in their liturgies but also in the program notes read by millions of concertgoers, because of all the musical settings of the Latin mass.[25] But the universal designation of *The Niceno-Constantinopolitan Creed* (which comes from 381) as *The Nicene Creed* (as though it had come from 325) does raise the historically and theologically important question: What can be the meaning of the verb "to abide, to remain in force [*menein*]," and of the adjective "sovereign, authoritative [*kyrian*]" in this decree of Constantinople I in 381 about the decree of Nicaea I in 325, terms that would seem to pertain not only in general to the doctrinal content but precisely to the *ipsissima verba* of *The Creed of Nicaea,* when the text of *The Creed of Nicaea* has not in fact remained in force as a functioning part of Christian confession and worship and is not authoritative or even familiar at all today, except for its inclusion in one or another collection of ancient creeds such as this one?

22. See chapter 17.3 below, "The Flowering of Creedal and Confessional Scholarship in the Modern Era."
23. Kelly, 296–331.
24. See chapter 7.4 below, "The Holy Spirit of Concord and the Sacrament of Concord: Two Ironic Case Histories," and Syndogmaticon 8.6.
25. See chapter 6.3 below, "The Place of Creed in Liturgy"; and chapter 6.4 below, "Councils and Confessions on Worship."

Ephesus (431).[26] Fifty years after the First Council of Constantinople, a council met at Ephesus in 431, which after some difficulty achieved recognition (after the fact) and "reception" as the third ecumenical council.[27] That is how it is still counted also by the Oriental Orthodox "non-Chalcedonian" or "pre-Chalcedonian" churches, which do not accept the authority of the councils after Ephesus and which have conventionally, though imprecisely, been labeled "Monophysite."[28] The Council of Ephesus included in its *Acts* the *Second Letter of Cyril of Alexandria to Nestorius,* in which Cyril expresses his resolve "to remove scandals and to expound the healthy word of faith to those who seek the truth." But "the most effective way to achieve this end," Cyril continues, "will be zealously to occupy ourselves *with the words* of the holy fathers [*en tois tōn hagiōn paterōn peritynchanontes logois*], to esteem *their words,* to examine our words to see if we are holding to their faith *as it is written* [*en tēi pistei kata to gegrammenon*]."[29] These formulas are a reference not only to the orthodox and catholic tradition in general but specifically to the creed as it was legislated and set down in writing by the First Council of Nicaea in 325, and to the very words of that first creed. And the Council of Ephesus itself, under the domination of Cyril, "decreed the following: 'It is not permitted to produce or write or compose any other creed [*heteran pistin*] except the one which was defined by the holy fathers who were gathered together in the Holy Spirit at Nicaea. Any who dare to compose or bring forth or produce another creed, . . . if they are bishops or clerics they should be deposed of their respective charges, and if they are laymen are to be anathematized.'"[30] But when the Council of Ephesus nevertheless went on in its *Formula of Union* to issue an additional affirmation of its own, beginning that affirmation with the solemn formulaic term that is employed for an official creedal statement, "We confess [*Homologoumen*]," it did so directly after having said that *The Creed of Nicaea* of 325 "is sufficient both for the knowl-

---

26. Hefele-Leclercq, 2–I:287–377; Vogt 1986; Vogt 1993.
27. See chapter 9.2 below, "Reception of Creeds, Councils, and Confessions as Ratification."
28. *Com Dec.*
29. *Eph 431* ep 2; italics added.
30. *Eph 431* decr.

edge of godliness and for the repudiation of *all* heretical false teaching,"[31] which included the new "heretical false teaching" of Nestorius that had precipitated the calling of the council.[32] In spite of all these vigorous espousals of creedal continuity, the third ecumenical council is far better known for its innovative change in having, with equal solemnity and formality, added to the deposit of the church's normative teaching the identification of the Virgin Mary as Mother of God or Theotokos.[33] The application of that title to her had probably begun at least a century earlier, though in the language of prayer rather than in the language of creed;[34] the first incontestable use of it seems to be in the statement of faith coming from Alexander, bishop of Alexandria (d. 328).[35] But only at the Council of Ephesus was it made official and binding.

Chalcedon (451).[36] The Synod of Ephesus of 449 (usually called "the Robber Synod of Ephesus") had made a point of refusing to issue any new affirmation of faith. Yet the antidote to it, the Council of Chalcedon of 451, which is counted as the fourth ecumenical council, is probably known best for having issued another "new creed," *The Definition of Faith of the Council of Chalcedon,* which would determine the shape of the doctrine of the person of Christ for the next fifteen centuries in both East and West.[37] Nevertheless Chalcedon, too, declared that in the area of creedal faith "preeminence belongs [*prolampein*] to the exposition of the right and spotless creed of the 318 saintly and blessed fathers who were assembled at Nicaea when Constantine of pious memory was emperor; and that those decrees also remain in force which were issued at Constantinople by the 150 holy fathers in order to destroy the heresies then rife and to confirm *this same* catholic and apostolic creed." There follow the texts both of *The Creed of Nicaea* and of *The Niceno-Constantinopolitan Creed;* and just

31. *Eph 431 Form Un;* italics added.
32. Lebedev 1904, 166–200.
33. See also chapter 12.2 below, "Popular Religion, the Rule of Prayer, and Tradition."
34. See chapter 12.1 below, "What Did the Laity Believe, Teach, and Confess?"
35. *Alex.*
36. Hefele-Leclercq, 2–II:649–857; Grillmeier and Bacht 1951–54; Gregorios, Lazareth, and Nissiotis 1981; Oort and Roldanus 1997.
37. See chapter 7.3 below, "Creeds and Confessions as Instruments of Concord."

as it is to the incorporation of *The Creed of Nicaea* in the *Acts* of the
Council of Ephesus of 431 that we owe what is generally regarded as
the most authoritative text of that creed, so it is likewise to the decrees of Chalcedon that we owe the preservation of the standard text of
The Niceno-Constantinopolitan Creed, because of the fate that befell the
manuscripts of the *Acts* of Constantinople I.[38] But it should be noted
that after reciting both of these creeds and calling them "the same [*ta
auta*]" in the plural, the decree of Chalcedon uses the singular, not
the plural, to declare, evidently referring thereby to the two together:
"This wise and saving creed [*symbolon*], the gift of divine grace, was
sufficient for a perfect understanding and establishment of religion."[39]
The two creeds, those of the Council of Nicaea from 325 and of the
Council of Constantinople I from 381, could be, and are, designated
by the most important successor of these two councils, the Council of
Chalcedon in 451, as though they were one and the same single *symbolon.* At the same time, it was not a "new" action but a repetition
of the decree of the second ecumenical council, when Chalcedon declared the see of Constantinople as "New Rome" to stand alongside
the see of Old Rome in church authority, on the grounds "that the city
which is honored by the imperial power and senate and enjoying [civil]
privileges equalling older imperial Rome, should also be elevated to
her level in ecclesiastical affairs and take second place after her."[40] This
decree, usually cited in the literature as the twenty-eighth canon of the
Council of Chalcedon rather than as also a canon of the First Council
of Constantinople, has remained highly controversial in the conflicts
over jurisdiction and primacy between East and West, to the point that
at Florence in 1439 the formula for reunion between Rome and the Armenians included the assertion that it was "by authority of Leo, bishop
of this holy see," that the Council of Chalcedon met."[41]

Constantinople II (553).[42] Without in any way contradicting the
decree of Chalcedon that equates the creeds of Nicaea and of Con-

38. Kelly, 296–331.
39. *Chal* def.
40. *Chal* can 28.
41. *Flor Arm* 9. See chapter 4.2 below, "Doctrines of Church Order East and
West."
42. Hefele-Leclercq, 3–II:1–156.

stantinople, the fifth ecumenical council, the Second Council of Constantinople in 553, produced a somewhat more nuanced formulation. Following upon *The Edict of Justinian* issued two years earlier,[43] this council met to condemn "the Three Chapters"—Theodore of Mopsuestia, source for an orthodox creed closely resembling *The Niceno-Constantinopolitan Creed*,[44] Theodoret of Cyrrhus, and Ibas of Edessa—who were being defended by Facundus of Hermiane.[45] Unfortunately, the only relatively complete text of it to have survived has come down to us in an ancient Latin version rather than in the original Greek, even though, once again, almost all the bishops attending the council were from the East. Constantinople II declared: "When we met together, we first of all made a confession of the faith [*congregati ante omnia compendiose confessi sumus fidem illam tenere*]. . . . We confessed that we believe, protect, and preach to the churches that confession of faith which was set out at greater length by the 318 holy fathers who met in the council at Nicaea and handed down the holy doctrine or creed [*sanctum mathema sive symbolum*]." Significantly, the Latin version uses not native Latin words but two technical terms of Greek theology, *mathēma* and *symbolon*,[46] which, it seems safe to presume, appeared in the lost Greek original of the decree and were transliterated rather than translated in the surviving Latin text. The decree of the council continues: "The 150 [bishops] who met in council at Constantinople also set out the same faith and made a confession of it [*eamdem fidei confessionem*]"; this time, however, the translation from Greek employed Latin terminology.[47]

　　Constantinople III (680-81).[48] The sixth ecumenical council, the Third Council of Constantinople in 680–81, was convoked to deal with the question of whether Christ had two wills (one for his divine nature and one for his human nature) or a single will (for his one divine-human person). It grounded its condemnation of the heresy of Monothelitism ("a single will") in the precedent of the formula of the Coun-

---

43. *Edict*.
44. *Thdr Mops*.
45. *Fac*.
46. Lampe, 819, 1282.
47. *CP II*.
48. Hefele-Leclercq, 3–I:472–538.

cil of Chalcedon in 451 about two natures, with the will being seen as
a function of the nature or *physis* and therefore dual rather than as a
function of the person or *hypostatis* and therefore single. *The Exposition
of Faith* of this sixth ecumenical council pledges its allegiance to the
doctrinal and creedal decrees of each of the five preceding ecumenical
councils one by one, "following without deviation in a straight path
after the holy and accepted fathers [*tēi tōn hagiōn kai enkritōn paterōn
aplanōs eutheiai tribōi katakolouthēsasa*]." Then, just as Chalcedon did
in 451, it specifies *The Creed of Nicaea* of 325 and *The Creed of Constantinople* of 381 as "the creed," once again employing the noun in
the singular and once again reciting both creeds, with the declaration:
"This pious and orthodox creed of the divine favor was enough for a
complete knowledge of the orthodox faith and a complete assurance
therein [*eis entelē tēs orthodoxou pisteōs epignōsin te kai bebaiōsin*]."[49]
Therefore the condemnation of Monothelitism, although it does not
appear as such in any of the earlier dogmatic legislation (whether or
not it may properly be seen as implicit in *The Definition of Faith of
Chalcedon*), is being presented as no more than a component part of
"following without deviation" the creed and the decrees of the first five
councils.

　　Nicaea II (787).[50] Although the agenda of the seventh ecumenical council, which met at Nicaea in 787 to restore images to the
worship of the church after they had been condemned and abolished
(and virtually annihilated) by iconoclasm, was addressing a question
that was seemingly quite different from the trinitarian and the christological issues that had been considered by the first six councils, it declared it to be its aim

> that the divinely inspired tradition of the catholic
> church should receive confirmation by a public decree.
> So having made investigation with all accuracy and
> having taken counsel, setting for our aim the truth, *we
> neither diminish nor augment, but simply guard intact
> [ouden aphairoumen, ouden prostithemen, alla . . . dia-*

49. *CP II* ecth.
50. Hefele-Leclercq, 3–II:741–98.

phylattomen] all that pertains to the catholic church. Thus, following the six holy universal synods, in the first place that assembled in the famous metropolis of the Nicaeans, and then that held after it in the imperial, God-guarded city [Constantinople].

Then follows the recitation of *The Niceno-Constantinopolitan Creed,* which is followed in turn by a catalog of the heresies, beginning with "Arius and those who think like him and share in his mad error" and continuing with the heresies anathematized by the five councils held in the four and a half centuries between Nicaea I and Nicaea II: "To summarize, we declare that we defend free from any innovations [*akainotomētous*] all the written and unwritten ecclesiastical traditions that have been entrusted to us." Among the traditions that are almost completely "unwritten," the council fathers include "the production of representational art," which is justified on the ground that "it provides confirmation that the becoming man of the Word of God was real and not just imaginary."[51] On the basis of the traditional principle enunciated by Gregory of Nazianzus, "That which [the divine Logos] has not assumed [in the incarnation] he has not healed [in the redemption] [*to gar aproslēpton atherapeuton*],"[52] that insistence on the genuineness and the integrity of the human nature of Christ was, in its own right, the thrust of the actions of the three preceding councils in their successive rejections of the teachings that the humanity of the incarnate Logos possessed either a "nature" (Chalcedon) or a "will" (Constantinople II) or an "action [*energeia*]" (Constantinople III) that was, as a consequence of the incarnation, different from the nature or will or action of the human race he came to save. For, in the words of *The Definition of Faith of Chalcedon,* "at no point was the difference between the natures taken away through the union, but rather the property of both natures is preserved."[53] At Constantinople II and Constantinople III the same had been said to be true of the difference between the wills and of the difference between the actions. From an application of this conciliar and creedal affirmation to the challenge now being posed by

51. *Nic II;* italics added. Giakalis 1994; Syndogmaticon 8.10.
52. Gregory of Nazianzus *Epistles* 101 (*NPNF*-II 7:440); see Wiles 1968.
53. *Chal* 19–20.

iconoclasm it necessarily follows, according to the Second Council of Nicaea, that this "real and not imaginary" humanity of the incarnate Logos can, and should, be depicted in the "representational art" of the icons that are part of the church's worship, even though none of the decrees of the preceding six councils had ever drawn such an inference in so many words.

At the end even of this brief recital of conciliar decrees, the question remains: Just what can the decrees of these seven ecumenical councils claim to be doing when they, at one and the same time, affirm an unchanged and unchangeable continuity, which is embodied above all in the very text of the creed adopted by the Council of Nicaea in 325, and yet repeatedly manifest such a remarkable capacity for change? This is demonstrated in the legitimation of sacred images by the Second Council of Nicaea in 787, but perhaps the most dramatically when *The Formula of Union of the Council of Ephesus* forbids "produc[ing] or writ[ing] or compos[ing] any other creed except the one which was defined by the holy fathers" in *The Creed of Nicaea*,[54] and nevertheless decrees the formula calling the Virgin Mary "Theotokos," which John Henry Newman acknowledges to have been "an addition, greater perhaps than any before or since, to the letter of the primitive faith."[55]

1.2. Patristic Thought on Continuity and Change

Yet the same development of the first seven ecumenical councils from Nicaea I in 325 to Nicaea II in 787 that raises this question of change and continuity in creeds also provides some of the historical resources that are needed for beginning to formulate an answer to it. For in one form or another, the relation between continuity and change has been a central concern of Christian thought from the beginning. All four evangelists, and above all Matthew, take great pains, in their descriptions of the events that have constituted what the apostle Paul calls "the *new* covenant,"[56] to affirm the continuity of the life and message of Jesus Christ with the revelation that had been given to Moses and

54. *Eph 431 Form Un;* see Marx 1977, 183–202.
55. Newman [1845] 1974, 319.
56. 1 Cor 11.25; italics added.

the prophets as part of the *old* covenant with Israel. Near the beginning of the Gospel according to Matthew, for example, a divine oracle in the book of the prophet Hosea, "Out of Egypt have I called my son," which, as the second half of a parallelism that begins with "When Israel was a child I loved him," clearly refers originally to the exodus from Egypt of the people of Israel as the "son" of God,[57] is applied, with the formula "This was to fulfil what the Lord had spoken by the prophet," to the flight of Jesus, Mary, and Joseph to Egypt to prevent King Herod from murdering the infant Christ.[58] In some passages such as this one, it is at least possible to conclude from the Greek conjunction *hina* not only that a prediction or a promise given long ago by the prophets of Israel has now been fulfilled but that the very purpose of the New Testament event was to carry out the Old Testament prophecy and thus to vindicate the faithfulness of God.[59] Near the end of his Gospel, therefore, Matthew describes Jesus as reacting to the effort of the disciples to spring to his defense against the arresting mob in the garden of Gethsemane by asking, "How then would the Scriptures be fulfilled, that it must be so?"[60]

The apostle Paul, above all in chapters 9 through 11 of his Epistle to the Romans, strives to establish both continuity and change between the two covenants, the covenant with Israel and the covenant with the church, characterizing the permanent place of the people of Israel within the divine economy, also after the coming of Jesus Christ, in language so strong that New Testament scholars are still struggling to come to terms with it.[61] The locus of continuity is the covenant with Israel: the coming of Jesus as the promised Messiah means not that Israel is being called upon to relinquish its covenant but that the Gentiles are being called to participate in that ancient and continuing covenant of God with Israel. The question of the relation between continuity and change becomes, if anything, even sharper in the dramatic narrative of the Book of Acts, which begins with its opening chapter in Asia, in Jerusalem, and concludes with its closing chapter in

57. Hos 11.1.
58. Mt 2.15.
59. Blass-Debrunner, 186–88.
60. Mt 26.54.
61. Stendahl 1976, 1–77.

Rome, in Europe.[62] In its one-sentence summary of what was preserved during the transition from the generation of the original disciples of Jesus to the generation that followed it as this generation was eventually represented by Paul, and what would be preserved also by all succeeding generations of the church, "And they remained faithful to the apostles' teaching and fellowship, to the breaking of bread and the prayers,"[63] the connections among those four constituent elements of faithfulness and continuity are not defined with any precision. Rather, they are left to the subsequent history of the church to make more specific through various "apostolic" structures of tradition, including eventually the creeds as well as the apostolic ministry, apostolic worship, and the apostolic writings that would ultimately be collected into the New Testament.[64]

The immediately ensuing battles with Marcion, with the Gnostics, and with the Montanists during the second and third centuries each raised the question of continuity and change in some fundamental way. With his exclamation "O wonder of wonders, . . . that one cannot compare the gospel with anything else!"[65] Marcion affirmed the utter novelty of the Christian message by denying the continuity of the Father of Jesus Christ with the Creator God of Israel, of the New Testament with the Old, of Paul with the (other) apostles, and of Luke with the (other) Gospels. The Gnostics posited a radical discontinuity between the common faith of the church and their "higher" understanding of divine mysteries. And the Montanists laid claim to the presence of the Paraclete and Counselor promised by Christ in the Gospel of John,[66] a presence that was denied to other so-called Christians. In response to these challenges to continuity, it fell to several of the ante-Nicene church fathers of the second and third centuries, among whom Ignatius of Antioch and then Irenaeus of Lyons were the most systematic spokesmen for the emerging creedal tradition,[67]

---

62. See chapter 11.1 below, "Cultus, Code, and Creed Across Cultural Boundaries."
63. Acts 2.42 (RSV plus NJB).
64. See chapter 13 below, "Rules of Faith in the Early Church."
65. Quoted in Harnack [1924] 1960, 2:256.
66. Jn 14.26, 15.26.
67. *Ign; Iren.*

to articulate the "criteria of apostolic continuity" in a form that was to go on being normative throughout the history of the church.[68] It is, nevertheless, only in the fourth century, after the recognition of the church by Constantine and after the Council of Nicaea, that the full implications of continuity-with-change are drawn for each of the four criteria of apostolic continuity in the passage quoted from the second chapter of Acts: doctrine, fellowship, the breaking of bread, and the prayers. In that century, the formulation of continuity and change quoted earlier from the opening words of the first church history by Eusebius of Caesarea, "the successions from the holy apostles,"[69] sets this apostolic continuity into conscious opposition with the "novelty-mongering [*kainotomia*]" of the Gnostics and other heretics.[70] Following up on that opening formulation, the entire *Ecclesiastical History* of Eusebius is concerned to document several kinds of continuity: in the various episcopal sees, for which he produces lists of bishops on which historians are still dependent; in the "catechetical school" of Alexandria, directed by a succession of theologians from Pantaenus to Clement to Origen;[71] and in the orthodox doctrines of the church, in spite of Eusebius's own deviation, as a Semi-Arian, from what comes to be formulated as orthodox teaching.[72]

This widely held view, that in a basic sense it is heresy rather than a changeless orthodoxy that has experienced development by a movement through time, has led to at least one lamentable by-product. As a result of it, we are in some sense far better informed by the documents of the church about the history of heresy during the first three centuries of the church than we are about the history of orthodoxy and its creeds during that same period—and this in spite of the almost total disappearance of the writings of the heretics themselves, which later historians are compelled to try to reconstruct on the basis of the lengthy but not always fair or representative quotations from them in the polemics of the orthodox heresiologies.[73] This imbalance between

---

68. *Chr Trad* 1:68–120.
69. Eusebius *Ecclesiastical History* 1.1.1 (*NPNF*-II 1:81).
70. Lampe, 693.
71. Eusebius *Ecclesiastical History* 5.10–11, 6.6 (*NPNF*-II 1:224–26, 253–54).
72. *Ant 341*.
73. Quasten, 1:256.

the history of heresy and the history of orthodoxy has been perpetuated in the work of many modern historians. In the nineteenth century, Ferdinand Christian Baur made the diversity of Christian teaching from its beginnings, as evidenced by the conflict between Peter and
Paul, the basis for a brilliant and profoundly influential reinterpretation of the history of the early church.[74] A century later, the work of
Walter Bauer concentrated on heresy and diversity in the first century,
sometimes stimulating among scholars and theologians a greater interest in these movements of thought than in what was to emerge as the
normative creedal doctrine of the catholic church.[75]

1.3. The Doctrine of the Trinity as Example
of Continuity and of Change

Nevertheless it would be quite superficial to conclude from this, as
some historians and theologians have, that none of the Christian writers and defenders of conciliar creeds in the fourth and following centuries, in their static concern for what Eusebius called "the successions
from the holy apostles," were paying any attention at the same time to
the dynamics of this issue of continuity and change. For the doctrines
legislated in the creeds and decrees of all of the first seven ecumenical councils just reviewed, first the dogma of the Trinity (at Nicaea I
in 325 and Constantinople I in 381) and then the related but distinct
dogma of the person of Jesus Christ (at Ephesus in 431, Chalcedon
in 451, Constantinople II in 553, and Constantinople III in 680–81)
and its application to the question of images at Nicaea II in 787, are
not only the dogmatic foundation for what was to become orthodox
worship and orthodox confession in both East and West ever since.
They are also a key to the early Christian interpretation of the relation between continuity and change in the creed and confession of the
church, thus of an understanding not only of the movement through
time that heresy has taken, as the concentration of many of the sources
on this issue might suggest, but especially of the historical course that
orthodoxy has taken.

74. Hodgson 1966.
75. Bauer 1971.

Much of the creedal history of the fourth century, exempli-
fied in *The Creed of the Dedication Synod of Antioch* of 341[76] and the
equally controversial synods of Sirmium,[77] can be read as an effort to
confront this very question of continuity and change in the doctrine
of the Trinity, as it was raised by the development and change that
went beyond the original *Creed of Nicaea* of 325. The language of *The
Creed of Nicaea*, for example, uses more or less as synonyms the Greek
technical terms *ousia* ["essence," "being," or "substance"] and *hypostasis* [sometimes rendered in English as "subsistence" or as "person"],
in its condemnation of those who teach that the Son of God is "from
another hypostasis or substance [*ex heteras hypostaseōs ē ousias*]."[78] It
is a principal contribution of the fourth-century debates, and of the
participation in them of "the three Cappadocians" (Basil of Caesarea,
Gregory of Nazianzus, and Gregory of Nyssa), to both the trinitarian
conceptualization and the trinitarian vocabulary of subsequent generations and creeds that, by contrast with this apparently nontechnical
sense of the two words, they introduce a greater measure of precision
by distinguishing between them and reserving *ousia* for the One and
hypostasis for each of the Three: *mia ousia, treis hypostaseis,* as the language of church and creed goes on affirming ever after.[79] The continuity and change in technical terminology was subsequently to become
an even more daunting assignment for the Councils of Ephesus, Chalcedon, Constantinople II, and Constantinople III, as they wrestled with
the ever greater terminological complexities of the doctrines of two
natures [*physeis*], then of two wills [*thelēmata*], and then of two activities [*energeiai*] in the one person or hypostasis of Christ the God-man
and incarnate Logos. But well beyond that, the most problematic substantive change beyond Nicaea was the doctrine of the Holy Spirit.
The problem begins with the confusion over the language of the New
Testament about the Holy Spirit, for example, Paul's puzzling identification of "the Lord [*ho kyrios*]," which is usually a title for the Son,
with "the Spirit [*to pneuma*]";[80] and the confusing usage continues dur-

76. *Ant 341.*
77. *Sirm 357; Sirm 359.*
78. *N* anath.
79. Prestige 1956, 179–96.
80. 2 Cor 3.17.

ing the centuries before Nicaea.[81] The Council of Nicaea itself did not
move much beyond that. At the council the issue raised by Arianism is
taken to be, in Adolf von Harnack's classic formulation, "Is the Divine,
which has appeared upon the earth and reunited man with God, identical with the highest divine Being who rules heaven and earth, or is
the same semi-divine?"[82] Clarifying both the doctrine about God the
Father and the doctrine about the Son of God, therefore, *The Creed
of Nicaea* specifies that the Son is "God from God, light from light,
true God from true God, begotten not made, consubstantial with the
Father."[83] But there is nothing about the Holy Spirit to correspond to
these clauses, simply the five words: "and in the Holy Spirit [*kai eis
to hagion pneuma*],"[84] by contrast, for example, with the more ample
statement about the Holy Spirit in *The Apostolic Constitutions* from the
second half of the fourth century.[85] The historical consequence was—
to quote not the relativistic judgment of some modern historian of doctrine but the quite surprising statement of Gregory of Nazianzus surnamed "the Theologian," one of "the Three Hierarchs," in his *Oration
on the Great Athanasius*—that during the quarter-century or so after
the Council of Nicaea, "to be only slightly in error [about the doctrine
of the Holy Spirit as God] was to be orthodox."[86]

Then suddenly the issue broke out. In about 360, Athanasius
wrote his *Four Letters to Serapion*.[87] A few years thereafter Gregory
of Nyssa delivered a *Sermon on the Holy Spirit* (whose authenticity
has been questioned, although it is probably his).[88] Perhaps in 375 his
brother, Basil of Caesarea, wrote the most influential of all the treatises on the subject, *On the Holy Spirit*.[89] In the second half of 380
Gregory of Nazianzus issued the fifth of his *Theological Orations*, dealing with the legitimacy of the use of the term "God" for the Holy Spirit
in spite of the absence of any unequivocal instance of such usage in the

---

81. Macholz 1902.
82. Harnack [1889–91] 1957b, 242.
83. *N* 2.
84. *N* 8.
85. *Ap Const*.
86. Gregory of Nazianzus *Orations* 21.33 (*NPNF*-II 7:279).
87. Quasten, 3:57–59.
88. Quasten, 3:259.
89. Quasten, 3:210–11.

Bible.[90] At about the same time Didymus the Blind composed a treatise *On the Holy Spirit* (in Greek, though it survives only in the Latin
translation by Jerome).[91] The Latin treatise by Hilary of Poitiers generally known as *On the Trinity* (whose original title seems to have been
On the Faith, De fide), which addressed the question of the place of
the Holy Spirit in the Trinity, was written during the years of Hilary's
exile in the East; for as has been pointed out, "only in the East could
Hilary have had any knowledge of this new question of which the West
would take cognizance only after a delay of many years."[92] And in 381,
Ambrose of Milan, with extensive borrowings from one or more of the
Greek treatises just listed, put out his own *De Spiritu Sancto*.[93] Also in
381 the First Council of Constantinople went beyond the brief formula
of Nicaea by attaching to its confession of the hypostasis of the Holy
Spirit a declaration about the procession of the Spirit from the Father,
and then a series of affirmations about the church, the sacrament of
baptism, and the Christian hope as the historical works of the Holy
Spirit, corresponding to the affirmations already made in *The Creed
of Nicaea* about the historical work of creation by the Father and the
historical work of redemption by the Son:

> And in the Spirit, the holy, the lordly and life-giving
> one, proceeding from the Father, co-worshiped and
> co-glorified with Father and Son, the one who spoke
> through the prophets; in one, holy, catholic, and apos-
> tolic church. We confess one baptism for the forgiving
> of sins. We look forward to a resurrection of the dead
> and life in the age to come. Amen.[94]

This creedal "change" resulted in the new measure of balance, if not
quite of symmetry, among the confessions of the three divine hyposta
ses that define Christian orthodoxy from then on.

At least by hindsight, it does seem necessary to ask why it took
so long before this process began. During those first three and a half

90. Quasten, 3:242.
91. Quasten, 3:87–88.
92. Quasten, 4:39–43.
93. Quasten, 4:169–70.
94. N-CP 8–12.

centuries the church was gradually drawing out the fuller implications of each of the four elements in the capsule summary quoted earlier from the second chapter of the Acts of the Apostles, "the apostles' teaching, fellowship, the breaking of bread, and the prayers."[95] That process was by no means unilinear, but involved continual struggles to find the best words for speaking what was ultimately "ineffable [*to arrēton*]" when articulating the faith of the church. The outcome of those struggles over language was highly complicated, and often almost counterintuitive. For example, a term like "fullness [*plērōma*]," which could claim impeccable credentials in key passages of the New Testament about the relation of the person of Christ to God, such as the statement of John that "from his *plērōma* have we all received, grace upon grace"[96] and that of Paul that "in him the whole *plērōma* of deity dwells bodily,"[97] nevertheless did not manage to find its way into the creeds, perhaps because of its prominence in the heretical vocabulary of the Gnostics about the divine abyss and its emanations.[98] Even the term *logos* did not make it into the creed, in spite of its prominence not only in the New Testament but in the subsequent theological development.[99] But the term *homoousios,* which had less than respectable origins and which had great difficulty shaking off an unmistakable odor of heresy, is enshrined forever in *The Creed of Nicaea* and then in *The Niceno-Constantinopolitan Creed.*[100] Yet through all of this creedal controversy about the second hypostasis of the Three, the official creedal formulation of the doctrine of the third hypostasis, the Holy Spirit, had to wait.

That phenomenon of delay and then change in the doctrine of the creeds about the Holy Spirit over a very long period of time, which refutes any static definition of the relation between continuity and change, did not remain unnoticed by the participants in the developments of the half-century between *The Creed of Nicaea* and *The*

95. Acts 2.42.
96. Jn 1.16.
97. Col 2.9.
98. Bauer-Arndt-Gingrich, 672; Lampe, 1094–95.
99. Jn 1.1–14; Bauer-Arndt-Gingrich, 477–79; Lampe, 807–11.
100. Prestige 1956, 197–218.

Niceno-Constantinopolitan Creed. Indeed, it elicited from Gregory of Nazianzus not only the admission quoted earlier, that even after the Council of Nicaea and its creed "to be only slightly in error was to be orthodox,"[101] but an interpretation of the progressive history of revelation that takes the doctrine of the Trinity both as its theological subject and as its historical modality, in a formulation that J. N. D. Kelly, a leading scholar of early creeds, has described as "a highly original theory of doctrinal development."[102] In endeavoring to explain why it is that the cardinal Christian doctrine of the Trinity, and specifically the doctrine of the Holy Spirit within the Trinity, was not revealed and set down all at once, Nazianzen contrasts this trinitarian development with the historical development of the requirements of the divine law from Moses to the New Testament:

> In the case by which I have illustrated it, the change is made by successive subtractions [for example, of circumcision and of the dietary regulations]; whereas here perfection is reached by additions. For the matter stands thus. The Old Testament proclaimed the Father openly, and the Son more obscurely. The New [Testament] manifested the Son, and suggested the deity of the Spirit. Now the Spirit himself dwells among us, and supplies us with a clearer demonstration of himself. For it was not safe, when the Godhead of the Father was not yet acknowledged, plainly to proclaim the Son; nor when that of the Son was not yet received to burden us further (if I may use so bold an expression) with the Holy Ghost; . . . but that by gradual additions, and, as David says, "goings up,"[103] and advances and progress from glory to glory,[104] the light of the Trinity might shine upon the more illuminated. For this reason it was, I think, that he *gradually* came to

101. Gregory of Nazianzus *Orations* 21.33 (*NPNF*-II 7:279).
102. Kelly 1958, 261.
103. Ps 83.6 (LXX).
104. 2 Cor 3.18.

> dwell in the disciples, measuring himself out to them
> according to their capacity to receive him.[105]

As Georges V. Florovsky has summarized this remarkable passage, "The spiritual experience of the Church is also a form of revelation."[106]

Or to put it another way: As the historical events of the life and teachings of Jesus recorded in the four Gospels provide the church with empirical information concerning the temporal and earthly career of the second hypostasis of the Trinity, on the basis of which *The Creed of Nicaea* formulates its confession about him and about the eternal and metaphysical relation of the Son to the Father as *homoousios;* so it is the events of the history of the church from the first century to the fourth century—missionary growth, persecution and martyrdom, apostasy and sainthood, orthodoxy and heresy, discipline and worship, and the consolation of the Holy Spirit in life and in death—that provide a kind of "database" concerning the temporal and earthly career of the third hypostasis, on the basis of which *The Niceno-Constantinopolitan Creed* can frame its confession about the eternal and metaphysical relation of the Holy Spirit to the Father and about the Spirit's functioning in the church. According to this statement of Gregory of Nazianzus, a failure to recognize that the tradition of divine revelation is a living reality and a dynamic force, driven by the Holy Spirit as "lordly and life-giving,"[107] is what produces heresy. But, he is arguing, the same divine logic that required a development from the doctrine of the *Logos* in the prologue of the Gospel of John to the *homoousios* of *The Creed of Nicaea* now necessitates a still further "change"—precisely in order to preserve the continuity. Or, to put the development into an even fuller context: there is obviously a radical change, but there is a no less demonstrable continuity, from the confession of the oneness of God voiced in *The Shema* of the Book of Deuteronomy to the confession of the triune oneness of God formulated in the *homoousios* of *The Nicene Creed* and *The Niceno-Constantinopolitan Creed.*[108] Thus continuity and change are to be seen not only as noncontradictory: they

---

105. Gregory of Nazianzus *Orations* 34.26 (*NPNF*-II 7:326); italics added.
106. Florovsky 1972–89, 7:156.
107. *N-CP* 8.
108. See chapter 11.4 below, "The Paradigm: *Shema* to *Homoousios*."

are to be seen as mutually supportive and as mutually affirming, by a process analogous in some respects to the transcendent *perichōrēsis* or "co-inherence" of the three divine hypostases in the Trinity.[109]

1.4. The Person of Christ as Exemplar of Continuity and of Change

Similarly, the movement that carried the dogma of the church from the consideration of the Trinity at Nicaea I and Constantinople I to the consideration of the person of Christ at Ephesus, Chalcedon, Constantinople II, and Constantinople III also implies that the doctrine of the person of Christ, like the doctrine of the Trinity, can serve as a key to the question of the relation between continuity and development. As the example of the doctrine of the Trinity, and of the Holy Spirit in the Trinity, provides Gregory of Nazianzus with the basic outline for his formulation of the doctrine of the development of doctrine, so also the identification of the person of Christ as the exemplar both of continuity and of change appears repeatedly in the *Exposition of the Song of Songs* by his fellow Cappadocian, Gregory of Nyssa. For Gregory of Nyssa, "progress [*prokopē*]" is, in its most obvious sense, a way of speaking about the movement of the human soul as it ascends to God: this "ascent [*anodos*] of the soul" he calls "progress [*prokopē*]."[110] But he is deeply concerned to insist that in speaking about it he is describing not some static condition or quiddity but a living reality that is dynamically changing and is constantly in motion. In one of the later discourses of the *Exposition of the Song of Songs*, therefore, he invokes a bold simile to make this point: as an actor changes costumes and characters, appearing now as a king and now as a commoner, so the movement of Christian virtue "from glory to glory"[111] is a genuine growth and development in relation to the changing opportunities and obligations of the Christian life; and even in the life to come it will never reach satiety.[112]

Yet even that audacious comparison does not quite measure

109. Prestige 1956, 291–300.
110. Gregory of Nyssa *Commentary on the Song of Songs* 4 (McCambley 1987, 97).
111. 2 Cor 3.18.
112. Gregory of Nyssa *Commentary on the Song of Songs* 6 (McCambley 1987, 132–33).

up to an earlier passage about *prokopē* in Nyssen's *Exposition of the Song of Songs*, citing the text in the Gospel of Luke, "And Jesus increased [*proekopten,* the verb corresponding to Gregory's noun *prokopē,* progress] in wisdom and in stature and in favor with God and men."[113] This text goes on serving as a standard proof for the growth and human development of Jesus: Augustine, quoting the creed as well, takes it as proof that Christ "not only gave the Holy Spirit as God, but also received it as man."[114] But for Gregory it becomes, as it is for his spiritual father Athanasius,[115] a demonstration not only that the dogma of the full deity of Christ is consistent with the assertion of his full and genuine humanity but that Jesus the God-man is the exemplar for all growth and development:

> The child Jesus born within us *advances by different ways* in those who have received him in wisdom, in age, and in grace. He is not the same in every person, but is present according to the measure of the person receiving him. He shows himself according to each one's capacity. He comes either as an infant, or a child advancing in age, or as one fully grown.[116]

Applied to the theologians of the church, and specifically to the history of their doctrines and to the history of the church's creeds, that christocentric definition of *prokopē* contains within it the possibility of affirming both continuity and development, and of doing so simultaneously.

But to understand this view of continuity-and-development, especially in the formulation given it by Gregory of Nyssa, it is helpful to read the theology of this fourth-century Greek theologian in the light of what has been said about a seventh-century Greek theologian and commentator on the Cappadocians, Maximus Confessor:

> It is the *idea of Revelation* which defines the whole plan

113. Lk 2.52.
114. Augustine *On the Trinity* 15.26.46 (*NPNF*-I 3:224).
115. Athanasius *Discourses Against the Arians* 3.28.50–53 (*NPNF*-II 4:421–22).
116. Gregory of Nyssa *Commentary on the Song of Songs* 3 (McCambley 1987, 86–87); italics added.

> of St. Maximus' reflections . . . . However, all the origi-
> nality and power of St. Maximus' new Logos doctrine
> lies in the fact that *his conception of Revelation is de-*
> *veloped within Christological perspectives.* . . . It is not
> that Christology is included in the doctrine of Reve-
> lation, but that the mystery of Revelation is discern-
> ible in Christology. It is not that Christ's person de-
> mands explanation, but that everything is explained in
> Christ's person—the person of the God-man.[117]

This statement that the "conception of Revelation is developed within
Christological perspectives" and that "the mystery of Revelation is discernible in Christology" should be viewed in connection with a statement quoted earlier, that "the spiritual experience of the Church is
also a form of Revelation,"[118] and with the quotation from Gregory of
Nazianzus on which that statement was a comment.[119] Taken together,
all of this suggests that the mystery of creedal continuity and the mystery of creedal development—and the mystery of how there can be both
continuity and development—are to be interpreted dialectically, in the
light of the doctrine of the person of Christ, confessed by the councils
and in the creeds, as the exemplar both of continuity and of change.

1.5. Change and the "Passing" of Creeds

The ancient problematic of change and of continuity in the history of
creeds, which has, of course, never been absent from the consciousness of those who studied that history, as for example the reflections
of Thomas Aquinas make clear,[120] moved into the center of scholarly
attention during the eighteenth and nineteenth centuries.[121] For the
purposes of this introductory chapter, three examples—all, as it happens, from British thought, although it would not be difficult to provide illustrations from elsewhere, above all from German thought and

117. Florovsky 1972–89, 9:216–17; italics original.
118. Florovsky 1972–89, 7:156.
119. Gregory of Nazianzus *Orations* 34.26 (*NPNF*-II 7:326).
120. Thomas Aquinas *Summa Theologica* 1a.36.2; see chapter 7 below, "Formulas
of Concord—And of Discord."
121. See chapter 17.3 below, "The Flowering of Creedal and Confessional Scholarship in the Modern Era."

scholarship[122]—may suffice to document the movement during those two centuries, from a static definition (and a consequent rejection) of continuity to a wistfully romantic portrayal of change and loss to an innovative effort at a redefinition of continuity that embraces change.

"The Greeks of Constantinople," according to Edward Gibbon's hostile account of what continuity meant in orthodox Christianity,

> held in their lifeless hands the riches of their fathers, without inheriting the spirit which had created and improved that sacred patrimony: they read, they praised, they compiled, but their languid souls seemed alike incapable of thought and action. Not a single idea has been added to the speculative systems of antiquity, and a succession of patient disciples became in their turn the dogmatic teachers of the next servile generation. Not a single composition of history, philosophy, or literature has been saved from oblivion by the intrinsic beauties of style or sentiment, of original fancy, or even of successful imitation. . . . The minds of the Greeks were bound in the fetters of a base and imperious superstition, which extends her dominion round the circle of profane science.[123]

That Enlightenment interpretation of the orthodox dogmatic and creedal tradition in Eastern Christendom, of which Gibbon is not the only example but is perhaps the most eloquent spokesman, was to dominate much of both Protestant and secular historiography.[124]

Being, if anything, even more aware of change and loss than Gibbon, Matthew Arnold reflected on it in his prose and in his poetry. His deeply moving lines about the ebb and flow of the tide have often been used to describe the change in modern attitudes toward religious beliefs and creeds:

122. *Chr Trad* 5:75–89, 265–81.
123. Gibbon [1776–88] 1896–1900, 6:107–8 (ch 53).
124. Benz 1952.

> The Sea of Faith
> Was once, too, at the full, and round earth's shore
> Lay like the folds of a bright girdle furl'd.
> But now I only hear
> Its melancholy, long, withdrawing roar,
> Retreating, to the breath
> Of the night-wind, down the vast edges drear
> And naked shingles of the world.[125]

Less familiar but no less apt, however, is a line from another of his poems, inspired by the reading of book 9 of Augustine's *Confessions*: "Creeds pass, rites change, no altar standeth whole."[126] The historical recognition that not only do "rites change," which anyone who knows the history of liturgies East and West has always acknowledged, and that "no altar standeth whole," which is so frequently documented in the history of modern persecution, but that "creeds pass," together with the historical description of the "melancholy, long, withdrawing roar" of that process, has been a major element in "the evolution of the historical," the modern enthronement of historical change as the primary category by which to understand doctrines and creeds, as well as many other phenomena.[127]

In that context, the *Essay on the Development of Christian Doctrine,* which was published in 1845 by Matthew Arnold's doppelgänger, John Henry Newman, represents a tour de force in the effort to capture that category of historical change for the orthodox cause and thus to vindicate creeds by the very fact that they do change. "In a higher world it is otherwise," Newman writes, "but here below to live is to change, and to be perfect [i.e., mature] is to have changed often."[128] He is speaking there about the church and its doctrine, which, he says, "changes . . . in order to remain the same," but what he says pertains also to himself. As he puts it elsewhere in defense of the changes in his religious opinions, "I have changed in many things:

125. Matthew Arnold "Dover Beach."
126. Matthew Arnold "Monica's Last Prayer."
127. Pelikan 1971, 33–67.
128. Newman [1845] 1974, 100.

in this I have not. From the age of fifteen, dogma has been the fundamental principle of my religion: I know no other religion; I cannot enter into the idea of any other sort of religion; religion, as a mere sentiment, is to me a dream and a mockery. . . . What I held in 1816, I held in 1833, and I hold in 1864. Please God, I shall hold it to the end."[129]

The chapters that follow are an introduction to the phenomenon of continuity and change in creeds and confessions over a period of twenty centuries, and the various collections and editions of creeds and confessions, including *Creeds and Confessions of Faith in the Christian Tradition,* are an extensive and detailed documentation of it: how creeds rise, and therefore also how they "pass," frequently with a "melancholy, long, withdrawing roar"—and, for that matter, how they sometimes rise again in a new form, even with what might at least occasionally be called a "triumphant, long, *returning* roar," but more often in a fashion far less dramatic but no less real.

129. Newman [1864] 1967, 54.

CHAPTER TWO

The Creedal and Confessional Imperative

CREEDS AND CONFESSIONS OF FAITH have their origin in a two-fold Christian imperative, to believe and to confess what one believes. The term *creed* comes from the first, the term *confession of faith* from the second. "Since we have the same spirit of faith as he had who wrote, 'I believed, and so I spoke,'" the apostle Paul quotes the words of the psalmist to explain to the Corinthians, "we too believe, and so we speak."[1] The English word *creed* is derived from *credo*,[2] which is the first person singular of the Latin verb for "I believe" and is the first word in the Latin text both of *The Niceno-Constantinopolitan Creed*[3] (traditionally, though not as it was originally adopted by the First Council of Constantinople in 381, which has "*We* believe") and of *The Apostles' Creed*.[4] Nevertheless, it signifies not only the isolated act or state of believing (which is never, of course, an isolated state or act at all) but, more specifically, the personal and the collective act of believing in combination with the personal and the collective act of confessing the faith that is believed.[5] It is also the apostle Paul who definitively sets down in his Epistle to the Romans, perhaps quoting an already existing Christian precreedal formula, the close correlation between these two acts of believing and confessing (with the classical literary figure of chiasm applied to the ordering of the two terms): "If you *confess* with your lips that Jesus is Lord and *believe* in your heart

1. 2 Cor 4.13; Ps 116.10.
2. *OED* 2:1156–57.
3. *N-CP* 1.
4. *Ap* 1.
5. Hein 1991.

that God raised him from the dead, you will be saved. For man *believes* with his heart and so is justified, and he *confesses* with his lips and so is saved."[6]

The confessions and the teachers of many traditions draw on these words of Paul in Romans to explain the meaning both of faith and of confession, as well as the relation between the two. Expounding the creed of the West, which he quotes in a variety of forms,[7] Augustine of Hippo opens one of his earliest treatises, *On Faith and the Creed,* with the assertion that "we cannot secure our salvation unless . . . we make our own the profession of the faith that we carry in our heart. . . . We have the catholic faith in the creed, known to the faithful and committed to memory, contained in a form of expression as concise as has been rendered admissible by the circumstances";[8] and in one of his last treatises, he defines faith as "thinking with assent [*cum assensione cogitare*]."[9] Similarly, his Western contemporary Rufinus of Aquileia points out in his commentary on the opening word of *The Apostles' Creed,* "*Credo,* I believe," that "it is only right that you should first of all confess that you believe."[10] In the East, *The Orthodox Confession of the Catholic and Apostolic Eastern Church* by *Peter Mogila* quotes these words of Paul to introduce its discussion of faith.[11] In the Lutheran confessions, they provide *The Apology of the Augsburg Confession* with the basis for its most extensive consideration of the relation between faith and confessing the faith.[12] In the Reformed confessions, they form the epigraph for *The Second Helvetic Confession* of 1556.[13] And in the confessions of Congregationalism, they are the first proof text from Scripture for *The Savoy Declaration* of 1668.[14]

6. Rom 10.9–10; italics added.
7. *No Afr.*
8. Augustine *On Faith and the Creed* 1 (NPNF-I 3:321).
9. Augustine *On the Predestination of the Saints* 5 (NPNF-I 5:499–500).
10. Rufinus *A Commentary on the Apostles' Creed* 3 (ACW 20:32).
11. *Mogila* 1.4.
12. *Apol Aug* 4.383–85.
13. Staedtke 1966, 313–15.
14. *Sav* pr.

2.1. Believing and Confessing

Believing and confessing, then, have always been correlatives:[15] a creedlike confession of the resurrection of Christ in the New Testament is followed by the formula, "So we preach and so you believed."[16] The correlation becomes clear in the reiterations and permutations of these two terms *believe* and *confess* (often in combination with the third term, *teach*, to which the next chapter will be devoted) in the language of creeds and confessions throughout Christian history. An early creedal fragment, usually assigned to the third or fourth century, opens with the words "[One] confesses the faith,"[17] and *The Western Creed of Sardica* at the middle of the fourth century, though rejected as heterodox, speaks of "the catholic and apostolic tradition and faith and confession."[18] "We believe [*Pisteuomen*]": *The Creed of Nicaea,* adopted at the first ecumenical council in 325,[19] and then *The Niceno-Constantinopolitan Creed,* associated with the second ecumenical council in 381,[20] say this as their very first word; and near its close the latter says, "We confess [*homologoumen*]."[21] At the third ecumenical council, the Council of Ephesus of 431, the formula written by Cyril of Alexandria declares "We confess [*homologountes*] the Word to have been made one with the flesh hypostatically";[22] and *The Formula of Union* of the Council of Ephesus likewise begins with the word "We confess [*Homologoumen*]."[23] *The Definition of Faith of the Council of Chalcedon* of 451 affirms that "following the saintly fathers, we all with one voice teach the confession [*homologein . . . ekdidaskomen*] of one and the same Son."[24] "If anyone will not confess [*homologei*] that the Father, Son, and Holy Spirit have one nature or substance . . . let him be anathema" is the first of *The Anathemas Against the "Three Chapters"* of the Second Council of Constantinople in 553, followed by similar formulas later

15. Arens 1989.
16. 1 Cor 15.3–11.
17. *Dêr Bal.*
18. *Sard.*
19. *N 1.*
20. *N-CP 1.*
21. *N-CP 10.*
22. *Eph 431* ep 3.
23. *Eph 431 Form Un.*
24. *Chal 1–4.*

in the *Acts* of that council and concluding with the summary: "Such, then, are the assertions we confess."[25] "When we met together," according to this council, "we first of all made a confession of the faith. . . . We confessed that we believe, protect, and preach to the churches that confession of faith which was set out at greater length by the 318 holy fathers who met in the council at Nicaea and handed down the holy doctrine or creed. The 150 [bishops] who met in council at Constantinople also set out the same faith and made a confession of it."[26] The Third Council of Constantinople of 680–81, which is numbered as the sixth ecumenical council, stated that, "following the five holy and universal synods and the holy and accepted fathers, and defining in unison, [it] professes [*homologei*]."[27] And the dogmatic decree of the seventh ecumenical council, held at Nicaea in 787 to condemn iconoclasm, reaffirms its loyalty to all six of its predecessors and to "the teaching of our holy fathers . . . , the tradition of the catholic church."[28]

Synods of the Middle Ages that were either purely Western or purely Eastern rather than ecumenical maintained this pattern of correlation between believing and confessing. *The Creed of the Eleventh Synod of Toledo* of 675, in response to recent errors in Spain,[29] reasserts the orthodox doctrine of the Trinity by opening its statement with the formula: "We confess and believe the holy and ineffable Trinity."[30] And when, four centuries later, at the Synod of Rome on 11 February 1079, *The Confession of Berengar* of Tours, obtained under duress, formulates the catholic doctrine of the real presence of the body and blood of Christ in the eucharist more precisely than any earlier official creed, confession, or council of the church ever had, it declares: "I, Berengarius, in my heart believe and with my lips confess."[31] Another century later, *The Profession of Faith of Valdes* is introduced with the formula: "Let it be known to all the faithful that I, Valdes, and all my brethren . . . believe in heart, perceive through faith, confess

25. *CP II* anath 1, 2, 8, 10, 14.
26. *CP II.*
27. *CP III.*
28. *Nic II.*
29. Cavadini 1993.
30. *Tol XI* 1.
31. *Brngr 1079.*

in speech, and in unequivocal words affirm."[32] In the East, *The Definition of the Synod of Constantinople* of 879–80, repeating *The Niceno-Constantinopolitan Creed,* declares: "This is how we affirm [*phronoumen*], and in this confession of the faith [*en tautēi tēi homologiai tēs pisteōs*] we have been baptized."[33]

With small variations, these ancient formulas of the seven ecumenical councils of the undivided church, and then, in keeping with the precedent set by them, of synods and confessions in both East and West, are followed by the later confessional statements both of Roman Catholicism and of Eastern Orthodoxy. At least on this point, the third session of the Council of Trent was speaking for this entire Western and Eastern tradition when it summarized the creedal and confessional imperative:

> That this loving care of the council may both begin and continue by the grace of God, it determines and decrees first of all to begin with a creed of the faith. In this it follows the example of the fathers of the more revered councils who, at the beginning of their proceedings, were accustomed to make use of this shield against all heresies, and in some cases by this means alone they have drawn unbelievers to the faith, defeated heretics, and strengthened the faithful. Hence the council voted that the creed which the Holy Roman Church uses as that basic principle on which all who profess the faith of Christ necessarily agree as the firm and sole foundation against which "the powers of death shall never prevail,"[34] should be expressed in the words in which it is read in all the churches.[35]

There follows the text of *The Niceno-Constantinopolitan Creed* in its *Western Recension.* At its fifth session, on 17 June 1546, *The Decree of the Council of Trent* says that it "determines, confesses, and de-

32. *Vald.*
33. *CP 879–80.*
34. Mt 16.18.
35. *Trent 3.*

clares [*statuit, fatetur ac declarat*]";[36] and, at its thirteenth session, on
11 October 1551, that it "teaches and openly and without qualification
professes."[37] Its creedal statement, *The Tridentine Profession of Faith* of
1564, opens with the formula, "I, N., with firm faith believe and profess [*firma fide credo et profiteor*] each and every article contained in the
symbol of faith which the Holy Roman Church uses," once more following this with the text of *The Niceno-Constantinopolitan Creed* in its
Western Recension.[38] *The Divine Liturgy According to Saint John Chrysostom* coordinates the two doctrines of the divinity of Christ and of
the real presence in the eucharist with the formula "I believe, O Lord,
and I confess [*pisteuō Kyrie kai homologō*]."[39] According to *The Confession of Metrophanes Critopoulos,* the sacrament of chrism confers on believers "power and boldness fearlessly and confidently to confess their
Christian faith," because "we may devoutly and correctly hold to the
faith, but if we do not confess it with boldness, we are not worthy of
the divine revelation."[40] *The Orthodox Confession of the Catholic and
Apostolic Eastern Church by Peter Mogila,* quoting the words of Romans
10.10 as cited earlier, defines "the orthodox catholic and apostolic
faith" as "to believe with the heart and confess with the mouth one
God in three persons."[41] Concerning the saints as "mediators and intercessors for us with God," *The Confession of Dositheus and of the Synod
of Jerusalem* declares that "we do not doubt, but rather unhesitatingly
believe and confess";[42] "and therefore," it summarizes its view of confessing the faith, "we are not only persuaded, but we confess as true
and undoubtedly certain, that it is impossible for the catholic church
to err, or to be deceived at all, or ever to choose falsehood instead of
truth."[43] "Let us hold fast to the confession," the Orthodox reply of
the patriarch of Constantinople accordingly admonishes his Protestant
correspondents.[44]

36. *Trent* 5.1 int.
37. *Trent* 13.1.
38. *Trid Prof* 1.
39. *Lit Chrys* 2.H.1; see *Mogila* 1.107.
40. *Metr Crit* 8.2, 9.16.
41. *Mogila* 1.4.
42. *Dosith* decr 8.
43. *Dosith* decr 12.
44. *Jer II* 1.4.

During the Reformation period, it is in the Protestant confessions of faith, more even than in the formularies of Roman Catholicism of that period, that this accent on believing and confessing, or on interpreting Scripture and "making confession," or on "believing, teaching, and maintaining,"[45] is especially prominent. *The First Helvetic Confession* of 1536 in its German text employs the formula "we confess [*bekennen wir*]," for which the Latin is "we assert [*asserimus*]."[46] *The Wittenberg Articles* of the same year declare: "We confess simply and clearly, without any ambiguity, that we believe, hold, teach, and defend."[47] *The French Confession* of 1559 begins with "We believe and confess [*Nous croyons et confessons*]."[48] *The Scots Confession* of the following year describes itself as "this brief and plain confession of that doctrine which is set before us, and which we believe and confess," and as "the confession of our faith, as in the following chapters"; and it proceeds to employ this phraseology throughout those following chapters: "We confess and acknowledge"; "We confess and believe"; "We believe and confess"; and "We affirm and avow."[49] Its supplementary confession, *The King's Confession or Second Scots Confession* of 1581, expands this phraseology to the full-blown "We believe with our hearts, confess with our mouths, subscribe with our hands, and constantly affirm before God and the whole world."[50] *The Belgic Confession* of 1561 opens with: "We all believe in our hearts and confess with our mouths."[51] The first chapter of *The Second Helvetic Confession* of 1566 begins with the words "We believe and confess [*Credimus et confitemur*]"; the third chapter begins with "We believe and teach"; and the eleventh chapter declares, "We further believe and teach" and "We believe and teach."[52] The Hussite *[Second] Bohemian Confession* of 1575 opens with the words: "We believe with our heart and confess with our mouth";[53] most of the following articles likewise open with some

45. *Fid rat* 10, con.
46. *Helv I* 20.
47. *Witt Art* 1.
48. *Gall* 1.
49. *Scot I* pr, 1, 19.
50. *Scot II.*
51. *Belg* 1.
52. *Helv II* 1.1, 3.1, 11.1, 11.11.
53. *Boh II* 1.

such formulation. Those same words open the Brownist *True Confession* of 1596.[54] The Lutheran *Formula of Concord* of 1577 repeatedly introduces its affirmations of various doctrines in successive articles with "We believe, teach, and confess."[55] The opening words of *The Reaffirmed Consensus of the Truly Lutheran Faith* of 1655 are repeated in each of its eighty-eight "points": "We profess and teach [*Profitemur et docemus*]."[56]

The Anabaptist *Hans Denck's Confession Before the Council of Nuremberg* likewise opens each article with the formula it employs at the beginning: "I, Hans Denck, confess";[57] and it concludes with the following coda: "All this I confess from the depth of my heart before the countenance of the invisible God, to whom through this confession I most humbly submit myself."[58] Almost every article of *The Mennonite Confession of Faith of Dordrecht* of 1632 invokes some variant on the formula "We believe and confess, according to Scripture."[59] Similarly, the confessions of nineteenth- and twentieth-century groups that arose outside the mainstream of Orthodox or Catholic or Protestant teaching nevertheless keep the traditional nomenclature of the creedal and confessional imperative. The confession entitled *The Fundamental Beliefs of the Seventh-Day Adventist Church,* issued in 1872, goes beyond the conventional identification of that church with the doctrine of the second coming and the doctrine of the Sabbath to include the principal components of faith and confession.[60] The Church of Christ Scientist in its *Science and Health with a Key to the Scriptures* includes a statement of 1879 with the heading: "Tenets of the Mother Church."[61] Already in 1842 the Mormons issued *Articles of Faith of the Church of Jesus Christ of Latter-Day Saints,*[62] and in 1887 the Quakers published *The Richmond Declaration of Faith of the Society of Friends.*[63] And in 1916

54. *True Conf* pr.
55. *Form Conc Epit* 1.2.
56. *Cons rep* pr, 1.1.
57. *Denck* 1.
58. *Denck* 3 con.
59. *Dordrecht* 2.
60. *Adv.*
61. *Chr Sci.*
62. *LDS.*
63. *Richmond.*

The Statement of Fundamental Truths of the Assemblies of God declares the common doctrinal faith shared by the several Pentecostal groups making up that newly created denomination.[64] *The United Church of Christ in Japan Confession of Faith* of 1954 introduces its reaffirmation of *The Apostles' Creed* with the formula: "Thus we believe, and with the saints in all ages we confess."[65] Inseparable though believing and confessing therefore are from each other in the concrete practice both of the church and of the individual, they are nevertheless distinct from each other in their meaning, already in the language of the New Testament and then in the development of the usage of the church.[66]

2.2. Faith Defined

It is a reflection of the difficulty of achieving consistency in Christian theological vocabulary to note that in contemporary English, including the English of various translations of the Bible, there is no verb that is an etymological cognate to the noun *faith*. Employing the noun, one can "have faith" or "come to faith," but the only simple verb for this is the verb *believe*. But the noun *belief* by itself does not, especially in the singular, correspond any longer to the noun *faith* as the word is used now: *The Oxford English Dictionary* rightly designates as "archaic" or "obsolete" the use of *belief* to refer to "trust in God, the Christian virtue of faith."[67] The plural *beliefs* does identify the particular tenets one believes, which, if they are the particular beliefs of some Christian orthodoxy or other (howsoever this orthodoxy may be specified by the believer or by the believer's church), may also be called "articles of faith," because of the way creeds and confessions of faith have conventionally been divided into discrete "articles": *The Apostles' Creed* into twelve, on the basis of the later tradition of its composition by the twelve apostles after the ascension of Christ; and (probably later) *The Niceno-Constantinopolitan Creed* also into twelve articles;[68] and then the Reformation confessions into many, as in the

64. *Assem.*
65. *Un Ch Japan* 5.
66. *ABD* 2:744–60 (Joseph P. Healey, Dieter Lührmann, George Howard); Cullmann 1949.
67. *OED* 1–II:782.
68. *Mogila* 1.5.

case of *The Thirty-Nine Articles of the Church of England,* preceded by *The Forty-Two Articles.*[69] The plural *faiths* now designates entire systems of belief or even what we now would call "world religions," as in "the true faith" or "the Jewish faith" or "the Christian faith."[70] The negative prefixes that are attached to these nouns add to the interest, and perhaps also to the confusion. *Unfaith* is defined as "lack of faith or belief, esp. in religion," but it is significant that fully half of the relatively few instances *The Oxford English Dictionary* provides for *unfaith* use the word as a direct antonym to the word *faith.*[71] *Unbelief,* however, is much better attested and often carries the connotation, as in a quotation provided there from Samuel Taylor Coleridge, of "heresies and unbelief."[72] Coleridge is likewise the author of the familiar phrase "willing suspension of disbelief," which, he says, constitutes "the poetic faith."[73]

Because of the debates in the Reformation confessions over the doctrine of justification by faith, it should be noted that this asymmetrical relation between the noun *faith* and the verb *believe* in English (corresponding to the asymmetrical relation between the noun *fides* and the verb *credere* in the Latin of the Vulgate and of many Western creeds and confessions, whether Protestant or Roman Catholic) is paralleled by a similarly asymmetrical relation, apparently unique to English, between the noun *righteousness* and the verb *justify* (meaning "make righteous")—two terms that reflect, respectively, the Germanic and the Latinate roots of the English language. In Greek and in Latin, the passive verbs corresponding to the nouns *dikaiosynē* and *iustitia,* *dikaiousthai* and *iustificari,* "to be justified," are perfect cognates to the nouns. In the Greek of the Bible and of the Eastern creeds and confessions, the noun for "faith," *pistis,* and the verb for "to believe," *pisteuein,* are also perfect cognates. It does perhaps deserve mention in this connection, moreover, that throughout the Gospel of John the Greek noun for "faith" never appears, only the verb for "to believe." This may seem somewhat surprising, because John's Gospel contains

69. *OED* 1–I:470.
70. *OED* 4–I:31–32.
71. *OED* 11–II:184.
72. *OED* 11–II:59.
73. Samuel Taylor Coleridge "Preface" to *Lyrical Ballads.*

what is probably the most frequently quoted verse of the Bible on the topic of faith and believing, "God so loved the world that he gave his only Son, that whoever *believes* in him should not perish but have eternal life."[74] That verse becomes part of the words of institution in the Anaphora or eucharistic prayer of the Eastern Orthodox *Divine Liturgy According to Saint John Chrysostom*.[75] The same text figures in the confessional controversies of Protestantism when the Arminian *Remonstrance* quotes it because of its apparently universalistic and therefore antipredestinarian implications,[76] which the article "Concerning Divine Predestination" of the Synod of Dort of 1618–19 denies by quoting it in support of the Calvinist doctrine.[77]

It is not surprising in the light of the emphasis on the doctrine of justification by faith that definitions of the word *faith* become a standard part of many Reformation confessions.[78] *The Geneva Confession* of 1536 describes faith as present when, "in certain confidence and assurance of heart, we believe in the promises of the gospel, and receive Jesus Christ as he is offered to us by the Father and described to us by the word of God."[79] Also coming from Swiss Protestantism, but from its German-speaking rather than its French-speaking cantons, *The First Helvetic Confession* of the same year defines it as "a sure, firm, and solid foundation for and a laying hold of all those things for which one hopes from God, and from which love and subsequently all virtues and the fruit of good works are brought forth."[80] *The Second Helvetic Confession* speaks of it as "not an opinion or human conviction, but a most firm trust and a clear and steadfast assent of the mind, and then a most certain apprehension of the truth of God presented in the Scriptures and in the Apostles' Creed."[81] *The Heidelberg Catechism* of 1563 defines it as "not only a certain knowledge by which I accept as true all that God has revealed to us in his word, but also a wholehearted

74. Jn 3.16; italics added. See, for example, *Madag* 5.
75. *Lit Chrys* F.3.
76. *Remon* 2. See also *New Hamp* 4.
77. *Dort* 1.1.2.
78. *Ans* 17.118; *18 Diss* 1; *Hub Chr Cat* 1.23. See Syndogmaticon 1.6.
79. *Genv Con* 11.
80. *Helv I* 13.
81. *Helv II* 16.1.

trust which the Holy Spirit creates in me through the gospel."[82] "By this faith," according to *The Westminster Confession of Faith* of 1647, "a Christian believeth to be true whatsoever is revealed in the word, for the authority of God himself speaking therein, and acteth differently upon that which each particular passage thereof containeth, yielding obedience to the commands, trembling at the threatenings, and embracing the promises of God for this life, and that which is to come"— all of these being functions of faith.[83] *The Westminster Shorter Catechism* of the following year defines faith in Jesus Christ as "a saving grace, whereby we receive and rest upon him alone for salvation, as he is offered to us in the gospel."[84] And *The Mennonite Short Confession of Faith* of 1610 contains the definition: "This faith is a certain heartfelt assurance or inner knowledge of God, of Christ, and other heavenly things received by grace out of the word of God."[85]

In an effort to classify these several meanings of *faith* in the language of the Bible and in the usage of the creeds and confessions of the churches, the systematic theologians of the Reformation tradition distinguish among three closely interrelated senses of the word: faith as knowledge, as assent, and as trust. It is necessary to know the doctrinal and historical content of the Christian message in at least some detail, to acknowledge that the message is true, and to have personal confidence in it as reliable in life and in death; the etymological root of the English word *confidence* is the Latin word for "faith," *fides,* and from it the verb *confidere*. When those same theologians also speak, as they do so often, about "justification *by faith*," it is chiefly the third of these, faith as trust and confidence, though of course in conjunction with a presupposed faith both as knowledge and as assent, that they have in mind—or, as *The Augsburg Confession* already puts it in 1530, "such true faith as believes that we receive grace and forgiveness of sin through Christ."[86] The definition of faith as trust also raises special questions for Calvinist confessions because of their doctrine of predestination. Defining certainty of grace and salvation as "not a bare

82. *Heid* 21.
83. *West* 14.2.
84. *West Sh Cat* 86.
85. *Ries* 20.
86. *Aug Ger* 20.23.

conjectural and probable persuasion . . . but an infallible assurance of faith," *The Westminster Confession of Faith* nevertheless insists that "this infallible assurance does not so belong to the essence of faith, but that a true believer may wait long, and conflict with many difficulties before he be partaker of it."[87] For it is experientially—as well as pastorally—obvious that not everyone who has faith attains existentially to the possession of this "infallible assurance" of having been eternally predestined to salvation; nevertheless, such Christians are not to doubt that they truly possess a saving "faith."[88]

But when these theologians of the Reformation, together with theologians of all the other Christian traditions up to the present day, speak about a "confession of *faith*," or about the creed as *fides*,[89] the chief emphasis lies on the first and second meanings of the word *faith*, faith as knowledge and faith as assent, rather than on faith as trust. So it does also in the use of the term *faith* in the title of each of the five historical chapters that form the final section of this volume (and in the heading of each of the five parts of *Creeds and Confessions of Faith in the Christian Tradition*): "Rules of *Faith* in the Early Church"; "Affirmations of *Faith* in Eastern Orthodoxy"; "Professions of *Faith* in the Medieval West"; "Confessions of *Faith* in the Reformation Era"; and "Statements of *Faith* in Modern Christianity." For each of these sets of texts, a "faith" that is confessed is an objective content, something to be learned, memorized, and known, and something to be accepted on authority, acknowledged as divine truth, and vigorously defended as such against "deniers of the faith"—as well as being of course, obviously and supremely, a personal and existential declaration of obedience and trust in God and in the revealed word of God.

Among the many references to "faith" and "believing" in the New Testament, two passages in particular stand out as documenting, and having contributed to, this "objective" or creedal and confessional sense of faith as knowledge and as assent, as distinct from the "subjective" or existential sense of faith as trust. One of the passages employs the verb with a proposition "that" something is true, the other the noun

87. *West* 18.2–3. See Syndogmaticon 11.2.
88. See chapter 12.4 below, "Code, Creed, and Folk Culture."
89. *Ad tuendam.*

with the definite article: from the Epistle of James, "You *believe* that God is one; you do well. Even the demons *believe*—and shudder";[90] and from the Epistle of Jude, "Beloved, being very eager to write to you of our common salvation, I found it necessary to write appealing to you to contend for *the faith* which was once for all delivered to the saints."[91] Neither of these passages appears as part of the two most powerful and most influential discussions of the topic of faith in the New Testament: the exposition of faith and justification in the third chapter of the Epistle to the Romans, which Reformation confessions cite over and over in support of the doctrine of justification by faith alone [*sola fide*];[92] and the "roll call of faith" in the eleventh chapter of the Epistle to the Hebrews, in which, locating Christian faith in the continuity of the first covenant with the people of God, one verse after another opens with the paean "By faith." The passage from the Epistle of James is often interpreted by New Testament scholars as having been provoked as a corrective on the Pauline explanations, in the Epistles to the Romans and to the Galatians, of the contrast between faith and works in justification, or at any rate as a corrective on how some early Christians were construing these explanations. As a result, the effort to prove, as *The Second Helvetic Confession* puts it,[93] that "James does not contradict anything in this doctrine of ours," a doctrine that is based primarily on the writings of Paul—and thus the effort to harmonize James and Paul in accordance with Reformation doctrine—becomes one of the more challenging assignments for the exegetical case being propounded in the Protestant confessions, to which, for example, *The Apology of the Augsburg Confession* devotes a lengthy dissertation.[94] In *The Orthodox Confession of the Catholic and Apostolic Eastern Church by Peter Mogila,* which is in part an Eastern Orthodox response to confessions shaped by the Protestant Reformation (including that of the sometime patriarch of Constantinople, Cyril Lucar), the first two proof texts come from James.[95] Taken together, these two statements of

---

90. Jas 2.19; italics added.
91. Jude 3; italics added.
92. *Apol Aug* 4.73; *Belg* 22; *Heid* 60; *Helv II* 15.4; *Form Conc Sol Dec* 3.12.
93. *Helv II* 15.6.
94. *Apol Aug* 4.244–53; also *Form Conc Sol Dec* 3.42–43.
95. *Mogila* 1.1.

James and Jude in the New Testament do seem to preclude any attempt
to restrict the terms *believing* or *faith* to the saving faith of the believer,
"subjective faith" as we have been calling it. For although the demons
do believe, and believe "correctly," that is to say, accurately, and could
therefore ironically be called "orthodox" in their doctrine, they are not
saved by that faith, because they have knowledge and assent but not
trust; and the faith that was "once for all delivered [*hapax paradotheisē*]
to the saints" in the past, for which it is necessary to contend against
its enemies in the present, does appear to have to be something "objective," a delivered content, what the Vulgate calls a *depositum* [*fidei*] that
needs to be guarded,[96] rather than exclusively a personal relationship
between God and the believer (which, as every believer knows from
repeated and bitter experience, also needs to be guarded no less zealously against the very same enemies). To make this distinction, it has
become customary in theological Latin to speak about this objective
faith as "the faith *which* one believes [*fides quae creditur*]" and about
subjective faith as "the faith *with which* one believes [*fides qua creditur*]." Such a clarification of terms is at work in the distinction of *The
Irish Articles of Religion* of 1615, that faith is "not only the common
belief of the articles of Christian religion, and the persuasion of the
truth of God's word in general," *fides quae creditur* as knowledge and
assent, "but also a particular application of the gracious promises of
the gospel . . . an earnest trust and confidence in God," *fides qua creditur* as trust.[97] On the basis of *The Niceno-Constantinopolitan Creed* and
of the Eastern Orthodox tradition associated with it, *The Confession of
Dositheus and of the Synod of Jerusalem* of 1672 combines the subjective
and the objective components when it defines faith as a "persuasion
within us [*en hēmin . . . hypolēpsin*]," but also specifies that this "persuasion" is to be *orthotatēn,* "as this is contained in the creed of the
first and the second ecumenical council."[98] Unlike Latin, which lacks
a definite article, present-day English has incorporated this distinction
into its usage by employing the definite article for the *fides quae creditur,* the faith which one believes, and calling it "*the* faith," as in the

96. 1 Tm 6.20 (Vulg); 2 Tm 1.14 (Vulg).
97. *Irish* 37. See Syndogmaticon 1.1, 1.6.
98. *Dosith* decr 9.

words of the Epistle of Jude, "*the* faith which was once for all delivered to the saints";[99] but it refers to *fides qua creditur,* faith with which
one believes, without an article, simply as "faith," as in the words of
the Epistle to the Romans, "a man is justified by faith."[100]

Reflecting their provenance in the catechetical and baptismal
pedagogy of the first Christian centuries, many of the earliest creedal
fragments that culminate in *The Apostles' Creed* are cast in the form of
question and answer: "Do you believe? I believe."[101] In another early
tradition, that associated with the doctrinal decrees of church synods
and councils, beginning with *The Creed of Nicaea* in 325[102] and *The
Niceno-Constantinopolitan Creed* defined by the council held at Constantinople in 381,[103] the standard formula is originally not singular
but plural: "We believe [*Pisteuomen*]." But that plural of the conciliar
decree likewise becomes a singular in *The Niceno-Constantinopolitan
Creed,* "I believe in one God," because, according to some scholars,
this creed originated as a baptismal creed. That is how it also goes
on being used in the East,[104] but the West uses it as the Credo for the
liturgy of the mass, and *The Apostles' Creed* for baptism.[105] The singular prevailed in most of the communions that continued to employ the
"Nicene Creed" in their eucharistic liturgies, including Eastern Orthodoxy, Roman Catholicism, Anglicanism, and Lutheranism. In the late
twentieth century, liturgical and theological reforms, particularly those
associated with the Second Vatican Council, brought about the restoration of the plural within Roman Catholicism and beyond.

Even more significant for creedal development than this oscil-
lation between singular and plural forms of the verb "to believe," however, is the variety of grammatical constructions for the verb and the
noun, in the Greek both of the New Testament and of patristic texts,
including also creeds—and, to the extent that a less inflected language

99. Jude 3.
100. Rom 3.28.
101. *Hipp;* see chapter 13.2 below, "The Kerygma and Baptismal Symbols."
102. *N* 1.
103. *N-CP* 1.
104. *Mogila* 1.103.
105. Kelly, 296–331.

can reflect such nuances, also in various vernaculars, including even English—to identify the object of the believing:[106]

 1. A simple noun, usually in the dative case, to denote the personal object of believing defined as trusting, most often God or Christ. It is employed most memorably in Romans 4.3, Galatians 3.6, and James 2.23, three passages of the New Testament that are based on the Septuagint of Genesis 15.6, "Abraham believed God [*theōi*]," which also employs the dative. Sometimes, particularly with the noun "faith" rather than the verb "to believe," the noun that is the object of the believing appears in the genitive case, for example, "through the faith of Jesus Christ [*dia pisteōs Iēsou Christou*]" in the Greek of Romans 3.22, which seems to mean the faith that believes in Jesus Christ rather than the faith by which Jesus Christ himself believed; grammarians often refer to this as an "objective genitive."

 2. A prepositional phrase, usually with "into" (*eis* with the accusative case for Greek, *in* with the accusative case for Latin), but also with other prepositions, such as *epi* and *en*.

 3. A dependent clause, believing "that [*hoti*] such and such is true or has truly happened," stating a doctrinal proposition that is declared to be accurate, or an event in the history of salvation that is said to have actually occurred. For in the New Testament and other Christian texts "verbs of believing, contrary to Attic usage, very commonly take *hoti*," to refer to believing that something has taken place in the past and/or that it is truly so in the present (or, in a conflation of believing and hoping, that it will be so in the future).[107] An example of both can be seen in the

106. Cf. Blass-Debrunner, 295.
107. Blass-Debrunner, 397 (1), 204.

words quoted earlier: "If you confess with your lips that [*hoti*] Jesus is Lord and believe in your heart that [*hoti*] God raised him from the dead."[108] A variant on this construction can be the use of the infinitive form of the verb.[109]

The grammatical constructions of *The Niceno-Constantinopolitan Creed* in Greek are a combination and an adaptation of the second and third of these. Each of the three persons/hypostases of the Trinity is made the object of a believing "in": *Pisteuomen eis hena theon patera . . . kai eis hena kyrion Iēsoun Christon . . . kai eis to pneuma to hagion.* Then the distinctive titles and attributes of each are set in apposition to this accusative proper noun, also as objects of believing, for example, "the Father all-powerful, maker of heaven and of earth."[110] Especially in the language of the creed about the temporal and earthly history of the second person of the Trinity as the only-begotten Son of God who became incarnate, believing "that" propositions or historical events are true takes the form of participles used as substantives in Greek, modifying, or in apposition to, the proper noun of the title (*ton . . . katelthonta ek tōn ouranōn*), which were turned into Latin with relative clauses (*qui . . . descendit de coelis*). In English, in spite of earlier more literal translations of these participial phrases or relative clauses,[111] current versions render them as separate declarative sentences: "He came down from the heavens."[112] The usage is somewhat different in the language about believing in the third hypostasis or person of the Trinity as "the lordly and life-giving" Spirit. The original Greek of that epithet, which is *to kyrion* in the neuter rather than *ton kyrion* in the masculine, is, strictly speaking, an adjective meaning "lordly, of the Lord," not a noun to be translated as "the Lord," as it is already with the Latin *Dominum et vivificantem* and would be in most subsequent translations into various languages.[113] Other "objects" of believing are appended,

108. Rom 10.9.
109. For example, Acts 15.11.
110. *N-CP* 1.
111. *Lit Chrys* II.E.
112. *N-CP* 3.
113. *N-CP* 8.

not as though they were on the same level with the Holy Spirit, but because they represent the actions of the Holy Spirit within the history of salvation, as the predicates appended to the Father and the Son do for them: "in one, holy, catholic, and apostolic church."[114] Sometimes these objects of believing appear with additional verbs of affirmation, as in "We confess [*homologoumen*] one baptism for the forgiving of sins" and "We look forward to [*prosdokōmen*] a resurrection of the dead and life in the age to come."[115]

2.3. Confessing the Faith

When Christian doctrine is defined at the beginning of volume 1 of *The Christian Tradition* as "what the church of Jesus Christ believes, teaches, and confesses on the basis of the word of God,"[116] the emphasis, in what the subtitle of that work as a whole calls "a history of the development of *doctrine*," is on the second member of that triad, teaching the faith (to which the next chapter of the present work will turn). But here in *Credo*, as well as throughout collections such as *Creeds and Confessions of Faith in the Christian Tradition*, the emphasis is above all on the third, confessing the faith. It should be evident by now that the relation between believing and confessing is at once very close and very complex. As Miroslav Volf has put it, "Without personal identification with Jesus Christ, cognitive specification of who he is remains empty; without cognitive specification of who Jesus Christ is, however, personal identification with him is blind."[117] But just as *believing* turns out to have multiple meanings, so it is also with *confessing*, which translates the Greek verb *homologein* and noun *homologia* and their various cognates. It is in the contrast and correlation between "believing" and "confessing" that much of this complexity is identified and clarifed.[118] Correlating the two terms and arguing, on the basis of the distinction between the "inner" and the "outward," that "just as inner thinking on the things of faith is as such the act of faith, so too is outwardly confessing them," Thomas Aquinas classifies these multiple meanings

114. *N-CP* 9.
115. *N-CP* 10–12.
116. *Chr Trad* 1:1.
117. Volf 1998, 148.
118. Campenhausen 1972; Arens 1989, 169–404.

by making the following threefold distinction among the definitions of the terms *confession* and *to confess, confessio* and *confiteri* in his Latin:

> 1. Confession of the truths of faith; . . . this is an act proper to the virtue of faith, bearing on the end of faith. . . .
>
> 2. A confession of thanks or praise; this is the act of the virtue of *latria* [adoration], since its aim is to show outwardly the honor due to God, the end of *latria*.
>
> 3. The confession of sins; the purpose of this is the wiping out of sins, the end also of the virtue of penance.[119]

Within this catalog, which Thomas is summarizing on the basis of the usage of the Latin Vulgate, it is "confession of the truths of faith" as specified in his first definition that occupies our primary attention here.

It is, however, a combination of his second definition, "a confession of thanks or praise," with the third, "the confession of sins," that gives to the term *confession* its most celebrated literary expression ever, in the title of the *Confessions* of Augustine of Hippo.[120] As Augustine himself puts it, *confessio* means "accusation of oneself; praise of God."[121] By the time the thirteen books of the *Confessions* are completed, there is also very much "confession of the truths of faith" and of various doctrines embodied in the book, for example, one of his most important confessions anywhere of the doctrine of creation, which forms the bulk of the closing book; but all of it is being seen and portrayed through the lens of Augustine's personal experience. Perhaps the most relevant contribution of Augustine's *Confessions* to the understanding of the term *confession* with which we are chiefly working here is the character of a "confession" as a public statement. For although in its form the book is one long personal prayer, addressed to God in the second person singular by Augustine in the first person singular, this is in fact not only one of the longest but also one of the most pub-

119. Thomas Aquinas *Summa Theologica* 2a2ae.3.1 (tr. Blackfriars).
120. Courcelle 1950.
121. Augustine *Sermons* 67.2, as quoted in Brown 2000, 169.

lic prayers ever uttered in the history of the church: new editions of it in Latin and new translations of it into various languages keep on appearing. The uniqueness of the *Confessions* of Augustine as literature becomes evident by contrasting it with the work most resembling it in late antiquity, the *Meditations* of Emperor Marcus Aurelius. But the title as a designation for a work of autobiography by a man of letters goes on to have a life of its own. In the eighteenth century Jean-Jacques Rousseau not only invoked but parodied it with his *Confessions,* written between 1766 and 1770, but published only in 1781 and 1788, after Rousseau's death in 1778. And Leo Tolstoy, passionately concerned as he was for the radical reformation not only of his own moral character but of traditional Christianity, combined (staying with the categories of Thomas Aquinas) "the confession of sins" with "the confession of matters of faith" in his anti-Orthodox *Ispoved'* [*Confession*] of 1882.

In the use of *homologia* and *homologein* in the New Testament, this "confession of matters of faith" seems to be seen consistently as an individual act, which it is proper to describe by a verb that is in the singular, as in the words of the apostle Paul quoted earlier: "if thou shalt confess [*ean homologēsēis*] with thy mouth the Lord Jesus."[122] Therefore it is apparently not, or at any rate not in the first instance, the sort of formal "creed, known to the faithful and committed to memory" of which Augustine speaks,[123] but a spontaneous and individual act. The second and third forms of "confession" in Thomas's catalog, "the confession of thanksgiving or praise" and "the confession of sins," while continuing to be individual as well, also acquired collective form and corporate language. The second, "the confession of thanksgiving or praise," flowered into the eucharistic liturgies of East and West: *eucharistia* means "thanksgiving," and the liturgies all contain "confessional" expressions of thanksgiving. The third, "the confession of sins," grew into the elaborate penitential systems of both the Eastern and the Western church.[124] As a result of this, at least in common parlance, the word *confess* refers primarily to penitential confession, as when Hamlet says to his mother, "Confess yourself to heaven; / Repent what's

---

122. Rom 10.9 (AV).
123. Augustine *On Faith and the Creed* 1 (*NPNF*–I 3:321).
124. M. Driscoll 1999.

past; avoid what is to come;"[125] and the noun *confessional* stands for
the booth in which penitent sinners make their confession to a priest
and are absolved by him.[126] In the usage of the Protestant churches and
confessions of faith, reaction against the medieval penitential system,
which begins already with the Lollards at the end of the fourteenth
century[127] and continues with Luther's attack on indulgences in the
ninety-five theses of 1517, leads, for example in *The Lausanne Articles*
of 1536[128] and more extensively in *The Second Helvetic Confession* of
1566, to a definition of confession in this third sense as "this sincere
confession which is made to God alone, either privately between God
and the sinner, or publicly in the church where the general confession
of sins is said."[129] The reason for this, according to *The Westminster
Confession of Faith*, is that "he that scandalizeth his brother, or the
church of Christ, ought to be willing, by a private or public confession, and sorrow for his sin, to declare his repentance to those that are
offended."[130] This emphasis leads as well to the joint recitation of the
"General Confession" that becomes a decisive component of the opening section of many Protestant orders of common worship. In successive editions of *The Book of Common Prayer*, for example, it is followed
by the "comfortable words our Savior Christ sayeth," which, without
being a formal pronouncement of absolution as such, are equivalent
to a general announcement of absolution.[131] The public confession and
general absolution are related to the unsuccessful attempt to retain private confession and absolution in some of the Protestant churches as a
possibility, though no longer as an absolute obligation. Thus *The Augsburg Confession* insists that "it is taught among us that private absolution should be retained and not allowed to fall into disuse,"[132] and *The
[First] Bohemian Confession* of 1535 likewise asserts "that the penitent
should approach a priest and confess their sins to God himself before

---

125. Shakespeare *Hamlet* 3.4.149–50.
126. *OED* 2:802.
127. *Loll* 9.
128. *Laus Art* 6.
129. *Helv II* 14.6.
130. *West* 15.6.
131. *BCP* (Blunt 384–85).
132. *Aug Ger* 11.1; also *17 Art* 8; *Witt Art* 7; *Marburg* 11; *Witt Conc* 5.

him."[133] Although Luther's *Seventeen Articles,* as well as the early Anglican *Ten Articles* of 1536,[134] concede that "penance is to be reckoned as a sacrament,"[135] the later Anglican *Thirty-Nine Articles of the Church of England* can be taken to be speaking for most of the Anglican and other Reformers, including Luther, when they define that "there are two sacraments ordained of Christ our Lord in the Gospel, that is to say, baptism and the supper of the Lord."[136] It is in response to this Protestant criticism as well as to late medieval developments that *The Decree of the Council of Trent* addresses the doctrine of penance and confession at the fourteenth session of the council in 1551.[137]

The predominance of the corporate and collective form for the confession of praise and the confession of sins comes to apply also, and preeminently, to the first species of confession in Thomas's list, "the confession of matters of faith," which is our chief business here. "To confess God," according to *The Christian Catechism of the Orthodox Catholic Greco-Russian Church* composed by Metropolitan Philaret Drozdov of Moscow in the nineteenth century, means "to acknowledge that he is our God, and not deny him, although for confessing him we may have to suffer, or even die."[138] Even when, as noted earlier, the creedal confession opens with the verb in the first person singular, "I believe"—as it does originally in *The Apostles' Creed*[139] and other baptismal creeds, and then eventually in *The Niceno-Constantinopolitan Creed,* which is *The Nicene Creed* of the liturgy[140] and the baptismal creed in the East—it turns out that what the individual professes as a personal statement of faith necessarily has to be expressed in the exact words of the church's creed, from which it is not permissible to deviate. This Roman Catholic and Eastern Orthodox usage of the terms *confess* and *confession* in the sense of a common and corporate confession of faith is shared by the Reformed and the Lutheran confessions

133. *Boh I* 5.3.
134. *10 Art* 3.1.
135. *17 Art* 7.
136. *39 Art* 25.
137. *Trent* 14; see Duval 1985, 151–208.
138. *Russ Cat* 507.
139. *Ap* 1.
140. *N-CP* 1.

of the Reformation era, as is evident in their very titles as well as in the passages that have been quoted from many of them. If anything, also perhaps because of the disappearance of the sacrament of penance and confession, the use of the term *confession* to mean "confession of faith," both as a title for individual statements of faith and as a general concept, is more typical of Protestant than of Roman Catholic or of Eastern Orthodox ecclesiastical usage. Within Eastern Orthodoxy, the term does appear in the title of the statement of faith and doctrine prepared by Metrophanes Critopoulos as *Confession* in 1625, in the one written by Peter Mogila as *The Orthodox Confession of the Catholic and Apostolic Eastern Church* in 1638, and in *The Confession of Dositheus and of the Synod of Jerusalem* in 1672 (as well as in the most tragic of all Eastern confessions, *The Eastern Confession of the Christian Faith by Cyril Lucar* in 1629). But three of these four Orthodox "confessions" were in some significant measure written as responses (and the other one as a concession as well as a response) to the Protestant "confessions" that had begun to appear in the century preceding them.[141]

The normative model for such acts of "confessing," whether by the individual or by the church, is none less than "Jesus, the apostle and high priest of our confession," as the Epistle to the Hebrews calls him,[142] who, as the First Epistle to Timothy says, "in his testimony before Pontius Pilate made the good confession [*tēn kalēn homologian*]."[143] As the Congregationalist *Savoy Declaration* of 1658 affirms on that basis, "Christ is the great and first confessor."[144] Yet in its form, the "good confession" of Christ certainly did not consist in reciting a creed! Rather, he was in his own person the One of whose suffering and crucifixion "under Pontius Pilate" both *The Niceno-Constantinopolitan Creed*[145] and *The Apostles' Creed*[146] would eventually speak, the one who did precisely what he said of himself in his testimony before Pontius Pilate: "For this I was born, and for this I have come into

---

141. See chapter 14.4 below, "The Eastern Confessions as Equal and Opposite Reactions."
142. Heb 3.1.
143. 1 Tm 6.13. See chapter 8.1 below, "Confessing as a Political Act."
144. *Sav* pr.
145. *N-CP* 4; see also *Ign*.
146. *Ap* 4; see the explanation in *Heid* 38.

the world, to bear witness to the truth."[147] The inescapably reciprocal relation between his own "good confession," not now before a mere Roman procurator but before his Father in heaven, and the "confession" of his followers in the church is the theme of another saying of Jesus in the Gospels, translated in the Authorized ("King James") Version as: "Whosoever therefore shall *confess* me before men, him will I *confess* also before my Father which is in heaven. But whosoever shall deny me before men, him will I also deny before my Father which is in heaven."[148] In the version of Luke, with the retention of "confess" but with some other significant variations (especially the reference to the angels), the saying is, as the Authorized Version translates: "Whosoever shall *confess* me before men, him shall the Son of man also *confess* before the angels of God: But he that denieth me before men shall be denied before the angels of God."[149] This relation between the disciple's "confessing" and the "confessing" by the Son of man before his Father is obscured when practically all modern versions of the English Bible render the Greek verb *homologein* there with some other English verb than "confess," with which they usually translate that verb at other places, including the clear parallel to these passages in the words of Christ in the Book of Revelation: "I will confess his name before my Father and before his angels."[150]

2.4. The Content of the Confession

For the New Testament, therefore, what is to be "confessed" as well as what is to be "believed" is Jesus Christ. That means above all his lordship, as in two familiar statements of the apostle Paul, the first of them quoted here earlier and the second to be considered later as a primary instance of creedlike elements in the New Testament:[151] first, "If you *confess* with your lips that Jesus is Lord and believe in your heart that God raised him from the dead, you will be saved";[152] second, "That at the name of Jesus every knee should bend, in heaven and on earth and

147. Jn 18.37.
148. Mt 10.32–33 (AV); italics added. See *Eun* 1; *Belg* 37. Also Bornkamm 1939.
149. Lk 12.8–9 (AV); italics added.
150. Rv 3.5 (RSV).
151. See chapter 5.1 below, "Creeds in Scripture."
152. Rom 10.9; italics added.

under the earth, and every tongue *confess* that Jesus Christ is Lord, to the glory of God the Father."[153] But already within the pages of the New Testament, that confession that Jesus Christ is Lord is undergoing further development, as the second quotation also suggests. Apparently in response to an early form of the Gnostic heresy, which New Testament writers perceived as a denial of the physical and human reality of the coming into flesh of the Son of God and as a dualism that, in the interest of such a denial, separated "Jesus" from "the Christ" as two different entities, it became necessary to introduce a greater specificity of teaching into both the believing and the confessing of the church: "Every one who believes that Jesus is the Christ," instead of separating Jesus from the Christ, "is a child of God," the First Epistle of John promises; and therefore also: "Every spirit which confesses that Jesus Christ has come in the flesh [or: confesses that Jesus is the Christ who has come in the flesh] is of God, and every spirit which does not confess Jesus is not of God. This is the spirit of antichrist."[154] From such a "believing that" and "confessing that" it is a substantial quantitative change, but really not much of a qualitative change, to the believing and confessing of all the later creeds and confessions of faith. Thus the first significant Christian Latin writer, Tertullian, addressing himself to the "rulers of the Roman empire" in defense of "our confession of the name of Christ," presents "an exhibition of what our religion really is" in the form of the confession: "The object of our worship is the one God."[155]

Through that development, "confessing the faith" becomes a "confession," a formal, official, public, and binding statement of what is believed and confessed by the church. Not only do the creedal statements of later councils—for example, of the Council of Ephesus in 431[156] and of the Council of Chalcedon in 451[157]—quote, and incorporate in their entirety, the creeds of earlier councils, above all *The Creed of Nicaea* as "the faith of the 318 fathers at Nicaea" and *The Niceno-Constantinopolitan Creed*, "the faith of the 150 fathers," to assert their

153. Phil 2.10–11; italics added.
154. 1 Jn 5.1, 4.2–3.
155. Tertullian *Apology* 2, 16–17 (*ANF* 3:19; 31); also *Tert.*
156. *Eph 431* ep.
157. *Chal* def.

continuity with them.[158] But later confessions in turn cite these creeds and councils with the same intent, and still later confessions cite earlier confessions, even within the confessional traditions of the churches of the Protestant Reformation. That is what *The Formula of Concord* of 1577 is doing when it identifies "the unanimous consent of our Christian faith" with "the symbol of our own age, called the First, Unaltered Augsburg Confession" of 1530.[159] In a similar vein, the conclusion of *The Canons of the Synod of Dort* of 1618–19, after having set forth "the clear, simple, and straightforward explanation of the orthodox teaching," affirms it "to be derived from God's word and in agreement with the confessions of the Reformed churches," and calls upon other Christians of other confessions to look both at the Reformed confessions of the sixteenth century and at the synod's own formularies, and thus "to form their judgment about the faith of the Reformed churches . . . on the basis of the churches' own official confessions and of the present explanation of the orthodox teaching which has been endorsed by the unanimous consent of the members of the whole synod, one and all."[160] The confessions of the Anabaptists and Baptists of the Reformation, too, find it necessary to set forth and expound "the articles which some brothers previously had understood wrongly and in a way not conformed to the true meaning."[161] The General Baptist *Faith and Practice of Thirty Congregations Gathered According to the Primitive Pattern* in England affirms "that God doth command men to speak or declare that which they have learned by the teaching of the creatures," to confess the doctrine they have learned.[162] And *The Assembly or Second London Confession* of the seventeenth-century English Baptists formulates this approach to the language of creeds and confessions as follows: "We have no itch to clog religion with new words, but to readily acquiesce in that form of sound words which hath been, in consent with the Holy Scriptures, used by others before us."[163]

158. See chapter 1.1 above, "Continuity *versus* Change in the Decrees of the Ecumenical Councils."
159. *Form Conc Epit* pr 3.
160. *Dort* con; De Jong 1968.
161. *Schleit* con.
162. *Gen Bap* 7.
163. *London II* pr.

But such declarations, together with the church law that requires confessional subscription as a prerequisite for ordination in the
church,[164] can easily confuse *confessing* and *confession*.[165] The relation
between the two was a central issue in the modern history of "confessionalism" in Germany.[166] It was such an equation of "our act of confessing" with subscribing "the confessions of the Reformation" whose
dangers Karl Barth was especially concerned to point out.[167] He was
doing so, moreover, in the very years in which, through *The Barmen
Declaration* of 1934 under his leadership, the adherents of diverging
"confessions of the Reformation" came together to carry out their own
new "act of confessing," and to produce their own new "confession,"
in response to the Nazi threat.[168] It is an indication of that equation of
"our act of confessing" with subscribing "the confessions of the Reformation" that in some languages—above all in German, but sometimes
also in English—the meaning of *confession* as "a formulary in which a
church or body of Christians sets forth the religious doctrines which
it considers essential; an authoritative declaration of the articles of belief; a creed" passes over, as *The Oxford English Dictionary* notes, into
the meaning: "the religious body or church united by one Confession
of Faith; a communion."[169] In contemporary German, therefore, the
word *Konfessionskunde* to designate a field of theological study means
not the study of "confessions" in the narrow sense of "statements of
faith" in which the term is being used here but the study of "denominations" or "communions," which includes their confessions of faith but
is by no means confined to these.[170] Yet in contemporary theological
English, perhaps because of the rapid increase of ecumenical contacts
during the twentieth century, the use of the word *confession* to refer to
"the religious body or church united by one Confession of Faith" cited
by *The Oxford English Dictionary* seems to have achieved considerable
currency even within those Protestant churches that are not themselves

164. See chapter 9.4 below, "Confessional Subscription as Legal Compliance."
165. Jüngel 1968; Link 1998.
166. Reese 1974.
167. Barth 1935.
168. Ahlers 1986; Burgsmüller and Weth 1983.
169. *OED* 2:802.
170. *PRE* 19:205–7 (Ferdinand Kattenbusch).

identified chiefly by a creedal confession of faith. It has been pointed out that "the concept of the Church as a confessional entity (Orthodox, Anglican, Lutheran etc.) is historically a late phenomenon," but that by now "confessionalism is deeply rooted in our history."[171]

Yet the indigenization and inculturation of creeds and confessions, which has taken a quantum leap during the nineteenth and twentieth centuries,[172] has also enabled, or compelled, the Protestant churches as "confessions" to reexamine the concept of "the confessional church" and the simplistic equation of "our act of confessing" with subscribing "the confessions of the Reformation" or even the creeds of the early church. Thus when, in 1951, the Protestant Christian Batak Church (H. K. B. P.) of Indonesia sought to explain itself to its Western mother and sister churches, both Lutheran and Reformed, as well as to the predominantly Muslim culture of Indonesia, it opened its statement with the declaration, "A 'confession of faith' is of the utmost necessity for establishing our faith and opposing heresy," and proceeded to explain that "the church, in opposing heresies which arise, continuously requires new confessions," one of which was this very *Confession of Faith,* setting forth what was believed, taught, and confessed by Indonesian Christian believers and churches in the twentieth century. For, they averred, just as their spiritual forebears so often had, "a Christian group cannot be called a 'church' if it has no confession."[173] This declaration continued to hold in Indonesian Christianity.[174] The other side of that declaration was the insistence of a twentieth-century theologian in India that a church that was born of the missions but that had now come of age should undertake "its own grappling with the problems of our Faith, without of course losing contact with all that comes to her through the age-long wisdom of the Church Universal,"[175] as this has been embodied also in the creeds and confessions of that faith.

171. Zizioulas 1985, 259–60.
172. See chapter 11 below, "Transmission of Creeds and Confessions to Other Cultures."
173. *Bat* pr 4.
174. Nortier 1941, 10–11.
175. Devadutt 1949, 43.

CHAPTER THREE

Confession of the Faith
as Doctrine

AS THE PRECEDING CHAPTER has pointed out, such phrases as "believing in," "believing that," and even "confessing that," according to the usage of the New Testament and of most of the Christian tradition through the centuries, do not have creedal propositions as their ultimate point of reference. Rather, they are directed to the personal God of biblical revelation, the God who has acted concretely in the events of biblical history and finally "in these last days"[1] in the history of Jesus Christ, therefore the God to whom believers pray and in whom believers trust and hope.[2] As a fourteenth-century Byzantine confession expresses this priority, "Whatever at any time is said by the saints concerning the divine doctrine, even if it is not very much fitted out with truth and theological precision, we rely on the God whom they teach."[3] But specifying just what such "relying on the God whom they teach" or "believing in" or "believing that" means, and then being obliged to "confess" what is believed, must finally lead to propositions and to a striving for "theological precision": the teaching of the faith, teaching the truth about God as well as about the authority of biblical revelation and biblical history.

Thus one of the earliest confessions of the Reformation speaks about "faith in the gospel," which it follows immediately with the insistence, in an attack on the medieval system of authority, that "in the gospel we learn that human doctrines and traditions are of no avail to

1. Heb 1.2.
2. See also chapter 17.4 below, "In Light of Their History, Do Creeds Have a Future as well as a Past?"
3. *CP 1351 25.*

salvation."[4] As the use of terms in this confessional statement makes clear, believing, even and especially a believing that sets itself apart from "human doctrines and traditions," is inseparable from doctrine and teaching. Faith and the confession of the faith must always be more than doctrine, of course. For they involve the whole of Christian obedience, both for the individual believer and for the church, including, for the church, polity and church order,[5] and, for the individual as well as for the church, a life of prayer and of conformity to the divine will.[6] But it is equally important to emphasize that confessing the faith can never be less than doctrine. When, in the interest of the authenticity of the "experience of Christ as my personal Savior" or of some other such redefinition, faith is drained of its doctrinal content, neither the personal Christian experience nor its authenticity can long endure.[7] *The French Confession* of 1559 automatically connects the two affirmations: "our Lord Jesus Christ to be our only Savior and Redeemer, and his doctrine to be the only doctrine of life and salvation."[8] The concluding words of the apostle Paul's hymn in praise of love in 1 Corinthians 13, "So faith, hope, love abide, these three; but the greatest of these is love,"[9] do put faith, not even to mention doctrine, in its proper rank, that is, below love, which is "the greatest" of all. This made it necessary for a Reformation confession, in its defense of the Protestant doctrines of faith and of justification by faith alone, to provide an explanation for this somewhat embarrassing apostolic priority of love over faith.[10] Nevertheless, these words also affirm that not only love but faith (as well as hope) will "abide."

When the New Testament describes the primitive Christian community after the resurrection and the ascension of Christ as having "remained faithful to the apostles' teaching and fellowship, to the

4. *67 Art* 15, 16.
5. See chapter 4 below, "Faith and Order."
6. See chapter 6 below, "The Rule of Prayer and the Rule of Faith"; and chapter 10 below, "Deeds, Not Creeds?"
7. Trilling [1950] 2000, 180; see chapter 17.1 below, "The Discomfort with Creed Caused by the Consciousness of Modernity."
8. *Gall* pr.
9. 1 Cor 13.13.
10. *Apol Aug* 4.225–28.

breaking of bread and the prayers"[11]—this time with "teaching" being assigned the first place among these four apostolic marks of identification—it is speaking about a time when the original apostles were still living and were therefore teaching in person. But by the time this description was written down by the evangelist Luke in the Acts of the Apostles, which was perhaps in the eighties of the first century, and therefore (according to early tradition) after all of the original twelve disciples of Jesus except John had died,[12] "the apostles' teaching" had already begun to take shape as a recognizable body of teachings, which were gradually being set down in several closely connected forms. These included the early kerygma, which had first been proclaimed orally and then was communicated in writing, through those Gospels that were eventually acknowledged as canonical, but also, as Luke's introduction to his Gospel attests, through "many" other compositions that did not become canonical,[13] some of which have surfaced only in modern times. Another repository of such teachings was the epistles that were sent to various churches and individuals by the apostles and then were gradually collected and circulated.[14] An important but elusive source of information is primitive orders of worship, although the details of these liturgies, particularly their creeds, were often kept secret.[15] And, in that context, there arise the first versions of expressions of faith that would eventually emerge as the early creeds, even though admittedly that entire process still had a long way to go.[16]

3.1. The Teaching of the Church

In this passage from the Book of Acts about "the apostles' teaching" and in others, therefore, the English word *teaching*—like the English word *instruction* and like the Latin word *doctrina,* but unlike the English word *doctrine,* at any rate in present-day usage[17]—can be taken

11. Acts 2.42 (RSV plus NJB); see chapter 13 below, "Rules of Faith in the Early Church."
12. Eusebius *Ecclesiastical History* 3.23, 3.31 (*NPNF*-II 1:150–52, 162–63).
13. Lk 1.1.
14. 2 Pt 3.15–16.
15. See chapter 6.3 below, "The Place of Creed in Liturgy."
16. See chapter 13 below, "Rules of Faith in the Early Church."
17. *OED* 3-I:572–73.

as a reference either to a process or to a content. When Cicero says that the intellectual formation of the complete orator requires *doctrina,* he means not a particular set of tenets, whether religious or philosophical, but, as the English translators have rendered the term, "theoretical training" or "art."[18] And when he says that the Roman orators excelled in *virtus* but the Greek rhetors in *doctrina,* "virtue" may be a satisfactory English equivalent for the first, but the second is, again quoting English translators, better rendered as "learning."[19]

The contrast between the two best-known books bearing the title *De doctrina christiana* illustrates this problem of how to translate *doctrina:* John Milton's ill-fated work (not published until the nineteenth century because of its heterodox, neo-Arian views on Christ and the Trinity) is a treatise on the major doctrines of Christianity and on the errors of traditional orthodoxy about them.[20] But Augustine's book under the same title, which he began in 397, a few years after his conversion to catholic Christianity, but did not complete until 427, shortly before his death, is not, as the usual English translation of its title would certainly lead the uninitiated reader to suppose, a treatise about the content of "Christian doctrine" or theology at all. Rather, it is about "Christian communication" as a process and as a skill. This is to be exercised through a soundly orthodox and catholic interpretation of Scripture, the application of the principles of semantics to the signs and meanings of the Bible (including the distinction between symbol [*signum*] and reality [*res*]), and the practice of Christian rhetoric as applied to preaching, which shares some of the methods of classical rhetoric but which also has special rules.[21] In the concrete life of the church, however, the two meanings of *doctrina* can come together. For the Christian communication of Augustine, as it is reflected in the hundreds of his sermons that have been preserved, including some that have been discovered or identified only recently,[22] has, as its required content and its unquestioned presupposition, the orthodox doctrine that has been confessed by the church catholic in its creeds

18. Cicero *Brutus* 29.111.
19. Cicero *De oratore* 3.34.
20. *Chr Trad* 5:25–35.
21. Quasten, 4:376–77.
22. Quasten, 4:398–400.

and councils.[23] Being a servant of the church, who is bound to its faith and pledged to its creed, the preacher is not called primarily to voice his private opinions, however brilliant these might be. As *The Second Helvetic Confession* states its Reformed position more than a millennium after Augustine, "the preaching and writings of the apostles . . . is also rightly called evangelical doctrine," so that "the true harmony of the church consists in doctrines [*dogmata*] and in the true and harmonious preaching of the gospel of Christ, and in rites that have been expressly delivered by the Lord."[24] This emphasis on the importance both of church order and of church discipline in relation to the other "notes" of the church, as well as in relation to doctrine, is characteristic of *The Second Helvetic Confession* and of other Reformed confessions.[25]

Implicit in the use of the term *teaching* in association with *believing* and *confessing* is such a distinction between the private opinion of the teacher and the public doctrine of the church. In the third century, the first great systematic theologian of Christian history, Origen of Alexandria, states the distinction for all time to come. He does so in a formulation that reflects, even in the absence of definitively legislated creeds, a widely held catholic consensus about those "certain points" that are "necessary," as distinguished from the things that are still questions open to exploration by those who have received "the gift of language, of wisdom, and of knowledge." It is a consensus for which Origen regards himself as a spokesman:[26]

> Now it ought to be known that the holy apostles, in preaching the faith of Christ, delivered themselves with the utmost clearness on certain points which they believed to be necessary to every one, even to those who seemed somewhat dull in the investigation of divine knowledge; leaving, however, the grounds of their statements to be examined into by those who should

23. Augustine *On the Trinity* 1.4.7 (*NPNF*–II 3:20).
24. *Helv II* 13.3; 17.17.
25. See chapter 4.3 below, "Polity as Doctrine in the Reformed Confessions"; and chapter 10.1 below, "Doctrines of Christian Discipline in the Reformation Confessions."
26. Daniélou 1955.

deserve the excellent gifts of the Spirit, and who, especially by means of the Holy Spirit himself, should obtain the gift of language, of wisdom, and of knowledge: while on other subjects they merely stated the fact that things were so, keeping silence as to the manner or origin of their existence; clearly in order that the more zealous of their successors, who should be lovers of wisdom, might have a subject of exercise on which to display the fruits of their talents—those persons, I mean, who should prepare themselves to be fit and worthy receivers of wisdom.[27]

He then goes on to summarize the faith of the church in the formulation that we have called *The Creed of Origen*.[28] (It deserves to be noted, however, that this preface is preserved only in the Latin translation by Rufinus of Aquileia, which on many points, including perhaps this one, there is some reason to suspect of inaccuracy—or worse.)

In subsequent controversy over Origenism there arose the accusation that Origen himself did not faithfully observe this distinction in his own views on eschatology and permitted his own immense "gifts of language, of wisdom, and of knowledge" to carry him outside the boundaries. That accusation became evident in great detail with the issuance of *The Edict of Emperor Justinian on the True Faith* in 551,[29] and then two years later without similar doctrinal specificity with the declaration of the Second Council of Constantinople that "if anyone does not anathematize [among others] . . . Origen, as well as their heretical books . . . let him be anathema."[30] Subsequent controversy about Augustine, or at any rate the criticism of him within Eastern Christendom, has raised similar questions about the intrusion of one of his private opinions, the procession of the Holy Spirit "from the Father and the Son" rather than only "from the Father" (the Filioque), into the public doctrine of the church as this is confessed in the Latin West-

27. Origen *De Principiis* pr 3 (*ANF* 4:239).
28. *Orig.*
29. *Edict*; see Diekamp 1899, 90.
30. *CP II* anath 11.

ern Recension of *The Niceno-Constantinopolitan Creed*,[31] and as it goes
on being confessed in the doctrinal formularies of the Protestant Reformation.[32] But as long as a private opinion or "theologoumenon" was
identified as such and did not go against the binding public doctrine
already being confessed by the church in its creeds and confessions
of faith, it has been able to make some claim to legitimacy, though a
strictly limited one. Nor does this criterion preclude the possibility that
it might in some sense go beyond this public doctrine or even, in some
instances, anticipate its later formulations.

Thus it is that one of the most persistent features of all creeds
and confessions of faith, including those collected in the volumes of
Creeds and Confessions of Faith in the Christian Tradition—so persistent as to be obvious and therefore in danger of being overlooked,
especially in the aftermath of the modern controversies over Liberal
theology—is the utter seriousness with which they treat the issues of
Christian doctrine as, quite literally, a matter of life and death, both
here in time and hereafter in eternity.[33] Many of these statements of
faith, including the conciliar documents of the early period and a large
number of the confessional documents of the Reformation period, also
deal with church order and discipline, with liturgical practice, and with
Christian morality, and not only with "doctrine" in the usual sense.[34]
Nevertheless, even without counting words or lines, it does seem safe
to classify virtually all of these texts as, in the first instance, doctrinal
declarations, and to identify many of them as exclusively that. When
studying each of these creedal or confessional documents in the context of its historical setting, a modern reader will be reminded over and
over again of their involvement, unconscious though it sometimes was,
in the political, cultural, intellectual, and scientific currents and presuppositions of their times, which must not be ignored in interpreting

31. *N-CP Occ* 8. See chapter 7.4 below, "The Holy Spirit of Concord and the
Sacrament of Concord: Two Ironic Case Histories"; and chapter 15.1 below, "The
Western Reception of the Catholic Creedal and Conciliar Tradition." See also Syndogmaticon 8.6.
32. See chapter 16.3 below, "Catholic Substance and Protestant Principle in Reformation Confessions."
33. Lindbeck 1984.
34. See chapter 4 below, "Faith and Order"; chapter 6 below, "The Rule of Prayer
and the Rule of Faith"; and chapter 10 below, "Deeds, Not Creeds?"

them.[35] But all such cultural and political references in these creeds and confessions put together can seem almost trivial by comparison with the attention they give to doctrine. Only a few of these texts—notably *The Social Creed of the Methodist Church* of 1908,[36] its successor statement adopted by the Federal Council of Churches, *The Social Creed of the Churches* of 1908 in the United States,[37] and *The Social Creed of the Methodist Church of Brazil* of 1971[38]—reverse this priority, putting social and political issues into the primary position and making doctrine secondary. As a consequence, even intensely political confessions deal chiefly with the central doctrines of the Christian faith, not primarily with their political situation as such apart from those Christian doctrines. That was true of *The Creed of Nicaea* of 325, which was sponsored and eventually enforced by the authority of the newly converted emperor, Constantine I. It applies also to *The Augsburg Confession* of 1530, which was delivered before the Diet of the Holy Roman Empire in the presence of Emperor Charles V. And almost exactly four centuries later, *The Barmen Declaration* of 1934, which was delivered against the heresies spawned by the official National Socialist ideology of the German government, takes its stand on Christian doctrine. Addressing the no less politically charged atmosphere of the First Council of Constantinople in 381, Gregory of Nazianzus summarized the traditional and orthodox assignment of priorities: "Nothing is so magnificent in God's sight as pure doctrine, and a soul perfect in all the dogmas of the truth."[39]

3.2. "The Sum of Doctrine"

For Christians and for the Christian church, faith has always been above all a personal loyalty to a personal God, who is revealed in Christ and who is present in the church by the Holy Spirit. But the Christ to whom the words of *The Niceno-Constantinopolitan Creed*,

---

35. See chapter 8 below, "The Formation of Confessions and the Politics of Religion"; and chapter 17.4 below, "In Light of Their History, Do Creeds Have a Future as well as a Past?"
36. *Soc Meth.*
37. *Soc Ch.*
38. *Meth Braz;* also *Chin Man* of 1950 and *PRCC* of 1977.
39. Gregory of Nazianzus *Orations* 42.8 (*NPNF*–II 7:388).

"And [I, or we] believe in one Lord Jesus Christ,"[40] affirm such a loyalty is not an abstract idea in the universe of the Platonic forms, nor is
he a fallen hero lost in the shadows of the historical past. He is, in an
apt formula that goes back at least to the first historian of the church,
Eusebius of Caesarea, "the only high priest of all, and the only king of
every creature, and the Father's only supreme prophet of prophets":[41]
therefore priest, king, and prophet at the same time. This concept of the
threefold office is shared also by confessions of the Radical Reformation, including for example *The Racovian Catechism*,[42] *The Short Confession* of the Mennonites by Hans de Ries,[43] and the Baptist *First London Confession*,[44] and appears as well in the catechisms and systematic
theologies of various communions such as the Eastern Orthodox, as
well as in the decrees of the Second Vatican Council.[45] But it is particularly the confessions in the Reformed tradition, including *The Geneva
Catechism, The Heidelberg Catechism,* and *The True Confession of Faith*
in the sixteenth century,[46] *The Westminster Confession of Faith* in the
seventeenth,[47] and, in the twentieth, *The Basis of Union of the United
Church of Canada* of 1925,[48] who speak of a *munus triplex,* to describe
Christ as uniquely combining in himself these three often conflicting
strains in the history of Israel and in the history of religion generally,
the prophetic, the priestly, and the kingly office. "Christ, as our Redeemer," *The Westminster Shorter Catechism* of 1648 says, "executeth
the offices of a prophet, of a priest, and of a king, both in his estate of
humiliation and exaltation."[49] As priest, the one and only eternal highpriest, an office that is ascribed to him above all in the typological interpretation of the Old Testament liturgy by the Epistle to the Hebrews,
Christ is seen as having "expiated our sins by the unique sacrifice of

40. *N-CP* 2.
41. Eusebius *Ecclesiastical History* 1.3.8 (*NPNF*–II 3:20).
42. *Rac* 5 int.; also *Pol Br* B.
43. *Ries* 9–18; also *Geloof* 13–16; *Menn Con* 5.1.
44. *London I* 10.
45. *Mogila* 1.34; *Vat II* 5.1.31, 34–36.
46. *Genv Cat* 34; *Heid* 31; *True Con* 12.
47. *West* 8.1.
48. *Un Ch Can: Union* 7.
49. *West Sh Cat* 23.

his own death,"[50] of which the sacrifices of the Levitical priesthood are seen as anticipations. That sacrifice is his own body and life, given up in death on the altar of the cross, and then, according to the Catholic tradition but decidedly not according to the Protestant tradition,[51] continued in the oblation of the mass. Therefore he is, in the words of the Fourth Lateran Council's confession of 1215, *On the Catholic Faith* (which was echoing an early medieval hymn), "both priest and sacrifice,"[52] or, as *The Liturgy of Saint John Chrysostom* calls him, "the offerer and the offered [*ho prospherōn kai prospheromenos*]."[53] As king, Christ announces the coming of the kingdom of God in his message and then accomplishes it in his own person, by his conquest of the devil and the other powers of evil who held the world and humanity in their thrall. And he promises the complete triumph of the kingdom through his return to judge the living and the dead at the end of history,[54] bidding his disciples and the church to pray in the second petition of the Lord's Prayer for the coming of the kingdom of God.[55] But of these three offices united in Christ, it is the first according to the customary numbering, the prophetic office, that especially pertains to doctrine. For, as *The Geneva Catechism* of John Calvin puts it, "Since this office [of prophet] was given to the Lord Jesus to be the Master and Teacher of his own, its end is to bring us the true knowledge of the Father and of his truth, so that we may be scholars [pupils] in the household of God. . . . We must continue to be disciples of Christ right to the end."[56] Or, as Calvin says even more directly in his *Institutes of the Christian Religion,* "the prophetic dignity in Christ leads us to know that in the sum of doctrine [*summa doctrinae*] as he has given it to us all parts of perfect wisdom are contained."[57] Loyalty to the person of Christ requires loyalty to that "sum of doctrine as he has given it to us."

At first reading, John Calvin's language about a *summa doc-*

50. *Tig* 4.
51. *Heid* 80.
52. *Lat 1215* 1; Raby 71. See Syndogmaticon 10.9.
53. *Lit Chrys* II.B.1.
54. *N-CP* 7.
55. *Heid* 123. See Syndogmaticon 7.2.
56. *Genv Cat* 44, 308.
57. Calvin *Institutes of the Christian Religion* 2.15.2 (McNeill 1960, 1:496).

trinae, echoing as it does the title of the *Summa Theologiae* of Thomas Aquinas, might sound as though it were making the presumptuous, indeed preposterous, claim that Christian "doctrine," in fact an entire "sum of doctrine as he has given it to us"—represented by the intricate reasonings and careful formulations of the four books and the many hundreds of pages of Calvin's masterwork, *The Institutes of the Christian Religion* in its final edition of 1559—came, as such, from Christ himself. Therefore it could lay claim to the status of revealed doctrine, what *The Heidelberg Catechism* calls "the articles of the Apostles' Creed, our universally [*allgemein*] acknowledged confession of faith."[58] But such an impression must be corrected by Calvin's demonstration, in many other passages of his works, of a much more subtle conception of the methodology of doctrine and of a more sensitive awareness of the complex paths of analysis and reflection by which the theologian, as well as the church, moves from Scripture to dogma.[59] For Calvin and Calvinism, the deposit of revelation is contained in the divinely inspired Holy Scripture, its words and the persons of whom it speaks and through whom the Holy Spirit speaks in it, the prophets and psalmists and apostles, and above all the person of Christ, through whom the definitive revelation of the will of God has come to the human race.[60] But throughout the history of the church the problem has been that "all things in Scripture are not alike plain in themselves, nor alike clear unto all," as *The Westminster Confession of Faith* is obliged to acknowledge.[61] From this it follows that "when there is a question about the true and full sense of any Scripture (which is not manifold, but one), it must be searched and known by other places that speak more clearly."[62] Clear passages are to explain obscure passages, rather than the other way around. The cautionary tale of the history of the interpretation of the Apocalypse has often proved that principle: in the early church, according to Eusebius, "the opinions of most men are still divided" about it, and its status was still to be "decided from the testimony of the

58. *Heid* 22; see also chapter 16.3 below, "Catholic Substance and Protestant Principle in Reformation Confessions."
59. Dowey 1952.
60. Heb 1.1–4, cited in *Gall* 2.
61. *West* 1.7.
62. *West* 1.9.

ancients";[63] in the Reformation it is the only book of the New Testament on which Calvin did not compose a commentary, and Luther did not compose one either. That methodology of explaining obscure passages on the basis of clear ones is based on the principle that Scripture interprets Scripture, because "the supreme judge, by which all controversies of religion are to be determined, and all decrees of councils, opinions of ancient writers, doctrines of men, and private spirits, are to be examined, and in whose sentence we are to rest, can be no other but the Holy Spirit speaking in the Scripture."[64] These other authorities, the Roman Catholic and the Eastern Orthodox understandings of ancient conciliar tradition, as well as the "private spirits" that are the authority for Enthusiasts, Quakers, and other left-wing Protestants, cannot be put on the same level with "the Holy Spirit speaking in the Scripture."[65] Ultimately, of course, that principle requires for its full application a commanding knowledge of the original Hebrew and Greek of the Bible.[66] Once such warnings and qualifiers are stipulated and consistently carried out, it becomes possible, as is amply shown by *The Westminster Confession of Faith,* to put together, in the name of the sole authority of Scripture, a confessional and theological "sum of doctrine" that is formidable indeed.

By implication, unfaithfulness to this sum of doctrine amounts to disloyalty toward Christ, because the history of the church shows that it is a theological anomaly, or at best a fortunate inconsistency, for a true personal faith as *fides qua creditur,* "the faith with which one believes," to rest on false teaching as *fides quae creditur,* "the faith which one believes."[67] That is at any rate the conviction underlying the sharp condemnations of false doctrine in so many creeds and confessions from all the major confessional traditions.[68] *The Syllabus of Errors of Pope Pius IX* of 1864 speaks of "the principal errors of our time, which are censured in consistorial allocutions, encyclicals, and other

---

63. Eusebius *Ecclesiastical History* 3.24.18 (*NPNF*–II 1:154).
64. *West* 1.10. Syndogmaticon 8.11.
65. See chapter 5.4 below, "Confessional Rules of Biblical Hermeneutics."
66. *West* 1.8.
67. See chapter 2.2 above, "Faith Defined."
68. See chapter 7.1 below, "Creedal Anathema and Polemics." Also Syndogmaticon 1.5.

apostolic letters of our Most Holy Father [*Domini*], Pope Pius IX,"
and then itemizes eighty such errors, with a great many more condemned by implication.[69] The Lutheran *Formula of Concord* of 1577,
after having all along identified the one or more erroneous antitheses
to each of the doctrines that it affirms in the positive statements of its
first eleven articles, devotes its twelfth article to an entire catalog of still
further errors, particularly among other Protestant groups.[70] Patriarch
Jeremias II of Constantinople concludes his first reply to the overtures
from these very same Lutherans with the stern admonition: "Let no
one undertake or think anything contrary to the decisions of the holy
apostles and the holy councils."[71] The Reformed *Second Helvetic Confession* of 1566 specifically lists as the heretical objects of its condemnation "the Jews and Mohammedans . . . . all heresies and heretics. . . .
the Monarchians, Novatians, Praxeas, Patripassians, Sabellius, Paul of
Samosata, Aetius, Macedonius, Anthropomorphites, Arius, and such
like,"[72] with a substantial number of additional names and errors of
heretics and heresies being supplied elsewhere throughout its chapters.

Both the affirmations and especially the condemnations, moreover, are often couched in language that grates harshly on many modern ears.[73] In the West, *The Athanasian Creed* threatens: "This is the
catholic faith. Unless one keeps it in its entirety inviolate, one will
assuredly perish eternally."[74] In the East, *The Synodical Tome of the
Synod of Constantinople of 1351* explains (in words spoken by Gregory
Palamas) why especially the positive formulation of doctrine in a formal confession of the church demands such care and accuracy: "Defense of orthodoxy is one thing and confession of faith is another. In
a controversy it is not necessary for the defender to speak with great
accuracy in his expressions, as the great Basil says; but in a confession
accuracy [*akribeia*] in all respects is preserved and required."[75] Particu-

---

69. *Syl ttl.*
70. *Form Conc Epit* 12.
71. *Jer II* 1.29.
72. *Helv II* 3.5.
73. See chapter 17.1 below, "The Discomfort with Creed Caused by the Consciousness of Modernity."
74. *Ath* 2.
75. *CP 1351* 7.

larly because this attitude toward "accuracy" in doctrinal truth claims seems so uncongenial to the spirit of the present day, it may be helpful to invoke the analogy of modern scientific and technological doctrine, where getting things exactly right is the goal, or at least the ideal, and where getting things wrong is seen as potentially dangerous. To the recipe for an explosive or the design for a bridge, the warning of *The Athanasian Creed* can be applied with minimal adaptation: "Unless one keeps it in its entirety inviolate, one [or some other 'one'] will assuredly perish," in this world if not "eternally," as a result of the use of false data or the incorrect interpretation and application of valid data. Presumably, everyone would expect and require pharmacists, at peril of excommunication from their profession, to understand correctly the Latin text of a prescription and then to prepare the dosage in literal obedience to the "authorial intent" of the prescribing physician; for otherwise the patient may "perish." The prominence of medical metaphors in Christian language lends additional force to this analogy. One term for the eucharist in very early Christian language is "medicine of immortality [*pharmakon athanasias*],"[76] and one of the most important early heresiologies, that of Epiphanius of Salamis, bore the title *Panarion* or *Medicine Chest.*[77]

Creeds and confessions of faith, therefore, are a response to the New Testament imperative to be "sound" and orthodox in doctrine,[78] an imperative that believers and confessors understand as a divine command. Having originated as such a response, creeds and confessions will then serve as the criterion for determining what true orthodoxy in doctrine is. The purpose of *The Thirty-Nine Articles of the Church of England* of 1562, labeled as "articles upon which it was agreed by the archbishops and bishops of both provinces and the whole clergy, in the convocation held at London in the year of our Lord God, 1562, according to the computation of the Church of England," is said to be twofold: "for the avoiding of the diversities of opinions, and for the establishing of consent touching true religion."[79] Positively,

76. Ignatius *Epistle to the Ephesians* 20.2 (ACW 1:68); *Metr Crit* 9.11.
77. Quasten, 3:384–86.
78. 1 Tm 1.10; Ti 1.9, 2.10.
79. *39 Art* pr.

then, it is the intent of confessions to "establish consent touching true religion." "Consent" refers to the doctrinal consensus that is sought and achieved, and that then the authorities of the church, and often the authorities of the state as well, enforce upon those who make the confession their own.[80] But it usually includes (as in the case of *The Thirty-Nine Articles of the Church of England*) an affirmation of consensus and continuity with at least some of the major voices of orthodoxy from the past, as these are documented above all in the historic creeds:[81] "The three creeds, Nicene Creed, Athanasius's Creed, and that which is commonly called the Apostles' Creed, ought thoroughly to be received and believed; for they may be proved by most certain warrants of Holy Scripture."[82] Negatively, confessions are drafted so as to "avoid the diversities of opinions." As noted earlier, not every diversity of opinion is taken to represent an automatic threat to orthodoxy, only those that publicly and pertinaciously contradict the official teaching of the church, as it is being reaffirmed and defined in this confession. But some kinds of "opinion" that had been acceptable at one period of history eventually came under condemnation by the church of a later period, sometimes through the issuance of an additional creed or confession. The net result was less and less "diversity"—or, especially since the Reformation, a still further division or schism to make room for this diversity (as well as to keep out other kinds of "diversities of opinions").[83]

3.3. "Doctrines" and Doctrine

Calvin's phrase "sum of doctrine," in which not only "sum" but also "doctrine" is in the singular, does raise a troubling if intriguing question about creeds and confessions, particularly those of the Reformation and the modern period, with their multiple articles and there-

80. See chapter 9 below, "Creedal Dogma as Church Law"; and chapter 8.2 below, "Civil Law on Adherence to Creeds."
81. See chapter 1.1 above, "Continuity *versus* Change in the Decrees of the Ecumenical Councils"; chapter 14.3 below, "The Sacred Tradition of the Seven Ecumenical Councils"; chapter 15.1 below, "The Western Reception of the Catholic Creedal and Conciliar Tradition"; and chapter 16.3 below, "Catholic Substance and Protestant Principle in Reformation Confessions."
82. *39 Art* 8.
83. See chapter 8.4 below, "The Politics of Confessional Diversity."

fore multiple doctrines: Just how many Christian doctrines are there that have to be confessed? In the usage of the New Testament, the word *doctrine* (which in the Revised Standard Version of the English Bible is the translation for the Greek vocables *didaskalia, didachē,* and *logos*) is always in the singular when it is used positively as a reference to "sound doctrine,"[84] or to "the good doctrine which you have followed,"[85] or to "the elementary doctrine of Christ."[86] So it is also with the noun *truth* (*alētheia*). There is no instance in the New Testament that would correspond completely to the formula of the American *Declaration of Independence,* "We hold *these truths* to be self-evident,"[87] by using the plural of the noun to refer to the individual "truths" of the gospel, although the plural of the adjective in the words of Paul "whatsoever things are true [*hosa estin alēthē*]"[88] does come quite close to doing so. In the New Testament the plural "doctrines" is reserved for what is called in the Gospels, on the basis of the words of Isaiah, "teaching as doctrines the precepts of men"[89]—a condemnatory passage that is quoted over and over in such Protestant confessions as *The Geneva Confession,*[90] *The First Helvetic Confession,*[91] *The Second Helvetic Confession,*[92] *The Scots Confession,*[93] *The [First] Bohemian Confession,*[94] *The Heidelberg Catechism,*[95] and *The Westminster Confession of Faith*[96] against the Roman Catholic (and Eastern Orthodox) view of the authority of church traditions, which are seen by these confessions as nothing more than "doctrines of men" in comparison with the divine authority of Holy Scripture. The plural "doctrines" appears likewise in such New Testament phrases as "human precepts and doctrines"[97]

84. 1 Tm 1.10; Ti 1.9, 2.10.
85. 1 Tm 4.6.
86. Heb 6.1.
87. Laqueur and Rubin 1989, 107; italics added.
88. Phil 4.8 (AV).
89. Is 29.13; Mt 15.9; Mk 7.7.
90. *Genv Con* 17.
91. *Helv I* 4.
92. *Helv II* 2.6, 16.5.
93. *Scot I* 14.
94. *Boh I* 7, 15.
95. *Heid* 91.
96. *West* 20.2.
97. Col 2.22.

and "deceitful spirits and doctrines of demons." [98] For the language of
the New Testament, then, the "sum of doctrine" apparently *is* the doctrine (in the singular) of Christ and the church, and only those on the
outside, false teachers whether demonic or human, have a plurality of
"doctrines."

From the doctrinal decrees of the ancient councils of the
church it is evident that, howsoever many other doctrines they may
contain or at least mention, they do assign the priority over all of these
to the doctrine of the Trinity and the related doctrine of the incarnation. For, as *The Athanasian Creed* formulates that widely held priority,
"Whoever desires to be saved must above all things hold the catholic
faith. . . . Now this is the catholic faith, that we worship one God in
Trinity and Trinity in unity. . . . It is necessary, however, to eternal salvation that one should also faithfully believe in the incarnation of our
Lord Jesus Christ." [99] In one way or another, therefore, each of the first
seven church councils can be seen as an attempt to give the church's
doctrinal response to the question asked by Jesus Christ in the Gospels:
"Who do you say that I am?" [100] First that question is answered by the
doctrine regarding the relation of his person to the person of the Father
and to the person of the Holy Spirit in the Trinity; that happens in the
first two ecumenical councils. When the question has been answered
on that basis, it then has to be answered further with the doctrine regarding the relation between the divine nature and the human nature
within his own person; that happens in the next four ecumenical councils. Even the defense of the use of images in the church, as this is confessed by the seventh ecumenical council, the Second Council of Nicaea
in 787, justifies the practice on the basis of the doctrine of the reality of
the incarnation. Consequently, "If anyone does not confess that Christ
our God can be represented in his humanity, let him be anathema." [101]

It is arguable, then, that for these seven ecumenical councils
of the church and for their definitions of the faith, the doctrine of the
Trinity and the doctrine of the incarnation are (in Calvin's phrase) "the

98. 1 Tm 4.1; *Tetrapol* 9.
99. *Ath* 1, 3, 29; also, for example, *Tol XI* 1.9.
100. Mt 16.15.
101. *Nic II* def, anath 1.

sum of doctrine." The other "doctrines" addressed in later confessions of faith stand in a derivative and therefore even, in some sense, in a secondary position by comparison. Perhaps most notable of all among these other doctrines, in the light of the subsequent development of doctrine especially in the West, already in the medieval period and then in the confessions of Protestantism, is the related doctrine of the atoning work of Christ.[102] As Georges V. Florovsky puts it in an essay that explicitly borrows its title "Cur Deus Homo" from the medieval Western "father of scholasticism," Anselm of Canterbury,[103] "the question about the *ultimate motive* of the Incarnation was never formally discussed in the Patristic Age"[104] or in the councils and creeds of that age. The teaching of the church deals with the doctrine of the *person* of Christ as true God and true man. The formulation of the doctrine of the *work* of Christ is a theme that is better left to the celebrations of the liturgy, the homilies of preachers, and the commentaries and speculations of theologians than spelled out in dogma and creed. That applies whether it is interpreted as a ransom paid to the devil, or as a redeeming sacrifice, or as an act of vicarious satisfaction rendered to God, or as the supreme example of faith and obedience to God, or as a demonstration to the world of divine love, or as the victory of the cross and resurrection over sin, death, and the devil—or as several or all of the above.[105] The patristic hesitation to legislate a dogma of the work of Christ on a par with the dogma of the person of Christ maintains itself in later times as well, at any rate to some degree. Yet there was a wide acceptance throughout Western Christendom, in Roman Catholicism but perhaps even more enthusiastically in mainstream and in Evangelical Protestantism, of the Anselmic doctrine of the death of Christ as a "substitutionary atonement" and satisfaction rendered by Christ the God-man to the violated honor of God.[106]

For example, the statement in the earliest confession of the Protestant Reformation in Part Four of *Creeds and Confessions of Faith*

---

102. *Pres USA* 9.09; also Dowey 1968, 49–53.
103. See chapter 15.3 below, "Scholastic Theology as Reasoning on the Basis of the Creed."
104. Florovsky 1972–89, 3:164; italics original.
105. As they have been reviewed in Aulén 1969.
106. *Camb Dec* 2, 4; *Chr Trad* 3:129–44, 4:161–63, 359–61, 5:95–101.

in the Christian Tradition, which is *The Sixty-Seven Articles of Ulrich Zwingli* of 1523, that "Christ has borne all our pain and misery," is not a doctrinal proposition in its own right but the presupposition for the polemical declaration that "whoever now attributes to works of penance what belongs to Christ alone, errs and blasphemes God."[107] The same is true of the formulations of the doctrine of atonement through Christ contained in other Reformation confessions. The Latin text of *The Augsburg Confession* employs the technical term of Anselm's treatise when it teaches that "Christ . . . by his death made satisfaction for our sins [*sua morte pro nostris peccatis satisfecit*]."[108] Zwingli's *Reckoning of the Faith* includes the phrase that Christ is "a mediator to make a sacrifice for us to divine justice."[109] "By offering up himself he made satisfaction to God for our sins and the sins of all believers," *The First Confession of Basel* says in German.[110] In an even more Anselmic Latin formulation, *The Belgic Confession* asserts that the relation between "the justice and mercy of God" was resolved when Christ "presented himself in our name before his Father, to appease his wrath with full satisfaction."[111] In such confessional assertions, this "satisfaction" through the death of Christ is being used to counter the medieval idea of a punishment or penitential "satisfaction" offered by the sinner in restitution to the *rectitudo* or honor of God for the damage caused by sins. Satisfaction is one of the three steps of the Roman Catholic sacrament of penance, which are contrition, confession, and satisfaction, by which, according to the Council of Trent, "we become like Christ Jesus, who made satisfaction for our sins."[112] For these Protestant confessions, by contrast, the three steps of true repentance are contrition, faith, and the new obedience.[113] Within a single article, *The First Helvetic Confession* of 1536 rings many of the changes of the doctrine of the work of Christ, describing it as "quicken[ing] us," as "a pure, unblemished sacrifice," as "a payment," as having "overcome and con-

---

107. *67 Art* 54; also Zwingli's statement in *Fid rat* 3.
108. *Aug Lat* 4.2, 24.25–27. Also *17 Art* 9; *Witt Art* 7; *Form Conc Sol Dec* 3.57.
109. *Fid rat* 2.
110. *Bas Bek* 4; see also *Laus Art* 1.
111. *Belg* 20–21.
112. *Trent* 14.1.3, 14.1.8.
113. *Witt Art* 4.

quered death, sin, and the whole power of hell," as the restoration of the image of God, and as "lead[ing] us into the fellowship of his divine nature."[114] *The Wittenberg Articles* of 1536 give a strong endorsement to Anselm by name for his definition of original sin, which "we particularly approve,"[115] but they do not make a corresponding reference to Anselm when they describe the atonement as satisfaction. *The Heidelberg Catechism* can speak about the necessity of "satisfaction," arguing for it in Anselmic fashion, but it puts this Anselmic vocabulary into the context of its own distinctive understanding of salvation.[116] Not in an exposition of the atoning work of Christ, but in a polemic against the Roman Catholic teaching about penitential satisfactions, *The Second Helvetic Confession* of 1566 cites the argument "that Christ alone by his death or passion is the satisfaction, propitiation, or expiation of all sins."[117] Going a significant step further in the same direction by devoting a special article to "The One Oblation of Christ Finished upon the Cross," *The Thirty-Nine Articles of the Church of England* argue that "the offering of Christ once made is the perfect redemption, propitiation, and satisfaction for all the sins of the whole world, both original and actual, and there is no other satisfaction for sin but that alone."[118] And more specifically still, *The Westminster Confession of Faith* in its article "Of Christ the Mediator" restates the Anselmic doctrine of the work of Christ as satisfaction: "The Lord Jesus, by his perfect obedience and sacrifice of himself, which he, through the eternal Spirit, once offered up unto God, hath fully satisfied the justice of his Father, and purchased, not only reconciliation, but an everlasting inheritance in the kingdom of heaven, for all those whom the Father hath given unto him."[119] Even in *The Mennonite Short Confession of Faith* of 1610 the obedience, suffering, and death of Christ are described as "the reconciliation and satisfaction [*genoechdoeninge*] for all our sins and the sins of the world."[120]

114. *Helv I* 11. Syndogmaticon 4.1.
115. *Witt Art* 2; see also *West Sh Cat* 18.
116. *Heid* 12–18; see Metz 1970.
117. *Helv II* 14.13.
118. *39 Art* 31; also *Meth Art* 20.
119. *West* 8.5; also *Dort* 2.1.1–4.
120. *Ries* 13; also *Am Bap* 6.

The "doctrine" of the Virgin Mary is in a position similar to that of the "doctrine" of the work of Christ. In the early creedal fragments there is the repeated confession that "in a daughter of man there dwelt the Son of God."[121] In the creedal decrees of the first seven ecumenical councils, even in those of the Council of Ephesus in 431 awarding her the honorific title of "Theotokos" or "Mother of God," Mariology does not stand on its own as a discrete subject of the church's teaching and confession but functions as a corollary proposition—indispensable and incontestable, but nevertheless corollary—to the doctrine and confession of the person of Christ. It occupies the same position in *The Divine Liturgy According to Saint John Chrysostom*.[122] She is not even mentioned in *The Creed of Nicaea* of 325, which simply says that the Son of God "became incarnate, became human," with no reference to her at all.[123] But *The Niceno-Constantinopolitan Creed* of 381 affirms, more amply, that he "became incarnate from the Holy Spirit *and the Virgin Mary,* became human."[124] The first anathema of the Council of Ephesus declares, making it quite clear by the term "therefore [*dia touto*]" that the second and mariological clause of the confession is a corollary of the first and christological clause: "If anyone does not confess that Emmanuel is God in truth, and *therefore* that the holy Virgin is the Mother of God [Theotokos] (for she bore in a fleshly way the Word of God become flesh), let him be anathema."[125] In its subsequent development both Eastern and Western, the confession of the doctrine of Mary does not occupy a doctrinal niche of its own, but pertains to the doctrine of Christ, and elsewhere to the doctrine of the church, of which she is seen as the archetype.[126] That holds true even in the promulgations of the dogma of her immaculate conception by Pope Pius IX in 1854, a privilege that is said to be "on the basis of the merits of Christ Jesus the Savior of the human race,"[127] and of

121. *Arist.*
122. See chapter 14.2 below, "The Liturgy as the Church's Preeminent Confession of the Faith."
123. *N 3.*
124. *N-CP 3*; italics added.
125. *Eph 431* anath 1.
126. Semmelroth 1963.
127. *Ineff.*

the dogma of her bodily assumption by Pope Pius XII in 1950, which is said to be "for the honor [*ad honorem*] of her Son."[128] Nor, for that matter, has there been a creedal and traditional "doctrine" of justification (much less of justification by faith alone), at any rate before the confessions of the Reformation, although *The Canons and Decrees of the Council of Trent* speak about "the true and sound *doctrine* on justification which . . . the Catholic Church . . . has always retained,"[129] and *The Thirty-Nine Articles of the Church of England* can declare: "That we are justified by faith only is a most wholesome *doctrine*."[130] The plenary inspiration and inerrancy of the Bible, while certainly presupposed in the creeds and confessions, does not rise to the status of a confessed "doctrine" either.[131] Similarly, there are recognized limits to what a church confession has authorization to say about the "doctrine" of angels.[132]

It is the purpose of "doctrine" in all the creeds and confessions of faith, and in all the periods of church history, to promote, strengthen, and regulate, but also and first of all to articulate, what a later chapter of this book, borrowing the title from Cardinal Newman, calls "the orthodoxy of the body of the faithful" in the church.[133] The examples of *The Niceno-Constantinopolitan Creed* and *The Apostles' Creed*, as well as of *The Small Catechism of Martin Luther* and *The Heidelberg Catechism*, even though they do not exhaust the function of confessional and creedal doctrine, are a documentation of the decisive place that "the teaching of the faith," both as process and as content, occupies in the ongoing life and practice of the church. Because of the emphasis of the Protestant Reformation simultaneously on the centrality of Christian doctrine and on the universal priesthood of all believers, the catechism became both a major genre of Christian doctrinal confession and a dominant force in the life of the churches: *The [First] Bohemian Confession* of 1535 makes "Of the Catechism" the title

128. *Munif* 44.
129. *Trent* 6.1 int; italics added.
130. *39 Art* 11; italics added.
131. See chapter 5.2 below, "Scripture in the Creeds and Confessions."
132. *Mogila* 1.20.
133. See chapter 12 below, "The Orthodoxy of the Body of the Faithful."

of its article 2, right after article 1 "Of the Holy Scriptures." [134] But even before the Reformation, the catechisms of every age had it as their purpose, as John Calvin's preface to *The Geneva Catechism* of 1541 explains, "to see that little children should be instructed in Christian doctrine. That this might be done, not only were schools opened in early times, and people enjoined to teach their families well, but it was also a public practice to examine children in the churches on articles of faith common to all Christians. That this might be carried out in order, a formulary was used which was called a catechism." [135] A comparison of this *Geneva Catechism* with his *Institutes of the Christian Religion,* particularly in its monumental final version of 1559—the fundamental outline of both works is supplied by *The Apostles' Creed*—makes clear both the similarities and the differences between the two styles of expounding Christian doctrine: a profound and learned statement of the Reformed faith on the basis of Scripture and in response to opponents, compared with an enchiridion intended "to see that little children should be instructed in Christian doctrine." For the purposes of such a comparison, what the catechism omits, by contrast with what the work of dogmatics contains, is in many respects at least as important as what it includes.

Yet there has always been an even more fundamental medium than the catechism for communicating the doctrine of the faith to the body of the faithful. For Calvin also insisted that "among the many excellent gifts with which God has adorned the human race, it is a singular privilege that he deigns to consecrate to himself the mouths and tongues of men in order that his voice may resound in them" through the preaching of the word of God.[136] At almost exactly the same time, the fifth session of the Council of Trent, in a conscious program of reform directed against the medieval abuses to which the Protestant Reformation had been pointing so dramatically and often so effectively, declared that "the preaching of the gospel . . . is the chief task of the bishops," and therefore that "all bishops, archbishops, primates, and all others who preside over the churches are personally bound, unless

134. *Boh I 2.*
135. *Genv Cat* pr.
136. Calvin *Institutes of the Christian Religion* 3.1.5 (McNeill 1960, 2:1018).

legitimately impeded, to preach the holy gospel of Jesus Christ." The
council warned, moreover, that "if anyone treats with contempt the
fulfilment of this duty, he is to be subjected to severe penalties."[137]
The correlation of the content of "teaching the faith" as doctrine with
the process of "teaching the faith" as preaching, thus the dual meaning of the Latin word *doctrina,* becomes clear when the Latin and the
German texts of *The Augsburg Confession,* which possess equal confessional standing and authority, are laid side by side at article 7:

> Latin: For the true unity of the church it is
> enough to agree concerning the teaching of the gospel
> [*consentire de doctrina evangelii,* rendered in earlier En-
> glish translations as "the doctrine of the gospel"] and
> the administration of the sacraments.
>
> German: For it is sufficient for the true unity
> of the Christian church that the gospel be preached
> in conformity with a pure understanding of it [*dass
> da einträchtiglich nach reinem Verstand das Evangelium
> gepredigt*] and that the sacraments be administered in
> accordance with the divine word.[138]

The same correlation appears when *The Second Helvetic Confession* states in successive chapters that "the preaching and writings of
the apostles . . . is also rightly called evangelical doctrine," that "the
doctrine of repentance is joined with the gospel," and that "the true
harmony of the church consists in doctrines [*dogmata*] and in the true
and harmonious preaching of the gospel of Christ, and in rites that
have been expressly delivered by the Lord."[139] Pressed to its consequences, the correlation requires that in its content the preaching of
the gospel be doctrinal, not simply moral (even when it is dealing with
morality),[140] and, at the same time, that doctrine be preachable and
not be identified with the speculations and the quarrels of the learned

137. *Trent* 5.2.9–10 decr; see Freitag 1991, 353.
138. *Aug* 7.2.
139. *Helv II* 13.3, 14.1, 17.17.
140. See chapter 10.1 below, "Doctrines of Christian Discipline in the Reformation Confessions."

theological professionals.[141] It also means, in the words of Zwingli's
Profession of the Faith, that preaching is "above any other duty" as "in
the highest degree necessary,"[142] and further, as *The [First] Bohemian
Confession* insists, that the celebration of the eucharist is not to be separated from the preaching of the word.[143]

3.4. Doctrine as Dogma

Such a use of the term *dogmata* for "doctrines," not only in the authoritative texts of the Roman Catholic and the Eastern Orthodox traditions but in an unequivocally and militantly Protestant affirmation like
The Second Helvetic Confession of 1566,[144] is a reminder that to ensure
that the doctrine being preached and taught in the church be sound
has been the purpose of what we have called earlier "a formal, official, public, and binding statement of what is believed and confessed
by the church" in its creeds and confessions of faith.[145] The technical
term for such a binding and official public doctrine is *dogma,* although
it has not been until comparatively modern times that the technical
significance of the term has become virtually the only definition of it.
Plato speaks in the *Republic* about the moral responsibility incumbent
on "the disciples of philosophy" to hold to *dogmata,* which according
to him are not mere subjective opinions but, as Benjamin Jowett translates the passage, "certain principles about justice and honor which
were taught us in childhood, and under their parental authority we
have been brought up, obeying and honoring them."[146] Eventually the
Greek word *dogma* came to refer to a "public decree." That is how it is
employed in biblical Greek (as well as sometimes in the Greek confessions).[147] The Septuagint version of the Book of Daniel speaks of how a
royal "decree [*to dogma*] went forth," and of "the decree of the Persians

141. See also chapter 12.1 below, "What Did the Laity Believe, Teach, and Confess?"; and chapter 16.4 below, "From Reformation Confessions to Confessional
Scholasticism."
142. *Fid rat* 10.
143. *Boh I* 13.10.
144. *Helv II* 17.17.
145. See chapter 2.4 above, "The Content of the Confession."
146. Plato *Republic* 538C.
147. For example, *Jer II* 1.19.

and Medes [*to dogma Persōn kai Mēdōn*]."[148] The Book of Esther reports the advice to King Artaxerxes that "if it seems good to the king, let him make a decree [*dogmatisatō*] to destroy" the Jews.[149] The definition of *dogma* as an official public decree of a ruling authority carries over into the New Testament, especially in Luke-Acts. In the Christmas story in his Gospel, Luke uses it for the "decree" that went out from Caesar Augustus that all the world should be enrolled,[150] and then he uses it in the seventeenth chapter of the Acts of the Apostles for "the decrees of Caesar."[151] By extension, the preceding chapter of the Book of Acts applies it not only to such royal and imperial decrees but also to "the decisions [*dogmata*] that had been reached by the apostles and elders who were at Jerusalem,"[152] referring to the decree on Christian observance and nonobservance of Jewish dietary laws that had been laid down at the apostolic council as it was described in the fifteenth chapter of Acts.[153] Applying by anachronism the distinction of later councils and confessions,[154] then, *dogma* here could be said to refer to "discipline" rather than to "doctrine." The same would seem to be true of the famous distinction invoked by Basil of Caesarea between *dogma* and *kērygma,* where "the first and most general example" of *dogma* that he cites is "to sign with the sign of the cross those who have trusted in the name of our Lord Jesus Christ" and the second example is "to turn to the East at the prayer."[155]

In ecclesiastical usage, therefore, as this passage from Basil illustrates, *dogma* continues to carry a variety of connotations for a long time.[156] But by a combination of the meaning of universally binding "principles," as *dogma* is used by Plato, with legislative "decrees," as *dogma* is used by the Septuagint and by Luke-Acts, the term eventually

148. Dn 2.13, 6.8 (LXX).
149. Est 3.9 (LXX).
150. Lk 2.1.
151. Acts 17.7.
152. Acts 16.4.
153. Acts 15.28–29.
154. See chapter 4 below, "Faith and Order"; and chapter 10 below, "Deeds, Not Creeds?"
155. Basil of Caesarea *On the Holy Spirit* 27.66 (*NPNF*–II 8:40–41).
156. Lampe, 377–78.

acquires the special and more technical sense that we associate with it now. Therefore *The Oxford Dictionary of the Christian Church* defines it as "a religious truth established by Divine Revelation and defined by the Church,"[157] and the *Dictionary of the Ecumenical Movement* as "communally authoritative truths of revealed faith essential to the identity or welfare of Christian community."[158] According to the *Dictionnaire de Théologie Catholique,* it is "a truth revealed by God and, as such, directly propounded by the church for us to believe."[159] Or, more amply, another Roman Catholic reference book defines it as "a proposition to be believed with divine and Catholic faith, that is, a proposition which the Church expressly teaches in her ordinary magisterium, or by a papal or conciliar definition, as divinely revealed; the denial of which is, therefore, heresy."[160] That latter definition of "dogma" by Karl Rahner and Herbert Vorgrimler is a summary and paraphrase of the declaration of *The Dogmatic Constitution on the Catholic Faith of the First Vatican Council* of 1870 (which does not however, it should be noted, use the term *dogma* itself): "By divine and catholic faith all those things are to be believed which are contained in the word of God as found in Scripture and tradition, and which are proposed by the church as matters to be believed as divinely revealed, whether by her solemn judgment or in her ordinary and universal magisterium."[161]

On a variety of grounds, some historical and others theological and polemical, Adolf Harnack's magisterial *History of Dogma,* the first volume of the first edition of which appeared in 1889, posited "the threefold issue of the history of dogma" in Roman Catholicism, the Radical Reformation, and mainline Protestantism.[162] If that restrictive definition of dogma and its history were to hold, the massive confessional efforts of Reformation and post-Reformation Protestantism, whether Reformed or Lutheran, to legislate its own versions of "a religious truth established by Divine Revelation and defined by the

157. *ODCC* 495.
158. *DEM* 305 (George A. Lindbeck).
159. *DTC* 4:1575 (Edmond Dublanchy).
160. Rahner-Vorgrimler, 133.
161. *Vat I* 3.
162. Harnack [1893] 1961b, 7:21–34.

Church,"[163] as those efforts are documented in the bulk of the texts collected in Parts Four and Five of *Creeds and Confessions of Faith in the Christian Tradition,* the two largest of the five parts of the set, would not qualify as "dogma" in the strict sense of the word. But as early as 1908, in the first volume of his four-volume history of dogma in Protestantism, *Dogmengeschichte des Protestantismus,* Otto Ritschl protested against the artificiality of such an exclusion, nevertheless dedicating the book "to Adolf Harnack in long-standing gratitude."[164] It does seem impossible, or at any rate arbitrary, to maintain, at least on historical grounds, a definition and distinction under which, for example, the Roman Catholic doctrine of transubstantiation qualifies as a dogma but the Protestant doctrine of justification by faith does not.

In Protestantism no less than in Eastern Orthodoxy and Roman Catholicism, there have been, and there continue to be, official processes for the creedal and confessional definition of doctrine by the church. These processes do differ from one church to another and, even within the same church, from one historical period to another. As the chapters that follow will seek to document, the formulation of doctrine and dogma in creeds and confessions of faith has taken place under various auspices and in diverse arenas. Church and state, council and pope, cloister and university, liturgy and controversy, biblical exegesis and systematic theology, learned speculation and lay spirituality, cultural imperialism and cultural indigenization—all of these, and sometimes other factors as well, have had influential roles in the development of creeds and confessions of faith. The forms of expression, too, have been multiple and diverse. But all have participated in the dynamic interrelation among believing, teaching, and confessing:

> Without setting rigid boundaries, we shall identify
> what is "believed" as the form of Christian doctrine
> present in the modalities of devotion, spirituality, and
> worship; what is "taught" as the content of the word
> of God extracted by exegesis from the witness of the
> Bible and communicated to the people of the church

163. *ODCC* 495.
164. Ritschl 1908–27, 1:1–51.

through proclamation, instruction, and churchly theology; and what is "confessed" as the testimony of the
church, both against false teaching from within and
against attacks from without, articulated in polemics
and in apologetics, in creed and in dogma.[165]

It is this third component of the definition of doctrine, "what is 'confessed,'" that is our concern here in *Credo*. It has shaped the texts collected in *Creeds and Confessions of Faith in the Christian Tradition* and
then, in turn, has determined their selection for inclusion there.

165. *Chr Trad* 1:4.

CHAPTER FOUR

Faith and Order

THE ECUMENICAL MOVEMENT OF the twentieth century, the most ambitious effort in Christian history to deal with the divisions among confessions and with the issues of church unity, owes much of its origin to the "World Conference on Faith and Order."[1] The inclusion of both "faith" and "order" in that name comes from the recognition that although there are many historic divisions among churches that have been brought about by disagreements over faith and doctrine, other divisions are primarily the consequence of differences over the proper ordering of the structure of the church and over the forms of its ordained ministry, while many others have arisen through conflicts over some combination of church order and church doctrine. To be theologically realistic, therefore, any hope for reconciliation among the historically divided churches must be concerned both with faith and with order. The World Conference on Faith and Order first met at Lausanne, Switzerland, in 1927, issuing a *Call to Unity*,[2] and again at Edinburgh, Scotland, in 1937, issuing an *Affirmation of Union* and a confessional statement entitled *The Grace of Our Lord Jesus Christ*.[3] The parallel Universal Christian Conference on Life and Work, in whose deliberations doctrine took a secondary position on the basis of the slogan that "service unites while doctrine divides," met at Stockholm in 1925 and then at Oxford in 1937.[4] Out of the meetings of these two "conferences" in the British Isles during 1937 came the proposal that they should merge to form a "council," which eventually became the World Council of Churches in 1948, with a brief quasi-creedal formulation

1. Skoglund and Nelson 1963; Vischer 1963.
2. *F&O Laus.*
3. *F&O Edin.*
4. *DEM* 612–14 (Paul Abrecht).

of its "doctrinal basis."[5] In many quarters, however, this confession of "Jesus Christ as God and Savior" proved to be controversial, either because it seemed to many to be theologically inadequate or because it seemed to others to err on the side of a dogmatic maximalism.[6] The International Missionary Council, which had been founded in 1921, was integrated with the World Council of Churches in 1961. But Faith and Order has continued to maintain a distinct existence as the "Faith and Order Commission of the World Council of Churches," which "provides theological support for the efforts the churches are making towards unity"[7] and functions as the principal forum of doctrinal and theological dialogue, not only among the churches that are members of the World Council of Churches but also with churches that do not belong to the World Council, including the Roman Catholic Church and some of the Eastern Orthodox and Oriental Orthodox bodies as well as certain Protestant groups.[8] A similar function of facilitating dialogue and study has been performed by the "Commission on Faith and Order of the National Council of the Churches of Christ in the USA."

In any such theological dialogue, however, as the name "Faith *and Order*" indicates, it would be a misconception, though one to which expositions of creeds and confessions have sometimes been vulnerable, to separate considerations of the confession of the faith as doctrine from considerations of church order. For many of the creeds, confessions, and dogmatic decrees that have been promulgated by local synods, ecumenical councils, and denominational assemblies, as well as by bishops, patriarchs, and popes, as these texts have been published in various editions (which are listed in the front matter under "Editions, Collections, and Reference Works") and as they are collected in the volumes of *Creeds and Confessions of Faith in the Christian Tradition,* have been parts of a much larger body of legislation enacted by those same authorities. This has been no less true of the Reformation churches than it has of Roman Catholicism and Eastern Orthodoxy, even though the technical vocabularies and the official agencies of such

5. *WCC.*
6. *DEM* 1096–98 (Paul Abrecht).
7. *BEM* pr.
8. Gassmann 1979; also the materials assembled in Gassmann 1993.

legislation have been very different for different communions over time. As one study has put it, in introducing a discussion of the first four ecumenical councils of the church, "These councils not only defined trinitarian and christological dogma in terms which ever since have been regarded as normative by the major Christian confessions of East and West. They also laid down canons and disciplinary decrees which constitute a milestone in the history of church order, signaling as they do a shift from the multifarious customary law of earlier centuries to a written law universally applicable throughout the Church."[9] What this author calls "the history of church order," which is the primary subject of his book, is, of course, quite distinct from the history of what he calls "trinitarian and christological dogma" or what we have called "the confession of the faith as doctrine,"[10] which is the primary subject of this book.

Nevertheless, the two histories have been closely intertwined, both in the very beginnings of creedal and confessional development and in its later stages, and for particular reasons especially in the texts of those confessions and church orders that belong to the "Reformed" or Calvinist branch of Protestantism. For in the definitional formula of Wilhelm Niesel, who edited the works of John Calvin as well as an important twentieth-century scholarly collection of the Reformed confessions in their original languages, it is an identifying feature of those churches that call themselves "Reformed in accordance with the word of God [nach Gottes Wort reformiert]," as distinguished from the Lutheran churches, that for them "church order, too, bears a confessional character."[11] Therefore Niesel's edition of *The Heidelberg Catechism* of 1563 has reconnected it with *The Church Order of the Palatinate* [*Kirchenordnung der Kurpfalz*] of that same year, of which the first edition of *The Heidelberg Catechism* was an integral part,[12] even though it later went on being printed by itself in various Reformed lands.[13] *The French Confession* [*Confessio Gallica*] of 1559, too, is "inseparable" from the *Discipline Ecclésiastique* of the same year; and therefore Niesel

9. L'Huillier 1996, ix.
10. See chapter 3 above, "Confession of the Faith as Doctrine."
11. Niesel, v. See Syndogmaticon 9.7.
12. Niesel, 136–218.
13. Heijting 1989, 1:84–85.

has also published these two French texts together in his edition of the Reformed confessions, restoring both to the "discipline" and to the "confession" in the titles of this text the connection with each other that is necessary according to the Reformed understanding of both.[14] "Faith" and "order" are likewise coupled in the full title of the English Congregationalist confession that is now generally known as *The Savoy Declaration* of 1658: *A Declaration of the Faith and Order Owned and Practiced in the Congregational Churches in England*. In its preface it distinguishes between "the necessary foundations of faith and holiness," on which agreement is a necessary obligation for Christians, and "all other matters extra fundamental, whether of faith or order."[15] Its second part is entitled "Of the Institution of Churches and the Order Appointed in Them by Jesus Christ." Williston Walker, its modern editor, has given this second part the title "The Platform of Church Polity,"[16] the term "polity" being synonymous with "order" or "church government." Similarly, the first chapter of the earlier Congregationalist declaration from New England, *The Cambridge Platform* of 1648, carries the title "Of the Form of Church-Government; and that it is One, Immutable, and Prescribed in the Word of God." It opens with the words: "Ecclesiastical polity, or church government, or discipline is nothing else but that form and order that is to be observed in the church of Christ upon earth, both for the constitution of it and all the administrations that therein are to be performed."[17]

As is evident from all four of these Reformed documents, two of which originated on the European Continent and two of which came from England and its North American colonies, the primary doctrinal nexus between faith and order is ecclesiology, the doctrine of the church and the ministry, which many (though by no means all) of the other creeds and confessions of faith in all periods of church history have also included in their recital of what was to be believed, taught, and confessed. The declaration that "I believe . . . the holy catholic church," as *The Apostles' Creed* has it,[18] or even that "We believe

14. Niesel, 65–79.
15. *Sav* pr.
16. Walker, 403.
17. *Camb Plat* 1.1.1.
18. *Ap* 9.

. . . *in* [*eis*] one, holy, catholic, and apostolic church," as *The Niceno-Constantinopolitan Creed* puts it more amply,[19] identifies the reality of the church as the object of faith and of confession. The confessions of Reformation Protestantism strive, in the name of biblical authority, to differentiate their ecclesiology from that of their Roman Catholic adversaries. According to some of these Protestant confessions from various denominations in the sixteenth and seventeenth centuries, and beyond, the first attribute to be ascribed to "the catholic or universal church" is that it "is invisible" or, in the more complete terminology of a later paragraph of *The Westminster Confession of Faith*, "sometimes more, sometimes less visible"[20] —which means, according to these Protestants, that it was less visible in the Middle Ages and is more visible now in the Reformation. That is affirmed, for example, by *The Evangelical Counsel of Anshach* of 1524,[21] *The Geneva Catechism* of 1541,[22] *The Scots Confession* of 1560,[23] *The Second Helvetic Confession* of 1561,[24] *The Irish Articles of Religion* of 1615,[25] *The Westminster Confession of Faith* of 1647,[26] *The Savoy Declaration* of 1658,[27] *The Philadelphia Baptist Confession* of 1688,[28] and *The "Commission" Creed* of 1883.[29] Nevertheless, the confessions of the Protestant Reformers all insist in one way or another, in the words of *The Apology of the Augsburg Confession*, that this church is "not . . . some Platonic republic" out there somewhere in the realm of forms and abstract ideas but a "church [that] actually exists, made up of true believers,"[30] who are, however, ultimately known only to God, which is why the church is hidden or invisible. But any church that "actually exists" within human history would seem to need to have a specific

19. *N-CP* 9.
20. *West* 25.4.
21. *Ans* 1.4.7.
22. *Genv Cat* 100.
23. *Scot I* 16.
24. *Helv II* 17.15.
25. *Irish* 68.
26. *West* 25.1.
27. *Sav* 25.1.
28. *Philad* 1.
29. *Com Cr* 10.
30. *Apol Aug* 7.20.

shape, and its ministry, being "ordained," needs to have a form and "order"—not just any shape or form or order, moreover, but one that may legitimately lay claim to an apostolic authenticity. And as soon as any such claim to apostolic authenticity and legitimacy is asserted for a church and its ministry, and of course especially as soon as it is controverted, church order is seen to be an unavoidably doctrinal and therefore confessional question, not simply an administrative or a jurisdictional one. The claim, on the basis of the four marks of the church in *The Niceno-Constantinopolitan Creed*,[31] to be not only "one" church, a "holy" church, and a "catholic" church, but also an "apostolic" church, either begs the question of what makes the church truly "apostolic" or it identifies and defines this particular church's order and ministry as an apostolic one—or even perhaps as the only permissible apostolic ministerial order, whichever of the several alternative historical possibilities that order may be.

Even more fundamentally, any creed or confession of faith—even one that deals only with doctrine or dogma in the strictest sense, as many affirmations of faith do, in speaking as they do, for example, exclusively about the Trinity or about the person of Christ, or about the Trinity and the person of Christ together, as *The Athanasian Creed* does in making acceptance of these two doctrines necessary for salvation[32]—is perforce making a statement about church order by its very existence. For when the writers and presenters of one or another of these affirmations of faith take it upon themselves to open with some such formula as "We believe"[33] or "We believe, teach, and confess,"[34] they are, in their opponents' eyes, arrogating to themselves and to their party or school of thought (or sect) the right to speak in the name of the true church. But because they are, in their own eyes, "competent to issue supplementary statements concerning the faith," as one twentieth-century confession from South India puts it,[35] they are thereby only appropriating what truly belongs to them and to their church in the form in which that church has been constituted. A doc-

31. *N-CP* 9. See Syndogmaticon 9.6–8.
32. *Ath* 1, 3, 29. See chapter 3.3 above, "'Doctrines' and Doctrine."
33. *N* 1; *N-CP* 1.
34. See chapter 2 above, "The Creedal and Confessional Imperative."
35. *CSI 1947* 1.

trine of church order does not have to be specified to be confessed, and typically it has not been specified in complete detail until it has been challenged. But even when it is some other doctrine that is being specified, church order is also being defined and confessed at the very same time, in the very act of confessing the "apostolic" faith. "Faith" and "order" belong together, therefore, as they have in one way or another ever since the New Testament.[36]

At the same time, church order or polity does, of course, remain an administrative and jurisdictional question as well as a confessional question, and one that can and should also be studied on its own. The confessional criteria of church polity are determined by the interaction of several theological principles. A doctrine of church order rests on a particular method of reading the New Testament, with its sometimes confusing array of church offices. For example, the apostle Paul explains: "And his gifts were that some should be apostles, some prophets, some evangelists, some pastors and teachers,"[37] a roster that follows the consistent practice of the New Testament in not referring to the holders of any of these offices as "priests." In the subsequent usage of the church, several of those titles, including "priest," came to mean something beyond what they seem to have meant *ex professo* in the New Testament. A doctrine of order depends as well on how the continuity of the church is defined and how it is said to be guaranteed; for, in what might appear from the outside to be a classic instance of an argument in a circle, the church is called into being by the word of God, but the word of God is proclaimed and preserved by the church, each acting as a warrant for the other. In addition, differences of church order, for example, those between the Eastern and the Western church as well as many others in modern times, certainly reflect deep-seated cultural differences and "the interference of extra-ecclesial interests,"[38] which are not exclusively doctrinal but also are not devoid of doctrinal significance.[39] Yet a confessional consideration of the doctrinal principle that "the rule of prayer establishes the rule

36. Campenhausen 1968.
37. Eph 4.11.
38. *Balamand* 8–9.
39. See chapter 11 below, "Transmission of Creeds and Confessions to Other Cultures."

of faith [*lex orandi lex credendi*]"[40] is possible without a discussion of
such technical issues of liturgy as its vocabulary or music or postures
and gestures, even in those cases when the liturgy is expressly seen as
the church's preeminent confession of faith.[41] So also, an examination
of church order and polity as a confessional question is not obliged to
go into the details of church structure and organizational behavior as
such.

4.1. Apostolic Creed and Apostolic Ministry

The descriptions of the primitive Christian community in the early
chapters of the Acts of the Apostles do not in so many words contain a specific and detailed prescription of church order. In one sense
they did not have to do so, because the community that this book of
the New Testament portrays was being governed in person directly by
the apostles, who are described as having found it possible and legitimate to speak quite naturally and unabashedly, as the apostle Peter
did, with the delegated authority and "in the name of Jesus Christ of
Nazareth."[42] When conflict had arisen between Peter and Paul about
the continuing enforcement upon Christians of the Mosaic ceremonial
law, the college of apostles in the narrative of the Book of Acts could,
in resolving the conflict by convoking a council of the apostles, even
invoke the formula, which later ecumenical councils would cite as a
precedent,[43] and to which still later confessions of faith by churches of
various confessional traditions would likewise refer:[44] "It has seemed
good to the Holy Spirit and to us."[45]

When the apostle Paul was writing to a church that he himself had founded, for example the congregation at Corinth, he opened
his letters by presenting his apostolic credentials as "Paul, called by the
will of God to be an apostle of Christ Jesus,"[46] and again as "Paul, an

40. See chapter 6.2 below, *"Lex orandi lex credendi."*
41. See chapter 14.2 below, "The Liturgy as the Church's Preeminent Confession
of the Faith."
42. Acts 3.6.
43. *CP II.*
44. *Gall* 32; *Helv II* 27.1; *Camb Plat* 1.4; *Mogila* 1.72.
45. Acts 15.28.
46. 1 Cor 1.1.

apostle of Christ Jesus by the will of God."[47] But those same apostolic credentials likewise authorized him to write the longest and doctrinally the most comprehensive of all his epistles to a church that he did not found, and had not yet even visited, although he was planning to do so:[48] "Paul, a servant of Jesus Christ, called to be an apostle, set apart for the gospel of God . . . to all God's beloved in Rome."[49] And when the authenticity of those apostolic credentials came under attack in a church that he had originally founded,[50] but that had more recently been subverted by his opponents, he opened his epistle to them by identifying himself as "an apostle—not from men nor through man, but through Jesus Christ and God the Father," and proceeded, by means of an *apologia pro vita sua,* to vindicate his apostleship, unique though it undoubtedly was in the circumstances of its conferral because he had not been one of the original twelve who had witnessed the earthly ministry of Jesus.[51] Paul's underlying assumption appears to have been that if he was truly an apostle, albeit one "untimely born,"[52] the churches that he founded were just as apostolic and just as legitimate as were other churches, which were founded by other apostles who had been disciples of Jesus during his earthly ministry and which acknowledged and heeded apostolic authority.

After the death of the last of the original disciples and apostles —who was, according to early tradition, the apostle and evangelist John surnamed "the Theologian," the only one of the twelve to die a natural death[53]—a church that could lay claim to having been founded by an apostle was thereby deemed apostolic.[54] But this did not become an exclusive definition, for a church could be deemed to be fully "apostolic" without any pretense to an apostolic foundation.[55] There was a *historical* definition of apostolicity, therefore, but there was also a *normative* definition of apostolicity. Normatively, what was believed

47. 2 Cor 1.1.
48. Rom 15.32.
49. Rom 1.1,7.
50. Acts 16.6.
51. Gal 1–2.
52. 1 Cor 15.8.
53. Eusebius *Ecclesiastical History* 3.23, 3.31 (*NPNF*-II 1:150–52, 162–63).
54. Irenaeus *Against Heresies* 3.3.1 (*ANF* 1:415).
55. Dvornik 1958, 39–105.

to make a church apostolic, on the basis of the formula about "the apostles' teaching and fellowship, the breaking of bread, and the prayers" in the Book of Acts,[56] was (in some combination) its acceptance of the apostolic Scriptures, its faithfulness to the apostolic tradition in its life, worship, and doctrine, and its preservation of the apostolic order and ministry of the church as represented by the apostolic succession of bishops. The first two of these three criteria and their connection with each other in the earliest creedal (or creedlike) formulations of the church will concern us later.[57] Here the attention will be on the third criterion, the apostolicity of the episcopal order of the church as simultaneously a component of the church's confession of the apostolic faith and a warrant of its apostolicity.

Already within the pages of the New Testament, the successor of an apostle is said to possess a "gift of God that is within you through the laying on of [an apostle's] hands."[58] The church is said to have been "built upon the foundation of the apostles and prophets, Christ Jesus himself being the chief cornerstone"[59]—though it should be noted that some interpreters, citing the parallel usage later in the same epistle,[60] take "apostles and prophets" in this passage as a reference to these continuing offices in the church rather than to the biblical apostles of the New Testament and prophets of the Old Testament.[61] By the second century, this apostolic order of ministry is being identified also as the guarantee of apostolic doctrine. For Irenaeus of Lyons, as Damien van den Eynde puts it, "the doctrinal authority of the church is concentrated in the person of the bishops," just as for Hippolytus of Rome, van den Eynde continues, the bishops are "the successors of the apostles and the appointed guardians of doctrine."[62] Eventually this apostolic tradition of doctrine is seen as embodied in one or another of the church's creeds,[63] for which Irenaeus is an important early

56. Acts 2.42.
57. See chapter 5 below, "Scripture, Tradition, and Creed."
58. 2 Tm 1.6.
59. Eph 2.20.
60. Eph 4.11.
61. Bauer-Arndt-Gingrich, 724.
62. Eynde 1933, 180, 213.
63. See chapter 5 below, "Scripture, Tradition, and Creed"; and chapter 13 below, "Rules of Faith in the Early Church."

witness.[64] Thus these three "criteria of apostolic continuity," which it would perhaps be more precise to call a single but threefold criterion of apostolicity,[65] come to be defined more specifically as, in their interrelation: the apostolic Scriptures of the New Testament, together with an Old Testament that is interpreted christologically according to its "spiritual sense," on the basis of apostolic precedent; the apostolic creed, though not necessarily the very one that is eventually designated in the West as *The Apostles' Creed;* and the apostolic succession of bishops in the monarchical episcopate, as documented in the several bishops' lists preserved for various dioceses, especially for Rome.[66]

After the stabilization of the monarchical episcopate in the second and third centuries, the gravest crisis to arise over the doctrine of church order and ministry was precipitated by the schism with Donatism in the fourth and fifth centuries.[67] Although it had implications also for the relation between the definitions of "schism" and of "heresy,"[68] the Donatist schism, together with the responses to it by Optatus of Mileve and especially by Augustine of Hippo, was responsible for an ecclesiological clarification that would become normative in Western theology both for faith and for order at least until the Protestant Reformation. An early Latin source for our knowledge of creeds,[69] Cyprian of Carthage—who in his interpretation of the first of what were to become in *The Niceno-Constantinopolitan Creed* the four attributes of the church as "one, holy, catholic, and apostolic,"[70] had played such an important part in the definition of the episcopacy as the bond and sign of unity in the church—had also, in dealing with the second attribute, laid great emphasis on the sanctity of the bishop as the guarantee of the holiness of the church and of the sacraments that the bishop administered.[71] Claiming to be able to cite the authority of Cyprian, Donatism charged that some Catholic bishops had sinned

64. *Iren.*
65. *Chr Trad* 1:108–20.
66. Caspar 1926.
67. Frend 1952.
68. See chapter 10.2 below, "Heresy and/or Schism."
69. *Cyp.*
70. *N-CP* 9.
71. Willis 1950, 145–52.

by betraying the faith under persecution or by other immoral acts and that anyone remaining in communion with them became party to their apostasy, with the result that the entire ministry and all the sacraments of the Catholic church had been vitiated. In response, Augustine emphasized what he took to be the Catholic implications of Cyprian's doctrine of the church as "one" in opposition to what the Donatists were taking to be the schismatic implications of Cyprian's doctrine of the church and the ministry as "holy." The outcome was the Augustinian formulation of an affirmation of the doctrine of "orders," that is, of ordination to the priesthood and to the episcopate, that stressed its objectivity as well as that of the other sacraments. Otherwise there could be no confidence in the grace of the sacraments.[72]

4.2. Doctrines of Church Order East and West

But the threat to the doctrine of church order by the Donatist schism, great and tragic as it was, has been greatly overshadowed in the history of Christianity by the threat that came from the schism between the Eastern and the Western church. In the realm of creed and dogma, the principal point of division between them was and is the Filioque:[73] the question of whether in the Trinity the Holy Spirit should be said to be "proceeding from the Father," as the original text of *The Niceno-Constantinopolitan Creed* declares, or "from the Father and the Son [*ex Patre Filioque*]," as the *Western Recension* of *The Niceno-Constantinopolitan Creed* eventually reads.[74] But no less prominent—and in the judgment of many historians, even more decisive—was the difference between the two churches, which at times was as much political as ecclesiastical, over the doctrine of church order. By contrast with the Protestant Reformation of the sixteenth century, in which the questions of the episcopacy and ordination became divisive, the difference between East and West took place within the framework of a shared "profession of apostolic faith, participation in the same sacraments, above all the one priesthood celebrating the one sacrifice of

72. *Chr Trad* 1:308–13. See Syndogmaticon 9.3, 10.12.
73. See chapter 7.4 below, "The Holy Spirit of Concord and the Sacrament of Concord: Two Ironic Case Histories"; also Syndogmaticon 8.6.
74. *N-CP* 8; *N-CP Occ* 8.

Christ, the apostolic succession of bishops"; but the question was: did this "apostolic confession" validate the claim to an "apostolic throne," as the East argued, or was it the other way around, that "the apostolic throne established dignity, and dignity confession"?[75]

It was not accidental that the most complete and most authoritative early lists of bishops should have been the ones that were preserved at Rome[76]—that church, as Irenaeus said, which had been "founded and organized at Rome by the two most glorious apostles, Peter and Paul," rather than by only one apostle, and which possessed "preeminent authority [*potiorem principalitatem*]."[77] The outcome of the evolution of what we have been describing as the two definitions of apostolicity, the "historical" and the "normative," was a comprehensive system of church order. Normatively, the principle enunciated by Cyprian, "The bishop is in the church, and the church is in the bishop,"[78] would appear to mean that every episcopal see of the catholic church regardless of who founded it, and therefore every orthodox and catholic bishop who has not lapsed from the faith and communion of the church, is defined as apostolic, indeed as Petrine. But the historical equation of apostolicity with apostolic foundation was also perpetuated, in the eventual development of the theory of "pentarchy," the designation of five special centers of apostolic authority, each of which acquired, though never exclusively, the title of "patriarchate" (listing them, for now, in an arbitrary and neutral alphabetical order, according to the English alphabet): Alexandria, Antioch, Constantinople, Jerusalem, Rome. Of these five, Jerusalem, though it received the official acknowledgment as a patriarchate only at the Council of Chalcedon in 451,[79] could lay claim to a special kind of primacy. For it was acclaimed early as "the church from which every church took its start, the capital city [*metropolis*] of the citizens of the new cove-

75. *Balamand* 13; *Vat II* 5.3.15; *Resp Pius IX* 11.
76. Caspar 1926.
77. Irenaeus *Against Heresies* 3.3.2 (*ANF* 1:415–16); only the Latin translation of this passage has been preserved, and both its meaning and its possible Greek original have been debated.
78. Cyprian *Epistles* 68.8 (*ANF* 5:374–75).
79. J. Meyendorff 1989, 179.

nant" for all Christian believers.[80] It had had not one apostle, as most did, nor only two, as Rome did, but all of the twelve as its founders, including Peter—or, ultimately, Jesus Christ himself in his life, death, and resurrection, all of which took place there. Therefore Jerusalem is still being honored in *The Orthodox Confession of the Catholic and Apostolic Eastern Church by Peter Mogila* in the seventeenth century, not without an implicit criticism of claims being made on behalf of the church of Rome, as "without doubt the mother and princess of all other churches," the church that "outshone all other churches in sanctity of doctrine and manners."[81] Antioch, too, had once been a "see of Peter."[82] And so, of course, had Rome, and in a special way, also because he was martyred there. But is the primacy of Peter, affirmed in the promise of Christ to him,[83] the basis for what Irenaeus calls the "preeminent authority"[84] of the church of Rome and of its bishop, and for its right to act as the primary arbiter and defender of orthodoxy?[85] Or is there, in addition, some connection between the "preeminence" of that authority and the position of Rome as the capital city of the Roman empire? And if there is some such connection between the status of the church of Rome and the status of the capital city of Rome, what are the ecclesiastical implications of Emperor Constantine's action of 330 transferring the capital city of the Roman empire from Old Rome to Byzantium or Constantinople as "New Rome"?

The most controversial of the official answers to that question is the so-called twenty-eighth canon of the Council of Chalcedon in 451.[86] Repeating the declaration that had already been promulgated by the First Council of Constantinople in 381, the decree of Chalcedon reads: "The fathers [at the Council of Constantinople in 381] rightly accorded prerogatives to the see of older Rome, *since that is an imperial city;* and moved by the same purpose the 150 most devout

---

80. Irenaeus *Against Heresies* 3.12.5 (*ANF* 1:431).
81. *Mogila* 1.84.
82. Pelikan 1980.
83. Mt 16.18–19.
84. Irenaeus *Against Heresies* 3.3.2 (*ANF* 1:415–16).
85. *Horm* 1.
86. Thomas Owen Martin in Grillmeier-Bacht 1951–54, 2:433–58; Kartašev 1963, 424–28.

bishops apportioned equal prerogatives to the most holy see of new Rome, reasonably judging that *the city which is honored by the imperial power* and senate and enjoying [civil] privileges equalling older imperial Rome, should also be elevated to her level in ecclesiastical affairs and take second place after her."[87] On both theological and jurisdictional grounds (if such a distinction may even be taken to be valid in this case), this twenty-eighth canon of Chalcedon has never been accepted by Old Rome; at most, as at the Council of Florence, it was willing to accord Constantinople second place "after the most holy Roman pontiff."[88] But having acknowledged the historical primacy of Jerusalem as "the mother and princess of all other churches," *The Orthodox Confession of the Catholic and Apostolic Eastern Church by Peter Mogila,* in the very same sentence, declares that "in aftertimes the emperors gave the precedency [*ta prōteia tēs timēs*] to Old and New Rome, for the honor of the empire, which they became the seats of," without differentiating between the two capitals or sees as to this "primacy of honor" or "precedency."[89] According to official Western teaching as it is formulated for example by the confession of the Council of Trent, it is equally mistaken to attach "precedency" to Constantinople as "the most holy see of new Rome . . . the city which is honored by the imperial power," and to "accord prerogatives to the see of older Rome" on the grounds that "that is an imperial city"; for that makes the ecclesiastical standing of either one dependent on its political standing rather than on the institution of Christ in his commission to Peter.[90]

4.3. Polity as Doctrine in the Reformed Confessions

When the Protestant Reformation of the sixteenth century is viewed from the perspective of this schism between East and West, it must be seen as having taken place within one part of a Christendom that was already divided.[91] But because the East-West schism was, as that very designation indicates, geographical in its setting and scope, there had in fact been relatively few places where the two segments of Chris-

87. *CP I* can 3; *Chal* can 28 (italics added).
88. *Flor Un* 14–15.
89. *Mogila* 1.84.
90. Mt 16.18; *Trent* 3.
91. *Chr Trad* 4:76–77.

tendom came into direct contact and continuing face-to-face conflict. Among the most important of these were the mission of Cyril-Constantine and Methodius to the Slavs in the ninth century with its aftermath in the Balkans and elsewhere, and then the most dramatic of all such encounters, the Western sack of Constantinople during the Fourth Crusade in 1204, together with the establishment of a Latin patriarchate of Constantinople. With the eruption of the Reformation, by contrast, Western Christianity witnessed fundamental divisions within one region and society (and even family) after another — initially between Roman Catholicism and Protestantism, but very soon also among the several species of Protestantism. Both of these divisions precipitated by the Reformation expressed themselves doctrinally and confessionally, as can be seen from many confessional texts, including the many in Part Four of *Creeds and Confessions of Faith in the Christian Tradition.*[92] But the divisions were also institutional, organizational, and political.[93] These institutional, organizational, and political differences expressed themselves in turn also as doctrine and confession, with the validity of church order an essential issue.[94]

For the principle quoted previously from Wilhelm Niesel, that "according to Reformed doctrine, church order, too, bears a confessional character,"[95] identifies — alongside the well-known controversies over the real presence of the body and blood of Christ in the sacrament, over the relation between the two natures in Christ, and over predestination — one of the most significant differences between the Reformed and the Lutheran versions of the Protestant Reformation.[96] In opposition to Roman Catholic claims that the papacy had been established by Christ in the person of Peter, the Lutheran confessions characterize "the church polity and various ranks of the ecclesiastical authority" as having been "created by human authority," even though *The Apology of the Augsburg Confession* reiterates the "deep desire to maintain" them, including the episcopacy, though not *iure divino* (which was, of course,

---

92. See chapter 16.1 below, "The Proliferation of Confessions in the Age of the Reformation."
93. See chapter 8.3 below, "Confessions and the Formation of Politics."
94. Freitag 1991.
95. Niesel, v.
96. See the detailed discussion in Ainslie 1940.

the real issue).[97] In the event, however, the Lutherans did not "maintain" the traditional polity. Rather, in keeping with this designation of the precise details of ecclesiastical order as a system "created by human authority," the several national Lutheran churches of Northern Europe that came out of the Reformation of the sixteenth century and those that followed elsewhere in later centuries manifested what seemed to many to be an almost cavalier indifference to doctrines of church order and a great variety in their polity, all the way across the spectrum of alternative systems: the retention of the historic apostolic succession of bishops in the Lutheran Church of Sweden; the founding of a Lutheran bishopric in Denmark by Luther's collaborator, Johann Bugenhagen, that deliberately interrupted the apostolic succession; the abolition of any episcopacy at all in the Lutheran Church of Germany in favor, eventually, of a consistorial form of church government, and then in modern times an episcopate without claims to apostolic succession in the traditional sense; and among some Lutherans in North America, a species of extreme congregationalism, in theory if not in practice, and among others eventually an episcopate similar to the German form. By contrast with the single sentence that constitutes the article "Order in the Church" in *The Augsburg Confession*,[98] the corresponding article in *The [First] Bohemian Confession* of 1535, to which Luther wrote a foreword, goes into great detail about the requirements and duties of ministers, including the preferability of the celibate estate.[99] *The Second Helvetic Confession* of 1566 in its first chapter specifies that Holy Scripture prescribes the rules not only for the "reformation [*reformatio*]" of the churches but also for their "government [*gubernatio*]."[100] In a later chapter it elaborates what it identifies as "the apostolic doctrine concerning ministers": they are called "apostles, prophets, evangelists, bishops, elders, pastors, and teachers," each of which the confession defines and puts on an equal level with the others, contrasting those New Testament titles with the later development of "patriarchs, archbishops, suffragans, metropolitans, archdeacons, deacons, subdeacons,

97. *Apol Aug* 14.1.
98. *Aug* 14.
99. *Boh I* 9; 19.
100. *Helv II* 1.3.

acolytes, exorcists, cantors, porters, and I know not what others, as cardinals, provosts, and priors; greater and lesser fathers, greater and lesser orders," all of which it dismisses as human inventions and therefore nonapostolic.[101] *The Belgic Confession* of 1561 sets it forth as the divinely instituted polity by which the church is to be governed that, in addition to "ministers or pastors to preach the word of God and administer the sacraments," there should also be "elders and deacons, along with the pastors, to make up the council of the church."[102] "As to the true church," *The French Confession* affirms, "we believe that it should be governed according to the order established by our Lord Jesus Christ."[103] In the fourth book of his *Institutes of the Christian Religion*, John Calvin argued the case for this multiple form of ministry and for the interchangeability of the titles "bishop" and "presbyter" in the New Testament and in the present structure of the church.[104] The Eastern Orthodox *Confession of Dositheus and of the Synod of Jerusalem* in the seventeenth century, responding to Calvinist claims that "the Eastern Church assents to this wicked notion," singles out these Calvinist views of bishops and ministry for its specific condemnation.[105]

The tendency of the Reformed confessions already on the European Continent during the sixteenth and seventeenth centuries to give church order what Niesel terms "a confessional character" was, if anything, intensified in the Anglo-Saxon milieu of the British Isles and then of North America. Although the Anglican Church did retain what *The Lambeth Quadrilateral* of 1888, in defining the conditions for church union, would call "the historic episcopate"[106] also after its break with Rome in the Reformation of the sixteenth century, its primary confession, *The Thirty-Nine Articles of the Church of England,* assumes the practice of ordination by bishops standing in the apostolic succession[107] but does not make any special doctrinal point of it as a particular requirement. Instead, it contents itself with the

101. *Helv II* 18.5–6.
102. *Belg* 30.
103. *Gall* 29.
104. Calvin *Institutes of the Christian Religion* 4.3.8 (McNeill 1960, 2:1060–61).
105. *Dosith* decr 10.
106. *Lamb Quad* 4.
107. *39 Art* 36.

general requirement that preaching and the sacraments conform "to Christ's ordinance in all those things that of necessity are requisite to the same,"[108] without specifying what "those things" are or whether ordination by a bishop standing in the apostolic succession is one of them. This requirement is followed by the insistence that "bishops, priests, and deacons" are permitted "to marry at their own discretion."[109]

Nevertheless it is significant that so many of the major Protestant church groups in Great Britain and North America have defined and denominated themselves neither by their liturgy nor by their doctrine nor by their confession (not to say by the name of their founder) but by their polity: *Episcopalians* are those who believe, teach, and confess that by divine right the church is to be governed by bishops in the succession of "the historic episcopate";[110] *Presbyterians* vest that authority in the elders of the presbytery;[111] *Congregationalists* see the local congregation of gathered Christian believers as the divinely instituted form of church order;[112] and even *Baptists,* in spite of that nomenclature, set themselves apart not chiefly by their doctrine of baptism as such but by their definition of how the church is constituted and organized, with believers' baptism by total immersion as the most prominent mark of that definition.[113] Within this range of English Protestant doctrines about polity and church order, there had arisen, as the Congregationalist *Savoy Declaration* of 1658 acknowledges, "this unhappy persuasion in the minds of some learned and good men, namely, *that there is no settled order laid down in Scripture;* but it is left to the prudence of the Christian magistrate, to compose or make choice of such a form as is most suitable and consistent with their civil government," a conclusion from which *The Savoy Declaration* vigorously dissents; as a later confession puts it, "This ministry is exactly described . . . by most perfect and plain laws in God's word."[114] A later Congregationalist

108. *39 Art* 19.
109. *39 Art* 32; also *Witt Art* 14.
110. *Lamb Quad* 4.
111. *Crg Sh Cat* 79–81.
112. *Sav* (1658) pr; *Eng Dec* (1833).
113. *Gen Bap* 50; *Bap Gr Br*; *New Hamp* 13–14; *Abst Prin*; *Bap Conf*; *Bap Assoc.*
114. *Sav* pr (italics original); *True Con* 20.

confession, too, makes it incumbent "to observe all divine ordinances, and maintain that church order and discipline which is either expressly enjoined by inspired institution, or sanctioned by the undoubted example of the apostles and of apostolic churches."[115] Nevertheless, although they differ vigorously from one another about just what that form of primitive and divinely instituted "apostolic" church order is, the confessions of these churches are all agreed that indeed there is such a "settled order," one that is no less authoritative and binding than is the doctrinal form of the faith (about the details of whose content some of these confessions are willing to agree to disagree).[116]

The Scotch Presbyterian *Craig's Shorter Catechism* of 1592, therefore, assigns "the order of discipline established in the word" to the authority of "the pastors and elders by their mutual consent and judgment," and it defines "the office of the eldership" as "to watch over their flock and exercise the discipline."[117] The British Congregational *Savoy Declaration* of 1658 affirms that "what we have laid down and asserted about churches and their *government*, we humbly conceive to be the *order* which Christ himself hath appointed to be observed, we have endeavored to follow Scripture-light; and those also that went before us according to that rule, desirous of nearest uniformity with *reforming churches*, as with our brethren in *New-England*, so with others, that differ from them and us."[118] The second part of this *Savoy Declaration*, "The Platform of Church Polity," identifies gathered congregations as "particular societies or churches," and it asserts that "to each of these churches, thus gathered . . . [Christ] hath given all that power and authority, which is any way needful for their carrying on that order in worship and discipline, which he hath instituted." Moreover, it characterizes "these particular churches" as "each of them as unto those ends, the seat of that power which he is pleased to communicate to his saints or subjects in this world," rejecting outright the teaching that Christ instituted "besides these particular churches . . . any church more extensive or Catholic entrusted with power for the administration of his

115. *Eng Dec* 2.20.
116. *Sav* pr.
117. *Crg Sh Cat* 79–81.
118. *Sav* pr; italics original.

ordinances, or the execution of any authority in his name."[119] A representative Baptist statement of faith and order, *The New Hampshire Confession* of 1833, states its definition of the church and of its polity: "We believe that a visible church of Christ is a congregation of baptized believers, associated by covenant in the faith and fellowship of the gospel; observing the ordinances of Christ; governed by his law, and exercising the gifts, rights, and privileges invested in them by his word," with the term "baptized believers" referring to those who have been baptized, not as infants, but only when they were mature enough to be able to make a personal profession of faith as prerequisite to being baptized.[120] The Baptist position on the church and definition of its nature continues to be asserted in such twentieth-century confessions as *The Statement of Faith of the American Baptist Association* of 1905.[121]

This insistence of Reformed confessions upon a linkage between faith and order, or between doctrine and polity, is of a piece in some respects with the distinctively Reformed inclusion of church discipline as the third of the "marks of the church [*notae ecclesiae*]," alongside the generally shared Reformation criteria of the preaching of the word of God and the administration of the sacraments.[122] Some of these confessions can equate "ecclesiastical polity, or church government, or discipline" with "that form and order that is to be observed in the church of Christ upon earth, both for the constitution of it and all the administrations that therein are to be performed."[123] *The Heidelberg Catechism* lists "the preaching of the holy gospel and Christian discipline" in one phrase.[124] What *The First Helvetic Confession* calls "a universal, public, and orderly discipline" is a decisive mark by which the presence of the true church can be known.[125] And *The Belgic Confession* identifies as "required" in the church the exercise of "excommu-

119. *Sav* 2.3–6.
120. *New Hamp* 13. See Syndogmaticon 10.3.
121. *Am Bap* 10.
122. See chapter 10.1 below, "Doctrines of Christian Discipline in the Reformation Confessions." See Syndogmaticon 9.4.
123. *Camb Plat* 1.1.1.
124. *Heid* 83.
125. *Helv I* 14.

nication, with all it involves, according to the word of God."[126] Now if, according to *The Heidelberg Catechism,* "the preaching of the holy gospel and Christian discipline" have to go together,[127] and if moreover, according to *Craig's Shorter Catechism,* it is "the office of the eldership . . . to watch over their flock and exercise the discipline,"[128] it necessarily follows for the Reformed confessions that the disciplinary and administrative authority of the church and of its leadership must be the right one—no less so, though for quite different reasons, than it does for the primarily sacramental and hierarchical definitions of ministry and church order that are characteristic of the Eastern Orthodox and the Roman Catholic traditions.

4.4. Faith and Order in the
Ecumenical Confessional Dialogue

Because the ecumenical dialogue of the nineteenth and twentieth centuries between Christian confessions arose first as a dialogue among several Protestant church bodies, including Reformed church bodies, and almost simultaneously as a dialogue between Anglicanism and other churches, the Reformed understanding of polity as doctrine and the Anglican doctrine of the historic episcopate have been an unavoidable item on the ecumenical agenda from the beginning. Therefore even those churches that did not regard church order as a doctrinal issue could not avoid eventual engagement with it when they participated in ecumenical confessional discussion.

In addition, the modern ecumenical movement coincided with, and was facilitated by, the rise of the critical-historical method of studying the New Testament. As a result of such study, it was increasingly perceived to be impossible to make absolute claims for the historically conditioned and particular doctrines of any one church or confession, which were said to be due to other factors as well. Some of the most influential theological leaders of the ecumenical dialogue came to it from biblical and historical studies that interpreted the doctrines and creeds of the church—even some of the most ancient and

126. *Belg* 32.
127. *Heid* 83.
128. *Crg Sh Cat* 79–81.

most cherished of these—as having evolved over time, rather than as having remained untouched from the beginning in a supposedly apostolic "deposit." As that was taken to be true of creedal teachings that were shared by all the churches, so it was seen as even more true of confessional teachings that were the distinctive doctrines of one or another particular and historic church. Thus modern biblical and patristic philology, which produced the critical editions of sacred texts (including creeds and confessions) on which scholarship must still rely,[129] also gave meticulous attention to the terminology of church order as we have been examining it here. The outcome of such investigation was the discovery, for example, that the Greek terms *episkopos, presbyteros,* and *diakonos,* which are sharply differentiated in the catholic church order of both the West and the East with its doctrine of the threefold office of the ministry,[130] are employed quite loosely, sometimes perhaps even interchangeably, in the New Testament and other early Christian sources.[131] As the "Lima Text" of Faith and Order from 1982, *Baptism, Eucharist, and Ministry,* puts it: "The New Testament does not describe a single pattern of ministry which might serve as a blueprint or continuing norm for all future ministry in the church. In the New Testament there appears rather a variety of forms which existed at different places and times."[132] But if central components of the traditional doctrine of church polity had now been historically relativized and brought into question, it seemed to many to be presumptuous to continue to make them a necessary condition for the reunion of the churches and a barrier to Christian fellowship, including eucharistic fellowship.[133]

Such a connection between biblical criticism and ecumenism becomes visible already in the thought of Friedrich Schleiermacher. He was one of the first to cast doubt on the traditional view that the apostle Paul was the author of the pastoral epistles, 1 Timothy,

129. See chapter 17.3 below, "The Flowering of Creedal and Confessional Scholarship in the Modern Era."
130. *Trent* 23.2; *Metr Crit* 11.2.
131. Extensive bibliographies in Bauer-Arndt-Gingrich, 299, 700, 184–85.
132. *BEM* 3.19; also *Ghana* 6.2.
133. See chapter 7.4 below, "The Spirit of Concord and the Sacrament of Concord: Two Ironic Case Histories."

2 Timothy, and Titus, in which the idea of succession from the apostles through the laying on of hands at ordination is set forth more clearly than it is in most of the rest of the New Testament.[134] Schleiermacher was also the most celebrated theologian of the Prussian Union, in which the Reformed and the Lutheran churches of Prussia were joined together, beginning in 1817 at the three-hundredth anniversary of Martin Luther's posting of the ninety-five theses. In the Prussian Union, questions of polity and order proved to be no less vexing than questions of liturgy and the question of the continuing authority of the Lutheran and the Reformed confessions in the new united church.[135] Acting as a spokesman of the Prussian Union in his dogmatics, *The Christian Faith*, Schleiermacher consistently appealed to the authority both of the Lutheran and of the Reformed confessions, even while putting upon his reading of both of them the highly individual, indeed idiosyncratic, stamp of his unique theological method. The service book or *Kirchenagende* of the Prussian Union sought to gloss over the differences between the Reformed and the Lutheran doctrines of the eucharist by prescribing the formula of distribution [*Spendeformel*], "Our Lord Jesus Christ says, 'This is my body,'" leaving a decision about the literal or the symbolic meaning of "body" and "blood" to the individual communicant.

Only a few decades later, in 1888, came *The Lambeth Quadrilateral* of the Anglican bishops, which makes "the historic episcopate locally adapted, in the methods of its administration, to the varying needs of the nations and peoples called of God into the unity of his church," a condition for Christian reunion.[136] That requirement is both an invitation to other churches by its acknowledgment that polity can be "locally adapted" and a rejection of the full legitimacy of any order that does not demonstrably stand in the apostolic succession of "the historic episcopate." When *The Lambeth Quadrilateral* was issued in 1888, some still hoped that the Roman Catholic Church would recognize the legitimacy of "the historic episcopate" as it had been main-

---

134. 2 Tm 1.6.
135. *PRE* 20:253–61 (Albert Hauck).
136. *Lamb Quad* 4; Wright 1988; Draper 1988.

tained in Anglicanism, and therefore the validity of Anglican holy orders. But those hopes were dashed five years later by the papal epistle *Apostolicae curae* issued on 13 September 1893 by Pope Leo XIII,[137] at a time when there was little prospect that less than a century later the Second Vatican Council could declare that "among those [communions] in which Catholic traditions and institutions in part continue to subsist, the Anglican communion occupies a special place."[138]

In keeping with the ecumenical intent of *The Lambeth Quadrilateral*, the Anglican Church of Canada had originally participated in the discussions that would eventually lead to *The Basis of Union of the United Church of Canada* of 1925. But that document succeeded in bringing together only Canadian Congregationalist, Methodist, and Presbyterian churches (and not all the members of these). It contains a special section entitled "Polity" that strives to reconcile these three traditionally conflicting systems of church governance. It also includes, in its section entitled "Doctrine," articles labeled "Of the Ministry" and "Of Church Order and Fellowship." Deliberately avoiding the issues in the doctrine of the ordained ministry that have been a source of controversy and division, *The Basis of Union* finds it sufficient in its article "Of the Ministry" to say that "Jesus Christ, as the supreme head of the church, has appointed therein a ministry of the word and sacraments, and calls men to this ministry; that the church, under the guidance of the Holy Spirit, recognizes and chooses those whom he calls, and should thereupon *duly* ordain them to the work of the ministry."[139] In the article "Of Church Order and Fellowship" it adds that the church's "worship, teaching, discipline, and government should be administered according to [Christ's] will by persons chosen for their fitness and *duly* set apart to their office."[140] But no specific content for the crucial requirement that this "ordaining" in article 17 and this "setting aside" in article 18 be carried out "duly" is provided.

Yet nowhere have the problems of church order been more

137. Denzinger 3315–19.
138. *Vat II* 5.3.13.
139. *Un Ch Can: Union* 17; italics added.
140. *Un Ch Can: Union* 18; italics added.

urgent, and the relation to these traditional definitions of order more
vexing, than in the churches that have come into being through Protestant missions, particularly when two or more such "younger churches"
have sought to unite across the boundaries of both the doctrine and
the order that they had received from their mother churches in Europe
or America.[141] The need for church order was compounded by the relation of these churches to their non-Christian milieus. "We confess,"
declares *The Confession of Faith of the Protestant Christian Batak Church
(H. K. B. P.)* of Indonesia of 1951, "there must be a church order which
is based upon the word of God, for it is an instrument which regu-
lates the life of the church and gives it peace."[142] But in the negotiations beginning in 1919, which led first to *The Scheme of Union of the
Churches of South India* of 1929, and ultimately to *The Constitution of
the Church of South India* of 1947, the ecumenism of the twentieth century produced one of its most elaborate concrete efforts to encompass
the problem of church order, which was not only a doctrinal issue but
a divisive one. *The Scheme of Union of the Churches of South India* of
1929 (which still uses the word "churches" in the plural in its title)
affirms its intention to maintain "the continuity of the historic episcopate" and its "intention that eventually every minister in the united
church will be an episcopally ordained minister."[143]

But *The Constitution of the Church of South India* as adopted
in 1947 (which is now using the word "church" in the singular in its
title), by its confession "that episcopal, presbyteral, and congregational
elements must all have their place in its order of life, and that the episcopate, the presbyterate, and the congregation of the faithful should
all in their several spheres have responsibility and exercise authority
in the life and work of the church, in its governance and administration, in its evangelistic and pastoral work, in its discipline, and in its
worship,"[144] identifies as "necessary elements" not the episcopate by
itself but the three doctrines of church order and systems of church

---

141. Nortier 1941; see chapter 11.2 below, "The Fate of Creeds in Missions and
Migrations."
142. *Bat* 11, citing 1 Cor 14.33.
143. *CSI 1929* 2; 5.
144. *CSI 1947* 4.

polity, "episcopal, presbyteral, and congregational." These have been seen as antithetical, not only in South India but in most of the history of British Protestantism, and beyond, since the Reformation. The constitution goes on to specify not only the "responsibility" and "authority" of each of the three for the exercise of ministry in the Church of South India but the doctrinal foundations for its version of the relation between faith and order. Not surprisingly, the most sensitive question, in the light of the preceding history, is the episcopate—seen not as simply an efficient system of management but as a doctrinal affirmation.

With echoes of *The Lambeth Quadrilateral* and other formularies, *The Constitution of the Church of South India* states its definition of the episcopate in more detail than it devotes in previous paragraphs to the presbyterate and the congregation combined:

> The Church of South India accepts and will maintain the historic episcopate in a constitutional form. But *this acceptance does not commit it* to any particular interpretation of episcopacy, or *to any particular view or belief concerning orders of the ministry,* and it will not require the acceptance of any such particular interpretation or view as a necessary qualification for its ministry.
>
> Whatever differing interpretations there may be, however, the Church of South India agrees that, as episcopacy has been accepted in the church from early times, it may in this sense fitly be called historic, and that it is needed for the shepherding and extension of the Church in South India. Any additional interpretations, though held by individuals, are not binding on the Church of South India.

Those whose previous ordination had been exclusively in one or another of the three "necessary elements" would now participate in all three, and all new ordinations would be "performed by the laying on of hands *by the bishops and presbyters.*"[145] A reflection of the South Indian

---

145. *CSI 1947* 4; italics added.

experience, but also of their own histories, can be seen in *The Scheme of Church Union in Ceylon* of 1963[146] and in that of *The Church of North India/Pakistan* of 1965.[147]

Both the persistence of the differences over church order and the progress that has been made during the nineteenth and twentieth centuries in the direction of some common understanding of it are clearly reflected in *Baptism, Eucharist, and Ministry,* which was issued by the Commission on Faith and Order at Lima, Peru, in January 1982.[148] As the title suggests, this "Lima Text" was assembled from three preliminary draft documents, one on each of its themes. The third and final section, "Ministry," which was developed considerably later than the first two, is characterized by an effort to get beyond the impasse between "Protestant" and "Catholic" (in this case, including in that latter term both Orthodox and Anglican) positions on the apostolic succession of bishops, by locating it in the larger and more comprehensive context of "apostolic tradition," of which the episcopate is seen as an important channel but only one among others. When it is seen within the context of this "apostolic tradition," the "episcopal succession" becomes for *Baptism, Eucharist, and Ministry* "a sign," but not in any juridical sense "a guarantee, of the continuity and unity of the church." Rather than being interpreted exclusively in clerical and professional terms as "*the* ministry," the entire definition of "ministry," too, is to be viewed in a larger context, which is nothing less than "the calling of the whole people of God" to ministry. Within that total ministry, the ordained ministry points to "the dependence of the church on Jesus Christ, who is the source of its mission and the foundation of its unity." This is, moreover, not exclusively the role of the episcopate; rather, "the threefold ministry of bishop, presbyter, and deacon may serve today as an expression of the unity we seek and also as a means for achieving it."[149]

These instances of the ecumenical confessional dialogue—two

---

146. *Sri Lanka* 7.2.
147. *CNI.*
148. Wainwright 1986; *DEM* 80–83 (Max Thurian).
149. *BEM* 3.21.

from the nineteenth century, and several more from the twentieth—
may reinforce the point that even (or especially) in the confessional
formulations of the modern period, as in those of earlier periods,
questions of faith have continued to be inseparable from questions of
order.

II

The Genesis of Creeds
and Confessions

The recurrent protest against creeds, especially as it comes from modern secular thought as well as from modern Protestantism, whether Liberal or Evangelical (albeit on quite different grounds),[1] does raise the question, at least in the abstract, whether Christianity could conceivably have come into being and could have developed through time without ever having felt obliged to invent fixed creeds and formal confessions of faith—or, at any rate, without having had to produce so many thousands of them. The paganisms of ancient Greece and Rome, which surrounded and challenged the church when it began, did not require a creed. As a modern translator of the works of Plato has explained, in a description that in this case applies to Rome as well as to Greece, "Athenian religion was not a matter of creed and dogma but of ritual observance, *dromena,* things done, rather than *legomena,* things said—and this was appropriate, given a polytheistic religion whose doctrinal content, to the degree it might be said to have any at all, consisted mainly in the myths of Homer and Hesiod."[2] The same was true of the original religions of the Germanic, Celtic, Slavic, and other "barbarian" peoples who were to become Christian during the Western and Eastern Middle Ages. Nor were there "creeds" in the religions of most of the other nations all over the globe to which Christian missionaries throughout the centuries have brought not only their gospel but their creeds.[3]

1. See chapter 17.1 below, "The Discomfort with Creed Caused by the Consciousness of Modernity."
2. Allen 1984, 1:74.
3. See chapter 11.2 below, "The Fate of Creeds in Missions and Migrations."

But the exclusivity of a faith in the one true God rather than in many gods, combined with the particularity of the faith that this one true God has been specifically revealed in a unique set of historical events as those events are authoritatively recorded in a definitive literary deposit and as this revelation has been entrusted to a structured and continuing community, does seem to require that there be some sort of formula for the confessing of that faith. As Alexander Penrose Forbes put it at the end of the nineteenth century, "the essence of a revelation is that it must be definite,"[4] which implies that it must be affirmed and must be capable of being confessed. With each of the other two monotheisms of the Book, Judaism and Islam, therefore, Christianity did share the imperative of confessing as well as the prior imperative of believing (and the imperative of teaching or preaching).[5] All three of these religions could have said with the New Testament, and actually did say in one version or another, that "if you confess with your lips . . . and believe in your heart . . . you will be saved."[6]

Thus there are creedlike formulations that occur at various places in the Hebrew Bible. The most notable of these is not so much a creed as a self-disclosure of the divine Name to Moses by the voice of God from the burning bush, "I am that I am."[7] There are also creedal declarations that can be found in the Talmud as well as in the writings of individuals and of groups at various times within the Jewish tradition, leading up to the medieval idea of "the thirteen articles of faith."[8] Nevertheless Judaism has, at least in principle, satisfied this confessional imperative with a single creed, the recitation of the confession of *The Shema,* "Hear, O Israel: the Lord our God, the Lord is one [*Shema' Yisraēl, Adōnai Elōheinū Adōnai echād*]."[9] Likewise, at least partly because in Islam, as William Montgomery Watt says, "there is nothing equivalent to the bishops and ecumenical councils of the Church, and thus no body to give creeds an official status such as the Apostles'

4. Forbes 1890, 129.
5. See chapter 2 above, "The Creedal and Confessional Imperative."
6. Rom 10.9.
7. Ex 3.14; see chapter 11.4 below, "The Paradigm: *Shema* to *Homoousios*."
8. Kellner 1986.
9. Dt 6.4; see chapter 5.1 below, "Creeds in Scripture"; and chapter 13.1 below, "The Primal Creed."

Creed and the Nicene Creed have in Christendom[, t]he Islamic creeds formulate the beliefs of an individual scholar or of groups of scholars," rather than those of the Muslim tradition as a whole.[10] An example of such a "creed" is that of the Shi'ite Ibn Bābawayh.[11] "Faith in Islam," sometimes translated "the Muslim creed," is one of the "five pillars of Islam," together with prayer, fasting, almsgiving, and pilgrimage as the other four requirements.[12] But for a "creed" in the official, communal, and binding sense in which we are using the word here when we speak about the many Christian creeds and confessions or about *The Shema* of Judaism, Islam has basically remained content with the confession of *The Shahādah,* "There is no God but God, and Muhammad is his messenger," which, though not part of the Qur'ān in so many words, does summarize its central message. Why, then, could it not have been sufficient for Christians also to go on confessing their own version of *The Shema* or *The Shahāda*—which is what the apostle Paul does with the formula "There is one God, the Father, from whom are all things, and for whom we exist, and one Lord, Jesus Christ, through whom are all things and through whom we exist"[13]—and simply to let it go at that?

Each of the four chapters that follow will attempt to provide one component of an answer to that question. They will examine four historical factors, which, taken together, help to explain the genesis of creeds and confessions in the Christian church, as well as their constant multiplication through the centuries of Christian history. It is probably unnecessary to point out that in the life of the church, as in its confessions, none of these four—exegesis, prayer, polemics, and politics—functions in isolation from the other three. Political action and prayer, whether individual or collective, may sometimes be seen, both by pietists and by activists, as though they were going on in different or even in opposite realms. But throughout the history of Christianity they have repeatedly intersected, for good or ill. In the confessions of individual churches and denominations just as elsewhere, the exegesis

10. Watt 1994, 3.
11. Fyzee 1942.
12. Wensinck 1932.
13. 1 Cor 8.5–6.

of Holy Scripture frequently provides the occasion for polemics against those who "have learned nothing from the sacred texts,"[14] or against those who can be accused of having allowed the dead hand of merely human traditions to interfere with what is taken to be the clear and sovereign meaning of the divine word.[15] On the positive side, confessions are often the instruments through which churches identify and spell out, more specifically than they do anywhere else, what they believe to be the proper methods of biblical interpretation, or the fundamental principles of worship, or the limits of theological speculation, or the duties of the state and the duties of Christians toward the state. Not only are these four factors involved in the genesis of creeds and confessions, therefore, but the influences have worked in the opposite direction as well. Each of the four has also taken some of its own historical genesis, as well as some of its eventual form, from creeds and confessions of faith. As a result, it would be as grave an oversight to overlook the creeds and confessions when writing or studying the history of exegesis or of liturgy or of polemics or of politics as it would be for the history of the genesis of creeds and confessions to ignore these forces.

14. *Tome* 1.
15. *Helv I* 4; *Helv II* 2.6; *Scot I* 14; *West* 20.2.

CHAPTER FIVE

Scripture, Tradition, and Creed

AS CREEDS AND CONFESSIONS have come into being, they have represented themselves as setting forth what is believed, taught, and confessed by those who subscribe them as their particular constituencies[1]—or, even more ambitiously, what is believed, taught, and confessed by no less universal an entity than "the entire church of Christ"[2] or "all Christians."[3] But by such a genesis they are also, explicitly or implicitly, pointing beyond themselves and beyond their particular constituencies, in what looks very much like an argument in a circle, as noted earlier: the Scripture is to be understood as the tradition and this particular creed interpret it, but this particular creed, as well as perhaps the tradition, is subject to the Scripture. This circular argument and the tensions it expresses have attended the processes of creedal and confessional formation throughout Christian history.

According to the orthodox catholic tradition (or all the several orthodox and catholic traditions), the final words of the risen Christ to his eleven disciples and apostles legislated, both for them and for "the successors of the apostles" through the centuries,[4] a total system, with his own person at its center, in what came to be called "the great commission":[5] "All authority in heaven and on earth has been given to me. Go therefore and make disciples of all nations, baptizing them in the name of the Father and of the Son and of the Holy Spirit, teaching them to observe all that I have commanded you; and lo, I am with you

1. For example, *Belg* 1; *Dosith* 1.
2. *Fid rat* pr.
3. *Ans* 3.40.
4. *Vat II* 5.2.24.
5. *ABD* 2:1090–91 (A. Boyd Luter, Jr.).

always, to the close of the age."[6] Ultimately, these words require that "every tongue confess that Jesus Christ is Lord, to the glory of God the Father."[7] All who have ever identified themselves as Christians, therefore, have been united in recognizing Jesus Christ as Lord, whether or not they happen to have done so by means of a formal confession of faith. Even when the reinterpretation of the tradition by the confessions of the Protestant Reformation takes these words of the great commission to mean that the church is to teach only what Christ has commanded, "not what you have imagined or made up" in church traditions,[8] it affirms, in the phraseology of *The Westminster Confession of Faith,* that by these final words, baptism is, "by Christ's own appointment, to be continued in his church until the end of the world."[9] Similarly, *The Second Helvetic Confession* uses these words of Christ to confess that "he that illuminates inwardly by giving men the Holy Spirit, the same one, by way of commandment, [requires the external preaching of the word]."[10] *The Belgic Confession* sees in these final words of Christ the "form . . . prescribed by Christ" for "the baptism of all believers,"[11] and goes on in a later article to use them to prove that Christ "has commanded that all those who belong to him be baptized with pure water."[12] *The Heidelberg Catechism* attributes to them "the institution of baptism," by analogy with "the institution of the holy supper."[13] And *The Doctrinal Statement of the American Baptist Association* of 1905 declares: "We believe that the great commission teaches that there has been a succession of missionary Baptist churches from the days of Christ down to this day."[14]

Nevertheless, especially in the centuries since the Reformation of the sixteenth century, the Christian churches have been anything but united in specifying the relation of this supreme lordship of Christ to creeds and confessions of faith—and sometimes even to visible, in-

6. Mt 28.18–20; also Mk 16.15; Acts 1.8.
7. Phil 2.11.
8. *Ans* 2.15.
9. *West* 28.1.
10. *Helv II* 1.6.
11. *Belg* 9.
12. *Belg* 34.
13. *Heid* 71, 77.
14. *Am Bap* 12.

stitutional churches. Does "baptizing them in the name of the Father and of the Son and of the Holy Spirit" necessitate a trinitarian baptismal creed such as *The Apostles' Creed,* in which that formula is explicated, so that this great commission can serve *The Second Helvetic Confession* as a proof text for a chapter entitled "Of God, His Unity and Trinity"?[15] Does the command of "teaching them to observe all that I have commanded" lead the church ineluctably to the teaching of something very much like *The Creed of Nicaea,* as Basil of Caesarea thought that it did,[16] or even, in the West, to *The Athanasian Creed*? But quite apart from those controversies, does this commission with its promise mean not only, as *The Barmen Declaration* urges on the basis of it in opposition to Nazi totalitarianism, that "the church's commission, upon which its freedom is founded, consists in delivering the message of the free grace of God to all people in Christ's stead,"[17] but still more? Is it also legitimate, in the formula of *The Canons of the Synod of Dort,* to apply that promise generally in the sense that it would "shine forth in all the periods of the history of the church," and specifically in the sense that Christ gives his blessing after the ascension to what those same *Canons of the Synod of Dort* identify as later "apostolic" councils and "holy synods" and their decrees and confessions (including itself in that company)?[18] Does the promise, moreover, still apply to such assemblies when they, on the basis of Scripture but going beyond the language of Scripture and even beyond the language of earlier tradition,[19] legislate doctrines and formulate still further creeds and confessions of faith, or does it apply only to some of these assemblies, or to none of them at all? Be they fallible or infallible, how does the genesis of what *The Westminster Confession of Faith* calls "all synods or councils, since the apostles' times, whether general or particular,"[20] whether early or late, whether "ecumenical" or Roman Catholic or Eastern Orthodox or Protestant, with all their creeds and confessions, square with the credentials, especially of the Bible, that

15. *Helv* II 3.4.
16. Basil of Caesarea *On the Holy Spirit* 17.43 (NPNF–II 8:27).
17. *Barm* 6.
18. *Dort* pr.
19. *Ecth* 5.
20. *West* 31.4.

certify the church as being legitimately "apostolic" in addition to being "one" and "holy" and "catholic"[21]—as being in truth "the household of God, built upon the foundation of the apostles and prophets, Christ Jesus himself being the cornerstone"?[22] In short, what is the relation of Scripture, tradition, and creed?[23] And how does kerygma turn into dogma?[24]

5.1. Creeds in Scripture

Yet putting the issue in such a way does certainly beg the question, or actually several questions. Anyone who, in the name of the New Testament, declares an opposition to the very notion of creeds is obliged to come to terms with the priority—the chronological if not also the logical priority—of creed within the teachings of Jesus himself and of his apostles, as these are reported in quotations from Old Testament creeds by the New Testament.[25] For in response to a challenge by his opponents, Jesus recites the primal creed of *The Shema:* "Hear, O Israel: the Lord our God, the Lord is one."[26] In response to another challenge, the apostle Paul also recites *The Shema,* in order then to be able to say that for him and his fellow believers (employing a formula that does sound as though it might itself have come from an earlier Christian creed or hymn), "there is one God, the Father, from whom are all things and for whom we exist, and one Lord, Jesus Christ, through whom are all things and through whom we exist."[27] The profession of faith of the first ecumenical council of the church, convoked at Nicaea in 325 likewise in response to a challenge, opens not with a passage from the Gospels or from any other portion of the New Testament but with a Christian version of the same primal creed of Israel, which preceded the New Testament: "We believe in one God."[28] And it does so as the foundation for everything that it then goes on to say

---

21. *N-CP* 9.
22. Eph 2.19–20.
23. Geiselmann 1966.
24. See also chapter 13.2 below, "The Kerygma and Baptismal Symbols."
25. Proksch 1936.
26. Mk 12.29, which quotes Dt 6.4 verbatim from the Septuagint.
27. 1 Cor 8.4–6.
28. *N* 1.

about the Son of God as "consubstantial with the Father [*homoousios tōi patri*]."[29] For nothing in any of its language about the Son is to be seen as in any way contradicting or compromising, but rather as vindicating, this primal Mosaic creed, the confession of faith in the oneness of God. According to Nicene orthodoxy, the monotheistic creed is compromised not by the doctrine of the Trinity, as its opponents inside and outside Christendom charged,[30] but by the doctrine of Arius and others that the Son of God or the Holy Spirit can be inferior to the Father and nevertheless be divine.[31] Therefore Athanasius of Alexandria, the principal defender of *The Creed of Nicaea*, also quoting *The Shema*, insists that "when we read that there is 'one God,'" this is "not said in denial of the Son."[32] In Eastern Orthodoxy (proceeding in chronological order), *The Confession of the Orthodox Faith by Gregory Palamas* opens by confessing: "There is one God";[33] *The Confession of Metrophanes Critopoulos* opens with the words: "The catholic and apostolic church teaches that the foundation of our salvation is God himself alone";[34] *The Orthodox Confession of the Catholic and Apostolic Eastern Church by Peter Mogila* quotes *The Shema*;[35] and *The Confession of Dositheus and of the Synod of Jerusalem* is echoing Nicaea—and *The Shema*—when it opens with the words: "We believe in one God."[36] In the West, too, *The Shema* dictates the language for the opening of one after another of the Reformation confessions of faith, all the way across the confessional spectrum from Roman Catholicism to Anabaptism (likewise citing them in chronological order): *The Marburg Articles* of 1529;[37] *The Augsburg Confession* of 1530;[38] *The First Confession of Basel* of 1534;[39] *The French Confession* of 1559;[40] *The Scots Con-*

---

29. N 2.
30. ap. *Gennad* 2.
31. Gregory of Nyssa *On "Not Three Gods"* (*NPNF*-II 5:331–36).
32. Athanasius *Discourses Against the Arians* 3.24.7 (*NPNF*-II 4:397).
33. *Greg Palam* 1.
34. *Metr Crit* 1.1.
35. *Mogila* 1.8.
36. *Dosith* decr 1.
37. *Marburg* 1.
38. *Aug* 1.
39. *Bas Bek* 1.
40. *Gall* 1.

fession of 1560;[41] *The Belgic Confession* of 1561, with the superscription
"The Only God";[42] *The Tridentine Profession of Faith* of 1564, which
incorporates *The Western Recension* of *The Niceno-Constantinopolitan
Creed;*[43] *The Second Helvetic Confession* of 1566, which quotes *The
Shema* verbatim;[44] *The Hungarian Confession* [*Confessio Czengerina*] of
1570;[45] *The Thirty-Nine Articles of the Church of England* of 1571,
opening its Latin version with the words "Unus est";[46] and the Mennonite *Concept of Cologne* of 1591,[47] together with *The [Mennonite]
Short Confession of Faith of Hans de Ries* from 1618.[48] It can still be
heard, to cite only a few examples among many, in the opening words
of the modern confession of the Unitas Fratrum of 1749, "I believe in
the one only God,"[49] also in the opening words of *The "Commission"
Creed* of American Congregationalism from 1883, a verbatim quotation of *The Niceno-Constantinopolitan Creed,*[50] in *The Korean Methodist
Creed* of 1930, "We believe in the one God,"[51] and in *The Masai Creed*
of twentieth-century African Christianity, with special significance because of the native polytheism and animism surrounding it, "We believe
in the one High God, who out of love created the beautiful world and
everything good in it."[52]

Nor is *The Shema* of the Old Testament the only already existing creed or creedlike statement found in the books of the New Testament, as becomes evident from the roster of other biblical confessions
found in collections of creeds,[53] including "Creedal Statements in the
New Testament" in Part One of *Creeds and Confessions of Faith in the
Christian Tradition*. Probably the most often quoted, also because of
the words of Christ in response, "You are Peter, and on this rock I will

41. *Scot I* 1.
42. *Belg* 1.
43. *Trid Prof* 1.
44. *Helv II* 3.2; see Koch 1968, 59–61.
45. *Czen* 1.
46. *39 Art* 1.
47. *Cologne* 1.
48. *Ries* 1.
49. *Morav* 1.
50. *Com Cr* 1; *N-CP* 1.
51. *Meth Kor; Philip UCC* 1.
52. *Masai* 1.
53. Schaff, 2:3–8; Leith, 12–16.

build my church," which became the fundamental proof text for the papacy, is the confession of Peter at Caesarea Philippi: "You are the Christ, the Son of the living God." [54] But one of the most extensive and "creedlike" is the passage in which the First Epistle to Timothy, evidently drawing on some prior source, incorporates *The Shema* and then expands it into a Christian rule of faith:

> There is one God;
>> there is also one mediator
>>> between God and
>>> humankind;
> Christ Jesus, himself human,
>> who gave himself a ransom for all. [55]

There is another such citation one chapter later in the same epistle:

> He [or: God] [56] was revealed in flesh,
>> vindicated in spirit,
>>> seen by angels,
> proclaimed among Gentiles,
>> believed in throughout the world,
>>> taken up in glory. [57]

Whether any of our Gospels were in existence at that time or not, it would seem plausible that it was neither from them nor from some previous collection of the sayings of Jesus but from very early confessions of Christian faith, oral or written, that this epistle was quoting in both of these passages.

Although the Pauline authorship of this Epistle to Timothy has been questioned, at least partly because of the very presence of such creedlike and traditional formulas (and of an advanced system of church order), [58] an even more extensive affirmation of a similar kind

54. Mt 16.16–18.
55. 1 Tm 2.5 (NRSV).
56. Depending on whether the opening Greek word is taken as the relative pronoun *hos* or as the noun *theos*.
57. 1 Tm 3.16 (NRSV).
58. *ABD* 6:560–71 (Jerome D. Quinn).

appears already in the Epistle to the Philippians, which is undeniably Pauline:

> Christ Jesus,
> who, though he was in the form of God,
>> did not regard equality with God
>> as something to be exploited,
> but emptied himself,
>> taking the form of a slave,
>> being born in human likeness.
> And being found in human form,
>> he humbled himself
>> and became obedient to the
>>> point of death—
>> even death on a cross.
> Therefore God also highly exalted him
>> and gave him the name
>> that is above every name,
> so that at the name of Jesus
>> every knee should bend,
>> in heaven and on earth and under the earth,
> and every tongue should confess
>> that Jesus Christ is Lord,
>> to the glory of God the Father.[59]

As *The New Jerusalem Bible* says in commenting on this passage, "this proclamation [Jesus Christ as Lord] is the essence of the Christian creed," even if we concede that, technically speaking, there was not yet a fixed "Christian creed" at the time. And the imperative "that at the name of Jesus every knee should bend," as Werner Elert has said, "is not a doctrine, but a liturgical action."[60] Whether creed or hymn, this is a primitive "rule of faith," one that antedates any of our Gospels and that is embedded in one of the very earliest of the books that were eventually collected to form our New Testament.

It was a recognition of the reciprocal relation among the three

---

59. Phil 2.6–11 (NRSV).
60. Elert 1957, 15.

interlocking forces that the title of this chapter is calling "Scripture, tradition, and creed," as that reciprocity is reflected in the relation between Scripture and this rule of faith quoted in the second chapter of Philippians, when Augustine referred to this passage from Philippians as a "rule for clearing the question [of the person of Christ] through all the Sacred Scriptures," and "for interpreting the Scriptures concerning the Son of God."[61] On that basis, he set down the rule in a more formal manner: "We hold most firmly, concerning our Lord Jesus Christ, what may be called the canonical rule, as it is both disseminated through the Scriptures and has been demonstrated by learned and Catholic handlers of the same Scriptures, namely, that the Son of God is understood to be both equal to the Father according to the form of God, in which he is, and less than the Father according to the form of a slave, which he took." Immediately after having stated this "canonical rule [*canonica regula*]," he felt compelled to acknowledge that "there are some things in the sacred text so put as to leave ambiguous to which [part of this] rule they are rather to be referred," whether to "the form of God" or to "the form of a slave."[62] As this use of the terms "form of God" and "form of a slave" in the formulation of Augustine's "canonical rule" shows, its immediate source was Philippians 2.5–11. Later he went on to link John 10.30, "I and the Father are one," and Exodus 3.14, "I am who I am," with Philippians 2.6, "He did not regard equality with God as something to be exploited," to provide the foundation for his trinitarian hermeneutics.[63] Thus a prior "creed" that had been embedded in the New Testament became the key to the catholic and orthodox interpretation of the rest of the New Testament, as well as to a trinitarian and christological interpretation of the Old Testament that had preceded the composition of the New Testament. Or, as the twentieth-century Protestant theologian Helmut Gollwitzer has conceded, "the New Testament writings already presuppose all the confessional formulas of the community as tradition [*Paradosis*] and expound them";[64] and the subsequent centuries go on doing the same even more consis-

---

61. Augustine *On the Trinity* 1.7.14, 1.11.22 (*NPNF*-II 3:24, 29–30).
62. Augustine *On the Trinity* 2.1.2 (*NPNF*-II 3:37–38).
63. Augustine *On the Trinity* 5.3.4 (*NPNF*-II 3:88).
64. Gollwitzer 1962, 156.

tently. For when the New Testament urges believers to "contend for the faith which was once for all delivered [*hapax paradotheisē*] to the saints,"[65] that is a faith delivered by "tradition [*paradosis*]"; the Greek noun comes from a Greek verb that could, if the verb were not so rare in English, be translated as "to tradition."[66] Therefore the Vulgate translates Jude 3 as: *pro semel tradita sanctis fide*. Teachers and synods who were condemned as heretical, no less than those who were acknowledged as orthodox, claimed to be adhering to a traditional "faith which we have from our forefathers."[67] It was altogether consistent with this view when, according to Gregory of Nyssa, Gregory Thaumaturgus in the third century received by revelation from the apostle John a rule of faith that affirmed: "Perfect Trinity: in glory and eternity and sovereignty neither divided nor estranged."[68]

5.2. Scripture in the Creeds and Confessions

But as there are creeds and confessions of faith in Scripture, to which Scripture refers and in accordance with which Scripture has been interpreted by the fathers and councils of the church and by its creeds and confessions, so in turn the creeds and confessions of faith of the church refer beyond themselves to the Scripture. The first synodal creed, at Antioch in 325, a few months before the Council of Nicaea, describes its confession as "the faith that was set forth by spiritual men . . . always formed and trained in the Spirit by means of the holy writings of the inspired books."[69] Also at Antioch, the ill-fated *Creed of the Dedication Council* of 341 closes with the formula, "Following the evangelical and apostolic tradition,"[70] which is later repeated elsewhere.[71] *The Niceno-Constantinopolitan Creed* identifies the Holy Spirit as "the one who spoke through the prophets,"[72] and, employing a formula of Paul,[73] confesses that Christ "rose up on the third day in ac-

---

65. Jude 3; see chapter 2.2 above, "Faith Defined."
66. Lampe, 1013–16; *OED* 11–I:225–26.
67. *Ar; Smyr.*
68. *Greg Thaum.*
69. *Ant 325.*
70. *Ant 341* con.
71. *Rom Syn* con.
72. *N-CP* 8.
73. 1 Cor 15.3–4.

cordance with the scriptures [*kata tas graphas*]."[74] These words of Paul and of *The Niceno-Constantinopolitan Creed* are a reference to various passages of the Old Testament, "beginning with Moses and all the prophets, [in accordance with which on the road to Emmaus after the resurrection, Christ] interpreted to [the disciples] in all the scriptures the things concerning himself."[75] Following that supreme precedent of the risen Christ, later confessions of faith, above all those coming out of the Protestant Reformation, fairly bristle with biblical quotations and references. The first edition of *The Heidelberg Catechism* of 1563 concludes with a "List of such important proof texts as have been explained in the preceding Catechism," which in later editions are appended to the individual questions. In *The Westminster Confession of Faith* of 1647, which promises on its title page to provide "the Quotations and Texts of Scripture Annexed" to prove its doctrines,[76] the number of such quotations and texts of Scripture comes to more than fifteen hundred. Even the Eastern Orthodox *Confession of Metrophanes Critopoulos* accumulates two hundred or so, in spite of its reliance on the authority of written and unwritten traditions alongside Holy Scripture.[77]

Yet the centrality of the Bible in these Reformation and post-Reformation confessions goes well beyond the practice of providing proof texts for other doctrines. The authority of Scripture eventually came to be seen both as the doctrine that underlay and authenticated all other doctrines and as the doctrinal stance that differentiated Protestantism from Roman Catholicism and Eastern Orthodoxy. "We affirm," says *The Scots Confession* of 1560, "that those who say the Scriptures have no other authority save that which they have received from the kirk are blasphemous against God and injurious to the true kirk, which always hears and obeys the voice of her own spouse and pastor, but takes not upon her to be mistress over the same."[78] In the nineteenth century, therefore, the doctrine of the authority of Scripture alone (*sola Scriptura*) and the doctrine of justification by faith alone

74. *N-CP* 5.
75. Lk 24.27.
76. *West* pr.
77. *Metr Crit* 7.10.
78. *Scot I* 19; see also *18 Diss* 8.

(*sola fide*) were identified as, respectively, the "formal principle" and the "material principle" of the Protestant Reformation.[79] Even without a complete census, it does seem to be the case that almost every Reformation confession that does not lead off with *The Shema* and the Trinity devotes its opening article to the authority of Holy Scripture. Among Reformed confessions, *The Geneva Confession* of 1536,[80] and both *The First Helvetic Confession* of 1536[81] and *The Second Helvetic Confession* of 1566,[82] make it their first article, as does *The Westminster Confession of Faith* of 1647,[83] which follows and expands this opening declaration of *The Irish Articles of Religion* of 1615: "The ground of our religion and the rule of faith and all saving truth is the word of God, contained in the Holy Scripture."[84] Although the Lutheran *Augsburg Confession* of 1530, unlike these Reformed confessions, does not open with the authority of Scripture, the Lutheran *Copenhagen Articles* of the same year do.[85] The Lutheran *Formula of Concord* of 1577 also opens its *Epitome* with a preamble to all its articles: "We believe, teach, and confess that the prophetic and apostolic writings of the Old and New Testaments are the only rule and norm according to which all doctrines and teachers alike must be appraised and judged."[86] *The [First] Bohemian Confession* of 1535 makes the authority and primacy of Scripture its first article;[87] *The [Second] Bohemian Confession* of 1575 does the same.[88] *Sola Scriptura*, the sole authority of Scripture over church and creed, represents, then, a consensus of the several confessional families of the Protestant Reformation. At best, the church is to be seen as, in the words of *The Thirty-Nine Articles of the Church of England,* "a witness and a keeper of the Holy Writ," which is not to be put on a level with Holy Scripture.[89]

79. *PRE* 16:146 (Ferdinand Kattenbusch).
80. *Genv Con* 1.
81. *Helv I* 1.
82. *Helv II* 1; see Thomas 1853, 155–63.
83. *West* 1.
84. *Irish* 1.
85. Andersen 1954, 67–128, 469.
86. *Form Conc Epit* pr.
87. *Boh I* 1.
88. *Boh II* 1.
89. *39 Art* 20.

5.3. The Confessions and the Problem of the Canon

Within this total body of Protestant statements of faith, however, one difference between Reformed and Lutheran confessions in their statements about Scripture, as well as between both of these and Roman Catholic formularies, lies in their treatment of the problem of the Old Testament canon.[90] Neither the decrees of the ecumenical councils of the first centuries nor the early creeds definitively resolve the problem of the status of the Apocrypha or deuterocanonical books of the Old Testament, which are included in the Greek text of the Septuagint but not in the Hebrew Bible.[91] Augustine, whom Protestant confessions feel able to cite in support of their position on canonicity,[92] was nevertheless one of those who favored the inclusion of the Apocrypha as Christian Scripture of the church in spite of their absence from Jewish Scripture as defined by the Palestinian Hebrew canon.[93] Jerome opposed it on the basis of a distinction between "canonical" and "ecclesiastical" books, though he did include both in his Latin translation. Augustine's view predominated, but Jerome's continued to appear; and the two Old Testament "canons" coexisted in the Latin West during the Middle Ages. In the confessions of the Eastern Orthodox Church (for which the Septuagint possesses special divine authority as the inspired and normative Old Testament of the church)[94] there is also some variety. *The Confession of Metrophanes Critopoulos* says of the Apocrypha that "the church of Christ has never accepted them as canonical and authoritative"; but *The Confession of Dositheus and of the Synod of Jerusalem* speaks for the Orthodox mainstream in accepting the more inclusive canon of biblical books, which is, however, slightly different from that in the West.[95]

Biblical canonicity became an issue of theological controversy in the confessions of the Reformation period for several reasons. The Roman Catholic teachings about the cult of the saints and about the efficacy of prayers for the dead, both of them opposed by the Re-

90. Sanders 1972.
91. *ABD* 1:837–61 (James A. Sanders, Harry Y. Gamble).
92. *Helv II* 1.9, quoting Augustine *City of God* 18.38 (*NPNF–I* 2:382).
93. Augustine *City of God* 18.36 (*NPNF–I* 2:382).
94. *Resp Pius IX* 21.
95. *Metr Crit* 7.8; *Dosith* q 3.

formers, were thought to have no support in the undeniably canonical books but to depend on passages in the Apocrypha, specifically 2 Maccabees.[96] Both Renaissance humanism and Reformation theology developed a new grasp of the Hebrew language, and therefore a new appreciation of Hebrew Scripture, and therefore a new sense of the priority of the Palestinian canon over the larger canon collected in the Septuagint, which was after all only a translation (though supposedly a divinely inspired one) and not the original. The right to decide which books belonged in the canon was an especially provocative test case for the debate between Protestantism and Roman Catholicism about the relative authority of church and Scripture.[97] For if it was the church that had authoritatively decided which books were to go into the canon of Scripture and which were not, the very Scripture that Protestant doctrine was pitting against church and tradition, did it not appear to follow that the church also had the right to decide about the proper interpretation of that Scripture—and had it not already done so in its postbiblical traditions, creeds, and decrees?[98]

In response to the Protestant challenge, the fourth session of the Council of Trent on 8 April 1546 "decided that a written list of the sacred books should be included in this decree in case a doubt should occur to anyone as to which are the books which are accepted by this council." It proceeded to publish the complete list to include the disputed books, pronouncing its anathema on anyone who "should not accept as sacred and canonical these entire books and all their parts as they have, by established custom, been read in the Catholic Church, and as contained in the old Latin Vulgate edition."[99] It is a response to this definition, in turn, when *The French Confession* in its third article publishes the more restrictive list of canonical books according to the text of the Hebrew Scriptures, without the Apocrypha. That catalog of canonical books is followed in the fourth article by the explanation: "We know these books to be canonical, and the sure rule of our faith, not so much by the common accord and consent of the church,

96. 2 Mc 15.12–16; 12.42. See Syndogmaticon 3.8, 8.9.
97. Möhler [1832] 1958, 1:432–36. See Syndogmaticon 8.11, 8.12, 8.13.
98. *Chr Trad* 4:262–67.
99. *Trent* 4.1.

as by the testimony and inward illumination of the Holy Spirit [*le tes-moignage et persuasion interieure du sainct Esprit*], which enables us to distinguish them from other ecclesiastical books upon which, however useful, we can not base any articles of faith."[100] Many other Reformed confessions contain the same list: *The Belgic Confession* of 1561, including the same validation of the canonical books on the experiential grounds "above all because the Holy Spirit testifies in our hearts that they are from God, and also because they prove themselves to be from God," rather than on the grounds of church authority;[101] *The Thirty-Nine Articles of the Church of England,* identifying them as "those canonical books of the Old and New Testament of whose authority was never any doubt in the church";[102] *The Irish Articles* of 1615;[103] *The Westminster Confession of Faith* of 1647, which makes a point of dismissing the Apocrypha with the characterization that "the books commonly called Apocrypha, not being of divine inspiration, are no part of the canon of the Scripture; and therefore are of no authority in the church of God, nor to be any otherwise approved, or made use of, than other human writings";[104] and *The Confession of the Waldenses* of 1655.[105] Eventually the British and Foreign Bible Society forbade the inclusion of the Apocrypha in its printed Bibles regardless of language, including therefore translations of the Bible that had always included them before. But no such catalog appears either in *The Augsburg Confession* or in *The Formula of Concord* of 1577, except perhaps implicitly in the reference by the latter to "the *prophetic and apostolic* writings of the Old and New Testaments" as "the *only* rule and norm according to which all doctrines and teachers alike must be appraised and judged."[106] Luther's German Bible has continued to include the Apocrypha, though in a separate section with the warning that although they are useful to read, they are not to be put on a level with Scripture.

100. *Gall* 3–4.
101. *Belg* 3–5.
102. *39 Art* 6; see Forbes 1890, 102–12.
103. *Irish* 2–3.
104. *West* 1.3.
105. *Wald* 3.
106. *Form Conc Epit* pr 1 (italics added).

5.4. Confessional Rules of Biblical Hermeneutics

At least as important a function of creeds and confessions in relation to Scripture is to define rules of biblical hermeneutics.[107] By asserting that the suffering and the resurrection of Christ took place "in accordance with the scriptures,"[108] *The Niceno-Constantinopolitan Creed*, quoting 1 Corinthians 15, is requiring an interpretation of the Old Testament Scriptures as a witness to Jesus Christ, thereby also requiring an interpretation of the Bible "in accordance with" the creed; for the two are seen as correlative and interdependent. Although the formula of that creed, "begotten not made, consubstantial with the Father,"[109] is best known for the *homoousion,* a term of nonbiblical, even of heretical, provenance,[110] both of the terms being joined and yet kept apart by negation in its phrase "begotten, not made [*gennēthenta ou poiēthenta*]" are eminently biblical:[111] *poieō* is the first verb in the Septuagint Bible (which was the "Old Testament" of the early church, in its canon, text, and translations), "In the beginning God *epoiēsen* heaven and earth";[112] and *gennaō* is the first verb in the New Testament, "Abraham *egennēsen* Isaac."[113] They can, moreover, be employed more or less synonymously.[114] Indeed, as applied to the relation between the Father and the Son, *gennaō* also had to be seen as possibly synonymous with a third verb, whose use for that relation was, if anything, even more problematical than either of these, the verb *ktizō,* the technical term for "to create," eventually even for "to create *ex nihilo*."[115] For in the eighth chapter of the Book of Proverbs, which is rivaled only by the first chapter of the Gospel of John in the frequency with which it was cited during these fourth-century debates,[116] personified Wisdom (identified by Christian interpreters as the preexistent Son of

---

107. *ABD* 3:149–54 (Bernard C. Lategan). See Syndogmaticon 8.15.
108. *N-CP* 5; 1 Cor 15.3–4.
109. *N-CP* 2.
110. Prestige 1952, 197–218.
111. On their patristic use, see Lampe, 311, 1108.
112. Gn 1.1 (LXX).
113. Mt 1.2.
114. Heb 3.2.
115. May 1994; Lampe, 782.
116. *Chr Trad* 1:191–97.

God) says that "the Lord created [*ektisen*] me at the beginning of his work . . . before the hills, he begot [*gennai*] me."[117] These words, apparently equating the divine "begetting" of Wisdom with divine "creating," became, as Athanasius was compelled to admit, a formidable mainstay of the Arian teaching that the Father had created/begotten the Son as the prime creature, through whom all the (other) creatures had been made. Athanasius insisted that, to the contrary, the passage "has a very religious and orthodox sense,"[118] and that *gennaō* and *ktizō* do not mean the same at all, even when applied to God's relation to human beings.[119] By codifying that distinction, *The Creed of Nicaea*, echoed by later councils and creeds, assigns to itself, and thus to creeds, the hermeneutical function of clarifying and classifying scriptural terminology.[120]

Similarly, when *The Niceno-Constantinopolitan Creed* declares that "his kingdom will have no end,"[121] it is quoting the prophecy of the angel Gabriel to Mary at the annunciation,[122] which, according to Basil of Caesarea, came to the angel by the inspiration of the Holy Spirit.[123] In keeping with Augustine's "canonical rule," its function here in the creed is to make more precise—even to find an orthodox interpretation for—a saying of the apostle Paul, which was much beloved of Origen:

> Then cometh the end, when [Christ] shall have delivered up the kingdom to God, even the Father . . . . For [the Son] must reign, till [the Father] hath put all [the Son's] enemies under [the Son's] feet. . . . But when he saith all things are put under him, it is manifest that [the Father] is excepted which did put all things under [the Son]. And when all things shall be subdued unto [the Son], then shall the Son also himself be sub-

117. Prv 8.22, 25 (LXX).
118. Athanasius *Defense of the Nicene Definition* 3.13–14 (*NPNF*–II 4:158–59).
119. Athanasius *Discourses Against the Arians* 2.59 (*NPNF*–II 4:380–81).
120. Person 1978.
121. *N-CP* 7. See Syndogmaticon 7.2.
122. Lk 1.33.
123. Basil of Caesarea *On the Holy Spirit* 16.38 (*NPNF*–II 8:24).

ject unto [the Father] that put all things under him,
that God may be all in all.[124]

Historically, the insertion of this clause from the message of the angel
of the annunciation into the creed is bound up with the complex and
controversial teaching of Marcellus of Ancyra, a vigorous defender of
The Creed of Nicaea, who taught that the kingdom of Christ was coextensive with the history of the world but that at the end of history it
would cease and would yield to the kingdom of God the Father as "all
in all."[125]

As summarized by Johannes Quasten, "In his attempt to prove
the Arian heresy no more than a poorly veiled polytheism, he himself
teaches a monotheism which knows only an economical trinity. . . . It
is this tendency which leads him to the heretical doctrine that before
the creation of the world the Logos was only in God and that at the
end he will be only in God."[126] Because of its obvious affinities with
Sabellianism, this teaching of Marcellus created difficulties for the defenders of Nicaea—significantly, more so in the East than in the West,
perhaps because of the differing theories of the Trinity that were already at work in the fourth and fifth centuries and that would break
into the open in the controversy over the Filioque.[127] Because of the
danger posed by this eschatological theory to the permanence and eternity of the distinction of Father, Son, and Holy Spirit and to the doctrine of their equality in essence, *The Niceno-Constantinopolitan Creed*
makes it a continuing part of the confession of the orthodox faith ever
after to go on declaring that Christ's "kingdom will have no end."[128]
The creed of 325 anathematizes "those who say 'there once was when
he was not.'"[129] Now, to be able to assert that there is no beginning
of the Logos-Son but that he has always been distinct from the Father,
also before creation and incarnation, the creed of 381 asserts, with the

124. 1 Cor 15.24–28 (AV).
125. *DTC* 9:1993–98 (Marie-Dominique Chenu).
126. Quasten, 3:199.
127. See chapter 7.4 below, "The Holy Spirit of Concord and the Sacrament of
Concord: Two Ironic Case Histories."
128. Seibt 1994; Feige 1991.
129. *N* anath.

first chapter of Luke, that there will likewise be no end of his kingdom and rule.[130]

Proceeding on the same basis, *The Tome of Pope Leo I* of 449 affirms the interdependency of Scripture and creed in its denunciation of Eutyches: "A man who has not the most elementary understanding even of the creed itself can have learned nothing from the sacred texts of the New and Old Testaments. . . . He had no desire to acquire the light of understanding by working through the length and breadth of the Holy Scriptures. So at least he should have listened carefully and accepted the common and undivided creed by which the faithful confess."[131] Then *The Tome* reviews the most crucial "sacred texts of the New and Old Testaments" in the light of "the common and undivided creed by which the faithful confess," specifying how various passages require a cross-reference to other passages—between New Testament and Old, epistle and Gospel, but also with equal ease from Scripture to creed and back again. Making its own this "letter of the primate of greatest and older Rome, the most blessed and most saintly Archbishop Leo, written to the sainted Archbishop Flavian," *The Definition of Faith of the Council of Chalcedon* likewise affirms this correlation of Scripture and tradition to be normative when it describes itself as "following the saintly fathers" and as teaching "just as the prophets taught from the beginning . . . and as the Lord Jesus Christ himself instructed us, and as the creed of the fathers handed it down to us."[132]

This hermeneutical function of the ancient creeds sets a pattern for later statements of faith in East and West to imitate. In the East, *The Orthodox Confession of the Catholic and Apostolic Eastern Church by Peter Mogila* takes the statement of *The Niceno-Constantinopolitan Creed* that the Holy Spirit "spoke through the prophets" to mean both that the Holy Spirit is the "real author [*heuretēs*]" of all of Scripture and that "whatsoever the holy fathers have decreed, in general and particular orthodox councils," came from the same origin and hence is permanently binding on the church;[133] therefore "neither are we to be-

130. Gregory of Nazianzus *Orations* 30.4–5 (NPNF–II 7:310–11); *Tol XI* 18; *Mogila* 1.34.
131. *Tome* 1.
132. *Chal* 1, 25–27.
133. *Mogila* 1.72.

lieve more nor ought we to believe less than is therein expressed."[134] In the West, the decree of the fourth session of the Council of Trent not only legislates a list of the Old Testament canon that includes the deuterocanonical books but, attacking the Protestant idea of the private interpretation of Scripture, warns that

> no one, relying on his personal judgment in matters of faith and customs which are linked to the establishment of Christian doctrine, shall dare to interpret the Sacred Scriptures either by twisting its text to his individual meaning in opposition to that which has been and is held by holy mother church, whose function is to pass judgment on the true meaning and interpretation of the Sacred Scriptures; or by giving it meanings contrary to the unanimous consent of the fathers.[135]

With a verbatim quotation from this decree of the Council of Trent, *The Dogmatic Constitution on the Faith of the First Vatican Council* paraphrases it to mean that "in matters of faith and morals, belonging as they do to the establishing of Christian doctrine, that meaning of Holy Scripture must be held to be the true one which holy mother church held and holds, since it is her right to judge of the true meaning and interpretation of Holy Scripture."[136]

The intricacies of this interdependence between Scripture and creedal tradition, and of the interdependence between both of these and the apostolic succession of bishops in the churches, achieved the beginnings of a comprehensive formulation in the writings of the same second-century theologian whose writings are such an important source both for our knowledge of the texts of early Christian creeds[137] and for the significance of the very concept and term "rule of faith," Irenaeus of Lyons.[138] Responding to the Gnostics, Irenaeus postulates this interdependence as a guarantee of continuity with the apostles

134. *Mogila* 1.5.
135. *Trent* 4.2 decr.
136. *Vat I* 3.2.
137. *Iren.*
138. See chapter 1 above, "Continuity and Change in Creeds and Confessions"; and chapter 4 above, "Faith and Order." See also Syndogmaticon 1.4.

and a refutation of heresies.[139] The truth is to be learned "from those who possess that succession of the church which is from the apostles." These are, in turn, the same ones who "preserve this creed of ours [*eam fidem nostram*] in one God who created all things," and also the ones who can be trusted to "expound the Scriptures to us without danger, neither blaspheming God, nor dishonoring the patriarchs, nor despising the prophets."[140] A little later he identifies "the doctrine of the apostles [*hē tōn apostolōn didachē*]" as the creed and "the church's complete system of doctrine [*to archaion tēs ekklēsias systēma*]," on the basis of which alone "an unadulterated exposition of the Scriptures" is possible.[141] And that creed is the "complete system" that he recites and affirms at the beginning of his treatise[142] and summarizes as "the drawing-up of our faith" in his *Proof of the Apostolic Preaching*.[143] Thus also Clement of Alexandria identifies the "deposit [*parathēkē*] rendered to God, according to the teaching of the Lord by his apostles" as "the understanding and the practice of the godly tradition," transmitted to "those who receive and observe, according to the ecclesiastical rule, the exposition of the Scriptures explained by him." "The ecclesiastical rule," he explains, "is the concord and harmony of the law and the prophets in the covenant delivered at the coming of the Lord."[144]

That assumption of the interdependence of Scripture, tradition, and creed in the church comes under fundamental challenge in the confessions of the Protestant Reformers of the sixteenth century, with their insistence that "one divine text is to be interpreted in the light of another,"[145] not in the light of church or tradition or creed. In one of the earliest of these confessions, Ulrich Zwingli's *Sixty-Seven Articles* of 1523, "all who regard another doctrine as equal to or higher than the gospel," meaning "all who say that the gospel is nothing without the approbation of the church," are condemned.[146] For *The Scots*

139. *Chr Trad* 1:108–20; Eynde 1933; Flesseman-Van Leer 1954.
140. Irenaeus *Against Heresies* 4.26.5 (*ANF* 1:498).
141. Irenaeus *Against Heresies* 4.33.8 (*ANF* 1:508).
142. Irenaeus *Against Heresies* 1.10.2 (*ANF* 1:330–31).
143. Irenaeus *Proof of the Apostolic Preaching* 6 (*ACW* 16:51).
144. Clement of Alexandria *Stromata* 6.15 (*ANF* 2:509), quoting 1 Tm 6.20, 2 Tm 1.14.
145. *Ans* 3.25.
146. *67 Art* 5, 1.

Confession, authority in the church is "neither antiquity, usurped title, lineal succession, appointed place, nor the numbers of men approving an error," but "the true preaching of the word of God."[147] More moderately, *The Second Helvetic Confession* affirms its loyalty to "whatever things are defined from the Holy Scriptures concerning the mystery of the incarnation of our Lord Jesus Christ, and are summed up in the creeds and decrees of the first four most excellent synods convened at Nicaea, Constantinople, Ephesus, and Chalcedon—together with the creed of blessed Athanasius, and all similar symbols."[148]

By hindsight, in the light of the controversies of the nineteenth and twentieth centuries over the historical-critical method of studying the Bible, a striking lacuna in the confessions of the sixteenth century is their silence, alongside their declarations of biblical authority, about the two interrelated doctrines of biblical inspiration and biblical inerrancy, upon which, in those later controversies, the authority of Scripture was thought to be dependent.[149] Although here, too, the axiom that "one does not define what is self-evident" applies,[150] that is only a limited explanation. Zwingli's *Sixty-Seven Articles* of 1523 make their confession "on the basis of the Scripture which is called *theopneustos* [that is, inspired by God],"[151] and *The Irish Articles of Religion* affirm the canonical books of the Bible "to be given by the inspiration of God, and in that regard to be of most certain credit and highest authority."[152] Such statements set forth, with lapidary brevity, the doctrines of authority, inspiration, and inerrancy in a single combined formula. When the greatly expanded successor of *The Irish Articles of Religion,* which is *The Westminster Confession of Faith* of 1647, after asserting that "all [canonical books of the Old and the New Testament] . . . are given by inspiration of God,"[153] and that "the Old Testament in Hebrew, . . . and the New Testament in Greek . . . , being immediately

---

147. *Scot I* 18.
148. *Helv II* 11.18; see also chapter 16.3 below, "Catholic Substance and Protestant Principle in Reformation Confessions."
149. Welch 1972–85, 2:165–71.
150. Florovsky 1972–89, 1:57.
151. *67 Art* pr, quoting 2 Tm 3.16.
152. *Irish* 2.
153. *West* 1.2.

inspired by God, and by his singular care and providence kept pure in all ages, are therefore authentical,"[154] goes on to declare that "the infallible rule of interpretation of Scripture is the Scripture itself,"[155] it almost, but not quite, says (keeping its phraseology but transposing the sequence) that "the rule of interpretation of Scripture is the inspired and infallible Scripture itself." Eight years after this Reformed *Westminster Confession of Faith*, a supplementary Lutheran confession, *The Reaffirmed Consensus of the Truly Lutheran Faith* of 1655, moves a considerably greater distance in that direction;[156] but it never managed to achieve normative confessional status. During the nineteenth and twentieth centuries, as Claude Welch has noted, the "most prominent in the biblical controversy . . . was the Presbyterian tradition,"[157] which produced a host of supplementary confessions in different countries during that period.[158] But both of the major traditions of the Reformation confessions, the Lutheran as well as the Reformed and Presbyterian, now addressed the issue with new confessional definitions about biblical inspiration and inerrancy, as for example:

> We teach that the Holy Scriptures differ from all other books in the world in that they are the word of God. They are the word of God because the holy men of God who wrote the Scriptures wrote only that which the Holy Ghost communicated to them by inspiration. . . . We teach also that the verbal inspiration of the Scriptures is not a so-called "theological deduction," but that it is taught by direct statements of the Scriptures. . . . Since the Holy Scriptures are the word of God, it goes without saying that they contain no error or contradiction, but that they are in all their parts and words the infallible truth, also in those parts which

154. *West* 1.8.
155. *West* 1.9.
156. *Cons rep* 2.6.
157. Welch 1972–85, 2:166.
158. See chapter 11 below, "Transmission of Creeds and Confessions to other Cultures."

treat of historical, geographical, and other secular matters.[159]

Other twentieth-century Protestant confessions do the same.[160] For example, *The Doctrinal Statement of the American Baptist Association* of 1905 lays down as its first article, "We believe in the infallible verbal inspiration of the whole Bible," and as its third, "The Genesis Account of Creation."[161] *The Lausanne Covenant* of 1974 in its second article speaks of the Bible as "the only written word of God, without error in all that it affirms, and the only infallible rule of faith and practice."[162]

All the Protestant confessions of the sixteenth and seventeenth centuries are agreed in principle that, in the words of *The Westminster Confession of Faith*, "all synods or councils, since the apostles' times, whether general or particular, may err, and many have erred. Therefore they are not to be made the rule of faith, or practice, but to be used as a help in both";[163] *The Scots Confession* says the same thing.[164] Concretely, nevertheless, they themselves do pass judgment on the correct interpretation of Scripture. Thus *The Belgic Confession*, rejecting the doctrine of an objective presence of the body and blood of Christ in the bread and wine of the sacrament apart from the faith of the communicant, interprets the narratives of the Gospels and Acts to mean that "Judas and Simon the sorcerer both indeed received the sacrament, but [did not receive] Christ, who was signified by it. He is communicated only to believers."[165] Distinguishing between *sacramentum* and *res sacramenti*, "the sacrament" and "the substance of the sacrament," *The Second Helvetic Confession* denies that such unworthy communicants receive the body and blood of Christ.[166] So do the Anglican *Thirty-Nine Articles*,[167] *The Belgic Confession*,[168] and *The Zurich Agree-*

---

159. *Br St Luth* 1.
160. *Naz* 4; *Bat* 4; *Camb Dec* 1.
161. *Am Bap* 1, 3.
162. *Laus Cov* 2.
163. *West* 31.4.
164. *Scot I* 20.
165. *Belg* 35; see also *Genv Cat* 370. See Syndogmaticon 10.6.
166. *Helv II* 21.9.
167. *39 Art* 29.
168. *Belg* 35.

ment [Consensus Tigurinus] of 1547 between Zwinglians and Calvinists, protesting against "those ridiculous interpreters who insist on what they call the precise literal sense of the solemn words of the supper," which "without question . . . are to be taken figuratively" and insisting "that God does not exert his power indiscriminately in all who receive the sacraments, but only in the elect." [169] Against this Reformed interpretation of the words of the New Testament, the Lutheran *Formula of Concord* likewise legislates an official interpretation of Scripture when it identifies "the chief question at issue" between the Reformed and the Lutherans as: whether "the true body and blood of our Lord Jesus Christ truly and essentially present. . . are received orally by all those who use the sacrament, be they worthy or unworthy, godly or godless, believers or unbelievers. . . . The Sacramentarians say No; we say Yes." [170] This official Lutheran interpretation of the Gospel narrative of the Last Supper is reinforced in *The Saxon Visitation Articles* of 1592.[171]

In the familiar formula of William Chillingworth, "The Bible, and the Bible alone, is the religion of Protestants." But for most Protestant confessions it has to be understood correctly, namely, in accordance with the confessions, as the preface to *The Canons of the Synod of Dort* specifies in so many words.[172] Confession and Scripture remained interdependent in practice even when the interdependence was negated in principle—negated by those very confessions. To justify this, *The Westminster Confession of Faith* of 1647 refines the principle of the sole authority of Scripture to mean the dual principle that "the whole counsel of God . . . is either expressly set down in Scripture, or by good and necessary consequence may be deduced from Scripture." [173] This specification of the "good and necessary consequences" that are to be invoked by the biblical exegete in arriving at "the whole counsel of God" makes it legitimate, and even requisite, to draw out the implications of a passage or group of passages in arriving at a doctrine that will then be just as entitled to be called biblical as is a doctrine that is expressed

---

169. *Tig* 16–17, 22.
170. *Form Conc Epit* 7.2.
171. *Sax Vis* 1.1.6.
172. *Dort* pr.
173. *West* 1.6.

in the *ipsissima verba* of a single passage of the Bible; the prime example is the doctrine of the Trinity. It also implies, however, that there is a necessary function of "deducing" by human reason in the hermeneutical process. When it comes to the dogma of the Trinity confessed in *The Niceno-Constantinopolitan Creed* and *The Athanasian Creed*, therefore, which the confessions of the Socinians and other Antitrinitarians reject on the grounds both of biblical authority and of reason,[174] *The Westminster Confession of Faith* presents as biblical doctrine, dependent not on church or tradition or council or creed but on the sole authority of Holy Scripture, the entire Western version of the dogma, complete with the vocabulary of "persons" and "substance," and even with the distinctively Western addition of the Filioque to the creed.[175] But even the trinitarian confessions within the Radical Reformation challenge the general Protestant consensus about the interpretation of Scripture. They do so by stressing the need for an inner illumination to correspond to the "lantern" of Scripture, which "cannot of itself . . . entirely remove the darkness."[176] But this subjectivist position of the Radicals could claim a measure of affinity with such mainstream Protestant confessions as *The French Confession,* which, as noted earlier, discriminates between the canonical books of the Bible and the Apocrypha "not so much by the common accord and consent of the church, as by the testimony and inward illumination of the Holy Spirit, which enables us to distinguish [the canon] from other ecclesiastical books."[177]

   The First Helvetic Confession of 1536 makes "Concerning the Interpretation of Scripture" the title of its article 2, immediately following article 1, "On Holy Scripture," but contents itself with the universally Protestant rule that "Scripture is to be interpreted in no other way than out of itself [*ex ipsa sola*] and is to be explained by the rule of faith and love."[178] *The Second Helvetic Confession* of 1566 expands this into one of the most detailed hermeneutical guides in any Refor-

174. *Trans; Rac;* but see *Socin.*
175. *West* 2.3. See also chapter 7.4 below, "The Holy Spirit of Concord and the Sacrament of Concord: Two Ironic Case Histories"; and chapter 16.3 below, "Catholic Substance and Protestant Principle in Reformation Confessions."
176. *Denck* 1.
177. *Gall* 3–4.
178. *Helv I* 2.

mation confession. "No prophecy of scripture is a matter of one's own interpretation"[179] is a warning that appears in everyone's Bible. *The Canons and Decrees of the Council of Trent* invoke this principle to attack the Protestant elevation of "personal judgment in matters of faith and customs which are linked to the establishment of Christian doctrine" over the right of the church to determine the correct interpretation of the Bible.[180] Confessions of the Radical Reformation quote it to prove that "it belongs to the Holy Spirit to interpret [it]," not to any human being or institution or tradition.[181] But *The Second Helvetic Confession* takes this New Testament prohibition to require that "we hold that interpretation of the Scriptures to be orthodox and genuine which is gleaned from the Scriptures themselves (from the nature of the language in which they were written, likewise according to the circumstances in which they were set down, and expounded in the light of like and unlike passages and of many and clearer passages) and which agrees with the rule of faith and love, and contributes much to the glory of God and man's salvation."[182] Confessionally, there are, then, several components of any sound Reformed exegesis of the Bible. The first is a grasp of the original languages of Scripture, as chapter 1 of *The Westminster Confession of Faith* puts it, "the Old Testament in Hebrew (which was the native language of the people of God of old), and the New Testament in Greek (which, at the time of the writing of it, was most generally known to the nations)."[183] But this insistence of the Renaissance and the Reformation on the original languages of the Bible had the possibility of clashing with the distinctive teaching of the Reformation,[184] stated in the same chapter of *The Westminster Confession of Faith,* that all believers, as priests, have the right and duty to judge matters of doctrine and therefore to interpret the Bible, the "right unto, and interest in the Scriptures, and are commanded, in the fear of God, to read and search them."[185] From this comes the claim that

179. 2 Pt 1.20.
180. For example, *Trent* 4.2.
181. *Denck* 1.
182. *Helv II* 2.1.
183. *West* 1.8.
184. Cf. *Trent* 4; *Dosith* q 1.
185. *West* 1.8.

"not only the learned, but the unlearned, in a due use of the ordinary means, may attain unto a sufficient understanding of them."[186] That implies that there must be trustworthy translations—trustworthy both philologically and doctrinally—into the several vernaculars. A second criterion is a consideration of the passage in question "according to the circumstances." This seems to require at least the following: a scholarly investigation of the historical context, together with a consideration of the analogies and differences between those "circumstances" and the present; a weighing of the "proportion [*ratio*]" of other passages, on the grounds, as stated in *The Thirty-Nine Articles of the Church of England,* that the church must not "so expound one place of Scripture, that it be repugnant to another";[187] and the implication of the passage for "the glory of God and man's salvation."

Perhaps the most momentous of all is the ambiguous formula, which *The Second Helvetic Confession* quotes verbatim from the language of *The First Helvetic Confession* of 1536,[188] that correct interpretations are those that "agree with the rule of faith and love [*cum regula fidei et caritate*]." Or, as *The Scots Confession* phrases it, "We dare not receive or admit any interpretation which is contrary to any principal point of our faith, or to any other plain text of Scripture, or to the rule of love."[189] The use of the conjunction "and" in the formulas of the two *Helvetic Confessions* and of the conjunction "or" in the formula of *The Scots Confession* could be seen as a reintroduction of the normative authority of some "rule of faith [*regula fidei*]" or other, alongside or in addition to that of Scripture—though not, indeed, the authority of "the interpretations of the holy Greek and Latin fathers," interpretations that are declared to be worthy of respect but not of deference.[190] The ambiguity of such references to "the rule of faith" as a norm for the interpretation of Scripture becomes especially acute at the very point under consideration here. Several Protestant confessions equate "the rule of faith" not with the creeds at all, either ancient or

186. *West* 1.7.
187. *39 Art* 20.
188. *Helv I* 2. See Syndogmaticon 1.4.
189. *Scot I* 18.
190. *Helv II* 2.2.

contemporary, but with Scripture alone. *The Belgic Confession* affirms that equation by giving its article 7 the heading: "The Sufficiency of Scripture."[191] And *The Westminster Confession of Faith* follows its listing of the canon of Scripture with the words: "All which are given by inspiration of God, to be the rule of faith and life."[192] *The Formula of Concord* calls "the prophetic and apostolic writings of the Old and New Testaments . . . the only rule and norm according to which all doctrines and teachers alike must be appraised and judged."[193] Because that assertion by the Protestant confessions of the sole authority—not merely the *supreme* authority but the *sole* authority—of Scripture could be taken to imply the rejection of the authority of the ancient creeds, it becomes necessary for the orthodox Protestant confessions to affirm their allegiance to the "creeds," which means "the three creeds, Nicene Creed, Athanasius's Creed, and that which is commonly called the Apostles' Creed."[194] When Luther's controversy with Zwingli over the real presence of the body and blood of Christ in the eucharist developed into a full-scale reconsideration of the doctrine of the two natures in Christ, a total apparatus not only of biblical exegesis but of conciliar and patristic quotations came into play, in the "Catalog of Testimonies" appended to *The Formula of Concord* of 1577.[195] This compilation of quotations even found its way into the corpus of the Lutheran confessions, although its status as a part of the normative *Book of Concord* remained a matter of some disagreement.

The vigor of this Protestant defense and the sharpness of this Protestant polemic could give the impression that the opposing Roman Catholic view of the relation between Scripture and creedal tradition was clear and consistent, but such an impression would be historically erroneous.[196] At the center of the unresolved issues in the Roman Catholic confessional position on the matter is the formula set down by the fourth session of the Council of Trent on 8 April 1546:

191. *Belg* 7.
192. *West* 1.2.
193. *Form Conc Epit* pr 1.
194. *39 Art* 8.
195. *Triglotta* 1105–49; *BLK* 1101–35.
196. Tavard 1959.

The council clearly perceives that this truth and rule
are contained *in written books and in unwritten traditions* which were received by the apostles from the
mouth of Christ himself, or else have come down to
us, handed on as it were from the apostles themselves
at the inspiration of the Holy Spirit. . . . The council
accepts and venerates with a like feeling of piety [*pari
pietatis affectu*] and reverence all the books of both the
Old and the New Testament . . . as well as the traditions concerning both faith and conduct, as either directly spoken by Christ or dictated by the Holy Spirit,
which have been preserved in unbroken sequence in
the Catholic Church.[197]

And *The Tridentine Profession of Faith* of 1564 expressly includes the
affirmation: "I most firmly accept and embrace the apostolic and ecclesiastical traditions. . . . I likewise accept Holy Scripture according to
that sense which holy mother church has held and does hold."[198] Do
these formulas, especially the coordination "in written books and in
unwritten traditions," mean that there are two parallel but distinct
sources of divine revelation, the Holy Scripture and the Holy Tradition,
which is both written and oral and is articulated in, though of course
not confined to, the creeds? The decree of the Council of Trent does not
answer that question, and it remained unanswered in official Roman
Catholic teaching amid vigorous debate over the centuries after the sixteenth.[199] Even the decrees of the First Vatican Council do not provide a
definitive solution.[200] In the wake of that council, *The Fourteen Theses of
the Old Catholic Union Conference with Greeks and Anglicans* at Bonn in
1874, affirming that tradition "is an authoritative source of teaching,"
add the unusual qualification, which echoes and criticizes the formula
of Trent, that it "is partly to be found in the consensus of the great
ecclesiastical bodies standing in historical continuity with the primitive
church, partly *to be gathered by scientific method* from the written docu-

197. *Trent* 4.1; italics added.
198. *Trid Prof* 2.
199. Geiselmann 1966.
200. *Vat I* 3.2.

ments of all centuries."[201] This seems to elevate historical and philological scholars to a normative role. In the twentieth century two Roman Catholic statements of faith address the problem, but somewhat differently. The promulgation of the dogma of the bodily assumption of the Virgin Mary by Pope Pius XII in 1950 is obliged to address the vexing problem of the silence of Scripture on the subject, and it could therefore be seen as an affirmation of the authority of nonbiblical tradition as a second source of revelation alongside Scripture.[202] But the Constitution "On Divine Revelation" of the Second Vatican Council does not legislate such an affirmation of two sources of revelation, as some had hoped and others had feared it might, but bypasses many of the questions by contenting itself with the declaration that "sacred tradition and Scripture are bound together in a close and reciprocal relationship. They both flow from the same divine wellspring, merge together to some extent [*in unum quodammodo coalescunt*], and are on course toward the same end. . . . Tradition and Scripture together form a single sacred deposit of the word of God entrusted to the church."[203]

201. *Bonn I* 9.1 (italics added); also *Leuen* 5; *Com Dec* 4; *LuRC Just* 14.
202. *Munif* 26, 38, 29.
203. *Vat II* 8.2.9–10.

CHAPTER SIX

The Rule of Prayer and the Rule of Faith

EVEN THE MOST STALWART champion of the crucial importance of creeds and confessions of faith for the life of the church would be obliged to acknowledge that among the different kinds of sacred text, prayer has to be ranked far above creed. This acknowledgment holds in spite of the presence within the New Testament of fragments that seem to be quoted from primitive Christian creeds or creedlike sources, as they are discussed elsewhere in this volume and as they are collected in Part One of *Creeds and Confessions of Faith in the Christian Tradition* under the heading "Biblical and Primitive Rules of Faith."[1] The earliest generations of disciples, and then all the generations of Christians who have come after them, remembered, as the New Testament says, that "Christ Jesus . . . in his testimony before Pontius Pilate made the good confession,"[2] which they strove to imitate as faithfully as they could when they in turn were called upon in their testimony to make their own "good confessions" before the long and dreary line of Pontius Pilate's successors for the next twenty centuries. The fact remains, nevertheless, that no confession or creed, not even *The Apostles' Creed* when it was widely regarded in the West as having been composed directly by the inspired apostles following the ascension of Christ,[3] can claim to trace the ancestry of its very words directly back to the person of Jesus Christ.

But prayer can and does. "Lord, teach us to pray, as John

---

1. See also chapter 5.1 above, "Creeds in Scripture"; and chapter 13 below, "Rules of Faith in the Early Church."
2. 1 Tm 6.13.
3. Rufinus of Aquileia *Commentary on the Apostles' Creed* 2 (ACW 20:29–31).

taught his disciples,"[4] the disciples implored Jesus according to the account in Luke's Gospel, and in response to their request he gave them the Lord's Prayer,[5] which in Matthew's Gospel appears instead as an integral part of the Sermon on the Mount.[6] As Augustine identifies the difference between the creed and the Lord's Prayer on the basis of the Pauline distinction between faith, hope, and charity,[7] "From this confession of faith, which is briefly summed up in the creed, . . . is born the good hope of the faithful, with holy charity as its companion. But of all the matters which are to be believed in the true spirit of faith, only those pertain to hope which are contained in the Lord's Prayer."[8] Therefore not the confession of the faith, but prayer, is to be the continuous activity of Christian believers. Not "Confess without ceasing" but "Pray without ceasing,"[9] the apostle Paul admonishes the Thessalonians, in words that are quoted by Eastern Orthodox confessions in support of "the Jesus Prayer";[10] this admonition, as Kallistos Ware has put it, describes "continual prayer as an implicit state."[11] Prayer is necessary for Christians, also according to *The Heidelberg Catechism* with all the strong emphasis it places on creed and doctrine, "because it is *the chief part* of the gratitude which God requires of us, and because God will give his grace and Holy Spirit *only* to those who sincerely beseech him in prayer without ceasing, and who thank him for these gifts."[12] And *The Christian Catechism of the Orthodox Catholic Greco-Russian Church* of Metropolitan Philaret Drozdov of Moscow identifies prayer, especially the inward prayer of the mind and heart but also the outward prayer of the mouth, as occupying the first place of all among "the means for attaining to a saving hope"; the confession of the faith in the creed, by contrast, is identified only as the first of the "duties which refer to the *outward* worship of God."[13]

4. Lk 11.1.
5. Lk 11.2–4.
6. Mt 6.9–13.
7. 1 Cor 13.13 (AV).
8. Augustine *Enchiridion* 30.114 (ACW 3:106).
9. 1 Thes 5.17 (AV).
10. *CP 1341* 48; *Mogila* 1.87.
11. Ware 2000, 81.
12. *Heid* 116 (italics added); see also *West* 21.3.
13. *Russ Cat* 388, 507; italics added.

It can, of course, be quite misleading and artificial to draw a disjunction between praying and confessing in this way, because, for one thing, the confessions of various traditions repeatedly deal with the meaning of prayer and its relation both to doctrine and to the confession of doctrine.[14] Thus *The Irish Articles of Religion* of 1615 exhort: "We ought to prepare our hearts before we pray, and understand the things that we ask when we pray."[15] More polemically, *The Geneva Confession* of 1536, citing the Lord's Prayer as the divinely given model of how to pray, goes beyond such universally shared views to assert, in opposition to Roman Catholic doctrine and practice: "We reject the intercession of the saints as a superstition invented by men contrary to Scripture, for the reason that it proceeds from mistrust of the sufficiency of the intercession of Jesus Christ."[16] *The French Confession* of 1559 makes the same point, and also cites the Lord's Prayer in substantiation: "We believe, as Jesus Christ is our only advocate, and as he commands us to ask of the Father in his name, and as it is not lawful for us to pray except in accordance with the model God has taught us by his word, that all imaginations of men concerning the intercession of dead saints are an abuse and a device of Satan [*abus et fallace de Satan*] to lead men from the right way of worship."[17] *The Augsburg Confession* of 1530 puts its criticism of the invocation of the saints somewhat more mildly, contenting itself with the objection that "it cannot be proved from the Scriptures that we are to invoke saints or seek help from them."[18] In explanation of this criticism, *The Apology of the Augsburg Confession* concedes, more mildly still, "that the saints in heaven pray for the church in general, as they prayed for the church universal while they were on earth"; but it insists that this prayer *by* the departed saints cannot be used to justify our prayer *to* the departed saints.[19] Nor is it only in such polemical contexts, but also in pastoral ones, that prayer arises as a topic for confessions, as can be seen, among many

---

14. *Tetrapol* 7. See *Syndogmaticon* 8.8.
15. *Irish* 48.
16. *Genv Con* 12–13; also *Genv Cat* 238. See *Syndogmaticon* 3.8.
17. *Gall* 24.
18. *Aug Ger* 21.2; also *Smal Art* 2.2.26.
19. *Apol Aug* 21.9.

examples, from the *Seventeen Articles for the Use of Visitors in Saxony* of 1527/28.[20] Therefore the decree of the Second Vatican Council of the Roman Catholic Church is expressing a pastoral concern that it has in common with every confession in every age when it prescribes that "there will be prayers, shared by the people, for the church, for those who have secular power over us, for those who are beset by needs of various kinds, and finally for all men and women, and the salvation and well-being of the whole world."[21]

6.1. The Lord's Prayer in the Confessions

Beyond these various references, whether polemical or pastoral, to the doctrine and the practice of prayer, the consideration of prayer becomes a major component in several confessions as a result of their devoting an entire unit to the exposition of the Lord's Prayer. "Faith, hope, and charity, these three"[22]—this Pauline triad serves, in Augustine's *Enchiridion* (whose alternate title was *On Faith, Hope, and Charity*) and then in the standard table of contents for catechisms in the Middle Ages as well as in the Reformation,[23] as the outline for a three-fold commentary. Faith—or, to be precise, "*the* faith" as the *fides quae creditur,* "the faith which one believes"[24]—is explained on the basis of the creed (which, for Western confessions and catechisms, including eventually the Protestant writers of catechisms and confessions, most often means *The Apostles' Creed,* but for the Eastern Orthodox writers of confessions and catechisms, *The Niceno-Constantinopolitan Creed*).[25] Hope is expounded on the basis of the Lord's Prayer, and love or charity on the basis of the Ten Commandments, which are prominently quoted in many confessions.[26] Through this device, an exposition of the Lord's Prayer, and thus of the topic of prayer as a whole, is incorporated into the public doctrine of all those churches that regard

20. *17 Art* 3.
21. *Vat II* 3.53 decr.
22. 1 Cor 13.13 (AV).
23. *Helv II* 25.1; see chapter 13.4 below, "Didache, Catechesis, and the Formulas of Exorcism."
24. See chapter 2.2 above, "Faith Defined"; also Syndogmaticon 1.1.
25. Compare, for example, *Heid* 23–58 with *Mogila* 1.4–126.
26. *Heid* 92–115; *Metr Crit* 6.1.

their catechisms not merely as pedagogical tools but at the same time as confessional statements.[27]

It should not be surprising that the doctrinal differences between the several communions and denominations, which figure so prominently in their other confessions of faith and are frequently the immediate provocation for them,[28] so often become marginal and sometimes become invisible when the sacred text under consideration is not a creed but a prayer, in fact, the prayer of Christ himself. Every day for twenty centuries its petitions have been prayed in more or less the same form by individual Christians and worshiping congregations everywhere, regardless of confessional affiliation. That underemphasis on doctrinal differences becomes clear from a comparison between two catechism-confessions containing commentaries on the Lord's Prayer that come from the Protestant Reformation with two that come from Eastern Orthodoxy (listing the four in chronological order): *The Small Catechism of Martin Luther* of 1529; *The Heidelberg Catechism* of 1563; *The Orthodox Confession of the Catholic and Apostolic Eastern Church* by Peter Mogila of 1643; and *The Christian Catechism of the Orthodox Catholic Greco-Russian Church* by Metropolitan Philaret Drozdov of Moscow of 1839. On some other issues the divergences between Protestantism and Eastern Orthodoxy, as well as the divergences between Lutheran and Reformed Protestantism, make themselves no less audible in these texts than they do in overtly polemical theological treatises. *The Orthodox Confession of the Catholic and Apostolic Eastern Church by Peter Mogila* teaches[29]—and the *Catechism* of Philaret agrees[30]—that in the consecration of the eucharist "the substance of the bread and the substance of the wine are changed into the very substance of the very body and blood of Jesus Christ." *The Orthodox Confession of the Catholic and Apostolic Eastern Church by Peter Mogila* (and then *The Confession of Dositheus and of the Synod of Jerusalem*), moreover, even employ the neologism of late Byzantine Greek for the

27. See chapter 3.3 above, "'Doctrines' and Doctrine."
28. See chapter 7.1 below, "Creedal Anathema and Polemics."
29. *Mogila* 1.107. On the entire issue, see Syndogmaticon 10.7.
30. *Russ Cat* 315.

Western scholastic term "transubstantiation," *metousiōsis*,[31] not simply the more usual and less technical participle "changing [*metabalōn*]" the bread and wine into the body and blood, which is used in *The Divine Liturgy According to Saint John Chrysostom*.[32]

On the same issue, *The Small Catechism of Martin Luther* makes a point of including his insistence that the Sacrament of the Altar "is the *true* body and blood of our Lord Jesus Christ, under the bread and wine,"[33] a formulation that is repeated the following year in the tenth article of *The Augsburg Confession* when it declares, employing in its Latin text the same terminology that is used in the decree of the Fourth Lateran Council of 1215,[34] that "the true body and blood of Christ are truly present [*vere adsint*] and are distributed to those who eat in the supper of the Lord."[35] The reply of the Roman Catholic *Confutation* to this formulation admits that "the tenth article gives no offense in its words."[36] Therefore *The Apology of the Augsburg Confession* can report with gratification: "They approve the tenth article, where we confess our belief that in the Lord's supper the body and blood of Christ are truly and substantially present [*vere et substantialiter adsint*] and are truly offered with those things that are seen, the bread and the wine, to those who receive the sacrament."[37] The sixth article of *The Wittenberg Articles* of 1536 between Anglicans and Lutherans repeats this tenth article of *The Augsburg Confession* verbatim.[38] Using some of the same words, the Anglican *Ten Articles* of that year teach "that under the form and figure of bread and wine . . . is verily, substantially, and really contained and comprehended the very selfsame body and blood of our Savior Jesus Christ, which was born of the Virgin Mary, and suffered upon the cross for our redemption."[39] This identification between the "body" in the eucharist and the "body" born of Mary is

31. *Mogila* 1.107; *Dosith* decr 16.
32. *Lit Chrys* 2.F.5; see *CP 1691*.
33. *Luth Sm Cat* 6.2; italics added.
34. *Lat 1215* 1.
35. *Aug Lat* 10.1. See *Def Plat* 1.5, 2.9.
36. *Confut* 10.1.
37. *Apol Aug* 10.1.
38. *Witt Art* 6.
39. *10 Art* 4.1.

a medieval Catholic formulation[40] in these preliminary confessions of Anglicanism that does not find its way into the eucharistic articles of its definitive confession, *The Thirty-Nine Articles of the Church of England* of 1571, which is more Protestant, and even Reformed, than they.[41] In opposition to such Catholic formulations, *The Heidelberg Catechism*, while modifying Zwingli's eucharistic teaching in some respects, incorporates into its final and definitive version the polemical statement: "The mass is fundamentally a complete denial of the once for all sacrifice and passion of Jesus Christ (and such an idolatry as to be condemned)."[42] Even its earlier versions include the insistence that "as the water in baptism is not changed into the blood of Christ, nor becomes the washing away of sins by itself, but is only a divine sign and confirmation of it, so also in the Lord's supper the sacred bread *does not become* the body of Christ itself, although, in accordance with the nature and usage of sacraments, it *is called* the body of Christ."[43] This parallelism between baptism and eucharist already appears in earlier Swiss Reformed confessions such as *The Ten Theses of Bern* of 1528,[44] Zwingli's *Reckoning of the Faith* of 1530,[45] *The First Confession of Basel* of 1534,[46] and *The Zurich Consensus* of 1549 between Zwinglians and Calvinists,[47] but now is being invoked in a catechism. But it is specifically rejected by the decree of the Council of Trent.[48] The parallelism is stated even more vigorously by *The Westminster Confession of Faith* when it specifies that the elements in the eucharist are "truly, yet sacramentally only, . . . sometimes called by the name of the things they represent . . . ; albeit in substance and nature they still remain truly and only bread and wine, as they were before."[49] In *The Thirty-Nine Articles of the Church of England* of 1571 any notion of a "change of

40. See chapter 15.2 below, "The Confessionalization of Western Sacramental Doctrine."
41. *39 Art* 28–29.
42. *Heid* 80; Beyer 1965; Syndogmaticon 10.9.
43. *Heid* 78; italics added.
44. *Bern* 4.
45. *Fid rat* 8.
46. *Bas Bek* 6.
47. *Tig* 22.
48. *Trent* 13.1.3 decr.
49. *West* 29.5.

the substance of bread and wine in the supper of the Lord" is also rejected; instead, there is the insistence that "the wicked . . . do not eat the body of Christ, in the use of the Lord's supper."[50]

But in the explications of the Lord's Prayer, and hence of the doctrine of prayer, by these four catechism-confessions there is no statement of doctrinal difference to match these polemics against the eucharistic teachings of other confessions. In *The Large Catechism of Martin Luther,* which like his *Small Catechism* also appeared in 1529 but was meant for clergy and more advanced laity, the opportunity does present itself, even while expounding the Lord's Prayer, to include the standard Protestant attack on "the kind of babbling and bellowing that used to pass for prayers in the church," at mass and at monastic prayers in observance of the canonical hours.[51] Here Luther's *Large Catechism* is joining, in spite of his profound disagreements with Zwingli on the Lord's supper, in the accusation that is voiced by *The Sixty-Seven Articles of Ulrich Zwingli* of 1523 against "that chanting and loud clamor which lack true devotion and are done only for the sake of reward,"[52] as well as in the polemic of *The French Confession* against ritualism.[53] By contrast, his *Small Catechism,* whose "chief parts" are intended for children and families, sets forth an explanation of the petitions of the Lord's Prayer "in the plain form in which the head of the family shall teach it to his household," which implies, it adds, that the Lord's Prayer should always be used in the same wording.[54] As a result, there is probably nothing in these questions and answers about prayer to which either his Roman Catholic or his Protestant opponents could fundamentally object. And the same would be true, or largely true, of the explanations of the Lord's Prayer in the *Catechism* of Heidelberg written by Zacharias Ursinus and in the *Catechism* of Metropolitan Philaret, as well as in the catechetical *Confession by Peter Mogila.* Such an ecumenical consensus would probably also include most other classic Christian commentaries on the Our Father, such as those of Gregory of Nyssa and Theodore of Mopsuestia in the

50. *39 Art* 28–29.
51. *Luth Lg Cat* 3.7.
52. *67 Art* 46.
53. *Gall* 24.
54. *Luth Sm Cat* 3.1; pr 7.

patristic era,[55] as well as those of the Protestant tradition, such as the brief summary-paraphrase of the Lord's Prayer in *The Anglican Catechism* of 1549,[56] as well as more recent commentaries.

6.2. *Lex orandi lex credendi*

Beyond these and other confessional and catechetical treatments of the doctrine of prayer and expositions of the Lord's Prayer, one very particular form of interaction between prayer and the confession of the faith has been a major force throughout the history of creeds and confessions and throughout the history of the development of Christian doctrine. That interaction is summarized in the ancient principle, "The rule of prayer is the rule of faith [*lex orandi lex credendi*]," or, more fully in its original formulation by Prosper of Aquitaine in the fifth century, "The rule of prayer should lay down the rule of faith [*ut legem credendi lex statuat supplicandi*]."[57] Therefore, as *The Encyclical Letter of Photius* puts it, "a little disregard for the things that have been handed down by tradition often leads into a complete disdain for doctrine [*pros holēn tou dogmatos . . . kataphronēsin*]."[58] A confession of the faith from each of the three major divisions of Christendom will illustrate this principle. A Protestant affirmation of doctrine that comes from a church tracing its ancestry to one of the "forerunners of the Reformation," *The Confession of the Waldenses* of 1655, for example, quotes extensively from the eucharistic prayer of the Waldensian liturgy as support, "to the end that every one may clearly see what *our belief* is as to this point."[59] From almost exactly the same time, *The Orthodox Confession of the Catholic and Apostolic Eastern Church by Peter Mogila* quotes a hymn of the liturgy to prove the doctrine of Christ's descent into Hades "although no mention is made thereof" in *The Niceno-Constantinopolitan Creed*.[60] And, to cite one of the more recent formulations of a rule of faith in relation to one of the more ancient expres-

---

55. Simpson 1965.
56. *Ang Cat.*
57. *Chr Trad* 1:339, 2:34–35, 3:66–80.
58. *Phot* 5.
59. *Wald* 30; italics added.
60. *Mogila* 1.49.

sions of the rule of prayer, the dogma of the bodily assumption of the Virgin Mary does not achieve formally defined dogmatic status in Roman Catholicism until 1 November 1950, with the issuance of the apostolic constitution *Munificentissimus Deus* by Pope Pius XII.[61] But long before the dogmatic and confessional promulgation of it, there are already liturgical observances of the Feast of the Assumption of the Virgin in the West—or, in the East, the Feast of the Dormition [*koimēsis*] of the Theotokos—for many centuries (although there is not evidence for them from the very earliest centuries of the church).[62]

Although the definition of the dogma of the assumption is one of the most recent instances of the application of the axiom that "the rule of prayer should lay down the rule of faith," the most ancient and most important documentation of this principle is the development of the dogma of the Trinity, specifically of the doctrine of the full and coequal divinity of the Son of God, and subsequently (though by a significantly different route) the development of the doctrine of the Holy Spirit as God. Even in a nineteenth-century Baptist confession, the baptismal formula and "the benedictions pronounced by the apostles, which are *acts of the highest religious worship*," continue to be the chief evidence for the doctrine of the Trinity.[63] The original *Creed of Nicaea* of 325 concludes its positive affirmations with the clause, "And [we believe] in the Holy Spirit,"[64] specifying no more about the Spirit than that. But *The Niceno-Constantinopolitan Creed* of 381 incorporates various explanatory appositions, including the liturgical declaration that the Holy Spirit is "co-worshiped and co-glorified [*synproskynoumenon kai syndoxazomenon*] with Father and Son."[65] That declaration about the worship of the Holy Spirit is simultaneously descriptive and prescriptive. For before the rule of faith in the creed was expanded in 381 to incorporate the several appositions ascribing to the Spirit an equality of "essence [*ousia*]" with the Father and the Son, the rule of prayer was already engaged in such an act of ascribing an equality of wor-

61. *Munif* 16; but see also *Munif* 20.
62. Jugie 1944; Daley 1998, 1–45.
63. *Free-Will Bap* 6.5; italics added.
64. N 8.
65. N-CP 8; see Syndogmaticon 8.7.

ship [*proskynēsis*] and an equality of glory [*doxa*] to the Holy Spirit. The most familiar instance of such "co-glorifying" is the Gloria Patri, "Glory be to the Father and to the Son and to the Holy Spirit," which puts the three on an equal level.[66] Therefore it is on the basis of the rule of prayer formulated in the Gloria Patri that Basil of Caesarea argues that the rule of faith formulated in *The Creed of Nicaea* requires a recognition of the full equality of the Spirit, and thus of the full equality of all three divine hypostases, in the triune Godhead. He does this in his treatise *On the Holy Spirit,* written shortly before the First Council of Constantinople of 381 made this a binding dogma of the church. Basil's version of the Gloria Patri contained several interesting (and, as he discovered, controversial) variations in the text, such as "Glory to the Father with [*meta*] the Son, together with [*syn*] the Holy Spirit," or "Glory to the Father through [*dia*] the Son in [*en*] the Holy Spirit." But he insisted against critics on various sides that the net doctrinal effect was the same.[67]

If by hindsight one uses later orthodoxy to judge the formal doctrinal language being employed during the first two or three centuries of Christian history, until the First Council of Nicaea and well after it, it is clear that even before this problem of the Holy Spirit in the Trinity arose,[68] there was a shocking diversity also in the concepts and terms with which Christian writers described the relation of the Son to the Father.[69] Certain formulas for the language of faith that eventually became suspect were still finding support among some of those Christian thinkers who were trying to develop a consistent terminology for the creeds and confessions of the church that would systematize the doctrine of the uniqueness of Jesus Christ without fundamentally compromising the oneness of God. Meanwhile, however, the language of prayer seemed much more intent on simply acknowledging Christ as God, even if it had to do so at the expense of conceptual precision and terminological consistency. In the opening words of the early homily

66. ODCC 682.
67. Pelikan 1993, 304–5.
68. See chapter 1.3 above, "The Doctrine of the Trinity as Example of Continuity and of Change."
69. See chapter 5.4 above, "Confessional Rules of Biblical Hermeneutics."

that came to be known as *The Second Epistle of Clement*, "Brethren, we ought to think of Jesus Christ as we do of God—as the 'judge of the living and the dead.'"[70]

It may seem to be an exception to this tendency when the injunction of Jesus in introducing the Lord's Prayer, "Pray then like this: Our Father,"[71] is taken by Origen of Alexandria in his treatise *On Prayer* to be an exclusionary principle, which requires "that we may never pray to anything generated—not even to Christ—but only to God and the Father of all, to whom even our Savior himself prayed."[72] But Eric Jay has pointed out "that Origen is not always consistent and that his devotion to Christ led him both himself to pray boldly to Christ, and to encourage others to do so, even though when he comes to write a treatise on the subject he is unable to justify the practice theologically."[73] Apparently, then, the rule of prayer has already moved far ahead of the rule of faith—or, perhaps better, the rule of faith is still lagging behind the rule of prayer—also for Origen. Elsewhere, therefore, Origen can be far less exclusionary, as when, responding to a pagan critic of the Christian message, he says that "we ought to pray to the supreme God alone, and to pray besides to the only-begotten Logos of God, the firstborn of all creation."[74] It has been the incurable habit of the usage of Christian prayer, and thus of the rule of prayer, that it regularly—one could almost say, blithely—violates the exclusionary principle articulated by Origen's version of the rule of faith, when it follows Origen's version of the rule of prayer by addressing prayer, praise, petition, and thanksgiving to the Son of God in worshipful terms that often are not significantly less extravagant than those being addressed to the Father. Arius and his followers, too, identified themselves with that tendency when the *lex orandi* of their liturgical language in praise of the Logos sometimes contradicted the theological formulas of subordination that they employed in their *lex credendi* to confess the inferiority of the Son to the Father.

70. *2 Clement* 1 (tr. Cyril Richardson).
71. Mt 6.9.
72. Origen *Prayer* 15 (ACW 19:57–60).
73. Jay 1954, 127.
74. Origen *Contra Celsum* 8.26 (Chadwick 1953, 471).

In defending *The Creed of Nicaea* of 325 as a normative state-ment of faith that does not clash with the practice of Christian prayer and devotion but in fact reinforces it—therefore as a rule of faith that does full justice to the rule of prayer—the opponents of Arianism, above all Athanasius of Alexandria, seize upon that Arian inconsis-tency.[75] They claim thereby to be speaking for "the orthodoxy of the body of the faithful" as this expresses itself chiefly in the language of prayer.[76] Many centuries after the Arian controversy, such inconsisten-cies between the rule of faith and the rule of prayer on the doctrine of the Trinity resurfaced when the Antitrinitarians of the Reforma-tion, who attacked the "traditions" and the metaphysical trinitarian language of Nicaea in Roman Catholicism and in the mainstream Ref-ormation confessions as a violation both of Scripture and of reason,[77] divided into two parties, the "Adorantists" and the "Non-Adorantists," over the propriety of addressing prayers and hymns to Christ as divine without becoming guilty of idolatry.[78] "We believe this same Jesus Christ is to be worshiped and adored, since the Father gave all things to the Son," *The Transylvanian Confession of Faith* of the Adorantist Uni-tarians confesses.[79] But *The Racovian Catechism* of 1605, in the title of its Latin translation of 1609, announced that the Socinians "acknowl-edge and confess no one other than the Father of our Lord Jesus Christ to be the true God of Israel; and no one before or after the man, Jesus of Nazareth, who was born of a virgin, to be the only-begotten son of God."[80]

This process of eventually conforming the creedal rule of faith to the liturgical rule of prayer in the treatment of the relation between the Father and the Son, as its outcome was definitively set down by the First Council of Constantinople of 381 in *The Niceno-Constantinopoli-tan Creed,* required a period of three centuries or so. Even more pro-tracted was the historical development by which such a conforming process took place with the Western doctrines of the seven sacraments

75. Athanasius *Discourses Against the Arians* 3.16 (*NPNF*–II 4:402–3).
76. See also chapter 12 below, "The Orthodoxy of the Body of the Faithful."
77. *Rac* 1.2.
78. G. H. Williams 1992, 504, 1128–33; Möhler [1832] 1958, 1:688–95.
79. *Trans* 2.
80. *Rac* ttl.

and of the real presence in the eucharist.[81] The early creeds seem to be largely silent on the doctrine of the sacraments. It has been suggested that in *The Apostles' Creed* the term *sanctorum communio* in Latin and *hagiōn koinōnia* in Greek,[82] which is now usually translated as "the communion of saints" referring to persons, should instead be translated "the communion/communication in holy things" referring to the sacraments of baptism and eucharist.[83] Even when it is read that way, however, the creedal term falls far short of a confession, in so many words, of the doctrine of the sacraments. And most of the time in subsequent centuries, above all when it comes to the fore as a subject for debate in the confessions of the Reformation era, it is not read that way at all.

For, interpreted as "the communion of saints," this phrase is taken by the confessions of Protestant Reformers of every stripe as a defining apposition and synonym for the preceding phrase of the creed, "the holy catholic church"[84]—or "holy *Christian* church," as Luther's version reads in both of his *Catechisms,* to avoid the confusion of "catholic" with "Roman Catholic"[85]—not as a reference chiefly to the saints in heaven, much less as a reference to the sacraments. "All who live in [Christ] the head," according to *The Sixty-Seven Articles of Ulrich Zwingli,* are "the church or fellowship [or communion] of the saints [*Gemeinschaft der Heiligen*]."[86] In the doctrine of *The First Helvetic Confession,* too, the church is "the fellowship and congregation of all saints [*die Gemeinschaft und Versammlung aller Heiligen*]."[87] Its successor, *The Second Helvetic Confession,* calls it "an assembly of the faithful called or gathered out of the world; a communion, I say, of all saints [*sanctorum inquam omnium communionem*], namely, of those who truly know and rightly worship and serve the true God in Christ the

81. See chapter 15.2 below, "The Confessionalization of Western Sacramental Doctrine."
82. *Ap* 9.
83. Elert 1966.
84. *Ap* 9.
85. *Luth Sm Cat* 2.3; *Luth Lg Cat* 2.34. The Latin of his *The Smalcald Articles* contains the formula: "I believe a holy catholic or [*sive*] Christian church" (*Smal Art* 3.12).
86. *67 Art* 8.
87. *Helv I* 14; *Bas Bek* 5.

Savior."[88] According to *The Scots Confession,* the church is "therefore called the communion, not of profane persons, but of saints."[89] In response to the question, "What do you understand by 'the communion of saints [*die gemeinschafft der Heiligen*]'?" *The Heidelberg Catechism* in its explanation of *The Apostles' Creed* is expressing a Reformation topos when it defines: "First, that believers *one and all,* as partakers of the Lord Christ, and all his treasures and gifts, shall share in one fellowship. Second, that each one ought to know that he is obliged to use his gifts freely and with joy for the benefit and welfare of other members."[90] The Mennonite *Concept of Cologne* of 1591 also speaks of the church as a "community of the saints [*gemeynschap der Heyligen*]."[91] Summarizing that Reformation topos, *The Westminster Confession of Faith* of 1647 entitles its chapter 26 "Of the Communion of the Saints." Thereby it extends this title to "all saints, that are united to Jesus Christ," rather than singling out those relatively few to whom traditional Roman Catholic and Eastern Orthodox usage, whether by formal canonization or not, awards the designation "saints."[92] But it also insists that "this communion which the saints have with Christ, doth not make them, in any wise, partakers of the substance of his Godhead, or to be equal with Christ, in any respect, either of which to affirm is impious and blasphemous."[93] Although it is possible for another Reformed confession to speak positively about "the fellowship of his divine nature,"[94] this insistence by *The Westminster Confession of Faith* does seem to be intended as a rejection of the Eastern Orthodox definition of salvation as *theōsis,* "unbegotten deification" or "the deification of our nature, the change into something better, the ecstasy and ascent to what is beyond nature,"[95] which bases itself on the New Testament phrase "partakers of the divine nature";[96] or perhaps it is

88. *Helv II* 17.1; also 24.3.
89. *Scot I* 16.
90. *Heid* 55; italics added.
91. *Cologne* 7.
92. *West* 26.1.
93. *West* 26.3.
94. *Helv I* 11.
95. *CP 1341* 26, 19; *Jer II* 1.10. See Syndogmaticon 8.2.
96. 2 Pt 1.4.

a rejection of the similar-sounding doctrine that, with quite another meaning, is affirmed in the confessions of the Radical Reformation.[97]

But in addition to these examples of the Trinity and the sacraments, the most dramatic instance of all in which Prosper's guiding principle, "the rule of prayer should lay down the rule of faith," was carried into conciliar and creedal legislation (as well as into large-scale political conflict) comes several centuries after Prosper, and in the Greek East rather than the Latin West: the question of the legitimacy of images in the church.[98] From the ambiguous testimony of earlier patristic tradition it is evident that, as it stood, the tradition of the rule of faith and its orthodox interpreters could not provide unequivocal justification for the Christian use of images, and that counting votes from the rule of faith might even lead to a negative verdict. But the tradition of the rule of prayer had meanwhile been following its own paths, and the icons became integral to Christian worship in the churches of the East. When the reading of the rule of faith put forth by the iconoclasts came into collision with the reading of the rule of prayer represented by the iconodules, the victory in the early battles belonged to the iconoclasts, and the icons were condemned and banished. But the victory in the war eventually went to the icons and their defenders. In the same city in which the dogma of the Trinity had achieved its initial conciliar acceptance and creedal formulation by the First Council of Nicaea in 325, the Second Council of Nicaea in 787 in its confession vindicated the use of icons on the grounds that "it provides confirmation that the becoming man of the Word of God was real and not just imaginary," thereby finally bringing the rule of faith into conformity with the rule of prayer.[99]

In a different form, iconoclasm returns in some sixteenth-century Protestant confessions, which take a stand against what *The Second Helvetic Confession* calls "not only the idols of the Gentiles, but also the images of Christians,"[100] while making it clear that "this does not mean that all sculpture or painting is universally forbidden, but

97. *Denck* 3; *Ries* 19.
98. Boespflug and Lossky 1987. See Syndogmaticon 8.10.
99. *Nic II*; Pelikan 1990a; Giakalis 1993.
100. *Helv II* 4.2.

only all images in the service of God, or in worshiping him in visible things." [101] Thus *The Heidelberg Catechism* declares: "God cannot and should not be pictured in any way. As for creatures, although they may indeed be portrayed, God forbids making or having any likeness of them in order to worship them, or to use them to serve him"—this term "creatures" clearly being intended to include (or, rather, to *exclude* as objects of veneration) the Virgin Mary and other saints.[102] Or, in the rhetorical question of *The Second Helvetic Confession,* "Since the blessed spirits and saints in heaven, while they lived here on earth, rejected all worship of themselves and condemned images,[103] shall anyone find it likely that the heavenly saints and angels are pleased with their own images before which men kneel, uncover their heads, and bestow other honors?" [104] Already in *The Ten Theses of Bern,* this rejection in principle of the tradition of images leads to the conclusion on practice that "when the setting up of images involves the danger of veneration, they are to be abolished." [105] And so they were, and with efficient rigor, especially in Reformed Switzerland.[106] To this new iconoclasm of the Protestant Reformation the decree of the twenty-fifth session of the Council of Trent responds by expressing its desire "to root out utterly any abuses that may have crept into these holy and saving practices," but at the same time by reiterating the teaching of both East and West "that images of Christ, the Virgin Mother of God, and the other saints should be set up and kept, particularly in churches, and that due honor and reverence is owed to them." [107]

As the Eastern definition of orthodoxy and its resolution in the conflict over iconoclasm would seem to suggest, the principle of *lex orandi lex credendi,* Western though it is in its origin and Latin though it is in its formulation, has in some respects been a special characteristic of the Eastern Orthodox tradition. At one level, the texts that are

101. *Genv Cat* 148. But see *Loll* 12.
102. *Heid* 97.
103. Acts 14.8–18; 17.22–25.
104. *Helv II* 4.3; also *Belg* 26.
105. *Bern* 8.
106. Wandel 1995.
107. *Trent* 25.2 decr; see also *Vat II* 5.1.51.

collected in Part Two of *Creeds and Confessions of Faith in the Christian Tradition* under the heading "Affirmations of Faith in Eastern Orthodoxy" can be taken as an extensive corroboration of the many agreements and analogies between Eastern Orthodox and Western Catholic confessions, also by contrast with Protestantism. But they make the profound differences no less unmistakable. For according to Eastern Orthodoxy, on one hand, the "confessional" place that is occupied in Roman Catholicism by such later declarations as *The Canons and Decrees of the Council of Trent* or *The Dogmatic Constitution on the Faith of the First Vatican Council* or *The Doctrinal Decrees of the Second Vatican Council,* and in Reformation Protestantism by such confessions as *The Augsburg Confession* or *The Second Helvetic Confession* or *The Westminster Confession of Faith,* belongs above all to the creeds and doctrinal decrees of the first seven ecumenical councils, which are shared with the rest of orthodox and catholic Christendom, rather than to any more recent or more distinctively Eastern statements of faith. And on the other hand, the most representative and normative summary affirmation of the Eastern Orthodox faith and of its doctrine is neither *The Orthodox Confession of the Catholic and Apostolic Eastern Church* by Peter Mogila nor *The Confession of Dositheus and of the Synod of Jerusalem* of 1672, honored though they both have been with official, synodal, and patriarchal approbation, but *The Divine Liturgy According to Saint John Chrysostom,* in Greek, Church Slavonic, and other liturgical languages, now including English, and the other Eastern orders of worship.[108] *The Liturgy According to Saint John Chrysostom* contains not only the confession of *The Niceno-Constantinopolitan Creed,* introduced with the admonition "Let us love one another, that with one mind we may confess Father, Son, and Holy Spirit,"[109] but the eucharistic confession and christological affirmation, "I believe, O Lord, and I confess that thou are truly the Christ, the Son of the living God. . . . I believe also that this is truly thine own pure body and that this is truly thine

108. See chapter 14.2 below, "The Liturgy as the Church's Preeminent Confession of the Faith."
109. *Lit Chrys* 2.D; see chapter 10.4 below, "Christian Love the Presupposition for Christian Confession."

own precious blood."[110] It is also included as a full-fledged confession in the standard collections of Eastern Orthodox confessions.[111]

Two other examples of texts for worship that perform a "confessional" function are *The Book of Common Prayer* of the Church of England and *The Easter Litany of the Moravian Church* of 1749. For Eastern Orthodoxy, Karmirēs's collection of confessions includes *The Liturgy According to Saint John Chrysostom* after the decrees of the councils and before the Eastern confessions [*homologiai*]. But for Anglicanism, the relationship is the other way around: editions of the Anglican *Book of Common Prayer* include *The Thirty-Nine Articles* (or its American revision) as an appendix. Therefore Charles Butler, an English Roman Catholic, could write in 1816 that "the symbolic books of the Church of England are the Thirty-Nine Articles and the Book of Common Prayer."[112] For most of its history going back to the Reformation of the sixteenth century, consequently, the system of doctrinal authority in the Anglican communion has held in tension the more Protestant and even Reformed accents in the definitive version of *The Thirty-Nine Articles*[113] and the more Catholic accents that are an outcome of the successive sixteenth-century revisions of *The Book of Common Prayer*.[114] It should, however, be noted that these latter continue to stand alongside some distinctly Protestant and Reformed language,[115] including the absence from the *Prayer Book* of any doctrine of "change" in the elements of the eucharist, as its Eastern Orthodox critics pointed out.[116] Simultaneously, therefore, Anglicanism required of its clergy, at the peril of suspension from office and sometimes even of imprisonment, subscription to "the *Articles*" and strict adherence to "the *Prayer Book*."[117]

The historical development of this tension, especially in the nineteenth and twentieth centuries, has made it, as one Roman Catho-

---

110. *Lit Chrys* 2.H.1.
111. Karmirēs, 1:246–70; Michalcescu, 277–98.
112. Butler 1816, 67.
113. Higham 1962.
114. On these revisions, see Daniel 1901.
115. Hague 1893.
116. *Resp Non-Jur* q 9–22; cf. *Lit Chrys* II.D.5.
117. See chapter 9.4 below, "Confessional Subscription as Legal Compliance."

lic reference book puts it, "difficult indeed" to answer the question: "What is the real doctrine of the Anglican Church now?"[118] The question has been a source of consternation especially for those textbooks of comparative symbolics that have sought to develop a taxonomy of the several churches on the basis of their confessions of faith.[119] Nevertheless, one such textbook in the nineteenth century found it possible to say of *The Thirty-Nine Articles:* "Its doctrinal system is a moderately Calvinist one; the clarity and precision in its exposition of this make this confession into one of the most excellent symbols of the Reformed Church."[120] And the most recent editor of *The Thirty-Nine Articles* asserts: "The theology of the Articles is uncompromisingly Protestant, and even Calvinist in tone. When Cranmer produced the 1553 edition [which we cite here under the title *The Forty-Two Articles*], it was the most advanced systematization of Protestant theology then in existence anywhere."[121] Therefore many collections that are devoted exclusively to Reformed confessions, such as those of Augusti, Böckel, and Niemeyer, include *The Thirty-Nine Articles of the Church of England.*[122] But at the same time, as *The Pullach Report* of 1972 declares, *The Book of Common Prayer* "has for a long time served as a confessional document in a liturgical setting."[123] This tension between *Articles* and *Prayer Book* also became a source of conflict for the minds and consciences of those Anglicans who came to see it as a contradiction.[124] In the event, however, their effort to subordinate the *lex credendi* of *The Thirty-Nine Articles* to the *lex orandi* of *The Book of Common Prayer* may be said to have had considerable success in the period since the second half of the nineteenth century, as the functional confessional authority of *The Thirty-Nine Articles* has steadily declined and has been largely overshadowed in practice by the authority, more or less precisely defined, of *The Book of Common Prayer.*

As the product of a history greatly different from the Angli-

---

118. *DTC* 1:1299–1301 (A. Gatard).
119. Mayer 1954, 273–90; on the problem, see also Schmidt 1966.
120. Hofmann 1857, 269.
121. Bray, 284.
122. Augusti, 126–42; Böckel, 664–79; Niemeyer, 601–11.
123. *A-L* 30.
124. Middleton 1951.

can development, *The Easter Litany of the Moravian Church* is textually, in spite of its title, at least as much a confession of faith as a litany in the strict liturgical sense of that word; in fact, it has been called, by more than one authority, "the principal confession of faith of the Bohemian Brethren."[125] It combines excerpts from *The Apostles' Creed* and *Luther's Small Catechism* with other elements of prayer service and statement of faith, opening with the creedal paraphrase: "I believe in the one only God, Father, Son, and Holy Ghost, who created all things by Jesus Christ, and was in Christ, reconciling the world unto himself"; to which the response is "This I verily believe."[126] It also contains an affirmation of baptism as the means by which "I am embodied a member of the church of Christ."[127] And for some reason, the article on the Holy Spirit reflects the Eastern Orthodox emphasis, over against the West, on the distinction between "proceeding" and "sending."[128] The same repossession of the principle of *lex orandi lex credendi* can be seen in a twentieth-century confessional restatement of the historic Reformed faith, issued in 1978, that takes the title: *Our Song of Hope.*[129]

6.3. The Place of Creed in Liturgy

This complementary relation between the rule of prayer in worship and the rule of faith in creeds and confessions of faith makes itself evident in other ways as well, for creeds have long been an integral component of worship and in several important instances have even originated there. Unfortunately, what the leading scholar of ancient creeds in the English-speaking world, J. N. D. Kelly, originally stated in 1950 in the first edition of his book, *Early Christian Creeds,* and could still repeat in its third edition of 1972, continues to be true: "There is no task in the field of liturgies which deserves higher priority to-day than the sorting out of the baptismal and associated rites, and the elaboration of a constructive theory of their evolution."[130] Nevertheless, there would

125. *ODCC* 522; Schaff, 3:799.
126. *Morav* 1.
127. *Morav* 4.
128. *Morav* 3; see chapter 7.4 below, "The Holy Spirit of Concord and the Sacrament of Concord: Two Ironic Case Histories."
129. *RCA.*
130. Kelly, 38.

appear to be scholarly agreement that *The Apostles' Creed* and its ante-cedent, *The Old Roman Creed,* took their start from the questions—three in number, corresponding to the Father, Son, and Holy Spirit in the baptismal command of Christ[131] and in the baptismal formula of the church—to which the candidate for baptism responded with "I be-lieve in [the Father, the Son, the Holy Spirit]." It remains less clear what roles, if any, were played by "declaratory creeds" alongside these "in-terrogatory creeds" in the various baptismal rites.[132] Even when infant baptism had become the normal practice and the candidates for bap-tism were therefore no longer able to respond in person to the creedal questions or to recite the creed in their own name but did so through their parents or godparents or sponsors or the witnessing congregation, the creed, which for the West meant *The Apostles' Creed* and for the East *The Niceno-Constantinopolitan Creed,* was a prescribed element in the administration of the sacrament of baptism.

The historical evidence about just when and by whom reciting or chanting *The Niceno-Constantinopolitan Creed* was introduced as a prescribed element also in the liturgy for the sacrament of the eucha-rist suggests that it was in the second half of the fifth century.[133] To quote again from Kelly, "an isolated, anonymous sentence which some-how found its way into the collected fragments of Theodore the Reader records that Peter the Fuller [d. 488], the runaway monk who sat four times on the patriarchal throne of Antioch, 'instituted . . . the recita-tion of the creed at every synaxis.'" But, Kelly continues, "the practice started by heretics in such a dubious atmosphere seems to have taken root at once, and not to have been displaced when orthodoxy once again gained the upper hand."[134] One of the earliest references to the place of the creed in the Byzantine liturgy is a passage from the *Ecclesi-astical Hierarchy* of Pseudo-Dionysius the Areopagite—in spite of "the many doubts raised about him"[135]—which identifies it as "that most universal song of praise. . . . This hymn is sometimes called a confes-

131. Mt 28.19–20.
132. Kinzig, Markschies, and Vinzent 1999; see chapter 13.2 below, "The Kerygma and Baptismal Symbols."
133. Brightman, 532 n 10; a recent discussion is Capelle 1955–67, 3:60–81.
134. Kelly, 348–49.
135. *Metr Crit* 1.11.

sion of praise, sometimes a symbol of adoration, sometimes—and here I think one is closer to things divine—a hierarchic thanksgiving [*hierarchikēn eucharistian*], for this hymn is a summary of all the blessed gifts which come to us from God. To me it seems that this song is a celebration of all the work of God on our behalf."[136] So according to this influential and pseudonymously "apostolic" authority, the creed is at one and the same time a "song of praise," a "hymn," a "confession of praise," a "symbol of adoration," and a "hierarchic thanksgiving"— all of these being references that apply more specifically to the rule of prayer than to the rule of faith, therefore to the second rather than to the third of the definitions of "confession" quoted earlier from Thomas Aquinas.[137]

The earliest reference to its use in the eucharistic liturgies of the West, with an acknowledgment of the already existing "use of the Eastern churches," also comes from the sixth century, from the canons of the Third Synod of Toledo in 589:

> Out of reverence for the most holy faith and to strengthen the vacillating minds of men, the holy synod has resolved, on the advice of the religious and glorious king Reccared, that in all the churches of Spain and Gaul the symbol of the council of Constantinople, that is, of the 150 bishops, shall be recited according to the use of the Eastern churches, so that before the Lord's Prayer is said the creed shall be chanted aloud by the congregation, testimony thereby being borne to the true faith and the people being enabled to draw near and partake of Christ's body and blood with hearts cleansed by the faith.[138]

Apparently it was only in the eleventh century that the Roman liturgy began to conform to this practice consistently. Thus the medieval order of the mass, which the Protestant Reformation inherited and, in the

136. Dionysius the Areopagite *The Ecclesiastical Hierarchy* 3.3.7 (*CWS* 217–18.).
137. Thomas Aquinas *Summa Theologica* 2a2ae.3.1; see chapter 2.3 above, "Confessing the Faith."
138. *Tol III* can, as translated in Kelly, 351.

case of the Lutheran and Anglican churches, heavily revised without altogether rejecting it, contained *"The Nicene Creed,"* that is, what we are calling here *The Niceno-Constantinopolitan Creed.* As *The Marburg Articles* of Luther and Zwingli confess in 1529, this affirmation of faith is "sung and read in the Nicene Creed by the entire Christian church throughout the world."[139] Therefore both Luther's Latin *Formula of the Mass* of 1523 and his *German Mass* of 1526 retain it, though with the substitution of "Christian" for "catholic" in the article on the church; *The Book of Common Prayer* also retains it, though with the omission of "holy" in the same article.[140] And in the twentieth century there was widespread ecumenical agreement that the liturgy of the eucharist should include a creed.[141]

6.4. Councils and Confessions on Worship

The prominence of creeds in the worship of the church has as its corollary the prominence of the worship of the church in creeds and confessions of faith. As a consequence, the order in the principle *lex orandi lex credendi* is sometimes reversed, with the law of prayer and worship following the lead of the law of faith and doctrine. As has been noted earlier, the oldest instance of this is the statement of *The Niceno-Constantinopolitan Creed,* issued by the second ecumenical council in 381, that the Holy Spirit is "co-worshiped and co-glorified with Father and Son,"[142] which is meant to voice the assurance that naming the Holy Spirit as "God" together with the Father and the Son in the language of Christian worship is not merely legitimate but obligatory as well as customary. In the debates leading up to that confession of 381, those who were defending the propriety of calling the Spirit "God" had been handicapped by the absence of individual liturgical prayers and hymns employing such language about the Holy Spirit, in marked contrast to the prayers and hymns about the Son, which Athanasius and other defenders of *The Creed of Nicaea* had been able to employ to such good advantage in making their case. The petitions of the church

139. *Marburg* 1.
140. *Luth Sm Cat* 2.3; *Luth Lg Cat* 2.34; *BCP.*
141. *BEM* 2.27.
142. *N-CP* 8.

prayed *for* the gift and presence of the Holy Spirit but not *to* the Spirit as such. Thus in the Epiclesis of *The Liturgy According to Saint John Chrysostom*—in a formula that went on being controverted between the Eastern and Western confessions because of the question of whether it was the recitation of the words of institution or the prayer for the Spirit that effected the change of the bread and wine into the body and blood of Christ[143]—the prayer of consecration in the eucharist reads, in words addressed to God the Father: "Send down thy Holy Spirit upon us and upon these gifts here presented. . . . And make this bread the precious body of thy Christ. And that which is in this cup the precious blood of thy Christ. *Making the change by thy Holy Spirit [metabalōn tōi Pneumati sou tōi Hagiōi]*."[144] But the entrance prayers of that liturgy, which appear to be later than most of the text, do open with the invocation addressed to the Holy Spirit as "Heavenly King, the Comforter [*paraklēte*], the Spirit of truth."[145] In the West, too, the two best-known hymns of prayer and petition *to* the Holy Spirit rather than merely *for* the Holy Spirit, the "Veni Creator Spiritus" usually attributed to the Carolingian theologian Rabanus Maurus and the "Veni Sancte Spiritus" probably composed by Stephen Langton,[146] arose long after the action of the Council of Constantinople in 381.

The same movement from the law of faith to the law of prayer takes place when, at the following ecumenical council, the Council of Ephesus in 431, the practice of calling "the Holy Virgin the Mother of God [Theotokos]" is legitimated as orthodox.[147] This gives creedal and confessional status to an already existing devotional (and perhaps liturgical) epithet. But the creedal and confessional legislation also becomes in turn a stimulus for the devotional and liturgical creativity of both East and West. The unique status of the Virgin Mary as Mother of God is reflected liturgically in the East in the development of the "Theotokion," which addresses to her the final stanza of a canonical

143. *Mogila* 1.107. See Syndogmaticon 10.7.
144. *Lit Chrys* 2.F.5; italics added.
145. *Lit Chrys* pr A.1.
146. *ODCC* 1686, with bibliographies.
147. See chapter 1.1 above, "Continuity *versus* Change in the Decrees of the Ecumenical Councils."

ode or hymn.[148] Her cult expanded during the three centuries between the Council of Ephesus and the outbreak of Byzantine iconoclasm, as became evident above all in the many icons and mosaics that were consecrated to her—and that were rejected and destroyed by the iconoclasts.[149] Under the attacks on this cult that came again, this time from the Protestant Reformation, Eastern Christendom, too, felt obliged to defend it in its confessions.[150] In the West, there was a direct linear connection between the decree of the Council of Ephesus in 431 and the reconstruction of the largest Marian church in the world, the basilica of "Saint Mary Major [Santa Maria Maggiore]" in Rome, which was rebuilt in 434 and dedicated to the Mother of God as an expression of the Western, Latin devotion to her that had already been articulated by Ambrose of Milan.[151]

One after another, the ecumenical councils, the regional synods, and the confessions of faith have debated and legislated liturgical forms as well as questions of doctrine, discipline, and church structure; very often, these latter questions, too, became issues of worship. But for Western Christendom at any rate, both Roman Catholic and Protestant, it was during the period of the Reformation that the rule of faith represented by confessions made its most significant and influential judgments about the rule of prayer represented by public worship. The emphasis of the Protestant Reformation on congregational singing included the singing of creeds. Martin Luther set *The Niceno-Constantinopolitan Creed* to words and music in the hymn "Wir glauben all an einen Gott," dating from 1524; it has been translated into English several times.[152] Johann Sebastian Bach elaborated on this hymn in a chorale prelude, but especially in the version that appears in his Catechism Preludes and its accompanying fughetta.[153] Eventually, the text of *The Niceno-Constantinopolitan Creed* would engage Bach at far greater length in the final years of his life, when he composed

148. *ODCC* 1677.
149. Pelikan 1990a, 121–51.
150. *Dosith* q 4.
151. Huhn 1954.
152. Julian [1907] 1957, 2:1287.
153. In the Schmieder catalog of Bach's works, *BWV* 437, 680, 681.

the *Symbolum Nicaenum* that was to be incorporated into his Mass in B Minor.[154] Bach's setting of *The Niceno-Constantinopolitan Creed* makes all the more intriguing the discovery in his library of a copy of the *Acroama Missale* of Giovanni Battista Bassani, which Christoph Wolff has interpreted as

> a study for the large movement from the B Minor Mass. . . . In both compositions it is the article of the creed, "Credo in unum Deum," the central thought that is constantly repeated and acquires "particular emphasis" through music. It becomes clear why Bach combines the *stile antico* with the *contrapunctus ostinatus:* the last validity of the ancient Christian formula of creed and the confessional reliance on belief are to be given symbolic musical expression.[155]

In this way, "the ancient Christian formula of creed and the confessional reliance on belief" and the liturgical theology of the Protestant Reformation reached not only into churches but into concert halls all over the world.

Similarly, as part of their legislation on the celebration of the mass, which condemns a variety of abuses in the pre-Reformation Western church, *The Decrees of the Council of Trent* order bishops to "keep out of their churches the kind of music in which a base and suggestive element [*lascivum aut impurum aliquid*] is introduced into the organ playing or singing."[156] Although it is, therefore, accurate in the strict sense to observe that these "instructions issued by the Council of Trent in the sphere of music amounted to hardly anything,"[157] this simple and apparently innocuous legislation, by the time it had been carried out, was also to have far-reaching effects both in churches and in concert halls. One composer after another advertised settings of the mass "in accordance with the reform of the Council of Trent." The most celebrated of all such settings, the *Missa Papae*

---

154. Wolff 1983, 107, 139–40.
155. Wolff 1991, 96.
156. *Trent* 22 decr.
157. François Lesure in Abraham 1968, 250.

Marcelli of Palestrina, one of more than a hundred settings of the mass that he composed, has even been credited with having "saved church music" within Roman Catholicism,[158] for the very reason that it achieved a harmonization of the rule of prayer with the rule of faith—and of the rule of musical creativity with both of them. One result of these sixteenth-century developments was that *The Niceno-Constantinopolitan Creed*, having become embedded in the liturgy of both East and West, has certainly been put to music more often, and in more varied musical settings, than all the other creeds of Christian history combined.

158. Quoted by Henry Coates and Gerald Abraham in Abraham 1968, 317; see also the bibliography there on Trent and church music.

CHAPTER SEVEN

Formulas of Concord—
And of Discord

HISTORICALLY, THE DESIGNATION *Formula of Concord* in the title of this chapter refers to the last of the officially approved Lutheran confessions, agreed upon in 1577 and incorporated into *The Book of Concord* of 1580.[1] But the term *concord* is often used not only as a definition of the purpose of a confession to "conduce to concord"[2] but as a title for such confessions as *The Wittenberg Concord* of 1536, *The Strassburg Concord* of 1563, and *The Swabian Concord* of 1574.[3] These "concords" belong to the group of confessions that Part Four of *Creeds and Confessions of Faith in the Christian Tradition* labels "Confessions of Attempts at Reconciliation and Alliance," but none of them was successful in its stated purpose of achieving an abiding inter-Protestant concord. Although the confession of 1577 calls itself a "formula of *concord*"—that is, of doctrinal concord among the several contending parties within Lutheranism, particularly in Germany, since Luther's death thirty years earlier—it could be described as a formula of discord as well. One modern study of it is appropriately titled *Discord, Dialogue, and Concord.*[4] For *The Formula of Concord* was a source of continuing discord between the Lutheran and the Reformed species of Protestantism, as well as of discord within Lutheranism.[5] *Concordia discors* (Zurich, 1607) was the title of a response to it thirty years later from the Swiss Reformed theologian Rudolf Hospinian.[6] To this,

1. *Form Conc.*
2. *Gall* 33.
3. Ritschl 1908–27, 4:116–19, 87, 119.
4. Spitz and Lohff 1977.
5. Dingel 1996 describes these debates as *Concordia controversa.*
6. *PRE* 8:392–94 (K. Sudhoff, E. F. Karl Müller).

in turn, the Lutheran theologian Leonhard Hutter wrote a rejoinder under the title *Concordia concors* (Wittenberg, 1614).[7] As this exchange (which was by no means the last) suggests, both "formula of concord" and "formula of discord" would be accurate names for many other creeds and confessions of faith, not only in the period of the Reformation but throughout Christian history. In what Welch has called "an age tired and disgusted with religious controversies,"[8] a deepening reaction against that persistent tendency of creeds and confessions to divide still further those whom they claimed to be uniting has also contributed in significant measure to the growing "discomfort with creed," outside the churches and even within them.[9]

The fifth ecumenical council was speaking for all councils and confessions in prescribing the role of doctrinal debate: "The holy fathers . . . dealt with heresies and current problems by debate in common, since it was established as certain that when the disputed question is set out by each side in communal discussions, the light of truth drives out the shadows of lying. The truth cannot be made clear in any other way than when there are debates about questions of faith, since everyone requires the assistance of his neighbor."[10] Or, as a characteristic aphorism of Alfred North Whitehead once put it, "Wherever there is a creed, there is a heretic round the corner or in his grave."[11] There is plenty of historical evidence for these generalizations, even though, strictly speaking, they do not quite hold for all the creeds. For example, *The Apostles' Creed,* the most universally accepted creed in Western Christendom, does not designate any heretics or heresies by name. But it has been suggested that when its opening declaration posits the equation, "God" = "the Father" = "the Almighty" = "the Creator of heaven and earth,"[12] it is by implication directing itself against the dualism of the heretic Marcion, the separation of the Father of Jesus Christ, the God of the Christian New Testament, from the

7. *PRE* 8:497–500 (Johannes Kunze).
8. Welch 1972–85, 1:31.
9. See chapter 17.1 below, "The Discomfort with Creed Caused by the Consciousness of Modernity."
10. *CP II* decr.
11. Whitehead [1933] 1942, 68.
12. *Ap* 1.

Creator of heaven and earth, the God of the Jewish Old Testament.[13]
The anti-Marcionite polemic of another early creed is more overt but
still affirmative: "We believe in one God, that is, in one First Principle
[archē], the God both of the law and of the gospel, who is both just
and good";[14] for Marcion also separated the just and wrathful Creator-
God of the Old Testament law from the good and loving Father-God
of the New Testament gospel. Yet even in this phraseology, as in that of
The Apostles' Creed to a greater extent, the formulation itself is a positive one. For, unlike many other creeds, *The Apostles' Creed* seems to
have been called forth, not by any heretic or heresy, but by the need of
the church for a succinct profession of faith to be used in connection
with the administration of baptism as a sacrament of initiation.[15]

The doctrine of the Holy Spirit as confessed in *The Western
Recension* of *The Niceno-Constantinopolitan Creed*, that the Holy Spirit
"proceeds from the Father and the Son [*ex Patre Filioque*],"[16] together
with the question, in response to Eastern criticism, of an addition to
the creed about the procession of the Holy Spirit, provides the occasion
for Thomas Aquinas to examine this problem, employing his familiar
logical distinction between the implicit and the explicit: "Every council
has set down some creed with a view to condemning a particular error.
Later councils, therefore, do not formulate a creed differing from one
more ancient, but, against emerging heresies, make explicit by added
phrases what was implicit in the earlier creed."[17] The underlying presupposition for Thomas here is the continuity of orthodox teaching
and therefore the presence already from the beginning, though only
implicitly, of doctrines that subsequently become explicit under challenge. In the terminology we have been employing,[18] such doctrines are
said to have been "believed" implicitly but not yet "confessed" (nor
perhaps even "taught") explicitly. Among the several alternative implications of the earlier formulation that might have been drawn, more-

---

13. Harnack [1924] 1960, 1:93–143.
14. *Meros* 2; also *Tol I* anath 8.
15. See chapter 13.2 below, "The Kerygma and Baptismal Symbols."
16. *N-CP Occ* 8; see chapter 7.4 below, "The Holy Spirit of Concord and the
Sacrament of Concord: Two Ironic Case Histories," and Syndogmaticon 8.6.
17. Thomas Aquinas *Summa Theologica* 1a.36.2 (tr. Blackfriars).
18. See chapter 2 above, "The Creedal and Confessional Imperative."

over, only the one that eventually achieves orthodox legitimacy can, according to Aquinas, properly be said to have been truly "implicit" in it all along. Thus the addition is said not to mean a new creed, in the sense of a substantive addition or even a modification, and there really is no change. But it is only by hindsight, after the heretical challenge and the orthodox response, that the implicit anticipations of such an orthodox response become discernible in the earlier recension of the creedal text. Moreover, only the authorized agencies of the church, howsoever they may be identified, have the right to draw out such implications and "define" them.

7.1. Creedal Anathema and Polemics

There is certainly no mistaking the prominence of anathemas against "empty and meaningless talk and error"[19] throughout the creedal and confessional tradition, beginning with each of the early ecumenical councils of the church. *The Creed of Nicaea* follows its positive affirmations with a list of propositions quoted from Arius and his followers, and then closes with the formula: "These the catholic and apostolic church anathematizes."[20] The letter of the council to the churches of Alexandria and Egypt explains, "it was unanimously agreed that anathemas should be pronounced against [Arius's] impious opinions and his blasphemous terms and expressions which he has blasphemously applied to the Son of God."[21] Although *The Niceno-Constantinopolitan Creed* of the second ecumenical council no longer includes these anathemas of *The Creed of Nicaea*—which, however, the two more or less contemporary *Creeds of Epiphanius* do include[22]—the council made it clear not only that the positive "profession of faith of the holy fathers who gathered in Nicaea in Bithynia is not to be abrogated, but is to remain in force," but that, negatively, "every heresy is to be anathematized" just as Nicaea anathematized it, including the new heresies on the doctrine of the Trinity that arose only after 325.[23] Speaking in the name of the Council of Ephesus, the twelve anathemas

19. *Polyc.*
20. *N* anath.
21. *Nic I* ep.
22. *Epiph.*
23. *CP I* can 1.

of Cyril of Alexandria against Nestorius, who was condemned and deposed by that council, begin with the condemnation of anyone who refuses the title "Theotokos" to the Virgin Mary by calling her merely "Christotokos," and close with the condemnation of anyone who does not identify the Logos as the one who "tasted death in the flesh."[24] Just before *The Definition of Faith of the Council of Chalcedon,* the decrees of the fourth ecumenical council respond to various errors by declaring that "it is opposed," that "it stands opposed," and that "it expels," and conclude by declaring, for good measure: "And it anathematizes."[25] This pleonastic form of anathema would be repeated in other eras, especially at the conclusion of a catalog of heretical doctrines, where only the heretical teaching is spelled out and the orthodox teaching is left implied.[26] After citing all four of these councils, the fifth ecumenical council "confessed that we held to be condemned and anathematized all those who had been previously condemned and anathematized by the catholic church and by the aforesaid four councils."[27] And so the refrain of anathema continues—from one council to another, from one creed to the next, in the East and in the West, before the Reformation and after it, in Protestantism no less than in Roman Catholicism and in Eastern Orthodoxy. Even those moderns who object to the use of anathemas can sometimes end up sounding stridently polemical in voicing their objections to any polemics.

In spite of such objections, the ancestry of the imprecatory formula of "anathema" pronounced by these councils and by later statements of faith issuing from other gatherings and church bodies—and the ancestry of the imperative that the corollary of the positive confession of a doctrinal truth of the gospel has to be the condemnation of any contrary teachings—can be traced directly to the New Testament.[28] "Let him be anathema [*ētō anathema* or *anathema estō*]" sounds out in Paul's epistles not only against "any one [who] has no love for the Lord,"[29] therefore against all those whose affections are wrong and

24. *Eph 431* anath 1–12.
25. *Chal* decr.
26. *Cum occas* con; *Syl.*
27. *CP II* act.
28. Bauer-Arndt-Gingrich, 54. See Syndogmaticon 1.5.
29. 1 Cor 16.22.

who sin against love, but no less vehemently against "any one [who] is preaching to you a gospel contrary to that which you received,"[30] therefore against all those whose doctrines are wrong and who sin against the faith. Elsewhere, too, the New Testament warns in unequivocal terms: "This is the antichrist, he who denies the Father and the Son. No one who denies the Son has the Father. He who confesses the Son has the Father also."[31] Although *The Apostles' Creed* does not in its text refer to the abjuration of any heresies, its context in the sacramental life of the church does carry such a connotation. For as part of the creedal interrogation out of which the declaratory form of *The Apostles' Creed* seems to have evolved, the candidate for baptism was required to renounce the devil and his "pomp."[32] The primitive ceremony is described by Tertullian, who is one of our earliest witnesses not only to the creeds[33] but to early Christian baptismal practice as well as to baptismal doctrine:[34] "When we are going to enter the water, but a little before, in the presence of the congregation and under the hand of the president, we solemnly profess that we disown the devil, and his pomp, and his angels. Hereupon we are thrice immersed, making a somewhat ampler pledge than the Lord has appointed in the Gospel," namely, in the baptismal formula.[35] It is clear from Tertullian's statements elsewhere that this profession "that we disown the devil, and his pomp, and his angels" refers, for the convert from paganism to Christianity, to the renunciation of the devil and the rejection of idolatry as the making and worshiping of false gods. "How have we *renounced* the devil and his angels," Tertullian asks rhetorically, "if we *make* them?"[36]

But it is evident already from such New Testament terminology as "deceitful spirits and doctrines of demons"[37] that "the devil, and his pomp, and his angels," disowned by the candidate for baptism as part

30. Gal 1.8–9.
31. 1 Jn 2.22–23.
32. Jürgens 1972, 1–2; see also chapter 13.2 below, "The Kerygma and Baptismal Symbols."
33. *Tert.*
34. *Chr Trad* 1:163–66.
35. Tertullian *The Chaplet, or De corona* 3 (*ANF* 3:94); Mt 28.19.
36. Tertullian *On Idolatry* 6 (*ANF* 3:64); italics original in the translation.
37. 1 Tm 4.1. See Syndogmaticon 1.11.

of the sacramental ritual of initiation, are seen as the instigators not simply of the worship of the false gods of paganism outside the church but of the false teachings and "the godless chatter and contradictions of what is falsely called knowledge [*tēs pseudōnymou gnōseōs*]" within professedly Christian ranks.[38] Renouncing the devil means *de*nouncing heresy—not only one's own, if any, but anyone else's, past, present, or future. And because of its context in the administration of baptism, such renunciation/denunciation obviously applies with special force to heresies that contravene the very meaning of the baptismal formula and the very charter of the church's trinitarian confession, which originated with Christ himself in commanding baptism, "the name of the Father and of the Son and of the Holy Spirit."[39] In these words of Christ to the apostles—so Basil of Caesarea argues in making the case for the full deity of the Holy Spirit in spite of the absence of any Scripture passage calling the Spirit "God" in so many words—"the Spirit is spoken of together with the Lord [the Son of God] in precisely the same manner in which the Son is spoken of with the Father. . . . According to the coordination of words delivered in baptism, the relation of the Spirit to the Son is the same as that of the Son to the Father. And if the Spirit is coordinate with the Son, and the Son with the Father, it is obvious that the Spirit is also coordinate with the Father."[40] The details of the language of such condemnations of heresy, as well as the structural juxtaposition of confession and condemnation, vary from one formula to another, even in the formulas that have come down to us. But a trinitarian creedal confession, and behind it a trinitarian baptismal formula coming from Christ himself, naturally becomes the basis for pronouncing an anathema on those who are seen as having contradicted the orthodox trinitarian faith confessed at baptism.

That is just what *The Creed of Nicaea* of 325 does. First it sets forth, largely in positive terms, what it is confessing as the orthodox faith of the church regarding the Trinity, and specifically regarding the relation between the Father and the Son (but, as has already been noted, without a similar elaboration regarding the Holy Spirit).

38. 1 Tm 6.20.
39. Mt 28.19.
40. Basil of Caesarea *On the Holy Spirit* 17.43 (*NPNF*–II 8:27).

Already as part of that positive declaration, the creed stipulates that the Son of God was "begotten not made," which is directed against the Arian equating of these two terms, according to which the Son is the first of the Father's creatures, through whom in turn he created all the other creatures.[41] The creed follows that affirmation with a catalog of quotations containing trinitarian errors attributable to Arius and other heretics: "Those who say 'there once was when he was not,' and 'before he was begotten he was not,' and that he came to be from things that were not, or from another hypostasis or substance [*ex heteras hypostaseōs ē ousias*], affirming that the Son of God is subject to change or alteration—these the catholic and apostolic church anathematizes."[42]

As we have already seen in the case of later councils, this procedure in the first conciliar creed sets the pattern for many subsequent statements of faith in the early church. But the pattern persists in various historical periods after the early church, including the Reformation. In this respect at least, the decree of the Council of Trent is speaking ecumenically and for its entire era when it asserts, "it is not enough to declare the truth unless errors are exposed and refuted."[43] As early as 1529, *The Marburg Articles* formulate in their first fourteen articles the teachings that the Lutheran and the Zwinglian parties hold in common. Only in the last do they address the differences between them over the doctrine of the Lord's supper, and even that, moreover, is spoken irenically.[44] A more successful and more durable "formula of concord" dealing with the same doctrine is the formula of intra-Reformed concord in the *Consensus Tigurinus* or *Zurich Consensus* of 1547 between Heinrich Bullinger, Zwingli's successor, and John Calvin. Here it is, at least in the first instance, the polemic that is said to unite the parties: against "not only the fiction of the papists about transubstantiation . . . , but also all stupid fantasies and worthless quibbles" of the Lutherans about the literal eucharistic presence,[45] which make it "particularly necessary to reject every idea of a local presence."[46] This

41. ap. Athanasius *Discourses Against the Arians* 2.50 (*NPNF*-II 4:575).
42. *N* anath. See *Ar.*
43. *Trent* 13.1 con.
44. *Marburg* 15.
45. *Tig* 24.
46. *Tig* 21. See Syndogmaticon 10.6.

became a formula of concord between the interpretation of the sacra-ments as "symbols," characteristic of the Zwinglian party, and the less drastic view of them as "instruments" of grace, to which Calvin in-clined.[47]

Even so undogmatic a confession as *The Savoy Declaration* of Congregationalism in 1658, which extends a sharing at the commu-nion table to those who disagree with its doctrines, including its doc-trine about the Holy Communion, does nevertheless present itself as "holding forth a professed opposition unto the common errors and heresies of these times," which, however, are not specified in detail or by name.[48] On the Reformed side, the five *Canons of the Synod of Dort* of 1619 follow the pattern of *The Creed of Nicaea*, positive articles and then rejections of error, by connecting the negative to the posi-tive with the formula: "Having set forth the orthodox doctrine, the synod rejects the errors of those who teach . . . ."[49] In the other prin-cipal Protestant tradition, the Lutheran, *The Saxon Visitation Articles* of 1592 present four articles reaffirming the "pure and true" Lutheran teachings "Of the Lord's Supper," "Of the Person of Christ," "Of Holy Baptism," and "On Predestination and the Eternal Providence of God," following these with four polemical articles condemning "the false and erroneous doctrines of the Calvinists" on the same points.[50] More than half a century later, *The Reaffirmed Consensus of the Truly Lutheran Faith* of 1655 (never adopted as an official confession of the Lutheran Church as a whole) divides each of its eighty-eight "points" into three parts: a positive reaffirmation of what it is presenting as "the truly Lutheran faith"; an anathema, using the formula "We reject [*Reiicimus*]," directed against contrary positions held by others who are also laying claim to the label of "Lutheran," especially George Calix-tus; and quotations to document those contrary positions.[51]

In an alternative but analogous format, *The Augsburg Con-fession* is divided into two parts. The first part, consisting of twenty-

47. *Tig* 12, 15.
48. *Sav* pr.
49. *Dort* 1–5; De Jong 1968.
50. *Sax Vis* 1–4.
51. *Cons rep.*

one articles, presents the doctrinal teachings of the Lutheran Reformation, largely in positive terms but with occasional identifications of what "we condemn [*damnamus*]."[52] The second part identifies various abuses, most of them abuses of praxis though with a doctrinal basis, against which the Reformation is protesting, "inasmuch as our churches dissent from the church catholic in no article of faith but only omit some few abuses which are new and have been adopted by the fault of the times although contrary to the intent of the canons."[53] And in the twentieth century, the preface to the Indonesian *Confession of Faith of the Protestant Christian Batak Church (H. K. B. P.)* of 1951 declares that "Roman Catholics . . . come again to spread their wings. Our doctrine stands in opposition to their teaching," as well as to many other perceived aberrations, non-Christian as well as Christian. In its first article as well as in most of those that follow, the confession states what it believes and then adds a paragraph beginning, "By means of this doctrine we reject and oppose . . . ."[54] That pattern of affirmation and then anathema is not quite a universal one, however, for sometimes the anathema can come first. For example, an early Protestant confession, Ulrich Zwingli's *Sixty-Seven Articles* of 1523, opens with the statement: "All who say that the gospel is nothing without the approbation of the church err and slander God." A later article declares: "Therefore all who regard another doctrine as equal to or higher than the gospel err and do not know what the gospel is."[55]

7.2. Direct and Indirect Censures

Although *The Niceno-Constantinopolitan Creed* does not incorporate the concluding anathemas of *The Creed of Nicaea* against heresy, it does contain several other clauses that are, in the terminology of Evenus, "indirect censures [*parapsogoi*]."[56] They condemn by implication, declaring not only that the Son of God is "begotten not made," in opposition to the Arian teaching that the Logos is a creature, but

---

52. Gensichen 1967.
53. *Aug Lat* 22 int 1.
54. *Bat* 1.
55. *67 Art* 1, 5.
56. Plato *Phaedrus* 267A (tr. Benjamin Jowett).

also, quoting the words of the angel Gabriel in the Gospel, that "his kingdom will have no end."[57] *The Christian Catechism of the Orthodox Catholic Greco-Russian Church* of 1839, invoking the ecumenically shared distinction between the kingdom of grace and the kingdom of glory,[58] reads this article of *The Niceno-Constantinopolitan Creed* as applying to the kingdom of glory because it is everlasting.[59] Such a reading, though not inconsistent with the article of *The Niceno-Constantinopolitan Creed,* does overlook its original polemical intent.[60] The identification of the missing footnotes to such polemical references in a creed is, therefore, in the first instance a historical assignment, but it may also illumine creedal and confessional statements that would otherwise remain obscure. Since the nineteenth century, historical theology has been especially assiduous in carrying out that assignment.[61]

In some cases, such an identification may be not only helpful but absolutely essential to explicating what a creed or confession means. Thus the confessions of the Reformation, reacting to the repeated charge of their Roman Catholic opponents that they are the recrudescence of ancient heresies, make it a point to condemn such ancient heresies by name, while at the same time condemning other and cognate heresies that have arisen more recently.[62] It is their strategy, then, to bracket together in their anathemas, as *The Canons of the Synod of Dort* put it, "various errors, some ancient and some new," in order, for example, to attack those who "summon back from hell the Pelagian error."[63] Subtly, or not so subtly, these rejections of ancient errors such as Pelagianism sometimes include their Roman Catholic opponents. For example, *The Augsburg Confession* in its statement of the doctrine of original sin condemns "the Pelagians *and others*."[64] These "others" may be meant to include Zwingli, but chiefly the term does seem to

57. N-CP 7; Lk 1.33.
58. See, for example, *West Sh Cat* 102, and Syndogmaticon 7.2.
59. *Russ Cat* 236–37.
60. See chapter 5.4 above, "Confessional Rules of Biblical Hermeneutics."
61. See chapter 17.3 below, "The Flowering of Creedal and Confessional Scholarship in the Modern Era."
62. See also chapter 16.3 below, "Catholic Substance and Protestant Principle in Reformation Confessions."
63. *Dort* pr, 2.2.3.
64. *Aug* 2.3; italics added.

refer to some of the medieval scholastics, whom both the Lutheran and the Reformed confessions consistently accuse of Pelagianizing tendencies in their teaching that God will not deny grace to an unaided human will that does whatever it can. *The Formula of Concord,* as the authorized commentary on *The Augsburg Confession,* fills in the details by identifying "the false dogma of the Semi-Pelagians," referring, among others, to those medieval scholastics.[65] In its doctrine of sin and the fall, *The Second Helvetic Confession* similarly identifies "Pelagius and all the Pelagians, together with the Jovinians," though without providing a historical commentary. But it also rejects as "curious questions" the speculations of otherwise unnamed recent theologians about whether God caused Adam to fall, adding the proviso: "unless perchance the wickedness of heretics or of other churlish men compels us also to explain them out of the word of God, as the godly teachers of the church have frequently done."[66] In a later chapter it links various errors, some ancient and some new, in a similar but less subtle fashion, anathematizing and identifying by name "the impious doctrine of Arius and the Arians . . . and especially the blasphemies of the Spaniard, Michael Servetus, and all his followers, which Satan through them has, as it were, dragged up out of hell."[67] Similarly, *The French Confession* attacks "the diabolical conceits of Servetus, which attribute a fantastical divinity to the Lord Jesus."[68] The reaffirmation of ancient anathemas and the formulation of new anathemas go hand in hand. Referring both to transubstantiation and to the definition of the mass as a sacrifice, *The Scots Confession* of 1560 speaks for other Reformation confessions of faith when it concludes: "This doctrine is blasphemous to Christ Jesus and would deprive his unique sacrifice, once offered on the cross for the cleansing of all who are to be sanctified, of its sufficiency; so we detest and renounce it."[69]

Also linking not simply transubstantiation but the doctrine of the real presence with the definition of the mass as a sacrifice, a particularly vehement instance of anathema and polemics in the Reforma-

65. *Form Conc Epit* 2.2.3.
66. *Helv II* 8.7, 8.10. See *Syndogmaticon* 1.11.
67. *Helv II* 11.3.
68. *Gall* 14.
69. *Scot I* 22.

tion confessions, and one that appears in a catechism rather than in a controversial treatise of polemical theology, is a question that was added to later editions of *The Heidelberg Catechism,* "What difference is there between the Lord's supper and the papal mass?" The answer is: "The mass teaches that the living and the dead do not have forgiveness of sins through the sufferings of Christ unless Christ is again offered for them daily by the priest, and that Christ is bodily under the form of bread and wine and is therefore to be worshiped in them. Therefore the mass is fundamentally a complete denial of the once for all sacrifice and passion of Jesus Christ, and such an idolatry as to be condemned."[70] This question 80 and its answer are not part of the original version of *The Heidelberg Catechism* of 1563, but appear in later editions as a supplementary polemical response to the decrees of the Council of Trent on transubstantiation and the sacrifice of the mass, decrees that were not published as a total collection until after the adjournment of the twenty-fifth and final session of the council on 3–4 December 1563.[71] Also directed against the "erroneous and bloody decrees made at Trent" and consisting of a recital and rejection of one decree of that council after another, including the "five illegitimate sacraments" and "processions and blasphemous litany," *The King's Confession* of 1581, which is intended to explain how "we abhor and detest all contrary doctrine and religion,"[72] provides a similar polemical supplement to reinforce the original *[First] Scots Confession* of 1560. Long before those decrees at Trent, Luther's *Smalcald Articles* of 1537, eventually a part of *The Book of Concord* of 1580, denounce the mass as "the greatest and most horrible abomination," and as a "dragon's tail" that has "brought forth a brood of vermin and the poison of manifold idolatries."[73] At about the same time, *The Geneva Confession* is calling "the mass of the pope . . . a reprobate and diabolical ordinance, subverting the mystery of the holy supper . . . , execrable to us, an idolatry condemned by God."[74] Even earlier, a long article of

---

70. *Heid* 80. See the detailed examination and defense of question 80 in Beyer 1965.
71. *Trent* 13.4. See Syndogmaticon 10.9.
72. *Scot II.*
73. *Smal Art* 2.2.1, 11.
74. *Genv Con* 16.

The Evangelical Counsel of Ansbach of 1524 calls the definition of the mass as sacrifice an affront to the sacrifice of Christ as the only true Highpriest.[75]

7.3. Creeds and Confessions as Instruments of Concord

Although creeds and confessions have so frequently had their origins in polemics and anathema and have also repeatedly been the occasion for still further polemics, it should be recalled that often they have succeeded in becoming instruments of concord as well. The modern era especially has seen a rapid increase in both the number and the extent of such instruments of concord. For example, all of the texts reproduced in the two volumes of *Growth in Agreement*, comprising nearly fifteen hundred printed pages, are from the final third of the twentieth century.[76] And those volumes include neither the many additional concords and agreements from this period and earlier in the twentieth century within confessional families rather than between them[77] nor the earlier twentieth-century union proposals across confessional lines and across several continents.[78] But to begin with the confession from which this chapter takes its title, *The Formula of Concord* of 1577 bears the subtitle: "a thorough, pure, correct, and final restatement and explanation of a number of articles of *The Augsburg Confession* on which for some time there has been disagreement among some of the theologians adhering to this confession."[79] In the seventh, eighth, and eleventh articles of the *Formula of Concord*, that intention "to deal *only* with those articles that were in controversy among the theologians of *The Augsburg Confession*,"[80] rather than with all the doctrinal controversies of Protestantism during the preceding half-century, is stretched to include the three doctrines of the Lord's supper, the person of Christ, and predestination. The differences of opinion over these

---

75. *Ans* 10.82.
76. See "Editions, Collections, and Reference Works" above.
77. *Pres Un* (Presbyterian) 1906; *Un Ref Ch* (Reformed) 1972, 1981, 1997; *Morav Am* (Moravian) 1995.
78. *Un Ch Can: Union* 1925; *Un Ch Japan* 1954; *Sri Lanka* 1963; *Ghana* 1965; *Zambia* 1965.
79. *Form Conc* pr.
80. *Form Conc Sol Dec* 7.1; italics added.

were not primarily a domestic dispute among the Lutheran adherents of the "unaltered" *Augsburg Confession*[81] but, beginning already with the polemics between Luther and Zwingli, a controversy between the two principal Reformation traditions, the Lutheran and the Reformed. Therefore *The Formula of Concord* even incorporates the conciliatory statement on the doctrine of the eucharist, *The Wittenberg Concord,* that both Luther and Martin Bucer accepted in 1536.[82] But the main body of *The Formula of Concord* does concentrate on the intramural quarrels among various parties of Lutheran theologians, putting itself forward as an expression and instrument of concord. On the doctrines of original sin and free will, for example, and then in each following instance of a disputed doctrine, it tries to identify the precise "status of the controversy," to distinguish sharply between differences of theological substance and mere differences of technical terminology, and to propose language that takes into account the underlying concerns of each of the contending parties but reconciles the differences by finding a vocabulary, often though not always from Scripture or tradition, in which the polarization is transcended.[83] As for its stated ambition of providing "a thorough, pure, correct, and final restatement," the history of theological controversy during the subsequent centuries, even within Lutheranism, does suggest that in some respects *The Formula of Concord* turned out to be more "thorough" than it was "final."

Another example from the later generations of the Reformation is *The Mennonite Confession of Faith of Dordrecht* of 1632, uniting the Old Flemish and the Young Flemish congregations of Mennonites and eventually becoming a formula of concord for most of the adherents of the Mennonite tradition. Speaking "in the name of and in behalf of the request of this, our as now united congregation at this place,"[84] the confession describes the conflicts within the Mennonite community during the generations after its founding. Quoting a catena of passages from Scripture that call for peace and harmony among believers, the confession acknowledges: "We found that we had strayed from [these

---

81. See chapter 9.4 below, "Confessional Subscription as Legal Compliance."
82. *Form Conc Sol Dec* 7.12–16; *Witt Conc* 1–3.
83. Schlink 1961, 41–52; Spitz and Lohff 1977, 38–57.
84. *Dordrecht* con.

passages] and, in so doing, had left the way of peace." To correct this, the confession expresses the resolve "to live and walk again in peace and love with each other, with the scattered sheep—of whom we were not the least—who are one with us in faith, doctrine, and practice." The path to reconciliation, according to the confession, is "a mutual, complete forgiving of, freeing from, and acquittal of all previous faults and mistakes, wrong actions, and restrictions."[85] In the first article, therefore, the confession declares: "We confess with the mouth and believe with the heart[86]—*in company with all devout men and women and in keeping with Scripture.*"[87] After reaffirming the essence of the orthodox and catholic tradition about the Trinity and declaring concerning Christ that "we confess *with all the saints* that he is the Son of the living God,"[88] the confession addresses some of the teachings in dispute between Anabaptists and that same catholic and orthodox tradition, but not in dispute among Anabaptists themselves, such as the duty "to marry among the chosen generation and the spiritual kindred of Christ (and none other),"[89] and the duty to rely neither on "baptism, nor the Lord's supper, nor church membership, nor any other outward ceremony."[90] In its own statement of the doctrine of the Lord's supper, therefore, *The Dordrecht Confession* emphasizes also "the unity and fellowship we have with God and each other, a unity represented and signified in the breaking of the bread."[91]

But in the history of Christian creeds and confessions of faith, the classic model of all time for a such a formula of concord is *The Definition of Faith of the Council of Chalcedon* of 451, particularly its confession of the one person of Jesus Christ as "acknowledged in two natures which undergo no confusion, no change, no division, no separation [*en duo physesin asynchytōs, atreptōs, adiairetōs, achōristōs gnōrizomenon*]."[92] All four of these predications, expressed by Greek ad-

85. *Dordrecht* pr.
86. Rom 10.10.
87. *Dordrecht* 1; italics added.
88. *Dordrecht* 4, quoting Mt 16.16; italics added.
89. *Dordrecht* 12.
90. *Dordrecht* 6.
91. *Dordrecht* 10.
92. *Chal* 17–18; Grillmeier and Bacht 1951–54, 1:389–418.

verbs with an alpha privative, are at one level quite polemical. By the first two terms, "no confusion, no change," as the creed goes on immediately to explain, it is insisting that "at no point was the difference between the natures taken away through the union."[93] This is directed against the christological tendency that issued in "Monophysitism" (*monē*=single, *physis*=nature), which was attacked for stressing the unity of the person of the God-man in such a way as to blur the abiding distinction between his divine nature and his human nature even after the incarnation, and which therefore taught that there was but "one theanthropic [divine-human] nature of the incarnate Logos," rather than two natures also after the incarnation and union.[94] But by connecting the third and fourth terms, "no division, no separation," inseparably yet distinctly with the first two, "no confusion, no change," the creed is attempting to assert in the same breath that "the property of both natures is preserved and comes together into a single person and a single subsistent being."[95] This in turn has as its polemical target the Christology of Nestorius, condemned two decades earlier by *The Definition of the Council of Ephesus:*[96] an emphasis on the permanent distinction between the human nature and the divine nature so sharp as to jeopardize the unity of the "single person and single subsistent being" of the one Lord Jesus Christ. When it is read in the light of these two (or more) conflicting Christologies,[97] therefore, the definition of the fourth ecumenical council at Chalcedon in 451 does represent an anathema, or rather a pair of anathemas, the second of them reinforcing the anathema of the third ecumenical council at Ephesus in 431 and the first of them anticipating the repeated anathemas of the fifth and sixth ecumenical councils at Constantinople in 553 and 680–81, which are directed against Monothelitism (the doctrine of a single will [*thelēma*] in the incarnate Logos) and Monenergism (the doctrine of a single center of activity [*energeia*] in the incarnate Logos), teachings that were seen, fairly or not, as refinements and extensions

93. *Chal* 19.
94. *Ecth.*
95. *Chal* 20–21.
96. *Eph 431* anath.
97. *Chr Trad* 1:226–77, 2:37–90.

of Monophysitism. That was why the Council of Chalcedon declared against both these Christologies that "it is opposed," that "it stands opposed," that "it expels," and that "it anathematizes."[98]

Yet *The Definition of Faith of the Council of Chalcedon*, standing though it does in the apostolic succession of anathemas, is intended to be a formula of concord at the same time.[99] For it is the special, though by no means unique, design of this *Definition of Faith of the Council of Chalcedon* to propound an overarching declaration of a doctrine of which each of the two—or several—alternatives is seen to be a correct but partial recognition (and not only a negation of the opposite doctrine), and thus to point each of them beyond itself to the dialectical truth. It can be argued that Christology is, even among Christian doctrines, not only uniquely paradoxical but uniquely dialectical. Even more than is the case with, for example, the dialectic between the doctrine of sin and the doctrine of creation in the image of God, as this dialectic demands attention from the Protestant confessions because the new emphasis of the Reformation on the Augustinian doctrine of original sin was seen by its opponents as veering in the direction of Manicheism,[100] Christology is subject to distortion by a weakening of the dialectic in either direction. The structure of *The Definition of Faith of the Council of Chalcedon* is aimed at achieving concord through simultaneously affirming the two natures as well as the one hypostasis or person. Both extremes are said to be wrong, yet both are acknowledged to be right—though only if each embeds its beloved formula in the total context of that dialectical affirmation. As became clear from the controversies before, during, and after the fifth and sixth ecumenical councils at Constantinople in 553 and 680–81, the ambition of Chalcedon failed, at any rate in the short run.[101] At least until the use of the terminology of Chalcedon in such twentieth-century formulas of concord as the *Common Declaration* of the Roman Catholic Church and the Armenian Apostolic Church of December 1996,[102] and *The Com-*

98. *Chal* decr.
99. Sellers 1940, 202–57.
100. *Helv I* 7–8; *Form Conc Epit* 1.1.
101. *Edict; Ecth.*
102. *Com Dec* 3.

mon Christological Declaration Between the Catholic Church and the As-syrian Church of the East of November 1994,[103] that failure is also evi-dent from the history of the Oriental Orthodox churches, which were labeled by their opponents as "Monophysite," and the history of the Assyrian Church of the East labeled "Nestorian," which have had a separate ecclesial existence ever since. But its standing for fifteen cen-turies as a statement of common faith in the West and in most of the East is an indication that in the long run *The Definition of Faith of the Council of Chalcedon* has indeed been a formula of concord,[104] at any rate until the attacks on it during the modern era.[105]

More profoundly, however, a consideration of *The Definition of Faith of the Council of Chalcedon* in the light both of the history that preceded it and of the history that followed it does demonstrate how a creed—and the "reception" of a creed[106]—can function as a formula of concord. The Latin word for boundary is *finis:* to "de-fine" is to set boundaries. As a definition of faith and doctrine, therefore, a creed is, in one sense, a line that is drawn to separate those who are within the boundary from those who are outside it: "These the catholic and apos-tolic church anathematizes," as *The Creed of Nicaea* declares.[107] But the line that *The Definition of Faith of the Council of Chalcedon* draws is more a circle than a straight line in the sand. There are still those on the inside and those on the outside, as the separation between the "Chal-cedonian" and the "non-Chalcedonian" churches until the present day shows. But when the council had spoken, it had still left room within the Chalcedonian circle for the traditionally "Antiochean" emphasis of looking at the person of Christ. It shared with this emphasis a pri-mary commitment to keeping the human nature of Christ from being impaired by the incarnation (which would have made Christ less than completely human), and thus to safeguarding the bond between the human race and the human nature of a Christ "who in every respect

103. *Chr Dec* 2.
104. See Gregorios, Lazareth, and Nissiotis 1981.
105. See chapter 17.1 below, "The Discomfort with Creed Caused by the Con-sciousness of Modernity."
106. See chapter 9.2 below, "Reception of Creeds, Councils, and Confessions as Ratification."
107. *N* anath.

has been tempted as we are, yet without sinning."[108] At the same time it also left room for the more "Alexandrian" emphasis of those who were bent on protecting, against the persistent tendency to exaggerate distinction into separation, the oneness of the incarnate Logos and thus the elevation not only of his human nature but of the human nature of all believers in him to "become participants of the divine nature,"[109] in the characteristically Eastern definition of salvation as *theōsis* or "deification."[110] *The Definition of Faith of the Council of Chalcedon* does both of these on the condition that each party acknowledge the authority of the circle and be willing to pursue its distinctive concerns only inside that Chalcedonian circle. Which has been, for most of the history of Christology since Chalcedon, precisely what they have done. In the East, for example, its formula appears as an acknowledged consensus in *The Confession of Metrophanes Critopoulos.*[111] In the West, both the Reformed rejection of the ubiquity of the human nature and body of Christ after the ascension and the Lutheran affirmation of such a ubiquity could invoke its authority and its very language in their claims to be orthodox by standing where Chalcedon had stood. Several Reformed confessions quote verbatim the adverbs of *The Definition of Faith of the Council of Chalcedon;*[112] and *The Formula of Concord* in its *Solid Declaration* cites "the ancient teachers of the church, both before and after the Council of Chalcedon," with the entire Chalcedonian creed being repeated in the catena of patristic texts entitled "Catalog of Testimonies" appended to *The Book of Concord.*[113]

7.4. The Holy Spirit of Concord and the Sacrament of Concord: Two Ironic Case Histories

As has been noted earlier, the *homoousios* of *The Creed of Nicaea,*[114] and then of *The Niceno-Constantinopolitan Creed,*[115] certainly became a for-

---

108. Heb 4.15.
109. 2 Pt 1.4.
110. *CP 1341* 26, 19; *Jer II* 1.10. See Syndogmaticon 8.2.
111. *Metr Crit* 17.7.
112. *Fid rat* 1; *West* 8.2; *Wald* 13; *Sav* 8.2.
113. *Form Conc Sol Dec* 8.18; *BLK* 1105–6.
114. *N* 2.
115. *N-CP* 2.

mula of enormous discord and controversy.[116] Likewise, as a twentieth-century ecumenical confession acknowledges, "the expression *sola gratia* . . . has been the subject of much controversy."[117] The same is true of the *sola fide* of the Reformation confessions. *The Tetrapolitan Confession* of 1530 states the polemical contrast: "Justification is to be ascribed to the good pleasure of God and the merit of Christ, *and to be received by faith alone*."[118] "We therefore teach and believe with the apostle," *The Second Helvetic Confession* asserts, "that sinful man is justified by faith alone in Christ [*sola fide in Christum*]."[119] *The Apology of the Augsburg Confession* indignantly rejects the criticism that the word "alone [*allein durch den Glauben*]," which Luther inserted into his German translation of Romans 3.28, is an unwarranted addition to the biblical text.[120] *The [First] Bohemian Confession* of 1535 joins these other Protestant confessions in declaring "that men are justified before God solely by faith or trust in Jesus Christ, without any of their efforts, merits, or works."[121] And *The Westminster Confession of Faith* calls faith "the alone instrument of justification."[122] In response to this doctrine of justification by faith alone, the decree of the Council of Trent condemns the *sola fide*.[123]

Ironically, however, the two most likely candidates for the dubious distinction of being the outstanding "formulas of discord" in the history of creeds and confessions of faith are not these two but the doctrine of the Holy Spirit, in spite of the admonition of the New Testament "to maintain the unity of the Spirit in the bond of peace,"[124] and the doctrine of the eucharist, which was originally intended to be the chief sacrament of concord.[125]

"And [I believe] in the Holy Spirit . . . who proceeds from the

---

116. Prestige 1956, 197–218.
117. *F & O Edin* 6.
118. *Tetrapol* 3; italics added; also *Heid* 61.
119. *Helv II* 15.4; also *Gall* 20.
120. *Apol Aug* 4.73–74.
121. *Boh I* 6.10.
122. *West* 11.2.
123. *Trent* 6.7–8; but see *LuRC Just* 25–27.
124. Eph 4.3.
125. 1 Cor 10.16–17.

Father and the Son [*qui ex Patre Filioque procedit*]":[126] no creedal or confessional formula in Christian history has been more of a formula of discord, and for a longer time, than this Western addition of the Filioque to the text of *The Niceno-Constantinopolitan Creed*.[127] The confessions of all sides to the controversy acknowledge, at least in principle, that "all languages and dialects are inadequate when it comes to giving a proper definition of divine things."[128] Even in comparison with the bitter disputes just mentioned over the *homoousios* and the *sola fide*, however, the Filioque has been for an entire millennium, and still is, the principal dogmatic point of division between Eastern and Western Christendom. At the same time, by gaining the allegiance of most of the classical Protestant confessions across the usual boundaries between Lutheranism, Calvinism, and Anglicanism, as well as between all of these and Roman Catholicism,[129] the Filioque, this formula of discord, ironically is also one of the most impressive cases of a formula of concord—at any rate as a teaching that is shared by confessions from all sectors of Western Christendom over against those of the Orthodox East.

The phraseology of the original text of *The Niceno-Constantinopolitan Creed* (before the Western addition), "the Holy Spirit . . . who proceeds from the Father [*to pneuma to hagion . . . to ek tou patros ekporeuomenon*],"[130] is taken over almost verbatim—except for the replacement of the Greek relative clause by a Greek participle, which is however translated by a relative clause in English—from the Gospel of John, where Jesus speaks of "the Spirit of truth, who proceeds from the Father [*to pneuma tēs alētheias ho para tou patros ekporeuetai*]." But those words of the Gospel are part of a longer sentence, in the first half of which Jesus describes the Holy Spirit also as "the Counselor, whom *I shall send* to you from the Father [*ho paraklētos hon egō pempsō hymin para tou patros*]."[131] In the preceding chapter of the same Gos-

126. *N-CP Occ* 8. See Syndogmaticon 8.6.
127. Oberdorfer 2001.
128. *Metr Crit* 1.6. See Syndogmaticon 1.3.
129. See chapter 16.3 below, "Catholic Substance and Protestant Principle in Reformation Confessions."
130. *N-CP* 8.
131. Jn 15.26; italics added.

pel, moreover, Jesus speaks of "the Counselor, the Holy Spirit, whom the Father will send in my name [*ho de paraklētos, to pneuma to hagion ho pempsei ho patēr en tōi onomati mou*]."[132] As the language of the Gospel stands, therefore, the "proceeding [*ekporeuesthai*]" of the Spirit is from the Father, but the "sending [*pempein*]" of the Spirit is by the Son from the Father or by the Father in the name of the Son. According to the Eastern reading of this language in the Gospel—and therefore of the language of the creed, which is derived from the Gospel—the term "proceeding" refers here to the mystery of the inner life of the Holy Trinity in the timeless realm of eternal being. It is, in the technical distinction, part of "pure theology [*haplē theologia*]," which *The Confession of Metrophanes Critopoulos* defines as "the knowledge of the one essence of God," rather than part of the "theology of the divine economy [*oikonomia*]" or historical dispensation.[133] The Son is "the only-begotten Son of God, begotten from the Father before all the ages, . . . begotten not made,"[134] and the Holy Spirit "proceeds" eternally, likewise from the Father.[135] Within the single divine "essence [*ousia*]" of the Trinity, therefore, the person or hypostasis of the Son is begotten eternally from the Father and the hypostasis of the Spirit proceeds eternally from the Father, not from "two causes [*dyo aitiai*]."[136]

But the "sending" of the Holy Spirit, like the incarnation of the Son "from the Holy Spirit and the Virgin Mary,"[137] is "to you," as the Gospel says (and is, in the technical term, "economic," part of the "theology of the divine economy" rather than part of "pure theology" or ontology).[138] It takes place within time and human history, the history of salvation, and therefore the East acknowledges that "there is no reason why we should not confess that this descent [*epiphoitēsis*] of the Holy Spirit is both from the Father *and from the Son*."[139] But that, according to the East, is not what is being confessed in this particular

132. Jn 14.26.
133. *Metr Crit* 1.2.
134. *N-CP* 2.
135. *N-CP* 8.
136. *Phot* 9.
137. *N-CP* 3.
138. *LTK* 4:1119 (Josef Schmid).
139. *Metr Crit* 1.7; italics added.

sentence of *The Niceno-Constantinopolitan Creed,* "who proceeds from the Father." *The Encyclical Letter* of 867 against the West by Patriarch Photius of Constantinople reports, as "blasphemy against the Spirit (or rather against the Holy Trinity as a whole)" and as "what must be the summit of evils," that some Western theologians "make the novel assertion [*kainologēsantes*] that the Holy Spirit proceeds not from the Father alone but also from the Son." It insists that quite apart from the dubious theological acceptability of the Filioque as such, it is extreme effrontery for the West "to adulterate with bastard ideas and interpolated words . . . the holy and sacred creed" by such an addition.[140] The *Condemnation* [*Apophasis kai Sēmeiōma*] in 1054 by the Synod of Constantinople, under the presidency of Patriarch Michael Cerularius, rejects the Filioque on the grounds that "they do not get this statement from the evangelists, nor does this blasphemous dogma derive from an ecumenical council," which had promulgated the creed originally.[141] The Filioque became a formula of discord in every subsequent encounter between East and West. In what has been called "the 'dogmatization' of the *Filioque* by the Latin West,"[142] *The Confession of the Second Council of Lyons* in 1274 anathematizes both those "who presume to deny that the Holy Spirit proceeds eternally from the Father and the Son" and those who "assert that the Holy Spirit proceeds from the Father and the Son as from two principles and not as from one."[143] The Filioque is a focal point for *The Confession of Faith of Gennadius II,* because it makes the doctrine of the Trinity vulnerable to the critiques of Muslim monotheists.[144] It occupies approximately one-fifth of the text of *The Confession of Metrophanes Critopoulos* of 1625.[145] And in its *Encyclical Against the Latin Innovations* issued in 1838, the Synod of Constantinople is still listing it first among the Western "novelties" to be condemned.[146] A century before the Reformation, at the Council of Florence in 1439, the formula "from the Father through the Son [*ex*

---

140. *Phot* 33, 8.
141. *CP 1054* 4.
142. Haugh 1975, 14.
143. *Lyons* anath.
144. Zēzēs 1980, 460–67.
145. *Metr Crit* 1.
146. *CP 1838* 1; *Resp Pius IX* 5.

Patre per Filium]" was proposed by the West, and temporarily accepted by most of the Eastern delegation, as a compromise.[147] It resurfaces in the wake of the First Vatican Council, when *The Old Catholic Agreement at Bonn on the Filioque Controversy* of 1875 between Old Catholics, Eastern Orthodox, and Anglicans, while acknowledging that "the addition *Filioque* to the symbol did not take place in an ecclesiastically regular manner," confesses that "the Holy Spirit proceeds from the Father through the Son."[148] But Florence did not gain acceptance, and except for such occasional references the formula did not prevail in East or West.[149] And therefore, when the Protestant Reformation broke out to claim the attention of the papacy, the Filioque was as firmly ensconced as ever in the Western text of the creed as part of the dogma of the Trinity. The Protestant confessions, virtually without exception, repeat it as orthodox doctrine, without even referring to the conflict between East and West over it.[150]

The ambiguous status of the doctrine of the Trinity in the Protestantism of the nineteenth century brought with it a loss of interest in such seemingly abstruse questions as the Filioque.[151] But the beginning of the renewal of Eastern Orthodox theological exchange not only with Roman Catholicism but with Anglicanism and Protestantism, which was brought about by the ecumenical movement, moved in the opposite direction, by making it clearer why, of all the issues that divided East and West, it should have been this abstruse question that divided the most. And the rebirth of interest in the doctrine of the Trinity within Western theology put it on the agenda once more. As an ecumenical issue, it was once again a creedal issue, an issue of "the three ecumenical creeds" as potential formulas of concord. But there was no avoiding the presence of the Filioque in two of these. It appears not only in the *Western Recension* of *The Niceno-Constantinopolitan Creed* but in the Western confession that was written in Latin but fathered on

147. *Flor Un.*
148. *Bonn II* 1.3, 2.3. See also *Cologne* 3.
149. On the Council of Florence, see chapter 9.2 below, "Reception of Creeds, Councils, and Confessions as Ratification."
150. See chapter 16.3 below, "Catholic Substance and Protestant Principle in Reformation Confessions."
151. Welch 1952 is a penetrating analysis of this process.

Athanasius of Alexandria, which confesses: "The Holy Spirit is from the Father and the Son [*a Patre et Filio*]."[152] And that has continued to make even these "ecumenical creeds" formulas of discord as well, even though theological discussions under ecumenical auspices have led to a deeper understanding on both sides (or on all the sides) of the underlying trinitarian and ecclesiological issues.[153]

A similar historical irony has plagued the doctrine of "the very sacrament which the Savior left in his church as a symbol of its unity and love, whereby he wished all Christians to be mutually linked and united. . . . this sign of unity, this bond of love, this symbol of concord [*hoc concordiae symbolum*]," but now a formula of discord and of "detestable schisms," as *The Decree of the Council of Trent* puts it.[154] In the context of the earliest consideration of the eucharist we have, which appears in Paul's First Epistle to the Corinthians and also includes the earliest account of its institution, its function and its effect are described this way: "The cup of blessing which we bless, is it not a participation [or: communion] in the blood of Christ? The bread which we break, is it not a participation [or: communion] in the body of Christ? Because there is one loaf, we who are many are one body, for we all partake of the one loaf."[155] Citing this passage, *The Westminster Confession of Faith*, speaking in this case for all other confessions, declares that for "true believers" the Lord's supper has been instituted by Christ to be "a bond and pledge of their communion with him, and with each other, as members of his mystical body."[156] But the same New Testament passage can also serve as a principal proof text for *The Heidelberg Catechism* in its second and third editions to declare in a polemical attack on the Council of Trent: "The mass is fundamentally a complete denial of the once for all [*einig*] sacrifice and passion of Jesus Christ, and as such an idolatry to be condemned."[157] Already in

152. *Ath* 23; see chapter 15.1 below, "The Western Reception of the Catholic Creedal and Conciliar Tradition."
153. Vischer 1981.
154. *Trent* 13.1.int, 13.1.8.
155. 1 Cor 10.16–17 (RSV); the alternate rendering "communion" comes from the translators of the RSV. See Syndogmaticon 10.8.
156. *West* 29.1; *Dordrecht* 10.
157. *Heid* 80; *Gall* 37.

the First Epistle to the Corinthians itself, moreover, it becomes painfully clear from Paul's complaint, "I hear that there are divisions among
you," and from his denunciation, "When you meet together, it is not
the Lord's supper that you eat,"[158] that the members of the congregation at Corinth, far from finding in the Lord's supper a sacrament
of concord, were using it as an occasion for all sorts of rivalry, party
spirit, and bitter discord.

Underlying this irony has been a fundamental circularity: a
sharing in the body and blood of Christ not only fosters and deepens
the unity of faith and love among believers in the church but also presupposes an existing unity in faith and in love. Does this unity in faith
require a unity in beliefs and in doctrine and confession, including
also a unity in the confession of the doctrine about the presence of
the body and blood of Christ in the eucharist? When 1 Corinthians
issues the warning that "any one who eats and drinks without discern-
ing the body eats and drinks judgment upon himself,"[159] this "discern-
ing" is taken by the Lutheran *Formula of Concord* to prove that "with
the bread and wine the body and blood of Christ are received not only
spiritually, by faith, but also orally," and that therefore "not only the
genuine believers and those who are worthy but also the unworthy and
the unbelievers receive the true body and blood of Christ."[160] This is
a conclusion that the Reformed confessions, such as *The French Confession* and *The Heidelberg Catechism* just cited, as well as *The Thirty-
Nine Articles of the Church of England*,[161] vigorously reject. On that
basis, then, the adherents of the two major Protestant confessional traditions, Reformed and Lutheran, could not take part together in the
sacrament of concord. Or, to cite an example often raised in the debates
of the twentieth-century ecumenical movement, Anglicans, Lutherans,
and Baptists—if all of them adhere strictly to their confessional standards—cannot share in the sacrament, but for quite divergent reasons:
Anglicans because the clergy of the Lutherans and Baptists have not
been ordained by bishops standing in the apostolic succession of what

158. 1 Cor 11.18, 20.
159. 1 Cor 11.29.
160. *Form Conc Epit* 7.6–7.
161. *39 Art* 29.

The Lambeth Quadrilateral calls "the historic episcopate,"[162] and therefore cannot confect a valid eucharist; Lutherans because the Anglicans and the Baptists do not subscribe to confessions of faith in which the doctrine of the real presence is unequivocally affirmed;[163] Baptists because the Anglicans and the Lutherans have been sprinkled as infants and therefore have not been, in the words of one Anabaptist confession, "baptized upon their faith according to the ordinance of Christ."[164]

The sixteenth-century efforts to resolve this irony also by means of confessions of faith began almost as soon as the doctrinal differences themselves did. *The Marburg Articles* of 1529—subscribed by "Martinus Luther, Justus Jonas, Philippus Melanchthon, Andreas Osiander, Stephanus Agricola, Johannes Brentius, Johannes Oecolampadius, Huldrychus Zwinglius, Martinus Butzerus, Caspar Hedio"—after reciting fourteen articles of faith on which there is doctrinal agreement, conclude:

> We all believe and hold concerning the supper of our dear Lord Jesus Christ . . . that the sacrament of the altar is a sacrament of the true body and blood of Jesus Christ, and that the spiritual partaking of this body and blood is especially necessary for every true Christian. . . . And although at present we are not agreed as to whether the true body and blood are bodily present in the bread and wine, nevertheless each party should show Christian love to the other, so far as conscience can permit, and both should fervently pray Almighty God that he, by his Spirit, would confirm us in the right understanding. Amen.[165]

In an attempt to address this impasse at Marburg, *The Wittenberg Concord* of 1536 between Luther and Bucer expresses a formula of agreement between Bucer and Luther: "We confess that, according to the

162. *Lamb Quad* 4.
163. *Aug Lat* 10.
164. *Ries* 33. See Syndogmaticon 10.3.
165. *Marburg* 15.

words of Irenaeus, the eucharist consists of two things, an earthly and a heavenly.[166] They hold and teach, therefore, that with the bread and wine the body and blood of Christ are truly and substantially present, offered, and received." The text adds that "by the sacramental union, the bread is the body of Christ," but at the same time rejects both "transubstantiation" and "local inclusion."[167] But the concord did not hold.

Nor was it only the difference between Lutheran and Reformed views of the eucharist that divided. Also within the Reformed camp itself, there were sharp differences. The most successful effort to bridge these was *The Zurich Consensus* of 1549 between John Calvin and Heinrich Bullinger, successor to Ulrich Zwingli, which clearly defines the use of a confession of faith as a formula of authentic concord: "We see no other way or more fitting course by which we may abolish religious controversy or suppress empty suspicions where now no division exists . . . than if those who seem to disagree, or do in fact disagree, explain their view openly and in turn, both by word of mouth and written document . . . , by making a declaration in definite, appropriate, and significant statements."[168] It teaches that "God grants within us by his Spirit that which the sacraments figure to our eyes and other senses," but that there is a distinction "between the signs and the things signified," therefore between the elements of bread and wine and the body and blood of Christ.[169] In *The Declaration of Thorn* of 1645 there was a vain attempt at an irenic formula about the eucharist.[170] But where the sixteenth and seventeenth centuries had failed, it remained for the twentieth century to invent some formulas of concord, first in *The Arnoldshain Theses* of 1957,[171] and then, following the lead of Arnoldshain, in *The Leuenberg Agreement* of 1973. *The Leuenberg Agreement,* however, insists without providing further explanation that, in its own words, it "leaves intact the binding force of the confessions within the participating churches" (irreconcilable

166. Irenaeus *Against Heresies* 4.18.5 (ANF 1:486); also cited in *Send*.
167. *Witt Conc* 1–2.
168. *Tig* con.
169. *Tig* 8–9.
170. *Thorn*; also *Send*.
171. *Arn* 4–5; Boelens 1964.

though these have historically been) and "is not to be regarded as a new confession of faith" but rather is to be seen as "a consensus . . . which makes church fellowship possible between churches of different confessional positions."[172] As a formula of concord going beyond the conventional Reformed-Lutheran and Anglican-Protestant antitheses, "the Lima Text," *Baptism, Eucharist, and Ministry* of 1982, puts the question of intercommunion into its total context by expressing the hope that "the increased mutual understanding expressed in the present statement may allow some churches to attain a greater measure of eucharistic communion among themselves and so bring closer the day when Christ's divided people will be visibly reunited around the Lord's table."[173]

172. *Leuen* 37; Rusch and Martensen 1989.
173. *BEM* 2.33.

CHAPTER EIGHT

The Formation of Confessions
and the Politics of Religion

Everything Is Politics but Politics Is Not Everything is the title of a book that was published in 1985 and translated into English in 1986.[1] That epigram applies to many areas of the history of the church, for example, to the tangled history of how bishops have been selected and by whom. The first Christian emperor of Rome, Constantine I, after he was converted but before he was baptized (which did not take place until just before he died), delivered an address to a group of bishops, in which, as reported by Eusebius, he "let fall the expression 'that he himself too was a bishop,' addressing them in my hearing in the following words: 'You are bishops whose jurisdiction is within the church; I also am a bishop, ordained by God to oversee whatever is external to the church.'"[2] The convoking of the Council of Nicaea in 325 and the espousal of "one in being [*homoousios*] with the Father" as the most important term in *The Creed of Nicaea*,[3] and then in *The Niceno-Constantinopolitan Creed*,[4] did make him and his imperial successors part of the history of creeds.

For the assertion of authority by the Christian emperor extended far beyond declarations governing "whatever is external to the church" to include much that was in fact "inside the church." For example, the Second Council of Constantinople in 553 could declare, in a simple coordination, at the beginning of its decrees: "We assembled in this imperial city, summoned here by *the will of God and the command of*

1. Kuitert 1986. See Syndogmaticon 7.3.
2. Eusebius *The Life of Constantine* 24 (NPNF–II 1:546).
3. *N* 2.
4. *N-CP* 2.

the most religious emperor."[5] As George Huntston Williams notes, "the fourth century resounded with the clamor of conciliar debate over the relation of the Son to the Father, but scarcely less important, behind the scenes, was the mounting concern over the proper relation of these very councils themselves to the Christian emperor."[6] Williams finds a correlation between the several confessional positions and the several political positions in the decades following the First Council of Nicaea:

> In insisting that the God of Creation, or Redemption, and the Final Assize is essentially one God, the Catholics were contending that the Lord of Calvary is also the Lord of the Capitol. But for this very reason the typical Nicenes were unwilling to accommodate revelation to reason purely in the interest of enhancing the cohesive value of Christianity for the Empire. In contrast, the Arians, having a comparatively low Christology, were pleased to find in their emperor a divine epiphany or instrument or indeed a demigod like Christ himself.[7]

In that light, the orthodox formulas of *The Creed of Nicaea*,[8] reaffirmed by *The Niceno-Constantinopolitan Creed*,[9] confessing the "one God" to be "the Father all powerful, maker of all things both seen and unseen," and the Son of God to be "one in being with the Father," can be taken to imply the radical subordination of all political authority, including even that of an orthodox Christian emperor, to the lordship of God the Father and of his coequal Son.

Long after Constantine, the juxtaposition between what Hans von Schubert calls "the formation of confessions and the politics of religion"[10] would continue to play a decisive role in the history not only of politics but of confessions. For the proper understanding of one Reformation confession after another, no less than for the understand-

5. *CP II* decr; italics added.
6. G. H. Williams 1951, 20–IV:12–13.
7. G. H. Williams 1951, 20–III:13–14.
8. N 1–2.
9. N-CP 1–2.
10. Schubert 1910.

ing of the councils and creeds of earlier centuries, it is necessary to pay attention to the political context. What were the power relations between the central political authority and the patrons of the confession? Is it possible to discern the political strategies at work in the presentation of the confession, and perhaps even in its composition? Does the confession espouse overtly political positions, and in what ways do its positions on questions of faith and morals carry political implications? How, if at all, did the political alignment change once the new confession was in place? Did some political parties and leaders switch allegiance from one confession to another, and why? These questions, and many others like them, are the stuff of any political history of the Reformation. But they must also not be overlooked by the history of creeds and confessions in the period of the Reformation (and in every other period of Christian history).

8.1. Confessing as a Political Act

It is not an accidental feature in the genesis of creeds and confessions, nor is it an incidental factor for their interpretation,[11] that so many of them bear the designation of political "powers that be,"[12] such as a nation, state, city, or ruler. In some instances that designation is no more than the identification of the geographical venue where the confession was issued or where the council met. Because of the relation of the Anabaptists to the government—any government—this would, obviously, apply in a special sense to the titles of such confessions as *The Schleitheim Confession* of 1527, *The Concept of Cologne* of 1591, and *The Mennonite Confession of Faith of Dordrecht* of 1632. But it is also the case with the confession adopted by the Council of Nicaea in 325, so that it would in some sense be more precise (but also more awkward) to refer to it as "the creed *at* Nicaea" rather than as *The Creed of Nicaea,* as we are calling it to distinguish it from the text that has usually been called *The Nicene Creed,* which we are calling *The Niceno-Constantinopolitan Creed.* But even in this case it was possible to find significance in the derivation of the Greek name of the city, *Nikaia,* from the Greek word for victory, *nikē,* Nike having also been a goddess

---

11. See also chapter 9.5 below, "Rules of Confessional Hermeneutics."
12. Rom 13.1 (AV).

in Greek paganism. That is what *The Decrees of the Second Council of Nicaea* of 787 seem to be doing with their play on words, "singing out with the prophets the hymns of victory [*tous epinikious hymnous*] to the church."[13] The practice of the World Council of Churches and of the Conference/Commission on Faith and Order to meet in a different city each time accounts for the use of the name of that city to identify the statement of faith issued there, such as Bangalore, India, for *A Common Statement of Faith* in 1978[14] or Lima, Peru, for *Baptism, Eucharist, and Ministry* of 1982, which is often called "the Lima Text."[15]

More often, however, the geographical identification of a creed or confession is its political identification as well. In the early centuries that applies with special force to the city of Constantinople, New Rome. Three of the seven councils universally (or almost universally) designated as ecumenical met there, those of 381, 553, and 680–81. Three others—Nicaea I in 325 and again Nicaea II in 787, and Chalcedon in 451—held their sessions just a few kilometers away from the capital city. Of the seven, therefore, only the Council of Ephesus of 431 met at some distance from Constantinople, though still in the East. And so it was both theology and politics, imperial as well as ecclesiastical politics, when the First Council of Constantinople in 381 (attended only by Eastern bishops), and then the Council of Chalcedon in 451, justified the standing of New Rome as a patriarchate of the church alongside Old Rome on the grounds of its standing as the new capital of the empire.[16] The schisms not only between Old Rome and New Rome but within each of their territories have proved over and over again that, employing the phraseology of John Meyendorff,[17] "Christian divisions," most of them bearing political connotations as well, could be more powerful than "imperial unity"—sometimes also more powerful, for that matter, than Christian unity as well.

This centrifugal force of politics and of doctrine would assert itself with even greater power in the Reformation and therefore in its

13. *Nic II* decr.
14. *F&O Ban.*
15. *BEM.*
16. *CP I* can 3; *Chal* can 28; also *Resp Pius IX* 21. See chapter 4.2 above, "Doctrines of Church Order East and West."
17. J. Meyendorff 1989.

confessions. Many of these confessions carry a country or city as part of their title, not only because of the place *at* which they became public (as was the case with *The Augsburg Confession*), but especially because of the political entity *of* which they became the confessional and the political voice. *The Heidelberg Catechism* was originally part of *The Church Order of the Palatinate* [*Kirchenordnung der Kurpfalz*], which was perforce a political document as well as an ecclesiastical one.[18] That political and national dimension of Reformation confessions became evident, for example, when, addressing themselves "to their fellow countrymen and to all other nations who confess the Lord Jesus with them," the spokesmen for "the Estates of Scotland" published *The Scots Confession* of 1560 under the complete title: "The Confession of the Faith and Doctrine Believed and Professed by the Protestants of Scotland, Exhibited to the Estates of Scotland in Parliament in August 1560 and Approved by Their Public Vote as Doctrine Founded upon the Infallible Word of God, And Afterwards Established and Publicly Confirmed by Various Acts of Parliaments, and of Lawful General Assemblies."[19] Churches in Asia and Africa during the twentieth century identified themselves by the rising political and national consciousness of their countries,[20] as for example in *The Statement of Faith of the Church of Jesus Christ in Madagascar* in 1958, reissued in 1968,[21] or in *The Scheme of Church Union in Ceylon* issued in Sri Lanka in 1963.[22]

Another index to the political context of confessions of faith is how often they were addressed directly to political rulers. *The Augsburg Confession* of 1530, presented to Emperor Charles V at the Diet of Augsburg, addresses him as "most serene, most mighty, invincible Emperor, most gracious Lord." It responds to his summons of "a diet of the empire to convene here in Augsburg," for two distinct but related purposes: "to deliberate concerning matters pertaining to the Turk, that traditional foe of ours and of the Christian religion," threatening Central Europe and attacking the gates of Vienna the previous year; and to deliberate "on what might be done about the dissension con-

18. See chapter 4 above, "Faith and Order."
19. *Scot I* pr.
20. *Un Ch Japan* 1954; *Ghana* 1965; *Zambia* 1965; *Togo* 1971.
21. *Madag.*
22. *Sri Lanka.*

cerning our holy faith and the Christian religion," which many feared
was weakening the common defense against the Turk.[23] In the same
year *The Tetrapolitan Confession* of Martin Bucer and his associates,
praising Emperor Charles V for "the unparalleled clemency and kind-
ness whereby thy Worshipful Majesty hath rendered himself so beloved
by the entire world," expresses the hope "that his Worshipful Majesty
will acknowledge the truth concerning all things which we have received for some time as Christ's doctrine and as the teaching of a purer
religion."[24] Also in that year, Zwingli's *Reckoning of the Faith* expresses
an even more optimistic hope to the emperor: "Whatever force, too,
you have heretofore exerted against the purity of the gospel may you
direct against the criminal attempts of ungodly papists."[25] *The French
Confession* of 1559 begins with a lengthy prefatory statement addressed
"Au Roy," expressing thanks that "hitherto having had no access to
your Majesty to make known the rigor of the persecutions that we
have suffered, and suffer daily," they are now finally able to "beseech
that you will see and hear our Confession of Faith," which confesses
"our Lord Jesus Christ to be our only Savior and Redeemer, and his
doctrine to be the only doctrine of life and salvation."[26] Christians,
moreover, are to remain subject to their magistrates "even if they are
unbelievers."[27] In the political atmosphere of the Cold War, that pattern was continued in the twentieth century with such a confession as
The Manifest of Korean Christians in 1973,[28] and under the special circumstances surrounding *The Credo from the Mass of the Marginalized
People* from Honduras in 1980,[29] *The Profession of Faith of the Salva-
doran Basic Ecclesial Communities* of 1984,[30] as well as *The Confession
of Faith of the Presbyterian-Reformed Church in Cuba* of 1977.[31] The full
title of the confession usually known as *The Westminster Confession of
Faith* of 1647 likewise makes its address to political authorities, calling

23. *Aug* pr 1–2.
24. *Tetrapol* pr.
25. *Fid rat* con.
26. *Gall* pr.
27. *Gall* 40.
28. *Korea.*
29. *Hond.*
30. *BEC.*
31. *PRCC.*

itself: "The Humble Advice of the Assembly of Divines, Now by Authority of Parliament sitting at Westminster, Concerning A Confession of Faith: With Quotations and Texts of Scripture annexed. Presented by them lately to both Houses of Parliament."[32]

Many of these confessions are addressed to hostile political authorities, and all could fittingly have made their own the biblical epigraph that heads *The Augsburg Confession:* "I will also speak of thy testimonies before kings, and shall not be put to shame."[33] In their experiences of opposition and even of persecution, moreover, they are making their own another biblical precedent as well, "Christ Jesus who in his testimony before Pontius Pilate made the good confession."[34] These confessors were ever mindful that Christ not only made a confession *before* Pontius Pilate but, as both *The Niceno-Constantinopolitan Creed* and *The Apostles' Creed*[35] affirm, also "suffered *under* Pontius Pilate." His confession "before Pontius Pilate" and his suffering "under Pontius Pilate" went together, with Pilate representing both an imperial regime that would persecute the church during the following centuries and a Greco-Roman paganism over against which the church would, during those same centuries, begin to define itself in its creeds. Therefore "as Jesus witnessed to the truth before Pontius Pilate, the representative of the Roman empire, so we are called today to speak the truth to the rulers."[36]

Every time an early creed opens by declaring its faith in "one God," as one after another of them does and as creeds and confessions go on doing throughout Christian history, echoing *The Shema,*[37] it is also defining the monotheism that distinguishes Christian belief (as well as Jewish belief) from the idolatry of Greek and Roman polytheism, of which the worship of Caesar was a particularly virulent expression. For in such creeds, one of the underlying issues at stake, whether theological or political, is "monotheism as a political prob-

32. *West* ttl.
33. Ps 119.46.
34. 1 Tm 6.13.
35. *N-CP* 4; *Ap* 4, italics added.
36. *Korea* 2.
37. See chapter 5.1 above, "Creeds in Scripture," and Syndogmaticon 1.7.

lem."[38] When, in the first postbiblical account of a Christian martyrdom, *The Martyrdom of Polycarp,* the Roman proconsul Statius Qua-
dratus, the political and spiritual descendant of Pontius Pilate and the
representative of Emperor Antoninus Pius, orders the aged Polycarp,
"Swear by the fortune of Caesar!" Polycarp instead confesses "with
boldness, 'I am a Christian. And if you wish to learn what the doctrines of Christianity are, appoint me a day, and you shall hear them.'"
And so he went to his death.[39] The twentieth century, which saw the
rise of both Nazi and Communist totalitarian regimes that were inimi-
cal to Christianity, also therefore produced several such confessions
that were political acts in this special sense. Preeminent among these,
both in its own time and in its subsequent role as a normative confession adopted by several Protestant churches in Germany and well beyond,[40] was *The Barmen Declaration* of May 1934, as a Christian confessional response to a twentieth-century revival both of polytheism
and of Caesar-worship no less virulent (though sometimes less overt)
in its opposition to the Christian gospel. Particularly in the fifth of its
six theses, protesting against the teaching that the church is "an organ
of the state" and that the state is "a total ordering of life,"[41] *The Barmen Declaration* became the rallying point, across confessional lines,
for the Christian rejection of National Socialism and of other ideolo-
gies of racial purity.[42] It has performed this function also for churches
engaged in the subsequent political-theological struggles of developing
"Third World" societies against colonialism, racism, and idolatrous
nationalism.[43] Although the persecution of the church by Communist
totalitarianism was at least as intense and destructive as Nazi persecution, producing many "confessors" and "new martyrs" and some reactions that could perhaps be called "confessional,"[44] it did not, for
some reason, evoke any assertive and unequivocal confessions of faith

38. Peterson [1935] 1951.
39. *The Martyrdom of Polycarp* 10 (*ANF* 1:41).
40. See the enumeration of these churches in Burgsmüller and Weth 1983, 68–77.
41. *Barm* 5.
42. Scholder 1988, 122–71; A. Cochrane 1962; Ahlers 1986.
43. *Bat* pr.
44. *Sheng Kung* 5.

against Marxism-Leninism that could be compared in their force to
the one at Barmen, and did evoke some vigorous confessional efforts
at accommodation.[45]

Yet confessing can be no less political an act when a regime is
friendly to the church, as the example of Constantine's direct involvement in the composition of *The Creed of Nicaea* demonstrates. In a different political context, the preface to *The Canons of the Synod of Dort*
of 1619 finds the parting promise of Christ to his church, "Lo, I am
with you always, to the close of the age,"[46] fulfilled and "documented
in the histories of the pious emperors, kings, and princes, whom the
Son of God stirred up for the support of his church."[47] That "support" of the church has taken many forms, but for the role of the
politics of religion in the formation of creeds and confessions one of
the most decisive has been the authority exercised by such "pious emperors, kings, and princes" in convoking the synods and councils that
have issued so many of the creeds and confessions. Repeating the formula of the Anglican *Forty-Two Articles,*[48] *The Thirty-Nine Articles of
the Church of England* can therefore state unequivocally, in opposition to medieval and Roman Catholic teaching, that "general councils
may not be gathered together without the commandment and will of
princes."[49] *The Westminster Confession of Faith* spells out this provision at greater length. To avoid misunderstanding, it begins by making
clear, in phraseology taken over from *The Irish Articles of Religion* of
1615,[50] that "the civil magistrate may not assume to himself the administration of the word and sacraments, or the power of the keys of the
kingdom of heaven." Nevertheless, it is his authority and duty "to take
order, that unity and peace be preserved in the church, that the truth
of God be kept pure and entire, that all blasphemies and heresies be
suppressed, all corruptions and abuses in worship and discipline prevented or reformed, and all the ordinances of God duly settled, admin-

45. *PRCC* 3.D–E; for a consideration of this difference, see Spinka and Reinhold
Niebuhr 1954.
46. Mt 28.20.
47. *Dort* pr.
48. *42 Art* 22.
49. *39 Art* 21.
50. *Irish* 58.

istrated, and observed." Therefore it does follow that the magistrate "hath power to call synods, to be present at them, and to provide that whatsoever is transacted in them be according to the mind of God."[51] A later chapter goes on to make it clear, however, that "if magistrates be open enemies to the church, the ministers of Christ of themselves, by virtue of their office, or they, with other fit persons upon delegation from their churches, may meet together in such assemblies," councils, and synods, and without governmental authorization, just as the apostles met together in the first council in Jerusalem without obtaining the permission of Pontius Pilate to do so.[52] But the confession also warns that "synods and councils . . . are not to intermeddle with civil affairs which concern the commonwealth," and it explains that "infidelity, or difference in religion, doth not make void the magistrates' just and legal authority, nor free the people from their due obedience to them, from which ecclesiastical persons are not exempt."[53]

8.2. Civil Law on Adherence to Creeds

A special instance of how the politics of religion can affect the formation of creeds and confessions as well as their perpetuation has been the legal dimension of adherence to creeds. In addition to the place of creeds and confessions, and of subscription to them, in the canon law of various churches,[54] civil law, too, has been decisive. For in the wake of the Constantinian settlement, *The Theodosian Code* decreed, in the edict that Emperor Theodosius I had issued on 27 February 380:

> We desire that all peoples who fall beneath the sway of
> our imperial clemency should profess the faith which
> we believe to have been communicated by the apostle
> Peter to the Romans and maintained in its traditional
> form to the present day, the faith which is observed
> likewise by the pontiff Damasus and by Peter of Alexandria, a man of apostolic sanctity; to wit, that according to apostolic discipline and evangelical teach-

51. *West* 23.3.
52. *West* 31.2, citing Acts 15.6–21.
53. *West* 31.5, 23.4.
54. See chapter 9 below, "Creedal Dogma as Church Law."

ing, we should believe in one deity, the sacred Trinity of Father, Son, and Holy Spirit, to be worshiped in equal majesty. And we require that those who follow this rule of faith should embrace the name of Catholic Christians, adjudging all others madmen and ordering them to be designated as heretics . . . condemned as such, in the first instance, to suffer divine punishment, and, therewith, the vengeance of that power which we, by celestial authority, have assumed.[55]

This was promulgated a year before the First Council of Constantinople, which adjourned in July 381 and was ratified by the same Emperor Theodosius I. But the "apostolic discipline and evangelical teaching" of the confession of "one deity, the sacred Trinity of Father, Son, and Holy Spirit," to which the edict refers and which as it stands is an assertion of the authority of *The Creed of Nicaea* of 325, was then equated with *The Niceno-Constantinopolitan Creed* of 381. To hold political office in the Christian Roman empire, and therefore in its continuations (which included the "Byzantine" Eastern Roman Empire and the "Holy Roman Empire" in the West), it was obligatory to adhere to that creed. For hanging over anyone who denied the creed was the threat not only of "divine punishment" but of political punishment by "the vengeance of that power which we [Theodosius I], by celestial authority, have assumed" and which his successors continued to wield.

Therefore, alongside the imperative doctrinal reasons for holding to the dogmas of the creed,[56] the Protestant Reformers of the sixteenth century had very good political reasons to defend themselves against the charge of their Roman Catholic adversaries that they did not accept these dogmas and that they had thereby jeopardized their political legitimacy. There may even be an echo of *The Theodosian Code* in the opening words of the Latin text of *The Augsburg Confession:* "Our churches teach with great unanimity [*magno consensu*] that the decree of the Council of Nicaea concerning the unity of the divine essence and concerning the three persons is true and should be believed

---

55. *Theodosian Code* 16.1.2.
56. See chapter 16.3 below, "Catholic Substance and Protestant Principle in Reformation Confessions."

without any doubting."[57] This dogmatic orthodoxy meant that there were no valid grounds for deposing the German "electors, princes, and estates" who were confessing here that "these things are preached, taught, communicated, and embraced in our lands, principalities, dominions, cities, and territories,"[58] which under imperial law they were claiming the right to reform. It was a grim vindication of that Protestant loyalty to the Nicene dogma when Michael Servetus was executed in 1553 for denying the orthodox doctrine of the Trinity.[59] Technically speaking, the execution of Servetus, like that of heretics under the Roman Catholic Inquisition, was carried out by the civil arm rather than by the Calvinist ecclesiastical authorities in Switzerland. But in both contexts the civil authorities were acting in their capacity as defenders of the faith who were subject to ecclesiastical discipline.[60] It is also striking to note that the unchallenged theological hegemony of the doctrine of the Trinity, beginning in the fourth century and ending in the eighteenth and nineteenth centuries,[61] was basically coextensive with the willingness and ability of civil authorities to go on enforcing it.

Just as the edict of Theodosius I in 380, according to Charles Norris Cochrane, marked "the process by which the New [Roman] Republic was to be transformed into the Orthodox [Roman] Empire,"[62] so also many confessions of the Reformation were not only affirmations of Protestant doctrine but expressions of the political coming-of-age of their sponsoring nations. On this score the Reformed confessions were further advanced than the Lutheran ones.[63] *The Augsburg Confession* was originally the expression of a German consensus, and *The Smalcald Articles* did present themselves as a statement of faith of the German princes and free cities who "accepted them, unanimously adopted them as their confession, and resolved that these articles should be presented publicly as the confession of our faith,"[64] also

57. *Aug Lat* 1.1.
58. *Aug* pr 6–8.
59. See chapter 7.1 above, "Creedal Anathema and Polemics."
60. Kamen 1998, 163–65.
61. Welch 1952.
62. C. N. Cochrane 1944, 327–29.
63. See also chapter 16.2 below, "Lutheran, Reformed, Roman Catholic, and Radical 'Confessionalisms.'"
64. *Smal Art* pr 2.

at any forthcoming church council. But it did not become the pattern, when for example the several nations of Scandinavia joined the Lutheran cause, for each of them to formulate its own confession. There was such a confession issued at Copenhagen in 1530, the *Confessio Hafniensis*.[65] But it soon yielded to *The Augsburg Confession* of the same year. The Lutheran folk churches of Scandinavia all accepted *The Augsburg Confession, Luther's Small Catechism,* and in some cases all or part of the rest of *The Book of Concord. The Second Helvetic Confession* of 1566 evoked a wide resonance also in the Reformed churches outside Switzerland,[66] and there was international participation of representatives from the Continent and from Great Britain in the Synod of Dort in 1619 and its doctrinal decrees, *The Canons of the Synod of Dort.*[67] But many, perhaps most, of the Reformed confessions, while sharing the Reformed faith being confessed in other lands, were largely confined to their own nationalities: *The First Helvetic Confession* of 1536; *The French Confession* of 1559; *The [First] Scots Confession* of 1560; *The Belgic Confession* of 1561; *The [Second] Bohemian Confession* of 1575; *The [Second] Scots Confession* of 1581. That made the Reformed communion, united though it was in mind and spirit, a confederation of churches that were (to use the Eastern Orthodox term) "autocephalous," not only administratively but confessionally, rather than being confessionally centralized, as both Lutheranism and Roman Catholicism were (though in drastically different ways).[68] During the modern period, this difference between Reformed and Lutheran churches would manifest itself as well in the negotiations about how, in the "younger churches" that came out of foreign missions, the several confessions of the sending churches were to be related to one another, both in their acculturation and in their political dimension.[69]

65. Andersen 1954.
66. Staedtke 1966, 81–202.
67. *Dort* con.
68. See also chapter 14.1 below, "The Ambivalence of the Orthodox Church Toward 'Symbolical Books.'"
69. Nortier 1941; see chapter 11.2 below, "The Fate of Creeds in Missions and Migrations"; and chapter 17.2 below, "Old and New Contexts of Christian Confessing."

8.3. Confessions and the Formation of Politics

The influence of the politics of religion on the formation of creeds and confessions has had, as its counterpart, the influence of creeds and confessions on the formation of politics, which is only part of all the various political, economic, and social influences exerted by the church. The New Testament writings do not deal in so many words with the possibility that political power could end up in the hands of Christian believers. Instead, the commandment in the Gospel, "Render therefore to Caesar the things that are Caesar's, and to God the things that are God's,"[70] as well as the commandment in the epistles, "Let every person be subject to the governing authorities. For there is no authority except from God, and those that exist have been instituted by God,"[71] pertain to the "Caesar" and the "governing authorities" of the pagan Roman empire, and in the latter case probably to Emperor Nero. It was in opposition to the claims of the Caesars to be divine "lords [kyrioi]" and worthy of divine worship that Christian martyrs such as Polycarp confessed the supreme lordship of Jesus Christ as the one *Kyrios*. As *The Niceno-Constantinopolitan Creed* declares, "[We believe] in *one Lord, Jesus Christ*,"[72] with no one else, not even the emperor whether pagan or Christian, being fully worthy of that title, except derivatively. But what would happen to such confessions with the advent of the unforeseen eventuality of Caesar's becoming a Christian[73] — and even acquiring the title "equal to the apostles [isapostolos]"?[74] *The Theodosian Code*, including the edict of 380 endorsing *The Creed of Nicaea*, illustrated what could and did happen, particularly with its ominous threats. But *The Theodosian Code* contained many other provisions as well, including legislation about both the church and the family, that showed the marks of their origin in Christian confession and practice.[75]

Yet just as in the fourth century "Athanasius moved . . . to an insistence . . . upon the complete independence of a council from

70. Mt 22.21.
71. Rom 13.1.
72. *N-CP* 2; italics added.
73. Tertullian *Apology* 21 (ANF 3:35–36).
74. Sophocles, 603.
75. Boyd 1905.

the emperor,"[76] so later councils and confessions of the Christian East repeatedly had occasion to articulate that insistence, specifically also against the authority of Christian emperors. In the sixth century, *The Edict of Emperor Justinian on the True Faith* of 551 had successfully prosecuted "the Three Chapters" even "after their death,"[77] so that they were condemned by the fifth ecumenical council two years later.[78] But in the seventh century, a similar attempt by the emperor Heraclius to close off debate over whether Christ had two "principles of action [*energaiai*]" or one[79] was countered by the sixth ecumenical council, which defined the doctrine that in Christ "two natural wills and principles of action meet in correspondence for the salvation of the human race."[80] And in the eighth century, the affirmation of the faith of Orthodoxy in opposition to iconoclasm by the seventh ecumenical council is at the same time an assertion of the authority of the church to regulate its own liturgy, in which that Orthodox faith is confessed.[81] Therefore in one and the same *Definition* the bishops at Nicaea II stated that they were decreeing "by the grace of God and by order of our pious and Christ-loving emperor and empress, Constantine [VI] and his mother Irene," but also made it clear that they themselves as bishops were "those responsible for the priesthood everywhere, in order that the divinely inspired tradition of the catholic church should receive confirmation by a public decree." Therefore "any election of a bishop, priest, or deacon brought about by the rulers is to be null and void."[82] In keeping with this, *The Divine Liturgy According to Saint John Chrysostom*, while it contains special prayers in support of "all civil authorities"—prayers that have continued without interruption whether those "authorities" were Eastern Orthodox, Roman Catholic, Protestant, Muslim, militarist, or Marxist—also contains a repetition of the warning of the Psalms, "Put not your trust in princes,"[83] and

76. G. H. Williams 1951, 20–IV:12–13.
77. *Edict* con.
78. *CP II* anath.
79. *Ecth* 5.
80. *CP III*.
81. See chapter 14.2 below, "The Liturgy as the Church's Preeminent Confession of the Faith."
82. *Nic II* can 3.
83. Ps 146.3.

thus confesses that all "princes" and governing authorities, whatever their religious faith or lack of it, are "mortal" and unworthy of an ultimate reliance.[84] Therefore *The Confession of Dositheus and of the Synod of Jerusalem* of 1672 warns that an archbishop is not "chosen by political rulers even if they are outstanding in virtue [*aretēi diapherousin*]" or in orthodoxy.[85]

In the West, too, most of the history of the politics of religion has been played out in struggles over the concrete areas of church and society rather than in creeds and confessions. Nevertheless, some of the medieval confessional documents do reflect those struggles. The opposition of Pope Gregory VII to the practice of the lay investiture of bishops and his excommunication of Emperor Henry IV, climaxing in their encounter at Canossa, are a major chapter in the political history of the Middle Ages. But in his *Dictatus Papae* Pope Gregory made it a confession of faith "that [the pope] has the right to depose emperors" and that "he himself ought to be judged by no one else."[86] Two centuries later, Pope Boniface VIII, in the bull *Unam Sanctam* of 1302, articulated, in the most unambiguous of terms, what has come to be seen as the normative medieval position, even while his own authority was crumbling under attack from the political rulers. According to *Unam Sanctam,* there are, as the Gospel specifies, "two swords," and no more, for Christ declared to the disciples, "It is enough."[87] These are the "spiritual" sword and the "material" sword, but "both are in the power of the church," the difference being that the spiritual sword is "to be used *by* [the church]" but the temporal sword "used *for* the church." The spiritual power of the church, as supremely vested in the pope, has the authority to judge all earthly powers, but it is not to be judged by any of them.[88]

Here again, however, the Reformation of the sixteenth century, particularly in its Reformed expression, brought on a quantum increase in the use of creeds and confessions to prescribe the duties of rulers and governments. *The Augsburg Confession* of 1530 confines

84. *Lit Chrys* I.A.2.
85. *Dosith* decr 10.
86. *Dict Pap* 12, 19.
87. Lk 22.38.
88. *Unam* 8; italics added.

itself to affirming the validity of civil government and, in opposition to Anabaptism, the legitimacy of its incumbency by Christians.[89] But one of the earliest Reformed confessions, *The Sixty-Seven Articles of Ulrich Zwingli* of 1523, grounds the power of government specifically in "the doctrine and work of Christ [*aus der Lehre und That Christi*]," as does a far later one in "the sovereign authority of Jesus Christ."[90] The meaning of "the doctrine of Christ" in that provision becomes clear when *The Sixty-Seven Articles* also require not only that the magistrates not command anything contrary to the will of God—which is a standard part of many different confessions from different periods,[91] often backed up by the New Testament injunction that "we must obey God rather than men"[92]—but also positively that "all their laws should conform to the divine will." From this it follows that "when they are unfaithful and do not act according to the rule [*regula*] of Christ, they may be deposed in the name of God."[93] As Philip Schaff's footnote to this formula puts it, "This article asserts the right of revolution."[94] The Zwinglian *First Basel Confession* of 1534 prescribes it as a duty of "every Christian government" to "do all in its power to see that God's name is hallowed among its subjects [and] God's kingdom extended."[95]

In the same vein, *The First Helvetic Confession* of 1536 makes it a duty that the civil government, "if it does not want to be tyrannical, is to protect and promote the true honor of God and the proper service of God by punishing and rooting out all blasphemy, and to exercise all possible diligence to promote and to put into effect what a minister of the church and a preacher of the gospel teaches and sets forth from God's word."[96] This means that although it is not the duty of "the minister of the church" to administer a civil office himself, it is the duty of the civil magistrate to learn the will of God from the minis-

89. *Aug* 16.
90. *67 Art* 35; *Un Pres* 37.
91. *Aug* 16.7; *Boh I* 16.6; *Jer II* 1.16, 1.28; *Cumb Pres* 72; *New Hamp* 16.
92. Acts 5.29.
93. *67 Art* 38–39, 42.
94. Schaff, 3:204.
95. *Bas Bek* 8.
96. *Helv I* 26.

ter's teaching and then to put it into action in the political order. Similarly, *The Second Helvetic Confession,* urging that "the care of religion belongs especially to the holy magistrate," assigns him the responsibility to "promote the preaching of the truth and sincere faith" and to "suppress stubborn heretics (who are truly heretics)."[97] *The Belgic Confession* of 1561 likewise lists "upholding the sacred ministry, with a view to removing and destroying all idolatry and false worship of the Antichrist" as an obligation of Christian rulers—a formulation that some of its heirs later repudiated as unbiblical.[98] *The Westminster Confession of Faith* of 1647 threatens those guilty of "publishing of such opinions, or maintaining of such practices, as are contrary to the light of nature, or to the known principles of Christianity, whether concerning faith, worship, or conversation," with being "called to account, and proceeded against by the censures of the church, *and by the power of the civil magistrate.*"[99] Significantly, this final phrase is omitted in the American edition of *The Westminster Confession.*[100] In the New World, *The Cambridge Platform* makes it "the duty of the magistrate to take care of matters of religion" but excludes from his purview "things merely inward, and so not subject to his cognizance and view, as unbelief, hardness of heart, erroneous opinions not vented."[101] Although the doctrinal position of *The Social Creed of the Methodist Church* of 1908 has far greater affinities with the confession of Arminianism,[102] it manifests affinities with these classic Reformed confessions when it concludes by stating as its goal "the recognition of the Golden Rule and the mind of Christ as the supreme law of society and the sure remedy of all social ills," also beyond the boundaries of the church, a statement of goal that was omitted when this text was revised to become *The Social Creed of the Churches* later the same year.[103]

The underlying assumption in such confessional prescriptions of the duties of Christian rulers toward the revealed "will of God," "the

97. *Helv II* 30.2–3.
98. *Belg* 36.
99. *West* 20.4; italics added.
100. *West Am* 20.4.
101. *Camb Plat* 17.6–7.
102. *Remon.*
103. *Soc Meth* 11; *Soc Ch* 14; *Meth Braz* 3.5.

rule of Christ," "the sovereign authority of the Lord Jesus Christ," and "the Golden Rule and the mind of Christ," and toward "the maintenance of the true religion, and for suppressing of idolatry and superstition," is not only the universal Christian acceptance of the authority of divine revelation as deposited in Holy Scripture. At work in these confessional prescriptions is the specific belief that this biblical revelation, as articulated by the preacher and the church, is applicable also to concrete political issues and should be "the supreme law of society and the sure remedy of all social ills." *The Exposition of Faith of the Third Council of Constantinople* of 680–81 hails "the faithful emperor" as "the new David" for having acted against heresy.[104] But when *The Augsburg Confession,* written in the midst of the political crises of 1529–30, prescribes that "His Imperial Majesty may in salutary and godly fashion imitate the example of David in making war on the Turk," it does not justify this by recourse to the authority of divine revelation but makes its reason clear. "Both [David and Charles V] are incumbents of a royal office which demands the defense and protection of their subjects,"[105] so that the example of a pagan Roman emperor (or even of a Muslim Turkish sultan) would have been no less applicable than that of a king of Israel. According to this confessional view of politics, which has been vigorously criticized in the wake of the history of the twentieth century, there are two divine realms, and it is by his "realm of the left hand" that God acts through government, even through King David (or Emperor Charles V or Elector Frederick the Wise).[106] By contrast, the examples of the monarchs of ancient Israel like David are proof for *The Scots Confession* of 1560 that "the preservation and purification of religion is particularly the duty of kings, princes, rulers and magistrates . . . to maintain true religion and to suppress all idolatry and superstition."[107] This characteristic application of the laws of the Bible, including those of the Old Testament, to political life and institutions is, however, significantly hedged in by the explanation of *The Westminster Confession of Faith* and of other Reformed confessions that not all bib-

104. *CP III* decr.
105. *Aug Ger* 21.1.
106. Schlink 1961, 226–69. See Syndogmaticon 7.2, 7.3.
107. *Scot I* 24.

lical laws can be applied directly to contemporary society. For to the people of Israel, "as a body politic, [God] gave sundry judicial laws, which expired together with the state of that people, not obliging any other now, further than the general equity thereof may require."[108]

Such references, also in Reformed confessions, to "general equity" or to "the light of nature" as a political principle express the belief, which they hold in common with most other confessions regardless of provenance, that even where "the rule of Christ" and the biblical revelation of "the will of God" in the divine law are regarded as politically normative, the formulation of civil law and the execution of public policy are, in some basic sense, the business of human reason in accordance with the natural law. *The Westminster Confession of Faith* opens with the acknowledgment that "the light of nature and the works of creation and providence do so far manifest the goodness, wisdom, and power of God, as to leave men inexcusable." It goes on to acknowledge that therefore "works done by unregenerate men . . . , for the matter of them, . . . may be things which God commands, and of good use both to themselves and others" in human society.[109] Although the revelation of God "in his word" is given "more clearly," there is, according to *The French Confession,* also a revelation "in his works, in their creation, as well as in their preservation and control." Even after the fall, a human being, though "totally corrupt," can nevertheless by the use of reason "still discern good and evil," also for society and government.[110] The condition of "man after the fall," according to *The Second Helvetic Confession,* is such that "his reason was not taken from him, nor was he deprived of will, and he was not entirely changed into a stone or a tree [*lapis et truncus*]." Therefore "in regard to earthly things, fallen man is not entirely lacking in understanding," including "the powers of the intellect" and "natural talents," politics being one of the "arts" that are in considerable measure accessible also to reason and understanding.[111]

Summarizing an estimate of fallen reason that is even more

108. *West* 19.4.
109. *West* 1.1, 16.7. See Syndogmaticon 1.2.
110. *Gall* 2, 9.
111. *Helv II* 9.2, 6. See Syndogmaticon 1.2, 1.3.

generous toward it than these Reformation confessions are, *The Dog-matic Constitution on the Catholic Faith of the First Vatican Council* of 1869–70 opens its decree on divine revelation with the declaration: "The same holy mother church holds and teaches that God, the source and end of all things, can be known with certainty from the consider-ation of created things, by the natural power of human reason." [112] In other words, divine revelation requires that reason, within its limits, is to be trusted. And so the authority of divine revelation teaches that there are truths that do not require the authority of divine revelation for their acceptance. This "understanding of earthly things remaining in man after the fall" of *The Second Helvetic Confession* and this "con-sideration of created things, by the natural power of human reason" of *The Dogmatic Constitution on the Catholic Faith of the First Vatican Council* do extend, in some measure, to politics and law, producing the possibility of what *The Apology of the Augsburg Confession* calls a "civil righteousness [*iustitia civilis*]." [113] Speaking for Eastern Orthodoxy, *The Confession of Metrophanes Critopoulos*, too, refers to "the natural light, which we are accustomed to call 'natural law [*emphytos nomos*].'" [114]

Often it is specific and concrete issues that provoke the politi-cal difficulties and conflicts to which the councils, creeds, and confes-sions are a response. Each in its own way, for example, both the state and the church have a stake in marriage. *The Christian Catechism of the Orthodox Catholic Greco-Russian Church* is expressing a Catholic and Orthodox consensus when, on the basis of the New Testament's desig-nation of marriage as a *mystērion,* the technical term for "sacrament" in Greek Christian theology,[115] it defines: "Matrimony is a sacrament, in which, on the free promise of the man and woman before the priest and the church to be true to each other, their conjugal union is blessed to be an image of Christ's union with the church." [116] That is also taught in other statements of faith emanating from the Eastern Orthodox tra-

---

112. *Vat I* 2.
113. *Apol Aug* 18.9; see chapter 10.1 below, "Doctrines of Christian Discipline in the Reformation Confessions."
114. *Metr Crit* 3.1.
115. Eph 5.32; Lampe, 892–93.
116. *Russ Cat* 361–62. See Syndogmaticon 10.15.

dition, such as *The Confession of Metrophanes Critopoulos*,[117] *The Ortho-dox Confession of the Catholic and Apostolic Eastern Church by Peter Mogila*,[118] and *The Confession of Dositheus and of the Synod of Jerusa-lem*.[119] Speaking for the Western Catholic tradition, *The Canons and Decrees of the Council of Trent* pronounce an anathema upon anyone who denies the sacramental status of matrimony or who "says that those same sacraments of the new law [including matrimony] are no different from the sacraments of the old law."[120]

That reaffirmation and condemnation became necessary in these Eastern Orthodox and Western Catholic confessions because of the confessions of the Protestant Reformation, which criticize the Catholic tradition for an estimation of marriage that is simultaneously not exalted enough and too exalted. Although at least one of them still teaches concerning voluntary celibacy "that he who gives himself to celibacy for the sake of the kingdom of heaven is acting more correctly and safely than if he involves and binds himself to marriage,"[121] these confessions join in denouncing compulsory celibacy for the clergy as "not only contrary to all divine, natural, and civil law, but also utterly opposed and contrary to the canons which the popes had themselves made and to the decisions of the most renowned councils."[122] Accord-ing to *The Thirty-Nine Articles of the Church of England*, "bishops, priests, and deacons are not commanded by God's law either to vow the estate of single life or to abstain from marriage."[123] Therefore the requirement of celibacy is, *The First Helvetic Confession* charges, "an abominable and dreadful thing invented and devised by men in opposi-tion to God's order."[124] While thus defending matrimony against celi-bacy, these confessions at the same time deny the sacramental status of matrimony. Again in the words of *The Thirty-Nine Articles of the Church of England*, they teach that matrimony is one of those "states of

117. *Metr Crit* 12.1.
118. *Mogila* 1.115.
119. *Dosith* decr 15.
120. *Trent* 7.1.1–2; also *Syl* 65–74 and *Lam* 51.
121. *Boh I* 19.2.
122. *Aug Ger* 23.13. See Syndogmaticon 10.13.
123. *39 Art* 32.
124. *Helv I* 27.

life allowed in the Scriptures, but yet have not the like nature of sacraments with baptism and the Lord's supper."[125] It is consistent with this denial when at least some of the Reformation confessions say not only that matrimony in the New Testament is no different from matrimony in the Old Testament but that it is primarily the business of the state rather than of the church. One of the most forthright statements of that position comes in *The Apology of the Augsburg Confession,* which asserts that "matrimony was first instituted not in the New Testament but in the very beginning, at the creation of the human race." Citing one of the several standard (and not entirely consistent) definitions of "sacrament," it concedes that matrimony "has the commandment of God and also certain promises" but insists that "these apply to physical life and not strictly to the New Testament."[126] Even those confessions that do not come out quite that flatly recognize that marriage, as *The Westminster Confession of Faith* puts it, is a matter of interest to both "church [and] civil magistrate."[127] Therefore, according to *The First Helvetic Confession,* a marriage is to be "confirmed in the presence of the church by a public exhortation and vow in keeping with its dignity," but "the government should also respect it and see to it that a marriage is legally and decently entered into and given legal and honorable recognition."[128]

This commonality of interest between the church and the civil magistrate in preserving the integrity of matrimony extends naturally to the area of education. *The Second Helvetic Confession* moves directly from a paragraph urging that "lawful courts be established in the church, and holy judges who may care for marriages" to a paragraph beginning with the words: *"Educentur quoque liberi."*[129] Educating their children is, in the first instance, the responsibility of the parents; but it is a requirement of the divine law in the Ten Commandments, according to *The Heidelberg Catechism,* "that the ministry of the gospel and Christian education be maintained."[130] Not only *The Hei-*

125. *39 Art* 25.
126. *Apol Aug* 13.14.
127. *West* 24.6.
128. *Helv I* 27.
129. *Helv II* 29.2–3.
130. *Heid* 103, explaining Ex 20.8.

delberg Catechism in the context of *The Church Order of the Palatinate,* but all other catechisms, both those that acquired formal confessional status and those that did not, were designed to be instruments for meeting that divine requirement. And if, as *The Second Helvetic Confession* teaches in its next article, the magistrate is to "promote the preaching of the truth and sincere faith,"[131] the education of the young in the catechism certainly belongs to his set of duties, too. Support for this position, with its considerable political implications, comes not only from other Reformed or Calvinist confessions but, somewhat surprisingly, from the preface to *Luther's Small Catechism.* The education of children, not in secular subjects alone but also in the catechism, is the responsibility both of parents and of "governing authorities [*Oberkeit*]," and neglecting it would "undermine and lay waste both the kingdom of God and the kingdom of the world." For "although we cannot and should not compel anyone to believe," it is nevertheless obligatory, for the sake of public morality and the civil order, to "insist that the people learn to know how to distinguish between right and wrong according to the standards of those among whom they live and make their living," which they can do from the teaching of the Ten Commandments in the catechism. Therefore if anyone refuses such instruction, "the prince is disposed to banish such rude people from his land."[132]

Matrimony and education had been high on the political and theological agenda of creeds, catechisms, and councils since the ancient church and throughout the Middle Ages. But it was in the period of the Reformation that a new agenda item began to appear in the confessions, what *The Twelve Conclusions of the Lollards* already in 1395 denounce as "manslaughter in battle or by pretended law of justice for a temporal cause."[133] This represented a challenge not only to the Catholic and Orthodox political consensus but to a political presupposition that the Magisterial Reformers had continued to share with that consensus: the legitimacy of the use of "the sword" by Christians. The political magistrate, according to the key proof text of the New Testament about government, "does not bear the sword in vain; he is the servant

---

131. *Helv II* 30.2.
132. *Luth Sm Cat* pr 19, 12–13; see Schlink 1961, 226–69.
133. *Loll* 10.

of God to execute his wrath on the wrongdoer."[134] But *The Schleitheim Confession* of the Mennonite Anabaptists in 1527 voices their insistence that "the sword is an ordering of God *outside the perfection of Christ*." Therefore when "many, who do not understand Christ's will for us, will ask: whether a Christian may or should use the sword against the wicked for the protection and defense of the good, or for the sake of love," the answer, "unanimously revealed," is that "it does not befit a Christian to be a magistrate."[135] One century—and many persecutions—later, after "flee[ing] from one city or country to another,"[136] *The Mennonite Confession of Faith of Dordrecht* of 1632 dissociates itself even more unambiguously from any doctrinal position that would "resist, despise, or condemn the state." But it continues to urge that for true believers, "with regard to revenge and resistance to enemies with the sword, we believe and confess that our Lord Jesus Christ as well as his disciples and followers have forbidden and taught against all revenge."[137] Yet at about the same time and with much of the same basic doctrinal orientation, an English Baptist confession feels obliged to defend itself against the opposite accusation of "intending to cut the throats of such as were contrary-minded to us in matters of religion."[138] In opposition to the Anabaptist interpretation of the sword, the confessions of the Magisterial Reformation teach that the prohibition of killing by the Decalogue does not forbid but actually requires, as *The Heidelberg Catechism* phrases it, that "the authorities are armed with the means to restrain murder," including among such "means" capital punishment.[139] They also teach that, in the language of *The Westminster Confession of Faith,* "it is lawful for Christians to accept and execute the office of a magistrate, when called thereunto," which includes "the power of the sword."[140] That teaching is also expressed in the anathema of *The Augsburg Confession* on the Anabaptist view of the sword and in its defense of the position "that Christians may without

---

134. Rom 13.4.
135. *Schleit* 6; italics added.
136. *Dordrecht* 14.
137. *Dordrecht* 13, 14; also *Ries* 37.
138. *Gen Bap* 25.
139. *Heid* 105.
140. *West* 23.2, 1.

sin . . . punish evildoers with the sword, engage in just wars, serve as soldiers,"[141] an anathema reiterated by *The Formula of Concord*.[142] Reformed confessions, too, denounce "the error of the Anabaptists [and] other anarchists,"[143] and with them "all those who would like to reject authority,"[144] and who, in the language of *The Second Helvetic Confession*, "when they deny that a Christian may hold the office of a magistrate, deny also that a man may justly be put to death by the magistrate, or that the magistrate may wage war, or that oaths are to be rendered to a magistrate."[145]

8.4. The Politics of Confessional Diversity

In his preface to the first confessional statement of Anglicanism, *The Ten Articles* of 1536, King Henry VIII describes it as his royal duty and charge "that unity and concord in opinion, namely in such things as doth concern our religion, may increase and go forthward, and *all occasion of dissent and discord touching the same be repressed and utterly extinguished*."[146] Almost a century later, *The Irish Articles of Religion* of 1615 present themselves as: "Articles of Religion, agreed upon by the Archbishops and Bishops, and the rest of the clergy of Ireland, in the convocation holden at Dublin in the year of our Lord God 1615, *for the avoiding of diversities of opinions, and the establishing of consent touching true religion*."[147] This confession was speaking from and to the political situation of the Irish Episcopal Church (which, though Protestant, called itself "the Church of Ireland") during the reign of James I, as well as the doctrinal situation of the Anglican Church and its Calvinism, already expressed in *The Lambeth Articles* of 1595,[148] shortly before *The Canons of the Synod of Dort* of 1619, which would be subscribed also by Anglican delegates. Later in the seventeenth century and also in Great Britain, the Quaker *Theses Theologicae of Robert Bar-*

141. *Aug Ger* 16.2–3.
142. *Form Conc Epit* 12.12–16.
143. *Belg* 36.
144. *Gall* 40.
145. *Helv II* 30.4.
146. *10 Art* pr; italics added.
147. *Irish* pr; italics added.
148. *Lamb Art* 1–4.

clay of 1675 protested that "all killing, banishing, fining, imprisoning, and other such things, which men are afflicted with, for the alone exercise of their conscience, or difference in worship or opinion, proceedeth from the spirit of Cain, the murderer, and is contrary to the truth."[149] The contrast between the emphasis of the first of these British confessions on repressing and utterly extinguishing "all occasion of dissent and discord," or of the second on "the avoiding of diversities of opinions," on one hand, and the defense by the third confession, on the other hand, of "the alone exercise of their conscience, or difference in worship or opinion" has been a leitmotiv of both the confessional and the political development of modern history, especially in Great Britain.[150] Eventually, at the end of the seventeenth century, Great Britain took a leading part in providing guarantees of religious liberty, but other countries and other confessions have likewise participated in that process. For there has been a duality also in the public, confessional attitude of the Roman Catholic Church and its popes and councils, as well as in the attitude of other confessions, toward the politics of confessional diversity.

The language of *The Theodosian Code* as quoted earlier precluded the very idea of any diversity of confessions. The only place for diversity would appear to be among those whom, according to *The Creed of Nicaea*, "the catholic and apostolic church anathematizes,"[151] where their very diversity was taken to be proof of their error.[152] For if heresy in the realm of doctrine was tantamount to sedition in the realm of politics, the integrity of the body politic required doctrinal unity through conformity to a single confession. Deviation from that confession was punishable by excommunication and exile. It was to this ideal of confessional—and therefore political—unity that the events of the sixteenth-century Reformation seemed to represent such a fundamental challenge. But the Holy Roman Empire, to whose imperial diet of 1530 *The Augsburg Confession, The Tetrapolitan Confession,* and Zwingli's *Reckoning of the Faith* were all presented, was not a mono-

149. *Friends II* 14.
150. See chapter 17.2 below, "Old and New Contexts of Christian Confessing."
151. *N anath.*
152. See chapter 1.2 above, "Patristic Thought on Continuity and Change."

lithic, integrated realm with a pyramid of authority reaching up to a single autocrat with absolute powers. It was virtually a federation of "estates," principalities, duchies, kingdoms, and free cities, in which, by the provisions of *The Golden Bull* of 1348, the emperor was chosen by a group of electors, princes both secular and ecclesiastical. One of the purposes of the diet at Augsburg, according to the summons issued by Emperor Charles V on 21 January 1530, was to determine "how in the matter of errors and divisions concerning the holy faith and the Christian religion . . . every care [may be] taken to give a charitable hearing to every man's opinion, thoughts, and notions, to understand them, to weigh them." But all of this had the intent "to bring and reconcile men to a unity in Christian truth" and thus "to see to it that *one single, true religion* may be accepted and held by us all, and that we all live in one common church and in unity, just as we all live and battle under the one Christ."[153] Quoting that imperial formula about living and battling "under the one Christ"—which, in the twentieth century, provides the title for a statement of conciliation between Roman Catholicism and Lutheranism in 1980[154]—the preface to *The Augsburg Confession* claims the right of the princes and free cities of Germany to carry out a reformation of the church within their own principalities.[155] Though not intended by anyone, the historical outcome of the process was confessional diversity—not, at least initially, within any single principality, but within the Holy Roman Empire: the principle that the religion of the prince should determine the religion of the principality (*cuius regio, eius religio*), which was eventually codified in the Religious Peace of Augsburg of 1555. As has frequently been observed, therefore, religious liberty was the product of the Reformation, but not of the Reformers. It was not the teaching of any one confession but the result of the presence of so many competing confessions.

One of the most far-reaching of all confessional statements about religious freedom and confessional diversity ever issued is *Dignitatis humanae*, the *Declaration on Religious Freedom* by the ninth session of the Second Vatican Council on 7 December 1965. It prefaces

153. Reu, 2:71–72; italics added.
154. *LuRC 4.*
155. *Aug* pr.

its statements about the freedom of conscience by invoking a creedlike formula that paraphrases *The Niceno-Constantinopolitan Creed*,[156] "We believe that this one and only true religion subsists in the catholic and apostolic church." But the declaration insists that it is not deviating at all from "the sacred tradition and teaching of the church from which it continually draws new insights in harmony with the old."[157] Nevertheless, one such strikingly "new insight in harmony with the old" (but also in contrast with the old) at this council is this: "The human person has a right to religious freedom. Such freedom consists in this, that all should have such immunity from coercion by individuals, or by groups, or by any human power, that no one should be forced to act against his conscience in religious matters, nor prevented from acting according to his conscience." This right is said to be based not on political expediency but (as is clear from the very title of the declaration, *Dignitatis humanae*) "on the dignity of the human person as this is known from the revealed word of God and from reason itself," therefore not from revelation alone; and it is to be recognized, by both church and state, as a civil right.[158] It is specifically in connection with this development of doctrine about religious freedom that *Dignitatis humanae* also admits that in the past Christian individuals and institutions of different confessions have been guilty of coercion and persecution, when "at times in the life of the people of God, as it has pursued its pilgrimage through the twists and turns of human history [*per vicissitudines historiae humanae peregrinantis*], there have been ways of acting hardly in tune with the spirit of the gospel, indeed contrary to it."[159] In thus making what "the sacred tradition of the church" simultaneously calls a "confession of sins" and a "confession of the truths of faith,"[160] the confession of the Second Vatican Council becomes, in this respect at any rate, a voice for other confessions as well.

156. *N-CP* 9.
157. *Vat II* 9.1.
158. *Vat II* 9.2.
159. *Vat II* 9.12.
160. Thomas Aquinas *Summa Theologica* 2a2ae.3.1 (tr. Blackfriars); see chapter 2.3 above, "Confessing the Faith."

III

The Authority of Creeds
and Confessions

The question of the authority of creeds and confessions is in many respects the obverse side of the question of their genesis. Above all, the examination of the connections between Scripture and tradition in the genesis of creeds compels attention both to the connection and to the distinction between these norms for Christian teaching (or these two aspects of a single norm, as the case may be), and to the relative authority exercised by them.[1] If it is legitimate even for Protestant confessions that vigorously assert a doctrine of *sola Scriptura* to legislate not only the particulars of the biblical canon and the general principles of biblical interpretation but specific rules for its practice as well as the correct doctrinal exegesis of individual passages that have been controverted, it does have to be asked which of the two, Scripture "alone" or Scripture as normatively interpreted in the context of the confessional tradition, is functioning as the real locus of doctrinal authority here.[2] It can become an authoritative tradition for a church to declare in its confession that "we have no articles of faith, creed, or discipline, aside from the Bible."[3]

That general question of creedal and confessional authority, however, takes special form not only in the tradition of churches but in their concrete structure and activity. To organize their life, regulate their worship, administer their organization, staff their programs, and pay their bills, all the churches have had recourse to authority and law,

1. See chapter 5 above, "Scripture, Tradition, and Creed."
2. See chapter 5.4 above, "Confessional Rules of Biblical Hermeneutics"; also Syndogmaticon 8.13, 8.15; Thompson et al. 1963, 124–56.
3. *Adv* pr.

because church law of some kind is an unavoidable feature of any institutional Christianity (or of any other institutionalized religion, whether Christian or not).[4] On 10 December 1520, when Martin Luther burned the bull of Pope Leo X, *Exsurge Domine,* which threatened him with excommunication for his disobedience to the church and the papacy, he burned with it the medieval collection of canon law by Gratian. That was an expression of the same personal defiance that was to declare at the Diet of Worms in the following year, "Here I stand, I cannot do otherwise!" But it also articulated a theological protest against what he, as an expositor of Paul's Epistle to the Galatians in 1519, in 1523, and again at great length in 1535, took to be the legalistic mindset of the medieval church. Speaking for him and his followers a few years later, *The Apology of the Augsburg Confession* was to call this the *opinio legis.*[5] A few years after burning the canon law, however, Luther and his colleagues on the theological faculty of the University of Wittenberg were called upon by the Protestant civil authorities of the duchy of Saxony to render an expert scholarly and judicial opinion, or *Gutachten,* on persistent issues of marriage practice and marriage law. For this he found himself obliged to consult, among other sources, the canon law of Gratian.[6] And eventually the Lutheran authorities of both church and state in the duchy of Saxony and elsewhere were to enforce subscription to *The Augsburg Confession* of 1530, and then to the entire *Book of Concord* of 1580, as a legal requirement.[7]

To be sure, it has been possible at certain points in the history of the churches to propound a creed or confession of faith as nothing more authoritative than a set of official suggestions or advisory guidelines about faith and doctrine, without binding authority and therefore without even ecclesiastical sanctions or enforcement, much less the sanctions or enforcement of the civil authorities. Thus, the Congregationalist *Savoy Declaration* of 1658 opens with the assertion that "confession of the faith that is in us, when justly called for, is so indispensable a due all owe to the glory of the sovereign God, that it is

4. See chapter 4 above, "Faith and Order."
5. *Apol Aug* 4.265.
6. Möhler [1832] 1958, 1:497–98.
7. See chapter 9.4 below, "Confessional Subscription as Legal Compliance."

ranked among the duties of the first commandment." But that supreme and "indispensable" confessional obligation of the first commandment to "have no other gods,"[8] and therefore to make the right confession, apparently does not carry with it any confessional authority or creedal enforcement. For the same *Savoy Declaration* also disavows "whatever is of force or constraint in matters of this nature."[9] This seems to be referring not only to constraint by the civil government,[10] which had persecuted English Congregationalism for its dissent from the Anglican establishment, but to constraint by other churches, at whose hands Congregationalism had also suffered, and to constraint by any church, including the Congregational Church, upon the beliefs of its members. Therefore a later Congregationalist confession, *The English Declaration* of 1833, "disallow[s] the utility of creeds and articles of religion as a bond of union, and protest[s] against subscription to any human formularies, as a term of communion." It asserts, not only concerning the creeds and confessions of the past such as its own *Savoy Declaration* (as well as the creeds and the decrees of ecumenical councils of the ancient church, even *The Apostles' Creed*) but also concerning itself, that "it is not intended that the following statement should be put forth with any authority, or as a standard to which assent should be required." The reason, as it explains later, is that "human traditions, fathers and *councils*, canons and *creeds*, possess no authority over the faith and practice of Christians."[11] As Williston Walker formulated this attitude in the opening sentences of his preface to *Creeds and Platforms of Congregationalism* of 1893, a standard collection of doctrinal statements that includes these two confessions as well as many others from Congregationalists in England and America, "Congregationalism has always accorded large liberty to local churches in their interpretation of doctrine and polity. Its creeds are not exclusively binding, and its platforms have always been held to be open to revision. They have been witnesses to the faith and practice of the churches rather than tests for subscription."[12]

8. Ex 20.3.
9. *Sav* pr.
10. See chapter 8.2 above, "Civil Law on Adherence to Creeds."
11. *Eng Dec* 1.5, 4, 3.2; italics added.
12. Walker, xv.

That tendency of according "large liberty" (and then an ever larger and larger liberty) in the "interpretation of doctrine and polity" and of eschewing any and all "tests for subscription" that were "exclusively binding" would grow much stronger not only within Congregationalism, especially in the United States (and within its successor denomination, the United Church of Christ), but beyond Congregationalism within Liberal Protestantism generally, during the century that was about to begin soon after Walker wrote those words in 1893.[13] But even the modern Protestant supporters of a minimalist interpretation of creedal and confessional authority would have to grant, in their case with deep regret, that this "large liberty" has not been typical of most of the Christian tradition. It is, rather, one of the characteristics that have set Liberal Protestantism apart not only from Roman Catholicism and Eastern Orthodoxy but even from its own Protestant predecessors and opponents back to the period of the Reformation, for all of whom the authority of creeds and confessions was—and is—a continuing preoccupation. As the ecumenical experience of the twentieth century would repeatedly show, even the most sincere interconfessional openness and charity can suddenly stumble over unexpected and deeply held differences of belief, and thus over the persistent authority of creed and confession.[14]

13. See chapter 17.1 below, "The Discomfort with Creed Caused by the Consciousness of Modernity."
14. See chapter 17.2 below, "Old and New Contexts of Christian Confessing."

CHAPTER NINE

Creedal Dogma
as Church Law

THE FIRST FOUR ECUMENICAL church councils, from Nicaea I in 325 to Chalcedon in 451, not only promulgated the dogmas of the Trinity and the person of Christ that are still the fundamental creedal and confessional content of normative Christian teaching but, as Peter L'Huillier has pointed out, "laid down canons and disciplinary decrees which constitute a milestone in the history of church order."[1] The canons and disciplinary decrees of these and subsequent church councils became the moral, administrative, and liturgical laws contained in the ever-growing body of ecclesiastical legislation. They formed the basis for canon law, which has become a theological science and a historical discipline on its own, above all in Roman Catholicism but also in Eastern Orthodoxy and to some considerable extent in various branches of Protestantism.[2] As such, canon law has traditionally been distinguished from church doctrine, as well as from the more closely connected field of Christian ethics and moral theology. Violation of the church's rules about fasting is indeed called a sin, but for the reason that it is an act of disobedience to the church, whose rules about fasting nevertheless vary from one nation to another.[3] Because the church has authority and "power, in administering the sacraments, of making dispositions and changes it judged expedient for the well-being of recipients,"[4] and not because there is anything intrinsically immoral or wrong in eating meat on Friday, disobedience to the church is tanta-

1. L'Huillier 1996, ix; see chapter 4 above, "Faith and Order."
2. Kuttner 1960.
3. *Metr Crit* 18.4.
4. *Trent* 21.2.

mount to disobedience to God. But the church also has the authority to change the rules. This became evident to many millions of church members when, after the Second Vatican Council, the regulations of the Roman Catholic Church regarding fasting and abstinence were drastically curtailed, as for that matter they had frequently been waived throughout history by the dispensation of the church under special circumstances.

More amply and more accurately understood, however, the concept of church law should be defined in such a way as to include also creedal dogma. That refers to the doctrines that the church—or *a* church—has made binding on its members as (in the Latin West) a *credendum,* "that which has to be believed," or (in the Orthodox East) "that doctrine which all Christians are bound to believe"[5] and, consequently, bound also, when necessary, to teach and to confess; therefore the *Ad tuendam fidem* of Pope John Paul II was, formally, a revision of canon law "by which certains norms are inserted into the *Code,*" but it had very much to do with doctrine.[6] The Latin term *lex credendi,* which we have been translating as "the rule of faith,"[7] means literally "the law of believing." But creedal dogma, at any rate as it has been understood by most of Christendom during most of its history, differs from disciplinary legislation in at least one important respect. It is not in its doctrinal content (as distinct from its language) subject to repeal or even amendment[8] but is, in the formula of the First Vatican Council about doctrines defined by papal infallibility, "irreformable."[9] This view of dogma is, moreover, not confined to Roman Catholicism and Eastern Orthodoxy. Even so recent a confession as *The Declaration of the Faith and Articles of Religion of the Philippine Independent Church* of 1947 opens its concluding article with the unequivocal prohibition: "The Declaration of Faith shall not be altered, amended, or repealed."[10] When this central distinction between discipline and dogma is ignored (as it often is, and on all sides), therefore,

5. *Aug Lat* 1.1; *Russ Cat* 66.
6. *Ad tuendam* ttl.
7. See chapter 6.2 above, *"Lex orandi lex credendi."*
8. See chapter 1 above, "Continuity and Change in Creeds and Confessions."
9. *Vat I* 4.
10. *Philip Ind* 2.21.

Roman Catholic legislation on marriage, for example, is fundamentally misunderstood. It would certainly be a revolutionary action, but not an unprecedented one—as is evident from *The Union of Brest* of 23 December 1595, by which several Orthodox dioceses in Poland and Lithuania came into full communion with the see of Rome[11]—for Roman Catholicism to repeal the law requiring that parish clergy be celibate and to adopt the Eastern Orthodox and early Christian practice of permitting the ordination of married men.[12] For that is a question of discipline and of "church law [*lex ecclesiastica*]," as the decree of Trent calls it in so many words even while it is defending compulsory clerical celibacy against Protestant attacks.[13] But it is simply inconceivable that some later Roman Catholic council or pope would ever rescind the definition of matrimony as "rightly to be counted among the sacraments of the new law [*merito inter novae legis sacramenta annumerandum*]," as this definition of "our holy fathers and councils and the universal tradition of the church" is reaffirmed by the same decree of the Council of Trent,[14] and as it is then made a part of *The Tridentine Profession of Faith* of 1564,[15] in response to the Protestant insistence on confining the term *sacrament* to baptism and the Lord's supper.[16] For that is a question of doctrine.

In spite of this distinction between disciplinary law and dogma, it remains essential to understand that these doctrines laid down by churches in their creeds and confessions of faith do nevertheless carry the force of law—not only sometimes of civil law as enforced by secular governments, as noted earlier,[17] but of church law, often, in the past, of church law and civil law in alliance. That status of creedal dogma as church law applies historically to the great majority of creeds and confessions in various collections, including the first four parts of *Creeds and Confessions of Faith in the Christian Tradition,* and to the churches that have made these creeds and confessions their own, either originally

11. Halecki 1958.
12. *Metr Crit* 11.6.
13. *Trent* 24.9 decr.
14. *Trent* 24.1 decr.
15. *Trid Prof* 3.
16. *Heid* 68; *39 Art* 25.
17. See chapter 8.2 above, "Civil Law on Adherence to Creeds."

or eventually—which includes most churches, not only Roman Catholic and Orthodox but also Protestant. Because creeds and confessions of faith, therefore, do constitute a body of law and do carry the force of law, it makes sense that they also participate in the nature of law. For every branch of jurisprudence secular or sacred and therefore also for canonical and creedal jurisprudence, this implies at least the following five issues: enactment, ratification, enforcement, compliance, interpretation. But each of these applies here in a special way. That is true both because of the fundamental differences between church law and civil law and because of the distinctive nature of creeds and confessions of faith as statements of what a church and its members are required to believe, teach, and confess on the basis of divine revelation.

9.1. Creedal Formulation as Enactment

The ecclesiastical analogue to legislative enactment in the area of civil law is creedal and confessional formulation. In the creedal process just as in the legislative one, an important preliminary to the formulation is the role played by debate. As one Protestant confession puts it, "those who seem to disagree, or do in fact disagree, [should] explain their view openly and in turn, both by word of mouth and written document . . . , by making a declaration in definite, appropriate, and significant statements."[18] Or, in the words of one ecumenical council, "the truth cannot be made clear in any other way than when there are debates about questions of faith, since everyone requires the assistance of his neighbor."[19] Therefore an important component in the later understanding of the confessional formulation of the results is the examination of the several sides in the preceding controversy, for the fingerprints that each of them may have left on the eventual text of the creed. Where the text explains its relation to the debates, as *The Creed of Nicaea* of 325 does when it concludes its affirmative confession by itemizing in a series of quotations those positions that "the catholic and apostolic church anathematizes,"[20] the foregoing debates provide

18. *Tig* con.
19. *CP II* decr.
20. *N* anath.

the context not only for these condemnatory clauses and anathemas but also for the positive affirmations. In such a case, the clarification of what legal scholars call the "original intent" of those affirmations depends in considerable measure on the identification of the position or positions being anathematized. It also depends, of course, on the determination (assuming that the surviving historical sources make this possible, which is not always the case) of the state of the doctrine before the debate broke out. But the debates were not, or not only, between those positions that eventually received condemnation as heretical and those that eventually emerged victorious as orthodox, but among positions that could all go on laying some claim to orthodox standing, also after the normative doctrinal formulation had been enacted in a creed or confession of faith. Here, too, the role of debate in creedal enactment and formulation is no less important, only more difficult. It is up to scholarly research into the history of doctrine to provide the missing footnotes.[21] *The Canons and Decrees of the Council of Trent* of 1545–63 may serve as one example among many. Many of the memoranda, letters, diaries, proposals, and draft decrees from the Council of Trent have been preserved and compiled in the multivolume collection *Concilium Tridentinum*, published by the Görres Gesellschaft beginning in 1901. Thanks to this treasure trove of primary source material, research has made it clear that the decree of the sixth session of that council on the doctrine of justification through both faith and works[22] is addressing not only the various Protestant versions of justification *sola fide*, to which it has conventionally been related in the older polemical and scholarly literature, but also the several divergent definitions both of justification and of faith inherited from medieval theology and espoused by one or another of the parties among the council fathers at Trent, including, most significantly, the Augustinian Girolamo Seripando.[23] Such a reinterpretation is in keeping with Trent's original definition of "the dual purpose on account of which the coun-

---

21. See chapter 17.3 below, "The Flowering of Creedal and Confessional Scholarship in the Modern Era."
22. *Trent* 6.7–8.
23. *Chr Trad* 4:279–89, which is based on the volumes of *Concilium Tridentinum*.

cil was primarily brought together," which was to be internal as well as external.[24]

Repetitive though many of their formulas of affirmation and of condemnation may be, both within and between the several periods of their history, creeds and confessions of faith manifest in their enactment a great variety of authors and sponsors—not to mention pseudonymous creeds (of which *The Athanasian Creed* is the best known). Even the broad categories of *personal, regional, synodal,* and *conciliar,* as they are being applied here to the creedal developments of the first several centuries,[25] do not begin to exhaust the list of the Christian agencies that have taken it upon themselves to formulate statements of faith at one or another time in the history of the church. The legitimacy and competency of such an agency to formulate a creed in response to controversy and to promulgate it as church law, moreover, has repeatedly itself become a major issue of controversy—and therefore eventually a topic for creedal and confessional assertion in its own right as well. Legitimacy and competency can become an especially delicate problem if some later reaffirmation of a creed or confession seems, paradoxically, to be accompanied by a challenge to the very authority under which that creed was originally formulated. Thus the Western church after its schism with the East continues to affirm as orthodox the trinitarian formulations of the First Council of Constantinople of 381 in *The Niceno-Constantinopolitan Creed* and the christological formulations of *The Definition of Faith of the Council of Chalcedon* passed in 451, even though the canons of both of these councils (erroneously, in Western eyes) rank the patriarchate of Constantinople as New Rome alongside the patriarchate of Old Rome.[26] A similarly delicate problem is the acceptance, by the Protestant confessions, of these trinitarian and christological dogmas. For they were legislated in the ecumenical councils of the fourth, fifth, sixth, and seventh centuries by bishops to whose successors in the sixteenth and later centuries these same Reformation confessions steadfastly refuse to ascribe

24. *Trent* 3.
25. See chapter 13 below, "Rules of Faith in the Early Church."
26. See chapter 4.2 above, "Doctrines of Church Order East and West," and *Flor Arm* 9.

a similar authority, to the point of identifying as "the real Antichrist" the *primus inter pares* among these bishops, the pope and bishop of Rome.[27] The Protestant confessions justify this apparent inconsistency on the grounds—invoking a disjunction between Scripture and tradition that Roman Catholicism and Eastern Orthodoxy find unacceptable—that it is not the conciliar authority but the scriptural correctness of *The Niceno-Constantinopolitan Creed* and *The Definition of Faith of the Council of Chalcedon* that makes them orthodox and binding. Therefore an acceptance of the orthodox creeds does not necessarily require an acceptance of bishops, popes, and church councils.[28] But in taking such a position, the Protestant confessions are, in their own way, raising the vexing question of canon law and theology about the "reception" of creeds, councils, and confessions as church law.

9.2. Reception of Creeds, Councils, and Confessions as Ratification

Most statements of faith have been enacted as occasional documents, which were initially drafted under the specific circumstances of one time and place to meet a particular need or to respond to a particular challenge, not always with an eye to the indefinite future. Just as a consideration of the historical circumstances surrounding the composition and the transmission of any book of the Bible (at least to the extent that these circumstances are knowable) is an indispensable element for its present-day interpretation,[29] so it must be with any creed or confession of faith. That is the reason for the historical materials that are being supplied both in this companion volume and in the introductions and notes throughout the volumes of *Creeds and Confessions of Faith in the Christian Tradition*. Yet as with the Bible, so also, though in appropriately lesser measure, with a creed or confession, the history that is sometimes the most interesting, and often even the most important, is what the confession has subsequently become both in the life and in the teaching of the church or churches. The process by which a confession or some other piece of ecclesiastical legislation that has been

---

27. *Smal Art* 2.4.10; *West* 25.6; *Sav* 26.4; *Philad* 4. See Syndogmaticon 11.3.
28. *Scot I* 20; *Helv II* 3.4, 11.18. See Syndogmaticon 1.4, 8.11, 8.12, 9.1, 9.8.
29. See chapter 5.4 above, "Confessional Rules of Biblical Hermeneutics."

written under particular circumstances graduates from the occasional to the normative has acquired the technical designation *reception*.[30]

Particularly since the Second Vatican Council of 1962–65, which stimulated new attention to the council as an authoritative force in church history and canon law, *reception* has been the object of growing theological and scholarly investigation.[31] In the development of literary criticism and literary history during that same period, the "reception history" of a work has been used to illumine both the work itself and subsequent periods. The term is likewise a common one in jurisprudence and the history of law, where an outstanding instance is the "reception" of Roman law in the medieval West and its relation to barbarian law codes.[32] When it is applied to confessions and councils, too, it remains the designation for a legal process. For it involves whatever mechanisms of decision-making and legislation a church—whether national or regional or local or denominational or, for that matter, universal—employs to adopt norms for its faith and teaching, its worship and practice. Or, as Yves Congar defines it, reception is "the process by means of which a church (body) truly takes over as its own a resolution that it did not originate as to its self, and acknowledges the measure it promulgates as a rule applicable to its own life. . . . It includes a degree of consent, and possibly of judgment, in which the life of a body is expressed which brings into play its own, original spiritual resources."[33] The analogous concept in civil law is ratification, as it was applied, for example, to *The Constitution of the United States,* on the basis of "the two cardinal principles that came to define the ideal standard: that a constitution should be proposed by a convention elected for that purpose alone [in this case, by a synod or council], and subsequently ratified through some mechanisms of popular consent."[34] Traditionally, the conclusion of *The Thirty-Nine Articles of the Church of England* contains a section that even carries the heading "The Ratification," which explains the reception of the confession: "This Book of

30. Hauck 1907.
31. Grillmeier 1970; Congar 1972.
32. See, for example, Hazeltine 1926, 754–55.
33. Congar 1972, 45.
34. Rakove 1996, 98; see his entire chapter, "The Concept of Ratification," 94–130.

Articles before rehearsed, is again approved, and allowed to be holden and executed within the realm, by the assent and consent of our Sovereign Lady Elizabeth. . . . Which Articles were deliberately read, and confirmed again by the subscription of the hands of the archbishop and bishops of the upper-house, and by the subscription of the whole clergy of the nether-house in their convocation."[35]

A particular version of the problem of ratification and reception became one of the issues in the conflict between East and West. It was an incontrovertible historical—and geographical—fact that all seven of the councils acknowledged to have been "ecumenical" were held in the East, all but one of them (Ephesus in 431) at or quite near New Rome, Constantinople. It is difficult to draw any firm statistical conclusions from the often imprecise, and sometimes even symbolical, reports of the number of bishops in attendance: "318" at Nicaea I because of the number of servants whom Abraham enlisted to fight in his rescue of Lot;[36] "630" at Chalcedon because of the numerical value of the first two consonants of the name "Chalcedon" in Greek, chi and lambda.[37] But at all seven of these councils there do seem to have been many more Eastern participants than Western (and at Constantinople I in 381, only Eastern bishops), although it would be a mistake to overlook the deference repeatedly accorded, also by Eastern bishops, to representatives of the bishop of Old Rome. The councils had, moreover, been convoked by the emperor, not by the bishops or patriarchs acting solely on their own authority, much less by the bishop and patriarch of Old Rome acting unilaterally on his own authority. But Pope Gregory the Great not only composed what we are calling here *The Creed of Pope Gregory I;*[38] but as part of his broadening definition of the authority of the bishop of Rome, he also formulated a special theory of the authority of the councils. On one hand, speaking about the first four councils, those of Nicaea I, Constantinople I, Ephesus, and Chalcedon, he affirmed: "In like manner all the four synods of the holy universal church we receive as we do the four books of the

35. *39 Art* con.
36. Gen 14.4.
37. See L'Huillier 1996, 85n. 10 on Nicaea, 303n. 48 on Chalcedon.
38. *Greg I.*

holy Gospels." But on the other hand he asserted that "without the authority and consent of the Apostolic See [i.e., of Rome], none of the
matters transacted [by a council] have any binding force," and he reserved to the Apostolic See of Rome the right on its own authority to
annul the acts of any synod or council, regardless of its auspices.[39] That
is what happened to the canons of the First Council of Constantinople
and of the Council of Chalcedon on the position of the patriarch of
Constantinople.[40]

It would appear, then, that reception always implies the possibility of nonreception.[41] Therefore the best way to clarify the process
and meaning of reception historically would seem to be by examining two statements of faith that have failed to achieve it. By contrast
with the assembly at Ephesus in 431, which came to be acknowledged
as the third ecumenical council, the "robber synod of Ephesus [latro-
cinium Ephesinum]" of 449 was given that epithet by Pope Leo I, and
the name has stuck.[42] Harnack's witticism about "the Council of Chalcedon, which to distinguish it from the Robber Council we might call
the Robber and Traitor Council,"[43] is certainly an extreme judgment.
Nevertheless there were, on the face of it, several noteworthy parallels,
not only between Ephesus 449 and Chalcedon 451, but especially between Ephesus 431 and Ephesus 449.[44] Both Ephesus 431 and Ephesus
449 were summoned by Emperor Theodosius II, the latter of them on
30 March 449, in response to an appeal that had been addressed to
"the holy council of the bishops of Rome, Alexandria, Jerusalem, and
Thessalonica." The number of bishops in attendance was nearly the
same: at the session of Ephesus 431 on 22 June, at which Mary was
declared to be "Theotokos," nearly 160; at Ephesus 449, about 140.
Both councils were dominated by the patriarch of Alexandria, who
was Cyril in 431 and Dioscorus in 449, and a plausible historical case
could be made for the thesis that Dioscorus acted no more highhand-

39. *Chr Trad* 1:335, 354.
40. See chapter 4.2 above, "Doctrines of Church Order East and West."
41. See O'Gara 1988 on the First Vatican Council.
42. Grillmeier-Bacht 1951–54, 1:213–42, 2:197–231.
43. Harnack [1893] 1961b, 4:196.
44. Vogt 1993 is a careful examination of Ephesus 431; Horn 1982 is a comparison of the role of Pope Leo at Ephesus 449 and at Chalcedon.

edly at the later council than Cyril had at the earlier one. Both councils condemned the bishop of Constantinople, who was Nestorius in 431 and Flavian in 449. In his appeal at the end of Ephesus 449, Theodosius II, exercising the traditional function of the emperor, confirmed its decrees and called upon all the bishops of his empire to reaffirm their subscription to *The Niceno-Constantinopolitan Creed* and to refrain from electing as bishop any supporter of the heretical patriarchs of Constantinople, Nestorius and Flavian. On purely procedural rather than doctrinal grounds, therefore—not to mention considerations of Realpolitik, whether civil or ecclesiastical—it seems difficult to explain why Ephesus 431 should stand on the books as the third ecumenical council and Ephesus 449 as the robber synod. As Congar wrily comments, "the history of the third Council was hardly such as to allow it to be considered as properly ecumenical."[45] But the fundamental juridical difference between 431 and 449 was in their reception, particularly the response of Pope Leo I, whose *Tome* of 449, addressed to Patriarch Flavian of Constantinople, whom the synod of 449 deposed, served as a foundation for *The Definition of Faith of the Council of Chalcedon* of 451.[46]

By comparison with Ephesus 449, or for that matter even with Ephesus 431, there was a far more massive preponderance of forces in attendance and initially in favor of the Eastern Orthodox reception of the decree promulgated by the Council of Florence on 6 July 1439, *Laetentur coeli*. They included on the Eastern side the patriarch of Constantinople, Joseph II, and the Byzantine emperor, John VIII Palaeologus. The issue of reception was, moreover, receiving careful attention from the Western proponents of conciliar authority at this very time.[47] Part of the case for the reception of a statement of faith issued by a council usually depends on the sense that the doctrines at issue have received thorough examination and therefore that there has not been a rush to judgment. On those grounds, the effort of Florence to cut through the controversies over the Filioque could be presented as the outcome of all those treatises over so many centuries on both sides of

45. Congar 1972, 46.
46. Grillmeier-Bacht 1951–54, 1:1–242, 389–418.
47. Krämer 1980.

the debates about the doctrine of the double procession of the Holy Spirit. The confession of the council substitutes the formula "from the Father *through* the Son [*ex Patre per Filium*]" for "from the Father *and* the Son" (which the East rejected as erroneous), but also for "from the Father" only (which the West regarded as incomplete, in spite of its having been the original language of *The Niceno-Constantinopolitan Creed*). Ephesus 431 under the dominance of the *Anathematisms* of Cyril, as well as Ephesus 449 with its lumping of the Nestorianism condemned in 431 and the entire school of Antioch, could be represented as the victory of a single theological party. But *The Creed of Florence* could be interpreted as having imitated *The Definition of Faith of the Council of Chalcedon* in bringing into one statement of faith the valid point being made by each party while rejecting the extremes at both ends of the spectrum.[48]

Yet *The Creed of Florence* failed of acceptance and reception by the Eastern church.[49] Like the Union of Florence itself, the opposition to the union was a composite of popular beliefs, theological scholarship, political realism, military strategy, and pragmatic concern.[50] The objections of the Church of Moscow to the union, by which its implementation was effectively blocked and which were followed not long thereafter by the establishment of the patriarchate of Moscow in 1589, constituted in some respects the most decisive veto of the reception of Florence.[51] Doctrinally, the most authoritative voice in opposition was that of Marcus Eugenicus, metropolitan of Ephesus, who wrote not only an *Encyclical Letter* against it, but a *Confession of Faith*.[52] But what Ihor Ševčenko has called the "repercussions" of the Council of Florence,[53] direct and indirect, were to continue for centuries, also in the Ukrainian *Union of Brest* in 1595, and a century later in *The Union of Užhorod*.

---

48. See chapter 7.3 above, "Creeds and Confessions as Instruments of Concord."
49. See also chapter 12.2 below, "Popular Religion, the Rule of Prayer, and Tradition."
50. Geanakoplos 1966.
51. *Prav Slov* 2:2446–54. Documents and analysis in Krajčar 1976.
52. *Mark Eph.*
53. Ševčenko 1955.

9.3. The Enforcement of Orthodoxy

Like any other law, a creedal law requiring orthodox teaching must be enforced to be effective. But historically, it should be noted in this connection that the authority of a creed or confession has not always been necessary for the achievement and the enforcement of doctrinal conformity. Thus it would be highly misleading to come to any conclusions about the doctrinal orthodoxy of Thomas and Alexander Campbell or of their followers, who eventually became the Disciples of Christ (or simply "Christians"), only on the basis of their "confessional principle," or rather their proclaimed lack thereof. For on paper, as in Thomas Campbell's *Propositions* of 1809,[54] they rejected the legitimacy of any dogmas and of any confessions or creeds, even of *The Apostles' Creed*, as "religious impositions practiced upon the credulity of less favored ages than the present," and hence as "both the cause and the effect of partyism, and the main perpetuating causes of schism." They urged instead the sole authority of the New Testament, in relation to which even the canonical Old Testament occupied a secondary position.[55] Opponents—Roman Catholic defenders of the inseparability of Scripture and tradition as well as those Protestants, both Reformed and Lutheran, who combined an insistence on *sola Scriptura* (which, in principle, they had in common) with the affirmation of confessions, both universal and particular—predicted that such independence from creeds would inevitably lead to doctrinal anarchy and to the "diversities of opinions" of which *The Irish Articles of Religion* of 1615 speak and which those articles are designed to "avoid."[56] Although Alexander Campbell, in turn, charged such confessional Protestants with fundamental inconsistency for affirming the sole authority of the Bible in theory but compromising it in practice, their dire predictions appeared to be coming true in the twentieth century, when some theologians belonging to the Disciples of Christ, with apparent impunity, did seem to deny such basic doctrines of the mainstream creedal and confessional tradition as the Trinity and the incarnation. But, whether or not it was

54. *Dec Addr.*
55. *Chr Trad* 5:269–70.
56. *Irish* pr; see chapter 8.4 above, "The Politics of Confessional Diversity."

in turn also inconsistent of them to do so, the early generations of the Disciples of Christ, together with a substantial part of the membership of that denomination in later generations, actually taught much of what the creeds taught. Eventually they even drafted a doctrinal statement that could almost be called a "confession."[57] On those same doctrines of the Trinity and the incarnation, therefore, they held to a doctrinal consensus that they shared with other Christians, whether Roman Catholics or Eastern Orthodox or Anglicans or confessional Protestants, who adhered to the historic creeds. Similarly, the English Congregationalists of Campbell's time felt able to boast in their confession "that, notwithstanding their jealousy of subscription to creeds and articles, and their disapproval of the imposition of any human standard, whether of faith or discipline, they are far more agreed in their doctrines and practices than any church which enjoins subscription and enforces a human standard of orthodoxy."[58]

The controversies over the verbal inspiration and the literal inerrancy of the Bible that ravaged several Protestant denominations, especially but not exclusively in the United States, during the nineteenth and twentieth centuries also manifested an ambiguous relationship with confessionalism. The earliest Reformation formularies of the sixteenth century fail to incorporate a doctrine of biblical inspiration and inerrancy, in part no doubt because this teaching was not a point of controversy and—with sometimes rather considerable variations of emphasis, as there had been already in the early church and the Middle Ages[59]—was the common property of all the contending parties. During the seventeenth century, several new confessions began to compensate for that inadequacy, some of them, such as *The Westminster Confession of Faith* of 1647, teaching in so many words that the books of the Bible "are given by inspiration of God" and that they are, in their original languages, "immediately inspired by God, and, by his singular care and providence kept pure in all ages."[60] When, during the nineteenth and twentieth centuries, the combined impact of the

57. *Design* (1968).
58. *Eng Dec* 1.7.
59. Kropatschek 1904, 423–35.
60. *West* 1.2; 1.8.

historical-critical study of the Bible and of perceived contradictions between the biblical account of creation and modern science made the
inspiration and inerrancy of the Bible the most burning of all doctrinal issues for several churches, some of these seventeenth-century affirmations, for example the Presbyterian *Westminster Confession of Faith,*
were still part of the corpus of confessional standards, although more
recent quasi-confessional statements had diminished their authority.[61]
Others, like *The Reaffirmed Consensus of the Truly Lutheran Faith* of
1655, which taught that Scripture was "written by the inspiration of
God, who provided the content and dictated the words [*Deo inspirante,
suggerente et dictante*],"[62] had not achieved such adoption. Hence there
appeared to be need for still further supplementation.[63] But it is not at
all clear that the presence of such confessional affirmations concerning
the Bible made the enforcement of the doctrine of inerrancy and the
exercise of discipline against those who were accused of denying it any
more effective in the Presbyterian and Lutheran churches of the United
States, which were overtly confessional in their doctrinal standards and
relatively centralized in their ecclesiastical administrations, than in the
less centralized and less confessional Southern Baptist Convention[64] or
in American Evangelicalism and Fundamentalism generally.[65]

Even though the absence of a detailed doctrine of the plenary
and verbal inspiration of the Bible in the classic confessions of the
Reformation period appeared to make confessional authority a blunt
weapon just at the time when it was needed most, the fact remains that
through most of the history of the creedal and confessional churches
their doctrinal discipline has been closely tied to the enforcement of
their confessions. As the procedures of doctrinal enforcement from the
age of Constantine to the time of the Protestant Reformation and well
beyond it demonstrate, the alliance between the spiritual and the secular arms provided some of the most efficient mechanisms of creedal
enforcement.[66] It is under its article entitled "On the Political Magis-

61. *Aub.*
62. *Cons rep* 2.6.
63. See chapter 5.4 above, "Confessional Rules of Biblical Hermeneutics."
64. *Abst Prin* 1; *Am Bap* 1, 3. See Syndogmaticon 8.14.
65. *Camb Dec* 1.
66. See chapter 8.2 above, "Civil Law on Adherence to Creeds."

tracy," not in its article on the church and ministry or in one on the confessions, that a post-Reformation Lutheran confession lays down the requirement of confessional conformity.[67] But even while that was going on, and especially with the gradual breakup of the alliance between church and state and their eventual separation, the churches developed additional instruments and legislation of their own to require legal compliance with their public doctrine. A special case of enforcement and of reception—or more precisely, of ongoing reception as distinct from initial reception—is the church law in many different Christian communions requiring the affirmation of loyalty to a confession and legal compliance with it, often referred to as confessional subscription, or, in the comprehensive phrase of *The King's Confession* of 1581, "our confession, promise, oath, and subscription."[68] It has been defined in English usage as "a declaration of one's assent *to* articles of religion, or some formal declaration of principles, etc., by signing one's name; *spec.* in the Church of England, assent to the Thirty-nine Articles."[69] Several specific historical examples may serve to highlight some of the theological, intellectual, and moral questions raised by confessional subscription.

9.4. Confessional Subscription as Legal Compliance

Many of the theological issues of confessional subscription were raised first by the Lutheran Reformation, and have continued to be of special concern to its heirs.[70] Partly this was so because *The Augsburg Confession* came so early, as one of the first (though not the very first) of the confessions of the Protestant Reformation. Another reason is that "the theologians of *The Augsburg Confession*," as they began calling themselves already in the sixteenth century,[71] were from the very beginning preoccupied with pure doctrine, to the point of making the *doctrina evangelii* and a pure understanding of it constitutive of the church and

67. *Cons rep* 16.78.
68. *Scot II.*
69. *OED* 10–II:44, with apposite quotations; italics original.
70. *Def Plat* 1.1; *Br St Luth* 45–48; Walther [1858] 1972; Friedrich Bente in *Triglotta* 1:7–9.
71. *Form Conc Epit* 1.

its unity.[72] Just as the names of princes and free cities appended to the original presentation of *The Augsburg Confession* to Emperor Charles V in 1530 belong to the initial reception of the confession, so also the developing use of *The Augsburg Confession* and then, after 1580, of the entire *Book of Concord* as a required norm for ordination and affiliation became the first, or nearly the first, instance of the requirement of confessional subscription.[73]

But the status of such subscription became more complicated, and in ways that presaged the later ramifications of the issues both of confessional subscription and of confessional hermeneutics in the nineteenth and twentieth centuries, as a result of the revisions in the text of *The Augsburg Confession* leading to the *Confessio Augustana Variata* of 1540. Some of the same irenic concerns that had inspired Philip Melanchthon in the original (and official) version of *The Augsburg Confession* to formulate the Lutheran teachings in such a way, as the confession itself says, that "nothing . . . departs from the Scriptures or the catholic church or the church of Rome, in so far as the ancient church is known to us from its writers,"[74] now produced a version of *The Augsburg Confession* that was *variata* in the opposite direction of accommodations to Reformed Protestantism at a number of crucial passages. The most important of these changes affected the doctrine of the real presence of the body and blood of Christ in the eucharist, over which Luther disputed much more vigorously and bitterly against other Protestants during the last two decades of his life than he did over the doctrine of transubstantiation against the scholastics and the followers of *The Lateran Creed*. For the original formulation of 1530, "Our churches teach that the body and blood of Christ are truly present [*vere adsint*] and are distributed to those who eat in the supper of the Lord. They disapprove of those who teach otherwise,"[75] the *Variata* substitutes the words "with the bread and wine the body and blood of Christ are truly shown forth [*exhibeantur*]," and it omits

---

72. *Aug Lat* 7.2; see chapter 3.3 above, " 'Doctrines' and Doctrine."
73. Ritschl 1908–27, 1:193–403.
74. *Aug Lat* con 1.
75. *Aug Lat* 10; see *Lat 1215* 3.

any condemnation of opposing doctrine.[76] It was, therefore, to *"The Confession of Augsburg,"* but "as it was explained by the author" as *The Confession of the Waldenses* of 1655 formulates the qualification,[77] that John Calvin and some of his followers were willing to affix their subscription.[78] But they were opposed by the insistence of the strictly confessional Lutherans on the authority of "the symbol of our time, the first and unaltered [*ungeänderte*] Augsburg Confession."[79]

A particularly intriguing version of confessional subscription during the sixteenth and seventeenth centuries is the status of *The Thirty-Nine Articles of the Church of England* of 1571. The so-called Royal Declaration of 1628, composed by Archbishop William Laud in the name of King Charles I and often attached to the printed text of *The Thirty-Nine Articles,* seems, on the face of it, to define the status of the confession and of subscription to it quite unequivocally:

> That for the present, though some differences have been ill raised, yet we take comfort in this, that all clergymen within our realm have always most willingly *subscribed to* the articles established. Which is an argument to us that they all agree in *the true, usual, literal meaning of the said articles,* and that even in those curious points, in which the present differences lie, men of all sorts take the Articles of the Church of England to be for them. Which is an argument again, that none of them intend any desertion of the articles established. . . .
>
> That if any public reader in either of our universities, or any head or master of a college, or any other person respectively in either of them, shall affix any new sense to any article, or shall publicly read, determine, or hold any public disputation, or suffer any such to be held either way, in either the universities or colleges respectively; or if any divine in the universities

---

76. *Aug Var* 10.
77. *Wald* 33.
78. See the brief discussion in McNeill 1957, 197–98.
79. *Form Conc Epit* pr 4.

shall preach or print any thing either way, other than
is already established in convocation with our royal assent, he, or they the offenders, shall be liable to our
displeasure, and the church's censure in our commission ecclesiastical, as well as any other. And we will
see there shall be due execution upon them.[80]

Not many years later, however, it was King Charles himself who suffered the ultimate kind of "due execution," on 30 January 1649, as
Archbishop Laud also had four years earlier on 10 January 1645. The
ambiguity of confessional subscription in the Church of England was
being further compounded at this same time by the problem of reception as applied to the ultra-Calvinistic *Canons of the Synod of Dort* of
1618–19, whose signatories included the delegates of the Church of
England as the first among the churches represented by groups of delegates from various nations.[81] Such Anglican "subscription" to Dort (if
it is fair to call it that) came in spite of the deep hostility of many
seventeenth-century Anglicans to the Calvinist doctrines of total de-
pravity, limited atonement, and double predestination that were at the
heart of *The Canons of the Synod of Dort*.

　　These two instances from the sixteenth and seventeenth centuries set much of the pattern of confessional subscription, whether
Lutheran or Anglican, and therefore defined many of the issues for
subsequent times. Nevertheless, the nineteenth and twentieth centuries
witnessed some of the most dramatic examples of how these issues
worked concretely in the life of the churches.[82] Karl Gottlieb Bretschneider, like many of his German Protestant contemporaries at the
end of the eighteenth and the beginning of the nineteenth century,
experienced grave personal doubts about the morality and intellectual honesty of subscription to the Reformation confessions but finally
did not permit these compunctions to deter him from studying theology, being ordained into the ministry, and even rising to the office
of *Generalsuperintendent*. One answer he found to the dilemma of subscription was the effort, as expressed in the Prussian Union, to bring

80. Forbes 1890, l–li; italics added.
81. *Dort* con.
82. On the issue as a whole, see Hall 1995.

about a reconciliation between the Lutheran and the Reformed confessions and a union between the two churches.[83] But in addition to
his participation in that effort to transcend the differences between
Reformed and Lutheran in the name of a single "Evangelical Church
[*evangelische Kirche*]" or "United Church [*unierte Kirche*]," Bretschneider also confronted the question of subscription head-on in a special
treatise on the subject, published in 1841. With quotations from the
confessions he strove to prove that in the context of Reformation theology the very idea of confessional subscription as legal compliance,
and therefore the idea of the enforcement of confessional orthodoxy
as "confessional coercion [*Symbolzwang*]," constituted a contradiction
in terms that ran contrary both to the spirit and to the letter of the
sixteenth-century formularies themselves.[84] In this he was articulating
a widely held position.

Another case study was supplied by the Modernist crisis in
the Roman Catholic Church. Different though they are in form and in
force from the Protestant confessions of faith, *The Doctrinal Decrees
of the Council of Trent* and *The Tridentine Profession of Faith*—and, in
considerable measure, even *The Dogmatic Constitution on the Catholic Faith of the First Vatican Council*—share the lacuna noted earlier,
a lack of detailed attention to the implications of historical and critical study as applied to Scripture and the Christian tradition. That lack
enabled several leading Roman Catholic scholars, usually identified as
Modernists, to advance the claim that they were not transgressing the
boundaries of official church teaching when they propounded radical
interpretations of Scripture.[85] When neither the usual course of theological controversy nor the ordinary magisterium of the church nor
doctrinal discipline succeeded in getting rid of such ideas but, on the
contrary, threatened to foment further scandals and divisions, Pope
Pius X in the decree *Lamentabili* of 1907 itemized eleven errors having
to do with the inspiration and inerrancy of Scripture.[86] In the encyclical *Pascendi dominici gregis* of the same year he condemned their re-

83. Bretschneider 1841, 15; *PRE* 3:389–91 (Karl Rudolf Hagenbach).
84. Bretschneider 1841, 40–49.
85. *Chr Trad* 5:298–99, 325–26.
86. *Lam* 9–19.

duction of the inspiration of the biblical writers to (qualitatively if not quantitatively) nothing more than the impulse by which "any believer is prompted to express his faith in word or writing [*verbo scriptove*]." [87] In *Sacrorum antistitum,* his *motu proprio* of 1 September 1910, therefore, he legislated the requirement that Roman Catholic teachers of theology take the following "anti-Modernist" oath: "I firmly embrace and accept, collectively and separately, everything that has been defined, affirmed, and declared by the inerrant magisterium of the church, especially those chief doctrines that are specifically directed against the errors of this time," which are then enumerated in detail and many of which pertain to the issues raised by the Modernists; in *Ad tuendam fidem* of 1998 this was expanded to include "the truths of the Catholic faith which the church, in the course of time and under the guidance of the Holy Spirit, 'who will teach the whole truth' (Jn 16.13), has even more deeply explored and will continue to explore." [88]

As many of the texts presented in later sections of Part Five of *Creeds and Confessions of Faith in the Christian Tradition* suggest, consideration of confessional subscription becomes especially pointed when those who have subscribed to historic confessions of faith engage in programs of union and reconciliation with others who have subscribed to the same confessions, or especially with those who have traditionally subscribed to other confessions. If the reconciliation takes place within a confessional family, [89] as was the case early in the twentieth century with *The Reunion of the Cumberland Presbyterian with the Presbyterian Church, U.S.A.* of 1906, [90] the reconciling parties must deal with the question of the adequacy of a confessional standard that each of them has hitherto regarded as sufficient, even though the confession and subscription to it had not managed to hold together or to bring together all who subscribed it. If the reconciliation brings together two or more parties who have been separated for several centuries, as for example *The Leuenberg Agreement* [*Konkordie reformatorischen Kirchen in Europa*] of 1973 does for Lutheran and Reformed churches

87. *Pasc.*
88. *Sacr ant; Ad tuendam* 2.
89. *Un Ref Ch* (Reformed) 1972/81/97/2000; *Morav Am* (Moravian) 1995.
90. *Un Pres; Pres USA.*

in Europe,[91] or for a great many centuries, as for example the *Common Christological Declaration Between the Catholic Church and the Assyrian Church of the East* of November 1994 at least begins to do,[92] those who have hitherto adhered to one of the confessions will be in the position of being obliged to explain to other members of their confessional family why the reconciliation does not represent a fundamental compromise of their previous confessional stance. Such is the claim being made by *The Leuenberg Agreement,* that it "leaves intact the binding force of the confessions within the participating churches" and "is not to be regarded as a new confession of faith," but "sets forth a consensus . . . which makes church fellowship possible between churches of different confessional positions."[93] And when, as in the successive documents coming out of the negotiations that led to the creation of the Church of South India and other such unions,[94] the participating groups have all been missionary daughters of mother churches, each of whom has its own particular confessional statements of one or another sort and most of whom have never succeeded in effecting similar concordats at home with their counterparts, there is no avoiding the problem of the potential contradiction between old and new confessional loyalties.[95]

These historical examples, which could easily be amplified by other instances from the history of creeds and confessions of faith as discussed throughout this volume, raise a host of questions about subscription, among which, in the present chapter, the theological questions are the most pressing. The first of these, like so many other theological questions, has been formulated in Latin, for example in one post-Reformation Lutheran confession,[96] and then again in a doctrinally similar twentieth-century reaffirmation.[97] Both of these neo-Reformation confessions require a "categorical" subscription to the

91. *Leuen.*
92. *Chr Dec.*
93. *Leuen* 37.
94. *CSI 1929; CSI 1947;* also *Ghana.*
95. See chapter 4.4 above, "Faith and Order in the Ecumenical Confessional Dialogue."
96. *Cons rep* 16.78.
97. *Br St Luth* 47.

Lutheran confessions, not a "conditional" one: not "*quatenus* [in so far as]" the confessions are in agreement with Scripture, but "*quia* [because]" they are. A *quia* would seem to imply that loyalty to the teaching of these confessions is tantamount to loyalty to the teaching of Scripture. Critics found this implication concerning the confessions to represent an inherent contradiction with the principle of *sola Scriptura*, as those very confessions of the Protestant Reformation vigorously espoused it in opposition to such formulas as that of *The Canons and Decrees of the Council of Trent:* "The council accepts and venerates with a like feeling of piety and reverence all the books of both the Old and the New Testament . . . as well as the traditions concerning both faith and conduct . . . which have been preserved in unbroken sequence in the Catholic Church."[98] Did the Lutheran *quia*-subscription to *The Book of Concord* (and the Reformed equivalents of such subscription, for example to *The Westminster Confession of Faith*) smuggle the authority of tradition back in—even when the tradition was the doctrine that only Scripture, and not tradition, was to be the authority? The reply to this objection was that a confessional subscription *quatenus* was meaningless and unenforceable.[99] It provided only an illusory protection against being "tossed to and fro and carried about with every wind of doctrine."[100] Subscribing to a creed only "to the extent that" it agreed with Scripture carried with it no specification of just what that extent was. After all, as the rhetorical argument put it, a Christian could subscribe even to the Qur'ān to the extent that it harmonized with the Bible, for example in teaching monotheism or ascribing authority to Moses and to Jesus.[101]

The other theological question, though not identical with the first, is generically related to it: Does subscription to a creed or confession extend only to the doctrines stated in it, or also to other matters, to its historical, political, scientific, and moral judgments, and above all to its interpretations of specific passages of the Bible?[102] Once again,

98. *Trent* 4.
99. Walther [1858] 1972, 64–70.
100. Eph 4.14.
101. Walther [1858] 1972, 58.
102. See chapter 5.4 above, "Confessional Rules of Biblical Hermeneutics."

the alternatives could be put in ways that were equally unpalatable.[103] If the interpretations of specific passages of the Bible were not covered by subscription, that seemed to mean that loyalty to the creed required acceptance of its doctrines even if the biblical exegesis leading to those doctrines proved to be unacceptable or at any rate inconclusive, as when a particular creedal doctrine was apparently dependent on an allegorical or typological reading of a biblical passage. For example, the strictly exegetical case for the doctrine of *Maria semper virgo*, the perpetual virginity of Mary, rested at least in part on the typological interpretation of such Old Testament passages as "This gate shall remain shut . . . ; for the Lord, the God of Israel, has entered by it."[104] The *semper virgo* was part of the Catholic tradition in both East and West,[105] and was repeated in those Latin words even by some Protestant statements of faith representing several confessional traditions, including the Lutheran *Smalcald Articles*,[106] the Hussite *[First] Bohemian Confession*,[107] Zwingli's *Reckoning of the Faith*,[108] and the Reformed *Second Helvetic Confession*.[109] To this interpretation, therefore, the literal meaning of all the references in the New Testament to "brothers" of Jesus was to be subordinated.[110] But if the scriptural exegesis of the creeds and confessions, and not only their doctrine, was normative, that seemed to undercut the imperative to "search the Scriptures,"[111] because such "searching" would be precluded a priori from finding anything that contradicted what is already in the confessions.

That issue, in turn, has raised serious moral questions for many. One of these is the compatibility of confessional subscription with the freedom of conscience, including academic freedom and the professional obligations of biblical scholars and other theological scholars, which are therefore also professional rights. The circumstances under which the medieval authorities extracted from Beren-

103. Bretschneider 1841, 66–94.
104. Ez 44.2.
105. Athanasius *Discourses Against the Arians* 2.70 (NPNF–II 4:386).
106. *Smal Art* 1.4.
107. *Boh I* 17.4.
108. *Fid rat* 1; also *Hub Chr Cat* 2.14.
109. *Helv II* 11.4.
110. Mt 12.46, 13.55; Mk 3.31; Jn 2.12, 7.3,5; 1 Cor 9.5; Gal 1.19.
111. Jn 5.39; cited, for example, in *West* 1.8.

gar of Tours the two confessions of faith headed *Ego Berengarius,*[112] which forever after bear his name, represented duress and even torture. But this is by no means an isolated case in Christian history. As noted earlier, *The Declaration on Religious Freedom of the Second Vatican Council* acknowledges, though without citing this or other specific instances, that "at times in the life of the people of God, as it has pursued its pilgrimage through the twists and turns of human history, there have been ways of acting hardly in tune with the spirit of the gospel, indeed contrary to it."[113] Closely related to freedom of conscience is the question of sheer honesty. In subscribing *The Thirty-Nine Articles of the Church of England,* according to one of the characters in John Henry Newman's autobiographical roman à clef (quoting Samuel Johnson, but without attribution), "we only sign the Articles as articles of peace; not as really holding them, but as not opposing them. Therefore, when we sign the Articles, we only engage not to preach against them."[114] As the author's personal experience had proved in the controversy over his "Tract Ninety," such an opinion about confessional subscription raised more questions of confessional hermeneutics than it solved.

9.5. Rules of Confessional Hermeneutics

The status of a creed or confession, or of any other law, depends in considerable measure on its interpretation, and therefore on the hermeneutical principles applied to it by later generations.[115] As there are confessional rules of biblical hermeneutics,[116] therefore, so there need to be rules of confessional hermeneutics. But as the early church had used its oral tradition and then the New Testament to determine its hermeneutics for the Old Testament, and then had used the tradition and its creeds and confessions to determine its hermeneutics for the New Testament, so the churches eventually had to develop rules of hermeneutics also for the creeds and confessions themselves. The need for such hermeneutical rules erupted already after 325, with the furi-

112. *Brngr 1059; Brngr 1079.*
113. *Vat II 9.12.*
114. John Henry Newman *Loss and Gain,* ch 15.
115. Garet 1985.
116. See chapter 5.4 above, "Confessional Rules of Biblical Hermeneutics."

ous controversies over the interpretation of *The Creed of Nicaea* that eventually led to the First Council of Constantinople of 381 and the issuance of *The Niceno-Constantinopolitan Creed*. The designation of a creed as unchangeable, and the consequent practice of reciting such an unchangeable creed, *The Niceno-Constantinopolitan Creed* in most cases, at later councils called to address theological questions that had not been, at least in this form, addressed in that creed, necessitated the development of hermeneutical principles for the interpretation of one creed by another.[117]

One of the most explicit confessional formulations of a hermeneutic for the interpretation of creeds and confessions of faith came in the opening words of *The Wittenberg Articles,* adopted jointly by Lutherans and Anglicans in 1536: "We confess simply and clearly, without any ambiguity, that we believe, hold, teach, and defend everything which is in the canon of the Bible and in the three creeds, i.e. the Apostles', Nicene, and Athanasian Creeds, *in the same meaning which the creeds themselves intend and in which the approved holy fathers use and defend them.*"[118] The primary confessions of those two communions, *The Augsburg Confession* of 1530 and *The Thirty-Nine Articles of the Church of England* of 1571, which, as has been noted earlier in this chapter, have been historically fundamental to the analysis of the problems of confessional subscription, have also been among the most vigorously contested texts in the debates over confessional hermeneutics. What did the juxtaposition of "Catholic substance and Protestant principle"[119] in the Reformation and its confessions imply for the interpretation of these two confessions: a "correction" of the more Protestant elements of *The Thirty-Nine Articles of the Church of England*[120] on the basis of the more Catholic substance still retained in *The Book of Common Prayer*? a "correction" of the more Catholic elements of *The Augsburg Confession*[121] in the light of the more radically Protestant

---

117. See chapter 1.1 above, "Continuity versus Change in the Decrees of the Ecumenical Councils."
118. *Witt Art* 1; italics added.
119. See chapter 16.3 below, "Catholic Substance and Protestant Principle in Reformation Confessions."
120. *39 Art* 20.
121. *Aug Lat* con 1.

principles by which, supposedly, "the young Luther" had become the Reformer in the first place?

There had long been a question about the hermeneutics of *The Book of Concord*, above all about the limitations that subscription to *The Formula of Concord* of 1577, the last of the confessional documents in the collection of *The Book of Concord* of 1580, placed on the interpretation of *The Augsburg Confession*, which was the first of the strictly confessional documents in it (although Luther's *Small Catechism* and *Large Catechism* had been written in the preceding year). Behind these lay the problem of the interpretation of *The Apostles' Creed*, *The Niceno-Constantinopolitan Creed* in its *Western Recension,* and *The Athanasian Creed*, which stand at the beginning of *The Book of Concord*. For the controversy over the *Confessio Augustana Variata* of 1540 concerned not only the legality of Melanchthon's largely unilateral changes as they affected the latitude of subscription to the original *Augsburg Confession* of 1530 by such Reformed theologians as John Calvin, but their implications for the interpretation of that fundamental text. One of the twentieth-century translators of *The Book of Concord* into English in 1959, Theodore G. Tappert, summarized a widely held consensus about the "three major points of reference" for the hermeneutics of the Lutheran confessions: Martin Luther, the pre-Reformation church, and the Bible.[122] Another member of this team of translators into English, Arthur Carl Piepkorn, stated what he saw to be the principle and procedure for its interpretation:

> We are to understand and confess the Symbols in their original historic sense—that is, in the sense which the words and terms had when the documents in question were formulated, and not in the sense which some of the words and terms may subsequently have acquired through the dialectic of controversy. Thus we must not read into the Catholic Creeds as pre-Reformation documents the sense with which the Reformers may have invested certain of their terms; similarly we must not read into the particular creeds of the sixteenth cen-

122. Tappert 1947, 359–65.

tury the sense with which subsequent systematizers of
Lutheran doctrinal insights invested certain terms.[123]

In both of these prescriptions, confessional hermeneutics and confessional subscription came together.

But a divergent hermeneutical method, which developed during the latter half of the nineteenth century and the first half of the twentieth, "reversed the long-established order and interpreted the creeds and confessions of the Reformation in the light of the teaching of the Reformers, instead of adapting the dynamic faith of the Reformation to the doctrines of the creeds."[124] That method strove to adjust the interpretation of the Lutheran confessions to what was regarded as a more "dynamic" interpretation of Reformation teaching in place of what was taken to be the "static" confessionalist one. New attention to Luther's works, not only to the three confessions of which he is the author (the two *Catechisms* and *The Smalcald Articles*), but especially to his early writings, above all the newly discovered *Lectures on Romans* of 1516, provided this hermeneutic with a powerful tool for an existential and dynamic reinterpretation of Luther, to which *The Augsburg Confession* and a fortiori *The Formula of Concord* were to be subordinated. Coinciding as it did with the efforts at confessional rapprochement between the Reformed and Lutheran churches of Germany during the century and a half that began with the Prussian Union of 1817 and closed with *The Barmen Declaration* of 1934, *The Arnoldshain Theses* of 1957, and *The Leuenberg Agreement* of 1973,[125] this reinterpretation of confessional authority led many to a reinterpretation of confessional hermeneutics as well. As a result, according to the confessionalist polemic of Werner Elert, there emerged the contrast between "two kinds of Lutheranism—the one, that which is contained in the confessions; the other, that which found its most fitting expression in the theology of the professors of the nineteenth century . . . , [which] has again set up an objective norm for what Lutheranism should mean in its original sense. This norm is the 'young Luther.'"[126]

123. Piepkorn 1993, 19–20.
124. Pauck 1961, 334.
125. *Barm; Arn; Leuen.*
126. Elert 1962, 9–10.

During the same period, an analogous hermeneutical effort, although one that moved in the opposite direction—not away from the vestigial catholic substance of the Reformation confessions but toward a supposed catholic consensus—was being applied to *The Thirty-Nine Articles of the Church of England*. One of the most celebrated of all the controversies anywhere over confessional hermeneutics erupted in response to John Henry Newman's "Remarks on Certain Passages in the Thirty-Nine Articles," which was published on 27 February 1841 as the ninetieth—and, as it turned out because of the storm it raised, the last—of the *Tracts for the Times*.[127] This series had been coming out from Newman and other "Tractarian" leaders of the Oxford Movement in Anglicanism since 1833.[128] Newman's purpose in "Tract Ninety," as he said in his introduction, was "to show that, while our Prayer Book is acknowledged on all hands to be of Catholic origin, our Articles also, the offspring of an uncatholic age, are, through God's good providence, to say the least, not uncatholic, and may be subscribed by those who aim at being catholic in heart and doctrine."[129] To this end, Newman strove, in "Tract Ninety," to give *The Thirty-Nine Articles* as catholic a reading as possible. "There was," he would explain in 1864, "no doubt at all about the elasticity of the Articles." On that basis he "wanted to ascertain what was the limit of that elasticity in the direction of Roman dogma" on a number of the questions in dispute between Protestantism and Roman Catholicism, specifically the doctrines of purgatory, veneration of images and relics, the invocation of the saints, and the mass.[130] Whatever else it did, "Tract Ninety" dramatically called attention to the equivocal status of confessional subscription to *The Thirty-Nine Articles of the Church of England*.[131] Its eventual personal outcome, four years later, was that Newman was received into the communion of the Roman Catholic Church. But the hermeneutical challenge has persisted, for this and other creeds and confessions.

127. Middleton 1951, with extensive quotations from contemporary sources.
128. Brilioth 1933.
129. Newman [1841] 1964, 150–51.
130. Newman [1864] 1967, 80. See Syndogmaticon 12.1, 8.10, 3.8, 10.9.
131. Schmidt 1966.

CHAPTER TEN

Deeds, Not Creeds?

IN EVERY PERIOD OF THE history of the church, the most persistent challenge to the authority of creeds and confessions has been the
widely shared perception of a danger to morality that can come from
any of the various disjunctions between the moral code on one hand
and the dogmatic creed or the closely related liturgical cultus on the
other. That perception is epitomized in the modern slogan "deeds, not
creeds," which Henry Wadsworth Longfellow set to verse:

> A Theologian, from the school
> Of Cambridge on the Charles, was there;
> Skilful alike with tongue and pen,
> He preached to all men everywhere
> The Gospel of the Golden Rule,
> The New Commandment given to men,
> Thinking *the deed, and not the creed,*
> Would help us in our utmost need.
> With reverent feet the earth he trod,
> Nor banished nature from his plan,
> But studied still with deep research
> To build the Universal Church,
> Lofty as is the love of God,
> And ample as the wants of man.[1]

This warning against the danger of emphasizing creeds about
Jesus Christ as the Second Person of the Trinity and the Son of God
incarnate at the expense of deeds in obedience to Jesus Christ as the

---

1. Henry Wadsworth Longfellow *Tales of a Wayside Inn*, Prelude; italics added.

moral teacher and example was also dramatically emphasized by the rhetorical questions of another nineteenth-century poet:

> Ah! what if some unshamed iconoclast
> Crumbling old fetish raiments of the past,
> Rises from dead cerements the Christ at last?
> What if men take to following where He leads,
> Weary of mumbling Athanasian creeds?[2]

The danger had been perceived and pointed out far earlier, not least by spokesmen for orthodox Christianity themselves in their statements of explanation and defense. The apologies of early Christians such as Clement of Alexandria and Augustine attack Greco-Roman paganism for its concentration on the minutiae of ritual propriety in complete disjunction from moral conduct.[3] In response to Muslim critiques, *The Confession of Faith by Gennadius II, Patriarch of Constantinople* specifies that "the souls and the bodies of those who believe rightly *and* live rightly will depart into Paradise."[4] But there has been a widespread impression that Christians have in fact concentrated on the fine points, not only of liturgical correctness, but also of doctrinal orthodoxy, at the price of morality. This has been a continuing problem for Christian creeds and confessions throughout their history. It was formulated in a parable of Jesus to his hearers: "What do you think? A man had two sons; and he went to the first and said, 'Son, go and work in the vineyard today.' And he answered, 'I will not'; but afterward he repented and went. And he went to the second and said the same; and he answered, 'I go, sir,' but he did not go. Which of the two did the will of his father?"[5] Obviously, the right answer is: the first son, whose deed ("he repented and went"), coming as it did better late than never, was more authentic than the doctrinally correct but morally sterile creed of the second son ("'I go, sir,' but he did not go"). The critique of creeds at the expense of deeds has become especially vigorous in the modern

2. Roden Noël "The Red Flag."
3. Clement of Alexandria *Exhortation to the Heathen* 3 (ANF 2:183–84); Augustine *City of God* 2.6 (NPNF–I 2:26).
4. *Gennad* 11; italics added.
5. Mt 21.28–31.

era, since the age of the Enlightenment.[6] The responses to this problem have varied between and even within different historical periods,
in different churches and confessions, and in diverse cultural contexts.[7]

10.1. Doctrines of Christian Discipline
in the Reformation Confessions

Yet it has not been only the critics of creeds and confessions inside
or outside the various churches since the Enlightenment, but the authors of the creeds and confessions themselves,[8] including the authors
of the confessions of the Protestant Reformation, who have voiced this
recurring concern over the peril of creeds without deeds. Among the
many different challenges that it addressed to medieval society and to
the historic claim of the Roman Catholic Church to occupy the role of
omnium ecclesiarum mater et magistra, "mother and teacher of all the
churches," as the decree of the Council of Trent calls her,[9] the Protestant Reformation of the sixteenth century, through the multitude of
confessions of faith that it produced, brought a new attention to questions about the connections between doctrinal confession, liturgical
observance, and moral conduct. The criticism of medieval worship in
The Sixty-Seven Articles of Ulrich Zwingli of 1523 charges that "chanting and loud clamor which lack true devotion and are done only for
the sake of reward, either seek the praise of men or material gain,"[10]
thereby singling out for attack the threat of empty ritualism perceived
to be present in the liturgy of the medieval church. But it is, of course,
quite understandable that the other side of the question, the issue of
works without faith, of deed without creed, should predominate in
texts that are addressed chiefly to the area of Christian doctrine, as
practically all of these confessions of the Reformation are,[11] that expound the doctrine of justification by faith alone without works, and

6. See chapter 17.1 below, "The Discomfort with Creed Caused by the Consciousness of Modernity."
7. See chapter 11 below, "Transmission of Creeds and Confessions to Other Cultures."
8. *Dosith* decr 13–14.
9. *Trent* 22.8.
10. *67 Art* 46.
11. See chapter 3.1 above, "The Teaching of the Church."

that attack a righteousness of works as vigorously as the Lutheran and Reformed confessions do. *The Westminster Confession of Faith* concedes that in some cases the works of Christians and the works of decent citizens who are not Christians—of those who, as it says elsewhere, are "diligent to frame their lives according to the light of nature, and the law of that religion they do profess" [12]—are, as to "the matter of them" and in their outward content, not obviously different from each other. In both of these groups of people such works are "things which God commands, and of good use both to themselves and others." The decisive difference between these two sets of works, both of which are "of good use," is that even when they are beneficial to society, "works done by unregenerate men . . . proceed not from a heart purified by faith, nor are done in a right manner according to the word, nor to a right end, the glory of God." [13] All three of these criteria of what sets good works apart as truly "good" in the scriptural and Christian sense of that word—faith as the basis of genuinely good works, the word of God as their norm, and the glory of God as their end or goal [14]—are the issues with which Christian doctrine, especially as this is being set forth here in such detail by *The Westminster Confession of Faith* in the name of the Protestant Reformation as a whole, uniquely deals and for which natural religion and natural morality are thought to be inadequate. For, in the familiar opening words of a companion work, *The Westminster Shorter Catechism,* "Man's chief end is to glorify God, and to enjoy him forever." As it adds later in explanation of what it means both to glorify God and to enjoy God, "the duty which God requireth of man, is obedience to his revealed will," an obedience that is to be expressed in God-pleasing deeds, but also in God-pleasing creeds, both of which are means of glorifying God. [15]

That doctrinal emphasis is responsible for the centrality of the question of motivation in the approach of the Reformation confessions to the two related issues of morality and of the distinctiveness of Christian obedience in contrast with mere civic respectability. Thus

12. *West* 10.4. See Syndogmaticon 1.2.
13. *West* 16.7.
14. See also, for example, *Gen Bap* 39.
15. *West Sh Cat* 1, 39.

The Belgic Confession attributes to human beings without grace an inability to "do a thing out of love for God but only out of love for themselves and fear of being condemned," a motivation that corrupts even those socially valuable and outwardly moral deeds of which such an unregenerate human nature is undeniably capable.[16] Summarizing for all the confessions this Reformation emphasis on the indispensability of a correct and Christian motivation for moral works, *The Apology of the Augsburg Confession* of 1531 declares:

> Therefore we may profitably distinguish between civil righteousness [*iustitia civilis*] and spiritual righteousness, attributing the former to the free will and the latter to the operation of the Holy Spirit in the regenerate. This safeguards outward discipline, because all men ought to know that God requires this civil righteousness and that, to some extent [*aliquo modo*], we can achieve it. At the same time it shows the difference between human righteousness and spiritual righteousness, between philosophical teaching and the teaching of the Holy Spirit; and it points out the need for the Holy Spirit.[17]

The definition of "civil righteousness" continued to be a way of teaching about the limited but genuine moral capacity of the fallen human will to contribute something good in the civil order, even though it could not achieve salvation by doing so.[18] But even where, as in the moral theology of medieval scholasticism, with its extensive reliance on the *Nicomachean Ethics* of Aristotle, the emphasis on such a distinction "between philosophical teaching and the teaching of the Holy Spirit" is perceived to be much less sharp than it is in the Reformation confessions, the acceptance of the true faith that is affirmed in the creed is still seen as a necessary prerequisite to the performance of any deed that is to qualify as an authentically Christian good work. "The pro-

16. *Belg* 24.
17. *Apol Aug* 18.9; see also *Confut* 18.1; *17 Art* 12 on "secular" goodness; and *Helv II* 16.9.
18. *Cons rep* 18.86.

logue of the II Part" of the *Summa Theologica* of Thomas Aquinas on ethics "expresses nothing but the very idea of 'the human' as revealed to us in Holy Scripture," a shrewd interpreter has noted, rather than, as a superficial reading of its heavily Aristotelian terminology has led many to conclude, a teaching that is predominantly philosophical.[19]

But as became painfully evident even to its partisan supporters when a confession of the second and third generations of the Protestant Reformation reached the absurd juncture of being obliged to condemn with equal force the teaching "that good works are necessary to salvation" and the teaching "that good works are detrimental to salvation,"[20] the clear and present danger of moral indifferentism was ever before the minds of the original Protestant Reformers and of their heirs in all subsequent generations.[21] Against the Lutheran formula of *satis est,* the contention of *The Augsburg Confession* that the "preaching [*Predigt*]" (German text) or "teaching [*doctrina*]" (Latin text) of the gospel and the administration of the sacraments are "sufficient" to assure the unity of the church, and by extension also the presence of the church,[22] it becomes the consistent requirement of the Reformed confessions that, in the words of *The Scots Confession* of 1560, "ecclesiastical discipline uprightly ministered, as God's word prescribes, whereby vice is repressed and virtue nourished," also must be listed among the "notes, signs, and assured tokens" of the true church. This "discipline" was not, of course, intended to take the place of the teaching and preaching of the word of God and the administration of the sacraments, on whose central importance the Reformed and the Lutheran confessions are agreed, at least in principle, in spite of their differences on the content of the sacraments,[23] but to be added to these, also because observance of the sacraments was itself an act of duty and discipline.[24] For "although this church and congregation of Christ is open and known to God's eyes alone" and therefore ultimately invisible to human scrutiny, *The First Helvetic Confession* explains, these marks—including "a uni-

19. Eschmann 1997, 166.
20. *Form Conc Epit* 4.1–2, 16–17; *Helv II* 16.8.
21. *Cons rep* 4.57.
22. *Aug* 7.2.
23. *Helv II* 17.11.
24. *Scot I* 18; *Cumb Pres* 103. See Syndogmaticon 9.4.

versal, public, and orderly discipline"—can make it "known" also on earth and to human eyes.[25] As *The Westminster Confession of Faith* explains a century later, the true church is "sometimes more, sometimes less visible" historically,[26] also because of the enormous fluctuations that have taken place in its practice of Christian moral discipline over time. Because all of these "marks" of the church are comprehended in the overall requirement "that all things are managed according to the pure word of God, all things contrary thereto rejected, and Jesus Christ acknowledged as the only head of the church," it follows, according to *The Belgic Confession*, that this requirement must include not only correct doctrine but "church discipline for correcting faults."[27] According to *The Heidelberg Catechism*, "the preaching of the holy gospel and Christian discipline [*die christliche Busszucht*]," taken together, are the two things by which "the kingdom of heaven is opened to believers and shut against unbelievers."[28] *The [First] Bohemian Confession* of the Hussite Unitas Fratrum, which was published with a foreword by Luther, somewhat softens their original position on the absolute necessity of discipline, in deference to Luther's fears that it might be reintroducing a moralistic righteousness of works.[29] But by 1575 the Hussites had meanwhile come under Reformed as well as Lutheran influence and had reaffirmed certain pre-Reformation traditions as well.[30] Therefore *The [Second] Bohemian Confession* lists "a due and legitimate obedience in the observance of all those things that the gospel and law of Christ commands" as "the third" among "the sure and infallible marks of the holy church," together with the preaching of the word and the administration of the sacraments.[31] That Reformed insistence on discipline as one of the "signs of the true church," together with the preaching of the gospel and the administration of the sacraments, can still be heard in the twentieth-century Indonesian *Confession of Faith of the Protestant Christian Batak Church (H. K. B. P.)*, a statement of faith drawn from

25. *Helv I* 14.
26. *West* 25.4.
27. *Belg* 29.
28. *Heid* 83.
29. *Boh I* 8.
30. David 1999, 324.
31. *Boh II* 11.

both Reformed and Lutheran sources,[32] reflecting the multiple origins of that united church in various Protestant missions.[33]

Creeds and deeds, faith and works, sacraments and discipline, the preaching of orthodoxy and the preaching of morality—all belong together for the Reformed confessions. "The Scriptures principally teach, what man is to believe concerning God, and what duty God requires of man," *The Westminster Shorter Catechism* explains in holding them together.[34] Therefore *The Second Helvetic Confession* on its first page affirms them both by describing the content of Scripture as "all that pertains to a saving faith, and also to the framing of a life acceptable to God [*cum ad salvificam fidem, tum ad vitam Deo placentem*]."[35] Later on, this confession makes it axiomatic that "discipline is an absolute necessity in the church [*quod oporteat esse in ecclesia disciplinam*]."[36] "To keep all in obedience to God," in the words of *The Belgic Confession* of 1561, "excommunication, with all it involves, according to the word of God, is required."[37] A later Congregationalist confession, while insisting, in opposition to most other confessions, Protestant as well as Roman Catholic, that "creeds possess no authority over the faith and practice of Christians," nevertheless requires "that no persons should be received as members of Christian churches but such as . . . attest a willingness to be subject to its discipline," regardless of their attitudes toward its creeds.[38]

The distinctive ecclesiology of the Mennonite and other Anabaptist confessions defines the church as a community that has been gathered in by the call of Christ to the discipleship of an "obedient following [*Nachfolge*]" of his will, example, and word.[39] Thereby the true church has been strictly set apart from the world, as well as from the church falsely so-called, from "popish and re-popish works and idolatry, gatherings, church attendance," and the like.[40] There-

---

32. *Bat* 8.
33. See chapter 11.2 below, "The Fate of Creeds in Missions and Migrations."
34. *West Sh Cat* 3.
35. *Helv II* 1.2.
36. *Helv II* 18.20.
37. *Belg* 32.
38. *Eng Dec* 3.2, 3.6.
39. Littell 1958.
40. *Schleit* 4.

fore *The Schleitheim Confession* of 1527 locates its discussion of "the ban" of excommunication as the second article, between its two sacramental articles, the first article "concerning baptism" and the third article "concerning the breaking of bread."[41] The Mennonite *Concept of Cologne* of 1591, quoting the admonition of Paul about the treatment of "any one who bears the name of brother if he is guilty of immorality,"[42] requires that "one is to have nothing to do with such persons, including not eating with them." But it warns no less solemnly, clearly on the basis of much practical experience over several generations, that this avoiding of the fallen brethren is to be carried out "with mature judgment," because its purpose is not to exclude anyone forever but to help bring it about that "those being disciplined" might "mend their ways" and return to the fold.[43] *The Short Confession of Faith of Hans de Ries* enumerates the duties of the ministry as: "teaching the divine word, administering the sacraments, and aiding the poor. Likewise God intended the servants of these offices to admonish the brethren, to chastise, and finally to separate the unrepentant from the brotherhood." But it warns that such separating and avoiding should not "ignore need and other requirements of daily living."[44] Similarly, *The Mennonite Confession of Faith of Dordrecht* of 1632 places special emphasis on this question of church discipline exercised on "those who are evil—whether in doctrine or in life." But all of this comes with the repeated pastoral warning that such discipline, including the "shunning [*Mydinghe*]" of the excommunicated, "ought to be used in Christian moderation so that it may have the effect not of destroying but of healing the sinner."[45]

It is especially because of the controverted doctrines of predestination and reprobation—which, though necessarily playing some role in many other Christian confessions both Eastern and Western,[46]

---

41. *Schleit* 2.
42. 1 Cor 5.11.
43. *Cologne* 7.
44. *Ries* 25, 36; also *Geloof* 27.
45. *Dordrecht* 16–17. See also *Camb Plat* 14.4.
46. *Metr Crit* 4.1; *Mogila* 1.26, 1.30; *Dosith* decr 3; *Form Conc Epit* 11. See Syndogmaticon 3.2, 1.13.

as they do in such portions of Scripture as the Epistle to the Romans,[47] are a special emphasis of the Reformed or Calvinist confessions — that the relation not only between creeds and deeds but between fate and free will as it pertains to moral deeds, also comes under fundamental scrutiny there, together with the Reformed attention to discipline. Therefore when *The Second Helvetic Confession* takes up these two doctrines, it immediately specifies: "We do not approve of the impious speeches of some who say, 'Few are chosen, and seeing I know not whether I am among the number of the few, I will enjoy myself.'"[48] *The Westminster Confession of Faith* opens its third chapter, "Of God's Eternal Decree," with the deterministic-sounding proposition that "God from all eternity did . . . unchangeably ordain *whatsoever comes to pass.*" But it immediately adds the clarification not only that "neither is God the author of sin," but also: "nor is violence offered to the will of the creatures, nor is the liberty or contingency of second causes taken away, but rather established."[49] *The Canons of the Synod of Dort* also unequivocally declare their account of predestination to be a doctrine that has been "proclaimed through the prophets, Christ himself, and the apostles, in Old and New Testament times, and has subsequently been committed to writing in the Holy Scriptures, so also today in God's church."[50] Predestination means that "before the foundation of the world, by sheer grace, according to the free good pleasure of his will, [God] chose in Christ to salvation a definite number of particular people out of the entire human race."[51] The inexorably corollary doctrine of reprobation, moreover, means that "God, on the basis of his entirely free, most just, irreproachable, and unchangeable good pleasure, made the following decision: to leave [those who have not been chosen or have been passed by in God's eternal election] in the common misery into which, by their own fault, they have plunged themselves; not to grant them saving faith and the grace of conversion."[52] This creedal insistence on such an unmitigated formulation both of the

47. Rom 9–11.
48. *Helv II* 10.6.
49. *West* 3.1; italics added.
50. *Dort* 1.1.14.
51. *Dort* 1.1.7.
52. *Dort* 1.1.15.

doctrine of predestination and of the doctrine of reprobation makes *The Canons of the Synod of Dort* especially insistent about proceeding to explain, in reference to Christian morality and in response to the gainsayers, that "this is far from saying that this teaching concerning election, and reflection upon it, make God's children lax in observing his commandments or carnally self-assured." In fact, the opposite is taken to be the case. Contrary to what the critics of Calvinistic predestinarianism, especially the Arminians regularly charged,[53] "by God's just judgment this [laxness and carnal self-assurance] does usually happen to those who casually take for granted the grace of election or engage in idle and brazen talk about it but are unwilling to walk in the ways of the chosen," rather than to those who accept the orthodox doctrine of election.[54] No "confession" of doctrine is to be permitted to invalidate the moral imperative, as is the case, according to *The Second Helvetic Confession,* with "the sloth and hypocrisy of all those who praise and profess the gospel with their lips and dishonor it by their disgraceful lives," lapsing into the fallacy of creeds without deeds, which is no better than the delusion of deeds without creeds.[55]

10.2. Heresy and/or Schism

Thus orthodoxy and morality, creeds and deeds, dogmatics and ethics, are affirmed to be inseparable by Christian confessions of all parties. One reason for their inseparability is that the true venue for both is not merely the faith and life of the individual but the faith and life of the church catholic. Heresy as a pertinacious violation of faith, and schism as a pertinacious violation of love, both are sins against the church. According to the formula of Basil of Caesarea, heretics such as the Manichaeans were "men who were altogether broken off and alienated in matters relating to the actual faith," while schismatics such as the Cathars or Valentinians were "men who had separated for some ecclesiastical reasons and questions capable of mutual solution."[56] Or, as Augustine put the same distinction in Latin, heretics (including the

53. *Remon.*
54. *Dort* 1.1.13.
55. *Helv II* 16.9; also *Lucar* 13.
56. Basil of Caesarea *Epistles* 188.1 (*NPNF*–II 8:223).

Manichaean sect, to which he himself had once adhered), "in holding false opinions regarding God do injury to the faith itself"; but
schismatics (including the Donatist sect, against which he contended in
North Africa), "in wicked separations break off from brotherly charity,
although they may believe just what we believe."[57] Or, in the words
of Augustine's mentor Ambrose, "though schismatics kept the faith
towards God, yet they kept it not towards the church of God."[58] Yet
such a way of speaking about *heresy* and *schism* and of distinguishing
between these terms can be misleading, because it seems to suggest a
considerably greater measure of consistency and precision in the usage
of these two words than is borne out by careful scrutiny of the patristic
sources, whether Latin or Greek.[59] Nevertheless, the content of the distinction as it was eventually formulated does reflect a way of thinking,
if not always a way of speaking, that is long established.

For example, the *Acts* of the First Council of Nicaea of 325,
in which "the catholic and apostolic church anathematizes" the Arian
heretics by laying down *The Creed of Nicaea*,[60] contain as well the following canon about dealing with schismatics, which has received far
less attention than have the dogmatic and creedal decrees of the council
about heretics:

> Concerning those who have given themselves the name
> of Cathars, and who from time to time come over pub-
> licly to the catholic and apostolic church, this holy and
> great synod decrees that they may remain among the
> clergy after receiving an imposition of hands. But be-
> fore all this it is fitting that they give a written under-
> taking [*homologēsai autous engraphōs*] that they will ac-
> cept and follow the decrees of the catholic church,
> namely, that they will be in communion with those
> who have entered into a second marriage and with
> those who have lapsed in time of persecution, and for
> whom a period [of penance] has been fixed and an

57. Augustine *On Faith and the Creed* 10.21 (*NPNF*–I 3:331).
58. Ambrose *On the Decease of Satyrus* 47 (*NPNF*–II 10:169).
59. Greenslade 1953, 15–34.
60. *N* anath.

occasion [for reconciliation] allotted, so as in all things to follow the decrees of the catholic and apostolic church.[61]

Not only does this canon of Nicaea also speak (twice), with reference to discipline and schism, about "the catholic and apostolic church," just as the anathematizing conclusion of *The Creed of Nicaea* does with reference to doctrine and heresy. But it invokes, in its requirement of "a written undertaking" from the schismatics, the verb *homologein*, the same technical term that has been employed in Christian Greek since the New Testament for "confessing" the faith.[62] Both schism and heresy, then, are violations of the catholic and apostolic church, and both require a *homologia* by the guilty parties to set things straight. The "Cathars" of whom it speaks—not to be confused with later medieval groups who acquired the same name because of a similar moral strictness but who were different in other respects[63]—were members of a rigorist sect. They agreed with Tertullian[64] in forbidding not only bigamy in parallel (as all Christians did) but bigamy in series, a second marriage after the death of one's spouse, and they refused to be in communion with anyone who was accused of having bought safety by compromise during the persecution of 249–51 under the emperor Decius. For the development of the distinction between schism and heresy it is important to bear in mind that the leader of these "Cathars" was the Roman presbyter Novatian. He was notable for two achievements that by hindsight could appear to have been mutually contradictory: the founding of this rigoristic sect, and the authorship of a scrupulously orthodox treatise *On the Trinity*, which opens with the words, "The rule of truth requires [*Regula exigit veritatis*],"[65] and which Quasten has called "the first great Latin contribution to theology."[66] Therefore, employing somewhat anachronistically the distinction made by Basil

61. *Nic I* can 8.
62. Bauer-Arndt-Gingrich, 568–69; Lampe, 957–58. See chapter 2.3 above, "Confessing the Faith."
63. *ODCC* 301.
64. Tertullian *On Monogamy* (ANF 4:59–72).
65. *Novat* 1.1 (*ANF* 5:611).
66. Quasten, 2:217; see DeSimone 1970.

and Augustine, which eventually established itself in the usage of the church, it can be said that Novatian and Novatianism were guilty of schism but not of heresy. Or, in the terminology being employed in the present context, they were to be accused of error not in the doctrinal creed but in the moral deed, even in their excessively stringent enforcement of morality.[67]

The rigorism of Novatian and the Cathars, particularly their demand for the exclusion of bishops and priests who had betrayed the faith under persecution, was to take a new and more massive form in the Donatist movement.[68] By uniting itself with social, political, and ethnic forces in North Africa, this protest constituted the most serious challenge yet to the catholic church and its unity, not only in North Africa but well beyond. It would thus become decisive for the standard ecclesiastical definition of *schism* in the same way that Arianism became decisive for the standard ecclesiastical definition of *heresy*. But because both *heresy* and *schism* meant what the catholic and apostolic church identified as such, the defiance of the authority of the established institutional church by the Donatists could be seen as a heretical distortion of the doctrine of the church as well as a schismatic violation of the fellowship of the church. That was what it was eventually declared to be.[69] Through the conflict with Donatism, Augustine was forced, to a degree that neither he nor anyone else had been before, to clarify the doctrines of the church, the ministry, and the sacraments. In opposition to the stress of the Donatists on the personal holiness of bishops and priests as a warrant for the grace and holiness of the sacraments administered by them, for which with some justification they were able to lay claim to the legacy of the martyr and orthodox bishop Cyprian of Carthage,[70] Augustine explained the attribute "holy" in the descriptions of the church by *The Niceno-Constantinopolitan Creed*[71] and *The Apostles' Creed*[72] as a reference, not in the first instance to the

67. *Metr Crit* 11.8.
68. Frend 1952.
69. Willis 1950, 129–30.
70. *Cyp*; Willis 1950, 145–52.
71. *N-CP* 9.
72. *Ap* 9.

empirical and subjective holiness of the individual members or of the clergy and the hierarchs of the church, but to the objective holiness that was conferred on believers through the sacraments of the church by the sanctifying grace of the Holy Spirit and by the institution of Christ, even through the ministry of clergy who had shown by their public actions that they were not holy men themselves.[73] Decisive as Donatism was, however, for the interpretation of the phrase "holy church" in *The Niceno-Constantinopolitan Creed* and *The Apostles' Creed* by Augustine and his disciples for a thousand years in the medieval Latin West, it acquired new importance when that standard Augustinian interpretation was put to the severest test it ever faced, as a result of what has been aptly termed "the rising tide of Donatism"[74] in the later Middle Ages and the Reformation. That "rising tide," therefore, also precipitated a major crisis for the traditional version of the relation between deeds and creeds.[75]

Although some version of the distinction between heresy and schism would therefore seem to possess a considerable validity, the distinction can be seen as artificial in several important respects. For, in the confessions of the Reformation no less than in the statements of faith coming out of Roman Catholicism or Eastern Orthodoxy, it is the church that does the confessing of the faith, not only the individual. It is also the church that does the defending—the defending of its faith and doctrine against heresy, the defending of its unity and love against schism. Likewise, the discipline of the church is obliged to deal with the violations of faith and doctrine as well as with the violations of unity and love. That was why the First Council of Nicaea not only published the first universally binding confession of faith and doctrine, which contains anathemas directed against heretics; but, speaking out against schismatics as well, its canons call upon them "to confess [*homologein*]" and to guarantee "that they will accept and follow the decrees of the catholic church" in both creed and deed.[76]

73. Pelikan 1986, 106–22. See Syndogmaticon 9.3.
74. Oberman 1963, 220–22.
75. See chapter 16.3 below, "Catholic Substance and Protestant Principle in Reformation Confessions."
76. *Nic I* can 8.

10.3. Orthodoxy and Asceticism

A special affinity between dogma-as-orthodoxy and discipline-as-*askēsis,* and thus between creeds and a particular class of deeds, has been documented by the history of the relation of orthodoxy to Christian monasticism in both East and West. Yet the affinity is by no means an automatic one. In a monograph of more than a hundred pages entitled "The Role of Eastern Monasticism in the Controversies of Church Politics over Chalcedon (431–519)," Heinrich Bacht has said about the circumstances surrounding *The Council ["Robber Synod"] of Ephesus* of 449: "Just as this imperial synod came into being in significant measure through the intrigues of particular circles of monks, so also from its very beginning it bore a strongly monastic stamp."[77] Therefore it must be remembered that there has been an impressive lineage of monastic heretics in both East and West. Two examples of this tendency should suffice to make the point briefly, one from each of those regions of the church. In the East, during the protracted conflicts over the eschatological teachings of Origen leading up to *The Edict of Emperor Justinian,*[78] the principal defenders of his controversial theories were monks.[79] Among these, Evagrius Ponticus was one of the most celebrated and profound, and he eventually also became one of the most notorious.[80] Although the anathema against "Origen [and others], as well as their heretical books" in *The Condemnation of the Three Chapters of the Second Council of Constantinople* in 553 does not mention Evagrius by name,[81] it is evident that he is included in it. Both *The Exposition of Faith of the Third Council of Constantinople* in 680–81[82] and *The Decrees of the Second Council of Nicaea* in 787 do identify him as the object of those anathemas of their predecessors at the fifth ecumenical council. The latter also calls him and others the authors of "mythical speculations [*mytheumata*]."[83] But in spite of these anathe-

---

77. Heinrich Bacht in Grillmeier-Bacht 1951–54, 2:227.
78. *Edict.*
79. Diekamp 1899.
80. On his monastic writings, see the commentary of J. Driscoll 1991.
81. *CP II* anath 11.
82. *CP III.*
83. *Nic II;* also *Greg Palam* 6.

mas, doctrinal aberrations continued to appear in the monastic circles
of Eastern Orthodoxy.

The most prominent ancient heretic native to the Western
Church—and the one whose name continues to be invoked as a cautionary tale more than a millennium later in the confessions of the
Protestant Reformation, whether Lutheran or Reformed[84]—was also
a monk. His asceticism, moreover, seems to have been at least partly
responsible for his heresy. Pelagius saw Augustine's doctrine of grace
as a threat to ascetic discipline, because, as Peter Brown has put it,
"Pelagius wanted every Christian to be a monk."[85] Therefore, "Whenever I have to speak of laying down rules for behavior and the conduct
of a holy life," he wrote in 413 in support of the decision of a young
patrician woman to become a nun, "I always point out, first of all, the
power and functioning of human nature, and show what it is capable
of doing."[86] It was that "power and functioning" inherent in human
nature, in all human nature, that seemed to him to be threatened or
even negated by the quietism and moral passivity that he took to be
implicit in Augustine's ideas about grace and original sin. Augustine
had expressed these ideas in the celebrated words of Book Ten of his
Confessions, "Give what thou commandest, and command what thou
willest,"[87] which Pelagius found to be so dangerous and offensive.[88]
Even when the Pelagian controversy was largely over and Augustinianism had emerged victorious, at least in principle, the "one vital area
[that] had not been touched" by it was, not surprisingly, the life of
"the monasteries."[89] They were therefore to become hotbeds for "semi-
Pelagianism" of various stripes during the next century or so.[90]

But it would be wrong to see these two heretics, Evagrius Ponticus and Pelagius, as typical of monks in either the East or the West.
Much more representative of the monastic spirit through most of its
history is the tradition associated with the name of the pioneer and

84. *Aug* 2.3; *Helv II* 8.7; *Form Conc Epit* 2.2.3; *Dort* 1.3.2.
85. Brown 2000, 348.
86. Pelagius *Epistle to Demetrias* 2 (*PL* 30:178), as translated in Brown 2000, 342.
87. Augustine *Confessions* 10.31.45 (*NPNF*-I 1:155).
88. ap. Augustine *On the Gift of Perseverance* 20.53 (*NPNF*-I 5:547).
89. Brown 2000, 400.
90. *Chr Trad* 1:319–24.

founding father of the Christian ascetic lifestyle, Antony of Egypt. As
its principles and practice were set forth in the widely influential *Life
of Antony*, almost certainly written by Athanasius, the asceticism of
Antony, although it was rooted in his own personality as this had manifested itself already in his youth, took definite form in church during a liturgy, when the words of Jesus were read: "If you would be
perfect, go, sell what you possess and give to the poor, and you will
have treasure in heaven."[91] In obedience to that imperative, he undertook a monastic life of self-denying discipline.[92] Eventually he attracted
others to the ascetic life, which for him was largely taken up with conflicts against the devil and other demons. According to Athanasius's
Life of Antony, however, his conflicts against schism and heresy were
no less vigorous. Because he shared the widespread Christian opinion
about the demonic origin of heresy and schism, the two conflicts ultimately became the same for Antony. He rejected any association with
the Meletian schism and the Manichaean heresy. But, as Athanasius
portrayed him, it was above all the Arian heresy that drew his opposition.[93] This opposition became all the more imperative for Antony
because, on some grounds or other, "the Arians lyingly asserted that
Antony's opinions were the same as theirs."[94] In response, he proceeded, at least as described in Athanasius's *Life of Antony*, to denounce
the Arian heresy with many of the same theological arguments that
Athanasius himself employed against it, paraphrasing the anathemas of
The Creed of Nicaea of 325:[95] "That the Son of God was not a created
being, neither had he come into being from non-existence, but that he
was the eternal Word and Wisdom [*Logos kai Sophia*] of the essence of
the Father. And therefore it was impious to say, 'There was a time when
he was not,' for the Word was always co-existent with the Father."[96]
The technical level of this theological discourse is all the more remarkable because Antony "had not learned letters," although it did have to

91. Mt 19.21.
92. Athanasius *Life of Antony* 1–4 (*NPNF–II* 4:195–97).
93. Athanasius *Life of Antony* 68 (*NPNF–II* 4:214).
94. Athanasius *Life of Antony* 69 (*NPNF–II* 4:214).
95. *N* anath.
96. Athanasius *Life of Antony* 69 (*NPNF–II* 4:214).

be granted that he "was a ready-witted and sagacious man." [97] These twin themes, the defense of orthodoxy and the espousal of asceticism, were blended and made mutually supportive in the double rhetorical question with which Antony challenged the pagan philosophers who had sought him out: "When has the knowledge of God so shone forth" at any time in classical Greek and Roman antiquity, as it was doing now because of the orthodox Nicene doctrine of the Trinity? "Or when has self-control [sōphrosynē] and the excellence of virginity appeared as now" among even the noblest spirits of paganism, as it was doing now because of the growing devotion and self-discipline of Christian ascetics, both male and female? [98]

The model of the Eastern monk as the champion of doctrinal orthodoxy was to reassert itself frequently in the centuries after Antony, for example in the character of Father Zosima the starec in F. M. Dostoevsky's The Brothers Karamazov. But perhaps never was monasticism as forceful and militant as it became in the defense of the Christian use of images, which achieved creedal definition in the dogmatic Decrees of The Second Council of Nicaea in 787 against the iconoclasm launched by the Byzantine emperor Leo III "the Isaurian." In his inimitable fashion, Edward Gibbon, who distributed his own ironic version of "unforgiving enmity" impartially and evenhandedly between orthodoxy and monasticism, described the contribution of the monks to this orthodox defense and eventual victory of the icons:

> In every act of open and clandestine treason, the emperor felt the unforgiving enmity of the monks, the faithful slaves of the superstition to which they owed their riches and influence. They prayed, they preached, they absolved, they inflamed, they conspired; the solitude of Palestine poured forth a torrent of invective; and the pen of St. John Damascene, the last of the Greek fathers, devoted the tyrant's head, both in this world and the next. I am not at leisure to examine how far the monks provoked, nor how much they have

97. Athanasius Life of Antony 72 (NPNF–II 4:215).
98. Athanasius Life of Antony 79 (NPNF–II 4:217).

exaggerated, their real and pretended sufferings, nor
how many lost their lives or limbs, their eyes or their
beards, by the cruelty of the emperor.[99]

The special importance of monasticism for orthodoxy in the Eastern
tradition has also been enhanced by Eastern canon law, which, unlike
the law of the Latin West, permits the ordination of married men to
the priesthood, but since the sixth century has restricted the episcopate to unmarried men. It is required, therefore, that the candidate be
a monk or that, if he is a widowed priest or an unmarried layman, he
take monastic vows before being consecrated bishop.[100] That was what
happened in the ninth century with Photius, who was a lay scholar
at the "university of Constantinople" before he rose to the patriarchal
throne of New Rome and composed *The Encyclical Letter of Photius* of
867 against the Filioque and other Western teachings.[101]

In the West, too, orthodoxy and asceticism have been mutually
supportive. A particularly brilliant example of such mutual support is
the career of Bernard of Clairvaux in the twelfth century. As monk and
mystic, he cultivated in himself and encouraged in others a highly personal and subjective spirituality, with a special devotion to the Virgin
Mary, which was celebrated in the lines of the *Paradiso,* based almost
verbatim on Bernard's writings, that climax Dante's *Divine Comedy.*[102]
But as abbot and theologian, he insisted on absolute obedience to the
objective authority of church and dogma. Both the subjectivity and the
objectivity were expounded in the name of the lordship of Christ and
the discipline of "the school of Christ."[103] In one of the most influential commentaries on the Song of Songs ever composed, Bernard led his
hearers through a series of deeply subjective meditations on the crucified Christ. "What is so effective for the healing of the wounds of
conscience and for the purification of the intention of the soul as constant meditation on the wounds of Christ?" he asked them. But when
Peter Abelard, from whose hand there would come, in his final letter

---

99. Gibbon [1776–88] 1896–1900, 5:254–55 (ch 49).
100. *Metr Crit* 11.7.
101. *Phot;* Dvornik 1948, 119–31.
102. Dante *Paradiso* 31–33.
103. *Chr Trad* 3:144–57.

to Héloïse, an orthodox if highly idiosyncratic creed,[104] seemed to him to be proposing an interpretation of the passion of Christ in which this sort of subjective meditation on the wounds of Christ and this experience of divine love as revealed in the cross actually appeared to have taken over as the complete definition of the content of the redemption and atonement achieved by the cross of Christ, he attacked Abelard and his pupils as "enemies of Christ."[105] For although there was not, strictly speaking, a defined church doctrine of the atoning work of Christ that would correspond to the doctrine of the person of Christ as this had been worked out by the ancient councils,[106] it was an incontrovertible truth of the faith for Bernard that Christ had come "not only to us [*ad nos*], but for our sakes [*propter nos*]." That is how the Latin text of *The Niceno-Constantinopolitan Creed* defines his work for all orthodox faithful to affirm and believe, saying that it was "for us humans and for our salvation [*propter nos homines et propter nostram salutem*]" that he came down from heaven, and "for us [*pro nobis*]" that he suffered under Pontius Pilate and rose from the dead.[107] Speaking at one and the same time with all the intense subjectivity of the first person singular possessive and with all the uncompromising objectivity of this orthodox creed of the catholic church, Bernard summarized his credo: "My God is what the catholic faith confesses him to be." The condemnation of Abelard by the Synod of Sens, at Bernard's urging, in 1140 or 1141[108] can be read as having put an official approval on the definition of orthodoxy that had been propounded by Bernard as theologian and monk.

But the definitive articulation of the combination of orthodoxy with asceticism in the Western Middle Ages came a century and a half later, and was the achievement of the Order of Friars Preachers founded by Dominic, and of its premier theologian, Thomas Aqui-

---

104. *Petr Ab;* see chapter 15.2 below, "The Confessionalization of Western Sacramental Doctrine."
105. See also chapter 15.1 below, "The Western Reception of the Catholic Creedal and Conciliar Tradition."
106. See chapter 3.3 above, "'Doctrines' and Doctrine."
107. *N-CP Occ* 3–4.
108. *Sens.*

nas.[109] So massive has been the philosophical and theological accomplishment of Thomas as to overshadow his spirituality in general, and his ascetic spirituality in particular. Textbooks all speak of his commentaries on Aristotle and quote from his *Summa contra Gentiles* and *Summa Theologica,* but Thomas the Dominican is often overshadowed by Thomas the Aristotelian. Yet it has become clear from twentieth-century research how fundamental his asceticism was for his moral and theological teaching.[110] For not only did he defend the dedication of the mendicant friars to poverty against their thirteenth-century (and latter-day) critics and detractors. But as Chenu has said,

> It is plain that Thomas's joining the Preachers—in
> spite of the violent opposition of his family (1244)—
> was, together with the religious orientation of his soul,
> the factor that fashioned all his activity, considered not
> only from an outward point of view but, especially,
> from that of doctrine and motivation. . . . Neither
> is it unimportant that Saint Thomas should join the
> Friars Preachers in the Christian world of Innocent III
> and that he should find in the midst of this new reli-
> gious family, at the most opportune time, an Albert the
> Great to be his master.[111]

The examples of these Eastern and Western monks suggest that the intellectual and theological obedience or self-restraint required to be orthodox is more than superficially analogous to the psychological and moral obedience or self-restraint required to be ascetic. The recognition of this analogy is not, moreover, restricted to the Eastern Orthodox and the Roman Catholic traditions. For example, while attacking monasticism as an institution, an orthodox Protestant confession such as *The Second Helvetic Confession* of 1566 strongly commends the ascetic practice of fasting,[112] as does the confession of the General Bap-

---

109. See chapter 15.3 below, "Scholastic Theology as Reasoning on the Basis of the Creed."
110. Weisheipl 1974; McInerny 1997.
111. Chenu 1964, 12, 14.
112. *Helv II* 18.7, 24.4–8; *Camb Plat* 9.1.

tists of England in 1651.[113] Both asceticism and orthodoxy could be described in words of the apostle Paul, which became a motto to later confessions both for life and for teaching:[114] "We destroy arguments and every proud obstacle to the knowledge of God, and take every thought captive to obey Christ, being ready to punish every disobedience."[115] Far from encouraging moral lassitude on the grounds that only true doctrine matters, as its modern opponents have sometimes charged,[116] a passionate zeal for orthodoxy has historically become a special cause for those who have consecrated their lives to poverty, chastity, and obedience.

10.4. Christian Love the Presupposition for Christian Confession

Beyond any of the differences among confessions about deeds and creeds that we have been describing, however, the fundamental relation of prayer to both creeds and deeds has been the twofold one already defined.[117] It has been one function of the creed to specify what the correct object of authentic ritual and worship is, and thus to define Christian confession as the presupposition for Christian love and prayer, lest one mistakenly address prayer and adoration to a false deity and thereby fall into idolatry. But in turn, the second function has been to affirm the inseparable bond between "deeds" and "creeds," between Christian love and Christian confession, and thus to interpret Christian love as the presupposition for Christian confession and Christian worship, "lest that by any means, when I have preached to [or worshiped with] others, I myself should be a castaway," as Paul says.[118]

Expressing an ecumenical consensus across confessional boundaries by bringing together all of these emphases into one formula of mutual dependence and reinforcement, *The Divine Liturgy According to Saint John Chrysostom* prefaces the recitation of *The Niceno-*

113. *Gen Bap* 73.
114. *Jer II* 1.28; *Mogila* 1.10.
115. 2 Cor 10.5–6.
116. See chapter 17.1 below, "The Discomfort with Creed Caused by the Consciousness of Modernity."
117. See chapter 6 above, "The Rule of Prayer and the Rule of Faith."
118. 1 Cor 9.27 (AV); *Friends I* 15.

Constantinopolitan Creed with the admonition: "Let us love one another, that with one mind we may confess [*Agapēsōmen allēlous hina en homonoiai homologēsōmen*] Father, Son, and Holy Spirit! The Trinity, one in essence and undivided."[119] With the principle, "The Creed belongs only to those who live it," Kallistos Ware has commented on this passage from the *Liturgy:* "This exactly expresses the Orthodox attitude to Tradition. If we do not love one another, we cannot love God; and if we do not love God, we cannot make a true confession of faith and cannot enter into the inner spirit of Tradition, for there is no other way of knowing God than to love Him."[120] According to *The Orthodox Confession of the Catholic and Apostolic Eastern Church by Peter Mogila,* the church, through the agency of the ecumenical council, has power over its members, including "patriarchs, popes, bishops, and all others,"[121] because it is, according to the New Testament, "the pillar and bulwark of the truth."[122] These words of First Timothy require, according to *The Confession of Dositheus and of the Synod of Jerusalem,* "holding the same doctrine of faith and always believing it identically and steadfastly."[123] Quoting those words of First Timothy again later, *The Orthodox Confession of Peter Mogila* draws from them the conclusion that the church's "precepts and doctrines are by no means human, but divine; not by man, but of God. When, therefore, we profess to believe in her, we profess to believe in the Scriptures delivered to her of God, and in the commands, which are inspired by God."[124] Both of these sets of "commands," those of Scripture and those of the church, make it a requirement, for example, that "a perfect reconciliation with all persons" is essential to the proper reception of the eucharist.[125]

This last point is a direct citation of the words from the Sermon on the Mount in which Jesus, decisively formulating that requirement of personal reconciliation for all time, warns his followers: "If you are offering your gift at the altar, and there remember that your

119. *Lit Chrys* II.D.
120. Ware 1997, 207.
121. *Mogila* 1.86.
122. 1 Tm 3.15.
123. *Dosith* decr 2.
124. *Mogila* 1.96.
125. *Mogila* 1.107.

brother has something against you, leave your gift there before the altar and go; first be reconciled to your brother, and then come and offer your gift."[126] In all periods of Christian history, the Christian critique of ritualism has therefore been able to attach itself to the attacks of the prophets, and then of Jesus himself in the Gospels, on any preoccupation with liturgical correctness at the cost of an authentic personal relation to God, which must always include a striving for moral purity. This perennial critique acquires distinctive force in the confessions from the period of the Protestant Reformation. Therefore *The French Confession,* citing additional warnings of this kind from the New Testament,[127] summarizes the case: "We reject all human inventions, and all laws which men may introduce under the pretense of serving God, by which they wish to bind consciences; and we receive only that which conduces to concord and holds all in obedience, from the greatest to the least."[128] Such human ritual inventions are prohibited, according to *The Westminster Confession of Faith,* because "God alone is Lord of the conscience, and hath left it free from the doctrines and commandments of men, which are in any thing contrary to his word, or beside it, in matters of faith or worship."[129] But in spite of the ecumenical consensus, there is one significant and ultimately decisive difference between *The French Confession* or *The Westminster Confession of Faith,* both of them Reformed, and *The Orthodox Confession of the Catholic and Apostolic Eastern Church by Peter Mogila,* speaking for Eastern Orthodoxy. For the Reformed confessions it is wrong not only to require something "contrary" to Scripture, but also to demand something additional to it or "beside it in matters of faith and worship." This includes, for example, the liturgical "commands" of the Orthodox Church, which for Peter Mogila carry a divine authority.

As they are expounded in the creeds and confessions of faith, with great diversity and often profound and fundamental disagreement, these expressions of Christian fidelity all nevertheless represent variations on the apostolic theme of "the obedience of faith," which

126. Mt 5.23–24; *Heid* 105.
127. Rom 15.17–18; 1 Cor 3.11; Col 2.6–8; Gal 5.1.
128. *Gall* 33.
129. *West* 20.2.

Augustine termed "the mother and guardian of all the virtues."[130] In the words of *The French Confession*, "we receive only that which conduces to concord and holds all in obedience, from the greatest to the least."[131] For at its core, the word *faith* and its cognates, in all the various languages with which we have been dealing here, means fidelity and loyalty: to be "faith-full" is to be "faithful." In the language of the Bible, that applies preeminently to the faithfulness of God:

> If we deny him, he will also deny us;
> if we are faithless, he remains faithful
> —for he cannot deny himself.[132]

Thus *faith* is above all an attribute of the faithful God, who made his covenant with the people of Israel, who renewed it and extended it (but did not abrogate it) through the coming of his Son, Jesus Christ, and who could not renege on the covenant without going against his very nature. But faith as faithfulness pertains as well to human beings, in their relation to the faithfulness of God and in their relation with one another. "Be faithful unto death," the writer of Revelation heard the divine voice promise, "and I will give you the crown of life."[133] In the best-known English poem to come out of the First World War, fallen soldiers warn their surviving comrades, "If ye break faith with us who die / We shall not sleep."[134] Therefore Abraham, who is, for the New Testament and for the subsequent history of the church, the outstanding paragon of faith as a trust even without knowledge, because in obedience to the commandment of God he set out for an unknown country,[135] is also the prime example of faith as fidelity, through his willingness to offer up Isaac, his beloved son, out of obedience and loyalty to the God of the promise.[136] In his Epistle to the Romans, which honors Abraham as "the father of all who believe,"[137] Paul the apostle

130. Augustine *City of God* 14.12 (*NPNF*-I 2:273).
131. *Gall* 33.
132. 2 Tm 2.12–13.
133. Rv 2.10.
134. John McCrae "In Flanders Fields."
135. Heb 11.8–10.
136. Lerch 1950.
137. Rom 4.11.

can speak at the opening about "grace and apostleship, for obedience to the faith among all nations, for [Christ's] name."[138] At the end of the epistle he returns to speak of a mystery "made known to all nations, for the obedience of faith."[139] On that basis, confessions sometimes link or even identify "faith" and "the obedience of faith,"[140] emphasizing in that single phrase the intimate connection between deeds and creeds. And even "holiness" churches, which emphasize the supremacy of the call to obedience, find it necessary to explain in the language of confession and doctrine what makes it the obedience *of faith*.[141]

10.5. A Modern Secular Parallel

Both as a moral code for modern civil societies and as a secular creed of sorts, *The Universal Declaration of Human Rights,* adopted by the General Assembly of the United Nations on 10 December 1948, is in some respects a parallel manifestation of this intimate connection between deeds and creeds.[142] The parallel is a limited one, even for such documents. *The American Declaration of Independence* of 4 July 1776 grounds its affirmation of "certain unalienable rights" in the endowing act of the "creator" and in "the laws of nature and of nature's God." Whatever the specific content of these terms may be in the context of the natural theology of the American Enlightenment and in the thought of their principal author, Thomas Jefferson, modern commentators often overlook their theistic point of reference. But *The Universal Declaration of Human Rights,* written in a twentieth-century context, avoids any theistic point of reference, indeed, any stated metaphysical presupposition at all. Nevertheless it does reaffirm the pledge of *The Charter of the United Nations* to promote "universal respect for and observance of human rights and fundamental freedoms," and it declares that "a common understanding of these rights and freedoms is of the greatest importance for the full realization of this pledge." On that basis *The Universal Declaration of Human Rights* presents itself as "a common standard of achievement for all peoples and all nations, to the

138. Rom 1.5 (AV).
139. Rom 16.26 (AV).
140. See, for example, *Apol Aug* 4.308–9; *Dort* 1.1.9.
141. *Naz* pr.
142. Glendon 2001.

end that every individual and every organ of society, keeping this Declaration constantly in mind, shall strive by teaching and education to promote respect for these rights and freedoms and by progressive measures, national and international, to secure their universal and effective recognition and observance."[143] In its quest for a "universal respect" and in its claim upon a "universality" of observance and application, *The Universal Declaration of Human Rights* bears a certain resemblance to the "catholic" and universal claims of the creeds and confessions of the churches. In its definition of itself as a code and "a common standard" that is intent on achieving "a common understanding," which is to be kept "constantly in mind," it aspires to function as a shared "rule of faith" and of conduct, much as the creeds do. And in its emphasis on "promotion" and on "teaching," as a process but implicitly also as a content, it exemplifies the fundamental and universal human impulse that is also articulated in a creedal formula shared by the Old and the New Testament and that underlies all the confessions: "I believed, and so I spoke."[144]

143. Laqueur and Rubin 1989, 197–98.
144. Ps 116.10; 2 Cor 4.13. See chapter 2 above, "The Creedal and Confessional Imperative."

CHAPTER ELEVEN

Transmission of Creeds and Confessions to Other Cultures

AMONG THE EARLIEST CHRISTIAN "creedal" affirmations to have come down to us—taking the chronology of the Gospels as it stands—are the confession of Simon Peter at Caesarea Philippi, "You are the Christ, the Son of the living God,"[1] and the confession of Thomas after the resurrection, "My Lord and my God!"[2] Probably spoken in Aramaic, they were then written down in Greek, then circulated throughout Europe chiefly in Latin, and eventually shared by all seven continents and by the islands of the sea in more than two thousand languages.

Similarly, as the texts in any collection such as Part One of *Creeds and Confessions of Faith in the Christian Tradition* will show, almost all of the early creeds of the church were originally written, and have been preserved, in Greek or Latin; the same is true of the dogmatic decrees of the first seven ecumenical councils. But some of those declarations in Greek and Latin of what the early church believed, taught, and confessed, notably *The Niceno-Constantinopolitan Creed* and *The Apostles' Creed,* have since been translated into many other languages, principally because of their function in worship,[3] as the church has been transplanted, and its faith transmitted, into other cultures across the globe, helping to realize the eschatological vision prophesied by the seer of the Apocalypse, of "every nation, all tribes and peoples and tongues."[4] Likewise, as the originals of the texts in

1. Mt 16.16.
2. Jn 20.28.
3. See chapter 6.3 above, "The Place of Creed in Liturgy."
4. Rv 7.9; *Morav Am 6.*

any collection of sixteenth-century formularies like Part Four of *Creeds and Confessions of Faith in the Christian Tradition* will show, most of the confessions of the Protestant Reformation were also composed in Latin, which (in addition to being the prescribed liturgical language during the Western Middle Ages) had been the universal language of scholarship, theology, and law, and which remained so during most of the Renaissance and the Reformation. But in keeping with the emphasis of the Reformation confessions on using the language of the people,[5] some Reformation confessions were originally written in one or another vernacular—most frequently, German, French, or English—or, in some instances, were rendered into these vernacular tongues from the original Latin, with the Latin and the vernacular versions sometimes possessing equal confessional authority in their churches.

Since the sixteenth century, some of these Protestant confessions, too, have been transmitted to other continents of the globe and in that process have also been translated into new languages. During the twentieth century, this process of transmission moved to the point that in Part Five of *Creeds and Confessions of Faith in the Christian Tradition*, which bears the title "Statements of Faith in Modern Christianity," it has seemed appropriate to employ the subtitle "The Twentieth Century: Globalization of Churches and Confessions." The international and intercultural "reception" of creeds and confessions of faith and the redefinitions of their authority in new settings are, therefore, a vital part of their history.[6] Presbyterianism, with its classic formation in *The Westminster Confession of Faith*[7] in the seventeenth century and its nineteenth-century statements like *The Declaration of Faith of the Cumberland Presbyterian Church* of 1814[8] and *The Auburn Declaration* of 1837,[9] is a leading example, producing during the twentieth century new confessions of faith in Cuba,[10] in Chile,[11] and in South

5. *Apol Aug* 24.2–5; *39 Art* 24; *Helv II* 23.1.
6. Sanneh and Wacker 1999; see also chapter 9.2 above, "Reception of Creeds, Councils, and Confessions as Ratification."
7. *West.*
8. *Cumb Pres.*
9. *Aub.*
10. *PRCC.*
11. *Chile.*
12. *Pres So Afr.*

Africa,[12] as well as *The Confessional Statement of the United Presbyterian Church of North America* in 1925[13] and a landmark *Confession* in 1967;[14] in addition, it has participated in the confessional productions of the United Church of Canada.[15] From such internationalism and interculturalism has come a new vindication of the claim, which in principle is made by all the creeds and confessions on behalf of their churches, to be truly "catholic"—even when some of those confessions at the same time identify "the catholic or universal church" as "some times more, sometimes less visible."[16]

This phenomenon of globalization and of internationalism and "multiculturalism" is, to be sure, by no means unique to Christendom. The rapid spread of Islam, within a century after the death of the prophet Muhammad in A.D. 632, from the Arabian peninsula through Asia Minor and North Africa to Spain and beyond, and its subsequent transplantation into Central and Eastern Asia, Subequatorial Africa, and eventually into Southeastern Europe and even the Western Hemisphere—creating what Marshall Hodgson has called "Islamdom," as a counterpart to "Christendom"—made the relation between the universally acknowledged sacred authority of Arabic as the inspired language of the Qur'ān and the particular languages of the several Muslim cultures, such as Turkish or Farsi or Urdu, always a problem and sometimes a resource to Muslim believers. Analogously, the global acceptance (in theory at any rate) of the tenets of liberal democracy has provoked continuing debate over the adaptability of democratic doctrine to the special needs and traditions of states and cultures where it and its original philosophical presuppositions were not native and still are not widely shared; as Bernard Lewis observes, "An Arabic loanword like *dimuqratiyya* lacks the resonance of *shari'a*," the Islamic law of the Qur'ān.[17] And the rise and fall of international Marxism-Leninism in the course of the twentieth century proved to be a political and philosophical laboratory, in which the experiment of an ideology that was aimed at overcoming class, transcending nationality,

13. *Un Pres.*
14. *Pres USA;* see Dowey 1968 and Rogers 1985.
15. *Un Ch Can: Union; Un Ch Can: Crd.*
16. *West* 25.3.
17. Lewis 1997, 8.

and abolishing religion collided with—and was eventually shattered by—stubbornly persistent cultural, regional, ethnic, and religious particularities. In each of these three movements, no less than in Christianity, those who have maintained that they believe, teach, and confess the true faith have repeatedly been compelled to probe for the "essence" of that faith within and beyond the accidents of its manifold historical manifestations, including the original manifestations; and they have sought to formulate that essence in propositions that seem quite "creedal."[18]

11.1. Cultus, Code, and Creed Across Cultural Boundaries

In the vocabulary of anthropology and other social sciences, the alliterative phrase "code, cultus, and creed," which could be an adaptation of the classical Greek triad of the Good, the Beautiful, and the True, is employed as a set of categories for describing the authority structures of religious institutions of many kinds. According to *The Oxford English Dictionary,* the term *code* applies primarily to the field of Roman law, where it refers to "one of the various systematic collections of statutes made by later emperors, as the *code of Theodosius, of Justinian;* specifically the latter."[19] Perhaps because of the close historical connection between Gratian's collection of canon law and the medieval reception of the Roman law,[20] *code* likewise carries some connotations of "church law," as it does, for example, in such a Western title as *The Code of Canon Law, Codex Iuris Canonici. The Oxford English Dictionary* goes on to point out that it can, however, also refer "by transfer" to "a system or collection of rules or regulations on any subject"; in spite of the inclusive term "any subject," all of the examples quoted for this latter usage pertain to the Christian "code" of conduct, thus to Christian ethics in obedience to the "code" of the divine law. And in the title of a magisterial volume of literary, philosophical, and theological reflection by Northrop Frye, the Bible itself becomes the "great code."[21]

18. See chapter 10.5 above, "A Modern Secular Parallel."
19. *OED* 2:582–83.
20. *NPNF*-II 14:xxix–xxxv.
21. Frye 1982.

Throughout Christian history, the variations of authority between code, cultus, and creed seem to have come out the most sharply
as a result of the confrontations between each of them and the phenomenon of cultural diversity, particularly when denominations and
their confessions have been transplanted to other cultures. This process is visible already within the pages of the New Testament, in "the
transmission of faith"[22] from a Jewish to a Gentile environment—or,
more accurately and fully, in the successive transmissions from a Palestinian Jewish to a Hellenistic Jewish environment, and then from a
Hellenistic Jewish to a Hellenistic Gentile environment (although the
boundaries between all three of these environments and between all
three of these transmissions were, and would remain, quite blurred). As
The Confession of Faith of Gennadius II declares, in explaining Christian trinitarian universalism to a Muslim audience, "through his Word,
the all-powerful and invisible God planted the truth in Jerusalem, but
through his Spirit he empowered his apostles to sow the truth in all the
world."[23] Therefore the Book of Acts—written, of course, in Greek—
opens in Jerusalem, reaches one of its first climaxes in the address of
Stephen to other Hellenistic Jews, and in its final chapter announces
momentously: "And so we came to Rome."[24] The question of which
elements of Judaism and of Jewish Christianity were to remain normative for observance by Gentiles who became Christian formed the
agenda for the first church council ever to have been held, the assembly of the college of the apostles likewise recounted in the Book of
Acts,[25] and therefore was the subject of the first "*dogmata* which had
been reached by the apostles and presbyters"—as its decisions or decrees were termed already in the Greek of the New Testament[26]—ever
to have been promulgated by a church council.[27]

What we are calling here the transmission of confessions to
other cultures and their indigenization is, therefore, closely related
to, though not identical with, the widely debated concepts of accul-

22. Walls 1996.
23. *Gennad* 4.
24. Acts 1.6, 6.8–7.53, 28.14.
25. Acts 15.22–29.
26. Acts 16.4.
27. Pokrovský 1914, 3–94.

turation, and more recently of inculturation.[28] The term *inculturation,* which is said to have come into the vocabulary of theology chiefly from anthropology, had been current for some time in other languages, including Spanish, Italian, and French,[29] from which it was introduced into English theological usage. It was defined in an authoritative essay of 1978 by the father general of the Society of Jesus, Pedro Arrupe, to signify: "the incarnation of the Christian life and of the Christian message in a particular cultural context, in such a way that this experience not only finds expression through elements proper to the culture in question, but becomes a principle that animates, directs, and unifies the culture, transforming and remaking it so as to bring about a 'new creation.'"[30] As the use of the term *incarnation* in this definition suggests, the divine action by which the Son of God, the Logos, "the Word, became flesh and dwelt among us"[31] in the person of Jesus Christ is seen here as the normative pattern for each subsequent "incarnation of the Christian life and of the Christian message in a particular cultural context."[32] This has led, for example, to the modern slogan, "We must Africanize Christianity, not Christianize Africa."[33] And the use of the Pauline term "a new creation [*kainē ktisis*]"[34] implies a metamorphosis by which an already existing reality, which had been part of the "old creation," has now been effectively redeemed and fundamentally transformed through radical renewal but without being annihilated.

Each time the Christian gospel is transplanted into a new culture, the definition of its authority must, initially or eventually, face those who bring the message, as well as those to whom it is brought, with a myriad of decisions about its indigenization and inculturation. After positing two definitions of *indigenization* in the context of the church in India as either "a missionary strategy" or "an indigenous response to a challenge from a foreign tradition," Bent Smidt Hansen dis-

---

28. Standaert 1994.
29. Lacoste, 565–68, with extensive bibliography.
30. Arrupe 1979–86, 3:172–81.
31. Jn 1.14.
32. Hillman 1993, 30–32.
33. *EC* 1:30 (George Evers).
34. 2 Cor 5.17; Gal 6.15.

tinguishes two patterns of indigenization corresponding to these definitions: "Indigenization as a missionary pursuit, or better termed as *external indigenization,* has mainly been a Protestant concern, concentrated on education and training of an Indian ministry. Hereby, however, the foundation stone was laid for an indigenous leadership, which in turn could take over from the missionaries and so inaugurate a new epoch of *internal indigenization.*"[35] These processes involve the cultus of Christian worship and prayer, the code of Christian behavior and morality, and the creed of Christian belief and teaching—all three. Because these three areas of cultus, code, and creed, though distinct, are also inseparable, any decisions about the relation of Christianity to its culture (or, more precisely, to its several cultures, including at least the culture in which it originated, the culture from which it has most recently been sent, and the culture to which it has now been transmitted) inevitably affects all three.

Of the three, it is *cultus,* though with some major exceptions, that has frequently tended to be the most accommodating to new and different cultures. In what Richard Fletcher has called "a deservedly famous letter sent to the English mission in the year 601," Pope Gregory I counseled Augustine of Canterbury and his missionary colleagues that in dealing with the pagan Anglo-Saxons, "the idol temples [*fana idolorum*] of that race should by no means be destroyed, but only the idols in them. Take holy water and sprinkle it in these shrines, build altars, and place relics [of Christian saints] in them. . . . When this people see that their shrines are not destroyed, they will be able to banish error from their hearts and be more ready to come to the places they are familiar with, but now recognizing and worshiping the true God."[36] The missionaries of medieval Western Christianity to other pagan peoples did not consistently follow this Gregorian principle; often they were much more drastically exclusivistic in their attitude not only toward heathen cultus but even toward heathen culture altogether. The most powerful force in this exclusivistic direction was the insistence of the Western church on preserving and enforcing Latin

35. Hansen 1986, 239–40; italics original.
36. Fletcher 1997, 253–54, quoting the Venerable Bede *Ecclesiastical History of the English People* 1.30.

as a uniform liturgical language and as the most palpable evidence of the participation of every new Christian nation, and of each individual parish, in the life of the universal catholic church with its center of authority in Rome. That insistence would lead to grave historical consequences in the ninth century, when the missionaries to the Slavs, Cyril and Methodius, who had come from Constantinople to Greater Moravia, translated the Byzantine liturgy from Greek into Slavonic, creating the Glagolitic alphabet (which was eventually superseded by the Cyrillic alphabet, named for Cyril, though it was not his invention). This evoked resistance from Western clergy, some of whom eventually formulated a doctrine that was labeled "trilingualism," according to which the only languages in which it was legitimate to carry on the public liturgical and eucharistic cultus of the church were the three languages that had appeared in the inscription composed by Pontius Pilate for the cross of Christ, "Jesus of Nazareth, the King of the Jews," which according to the Gospel of John was written "in Hebrew [Aramaic], in Latin, and in Greek."[37] That conflict over opposing views of liturgical indigenization contributed to the eventual schism between the Eastern and the Western churches and to the permanent division of the various Slavic peoples between Eastern Orthodoxy and Roman Catholicism.[38] Once again seven centuries later, in reaction against vernacular worship, which was one of the major demands of the Reformation confessions[39] and which became standard in the Protestant churches, the Council of Trent at its twenty-second session reaffirmed the supremacy of Latin as the language of the mass,[40] just as at its fourth session it had assigned a special authoritative standing also to the translation of the Bible that it called "the old well-known Latin Vulgate [*haec ipsa vetus et vulgata editio*]."[41]

Therefore it came as a sharp contrast to this strategy of Latinization, which had dominated Roman Catholic missionary policy and liturgical practice for so many centuries and in so many parts of the

37. John 19.19–20.
38. Dvornik 1970.
39. *Aug 24.2–4*; *Apol Aug 24.2–5*; *Genv Cat 247*; *Helv II 22.4, 23.1*; *39 Art 24*; *18 Diss 10*; *Meth Art 15*.
40. *Trent 22.8*.
41. *Trent 4.2*.

world, when the Second Vatican Council, echoing Pope Gregory the Great, not only, at its very first session, authorized the use of various local vernaculars for the liturgy of the mass, but at its third session formulated a decree, which dealt specifically with church music but carried far broader implications for the entire liturgical life of the church and for the relation of Christian cultus to indigenous culture:

> In some parts of the world, especially mission areas, peoples are found who have a musical tradition of their own, a tradition which has great importance for their religious and cultural way of life [*magnum momentum in earum vita religiosa ac sociali*]. This music must be taken with due seriousness; suitable scope is to be given for it to contribute both to their development of their sense of the religious, and to the adaptation of religious worship to their particular temperament.[42]

This policy is reflected in the hope of the Ghana Church Union Committee in 1965 "to develop forms of worship in which the distinctive gifts which God has given to the people of Ghana may be reverently used and offered."[43] It has repeatedly been applied to worship throughout the history of Christian missions by various groups, including also Eastern Orthodox monastic missionaries and the Protestant missionary societies. Its liturgical and hymnological results became visible—and audible—at most of the great international ecumenical gatherings of the twentieth century, which their participants therefore often likened to a new Pentecost, undoing by its harmony-in-diversity the linguistic and cultural chaos of the Tower of Babel, while at the same time avoiding the equation of unity with uniformity.[44] In some countries and churches, consequently, Pentecost is also the designated season of the church year to offer special prayers for Christian unity beyond cultural and confessional boundaries.[45]

This complicated historical background of Roman Catholic at-

42. *Vat II* 3.36, 3.119.
43. *Ghana* 11.2; *Laus Cov* 10.
44. Acts 2.1–13; Gn 11.1–9.
45. *DEM* 791 (Geoffrey Wainwright).

titudes toward the indigenization of cultus provides a context to examine the missionary activity of the Italian Jesuit Matteo Ricci in China during the sixteenth and early seventeenth centuries. As teacher and author, Ricci brought Western science and technology to the Chinese, and in a series of apologetic works he strove to identify the natural affinities of Confucianism for the gospel.[46] Adopting the lifestyle of a Confucian sage, he sought to adapt native Chinese religious rites—the traditional Chinese devotion to the person of Confucius, the practices of ancestor worship, and inherited religious terminology, particularly the Chinese words for "Heaven" and "God" (or "god")—to Roman Catholic worship. It was Ricci's contention that idolatry and polytheism were not integral to such Chinese rites as the piety toward ancestors and that therefore these pagan rites could be seen as compatible with monotheism; he even found monotheism at the origins of the Confucian system itself. Such rituals could therefore be accommodated to Christian and Catholic cultic practice, in whose reverence for the saints he found remarkable similarities to Chinese ancestor worship. Ricci's policies helped to provoke the "Chinese rites" controversy over accommodation or "missionary adaptation" to paganism.[47] Although the case of the Chinese rites was unique in many respects, the reactions of the Holy See to this bold program of liturgical and apologetic experimentation—initially supportive if cautious, then unequivocally condemnatory, and then much more affirmative beginning with the pontificate of Pope Pius XII—called attention to the many unresolved issues that remained for the indigenization of the Christian cultus in other cultures.[48]

When it has come to *code,* such "missionary adaptation" has been fraught not only with practical difficulties but with theological ones. The New Testament calls Abraham "the father of all who believe," who is said to have "rejoiced that he was to see" the day of Christ;[49] and a Christian confession of faith can hold him up as the model Christian husband.[50] Nevertheless he is described in the Book of

46. Spence 1984.
47. Mungello 1994.
48. *DTC* 2:2364–91 (J. Brucker).
49. Rom 4.11; Jn 8.56.
50. *Metr Crit* 12.2.

Genesis as both a slaveholder and a polygamist.[51] Yet when the Christians took over the control of Roman society and the administration and revision of its laws under the Christian emperors Constantine I, Theodosius I, and Justinian I, they proceeded in a manner that appeared to be fundamentally inconsistent. As Ernst Troeltsch has put it, they "changed nothing whatever in the laws affecting slaves"; but they insisted that "according to the religious philosophy of the Church, which was based upon that of the Bible, the monogamous family is the basis of Society and of the State," and therefore that henceforth polygamy was to be prohibited by imperial law, not only by ecclesiastical law.[52] Troeltsch's description is, however, less than adequate in several crucial respects; for eventually not only "the laws affecting slaves" but the teaching and practice of the church with regard to slavery would be "changed" drastically, though only after many centuries of delay, development, and controversy.[53] At the same time, the evolution of the Christian marriage ethic, in relation to "the monogamous family" of which Troeltsch speaks, but also in relation to such complicated problems as the grounds of divorce (also when applied to an existing polygamous family) or the definitions of impediment and incest and of permissible degrees of consanguinity or affinity, presents a convoluted study in the history of the cultural settings of Christian morality, doctrine, and canon law. For in those developments there arose tensions, not only among the Levitical code of the law of Moses, the Roman law, and the marriage practices of each successive tribe and nation to which Christianity was brought by missionaries, but between all of these and the ecclesiastical definition, within Roman Catholicism and Eastern Orthodoxy, of matrimony as one of the seven sacraments, as well as the requirement of celibacy for bishops and, in the West, for all other clergy.[54] In the several confessions of the Western tradition, these tensions led to the "four models of marriage—each with multiple variants—[that] lay at the heart of Western marriage law": "the Catho-

51. Gn 17.23, 16.1–3.
52. Troeltsch [1931] 1960, 1:133, 130.
53. Maxwell 1975.
54. *Trent* 7 can 1; *Mogila* 1.115.

lic sacramental model"; "the Lutheran social model"; "the Calvinist covenantal model"; and "the Anglican commonwealth model." [55]

Where does the transplantation of *creed* to other cultures belong in comparison with these historical patterns of adaptation and controversy in the indigenization of cultus and code? [56] Superficially, it might appear that creeds and confessions should be far less subject to change and adaptation through transplantation than are liturgical customs and moral practices. After all, a creed, like Scripture itself, would seem to require no more than translation into a new language (theologically and linguistically formidable though such an assignment has often proved to be) in order to be successfully transplanted, and eventually perhaps even indigenized, in the new culture. The Vulgate, Luther's German Bible, and the Authorized Version of the English Bible are only three examples among many of how successful this process can be in the case of the Scriptures, each of them having gone on to become the model for a literary language that would shape an entire culture for centuries. Just as the church did not write a new Bible for each new nation of converts, but only made the same canonical Scriptures available to them (even if that process necessitated, as it sometimes has, the invention or adaptation of an alphabet for a language that had previously been only oral), so also those converts were to be taught the orthodox "faith which was once for all delivered to the saints" [57] in tradition and creed, and without any alteration or "adaptation" at all in its substantive content. That principle of translation without change is precisely the norm that the churches have applied to *The Niceno-Constantinopolitan Creed* and *The Apostles' Creed* in one mission field after another from early times, and the process continues. But the myriad texts, from many centuries and originally in many languages, that are collected in *Creeds and Confessions of Faith in the Christian Tradition*, especially in Part Five, "Statements of Faith in Modern Christianity," are evidence that, historically as well as theologically and strategically, the transplanting of creeds and confessions to other

55. Witte 1997, 10.
56. Devadutt 1949.
57. Jude 3.

cultures has in fact proved to be far more complicated an assignment than a superficial judgment might have anticipated. For the emphasis of one Reformation confession on the legitimacy and the necessity of "the profession of good arts and all honorable branches of learning"[58] implies that the arts and the learning of other, newer cultures, too, can be "honorable" and can become a medium for confessing the faith. Even translation, whether of the Scriptures or of the creeds, is never a simple one-to-one transposition; for it has been observed that "much of the Western theory and practice of translation stems immediately from the need to disseminate the Gospels, to speak holy writ in other tongues," a need that applies also to liturgies and to creeds and confessions.[59] Moreover, the translation of creeds at its best has repeatedly proved to be a strategy that is, though necessary, not in itself sufficient to the challenge of transplanting the content of the faith and to the need for defining the authority of the creed in the setting of a new culture.

11.2. The Fate of Creeds in Missions and Migrations

The two principal agencies of transplantation and indigenization in the history of the church have been missions and migrations, in both of which code, cultus, and creed have all been decisive. In each of the seven volumes of his monumental *History of the Expansion of Christianity,* historian of missions Kenneth Scott Latourette uses his summary to ask: "What effect did Christianity have upon its environment; what effect did the environment have upon Christianity; what bearing did the processes by which Christianity spread have upon the effect of Christianity on its environment and of the environment upon Christianity?"[60] Each of Latourette's three questions involves creed as well as cultus and code. Similarly, a collection of scholarly essays published in 1939 to honor the historian of early Christianity Shirley Jackson Case is entitled *Environmental Factors in Christian History.* It includes an essay by Massey H. Shepherd dealing with the significance of the barbarian invasions for the history of the Western liturgy (*cultus*), one by Wilhelm Pauck concerned with the importance of nationalism for

---

58. *Tetrapol* 6; but see also *Loll* 12.
59. Steiner 1992, 257; *RCA* 6.
60. Latourette 1937–45, 7:416.

the Protestant Reformation (*code*), and one by Richard P. McKeon addressing the role of Aristotelianism in the history of Western Christian theology, especially during the period of medieval scholasticism, as it affected such doctrines as creation (*creed*).[61]

A particularly fascinating instance of transplantation through the interaction between mission and migration, as these two factors together have shaped the fate of creeds in a new culture as well as the new culture itself, is the history of "the apostle of the Goths," Ulphilas (or Wulfila). The most frequently cited example of cultural adaptation in this history is the report of the Arian historian Philostorgius (if it is accurate) that in translating the Bible into Gothic, Ulphilas omitted the Books of Kings, on the grounds that the Goths were already warlike enough without receiving any further encouragement from the Holy Writ of their new faith. Many other specific details of the biography of Ulphilas are equally unclear, including the question of whether he had initially been an adherent of *The Creed of Nicaea* and then became an opponent of it, or had affirmed the Arian doctrines of Christ and the Trinity all along. It is clear in any case that at the Second Synod of Antioch or "Dedication Council" of 341,[62] Ulphilas was consecrated bishop by Eusebius of Nicomedia, leader of the Arian party, and that therefore when he came from Constantinople to undertake the mission to the Goths in the early 340s, it was not Nicene orthodoxy but Arianism that he preached and taught and that the Goths accepted. He also subscribed to *The Creed of the Synod of Constantinople* of 360.[63] Nor was he merely a passive disciple of the Arian heresy. "Wulfila," it has been said, "can be considered as the master and motivating figure in a more or less direct manner of all the Arian writers active on the doctrinal plane whose works are extant today."[64]

This Arian tendency would seem to be evident even from the imperfect text of *The Confession of Ulphilas* (said to have been inscribed on his tombstone), which declares concerning the Holy Spirit that he is "neither God nor our God, but the minister of Christ, subject and

61. McNeill, Spinka, and Willoughby 1939.
62. *Ant 341.*
63. *CP 360.*
64. Quasten, 4:97.

obedient in all things to the Son."[65] This subordination of the third hy-postasis is an Arian teaching that *The Niceno-Constantinopolitan Creed* of 381 counters when it not only reaffirms *The Creed of Nicaea* in at-tributing to the Son "identity of being" with the Father but goes be-yond Nicaea to insist that the Holy Spirit is both God and Lord in the full sense.[66] Therefore it was as Arians—as Christians rather than pagans, but as heretics rather than orthodox Catholics—that the Goths migrated into Europe, the Ostrogoths moving chiefly to Italy and the Visigoths primarily to Spain. Because of his adherence to Christianity, though in the heretical Arian form, the king of the Visigoths, Alaric, spared the Catholic Christians when his army sacked the city of Rome in the year 410. But this adherence to Arian heresy did eventually bring them into conflict with the resident Catholic population, espe-cially in Italy. The most notorious instance of that conflict occurred when, for reasons that are still not entirely clear, the Arian Ostrogothic king Theoderic imprisoned the greatest scholar of the West, the Catho-lic theologian and philosopher Anicius Manlius Torquatus Severinus Boethius, who while in prison wrote his *Consolation of Philosophy,* one of the most beloved books of the Latin Middle Ages. The execution of Boethius was commemorated as a martyrdom for the orthodox Catholic creed and for the doctrine of the Trinity; Boethius had writ-ten highly influential creedal treatises on both of these topics, *De fide catholica* and *De Trinitate.*[67]

By contrast with the Arian Goths, another Germanic people, the Franks, came into Western Europe as pagans. In their case, there-fore, the sequence of mission and migration was the reverse of the pat-tern followed by the Goths: migration came first, and then mission. But when they were converted, it was to the Catholic orthodoxy of *The Niceno-Constantinopolitan Creed* rather than to the Arian heresy of *The Confession of Ulphilas;* and the Catholic Franks rather than the Arian Goths were the ones who became the natural allies of the papacy, the chief nation in the medieval Holy Roman Empire. The alliance was founded through the conversion of the king of the Franks, Clovis, to

65. *Ulph.*
66. N-CP 2, 8.
67. *Fid cath;* Chadwick 1992, 52–56, 175–80, 211–22.

orthodox Catholic Christianity, which according to the historian of the Franks, Gregory of Tours, took place in 496. Once converted to the Catholic faith, Clovis battled not only against the paganism out of which he had come, in keeping with the celebrated admonition that he was now to worship what he had been burning and to burn what he had been worshiping,[68] but against Germanic Arianism, which was eventually extirpated (though it took a long time). The alliance of the papacy and the Franks reached its climax in the year 800, when another Frankish king, Karl/Charles (known to history as Charlemagne), was crowned Roman emperor by the pope. This papal encouragement of a Western rival to the incumbent of the Christian "Roman" imperial throne in Constantinople was a major cultural and political factor in the estrangement between the two churches.[69] There is even some reason to believe that the insistence by Charlemagne, the king of the Franks who became the Roman emperor of the West, on the doctrine of Filioque and on its inclusion in the *Western Recension* of *The Niceno-Constantinopolitan Creed*[70] may be attributed to his sense that there was need for a stronger stand in favor of the doctrine of the Trinity, against the lingering Germanic Arianism that had come into Western Europe as a consequence of the mission of Ulphilas. The original creedal doctrine of the procession of the Holy Spirit only from the Father could, by an argument from silence, appear to smack of subordinationism.[71] To that extent, the process of transplanting the Christian creed to other cultures through mission and migration, or through migration and mission, can also be said to have had a share in shaping the most momentous creedal change in Christian history.[72]

Coinciding as it did with the missionary expansion of the nineteenth and twentieth centuries and the coming-of-age of "the younger churches,"[73] the unprecedented scale of migration into many new parts

68. Gregory of Tours *History of the Franks* 2.31.
69. Ostrogorsky 1969, 182–86.
70. *N-CP Occ* 8; *Fréjus* 4.
71. Cavadini 1993.
72. See chapter 7.4 above, "The Holy Spirit of Concord and the Sacrament of Concord: Two Ironic Case Histories"; and chapter 15.1 below, "The Western Reception of the Catholic Creedal and Conciliar Tradition."
73. Nortier 1941.

of the world during the same period likewise had great confessional implications. These were particularly challenging in the various attempts at mergers both within and across denominational and confessional lines,[74] also for groups that had not always resorted to the formal confession as an expression of their doctrinal identity. "Already the mission field," as the *Call to Unity* at Lausanne in 1927 observed, "is impatiently revolting from the divisions of the Western Church to make bold adventure for unity in its own right."[75] An outstanding instance, involving as it did both the practical issue of church polity and the doctrinal basis of polity, was the creation of the Church of South India.[76] Within the Baptist tradition, separation from the Lutheran establishment produced *The Confession of Faith of the Swedish Baptists.*[77] And *The Doctrinal Basis of the Baptist Union of Victoria, Australia* of 1888, in addition to confessing the "many phases of Christian truth in common with other denominations," such as "the divine inspiration" of the Bible, affirms a "distinctive emphasis upon the following fundamental principles of the Christian faith, as revealed in the New Testament."[78] At about the same time in New Zealand, a similar document, *The Doctrinal Basis of the New Zealand Baptist Union* of 1882, likewise opens with "the inspiration of the Bible and its authority in all matters of faith and practice."[79] But such a text as *The Confession of the Korean Methodist Church* of 1930 expresses the new and growing awareness of churches originally brought to Asia by evangelists from Great Britain and the Continent that confessional expressions originally formulated in the mother countries do not necessarily continue to meet the needs of a new cultural context.[80] Also in East Asia, in 1927, *The Bond of Union of the Church of Christ in China* expresses the deepening consciousness of fellowship among Chinese Christians,[81] and *The Confession of Faith of the United Church of Christ*

74. *Ghana; Un Ref Ch; Morav Am; Un Ch Can: Crd; UCC; Sri Lanka; Zambia.*
75. *F&O Laus* 1; also *Sri Lanka* 12.
76. See chapter 4.4 above, "Faith and Order in the Ecumenical Confessional Dialogue."
77. *Swed Bap.*
78. *Bap Aus* 1.
79. *Bap NZ* 1.
80. *Meth Kor.*
81. *Chin Un.*

in Japan of 1954 seeks to find a confessional formula for their faith and doctrine.[82]

11.3. Patterns of Creedal Indigenization

Transporting a confession of faith from one country or continent to another in this manner, whether through mission or migration or some other (sometimes related) channel such as imperial conquest or economic trade, or in modern times through printing or broadcasting, has necessitated not only translating the text into a new language and a new culture, but sometimes reconsidering the political context of the confession. Quite often, this reconsideration has proved to be the most prominent and the most controversial aspect of creedal indigenization. It has become especially necessary in the case of those confessions of faith that had depended for their origin and their enforcement upon an established church, supported by the state and supporting it in turn, but that were now to be reaffirmed under radically different political conditions. Because the United States of America as a new republic had waged and won the Revolutionary War to secure its independence from the kingdom in which Anglicanism was the established church, *The American Revision* of the Anglican *Thirty-Nine Articles* in 1801 was obliged to dissociate itself from the mother country. In reference to the *Homilies*, which are an authority for *The Thirty-Nine Articles of the Church of England* because of their "godly and wholesome doctrine,"[83] *The American Revision* specifies that "all references to the constitution and laws of England are considered as inapplicable to the circumstances of this church,"[84] just as in the revision of *The Anglican Catechism* the original "to honor and obey the king" is changed to "the civil authority."[85] *The American Revision of the Thirty-Nine Articles* in a later article substitutes the statement: "The power of the civil magistrate extendeth to all men, as well clergy as laity, in all things temporal; but hath no authority in things purely spiritual."[86] One article of the *Thirty-Nine Articles* also states, over against the assertions of papal au-

82. *Chin Outl.*
83. *39 Art 35.*
84. *39 Art Am 35.*
85. *Ang Cat.*
86. *39 Art Am 37.*

thority, that "general councils may not be gathered together without the commandment and will of princes";[87] but *The American Revision* of 1801 omits that article entirely.[88] Similarly, *The American Revision of the Westminster Confession of Faith* of American Presbyterianism drops the doctrine that the civil magistrate "hath power to call synods, to be present at them, and to provide that whatsoever is transacted in them be according to the mind of God."[89]

But when the revision of the Anglican *Thirty-Nine Articles* for the Protestant Episcopal Church in the United States also drops *The Athanasian Creed* from the original list of the three ancient creeds that are binding on Anglicans, leaving only *The Nicene Creed* and *The Apostles' Creed*,[90] the principal reason for that revision was probably not these political differences. Instead, it is to be explained by other cultural forces, above all the growing hostility, which was at work in Great Britain at least as widely as in the United States,[91] toward what was perceived as the harsh language of *The Athanasian Creed*, particularly its "damnatory clauses": "This is the Catholic faith. Unless one keeps it in its entirety inviolate, one will assuredly perish eternally."[92] Similar cultural or theological forces, rather than political ones, seem to have been responsible for transforming the exclusionary implications of the language of the British Presbyterian *Westminster Confession of Faith* of 1647 and *The Savoy Declaration* of 1658, "*Elect* infants, dying in infancy, are regenerated and saved by Christ,"[93] into the inclusionary language of the American *Confession of the Cumberland Presbyterian Church* of 1829: "*All* infants dying in infancy are regenerated and saved by Christ."[94] In the same way, the "American Lutheranism" set forth in the *Definite Platform* of 1855 showed that it was "American" not so much by its strong acceptance of the American proposition of religious liberty as by its accommodation of the Lutheranism of *The*

87. *39 Art* 21.
88. *39 Art Am.*
89. *West* 23.3, 31.2; *West Am* 23, 31.
90. *39 Art* 8; *39 Art Am* 8.
91. See chapter 17.1 below, "The Discomfort with Creed Caused by the Consciousness of Modernity."
92. *Ath* 2.
93. *West* 10.3; *Sav* 10.3; italics added.
94. *Cumb Pres* 54; italics added.

Book of Concord of 1580 to other communions of American Protestant-ism on such issues as the eucharist and private confession, an accom-modation that likewise entailed dropping *The Athanasian Creed*.[95]

Yet if, as all of these historical instances show, it takes a great deal more than mere translation to make a creed truly indigenous in a new culture, the insistent questions are, as they always have been: Which elements of a received statement of faith are accidental marks of the cultural matrix in which the creed or confession originally arose, rather than belonging to its essence? Which components of any par-ticular culture are sufficiently malleable and neutral to be taken over into a statement of the Christian faith? And which elements of that culture are so inherently alien to the gospel, even demonic, that they cannot be baptized but only exorcised?

Those questions are as old as the Christian faith itself.[96] The apostle Paul not only appealed in his epistles to the authority of Jew-ish Scripture (usually in the Greek of the Septuagint) and argued from the grammatical details of its very words to authenticate his message that Jesus was the promised Messiah.[97] But when he was facing a Greek audience in Athens, to which the authority of the Old Testament and the expectation of the Messiah voiced in it would have seemed like nonsense,[98] he felt free to switch from citing the Old Testament to quoting an inscription "To an unknown god" and "some of your poets," who had said, "In him we live and move and have our being" and "For we are indeed his offspring [*Tou gar kai genos esmen*]."[99] There was, then, apostolic legitimation for appropriating the language of Greek polytheists about their pagan deities—not, it should be noted, the proper name of such deities, except for "the Unknown"—and for transferring that possessive pronoun "his [*tou*]" to the one God of Jew-ish and Christian monotheism, the Creator of heaven and earth and the God and Father of the Lord Jesus Christ. A century or so later, Clem-ent of Alexandria exercised even greater freedom in appropriating, not only the language and literature of Greek culture, but specifically its

95. *Def Plat* 1.5, 2.9, 1.2, 2.3.
96. Harnack [1908] 1961a, 44–72.
97. Gal 3.16.
98. 1 Cor 1.23.
99. Acts 17.22–31.

philosophy, for the gospel. In a famous parallelism he extrapolated from the words of Paul, "The law was our schoolmaster [*paidagōgos*] to lead us unto Christ,"[100] to suggest a bold argument from analogy:

> God is the cause of all good things; but of some primarily, as of the Old and the New Testament; and of others by consequence, as philosophy. Perchance, too, philosophy was given to the Greeks directly and primarily, till the Lord should call the Greeks. For this was a schoolmaster [*paidagōgos*] to bring "the Hellenic mind," as the law [brought] the Hebrews, "to Christ." Philosophy, therefore, was a preparation, paving the way for him who is perfected in Christ.[101]

In the apologetics and "natural theology" of both the Greek East and the Latin West during the Middle Ages, such appropriation and adaptation led to the interpretation of the creed as "faith in search of understanding [*fides quaerens intellectum*]."[102]

But when the confessions of the Protestant Reformation attack various of the traditions of the medieval church, they single out for special criticism this sort of accommodation to non-Christian teachings and practices, by insisting that it overlooks the fundamental and nonnegotiable "difference . . . between philosophical teaching and the teaching of the Holy Spirit."[103] The cultus, code, and creed of the Middle Ages are all accused by the Protestant confessions of having fatally obscured that fundamental difference. In cultus, the veneration of the saints and of their images, even the veneration of the Virgin Mary, is denounced as an imitation of polytheistic worship, a product of "the imaginations and devices of men, or the suggestions of Satan."[104] In code, the reliance of scholastic moral theology on church tradition and on Aristotle's *Nicomachean Ethics* is accused of having

---

100. Gal 3.24 (AV).
101. Clement of Alexandria *Stromata* 1.5 (*ANF* 2:305).
102. *Chr Trad* 2:242–52, 3:255–67; see chapter 15.3 below, "Scholastic Theology as Reasoning on the Basis of the Creed." Also Syndogmaticon 1.2.
103. *Apol Aug* 18.9; see chapter 10.1 above, "Doctrines of Christian Discipline in the Reformation Confessions."
104. *West* 21.1–2. Syndogmaticon 3.7–8.

seriously dulled the edge of the distinctive obedience of faith to the revealed law of God, as the only complete norm of truly good works.[105]
And in creed, "the many-sided, refined and fastidious, but a little too
esoteric learning" of various theologians past and present is blamed
for their having subsumed the central doctrines of the Christian creed
under philosophical abstractions.[106] Inspired by the Pietism of the eighteenth and nineteenth centuries, Protestant Evangelicalism became even
more insistent than these Reformation confessions had been on the
uniqueness of the gospel and of the Christian creed in relation to other
cultures and systems of thought.[107] That set it apart not only from Roman Catholicism and Eastern Orthodoxy but from some earlier stages
of Protestantism.[108] Because this Pietist Evangelicalism played such a
major part in motivating the phenomenal growth of the European Protestant missionary enterprise during the nineteenth century, its "great
century,"[109] the problem of identifying the potential point of contact, if
any, between the Christian creed and other cultures forced itself upon
those in the twentieth century who were striving to confess the faith in
new cultural contexts where it had not been believed, taught, and confessed before. These cultural contexts were new either because the gospel had not penetrated to those regions earlier or because a historically
Christian culture had been fundamentally altered in the modern era.

Two statements of faith composed during the twentieth century may serve as dramatic illustrations of this vital issue, one by its
affirmations and the other by its negations: *The Masai Creed* and *The
Barmen Declaration*. Each is consciously responding to a system of
thought and belief that it regards as new in the experience of the
church. Therefore each presents itself to its culture as in some sense a
response to that culture's deepest needs or deepest traditions. At the
same time each, albeit in its own way, locates itself within the continuity of the creedal and confessional traditions of the churches. But
given these similarities, we must inquire even more after the differences
between them, for it is in such differences that criteria for any work-

105. *Heid* 91. Syndogmaticon 8.5.
106. *Helv II* 18.9.
107. Hutchison 1987, 62–90.
108. Troeltsch 1891.
109. Latourette 1937–45, 4–6.

able theory or practice of creedal indigenization may be found.[110] Such criteria in these twentieth-century formularies, moreover, ought themselves to manifest a demonstrable continuity with the creedal tradition and with the way earlier Greek and Latin creeds simultaneously reflect their culture and set themselves in opposition to it.[111]

Africa was a crucible during the twentieth century for the creedal relation between inculturation and the Christian determination to remain traditional.[112] That became evident in the creation of the "African Orthdox Church" in 1921[113] and in confessional statements from states that were emerging from colonialism during the second half of the twentieth century, nowhere more explicitly than in the catalog of idolatrous beliefs and practices condemned by the *Statement of Faith* of the Church of Jesus Christ in Madagascar in its first article.[114] *The Masai Creed,* prepared in the 1960s by the Holy Ghost Fathers in East Africa, was part of their conscious effort at what was called "inculturation applied" in a movement "toward an African Christianity."[115] Some adherents of ancient Christian traditions might find its formulations naive when they are viewed in the light of the trinitarian and christological controversies and creeds between the fourth and the seventh century. At first glance *The Masai Creed* might seem to be little more than a repetition or paraphrase of some of the earliest Greek and Latin creeds, as these appear in Part One of *Creeds and Confessions of Faith in the Christian Tradition.* But on closer inspection it demonstrates its indigenization in African ethnic tradition when it describes Jesus Christ as having been "always on safari doing good, curing people by the power of God, teaching about God and man, showing that the meaning of religion is love."[116] This summarizes—in fact, more amply than the Greek and Latin creeds of the early church do when they move directly from his being "born of the Virgin Mary"

110. See the taxonomy in H. Richard Niebuhr 1951.
111. C. N. Cochrane 1944; Pelikan 1993.
112. Sanneh 1983.
113. *Afr Orth.*
114. *Madag* 1; *Ghana; Togo.*
115. Hillman 1993.
116. *Masai* 2.

to his having "suffered under Pontius Pilate"[117]—the narratives of his
ministry of teaching and healing in the Gospels. Even more indigenized
is its declaration that after Christ died, "he lay buried in the grave,
but the hyenas did not touch him, and on the third day, he rose from
the grave."[118] This paraphrases the New Testament's application to the
burial of Christ of the verse from the Psalms,[119] as cited in other confessions:[120] "Thou wilt not . . . suffer thine Holy One to see corruption."
It is all the more authentic and primitively Christian because scaveng-
ing wild animals that ravaged graves were a problem in first-century
Palestine as well as in twentieth-century Africa. That is evident from
the practice of entombing the dead, including the body of the crucified
Christ, in a sepulcher "which had been hewn out of the rock," and of
"roll[ing] a stone against the door of the tomb."[121] The first edition of
Vincent J. Donovan's *Christianity Rediscovered* bears the subtitle "An
Epistle from the Masai."

It was, nevertheless, over the hard-won affirmation of the orthodox and catholic tradition of the church generally, as this is confessed in the formula of *The Masai Creed* that "God loves . . . *every
nation* and tribe on the earth,"[122] that the fiercest conflict of the twentieth century about cultural adaptation would break out. This happened,
not in Africa or any other developing region or mission field, but in the
heart of Western European Christendom, the land of the Holy Roman
Empire and the Reformation, and the site of the church's resistance
to the state in the nineteenth-century *Kulturkampf*.[123] Ironically, it was
also the capital of scientific theological, biblical—and creedal and confessional—scholarship.[124] The "German Christians," carrying out what
they presented as a logical extension and completion of Luther's Reformation, pressed for the accommodation of Christianity to the spirit

117. *Ap* 3–4; *N-CP* 3–4; cf. *Genv Cat* 55.
118. *Masai* 2.
119. Ps 16.10 (LXX); Acts 2.27, 13.35.
120. *Metr Crit* 3.9.
121. Mk 15.46.
122. *Masai* 1; italics added.
123. Reese 1974.
124. See chapter 17.3 below, "The Flowering of Creedal and Confessional Scholarship in the Modern Era."

of the Third Reich. This policy included deemphasizing or even elimi-
nating many of the Jewish components in Christian teaching, above all
the authority of the Jewish Scriptures of the Old Testament, as well
as prohibiting the ordination to the Christian ministry of anyone who,
like the original twelve apostles of Christ (and like Christ himself), had
Jewish blood.[125] Claiming to have found a deep spirituality in Nazi
mysticism about the führer and a compatibility and renewing power
in a revitalized Nordic ideology, the German Christians succeeded in
appealing also to many in all the churches who, while rejecting some
of its excesses, claimed to sense a genuine affinity with key elements
of the new faith.[126]

　　　This use of a new natural theology to achieve creedal indigenization evoked a response in *The Barmen Declaration* [*Theologische Erklärung zur gegenwärtigen Lage der Deutschen Evangelischen Kirche*] of
May 1934. Its opening thesis, therefore, is a rejection of the alluring
proposal that the message of the church should be accommodated to
natural theology, be it Greek or Nordic, and to the spirit of the time.
Even more emphatically than *The Masai Creed* with its confession "We
have known this High God in the darkness, and now we know him in
the light,"[127] *The Barmen Declaration* insists that the church must believe, teach, and confess Christ as "the single word of God [*das eine
Wort Gottes*]," the unique and ultimate revelation of the reality and will
of God.[128] The Christian church had confessed this in its creeds over
against the earlier paganisms of Greeks and Romans—and the paganisms of earlier Germans—and now it was called upon to confess it
again, and to accept the consequences of that confession in its total life
and message.

11.4. The Paradigm: *Shema* to *Homoousios*

Nevertheless, the most radical and the most far-reaching case of successful creedal indigenization-cum-differentiation in a new culture during all of Christian history, and the one that has served as a con-

125. Gutteridge 1976, 69–313.
126. Ericksen 1985; Lewy 1964.
127. *Masai* 1.
128. *Barm* 1.

scious or unconscious paradigm for all the others, was the transition from *The Shema* of the Book of Deuteronomy to the *homoousios* of *The Nicene Creed* and *The Niceno-Constantinopolitan Creed*.[129] For in Bernard de Margerie's formulation of the historical paradox, "in order to fight efficaciously against a rebirth of pagan syncretism, the council [of Nicaea in 325] judged it indispensable to use a term that came to it through Clement of Alexandria from the syncretist literature of the Gnostics."[130] The legitimacy of that transition raises all of the important questions to which all subsequent experiments in indigenization and inculturation would be obliged to pay attention, and the answers of fourth-century orthodoxy to those questions, as formulated for example by Athanasius of Alexandria,[131] were to become normative for such experiments. As John Courtney Murray once put it, commenting on the modern impasse between Christian confessions, "I do not think that the first ecumenical question is, what think ye of the church? Or even, what think ye of Christ? The dialogue would rise out of the current confusion if the first question raised were, what think ye of the Nicene homoousion?"[132] For if it was legitimate to borrow such a term from heretics or pagans and thereby to "use well what they invented badly,"[133] then the reformulation of the gospel in a new culture through the development of doctrine beyond the *ipsissima verba* of the New Testament and through the use of an indigenous creedal vocabulary can also be legitimate.

A decisive component of the transition was the simple linguistic one (which was, of course, really not so simple at all): *Shema* is a Hebrew word, *homoousios* a Greek word. The first large-scale attempt in history to bridge that particular linguistic gap had been the Septuagint, the translation of the Hebrew Bible into Greek by a group of Jewish scholars (traditionally, seventy-two in number) in Alexandria during the second and third centuries B.C. The Septuagint was *the* Bible for most of the writers of the New Testament, including the apostle Paul, and for most subsequent Greek-speaking Christians to

129. *Shema;* N 2; N-CP 2; see also chapter 13.1 below, "The Primal Creed."
130. Margerie 1982, 91.
131. Athanasius *Defense of the Nicene Definition* 6.27 (*NPNF*–II 4:168–69).
132. Murray 1964, 53.
133. *CP 1341* 50.

the present day. Its standing among them was so authoritative, even by comparison with the original Hebrew, that when Gregory of Nyssa in the fourth century speaks of "the original language of the Scripture [*ho prōtotypos tēs graphēs logos*]" of the Old Testament, he is in fact referring, not to the Hebrew original, but to the Greek translation in the Septuagint.[134] The historical transition from *Shema* to *homoousios*, therefore, participated in the momentous shift represented by the Septuagint, whose Jewish translators had evidently felt able to proceed on the assumption that the content of the biblical message could be carried over from Hebrew to Greek without loss.

Most immediately, the linguistic question had to be addressed in the area of vocabulary. When the Septuagint rendered *The Shema* with the Greek, "*Akoue, Israēl: kyrios ho theos hēmōn kyrios heis estin,*"[135] it was putting both of these central components of the Greek religious vocabulary—*ho theos hēmōn*, "our God," as a translation of the Hebrew *elōhēinu*; and *ho kyrios*, "the Lord," as a translation of the Hebrew *adōnai*, in place of the ineffable divine name *JHWH*—into the service of biblical teachings. Was it also claiming to have drained these Greek terms of all their original pagan meanings and to have refilled them with the faith of Israel? It is a clear reference to the problem of those two central elements of Greek religious vocabulary, perhaps also specifically to the Septuagint of *The Shema*, when the apostle Paul can declare, in creedlike language that is eventually echoed in the titles "one God [*hena theon*]" and "one Lord [*hena kyrion*]" of *The Niceno-Constantinopolitan Creed*:[136] "Although there may be so-called gods in heaven or on earth—as indeed there are many 'gods' [*theoi polloi*] and many 'lords' [*kyrioi polloi*]—yet for us there is one God [*heis theos*], the Father, from whom are all things, and for whom we exist, and one Lord [*heis kyrios*], Jesus Christ, through whom are all things and through whom we exist."[137]

As the linguistic aspects of the transition do in some ways

134. Gregory of Nyssa *Against Eunomius* 3.9.33 [11.3] (*NPNF*–II 5:234).
135. Dt 6.4 (LXX).
136. *N-CP* 1–2.
137. 1 Cor 8.5–6.

reflect, the difference between *Shema* and *homoousios* is between two ways of speaking, the first concentrating on history and the second on ontology. The larger context of *The Shema* is the extensive discourse of Moses that makes up the whole of the Book of Deuteronomy. Therefore *The Shema* is formulated as it is in order to root it in the history of Israel as the chosen people of God and in the history of the exodus as the event in which that special status of Israel through the covenant is made evident and by which it is constituted. *"Hear, O Israel,"* the text says, "The Lord *our* God, the Lord is one." [138] Thus the summons to Israel to hear and to pay attention precedes—and frames—the monotheistic confession itself. The God who is confessed by this primal creed to be "one" is first confessed to be "our" God, the one whose mighty deeds in the exodus of the people of Israel from Egypt, through the giving of the covenant and of the law at Sinai, and during the wanderings in the wilderness are the subject matter of the entire discourse of Moses. So already in the giving of the Ten Commandments at Sinai, the law is also framed by the history of the covenant: "I am the Lord your God, who brought you out of the land of Egypt, out of the house of bondage. You shall have no other gods before me." [139] The indicative narrative statement leads to the imperative prohibition by an implied "therefore."

This also dramatizes the contrast between *Shema* and *homoousios*. As the creeds and confessions of the fifth century were to emphasize even more strongly,[140] the predicate "one in being with the Father [*homoousios tōi patri*]" here is intended to pertain also to the history of the one who, a few phrases later, is said to have "suffered under Pontius Pilate." [141] But the emphasis of the *homoousios* is in the first instance on his eternal being—in the confessional distinction introduced earlier,[142] on "pure theology [*haplē theologia*]," which is "the knowl-

138. Dt 6.4; italics added.
139. Ex 20.2–3.
140. *Tome* 10; *Chal* 9.
141. *N-CP* 2, 4. See *Patr* as a sample of how this trinitarian faith was exported in the creeds employed by early missionaries.
142. See chapter 7.4 above, "The Holy Spirit of Concord and the Sacrament of Concord: Two Ironic Case Histories."

edge of the one essence of God," not on the "theology of the divine economy [*oikonomia*]" or historical dispensation.[143] What is at issue in the controversy leading up to the Council of Nicaea of 325 and beyond is the "being [*ousia*]" of the Son of God in relation to the "being [*ousia*]" of God the Father, whether the *ousia* of the Son is identical to that of the Father or only "similar [*homoios*]" to it: not merely the conformity of the will of the incarnate Son to the will of the Father, as in his prayer, "Not as I will, but as thou wilt,"[144] but the oneness of his very essence with the very essence of the one true and living God who is confessed as "one" in *The Shema*. Following its predecessor of two years earlier,[145] *The Creed of the Fourth Synod of Sirmium* of 359 rules out the term *ousia* on the grounds that it "gives offense as being unknown to the people, because it is not contained in the Scriptures."[146] (Actually, it does appear in one passage of the New Testament,[147] but as a term for the property squandered by the prodigal son in Christ's parable.) To both sides there was, therefore, vastly more than an "iota of difference" between calling the Son *homoousios* and calling him *homoiousios*.[148]

The biblical line leading from *Shema* to *homoousios* is the revelation given to Moses by the voice of God from the burning bush, as this is rendered in the Septuagint translation, in which it was known and transmitted by the early church: "I am the One-who-is [*Egō eimi ho ōn*]."[149] For in this "towering text,"[150] the origins of the ontological title *ho ōn* are traced not to the metaphysical speculations of the philosophers, where of course it is also present, but to the voice and word of the same God who gave his people *The Shema* through his servant Moses. The confessions and theologians of the church use this passage to legitimate the theological appropriateness of the idea of "essence, being [*ousia*]" (derived from the same verb as the substan-

143. *Metr Crit* 1.2.
144. Mt 26.39.
145. *Sirm 357*.
146. *Sirm 359*.
147. Lk 15.12–13.
148. *Chr Trad* 1:209–10.
149. Ex 3.13 (LXX).
150. Murray 1964, 5.

tive participle *ho ōn*) in trinitarian vocabulary, as well as the correctness of the *homoousios,* therefore also the necessary connection between *homoousios* and *Shema*.[151] On the basis of New Testament precedent,[152] icons label the Son of God with the inscription spoken from the burning bush, "the One-who-is [*ho ōn*]."[153] Therefore the burning bush itself, out of which these words came and which "was not consumed,"[154] is typologically "interpreted as Mary's virginal maternity."[155] And consequently Moses is seen, in both Eastern and Western theology, as the one whose inspired authority confirms not only the *Shema* of Deuteronomy in the creed of Israel but the *ho ōn* of Exodus, and therefore *ousia,*[156] and therefore the *homoousios* in *The Creed of Nicaea*.[157] That makes it a fitting model for every act of transplanting the creed to another culture. For it was the same Moses who "was instructed in all the wisdom of the Egyptians,"[158] and who was therefore seen as an adept in Gentile philosophy,[159] who also transcended all of that when he brought the law of God down from Mount Sinai, taught the people of Israel to recite *The Shema* of monotheism, and led them to the Promised Land.

151. Athanasius *Defense of the Nicene Definition* 3.6 (NPNF–II 4:396).
152. Rv 1.4, 7.
153. Onasch and Schnieper 1977, 133.
154. Ex 3.2.
155. Daniélou 1960, 224.
156. Augustine *On the Trinity* 5.2.3 (NPNF–I 3:88).
157. Athanasius *Defense of the Nicene Definition* 5.22 (NPNF–I 4:164–65).
158. Acts 7.22.
159. Pelikan 1993, 31–32.

CHAPTER TWELVE

The Orthodoxy of the Body
of the Faithful

ON THE FACE OF IT, THE authority of creeds and confessions would appear to be the ultimate tool for the repression of the common people by various upper-class elites, be they social or economic, political or ecclesiastical. It certainly seems to represent the suppression of the indigenous religious beliefs and practices of the proletariat of serfs and peasants, especially of those beliefs and practices that can be accused of being elements surviving from pre-Christian paganism. As a powerful weapon in the hands of priests and prelates, the authority of a creed threatens the members of the laity with the sanctions of excommunication and the denial of the grace of the sacraments here in time, as well as with damnation throughout eternity, for any failure to conform fully to the imposed doctrinal orthodoxy. "This is the Catholic faith," the conclusion of *The Athanasian Creed* intones, solemnly but ominously. And it adds for all to hear, from the highest to the lowest: "Unless one believes it faithfully and steadfastly, one will not be able to be saved."[1] When the imposed doctrinal orthodoxy is also, as it has been throughout most centuries of Christian history until relatively modern times,[2] the official creed not merely of the established church but of the political "powers that be,"[3] the intimidation of religious dissenters through punishment by torture, imprisonment, exile, and even death can be added to these religious sanctions.

It should not be surprising, therefore, that the rise of social

1. *Ath* 42.
2. See chapter 8.2 above, "Civil Law on Adherence to Creeds"; and chapter 17.2 below, "Old and New Contexts of Christian Confessing."
3. Rom 13.1 (AV).

history, as a methodology that is intended to accord a fairer share of
historical attention to major segments of society that have heretofore
been neglected or overlooked by historians on grounds of gender or
race or class, has brought with it a substantial scholarly effort to view
the history of the institutional church, specifically also of Christian beliefs, doctrines, and creeds, "from below," as the saying goes, by teas-
ing out the evidence from source materials that were, more often than
not, originally written to reflect and support the church establishment.[4]
As even a random sampling of scholarship from the second half of the
twentieth century will document, this innovative historiography has
brought many new insights into the religious faith and practice of "the
silent in the land" during various historical periods, insights that have
important implications for the history of spirituality and for the history
of creeds and confessions.

Thus the history of North African Christianity in late antiquity
and the early Middle Ages, which produced special creedal forms that
are best known to us on the basis of the works of Augustine of Hippo,[5]
has received a careful examination, on the basis also of archaeological
evidence that had hitherto been largely neglected, in what Peter Brown
calls "a grandiose and alluring hypothesis on the social and cultural
foundations of the Donatist movement"[6] by W. H. C. Frend. This "hypothesis" leads Frend to the conclusion that "in the fifth and sixth centuries, Catholicism had no appeal for the masses of the native population . . . . no message of effective social reform." As a result, "the
Catholic Church in Africa ultimately suffered the fate of its counterpart, the Melkite Church in Egypt," descending into virtual oblivion.[7]
In the sixth century, as *The Edict of Emperor Justinian* shows,[8] Justinian would claim to be acting, not in his own name and that of the
patriarchs and bishops alone, but in the name of "all believers" and of
the body of the faithful, when, in his capacity as the imperial defender
of orthodoxy, he participated in *The Anathemas Against the "Three*

4. Vauchez 1993.
5. *No Afr.*
6. Brown 2000, 484.
7. Frend 1952, 334.
8. *Edict.*

Chapters" at the Second Council of Constantinople in 553.[9] But "because he was the son of a peasant," his reconstruction of the basilica of Hagia Sophia after the Nika Revolt in 532 had been an expression of the populist inclination of Justinian to "blame it more on the senators than on the people" or "ordinary citizens."[10] Again, a seemingly bizarre aberration like the phenomenon of "sacred theft [*furta sacra*]," the stealing of the relics of saints during the Middle Ages in the Western church, has been imaginatively exploited to show that for "the masses of incompletely Christianized laity and ecclesiastical 'proletariat' . . . at the close of the eighth century Frankish religion was and had long been essentially one of mediation through the saints."[11] And the Hussite Reformation of the fifteenth century, from which there would eventually issue *The [First] Bohemian Confession* of 1535 and *The [Second] Bohemian Confession* of 1575,[12] has been traced by the Czech social historian František Graus to "popular feelings of being threatened and the consequent decision to do something about it[, which] gave the Hussite movement a special impetus, a grass-roots foundation which lent importance to its actions."[13] Unfortunately, this provocative new methodology has also led to some extremes of oversimplification and reductionism, which interpret "ancient heresies" as if in fact they had been nothing more than "disguised social movements" reflecting popular unrest. Popular religion, consequently, is seen as almost always standing in antithesis to the official creedal orthodoxies of church and state.[14]

But it is also possible to interpret the history of the religion of the people in quite the opposite direction. Such an interpretation was espoused in an article of 1859 by John Henry Newman, originally published in *The Rambler* and entitled "The Orthodoxy of the Body of the Faithful During the Supremacy of Arianism." It was subsequently reprinted as an appendix to the later editions of Newman's first book, *The Arians of the Fourth Century* (which had originally

9. *CP II* anath 1–12.
10. Treadgold 1997, 181–82.
11. Geary 1990, 31.
12. *Boh I; Boh II.*
13. Graus [1969] 1971, 83–84.
14. See the critical discussion in Jones 1966.

come out in 1833, while the author was still an Anglican). The article carries, throughout, some marks of what Stephen W. Sykes, speaking about Newman's *Essay on Development* of 1845, calls "enough confusion, perversity, and sheer prejudice, along with profound originality and brilliance to keep controversialists occupied for decades."[15] Its arresting opening sentences read: "The episcopate, whose action was so prompt and concordant at Nicaea on the rise of Arianism, did not, as a class or order of men, play a good part in the troubles consequent upon the Council; and the laity did. The Catholic people, in the length and breadth of Christendom, were the obstinate champions of Catholic truth, and the bishops were not."[16] Newman did concede the presence on both sides of certain "exceptions" to these sweeping generalizations. In a carefully framed postscript that he felt obliged to add later, he responded to Roman Catholic critics who had charged him with having underemphasized the doctrine of papal infallibility (which had meanwhile been promulgated, to mixed reactions from Newman, by *The Dogmatic Constitution on the Catholic Faith of the First Vatican Council* on 18 July 1870). "In drawing out this comparison between the conduct of the Catholic Bishops and that of their flocks during the Arian troubles," Newman explained, "I must not be understood as intending any conclusion inconsistent with the infallibility of the Ecclesia docens, (that is, the Church when teaching) and with the claim of the Pope and the Bishops to constitute the Church in that aspect."[17] Interestingly, he was still attributing the infallibility primarily to the church, and only then to "the Pope *and the Bishops*," whereas *The Dogmatic Constitution on the Catholic Faith of the First Vatican Council* overtly declares that "such definitions of the Roman pontiff are *of themselves, and not by the consent of the church, irreformable.*"[18]

For Newman, therefore, the authority of creeds, councils, and confessions of faith, as statements of what the church believes, teaches, and confesses, is part of the authority of the church. The church whose authority the creeds express is, while of course hierarchical in its juridi-

15. In Ker and Hill 1990, 355–56.
16. Newman [1859] 1901, 445.
17. Newman 1901, 464.
18. *Vat I* 4; italics added.

cal structure and administration, a church that is made up of the body of the faithful, not as customers or passive subjects who "pay, pray, and obey," but as "members one of another." [19] Because the relation of creeds and confessions to popular religion and the faith of the people is a topic that in a special sense cuts across the topics of all preceding eleven chapters of this book, instead of being one in a series of such topics, the present chapter will review, and in the same sequence, some of the materials and issues that have previously been presented in those chapters.

12.1. What Did the Laity Believe, Teach, and Confess?

From the "*We* believe" of *The Creed of Nicaea* of 325 and of *The Niceno-Constantinopolitan Creed* of 381,[20] to "the common and undivided creed by which *the faithful confess*" of *The Tome of Pope Leo I* of 449,[21] to the "*We unanimously* hold and teach, in accordance with the decree of the Council of Nicaea" of *The Augsburg Confession* of 1530,[22] to the "*We all* believe in our hearts and confess with our mouths" of *The Belgic Confession* of 1561,[23] to "the common name of all Christians subject to our apostolic throne" of *The Confession of Dositheus and of the Synod of Jerusalem* of 1672,[24] Christian creeds and confessions in many languages (in these cases, Greek, Latin, German, French, and Greek again) and from all the major traditions consistently represent themselves as speaking in the name of what Newman calls "the body of the faithful." Even *The Eastern Confession of the Christian Faith by Cyril Lucar* claims to be speaking "in the common name of all Christians,"[25] although it was eventually repudiated even by its own church. Such claims imply at the very least that, in the words quoted from Augustine earlier, "the catholic faith in the creed [is] known to the faithful and committed to memory, contained in a form of expression as concise

19. Eph 4.25.
20. *N* 1; *N-CP* 1; italics added. See Syndogmaticon 1.1.
21. *Tome* 2; italics added.
22. *Aug Ger* 1.1; italics added.
23. *Belg* 1; italics added.
24. *Dosith* pr.
25. *Lucar* 1.

as has been rendered admissible by the circumstances."[26] But by employing such language, the creed or confession appears to be making a far more ambitious claim, which could in some limited sense even be characterized as "democratic." Its teaching is not replacing or even correcting or revising or amplifying what the laity have in fact been believing and teaching all along, though perhaps without really knowing it. It is simply articulating and defending this against recent heretical adversaries, or it is making it more precise by the adoption of a more technical theological vocabulary, or it is transposing it from the implicit to the explicit and from the unconscious to the conscious. Therefore the laity are still confessing their own faith in this text. Addressing the questions "Whether a person is bound to believe explicitly in anything" and "Whether all are equally bound to have an explicit faith," Thomas Aquinas concludes: "Just as one is obliged to have faith, so too one is obliged to believe explicitly in its primary tenets, i.e. the articles of faith. With regard to other points, no one is bound to an explicit but only to an implicit belief or readiness to believe, i.e. to be prepared to believe whatever is contained in the Scripture. Even so, one is held to explicit belief in such matters only when it is clear to him that they are in truth contained in the teaching of faith." From this it follows, according to Thomas, that "explicitness in belief is not a matter of salvation uniformly for all; those who have the office of teaching others are held to an explicit belief in more things than others are."[27]

Nevertheless the historical fact remains that almost all the creeds and confessions of faith in all the churches have been produced by the pens of theologians, clergy, and prelates, "those who have the office of teaching others," as Aquinas terms them. Moreover, many of them bear unmistakable evidence of having been composed in the scholar's study. Therefore *The Apostles' Creed*—as well as *The Small Catechism of Martin Luther* of 1529 and *The Heidelberg Catechism* of 1563, both of which expound *The Apostles' Creed*—certainly cannot be seen as typical of the language and the learning evident in many of the other confessions of both East and West. One example from the

---

26. Augustine *On Faith and the Creed* 1 (*NPNF*-I 3:321).
27. Thomas Aquinas *Summa Theologica* 2a2ae.2.5–6 (tr. Blackfriars).

East is *The Synodical Tome of the Synod of Constantinople of 1351*, a defense of the controverted notions of Gregory Palamas about divine and human *energeia* and about "uncreated light," in which the patristic quotations, some of them highly abstruse, greatly outnumber the biblical citations.[28] Examples from the West include above all those from the second and later generations of the Reformation.[29] *The Formula of Concord* of 1577 represents itself as standing in continuity with *The Small Catechism of Martin Luther*, which it even calls "the layman's Bible."[30] In the Netherlands, *The Canons of the Synod of Dort* of 1618–19, by their appeal to the authority of "the confessions of the Reformed churches," are doing the same in relation to *The Heidelberg Catechism*, though without naming it.[31] This catechism-confession was widely distributed among the body of the Reformed faithful, in sixty-two editions in the Netherlands alone before 1585.[32] *The Canons of the Synod of Dort* and *The Belgic Confession* were eventually linked with it as the confessional standard of the Dutch Reformed Church. But article 8 of *The Formula of Concord* dealing with "The Person of Christ," especially in its *Solid Declaration*,[33] and the "First Head of Doctrine" of *The Canons of the Synod of Dort* entitled "Concerning Divine Predestination"[34] both proceed at a level of abstraction and with a degree of dogmatic and philosophical erudition that could be fully comprehensible only to a highly trained elite. Not even everyone who came out of a theological education at the university that was based on the classical preparation in the humanistic *Gymnasium* could be expected to be able to follow the heavily Greek and Latin technical vocabulary of the schematization of "the interchange of attributes [*idiomatum communicatio*]" in *The Formula of Concord*.[35] According to this doctrine, which is affirmed (though with divergent conclusions) also in some Re-

---

28. *CP 1351*.
29. See chapter 16.4 below, "From Reformation Confessions to Confessional Scholasticism."
30. *Form Conc Epit* 1.5.
31. *Dort* con.
32. Heijting 1989, 1:84–85.
33. *Form Conc Sol Dec* 8.
34. *Dort* 1.1.
35. *ODCC* 386.

formed confessions,[36] the attributes of one of the natures of Christ, including the omnipresence or "ubiquity" of his divine nature, are shared with the other nature through being communicated to his single divine-human person in the incarnation. The result of this interchange of attributes is, according to the *Epitome* of the *Formula* (which is intended to be more generally intelligible, even to laymen), that Christ can, "and indeed most easily, being present [everywhere], does impart his true body and his blood in the holy supper."[37] This seems to be making the doctrine of the real presence in the eucharist dependent on the metaphysics of a particular version of Christology. Originally, of course, the Christology became a matter of controversy between Reformed and Lutheran theology as a by-product of their controversy over the real presence, rather than the other way around. It is, moreover, clear from other confessions, neither Reformed nor Lutheran, that an unequivocal affirmation of the doctrine of the real presence is not necessarily tied to the christological concept of ubiquity at all, even while this concept of "the way of exchange [*tropos antidoseōs*]" is being affirmed.[38] Similarly, the clarification of the doctrine of justification by the Council of Trent is cast in the Aristotelian vocabulary of final cause, efficient cause, meritorious cause, instrumental cause, and formal cause.[39]

To comprehend the highly technical vocabulary of such schematizations in these various confessions and to follow their theological argumentation, it is helpful to know at first hand the other writings of the theologians who composed them, as well as the earlier patristic and scholastic sources on which they drew or against which they were contending. That is true even when, as is often the case, these sources are not identified in the texts (or even in modern critical editions). For that matter, such preparation is also needed to translate the terminology of such confessions into another language, as the history of the process of the indigenization of creeds and confessions into new languages by missionaries and converts demonstrates,[40] and as the preparation of the

---

36. For example, *Helv II* 11.10.
37. *Form Conc Epit* 8.12.
38. *Mogila* 1.56; *Metr Crit* 3.5; *Dosith* decr 17. See Syndogmaticon 10.6.
39. *Trent* 6.1.7; Aristotle *Physics* 2.3 (194b–95b).
40. See chapter 11.2 above, "The Fate of Creeds in Missions and Migrations."

volumes of *Creeds and Confessions of Faith in the Christian Tradition* has repeatedly shown. From both the form and the content of *The Canons of the Synod of Dort, The Westminster Confession of Faith,* and *The Formula of Concord* it would be easy, but mistaken, to conclude that "confession" or "creed" should be defined as the matter with which the learned caste of the theologians dealt.[41]

Yet the church has never been—or at least has never been *only*—a school, and the teaching of the church has never been only the business of scholars or theologians, or even only of the clergy. Because Christian doctrine is and must be the concern of the church, of the entire church, creeds and confessions of faith do claim to be speaking for their entire church, indeed, for "all Christians."[42] In much the same way, not all of the delegates from the thirteen colonies who attended the fateful deliberations that produced the American *Declaration of Independence* at Philadelphia on 4 July 1776—much less all of the citizens of the colonies, who had sent them there—could have written what Thomas Jefferson wrote. But Jefferson did insist strongly that when he wrote, he was consciously speaking not in his own name but in the name of all. What these delegates said in the conclusion of their *Declaration of Independence* about their political situation, therefore, the Christian framers of the creeds and confessions of faith in different ages could have said (and, using somewhat different words, often did say) about their doctrinal declarations: "And, for the support of this declaration, with a firm reliance on the protection of Divine Providence, we mutually pledge to each other our lives, our fortunes, and our sacred honor."[43] As the preface to *The Scots Confession* of 1560 puts it, "Long have we thirsted, dear brethren, to have made known to the world the doctrine which we profess and for which we have suffered abuse and danger."[44] In Western Christendom, therefore, *The Apostles' Creed* is confessed by (or, in the case of infants, *for*) individual candidates for baptism, as well as by a congregation. *The Niceno-Constantinopolitan Creed* is eventually embedded in the liturgi-

41. See also chapter 16.4 below, "From Reformation Confessions to Confessional Scholasticism."
42. *Ans* 3.40.
43. Laqueur and Rubin 1989, 109.
44. *Scot I* pr.

cal celebration of the eucharist by both East and West, as well as being used for baptism in the East.[45] Such confessions as Luther's *Small Catechism* of 1529 or *The Heidelberg Catechism* of 1563 are addressed to the ignorance of Christian doctrine among the common people,[46] and are presented "in the plain form in which the head of the family shall teach it to his household,"[47] to be studied and memorized by the children of the church and to be recited and pondered for a lifetime by lay believers as they consider (in the words of the opening question of the latter catechism) their "only comfort, in life and in death."[48] All of that applies regardless of whose pen may have been responsible for the original literary composition and the doctrinal phraseology of these creeds, catechisms, and confessions.

12.2. Popular Religion, the Rule of Prayer, and Tradition

At least to some degree, such an identification of creeds and confessions of faith as the vindication of the orthodoxy of the body of the faithful, and therefore such an interpretation of the authoritative confessional tradition as an apologia for "popular religion" (though not perhaps in the conventional sense of that term) are borne out even by the history of polemics and anathema. In answer to the question raised earlier about why some councils (for example, Ephesus 449) were not accorded recognition and "reception" even though they appeared to have met the formal criteria for an ecumenical council,[49] the Russian lay theologian Aleksej Stepanovič Chomjakov quoted the recent assertion of the Eastern Orthodox prelates that "the protector of religion is the very body of the church, even the people themselves [*auto to sōma tēs ekklēsias, ētoi autos ho laos*]"; and he declared that it was "solely because their decisions were not recognized as the voice of the church by the entire ecclesial people [*cerkovnom narodom*], by that people and within that world where, in questions of faith, there is no difference between the scholar and the unlearned, cleric and lay person, man and

45. See chapter 6.3 above, "The Place of Creed in Liturgy."
46. *17 Art* pr.
47. *Luth Sm Cat* 1 (and in the title of each of the other "chief parts").
48. *Heid* 1; Barth 1964.
49. See chapter 9.2 above, "Reception of Creeds, Councils, and Confessions as Ratification."

woman, and king and subject, . . . and where . . . the heresy of a learned bishop is refuted by an illiterate shepherd, so that all might be joined in the free unity of living faith, which is the manifestation of the Spirit of God." [50] The period of "the supremacy of Arianism" (as Newman's essay labels it) during the fourth century can be used, and was used by him, to support this thesis. The First Council of Constantinople in 381 and its *Niceno-Constantinopolitan Creed* was for him the vindication of the orthodoxy of lay spirituality, which, in this case, may be said to have known all along that in experiencing the gifts of the Holy Spirit believers were receiving, not some created "thing," but the presence of none less than the one true God. This is what the council's creed finally got around to confessing formally in 381.

Yet there is an even more fascinating example in the following century. Judging on the basis of the state of the surviving primary sources, it is also probably more verifiable. It was not until the third ecumenical council, the Council of Ephesus in 431, that the church by decree made the teaching official "that the holy Virgin is the Mother of God [Theotokos]." Nestorius, bishop of Constantinople, "New Rome," was condemned as a heretic and deposed from his episcopal throne for denying that title to the Virgin Mary and for refusing to call her more than "Mother of Christ [Christotokos]." [51] So it was that this Marian title became part of the rule of faith, remaining so even for some Protestant confessions, both Reformed and Lutheran. [52] All of that was going on at the official level of authoritative conciliar and creedal dogma, to which, as to every dogma, the beliefs and prayers of ordinary believers forever after were obliged to conform, under threat of the dire punishments both temporal and eternal that have been enumerated earlier.

But the doctrine of the Virgin Mary as Theotokos cannot be treated as simply another example of a dogma imposed from above on popular religion. We know this from an extremely unsympathetic source, which may for that reason be regarded as objective: Emperor Julian "the Apostate," who had once been a church member but had

50. *Resp Pius IX* 17; Chomjakov [1907] 1995, 2:91 (tr. Vera Shevzov).
51. *Eph 431.*
52. *Tetrapol* 11; *Form Conc Epit* 8.12.

rejected Christianity. He tells us that a century or so before the Council of Ephesus and without the pressure from above of any authoritative conciliar and creedal dogma or any imperial edict, Christians "would not desist in calling Mary the Mother of God [*Theotokon de hymeis ou pauesthe Marian kalountes*]," in their private prayers and perhaps in their public hymns, though they and the orthodox church were not yet doing so in their official dogmas and creeds. It would seem from the context that he was not referring to priests and prelates, or at least not only to them, but to lay Christians.[53] This is, moreover, sometimes taken by scholars to be the earliest absolutely uncontested instance of the word *Theotokos*, which does appear in *The Creed of Alexander of Alexandria* (d. 328),[54] but only as preserved in the *Ecclesiastical History* of Theodoret, written a century later,[55] and the use of the term in the writings of Athanasius and other earlier writers is textually doubtful.[56] Therefore the title may be said to have moved upward rather than downward, from the practice and prayer of the faithful in the fourth century or even earlier to the agenda of an ecumenical council in the fifth century, following the principle that "the rule of prayer should lay down the rule of faith"[57] and toppling even the bishop of New Rome on its way up. Some modern scholars have attempted, on considerably shakier grounds, to use this title to document an even longer continuity in the popular religion of the city of Ephesus, starting with devotion to the Mother Goddess Artemis and ending with devotion to the Mother of God Mary.[58] For during the missionary journeys of the apostle Paul, Ephesus had been the site of a popular uprising, stirred up by the goldsmiths and artisans of idols, who saw their livelihood threatened if idolatry were to be abolished and who therefore raised the cry, "Great is Artemis of the Ephesians!"[59] Less than four centuries later, the double Church of Saint Mary in the same city of Ephesus was the site for the vindication of the cult of the Blessed Virgin Mary as

53. Julian *Against the Galileans* 262D (*LCL* 157:399).
54. *Alex* 3.
55. Theodoret *Ecclesiastical History* 1.3 (*NPNF*-II 3:40).
56. Lampe, 639–41.
57. See chapter 6.2 above, "*Lex orandi lex credendi.*"
58. Jenny-Kappers 1986.
59. Acts 19.23–41.

348

Theotokos. Even if on balance one concludes, with many historians, that the condemnation of Nestorius was unjust, both doctrinally and legally, its importance for the question at hand is this: in addition to all the other personal maneuvers and political rivalries that were so obviously involved on all sides of this conflict, it does present us with the quite remarkable spectacle of the bishop of Constantinople being condemned for refusing to teach and to pray as the common people had been doing when they called Mary "Theotokos."

This was not, moreover, an isolated instance of the power of popular opinion, as can be seen from the reaction of the people of Constantinople against the Council of Florence.[60] In Byzantium, as one study of the reception of *The Decree of Union with the East* at Florence and of "the popular opposition" to it has put it, "the popular opposition was based . . . on the belief that union had been obtained under duress, that the military aid agreed to by the Holy See would, like previous papal promises, be ineffectual, and, finally, on the conviction that the Byzantine people themselves would suffer the judgment of God if the purity of the faith were altered."[61] But the most dramatic such case in the East, though it was not as directly attributable to "the popular opposition," did involve the orthodoxy of the body of the faithful as well as the ongoing question of the reception of the Council of Florence: the rejection of *The Eastern Confession of the Christian Faith by Cyril Lucar,* which had been issued in 1629. He was elected patriarch of Constantinople in November 1620; and, as Colin Davey has pointed out, "though he was four times deposed from and restored to the throne, he was Head of the Greek Church for fifteen out of the next eighteen years."[62] His *Confession* was published not only in his own name (which, in the light of the office he held, would already have been a prestigious credential) but "in the name and with the consent of the patriarchs of Alexandria and Jerusalem." Thus its espousal of such Reformed doctrines as the sole authority of Scripture[63] and double pre-

60. Marx 1977, 341–48; see chapter 9.2 above, "Reception of Creeds, Councils, and Confessions as Ratification."
61. Geanakoplos 1966.
62. Davey 1987, 98.
63. *Lucar* 2.

destination[64] appeared to carry the presumed canonical authority of three of the five incumbents of the ancient "pentarchy"[65]—Constantinople, Alexandria, and Jerusalem, though not Antioch, and of course not Rome—as well as the intellectual force and the prestige of "the first important theologian of the Eastern Church since the fall of Constantinople in 1453 . . . , the most brilliant and politically outstanding Greek Patriarch and national leader ('ethnarch') of the 17th century."[66] Some have even advanced the controversial hypothesis that Orthodox faithful in Ukraine, Ruthenia, and Eastern Slovakia were willing to reaffirm the Union of Florence and to give their allegiance to the Union of Brest of 1595/96 and the Union of Užhorod of 1646,[67] reuniting them with Rome but seeking to preserve Eastern spirituality and liturgy, because of their more or less clear perception that the Orthodox faith had been compromised by its most prominent official spokesmen. The only way for them to remain "Byzantine," paradoxically, seemed to be to break with "Byzantium." As Eastern and Western representatives have now acknowledged together, this happened "not without the interference of extra-ecclesial interests,"[68] political and nationalistic. But Cyril's *Confession* was condemned, and so was the patriarch who had been identified as its author, coming to a tragic personal end. It does seem fair to view several of the seventeenth-century Eastern Orthodox "confessions [*homologiai*]" as an equal and opposite reaction also to this quixotic effort at an *Orthodox Confession*, as well as to the Protestant confessions themselves.[69]

Nor would it be correct to conclude from the tragic histories of Nestorius, the Council of Florence, and Cyril Lucar that it was only New Rome that came in for such condemnation in the name of the orthodoxy of the body of the faithful. In fact, the most controversial such condemnation ever issued, which has had far-reaching historical repercussions into modern times, included a patriarch of Old Rome,

64. *Lucar* 3.
65. See chapter 4.2 above, "Doctrines of Church Order East and West."
66. *ODCC* 1001.
67. Halecki 1958, 199–419; Lacko 1966.
68. *Balamand* 8–9.
69. See chapter 14.4 below, "The Eastern Confessions as Equal and Opposite Reactions."

in the person of Pope Honorius I. The condemnation also cited patriarchs of New Rome, Alexandria, and Antioch. Thus, of the five ancient patriarchates of "pentarchy," only Jerusalem was spared in this case. Against the heresy of Monothelitism *The Exposition of Faith of the Third Council of Constantinople* of 680–81 affirms the dogma that the one person of Jesus Christ the incarnate Logos possessed two distinct wills in their integrity, one divine and one human, rather than a single and composite divine-human will. Believers are to be assured that their Savior assumed a human will like their own in all respects, "yet without sin,"[70] and that therefore their wills can be healed by his. In doing this, *The Exposition of Faith of the Third Council of Constantinople* labels and anathematizes, in addition to "Theodore, who was bishop of Pharan," the following patriarchs as errorists on this doctrine: "Sergius, Pyrrhus, Paul, and Peter, who were bishops of this imperial city [Constantinople]; and further Honorius, who was pope of elder Rome [*papan tēs prebyteras Rōmēs*]; Cyrus, who held the see of Alexandria; and Macarius, who was recently bishop of Antioch, and his disciple Stephen."[71] By condemning Pope Honorius for teaching falsely about the two wills of Christ, the council (the sixth ecumenical council, according to both Eastern and Western systems of counting) created the most difficult historical obstacle that would have to be faced twelve centuries later by *The Dogmatic Constitution on the Catholic Faith of the First Vatican Council* of 1869/70 (the twentieth ecumenical council, according to the Western, but not the Eastern, system of counting). This confession decrees that "when the Roman pontiff speaks *ex cathedra,* that is, when, in the exercise of his office as shepherd and teacher of all Christians, in virtue of his supreme apostolic authority, he defines a doctrine concerning faith or morals to be held by the whole church, he possesses, by the divine assistance promised to him in blessed Peter, that infallibility which the divine Redeemer willed his church to enjoy in defining doctrine concerning faith or morals."[72] For if at any time in history even one pope had erred in his official and public teaching, as *The Exposition of Faith of the Third Council of Con-*

70. Heb 4.15.
71. *CP III* anath; *Lat 649* 18.
72. *Vat I* 4.

stantinople does appear to say that Honorius had, that seemed sufficient to impeach papal infallibility as a doctrine, which was not a statement of average but a matter of all or nothing at all.[73] Therefore *The Old Catholic Declaration of Utrecht* of 1889, in the wake of the First Vatican Council, simultaneously asserts the authority of tradition alongside that of Scripture, but repudiates papal infallibility.[74]

Interpreters of *lex orandi lex credendi*, the principle that, in the words of Prosper of Aquitaine quoted earlier, "the rule of prayer should lay down the rule of faith,"[75] have been careful to emphasize that it is not to be applied indiscriminately, so as to elevate every vagary of poetic language or lay piety or popular superstition (any more than every vagary of theological speculation and scholarly erudition) to the status of doctrine and the rule of faith.[76] In the controversy over images, Alain Besançon has said, "the iconoclasts had no difficulty vituperating against the abuses of popular religion."[77] Therefore, even as the iconodule *Decree of the Second Council of Nicaea* of 787 is declaring that it is legitimate also for the common people "to pay these images the tribute of salutation and respectful veneration [*aspasmon kai timētikēn proskynēsin*]," it simultaneously insists, because of abuses both potential and real, that "certainly this is not the full adoration in accordance with our faith [*tēn kata pistin hēmōn alēthinēn latreian*], which is properly paid only to the divine nature" and which is therefore not properly paid to icons or to saints, nor even to the person of the Virgin Mary as Theotokos.[78] The veneration of the icons is not directed to them as such but "on the basis of their relationship [*schetikōs*]" to their prototypes.[79] On the Western side, *The Canons and Decrees of the Council of Trent* similarly express the determination "to root out utterly any abuses that may have crept into these holy and saving practices."[80] Orthodox confessions of the East and Catholic confes-

73. *Chr Trad* 2:67–68, 150–53, 5:250–59.
74. *Utrecht* 1–2.
75. *Chr Trad* 1:339, 2:34–35, 3:66–80.
76. *Munif* 20. See Möhler [1832] 1985, 1:22–23.
77. Besançon 2000, 124.
78. *Nic II*.
79. *Greg Palam* 4.
80. *Trent* 25 decr.

sions of the West are therefore agreed that not "adoration [*latria*]" but only "veneration [*dulia*]" (or in the case of the Virgin, *hyperdulia*) is the "worship [*proskynēsis*]" that is appropriately addressed to the saints, and hence to their images.[81] But, they complain, "the swarm of the heretics mistakenly equates honor with adoration."[82] Such Eastern Orthodox and Roman Catholic caution about the possibility that the popular religion of the faithful might ignore and blur the edge of these distinctions between the "full adoration" that pertains only to the Holy Trinity and the "salutary and respectful veneration" that pertains to Mary and the other saints and to their images is sharply intensified in the polemics of the confessions of the Protestant Reformation. Representative Protestant expressions of such prohibitions come from *The Second Helvetic Confession,* which prescribes: "In all crises and trials of our life we call upon [God] alone."[83] Again, it admonishes: "Let all the prayers of the faithful be poured forth to God alone, through the mediation of Christ only, out of faith and love. The priesthood of Christ the Lord and true religion forbid the invocation of saints in heaven or to use them as intercessors."[84] But that was just what the common people of the church (as well as the clergy) in both East and West had been doing "from the earliest times of the Christian religion," as its defenders could argue.[85] No less vigorously, *The Westminster Confession of Faith* declares: "Religious worship is to be given to God, the Father, Son, and Holy Ghost; and to him alone; not to angels, saints, or any other creature, . . . nor in the mediation of any other but of Christ alone."[86] This is aimed also against the traditional devotion of the faithful to the mediation of Mary as the Mother of God, who (also according to Roman Catholic and Eastern Orthodox teaching) remains a creature even though she is "more honorable than the cherubim, and more glorious beyond compare than the seraphim."[87]

81. Thomas Aquinas *Summa Theologica* 3a.25; *Metr Crit* 15.3, 17.9.
82. *Dosith* q 4.
83. *Helv II* 5.3.
84. *Helv II* 23.1.
85. *Trent* 25; *Metr Crit* 17.4.
86. *West* 21.2; *Cumb Pres* 75.
87. *Lit Chrys* F.6.

12.3. Conformity by the People of the Church
to Civil and Creedal Law

The problem of the relation between church and state, and therefore of the interrelation between creedal norms and social conformity, has often been in fact a conflict at the highest levels, between the ecclesiastical elite and the political elite. The confrontations of these two elites, as at Canossa on 28 January 1077 between Pope Gregory VII of the Holy Roman Church and Emperor Henry IV of the Holy Roman Empire, have served as its most dramatic symbols. "We are not going to Canossa!" Otto von Bismarck was said to have declared during the *Kulturkampf* of the nineteenth century between the Vatican and the newly reconstituted German *Reich*. But it seems safe to conclude that it was in the areas of what our earlier chapters have called "the forming of confessions and the politics of religion" and "creedal dogma as church law"[88] that the laity, also of other classes than the ruling elites, have had to experience much of their sharpest awareness of the interrelations between creedal norms and social conformity.

The Barmen Declaration [*Theologische Erklärung zur gegenwärtigen Lage der Deutschen Evangelischen Kirche*] of May 1934, by its attack on the claims of National Socialism that the church was to be downgraded to the status of "an organ of the state" and that the state was to be elevated to the status of a system for "a total ordering of life,"[89] was speaking not only *to* the Protestant laity of Germany (as well as to the Nazi regime, and to such church leaders as were tempted to collaborate with the regime), but *for* the Protestant laity, in their name and on their behalf. This specification applies, moreover, regardless of what a public opinion poll in 1934 might have revealed about the presence of anti-Semitism, Nazism, and racism among either the laity or the clergy or the theologians or the hierarchy of the various churches of Germany, whether Protestant or Roman Catholic.[90] Not only National Socialism but also Communism evoked from Christians and Christian churches new confessions for new situations, as it be-

88. See chapters 8 and 9 above; also Syndogmaticon 7.3.
89. *Barm 5*.
90. See Ericksen 1985; Dietrich 1988; Ericksen and Heschel 1999.

came evident yet once more that, in the words of James Russell Lowell's poem of 1844, "new occasions teach new duties."[91] In a pastoral letter of 1950, voicing its critical response to a vigorous declaration of support for the Chinese Communist regime that had been entitled "Direction of Endeavor for Chinese Christianity in the Construction of New China," or *The Christian Manifesto* that was issued by the China Christian Three-Self Patriotic Movement,[92] the House of Bishops of the Sheng Kung Hui, the Anglican Church in China, sought, on behalf of the faithful, to acknowledge what it took to be the valid points in that statement of faith and purpose, but to correct what it took to be its excessive compromises: "Hereafter our church should on the one hand positively promote spiritual life and religious education, so as to enable us all to have the Christlike personality and family, and on the other hand pay attention to productive labor and social service."[93]

Those responses likewise make clear that, not only in these Nazi and Communist societies, but also in many other societies throughout the history of Christianity, including secular democratic societies, no area of the interrelation between creedal norms and social conformity has been more crucial, or more vulnerable, than Christian education. Education has also been an area of central importance for the church's creeds and confessions of faith. Some of the most important of these have been prepared primarily for educational purposes, and many others have been obliged to address directly the responsibility of teaching the laity, both adults and children. *"Educentur quoque liberi,"* the Latin formula quoted earlier from *The Second Helvetic Confession,*[94] would be an accurate prescription, at least by implication, for most creeds and confessions. As *The Heidelberg Catechism* urges, it is obligatory "that the ministry of the gospel and Christian education be maintained."[95] It is for the sake of "the more uncultivated" and "so that the inexperienced may be instructed" that *The Wittenberg Concord* states the consensus among various parties of Protestants "that

---

91. James Russell Lowell "The Present Crisis," st 3.
92. *Chin Man;* see also *PRCC* of 1977 in Cuba.
93. *Sheng Kung* 5.
94. *Helv II* 29.3; see chapter 8.4 above, "The Politics of Confessional Diversity."
95. *Heid* 103.

private absolution also be preserved in the church, both on account of the consolation to consciences and because the discipline is very useful to the church."[96] The institutional structures for Christian education have varied widely in different societies and churches. Similarly, the emphases of the several confessions on the means and the methods for the Christian education of the laity, young and old, also reflect the distinctive character, ethos, liturgy, and theology of each of the different churches and confessions. These would include the place of the Bible in Protestant schools at all levels,[97] the role of the liturgy and of icons as primary teaching tools for Eastern Orthodox religious education,[98] and the use of "the mass [as] full of instruction for the faithful people" in Roman Catholicism.[99] But beyond all these differences among the churches and confessions, an important tool in almost all of them, both for expressing and for nurturing "the orthodoxy of the body of the faithful," has continued to be the catechism, "the layman's Bible,"[100] because of all the reciprocal linkages described earlier between creed and catechism.[101]

The Roman Catholic Church—with its long history of attention to education at all levels, particularly its attention to programs for the education of the young, and with its networks of women's and men's religious orders to staff those programs—has also addressed these issues in considerable detail through its official and confessional declarations. Therefore *The Syllabus of Errors of Pope Pius IX* of 1864 singles out, as one of the most dangerous among all the recent "errors" to be condemned, the claim of modern political secularism that "the absolute will of the civil and political authority" over education, even over the education of Christian and Roman Catholic children, takes precedence over the educational authority and responsibility of the church and of Christian parents.[102] A century later, *The Declaration on*

---

96. *Witt Conc* 5.
97. *Heid* 103; *So Bap* 12.
98. *Nic II*.
99. *Trent* 22.1.8.
100. *Form Conc Epit* pr.5; see *Helv II* 18.18, 25.1.
101. See chapter 3 above, "Confession of the Faith as Doctrine"; and chapter 6.1 above, "The Lord's Prayer in the Confessions."
102. *Syl* 45–48.

Christian Education of the Second Vatican Council, having "attentively and carefully weighed the supreme importance of education in human life and its ever greater influence on the social progress of this age," affirms "certain basic principles about Christian education, especially in schools." Therefore "true education," as the *Declaration* defines it, "aims at a formation of human persons which is directed towards their final end and at the same time towards the good of society," but not exclusively toward the latter, as not only totalitarianism but any other this-worldly secularism, even a democratic one, tends to claim. For it is not a privilege, but a "right [*ius*]," of children and adolescents "to be stimulated to weigh moral values with a correct conscience, to embrace them with personal commitment, and to know and love God more perfectly." From these principles there follows the operational conclusion that the parents of children "are to be acknowledged as their primary and principal educators," with "true freedom in choosing schools," which includes of course the schools of the church, and without unwarranted intrusion by the state into such choices.[103]

For Eastern Orthodoxy, the reinstatement of icons by the Second Council of Nicaea in 787 ratified the devotion of the laity as an argument in favor of images, and it interpreted images as "confirmation that the becoming man of the Word of God was real and not just imaginary." On that basis the council decreed that "like the figure of the honored and life-giving cross" (of which the iconoclasts, too, had continued to approve), images were to appear not only in churches and on priestly vestments but "in houses and by public ways." For, as it declared concerning the pedagogical value of the images of Christ, Mary, and the other saints, "the more frequently they are seen in representational art, the more are those who see them drawn to remember and long for those who serve as models, and to pay these images the tribute of salutation and respectful veneration."[104] Quoting these canons of the Second Council of Nicaea as having "established and confirmed to all ages the worship of holy and venerable images," *The Orthodox Confession of the Catholic and Apostolic Eastern Church by Peter Mogila* emphasizes that there is an immense and unbridgeable qualitative dif-

103. *Vat II* 7 act.
104. *Nic II* can. See Syndogmaticon 8.10.

ference between such a worship of icons by the Christian faithful and the pagan worship of idols.[105] Similarly, but quoting this time from a Western source, namely, the explanation of Pope Gregory the Great in his *Epistle to Serenus* that "pictorial representation is made use of in churches for this reason, that such as are ignorant of letters may at least read by looking at the walls what they cannot read in books,"[106] *The Christian Catechism of the Orthodox Catholic Greco-Russian Church* of 1839 explains that it is not contrary to the Ten Commandments "to honor icons as sacred representations, and to use them for the religious remembrance of God's works and of his saints; for when thus used, icons are books, written with the form of persons and things instead of letters." They are, therefore, to be a fundamental component in Christian education at all levels.[107] *The Second Helvetic Confession*, setting forth the Reformed rejection of sacred images, responds to both of these defenses in the name of what it regards as the authentic orthodoxy of the body of the faithful. To the christological defense of Christian icons for the laity it retorts that "although Christ assumed human nature, yet he did not on that account assume it in order to provide a pattern for carvers and painters." To the pedagogical defense it replies that Christ "commanded the preaching of the gospel—not to paint and to teach the laity by means of pictures."[108]

That insistence of *The Second Helvetic Confession* on Christ's command to preach the gospel as primary among the divinely ordained means for instructing the laity is decisive for all of the confessions of the Protestant Reformation. It is, according to *The Sixty-Seven Articles of Ulrich Zwingli*, the duty of both the laity and the clergy, indeed of "all Christians," to "do their utmost that everywhere only the gospel of Christ be preached."[109] Both of the major Protestant confessions issued in 1530 sound this note. *The Augsburg Confession* teaches that "the gospel [is to] be preached in conformity with a pure understanding of it."[110] *The Tetrapolitan Confession* puts such a strong emphasis

105. *Mogila* 3.55–56.
106. Gregory I *Epistles* 9.15 (NPNF–II 13:23).
107. *Russ Cat* 521.
108. *Helv II* 4.2–4.
109. *67 Art* 14.
110. *Aug Ger* 7.2.

on the preaching of the word of God to the laity that it makes "Of the Subject-Matter of Sermons [*De materia concionum*]" the title of its first article.[111] "The authority to preach God's word and to tend the flock of the Lord," according to *The First Helvetic Confession* of 1536, "properly speaking is the office of the keys." Therefore, it continues later, "the highest and chief thing in this office is that the ministers of the church preach repentance and sorrow for sins, improvement of life, and forgiveness of sins, and all through Christ."[112] Its greatly expanded successor of 1566, *The Second Helvetic Confession,* describes "the true harmony of the church" as consisting above all "in the true and harmonious preaching of the gospel of Christ."[113] *The Westminster Confession of Faith* of 1647 is summarizing most of the Protestant creeds and confessions of the century leading up to it, whether Reformed or Lutheran, when it prescribes, at the head of the list of the duties of "religious worship" applicable to all Christians, both clergy and laity, "the reading of the Scriptures with godly fear; the sound preaching and conscionable hearing of the word, in obedience unto God, with understanding, faith, and reverence."[114] Its companion work, *The Westminster Shorter Catechism,* sharpens this when it speaks of "the reading, but *especially* the preaching, of the word."[115] Reflecting the new attention in sixteenth-century Rome to issues of Christian communication,[116] and acknowledging, at least in some measure, the validity of this unanimous Reformation criticism of the late medieval church for having gravely neglected the instruction of the faithful through preaching and thus for having helped to bring on the Protestant Reformation, *The Canons and Decrees of the Council of Trent,* promulgated by its fifth session, on 17 June 1546, four months after Luther's death, prescribe that "the preaching of the gospel . . . is the chief task of the bishops."[117] The Eastern Orthodox *Confession of Dositheus and of the Synod of Jeru-*

111. *Tetrapol* 1.
112. *Helv I* 16; 19.
113. *Helv II* 17.17.
114. *West* 21.5.
115. *West Sh Cat* 89; italics added.
116. O'Malley 1979.
117. *Trent* 5.2.9–10 can; see also chapter 3.3 above, "'Doctrines' and Doctrine."

salem of 1672, too, in listing the duties of a bishop, prescribes that "he preaches the sacred gospel and contends for the Orthodox faith."[118]

12.4. Code, Creed, and Folk Culture

One direct implication of such an emphasis on "the orthodoxy of the body of the faithful" is to reject out of hand any version of the difference between the clergy and the laity that would reduce the popular religion of Christians to nothing more than morality, relegating questions of doctrine to the clerical and theological professionals, as though the common people cared only about how they behave but not about what they believe. As stated earlier, "doctrine" is the particular form that "faith" or "beliefs" take when they are articulated or defined.[119] Therefore the difference between the clergy and the laity can be taken to be, not that the laity are occupied only with the moral consequences of beliefs and do not concern themselves with the content of the beliefs, but rather, in the distinction quoted from Thomas Aquinas, that formal and official doctrine or "explicitness in belief is not a matter of salvation uniformly for all," but that "those who have the office of teaching others are held to an explicit belief in more things than others are."[120] And if there is any firm conclusion to be drawn from the social history of popular religion, a few examples of which were cited at the beginning of this chapter, it is that the ordinary people of the church do care, not only about conduct but about matters of their "faith" or "beliefs," even though the centrality of prayer and ritual in the modality of such caring may sometimes be dismissed as superstition by the condescension of the skeptic or the snobbery of the elitist or the cynicism of the Grand Inquisitor.

Two questions raised in Chapter 10, "Deeds, Not Creeds?" may serve as illustrations for the distinction—and for the close connection—between moral actions and doctrinal beliefs as these have affected "the body of the faithful." Augustine's contention, in opposition to Donatism, that the sacraments of a wicked priest are never-

---

118. *Dosith* decr 10.
119. See chapter 2.1 above, "Believing and Confessing"; chapter 3 above, "Confession of the Faith as Doctrine."
120. Thomas Aquinas *Summa Theologica* 2a2ae.2.5–6 (tr. Blackfriars).

theless valid because of the objectivity of his office as secured by the
sacrament of ordination was formulated with the faith of the people
in view. For if ordinary laypeople cannot rely on the sacraments as
vehicles of divine grace regardless of the moral condition of a priest
or bishop, but are obliged to investigate his sincerity in order to validate their having genuinely received baptism or chrism or absolution or
Holy Communion at his hands, the very credibility of the entire sacramental structure of the church is in fundamental jeopardy. On the basis
of Frend's contention, quoted earlier, that "in the fifth and sixth centuries, Catholicism had no appeal for the masses of the native population,"[121] it might well be the case historically that Augustine's defense
of the objective validity of the sacraments against Donatist objections
did fail to convince the masses. Statistical verification one way or the
other is impossible to obtain, and there is plenty of anecdotal evidence
on both sides. The statement of Graham Greene's immoral "whisky
priest," that nevertheless "I can put God into a man's mouth just the
same — and I can give him God's pardon,"[122] is an idiosyncratic version
of the Augustinian argument. Frend's reading of the beginning of the
Middle Ages, showing trends in popular religion that questioned the
efficacy of the Augustinian arguments, would appear to be even more
plausible for the end of the Middle Ages, when what Heiko Oberman
has called "the rising tide of Donatism"[123] became an issue, and then
especially for the period of the Reformation.

      The persistence with which the confessions of the Magiste-
rial Reformation, one after another, take such pains to repeat their
adherence to the Augustinian position against Donatism may demonstrate not only the impact of the constantly reiterated charge by Roman
Catholic polemics that Protestant reform was a revival of the ancient
schism and heresy of the Donatists but also the pastoral concern that
within the Protestant churches, too, there could be lay people in the
pew who were harboring Donatist suspicions about the clergy, even
about their own Protestant clergy.[124] It is symptomatic of the distinc-

121. Frend 1952, 334.
122. Graham Greene *The Power and the Glory,* part 3, ch 3.
123. Oberman 1963, 220–22.
124. See chapter 10.2 above, "Heresy and/or Schism," and chapter 16.3 below,

tive emphasis of the Protestant confessions, however, that although the validity of the eucharist even when it is received from the hands of "wicked ministers" continues to be a factor also for them,[125] the objectivity at issue for them is primarily that of the preaching of the word of God, and only secondarily or derivatively that of the sacraments (which it was for Augustine, master preacher though he was). Because of the unavoidably subjective nature of any sermon as it is being delivered from the pulpit, a lack of personal conviction might seem to be in a position to taint the proclamation (and interpretation) of the biblical word more readily than it does the administration of the sacraments. As Augustine had put it in the Christian rhetoric that forms the fourth book of his *On Christian Doctrine,* "They do good to many by preaching even when they do not live up to it; but far more would they do good by practicing what they preached."[126] Thus *The Second Helvetic Confession* in its first article contains the assurance to the people of the church that "the word itself which is preached is to be regarded, not the minister that preaches; for even if he be evil and a sinner, nevertheless the word of God remains still true and good."[127] In a later chapter it condemns "the error of the Donatists" in the strongest of terms as worthy of being "detested."[128] And *The Westminster Confession of Faith,* even in its chapter bearing the title "On the Sacraments," bases its rejection of Donatism on the doctrine of the objectivity of the word of God, not the objectivity of ordination: "Neither doth the efficacy of a sacrament depend upon the piety or intention of him that doth administer it; but upon the work of the Spirit, and *the word of institution,* which contains, together with a precept authorizing the use thereof, a promise of benefit to worthy receivers," which words, of institution and of precept and of promise, are to be believed regardless of the person of the minister.[129]

For the writers of those same Reformed confessions, it was,

"Catholic Substance and Protestant Principle in Reformation Confessions." Also Syndogmaticon 9.3.
125. *Cons rep* 10.69.
126. Augustine *On Christian Doctrine* 4.27.60 (NPNF–I 2:595–96).
127. *Helv II* 1.4.
128. *Helv II* 18.21.
129. *West* 27.3; italics added.

perhaps above all, the Calvinist doctrine of election and predestination that needed to be formulated with sensitive attention to what *The Augsburg Confession* also calls "God-fearing and anxious consciences,"[130] and to the faith and piety of the people of the church, as Roman Catholic and Eastern Orthodox confessions on this subject likewise warn.[131] In 1610 *The Remonstrance* of the Arminian party includes this assurance to all believers, with an "indirect censure" against Calvinist predestinarianism and a response to the charge that Arminianism neglects divine grace: "Those who are grafted into Christ by a true faith, and have thereby been made partakers of his life-giving Spirit, are *abundantly endowed* with power to strive against Satan, sin, the world, and their own flesh, and *to win the victory;* always, be it understood, with the help of the grace of the Holy Spirit."[132] In opposition to this confession of *The Remonstrance,* the classic confessional formulation of the Calvinist doctrine of predestination in all its rigor is the definition of *The Canons of the Synod of Dort* of 1618–19.[133] Directly upon articulating the definition of the two-edged doctrine of election and reprobation, these *Canons* address the existential and the pastoral dimensions of the doctrine, the predicament of "those who do not yet actively experience within themselves a living faith in Christ or an assured confidence of heart, peace of conscience, a zeal for childlike obedience, and a glorying in God through Christ." Such persons are counseled "to continue diligently in the use of means, to desire fervently a time of more abundant grace, and to wait for it in reverence and humility." But this is accompanied by a warning against "inquisitive searching into the hidden and deep things of God," and against relying on "some private revelation beyond or outside the word."[134] In an especially poignant address to the body of the faithful about the potentially devastating personal and pastoral implications of the doctrine of divine reprobation, *The Canons of the Synod of Dort* make it a special point to urge

130. *Aug* 20.15; *Form Conc Sol Dec* 2.47.
131. *Trent* 6.1.12–13 decr, 6.2.15–17 decr; *Dosith* decr 3. On the entire subject, see Syndogmaticon 3.2.
132. *Remon* 5; italics added. See Syndogmaticon 11.2.
133. See chapter 10.1 above, "Doctrines of Christian Discipline in the Reformation Confessions."
134. *Dort* 1.1.16, 1.1.12, 5.1.10.

that "godly parents ought not to doubt the election and salvation of their children whom God calls out of this life in infancy."[135]

From one Reformed confession to another, these notes are sounded. "God from eternity has predestined some men to life, and reprobated some to death" are the words with which the Calvinistic Anglicanism of *The Lambeth Articles* of 1595 opens. But a later article addresses the problem of certainty and assurance head-on: "The truly faithful man—that is, one endowed with justifying faith—is sure by full assurance of faith of the remission of sins and his eternal salvation through Christ."[136] "All those whom God hath predestinated unto life, *and those only*," according to *The Westminster Confession of Faith*, "he is pleased in his appointed and accepted time effectually to call."[137] That includes "elect infants, dying in infancy," without any reference to whether they have been baptized.[138] This applies as well to "all other elect persons who are uncapable of being outwardly called by the ministry of the word."[139] But, whether they are infants or adults, "others, not elected, although they may be called by the ministry of the word, and may have some common operations of the Spirit, yet they never truly come unto Christ, and therefore *can not be saved*."[140] Devoting an entire later chapter to the unavoidable anxious questioning about this "effectual calling," *The Westminster Confession of Faith* holds out the promise that "such as truly believe in the Lord Jesus, and love him in sincerity, endeavoring to walk in all good conscience before him, may, in this life, be certainly assured that they are in a state of grace."[141] But it also concedes that "this infallible assurance doth not so belong to the essence of faith, but that a true believer may wait long, and conflict with many difficulties before he be partaker of it. . . . And therefore it is the duty of every one to give all diligence to make his calling and election sure."[142] For those reasons, also according to *The Westminster*

135. *Dort* 1.1.17.
136. *Lamb Art* 1, 6.
137. *West* 10.1; italics added.
138. Cf. *Dosith* decr 16.
139. *West* 10.3.
140. *West* 10.4; italics added.
141. *West* 18.1.
142. *West* 18.3.

Confession of Faith, "the doctrine of this high mystery of predestination is to be handled with special prudence and care," among clergy and theologians but especially among the faithful.[143]

Above all, those who have to "conflict with many difficulties" over the doctrines of election and reprobation are to focus their attention on Christ and his cross. In the words of *The Second Helvetic Confession,* "Let Christ, therefore be the looking glass [*speculum*], in whom we may contemplate our predestination. . . . In the temptation in regard to predestination, *than which there is scarcely any other more dangerous,* we are comforted by the fact that God's promises apply to all the faithful."[144] It is a result of the continuing struggle of Reformed theology with the implications of election and reprobation for the faithful when *The Confession of the Cumberland Presbyterian Church* of 1829, following in this respect Zwingli's *Reckoning of the Faith,*[145] changes the original language of *The Westminster Confession of Faith* of 1647, "*Elect* infants, dying in infancy, are regenerated, and saved by Christ,"[146] to read: "*All* infants dying in infancy are regenerated and saved by Christ."[147] And it has been concluded from the history of popular religion in the orthodox Calvinism and Puritanism inspired by such confessions as *The Canons of the Synod of Dort, The Westminster Confession of Faith, The Second Helvetic Confession,* and *The Confession of the Cumberland Presbyterian Church,* as this popular religion has expressed itself in the life of human society, that here, too, in a sense of the word *orthodoxy* that Cardinal Newman certainly did not include in his phrase, it is possible to speak about "the orthodoxy of the body of the faithful."[148]

143. *West* 3.8.
144. *Helv II* 10.9; italics added.
145. *Fid rat* 5.
146. *West* 10.3; italics added.
147. *Cumb Pres* 54; italics added.
148. Weber [1930] 1992.

IV

The History of Creeds
and Confessions

Almost all collections and individual editions of creedal and confessional texts include historical introductions; these editions are identified for each text in the front matter of this work under "Abbreviations," and bibliographical descriptions of the editions are provided under "Editions, Collections, and Reference Works." Although these five historical chapters, therefore, are meant to be equally helpful to those readers who do not happen to be using our edition, they do correspond both in title and in subject matter to the five parts of *Creeds and Confessions of Faith in the Christian Tradition* and to the epochs of the history of the Christian tradition that are represented by them: the Early Church; Eastern Orthodoxy; the Medieval West; the Reformation Era; Modern Christianity. An adapted version of the substance of each chapter also appears there as an introduction to each of those parts. These chapters are not intended, however, either to replicate or to replace the history contained in the separate introductions to individual texts of creeds and confessions from all five of those periods. Rather, they seek, on the basis of the history and the texts, to single out principal motifs and distinctive characteristics of each epoch as these have affected the making of creeds during that time and as they have set that era in the history of creeds and confessions apart from other eras. As a result, each chapter contains, not only many citations from the creeds and confessions of its own era, but, for purposes of comparison and contrast, numerous references to those from other eras, many more such references than can be found, for example, in most collections of creeds and confessions that are devoted to only one period or one confessional tradition.[1]

1. See "Editions, Collections, and Reference Works" above.

For the historiography of creeds and confessions of faith in the Christian tradition, and therefore for the organization and classification of the texts of creeds and confessions as well (just as for the historiography of the institutional church or of Christian doctrine or of Christian ethics or of Christian worship), the problem of periodization inevitably raises questions and presuppositions of theology and philosophy that go far beyond the immediate subject matter of the historian's research as such.[2] In the words of Mandell Creighton—who was the author of a multivolume *History of the Papacy* and first editor of the *English Historical Review* (and eventually Anglican bishop of London)[3]—in his "Introductory Note" on "Division of history into periods" for the original edition of *The Cambridge Modern History,*

> Any division of history is doubtless arbitrary. But it is
> impossible for history to discharge all the obligations
> which, from a strictly scientific point of view, are in-
> cumbent upon it. If we accept the position that history
> is concerned with tracing the evolution of human af-
> fairs, we are continually being driven further back for
> our starting-point. . . . A pause must be made some-
> where. Humanity must be seized at some period of its
> development, if a beginning is to be made at all. The
> selection of that point must be determined by some
> recognizable motive of convenience.[4]

An extreme example of this "arbitrariness," though probably not of the "motive of convenience," was a brilliant and learned monograph on the history of the Christian doctrine of reconciliation and atonement, published in 1838 by Ferdinand Christian Baur of Tübingen, one of the founders of modern historical theology.[5] Baur's book divided that entire history into three quite uneven periods: from the beginnings of Christianity to the Reformation (about fifteen centuries); from the Reformation to Immanuel Kant (almost three cen-

2. Pelikan 1971, 120–28.
3. *ODCC* 430–31.
4. Creighton 1902, 1–2.
5. Hodgson 1966.

turies); and since Kant (thirty-four years, Kant having died in 1804). Baur's masterful analytic survey, *The Epochs of the Writing of Church History* [*Die Epochen der kirchlichen Geschichtsschreibung*], manifested the same concentration on the eighteenth and nineteenth centuries, as the beginning of the "scientific [*wissenschaftlich*]" writing of church history, at the expense of earlier historiography.[6] But it does seem to provide justification for the generalization that each of the major alternative philosophies of history has helped to shape one or another account of the history of Christianity, and therefore one or another system of historical periodization: the conception of historical cycles espoused in classical antiquity; the Augustinian-medieval conceptualization of "the two cities"; the Enlightenment doctrine of progress; the Hegelian dialectic of thesis-antithesis-synthesis (favored and creatively applied by Baur); Thomas Carlyle's "great man theory"; twentieth-century social history.[7]

The question of the relation between Scripture and tradition—which, as almost every confession from the period of the Reformation shows regardless of its denomination,[8] has always been a dividing issue between Protestantism and Roman Catholicism—has likewise impinged directly on how historians on both sides have organized their narrative material. This is reflected also in how they have included the New Testament simultaneously as the first period of church history and as the source and norm for all later periods. Likewise, the historiography of the Reformation (or of the several Reformations) of the sixteenth century, both Protestant and Roman Catholic, has been an especially productive and provocative area for fundamental questions about the problem of periodization.[9] Nor are the boundaries and categories of periodization quite the same from one subject area of Christian history to another. The history of creeds and confessions of faith is not unrelated to any of the other areas of the history of Christianity, having especially close connections with the history of doctrine and of

6. Baur [1852] 1962, 152–246.
7. See chapter 12 above, "The Orthodoxy of the Body of the Faithful."
8. See chapter 5 above, "Scripture, Tradition, and Creed;" Syndogmaticon 8.11–12.
9. Jedin 1946, 39–49.

the liturgy and of church law.[10] Nevertheless, in its schematization of periods it does seem to demonstrate above all its close ties with the history of Christian doctrine,[11] whose periodization (whatever arrangement of the historical material one elects to adopt) may therefore also be applied to the history of creeds and confessions of faith. That is the case here, employing the organizational structure of the five volumes of *The Christian Tradition: A History of the Development of Doctrine* (1971–89).

Some of these same considerations of historiography and of periodization have also shaped the arrangement of the texts not only between but within each of the five parts of *Creeds and Confessions of Faith in the Christian Tradition*. A basically chronological arrangement has turned out to be the most convenient one for Parts Two, Three, and Five: the creeds and confessions of faith from Eastern Orthodoxy, those from the medieval West, and those from modern Christianity. These latter have been subdivided into "The Seventeenth and Eighteenth Centuries: Confessionalizing the Outcome of the Reformation"; "The Nineteenth Century: Putting Confessionalism and Denominationalism to the Test"; and "The Twentieth Century: Globalization of Churches and Confessions." But chronology breaks down very soon in presenting or in interpreting the creeds of the early church. For one thing, it is simply impossible to date with precision many of these creeds, including some of the most important ones. In addition, the written form of many creeds as they have come down to us points behind itself to an earlier form, whether written or oral, that is now lost. Nevertheless, we have employed chronology wherever we could. Chronology proves to be inappropriate for the Reformation era, too, because it was in this period that the differences among confessions-as-creeds uniquely determined, and were uniquely determined by, confessions-as-denominations. These have therefore provided the obvious rubrics under which to group the texts. Within each of these several confessional groups of statements of faith, however, we have followed a basically chronological order.

10. See chapter 6 above, "The Rule of Prayer and the Rule of Faith"; and chapter 9 above, "Creedal Dogma as Church Law."
11. See chapter 3 above, "Confession of the Faith as Doctrine."

CHAPTER THIRTEEN

Rules of Faith in the Early Church

THE PROBLEM OF HISTORICAL periodization, discussed in the introduction to this final section, is especially acute in the consideration of the early church. For it is in the nature of the case that the term *early church,* as used in the title of this chapter and of the collection of creedal texts in Part One of *Creeds and Confessions of Faith in the Christian Tradition,* should have a cutoff point in one realm of Christian activity that is somewhat different from that which would be correct for another one. In a study of the history of the relations between church and state—without which much of the history of creeds and confessions of faith in any period is unintelligible[1]—it makes good sense to say that the period of "the early church" (or at any rate, of "the ancient church") closed with the acceptance of Christianity as a "legally permissible religion [*religio licita*]" by Emperor Constantine I in 313, and then its legal adoption as the official established religion of the Roman empire by Emperor Theodosius I in 380. For the history of Western monasticism, which has also played a role in the development of creeds especially in certain periods,[2] "the early church" should probably be taken to be the entire period of ascetic practice, eremitic activity, and cenobitic experimentation that concluded with the founding of the monastery at Monte Cassino by Benedict of Nursia in 529. This event launched the medieval or Benedictine period, which continued until the rise of the new orders of Dominicans and Franciscans during the later Middle Ages and the crisis of Western monasticism as a conse-

1. See chapter 8 above, "The Formation of Confessions and the Politics of Religion"; Syndogmaticon 7.3.
2. See chapter 10.3 above, "Orthodoxy and Asceticism"; Syndogmaticon 10.14.

quence of the Protestant Reformation. And for the history of Christian doctrine in both East and West, the careers of Pope Gregory I in the West and Maximus Confessor in the East make the beginning of the seventh century a convenient point to draw together the lines of development characteristic of "the early church," after which the doctrinal developments in the Eastern and the Western Middle Ages began to go their separate ways even more decisively than they had already been doing.[3] In the closely related realm of "dogma" in the strict and formal sense of the word,[4] a slightly later *terminus ad quem* is the appropriate one, namely, the seventh ecumenical council, the Second Council of Nicaea in 787,[5] the last council whose authority is recognized by both East and West.

In the realm of creeds, a related case can be made for identifying the early church as that period in the history of the church during which there arose the only statements of faith, whether creedal or conciliar, that have been and still are acknowledged as binding—though often in conjunction with later and more particularistic formularies— by the majority of those Christians and church bodies who would be willing to acknowledge any statements of faith at all to be binding. As a result of that development, several of the principal creeds that are included under Part One of *Creeds and Confessions of Faith in the Christian Tradition*, notably the doctrinal decrees of the first seven "ecumenical" councils, will figure prominently in each of the chapters dealing with later periods, for which they continued to be regarded as normative. To be complete as a collection standing on its own, therefore, the texts assembled in Parts Two, Three, or Four would have to include some of these earlier statements of faith.[6] These universally—or almost universally—acknowledged affirmations of faith actually represented no more than a tiny percentage of the survivors from the plethora of symbols, creeds, decrees, and rules of faith coming out of those early Christian centuries, as will become evident from the table of con-

3. *Chr Trad* 1:332–57.
4. See chapter 3.4 above, "Doctrine as Dogma."
5. *Nic II.*
6. See chapter 14.3 below, "The Sacred Tradition of the Seven Ecumenical Councils"; and chapter 16.3 below, "Catholic Substance and Protestant Principle in Reformation Confessions."

tents of any of the compilations of early creeds listed under "Editions" above.[7] That is one reason for our having assembled so many disparate texts from so many different sources in Part One of *Creeds and Confessions of Faith in the Christian Tradition,* under the general rubric "Rules of Faith in the Early Church." The reality of this creedal diversity has sometimes been denied or at least ignored, for a variety of theological and historical reasons. But the genuine necessity of showing that the phenomenon of creedal diversity, so characteristic of later periods and especially of the period of the Reformation and the modern era, was at work already in the first several centuries of church history serves in a curious way to call even greater attention to the continuing normative status of these few more or less universal rules of faith. Unique among these is *The Niceno-Constantinopolitan Creed,* because of its privileged status—allowing for the portentous divergence between its original version of 381 and its *Western Recension* on the doctrine of the double procession of the Holy Spirit, the Filioque[8]—in the Eastern Orthodox Church, the Oriental Orthodox Churches, the Roman Catholic Church, and several of the major Protestant churches. *The Niceno-Constantinopolitan Creed* and, for the West, *The Apostles' Creed* are likewise the creeds whose words and texts occurred and recurred, and whose authority was cited and recited, by later councils and confessions in all of the subsequent periods of Christian history and therefore in all of the subsequent four parts of *Creeds and Confessions of Faith in the Christian Tradition.* They were as well the creeds employed as liturgical confessions of the faith.[9]

Histories and collections of early Christian creeds since the eighteenth century[10] have grouped them in different ways, each having certain advantages but also displaying corresponding disadvantages. The complexity of the literary as well as the theological interdepen-

7. Caspari; *COD/DEC* 1–156; Denzinger, 1–615; Gerrish, 49–65; Hahn; Leith, 16–56; Schaff, 2:11–73.

8. See chapter 7.4 above, "The Holy Spirit of Concord and the Sacrament of Concord: Two Ironic Case Histories"; and chapter 15.1 below, "The Western Reception of the Catholic Creedal and Conciliar Tradition."

9. See chapter 6.3 above, "The Place of Creed in Liturgy."

10. See chapter 17.3 below, "The Flowering of Creedal and Confessional Scholarship in the Modern Era."

dence of Scripture, tradition, and creed[11] makes it obligatory to begin the collection of texts with what we are calling "*biblical and primitive rules of faith.*" Within this category of "primitive" as lumped together with "biblical" are comprehended the first two centuries of the history of Christianity. Taking those two centuries as a subperiod unto itself follows the lead not only of the standard four-volume Roman Catholic *Patrology* of Johannes Quasten, for which these two centuries set the borderline for the content of volume 1, but also of the leading Protestant edition of the church fathers in English, in which "the Apostolic Fathers are here understood as filling up the second century of our era" and therefore as including, beyond the usual collection of texts that are grouped under this relatively modern category of "apostolic fathers," the writings of Justin Martyr and Irenaeus.[12] It would be attractive to adopt a geographical taxonomy, not only according to the incipient and eventually fateful distinction between East and West (which is related to, though by no means precisely congruent with, the distinction between Greek creeds and Latin creeds), but according to the various regions within each of these two, such as Greek-speaking Asia Minor or Latin-speaking North Africa, that produced special and sometimes idiosyncratic creeds. But creeds moved about constantly, across the boundaries of space as well as those of time and those of language, and for many of them the present state of the source material permits us to identify only where they ended up, not where they started. Nevertheless the category of *regional* creeds has a certain value, too.

Because of early Christian secrecy about creeds, often called the *disciplina arcani,*[13] and because of the historical accidents of translation as well as of the preservation and transmission of manuscripts, many of these creeds have become available to us only as they were embodied (or, at any rate, partially quoted) in the writings of individual councils and theologians. As a result, in many instances there is no way of knowing any longer just how individual and personal the phraseology of these particular formulations was or whether the texts were being quoted verbatim from earlier sources that no longer exist for

11. See chapter 5 above, "Scripture, Tradition, and Creed."
12. Quasten, 1; *ANF* 1:vii.
13. Cyril of Jerusalem *Catechetical Lectures* 5.12 (*NPNF*–II 7:32); *ODCC* 488.

us. To cite a somewhat later but celebrated example, Augustine in the first book of his *On the Trinity* recites a creed that closely resembles or paraphrases the standard Latin text of *The Niceno-Constantinopolitan Creed* but in its exact words is not identical with it at all.[14] Elsewhere, moreover, both later in this treatise[15] and in other works,[16] Augustine quotes as the creed of the church yet other variant texts. Not only for Augustine, therefore, but for many other early Christian writers, there does need to be a category of more or less *personal* creeds, also because some of these seem to have become the basis for the formulation of later and more official creeds. Yet it is not to individual theologians or bishops but to gatherings of bishops in synods that we owe some of the most important creedal texts, even when their authority did not eventually achieve universal acceptance; hence the category of *synodal* creeds. So intrinsically powerful was the original impulse to confess the faith,[17] and so increasingly dominant the eventual creedal tradition, that those individuals and assemblies whose orthodoxy was acknowledged—or, as the case may be, vindicated—were not the only ones who took it upon themselves to formulate creeds, and we are able to recover, usually from the polemics of their orthodox opponents, heretical synodal creeds such as *The Creed of the Second ["Blasphemy"] Synod of Sirmium* from 357,[18] preserved by Hilary of Poitiers,[19] or heretical personal creeds such as that of the Arian theologian Eunomius,[20] to whom both Basil of Caesarea and his brother, Gregory of Nyssa, wrote lengthy responses.[21]

The Greek word *synodos* and the Latin word *concilium* were synonymous in the church and were used to translate each other, although ecclesiastical Latin also employed the loanword *synodus,* which appears already in non-Christian Latin as a term for a religious assembly.[22] But in keeping with English practice as it has developed (inconsis-

14. Augustine *On the Trinity* 1.4.7 (*NPNF*-II 3:20).
15. Augustine *On the Trinity* 15.14.23 (*NPNF*-I 3:213).
16. Augustine *On Faith and the Creed* (*NPNF*-I 3:321–33).
17. See chapter 2 above, "The Creedal and Confessional Imperative."
18. *Sirm 357.*
19. Hilary of Poitiers *On the Councils* 38 (*NPNF*-II 9–I:14–16).
20. *Eun.*
21. Quasten, 3:306–9.
22. Lampe, 1334–35; Blaise-Chirat, 188, 806.

tent though the usage has continued to be), we have striven for consistency here in distinguishing between "synod" and "council." We define as *synodal* creeds those originating in an assembly, whether orthodox or heretical, that was local and regional in provenance and that remained so in authority. *Conciliar* creeds are those decreed by an assembly that was, or was "received" after the fact as having been,[23] *ecumenical*. This category, too, is ambiguous because of the fundamental difference between the East and the West on the status of the fourteen so-called ecumenical church gatherings that have met in the West since 787.[24] For from among these assemblies during the early centuries of the church's history, only seven have been awarded the designation of "ecumenical council" (and have had their doctrinal decrees and creeds designated as "ecumenical") by both East and West: Nicaea I (325), Constantinople I (381), Ephesus (431), Chalcedon (451), Constantinople II (553), Constantinople III (680–81), and Nicaea II (787).

13.1. The Primal Creed

Behind and beneath all the primitive creeds of the apostolic and subapostolic era there stands the primal creed and confession of the Christian church, *The Shema*: "Hear, O Israel: The Lord our God is one Lord."[25] *The Shema* did not, of course, arise from within the history of Christendom at all; rather, the history of Christendom may in a real sense be said to have arisen from it. When Jesus was asked, in the narrative of the Gospel of Mark, usually regarded by New Testament scholars as the earliest of the four Gospels, "Which commandment is the first of all?" he responded with the words of *The Shema*, "The first is, 'Hear, O Israel: the Lord our God, the Lord is one; and you shall love the Lord your God with all your heart, and with all your soul, and with all your mind, and with all your strength.'"[26] That explicit reference is reinforced by what would seem to be a valid use of the argument from silence. Seeking to explain the curious circum-

23. See chapter 9.2 above, "Reception of Creeds, Councils, and Confessions as Ratification."
24. See chapter 14.3 below, "The Sacred Tradition of the Seven Ecumenical Councils."
25. Dt 6.4, 6.5–9, 11.13–21; Nm 15.37–41.
26. Mark 12.28–30.

stance "that Philo never directly quotes in support of [biblical mono-theism] that classical scriptural proof-text," *The Shema*, Harry A. Wolf-son proposed the explanation that "this principle was so commonly well known among those of his contemporaries to whom he addressed himself in his works," both in Palestine, "where this belief in the unity of God constituted a principle of faith which was twice daily confessed by the recitation," and in the Jewish Diaspora, including Philo's Alex-andria, where "undoubtedly the same confession of the belief in the unity of God was also followed twice daily by Hellenistic Jews," that Philo did not have to refer to it.[27] It certainly would appear to be legiti-mate to apply this argument also to Philo's Jewish contemporaries, Jesus and his early disciples in Palestine as well as Paul the Hellenis-tic Jew in Tarsus. One of the most moving tributes to the power of *The Shema* as a creedal affirmation comes at the conclusion of a mas-sive historical novel about the Second World War by Herman Wouk. A twentieth-century Diaspora Jew, Aaron Jastrow, confesses in his final testament, written in the death camp, that for much of his life he had been "an apostate. I dropped my Jewishness outside and inside. . . . Here under the Germans I resumed my Jewishness." He makes his final testimony to that reaffirmation of the faith of his childhood when, in the gas chamber, "he gasps out a deathbed confession, or tries to, with congesting lungs, swelling mouth tissues, in breath-stopping pain: '*The Lord is God. Blessed be His name for ever and ever. Hear, O Israel, the Lord our God is One God.*' He falls to the cement."[28]

Sometimes under pressure from threats and tortures fore-shadowing those that were to be inflicted on Aaron Jastrow and his kindred in the Jewish Holocaust of the twentieth century, the early gen-erations of Christian believers from whom these primitive rules of faith have come saw themselves, too, as witnesses to the oneness of God as confessed in that biblical creed, *The Shema*.[29] The Greek word for "witnesses" is *martyres*, which eventually became a technical term for those who died for their faith, while one who had suffered but had not actually died at the hands of persecutors received the title of "confes-

27. Wolfson 1947, 2:95.
28. Herman Wouk *War and Remembrance*, ch 89, 93; italics original.
29. Irenaeus *Against Heresies* 2.1.1 (*ANF* 1:358).

sor [*homologētēs*]." [30] The history of the primitive rules of faith during
the first and second centuries (and, by extension, of most of the creeds
and confessions that were to follow throughout Christian history) may
without exaggeration be regarded as the developing effort of the Christian community to square this primal and untouchable affirmation of
the ancient *Shema,* which no amount of theological speculation about
the doctrine of the Trinity could ever be allowed to jeopardize, compromise, or modify,[31] with the new realities of the history of salvation
and with the new traditions of the revelation in Christ that were being
celebrated in the liturgy and that had been recorded in the pages of
the New Testament.[32] For the same Gospel of Mark in which Jesus is
quoted as having appealed to the supreme authority of *The Shema*[33]
carries in earlier chapters the accounts of the baptism of Jesus and then
of the transfiguration of Jesus. Both occasions were punctuated by the
voice of God the Father from heaven, declaring Jesus to be his beloved
Son, in whom he is well pleased and to whom it is obligatory upon all
to listen.[34] If it is appropriate to refer to *The Shema* as a creed, as we
have been doing here, it would seem almost as appropriate to see in
this repeated divine declaration of the sonship of Jesus Christ a prox-
imate source—and, by the time these words were written down in our
Gospel of Mark, perhaps even a quotation as well[35]—of something
like a primitive creed that confessed, as almost all of them did, a faith
in "Jesus Christ, the Son of God." The linkage of believing in God
the Father "and [*kai*]" believing in Christ the Son "and [*kai*]" eventually also believing in the Holy Spirit, while at the same time keeping the monotheism of *The Shema* intact and inviolate, was the root
assumption from which the doctrine of the Trinity developed, as well
as the fundamental outline of many Christian creeds and confessions
throughout history.[36] On the basis of the words of Christ, "in the name

30. Lampe, 828–33, 957.
31. Gregory of Nyssa *On Not "Three Gods" to Ablabius (NPNF*–II 5:331–36).
32. See chapter 1.3 above, "The Doctrine of the Trinity as Example of Continuity
and of Change."
33. Mk 12.29.
34. Mk 1.11, 9.7; see *Tol I* 7.
35. The discussion in Feine 1925 is still helpful.
36. *CP 1351* 1.

of the Father and of the Son and of the Holy Spirit,"[37] defenders of *The Creed of Nicaea* such as Basil of Caesarea saw this conjunction "and [*kai*]," in the context of the use of the singular noun "the name," as proof for the equality and coordination, rather than an inequality and subordination, between the Father, the Son, and the Holy Spirit, as the three were named in the creed or in the baptismal formula or in the trinitarian doxology.[38]

That fundamental outline of the creeds[39] was tied to several closely related (indeed, overlapping) themes and activities of the followers of Jesus, as these may be seen to be enumerated in one of the first descriptive summaries we have of the life of the early church, from the second chapter of the Acts of the Apostles: "So those who received *his word* were *baptized*. . . . And they remained faithful to the apostles' *teaching* and *fellowship*, to *the breaking of bread* and *the prayers*."[40]

13.2. The Kerygma and Baptismal Symbols

From this declaration of the Book of Acts that "those who received his word were baptized" we may infer that there was a close connection between the early creeds and the preaching of this "word," the primitive Christian proclamation—or, as it has come to be called also in modern English, the "kerygma"[41]—to the church and by the church. The painstaking efforts of New Testament scholars to reconstruct this kerygma of the early church, as the kerygma is reflected above all in the Gospels but also in other books of the New Testament and of early Christian literature, has led to the recognition of these elements:

> the one true God, Creator of heaven and earth;
> his only Son, born of the Virgin Mary, divinely
>   powerful in word and deed, crucified under
>   Pontius Pilate, raised from the dead, and returning
>   to judge the world;

37. Mt 28.19.
38. Anderson 1980, 11.
39. See, for example, *Ep Apost.*
40. Acts 2.41–42 (RSV plus NJB); italics added. These motifs also appear, though in a different arrangement and without explicit reference to this passage in Acts, in Kelly, 13–14.
41. *OED* 5-IV:679.

> the Holy Spirit, who inspired the ancient prophets
> and whose breath is the life of the holy church.

Because so many of the texts that have survived from the most ancient of Christian writers after the New Testament were addressed chiefly to those on the outside of the church rather than to those on the inside, the discovery, during the twentieth century, of even one very early formulation of this kerygma that apparently was addressed orally to Christian believers in an assembled congregation, the papyrus of the *Homily on the Pasch* of Melito of Sardis from the second half of the second century, confirms especially the centrality in the message of the events of the "passion [*pathos*]" of Christ, climaxing in his resurrection.[42] It does not appear to be stretching the available evidence to suggest, therefore, that there was some such stock outline at the foundation of Christian preaching, which was passed on from one preacher to the next both by the laying on of hands at ordination and by a system of apprenticeship. As has been their wont in every age, preachers would concentrate a particular homily now on one component part of that outline, now on another, often on the basis of a particular passage from the Septuagint Greek translation of the Hebrew Bible.

Nor is it a great leap to suppose that this stock outline of the kerygma bore a distinct enough resemblance to the creeds that we now have, in whole or in part, to justify our viewing them as reflecting that outline, even though it would be unwarranted to identify it with their texts in every particular, as has sometimes been tried. The decisive role of the kerygma in determining the content and shaping the outline of the early creeds was, moreover, not confined to the primitive rules of faith. In fact, a case could be made for the thesis that one of the significant factors in the evolution of the early creeds (employing the categories of Part One of *Creeds and Confessions of Faith in the Christian Tradition*) from the "Biblical and Primitive Rules of Faith" of the first two centuries to the "Regional, Synodal, and Personal Symbols" of the third, fourth, and fifth centuries and finally to the "Conciliar and Ecumenical Decrees: From Nicaea I to Nicaea II" of the fourth to the eighth century, was the authority of the kerygma, as this was now

42. Quasten, 1:242–48.

being set down in more and more definitive and prescriptive forms, also through the gradual definition of the New Testament canon. That was what Athanasius maintained when he defended the doctrine of the Trinity, as *The Creed of Nicaea* had formulated it in 325, against the charge of unscriptural innovation. He argued that Nicaea, "the ecumenical council, commit[ted] to writing . . . that which from the beginning those who were eyewitnesses and ministers of the word[43] have handed down to us. For the faith which the council has confessed in writing, that is the faith of the catholic church."[44]

Because the proclamation of the kerygma and the administration of baptism belonged together, creeds were made necessary also by the demands of Christian baptism "in the name of the Father and of the Son and of the Holy Spirit,"[45] or "in the name of Christ,"[46] as becomes evident already from the New Testament. The association of a hypothetical primitive creed with baptism is borne out not only by these final and formulaic words of Christ to the disciples, "baptizing them in the name of the Father and of the Son and of the Holy Spirit," but by a highly revealing textual variant in the Acts of the Apostles, which is part of the account of the encounter between the apostle Philip and the Ethiopian eunuch. Following the question of the eunuch (which is universally attested in all the manuscripts), "See, here is water! What is to prevent my being baptized?" the "Western text" of the Book of Acts has the narrative continue: "And Philip said, 'If you believe with all your heart, you may.' And he replied, 'I believe that Jesus Christ is the Son of God.'"[47] This reading is represented by weighty manuscripts and early versions of the New Testament and is followed by the Vulgate, the Authorized Version of the English Bible, and other translations into various languages. Its closing affirmation about Christ, "I believe that Jesus Christ is the Son of God," does indeed sound distinctly like a "creedal" progression from the confession of Peter to Christ, "You are the Christ, the Son of the living God."[48] The author of

43. Lk 1.2.
44. Athanasius *Defense of the Nicene Definition* 6.27 (*NPNF*-II 4:168–69).
45. Mt 28.19.
46. Acts 2.38, 8.16, 19.5.
47. Acts 8.36–37 (var).
48. Mt 16.16.

Luke-Acts may be attributing to this candidate for baptism the words of an existing statement of faith, perhaps an oral rather than a written one. As this example indicates, some of these primitive formulas were binitarian rather than trinitarian in their verbal form, linking God the Father with Jesus Christ the Son, but not explicitly with the Holy Spirit.[49] The apostle Paul, who elsewhere uses the same prepositions in a formula that is triadic (whether or not it is intended to be "trinitarian"), "From [*ex*] him and through [*dia*] him and to [*eis*] him are all things,"[50] can confess, in language that also has a "creedal" ring to it: "For us there is one God, the Father, from [*ex*] whom are all things and for [*eis*] whom we exist, and one Lord, Jesus Christ, through [*dia*] whom are all things and through whom we exist," with no reference at all to the Holy Spirit.[51] Even the original *Creed of Nicaea* of 325, after affirming in considerable detail that the Son is "the only-begotten begotten from the Father, that is from the substance of the Father, God from God, light from light, true God from true God, consubstantial with the Father," concludes its affirmative portion with "And in the Holy Spirit," and not a word more about that.[52] The condemnatory clauses against heresy that follow, moreover, revert to the relation between the Father and the Son, saying nothing about the Holy Spirit.

But the trinitarian force of the baptismal formula—and, apparently on that basis, of the Gloria Patri—prevailed over any binitarian formulas even though these could claim biblical provenance. Many early Christian writers affirm this. *The Apostolic Tradition*, generally attributed to Hippolytus of Rome, describes baptism this way:[53]

> When the person being baptized goes down into the water, he who baptizes him, putting his hand on him shall say: "Do you believe in God, the Father Almighty?" And the person being baptized shall say: "I

49. Macholz 1902.
50. Rom 11.36; see Augustine *On the Trinity* 2.15.25 (*NPNF*-I 3:49).
51. 1 Cor 8.6.
52. See chapter 1.3 above, "The Doctrine of the Trinity as Example of Continuity and of Change."
53. Quasten, 2:191–92.

believe." Then holding his hand on his head, he shall baptize him once.

And then he shall say: "Do you believe in Christ Jesus, the Son of God, who was born of the Holy Spirit and the Virgin Mary, and was crucified under Pontius Pilate, and was dead and buried, and rose again the third day, alive from the dead, and ascended into heaven, and sat down at the right hand of the Father, and will come to judge the living and the dead?" And when the person says: "I believe," he is baptized again.

And again the deacon shall say: "Do you believe in the Holy Spirit, in the holy church, and in the resurrection of the body?" Then the person being baptized shall say: "I believe," and he is baptized a third time.[54]

Basing himself on this long-established usage throughout the church in both East and West, Ambrose of Milan gives an account both of baptismal practice and of an interrogatory trinitarian creed:[55]

You were questioned, "Do you believe in God the Father Almighty?" You said, "I believe," and were immersed, that is, were buried.

Again you were asked, "Do you believe in our Lord Jesus Christ and his cross?" You said, "I believe," and were immersed. Thus you were buried along with Christ; for he who is buried along with Christ rises again with him.

A third time you were asked, "Do you believe also in the Holy Spirit?" You said, "I believe," and a third time were immersed, so that your threefold confession wiped out the manifold failings of your earlier life.[56]

---

54. *Hipp;* a similar formula in *Test Dom.*
55. See Kinzig, Markschies, and Vinzent 1999.
56. Ambrose *De sacramentis* 2.7.20, as translated in Kelly, 36–37.

On this basis, the treatise *On the Holy Spirit* by Basil of Caesarea
—on which Ambrose's treatise *On the Holy Spirit,* written in Latin,
is highly dependent[57]—argues (as David Anderson, who translated it
from Greek into English, has summarized it): "If saving regeneration
begins through baptism in the name of Father, Son, and Spirit, with
name in the singular, then Father, Son, and Spirit form a coordinate
series, with all three sharing equal rank."[58]

Therefore an entire class of primitive creeds is often identified
as "baptismal symbols." This category includes the hypothetical reconstruction that August Hahn has presented as "the presumable original
form of the Eastern baptismal creed":

> We believe in one God, the Almighty, Maker of all
> things visible and invisible.
>
> And in one Lord Jesus Christ, his only-begot-
> ten Son, begotten of the Father before all ages; through
> whom also all things came to be; who for us came
> down from heaven and became incarnate, was born of
> the Virgin Mary and was crucified under Pontius Pilate
> and was buried, and rose on the third day in accor-
> dance with the Scriptures, and ascended into heaven,
> and is seated at the right hand of the Father, and will
> come in glory to judge the living and the dead; of his
> kingdom there will be no end.
>
> We believe also in one Holy Spirit, the giver of
> life, and in one holy catholic and apostolic church, one
> baptism of repentance for the forgiveness of sins, in
> the resurrection of the dead, in the kingdom of heaven,
> and in life everlasting. Amen.[59]

It is obvious that Hahn's reconstructed text comes very close to the
eventual text of *The Niceno-Constantinopolitan Creed* and to the presumed baptismal creed on which this may have been based.[60]

57. Quasten, 4:169–70.
58. Anderson 1980, 11; italics original.
59. Hahn, 122.
60. Kelly, 296–331.

As a consequence, even a historian of creeds and confessions who was committed to the authority of *sola Scriptura* as the only "rule of faith"[61] was constrained by the evidence to propound the following six conclusions:

> that *from the very beginning of the Christian Church* the candidates for Baptism everywhere were required to make a confession of their faith;
>
> that from the beginning *there was existing in all the Christian congregations a formulated confession,* which they called the rule of faith, the rule of truth, etc.;
>
> that this rule was identical with the confession required of the candidates for Baptism;
>
> that it was declared to be of apostolic origin;
>
> that the summaries and explanations of this rule of truth, given by these writers, tally with the contents and, in part, also with the phraseology of the Apostles' Creed;
>
> that the scattered Christian congregations, then still autonomous, regarded the adoption of this rule of faith as the only necessary condition of Christian unity and fellowship.[62]

Likewise, in a frequently quoted generalization, a leading historian of the early church, Hans Lietzmann, felt able to assert: "It is indisputable that the root of *all* creeds is the formula of belief pronounced by the baptizand, or pronounced in his hearing and assented to by him, before his baptism."[63]

13.3. The Deposit of the Faith, Evangelism, and Apologetics

That those who came after the first apostles "remained faithful to [*ēsan proskaterountes*] the teaching of the apostles" carried with it the

---

61. See chapter 5.2 above, "Scripture in the Creeds and Confessions."
62. Friedrich Bente in *Triglotta* 1:10; italics added.
63. Kelly, 30; italics added. See also Lietzmann 1966.

supreme obligation to "guard the deposit [*depositum custodire*]"[64] of
the faith against all its enemies, foreign and domestic, and to follow
the example of the apostles as evangelists and apologists. The prominence of that obligation not only in the pastoral epistles, whether these
are to be taken as Pauline or not, but in the other epistles bearing the
name of Paul and unquestionably written by him, appears to presuppose the existence of such a "deposit [*parathēkē*]," at least in some
primitive form or other. All or most of these epistles, it would seem,
were composed before any of our four Gospels had attained their final
written form. In his indubitably authentic First Epistle to the Corinthians, which seems to have been written during the early fifties of the
first century, Paul could refer in writing to "the gospel [*to euangelion*]"
about the suffering, death, and resurrection of Christ that he had "delivered to you [*paredōka hymin,* the verb corresponding to the noun
paradosis, tradition]" in oral form when he had visited the Corinthian
congregation in person earlier. He had in turn "also received it [*ho kai
parelabon*]" from the Lord Jesus Christ (and, it seems clear, *through*
the tradition of the church) earlier still, after his conversion from per-
secutor to apostle.[65] That carries the ultimate point of reference back
to only a very few years after the events themselves. As a "deposit,"
the gospel tradition that Paul had received and then had transmitted
orally and now was confirming by his epistles seems to have contained
(though it was not necessarily restricted to) the account of these saving
events of the suffering, death, and resurrection, including the institution of the eucharist, for which he had employed the same formulaic
introduction a few chapters earlier: "I received from the Lord what I
also delivered to you [*paredōka hymin*]."[66] Already in these two epistles
to the Corinthians, and then in his other epistles, Paul urged believers,
as he would put it at the conclusion of his letter to the Romans, "to
take note of those who create dissensions and difficulties, in opposition to the doctrine which you have been taught [*para tēn didachēn hēn
hymeis emathete*]."[67] Believers were to be "of the same mind, having the

64. 1 Tm 6.20 (Vulg); 2 Tm 1.14 (Vulg). See the use of these two passages by
Tertullian *The Prescription Against Heretics* 25 (ANF 3:254–55).
65. 1 Cor 15.1–7.
66. 1 Cor 11.23–25.
67. Rom 16.17.

same love, being in full accord and of one mind."[68] Not only for the preaching of the word within the congregation of the faithful, but for the defense of the deposit of the faith when it was under attack from those who distorted it "in opposition to the doctrine which you have been taught," it was necessary to give the deposit a structured form as a received *didachē* whose authority it was possible to cite. By the time we encounter such structured forms, among other places in the writings of Irenaeus of Lyons at the end of the second century,[69] they may be regarded as firm even though they are not completely fixed.[70]

For some of the earliest creeds, we are obliged to surmise the part that this polemical imperative of "guarding the deposit" of the faith may have played in their composition and choice of language.[71] In most cases, however, such surmises about the false teachers and false teachings being addressed by a creed are unnecessary even for those creeds that we have labeled "synodal" or "personal," but especially for those that we are calling "conciliar," where the polemical intent is stated, often at great length, either in the surrounding conciliar texts, including the private writings of prominent participants, or sometimes even in the text of the creed itself. That pattern is set already by the first of these conciliar creeds, *The Creed of Nicaea* of 325. It follows its positive affirmations about Father, Son, and Holy Spirit with these condemnatory declarations (which do not, however, identify by name the heretical authors of the quotations, probably because they do not have to): "Those who say 'there once was when he was not,' and 'before he was begotten he was not,' and that he came to be from things that were not, or from another hypostasis or substance, affirming that the Son of God is subject to change or alteration—these the catholic and apostolic church anathematizes."[72] This polemical accent becomes a persisting, even an increasing, dimension of creeds and confessions in later periods, above all in those from the period of the Reformation.

In the original Greek of the Gospel of Matthew, the parting commands of the risen Christ to the apostles before his ascension, to

68. Phil 2.2.
69. *Iren.*
70. Eynde 1933.
71. See chapter 7.1 above, "Creedal Anathema and Polemics."
72. *N* anath.

"baptize [*baptizontes*] in the name of the Father and of the Son and of the Holy Spirit" and to "teach [*didaskontes*] . . . all that I have commanded you," both take the grammatical form of participial phrases modifying the imperative "Make disciples of all nations [*mathēteusate panta ta ethnē*]."[73] In carrying out this imperative, the early church developed a twofold strategy toward those outside its membership: on the positive side, evangelism and missionary preaching first to Jews, and then increasingly to Gentiles, as distinct from preaching to the Christian congregation; and on the negative side, apologetics and defense against external attacks, as distinct from polemics against false teachings claiming to be Christian. It involved the task of evangelism, because the presentation of the kerygma to those who had not yet heard and believed required a different emphasis, though not a different content, from the proclamation of the message to the congregation of those who were already believers. But it also included the program of apologetics, because it was felt necessary to meet the objections of the cultured among the despisers of the gospel by seeming to stand on their ground and sometimes by taking a starting text not from Christian Scripture but from pagan philosophy or poetry. For this twofold apostolic strategy, too, there developed standardized creedlike formularies, which manifested certain parallels to those that were at work in congregational preaching, baptism, and antiheretical polemics. Some examples of such formularies for both activities are visible already in the sermons attributed to the apostles in the Book of Acts. For evangelism, there are the sermon of Peter at Pentecost and the summary of the history of Israel by Stephen the deacon and protomartyr, both of these presented as having been addressed in Greek to audiences of Hellenistic Jews.[74] For apologetics, we have the discourse of Paul and Barnabas after they had been taken for pagan deities in Lystra, and the discourse of Paul on the Areopagus in Athens. Both of these, and especially the second of them, made direct use of quotations from pagan Greek sources.[75]

73. Mt 28.19.
74. Acts 2.14–36, 7.2–53.
75. Acts 14.11–18, 17.22–33. See Wilckens 1961, especially 86–91; and Syndogmaticon 1.2.

Although the plot line of the narrative in the Acts of the Apostles required that the evangelistic discourses precede the apologetic discourses, the transition from the first to the second having been provided by the decision of Paul and Barnabas to "turn to the Gentiles" from the Jews, although not completely,[76] the standard pattern, as early as the second century, became the reverse of that order. It would remain so, for example in the *Orthodox Faith* of John of Damascus for the Eastern church and the *Summa Theologica* of Thomas Aquinas for the Western church: first apologetics, including eventually rational proofs for the existence of God and other components of what came to be called, more or less satisfactorily, "natural theology"; and only then the systematic exposition of the faith of the church. This later pattern was justified on the grounds that it followed the sequence set by Paul's Epistle to the Romans. There Paul opens with the statement on which, more than on any other, the natural theology of the apologetic enterprise would ever after depend for its apostolic credentials: "Ever since the creation of the world [or perhaps: On the basis of the creation of the world, *apo ktiseōs kosmou*] his invisible nature, namely, his eternal power and deity, has been clearly perceived in the things that have been made."[77] Then the Epistle to the Romans goes on in its remaining chapters to expound the apostolic kerygma about Christ and salvation in detail. Such is the sequence, for example, that is followed in the early diptych of Athanasius, which is divided in the manuscripts and editions as *Against the Heathen* and *On the Incarnation of the Word*. But if the generally accepted dating is correct, the two are best read as a single work in two volumes. Significantly, there are no creedal allusions until almost the very end of the first volume, to be followed by creedal references at considerably greater length in the second.[78] Similarly, it had been specifically in an apologetic context, addressing himself to the Roman emperor Antoninus Pius, that Justin Martyr, around the middle of the second century, affirmed an early and trinitarian creed:

76. Acts 13.48–51, 17.17.
77. Rom 1.20; Pelikan 1993, 65–66.
78. Athanasius *Against the Heathen* 46–47 (NPNF-II 4:28–30); *On the Incarnation of the Word* 20–32 (NPNF-II 4:46–53). Kannengiesser 1970 has argued against the traditional dating.

> That we are not atheists, since we worship
>   the creator of this universe . . .
> and that we with good reason honor
>   Him Who has taught us these things
> and was born for this purpose,
> Jesus Christ,
> Who was crucified under Pontius Pilate, the governor
>   of Judaea in the time of Tiberius Caesar,
> having learned that He is the Son of the true God
> and holding Him in the second rank,
> and the prophetic Spirit third in order, we shall
>   proceed to demonstrate.[79]

The sources permit us only to know for certain that the language of the creeds, once it had been formulated and established, helped to set the agenda for the evangelism and the apologetics. But as with the polemical attacks on those who claimed to be standing inside the Christian movement but who were seen as having denied and subverted its message, so with the defensive responses to those who were outside it, we may surmise from these and other examples that evangelistic and apologetic considerations likewise affected the language of the creeds.

13.4. Didache, Catechesis, and Formulas of Exorcism

"Teaching [*didachē* in Greek, *doctrina* in Latin]," as has been noted,[80] can refer both to process and to content. But for our purposes here it can be applied specifically to the Christian catechesis of the church, both as a content and as a process. The intimate connection between catechesis and baptism has sometimes been overlooked in the search for primitive creeds. Yet as J. N. D. Kelly has stated with regard to declaratory creeds as distinct from interrogatory creeds, "their roots lie not so much in the Christian's sacramental initiation into the Church as in the catechetical training by which it was preceded."[81] *The Teaching of the Twelve Apostles* [*Didachē tōn dōdeka apostolōn*]," or more fully

---

79. Justin Martyr *First Apology* 13 (*ANF* 1:166–67), following the translation and structure in Kelly, 72. See also *Patr.*
80. See chapter 3.1 above, "The Teaching of the Church."
81. Kelly, 50.

and more accurately, *The Lord's Instruction to the Gentiles Through the Twelve Apostles* [*Didachē tou kyriou dia tōn dōdeka apostolōn tois ethnesin*]," or simply *Didache,* is the title of what Quasten calls "the most important document of the subapostolic period, and the oldest source of ecclesiastical law which we possess." It was discovered only at the end of the nineteenth century, having therefore remained unavailable throughout most of Christian history (as well as throughout most of the history of patristic scholarship). As Quasten continues, it "has since enriched and deepened, in an amazing way, our knowledge of the beginnings of the Church." In spite of its title, however, it clearly "does not go back to apostolic times." Rather surprisingly, moreover, there are in it "no traces to be found of a universal creed formula," which both its title and later creeds would have led one to expect and which might also be surmised from the report that "it was used, as Athanasius tells us, for the instruction of catechumens."[82] It does, however, include the trinitarian baptismal formula.[83] Other evidence, however, substantiates the thesis of an important but often neglected book entitled *The Catechism of Primitive Christianity* [*Der Katechismus der Urchristenheit*], which was published in 1903 by Alfred Seeberg. He claimed to be able to discern in the body of the New Testament itself and in subsequent texts the presence of a primitive body of material that had been used, almost from the very beginning, for the instruction of catechumens. "The primitive Christian creeds," he concluded, in a summary quoted approvingly by Kelly (and as translated by him), "are simply and solely the recapitulation, in a formula based upon the Trinitarian ground-plan, of the basic catechetical verities."[84] It has been argued, moreover, that there is even some such "catechetical" structure already behind the language of the Pauline and other New Testament epistles.[85]

Eventually the Christian catechism would, on the basis of the New Testament enumeration of "faith, hope, love, these three,"[86] link three components: the Creed, *The Apostles' Creed* in the West, *The*

---

82. Quasten, 1:30, 36, 37; see Athanasius *Festal Letters* 39.7 (*NPNF*-II 4:552).
83. *Did* 7.
84. Seeberg [1903] 1966, 271; Kelly, 50.
85. Carrington 1940.
86. 1 Cor 13.13.

Niceno-Constantinopolitan Creed in the East;[87] the Lord's Prayer;[88] and the Ten Commandments. The latter two were biblical in origin, with the Lord's Prayer only gradually being stabilized in church usage on the version in the sixth chapter of the Gospel of Matthew, and the Ten Commandments being fixed in the wording of chapter 20 of the Book of Exodus. As integral components of catechetical pedagogy both for adult converts and then increasingly also for the children of those who already belonged to the church, the Lord's Prayer and the Ten Commandments were committed to memory for instruction as well as for worship. Therefore it would be surprising if there had not been pressure to achieve some similar fixity of wording for "faith" as well as for "hope" and "love." Augustine seems to indicate as much when he says, in words quoted earlier: "We have the catholic faith in the creed, *known to the faithful and committed to memory,* contained in a form of expression as concise as has been rendered admissible by the circumstances."[89] Augustine's own treatise *On the Catechizing of the Uninstructed* [*De catechizandis rudibus*] was not a catechism as such, nor an address to catechumens, but a handbook for the catechist.[90] The same was true of *The Great Catechism* of Gregory of Nyssa. Its prologue, with its warning that "the same method of instruction will not be suitable in the case of all who approach the word," makes it clear that, in spite of its title, it was meant to prepare the ministers of the word not for their "catechetical" task in the usual sense of that word, as instruction for the faithful, but for something closer to what is being called here their "apologetic" task, as defense and explanation addressed to outsiders.[91] The most celebrated demonstration of the connection between creed and catechesis, indeed "the first and only complete example of the course of instruction given in the early centuries to candidates seeking admission to the full privileges of the Christian Church,"[92] is found in *The Catechetical Lectures,* the last five of which

87. Compare, for example, *Heid* 23–58 with *Mogila* 1.4–126.
88. See chapter 6.1 above, "The Lord's Prayer in the Confessions."
89. Augustine *On Faith and the Creed* 1 (NPNF-I 3:321); italics added.
90. Augustine *On the Catechizing of the Uninstructed* (NPNF-I 3:282–314).
91. Gregory of Nyssa *The Great Catechism* pr (NPNF 5:473).
92. Edward Hamilton Gifford in *NPNF*-II 7:xlvi; see also Quasten, 3:363–67, with bibliography.

are also sometimes entitled *The Mystagogy*, delivered by Cyril of Jerusalem perhaps during Great Lent of 348. From these it is possible to reconstruct *The Baptismal Creed of Jerusalem* that underlay the lectures.[93] "This summary," Cyril said to his hearers, "I wish you both to commit to memory when I recite it, and to rehearse it with all diligence among yourselves, not writing it out on paper, but engraving it by the memory upon your heart."[94] This was because of the persisting danger of disclosing the mysteries of the faith to its enemies.[95]

The primitive Christian community is described in the Acts of the Apostles as having been faithful not only to the teaching of the apostles, but to the "fellowship [*koinōnia*]" of the apostles. *The Apostles' Creed* even makes "the fellowship or communion of the saints [Greek, *hagiōn koinōnia*; Latin, *communio sanctorum*]" an object of faith.[96] But always implicit in any such description or affirmation of the fellowship within the church and of the fellowship with the apostles is not only the primary fellowship both of the apostles and of the saints with Christ as its ground, but also the irreconcilable antithesis between the fellowship with Christ and the fellowship with demons. Because of conditions prevalent in Corinth, the antithesis of Christ and demons was especially prominent in both of the epistles addressed to the Corinthian congregation by the apostle Paul. It was an issue with regard to the eucharist: "I do not want you to be partners with demons. You cannot drink the cup of the Lord and the cup of demons. You cannot partake of the table of the Lord and the table of demons."[97] But he made it a more general issue when he warned the Corinthians again in his second epistle: "What fellowship [*koinōnia*] has light with darkness? What accord [*symphōnēsis*] has Christ with Belial? Or what has a believer in common with an unbeliever? What agreement has the temple of God with idols?"[98]

Because these developing formulas for affirming "the communion of saints," as in *The Apostles' Creed,* or "the fellowship of the

93. *Cyr Jer.*
94. Cyril of Jerusalem *Catechetical Lectures* 5.12 (*NPNF*-II 7:32).
95. *Lit Chrys* 2.H.1.
96. *Ap* 9; see also chapter 6.2 above, "*Lex orandi lex credendi.*"
97. 1 Cor 10.20–21.
98. 2 Cor 6.14–16.

apostles," as in the passage quoted from the Book of Acts, seem to have had as their counterparts some developing formulas for abjuring fellowship with demons and with Belial, there was a close verbal affinity between the positive confession expressed by means of the creed and the negative confession expressed by means of these formulas of exorcism. For example, arguing against the claims of Judaism and for the superiority of the power of Christ as this was demonstrated in the power over demons manifested in the Christian practice of exorcism, Justin Martyr,[99] whose *First Apology* addressed to Emperor Antoninus Pius was the source for another creedal fragment quoted earlier,[100] invoked a series of clauses, which would eventually become familiar through their incorporation in *The Niceno-Constantinopolitan Creed* and *The Apostles' Creed*, when he declared in his *Dialogue with Trypho:*

> In the name of this very Son of God and
>   first-begotten of all creation,
> Who was born through the Virgin,
> and became a passible man,
> and was crucified under Pontius Pilate by your
>   people,
> and died,
> and rose again from the dead,
> and ascended to heaven,
>   every demon is exorcised, conquered, and subdued.[101]

Later in this same dialogue of Justin with Trypho similar formulations occur, at least one of them including a reference to "blaspheming" that could also suggest a connection with exorcism.[102] Two centuries or so later, and after there was a fixed standard of orthodoxy as defined in *The Creed of Nicaea*, Athanasius likewise affirmed a close causal connection between the orthodox creed of the confessor and the power of the exorcist over demons when, in his hagiographic *Life* of Antony

---

99. *Just.*
100. Justin Martyr *First Apology* 13 (*ANF* 1:166–67).
101. Justin Martyr *Dialogue with Trypho* 85.2 (*ANF* 1:241), as translated in Kelly, 74.
102. Justin Martyr *Dialogue with Trypho* 126.1; 132.1 (*ANF* 1:262–63; 1:266).

of Egypt, the father of Christian monasticism, he portrayed Antony's blend of orthodoxy and asceticism as the performance of the dual task of combating the heretics and exorcising the demons.[103] Athanasius described how Antony, on the basis of the words just quoted from 2 Corinthians, "What fellowship has light with darkness?"[104] urged his hearers to have no fellowship with the Arian deniers of *The Creed of Nicaea*.[105] In the same context he also described in highly graphic language Antony's special powers as an exorcist and his victorious conflicts with demons.[106]

13.5. Prescribed Forms of Praying and of Confessing

Together with the death and resurrection of Christ, the institution of the eucharist by Christ is one of the two specific events in the life of Christ to be recorded both in all three Synoptic Gospels and in the First Corinthian Epistle of Paul.[107] Therefore, because the composition of First Corinthians probably antedates the writing down of any of the canonical Gospels, the first saying of Jesus ever to have achieved permanent written form was neither a parable nor the Sermon on the Mount nor even the Lord's Prayer, but these words, as quoted by Paul: "This is my body. . . . This cup is the new covenant in my blood."[108] The four accounts of the institution of the eucharist vary from one another in several significant details, most of all in the sequence of the bread and the (two) cups in Luke's version: "And he took a cup . . . . And he took bread. . . . And likewise the cup after supper."[109] The manuscript history of each of the four accounts (for example, the addition of the Pauline words "*new* covenant" instead of the simple term "covenant" in some manuscripts of the Gospels) provides further evidence both of the textual diversity in the biblical and liturgical traditions of the churches and of the countervailing desire to make these textual tra-

103. See, at greater length, chapter 10.3 above, "Orthodoxy and Asceticism."
104. 2 Cor 6.14–16.
105. Athanasius *Life of Antony* 69 (*NPNF*-II 4:214).
106. Athanasius *Life of Antony* 63–64 (*NPNF*-II 4:213).
107. For the eucharist: Mt 26.26–29; Mk 14.22–25; Lk 22.19–20; 1 Cor 11.23–25. For the death and resurrection: Mt 26–28; Mk 14–16; Lk 22–24; 1 Cor 15.1–8 (also Jn 20–21).
108. 1 Cor 11.23–25.
109. Lk 22.17, 19, 20.

ditions harmonious, perhaps even homogeneous. Behind that textual diversity, however, there is perceptible a common core, in that sense a single tradition within the several traditions. It was, moreover, a "tradition [*paradosis* in Greek]" that this, like the tradition about the resurrection in the fifteenth chapter of 1 Corinthians, Paul had in turn "handed on [*paredōka*]" to the church at Corinth after he had earlier received it himself.[110]

Any hasty conclusions or hypotheses regarding the association of the earliest creeds with the eucharist, however, must be restrained by two closely related cautions. In our surviving sources this association is simply not as ample for the eucharist as it is for baptism.[111] There was, moreover, for creeds and if anything even more for liturgies, such as that bearing the name of John Chrysostom,[112] a widespread practice throughout the church of attributing a later form to a leading figure or figures from an earlier time. Taken together, these circumstances make it virtually impossible to assign a date to the liturgy of what Acts calls "the breaking of bread" as it became a factor in the evolution of creeds. But by the end of the period being covered in the present chapter, at any rate, *The Divine Liturgy According to Saint John Chrysostom* of the Eastern Church or its predecessors,[113] and subsequently the Latin mass of the Western Church, had incorporated the recitation of *The Niceno-Constantinopolitan Creed* into the eucharistic service as a canonical requirement.[114] This development, as a result of which the association of the creed with the eucharistic liturgy became a permanent fixture, had as its counterpart the creedal and confessional function of the liturgy as such. But it does seem safe to hypothesize that the processes of textual stabilization that were at work in liturgy and in creed were certainly parallel, and that in some cases they were even identical.

Without straining the force of the definite article "*the* prayers [*tais proseuchais*]" in the language of Acts, therefore, it may be permissible to see here at least an inchoate reference to fixed forms of

110. 1 Cor 11.23.
111. See chapter 6.3 above, "The Place of Creed in Liturgy."
112. *Lit Chrys* ttl.
113. See chapter 14.2 below, "The Liturgy as the Church's Preeminent Confession of the Faith."
114. Brightman, 574.

praying, and, by derivation, also to fixed forms of confessing the faith. Among all these fixed forms of praying and of confessing, the Lord's Prayer was in a class by itself, and it always would be.[115] There are in the period up to A.D. 200 three very early witnesses to its text: the Gospels of Matthew and of Luke, and *The Didache* (which seems to be dependent on Matthew), to which Tertullian's version needs to be added as only a slightly later witness. A comparative table of these first three very early witnesses reveals a set outline and structure, but one that allowed for striking diversity, an impression that is corroborated further by the evidence from Tertullian.[116] The transmission and use of the text of the Lord's Prayer is a subject of vital importance in itself, also because it provided such ancient Christian writers as Origen and Gregory of Nyssa with the basis for their expositions of the meaning of prayer.[117] But its importance here lies chiefly in its bearing on the elusive problem of the relation between stability and variation in the transmission of the various sacred formulas of the church. For even a prayer—*the* prayer—attributed by both tradition and Scripture to the Lord of the church himself could be handed down, already within the pages of the New Testament, in two significantly variant formulations. These, moreover, continued to undergo further variations and developments even after the last book of the New Testament had been written. The process of variation culminated in the addition of an entire new conclusion, with the doxology "For thine is the kingdom and the power and the glory."[118] Because this was included in the Greek *textus receptus,* on the basis of the manuscripts available at the time, it was incorporated into the Reformation translations of the New Testament, such as Luther's Bible and the Authorized Version of the English Bible. Therefore it became, and still is, an integral part of the prayer for Protestants, in spite of its dubious attestation in the biblical text.[119] Hence it should not be surprising that the confession of the faith of the church, attributed only by a relatively late Western tradition to the twelve apostles, displayed even greater variations. But in *the* creeds as

115. See chapter 6.1 above, "The Lord's Prayer in the Confessions."
116. *ABD* 4:357 (J. L. H. Houlden).
117. Simpson 1965.
118. Mt 6.13 var.
119. *Heid* 128.

in "*the* prayers," including the Lord's Prayer, the variations do not obscure the continuity of a common core that justifies the use of the definite article in speaking of both.

The overwhelming changes in every aspect of the life of the church that were associated with the conversion of Constantine included the increasing fixed forms of the liturgy that would be celebrated in the new basilicas created by Constantine the builder.[120] Even without having to credit the traditional attributions of *The Gelasian Sacramentary* to Pope Gelasius or of *The Divine Liturgy According to Saint John Chrysostom* to John Chrysostom of Antioch and Constantinople,[121] it does seem safe to conclude that some individual portions of these orders of worship, and specifically collects and prayers, are quite early. The formal adoption of a rule of faith binding on all orthodox Christian believers in *The Creed of Nicaea* had its parallel and counterpart in such collects and prayers. Both developments were contemporary and belong together, along with the definition of the canon of the New Testament, evident in the Muratorian Canon and in Athanasius, as well as the evolution of the monarchical episcopate into a theory of church governance that would eventually assign supreme authority to the ecumenical council, and continuing authority, both at and especially between ecumenical councils, to a "pentarchy" consisting of the patriarchs of Rome, Constantinople, Alexandria, Antioch, and Jerusalem.[122] The idea of a prescribed creed and confession of faith—which eventually (that is, by the time of the Council of Chalcedon, in 451, and later) referred to *The Niceno-Constantinopolitan Creed*, although it would sometimes take the name "The Nicene Creed" or "The Faith of the 318 Fathers of the Council of Nicaea"—thus took its place with "the prayers" and with the "apostolic" canon and the "apostolic" episcopate/patriarchate in a comprehensive system of orthodox catholic authority.

120. Eusebius *The Life of Constantine* 2.45–46, 3.25, 29–43, 4:58–60 (*NPNF*-II 1:511–46, 526–27, 528–31, 555); Eusebius *Panegyric on Constantine* 9.12–19 (*NPNF*-II 1:593–94).
121. *Lit Chrys*.
122. See chapter 4.1 above, "Apostolic Creed and Apostolic Ministry."

CHAPTER FOURTEEN

Affirmations of Faith
in Eastern Orthodoxy

THE HISTORY OF THE EARLY creeds as it has been discussed in the preceding chapter of this volume,[1] as well as the creeds collected in various editions, including Part One of *Creeds and Confessions of Faith in the Christian Tradition* under the title "Rules of Faith in the Early Church," all reflect documents and events from the first several centuries of Christian history. Because these rules of faith set both the pattern and the content of creeds and confessions for all subsequent centuries of the Christian tradition up to the present time, the present chapter on the Orthodox East and the following chapter on the Medieval West, to be accurate and complete, would have to repeat a substantial portion of what has already been said there. The authoritative "conciliar" texts from the earlier period, moreover, would have to be reprinted in the collections for both of those periods, as belonging to the total body of normative confessions for each of them. All of this is, if anything, even truer for the Eastern view of the tradition than it is for the Western. Therefore if an individual scholar or a class of students attempted to study the doctrines of Eastern Orthodoxy on the basis solely of the formal and official Eastern Orthodox "confessions" as these are identified in the volumes of Michalcescu or Karmirēs[2] or in Part Two of *Creeds and Confessions of Faith in the Christian Tradition*— which is what Western authors of manuals on "comparative symbolics," both Roman Catholic and Protestant, have sometimes done—that would lead to a fundamental distortion of Eastern Orthodox teaching,

1. See chapter 13 above, "Rules of Faith in the Early Church."
2. See "Editions, Collections, and Reference Works" above.

as the writers of those later Eastern confessions would have been the first to point out.

The Synodical Tome of the Synod of Constantinople of 1341, quoting the Book of Proverbs,[3] formulates the criterion of Orthodoxy as: "respecting the eternal boundaries of the fathers."[4] Describing a boldness to the point of rashness that the Byzantines manifested as sailors and as warriors when they ventured forth into the unknown, and contrasting it with their attitude of caution to the point of timidity about crossing the boundary lines of ancient religious tradition, whether liturgical or dogmatic, one of them, the twelfth-century theologian Theorianus, in his *Disputation with Nerses the Armenian*, commented that they "are exceedingly manly in other respects; but when it comes to transgressing the boundaries of the holy fathers, they are extremely cowardly."[5] That observation, which the Byzantines accepted with pride, applied to their attitude toward "new" confessions. The ideals of originality and creativity, so cherished by much of modern theological thought, have since early times been dismissed by Greek-speaking Christian thinkers as the trendy "novelty-mongering [*kainotomia*]" and "lust for innovation [*neōteropoia*]" that are characteristic of heretics, by contrast with the continuity and "successions [*diadochai*] from the holy apostles" that mark authentic orthodoxy.[6]

The use of the term *confessionalism* with reference to the Eastern Orthodox Church,[7] therefore, would be intelligible, if at all, only in the framework of the overarching authority of ancient apostolic tradition, "without break or change, [in] both her doctrine and the succession of gifts of the Holy Ghost."[8] Then, on that basis, the "confessionalism" would be found in the dialectic between the two continuing apostolic imperatives cited earlier:[9] first, to "confess with your

---

3. Prv 22.28; see also *Lat 649* 20; *Resp Non-Jur* 1–5.
4. *CP 1341* 1.
5. *Chr Trad* 2:8–10.
6. Eusebius of Caesarea *Ecclesiastical History* 1.1.1 (*NPNF*–II 1:81).
7. On the applicability or inapplicability of this term to various Christian traditions, see also chapter 16.2 below, "Lutheran, Reformed, Roman Catholic, and Radical 'Confessionalisms.'"
8. *Russ Cat* 274.
9. See chapter 2 above, "The Creedal and Confessional Imperative."

lips that Jesus is Lord";[10] and, second, by such a confession "to contend for the faith which was once for all delivered to the saints"[11]—a faith not in need of redelivering, much less of reinventing. When the First Council of Constantinople in 381 legislated that "the profession of faith of the holy fathers who gathered in Nicaea in Bithynia [in 325] is not to be abrogated, but is to remain in force,"[12] the council fathers were locating themselves in a continuity of faith and of confession not only with those predecessors from half a century earlier but with the apostles and their successors in the almost three centuries that had led up to the First Council of Nicaea. They also set down, as normative for the centuries that were to follow, a submission to the authority of tradition that later generations would in turn apply also to them.[13]

14.1. The Ambivalence of the Orthodox Church Toward "Symbolical Books"

Several factors in Christian history have often led to the issuance of confessions of faith, including the challenge from a hostile environment, the crisis of doctrinal schism, and the necessity of indigenization. A review of these would show that they have been at least as powerful within Eastern Christendom since the schism between East and West as they have been in the West, even in the West since the Reformation with its plethora of confessions. And yet, during most of the history of Eastern Orthodoxy, those factors did not produce a vast corpus of confessions of faith, as they had done in the early church and as they went on doing in the West especially during and since the Reformation, but only a select few statements of faith that became more or less official (and usually "less" rather than "more" official). As a result, to a degree that would not be true of most other communions that have official confessions, it is possible for two scholars almost exactly a century

10. Rom 10.9–10.
11. Jude 3. See also chapter 2.2 above, "Faith Defined"; and chapter 5.1 above, "Creeds in Scripture."
12. *CP I* can 1; see chapter 1.1 above, "Continuity versus Change in the Decrees of the Ecumenical Councils."
13. *Chal* 1, 27.

apart to speak about the "identity" of Orthodoxy without so much as mentioning these statements of faith.[14]

The confessional imperative has acquired special urgency whenever the church and its members have lived in a hostile environment and under a hostile political regime.[15] Yet the longest continuing experience of the church with political regimes professing an opposing religious faith has been with the uncompromising monotheism of Islam. Its dominion over many formerly Christian lands and populations—in what one Eastern confession calls "those places where the tyranny of Antichrist prevails," even while the same confession admits that Islam often extends a generous tolerance to Christians[16]—has maintained itself now through fully two-thirds of Christian history, from the seventh century to the present. The venues of all seven of the universally acknowledged ecumenical councils, once the territory of Greek-speaking Christendom, are now Muslim. The West, too, had its violent military confrontations with Islam, in the conquest of Latin North Africa and Spain and then in the Holy Land during the Crusades, but also in Central Europe. "Matters pertaining to the Turk,"[17] for example, were a major concern for the Holy Roman Empire at the same Diet of Augsburg in 1530 to which *The Augsburg Confession, The Reckoning of the Faith* of Zwingli, and *The Tetrapolitan Confession* were presented. But it was Eastern theologians who bore the brunt of the Christian encounter with Muslim doctrine, especially in the earlier centuries of that encounter, before Thomas Aquinas and his generation encountered "Averroism." Therefore it might have been expected that these theologians would have written many confessions of faith as the church's response to the religion of the Qur'ān. There does exist an undated *Confession of the Christian Faith Against the Saracens* in Greek, but it is thought to be of Western origin.[18] In the library of treatises, disputations, dialogues, polemical poems, and other texts, especially in Greek and Arabic, coming out of the Eastern Orthodox confrontation with Islam, the most celebrated being those of John of Damas-

14. Schwarzlose [1890] 1970, ttl; Kallis 1989, ix.
15. See chapter 8.1 above, "Confessing as a Political Act."
16. *Metr Crit* 10.4, 23.2, 23.5.
17. *Aug* pr.
18. *PG* 154:1152.

cus and Theodore Abu Qûrra,[19] the only response to Islam to have achieved a certain official standing as a formal confession of faith came more than eight centuries after the Hegira. *The Confession of Faith by Gennadius II, Patriarch of Constantinople* was composed in 1455–56 as a response to the question of Mehmed the Conqueror, "What do you Christians believe?" by the philosopher-theologian George Scholarius, who became patriarch of Constantinople, with the name Gennadius II, shortly after its fall in 1453.[20]

Similarly, doctrinal schism between churches has frequently been the most important occasion for creeds and confessions. The controversy between the Eastern Church and the Western Church over the doctrine of the Holy Spirit and over the addition of the Filioque to *The Niceno-Constantinopolitan Creed* is, in turn, evidence of the role of creeds in such schisms,[21] as is their controversy over the claims to supreme authority by the bishop of Rome.[22] Taken together, as they need to be, these two questions are rightly seen by clergy and scholars alike as the chief points of religious difference between the two churches, beyond all the "linguistic, cultural, and political factors,"[23] all of which undoubtedly played an important part in dividing them.[24] A similar configuration of dogma and authority, in this case the dogma of justification by faith and the authority of *sola Scriptura* above church and tradition,[25] occupied a decisive position in the various schisms between Roman Catholicism and the several branches of Protestantism during the sixteenth and seventeenth centuries.

But the similarity between these two schisms breaks down at the point of confessional definition. For in the sixteenth and seventeenth centuries, each of the several parties to the Catholic-Protestant schism resorted, and repeatedly, to the confession of faith as a primary

19. *Chr Trad* 2:227–41.
20. *Gennad* ttl; Pharantos 1969, 42–71.
21. See chapter 7.4 above, "The Holy Spirit of Concord and the Sacrament of Concord: Two Ironic Case Histories"; chapter 15.1 below, "The Western Reception of the Catholic Creedal and Conciliar Tradition"; and chapter 16.3 below, "Catholic Substance and Protestant Principle in Reformation Confessions."
22. See chapter 4.2 above, "Doctrines of Church Order East and West."
23. *Com Dec* 4; also *Balamand* 8–9.
24. *CP 1054* 6; *Metr Crit* 3.8.
25. See chapter 5.2 above, "Scripture in the Creeds and Confessions."

weapon for both attack and defense in the conflicts over dogma and authority, with confessional responses to the opponents' confessions and then confessional replies to those responses helping to create during those two centuries a body of doctrinal literature that was distinctive and in some respects quite new.[26] During the far longer duration of the East-West schism, however, the no less bitter and passionate controversialists on both sides of those disputes over dogma and authority exchanged many polemical theological treatises—and even excommunications—but relatively few creeds or confessions. As they stand, only *The Encyclical Letter of Photius* of 867[27] and *The Edict of Michael Cerularius and of the Synod of Constantinople of 1054*[28] from the formative period of the schism hold a position even resembling "confessional" standing in Eastern Orthodox teaching and canon law. On the Western side, too, for that matter, there are fewer such texts than one might expect, at any rate before the Councils of Lyons (1274) and Florence (1439).[29] The latter of these did evoke *The Confession of Faith of Mark of Ephesus* of 1439.[30]

Perhaps the most striking contrast of all between the confessional development of the West and that of the East emerges from a consideration of the process of "indigenization."[31]An initial comparison suggests a similarity between West and East that is intriguing but probably misleading.[32] For in its administrative and juridical structure, contrasting with the pyramid of a single standard and locus of supreme authority in the papacy for Roman Catholicism, Eastern Orthodox Christendom has no one single supreme ruler but a series of "separate and independent"[33] or (to use the standard term of Eastern Orthodox canon law) "autocephalous" national churches. In that respect it resembles the Reformed confessional pattern rather than the

26. See chapter 16.1 below, "The Proliferation of Confessions in the Age of the Reformation."
27. *Phot.*
28. *CP 1054.*
29. *Lyons; Flor Un.*
30. *Mark Eph;* see the account of the Council of Florence in Gill 1959, and in Vasileiadēs 1983, 111–41.
31. See chapter 11.3 above, "Patterns of Creedal Indigenization."
32. See chapter 8.2 above, "Civil Law on Adherence to Creeds."
33. *Russ Cat* 261.

Lutheran.[34] But that system of governance has not been reflected, as might initially be supposed on the basis of the parallel with the Reformed pattern, in the composition of an individual confession by each autocephalous Orthodox church. In the case of *The Christian Catechism of the Orthodox Catholic Greco-Russian Church* by Metropolitan Philaret Drozdov of Moscow, a statement of faith that had been prepared as much for pedagogical as for strictly confessional purposes has, after some controversy over its allegedly "Westernizing" tendencies, achieved standing within one such autocephalous church, while being accorded a mixed reception in others.[35] On the other hand, *The Orthodox Confession of the Catholic and Apostolic Eastern Church by Peter Mogila* did gain acceptance well beyond Ukraine and Russia, having been endorsed by the Orthodox patriarchs of Constantinople, Alexandria, Antioch, and Jerusalem, thus by four of the five members of the original definition of "pentarchy."[36] Yet Mogila, too, was charged with Westernizing, in spite of his controversies with the "Uniates [Eastern Rite Catholics]" in Kiev.[37] Moreover, one twentieth-century dictionary of the Orthodox Church has characterized his *Confession* as follows: "Although the *Confession* (i.e., a statement of faith) was approved by the Synod of Jassy (1642), four patriarchates, and other councils that condemned Lukaris, it is not 'considered one of the primary witnesses to orthodox doctrine'[38] by the Orthodox today, or in the recent past. The *Confession* is one of the many unfortunate examples of the use of Roman Catholic polemics against problematical Calvinist influences within Orthodoxy, especially during this period in the Kievan and Muscovite churches."[39] By contrast, the same work describes *The Confession of Dositheus and of the Synod of Jerusalem* of 1672 as "a more balanced and traditionally Orthodox document than Mogila's."[40]

34. See chapter 16.2 below, "Lutheran, Reformed, Roman Catholic, and Radical 'Confessionalisms.'"
35. *Prav Slov* 1229–31, 2231–32.
36. *Mogila* pr; on the theory of pentarchy, see chapter 4.2 above, "Doctrines of Church Order East and West."
37. Golubev 1883–98, 1:543–53; Jobert 1974, 395–400.
38. *ODCC* [1099].
39. Prokurat, Golitzin, and Peterson 1996, 222.
40. Prokurat, Golitzin, and Peterson 1996, 110.

During the nineteenth and twentieth centuries, the high point of the scholarly publication of collections of confessions and symbolical books for all the Christian traditions of the West,[41] some Orthodox scholars as well as some Western scholars undertook the assignment of preparing parallel collections of Eastern Orthodox confessions. In 1843, E. J. Kimmel edited *The Symbolical Books of the Eastern Church*, which was augmented in 1850 by H. J. C. Weissenborn's *Appendix to the Symbolical Books of the Eastern Church*, and followed by the Eastern portion of Philip Schaff's *Creeds of Christendom* in 1877. In 1904 the Romanian scholar Jon Michalcescu published his *Thēsauros tēs Orthodoxias*, subtitled "The Confessions and the Most Important Testimonies to the Faith of the Greek-Oriental Church." But the standard collection of this sort is undoubtedly the comprehensive two-volume work edited by the twentieth-century Greek scholar Ioannēs Karmirēs, *The Dogmatic and Symbolic Monuments of the Orthodox Catholic Church*, which was published in Athens in 1952; it has since appeared in Graz, Austria, in a new and revised edition (1968), with several additions. Through the circulation of these collections it became customary, especially in the West, to speak rather loosely, as Kimmel and Weissenborn had and as Karmirēs also did, about "the symbolical books of the Eastern Church," as though they were the Eastern counterpart of the texts collected for the Reformed churches by August Hermann Niemeyer or Ernst Gottfried Böckel or Wilhelm Niesel.[42] The ambivalence of Eastern Orthodoxy toward its confessions becomes evident when the Greek Orthodox theologian Chrēstos Androutsos in his *Dogmatics of the Eastern Orthodox Church*, while acknowledging their authoritative standing, refers to them only as the "*so-called* symbolical books" of Orthodoxy,[43] but in his *Symbolics from an Orthodox Perspective* is willing to head the chapter on them simply as "*The* Symbolical Books of the Eastern Church."[44]

41. See chapter 17.3 below, "The Flowering of Creedal and Confessional Scholarship in the Modern Era."
42. See Hofmann 1857, 130–41.
43. Androutsos 1956, 20; italics added.
44. Androutsos 1930, 37–45; italics added.

14.2. The Liturgy as the Church's
Preeminent Confession of the Faith

A principal reason for this ambivalent position of "symbolical books" within Eastern Orthodoxy lies, however, in the distinctively Eastern version, articulated in a special way in the *Philokalia,* of the inseparable connection between "the rule of prayer [*lex orandi*]" and "the rule of faith [*lex credendi*]." That connection has been important throughout Christian history, across the various boundaries of denomination and confession, also in the West. But interpreters of the Eastern Orthodox tradition, whether sympathetic or critical, are agreed on the proposition that within Eastern Orthodoxy *The Divine Liturgy According to Saint John Chrysostom* is an especially forceful illustration of the universal principle of *lex orandi lex credendi;*[45] as noted earlier, it differs from the liturgies of other traditions, including even *The Book of Common Prayer* of Anglicanism, by being accorded a special position among the Eastern Orthodox confessions in the standard published collections of "symbolical books."[46] Anastasios Kallis, who has prepared a trilingual edition of it with parallel columns in Greek, Church Slavonic, and German, and whose versification of its text we have employed here, introduced his edition of the liturgy with the explanation: "The identity of Orthodoxy consists neither in a doctrine nor in an organizational system, but in the correct praise of the Triune God, which has its center in the celebration of the Eucharist, or simply in the *Liturgy,* through which the one congregation assembled in the name of Christ becomes his body, the church."[47] Adolf von Harnack, pronouncing the judgment that "it was to destroy this sort of religion that Jesus Christ suffered himself to be nailed to the cross!" characterized the Eastern Orthodox liturgy as consisting in "the cult of a mystery . . . , hundreds of efficacious formulas small and great, signs, pictures, and consecrated acts, which, if punctiliously and submissively observed, communicate divine grace and prepare the Christian for eternal life. Doctrine as such

45. J. Meyendorff 1982, 122–23.
46. Karmirēs, 246–70; Michalcescu, 277–98. See chapter 6.2 above, *"Lex orandi lex credendi."*
47. Kallis 1989, ix.

is for the most part something unknown; if it appears at all, it is only in the form of liturgical aphorisms."[48]

But doctrine is far from being "in the most part something unknown" in this liturgy, and the "liturgical aphorisms" are confessions of faith. As Paul Meyendorff has put it, "Liturgy is itself a source of theology. Just like Scripture, the liturgy is a revelation, which implies a multiplicity of meanings, and indeed offers the possibility for participation in divine life."[49] The relation between doctrine and liturgy in Eastern Orthodoxy is reflected in the dual meanings both of the word *confession* and of the word *orthodoxy*. As we have noted earlier on the basis of Augustine, the Latin noun *confessio* can refer either to "accusation of oneself" or to "praise of God," thus to the "confession" of sins or to the "confession" of the glory of God as made known in the revelation of divine truth.[50] The Greek counterparts of *confessio,* together with their cognate verbs, can likewise carry either meaning, although patristic and Byzantine Greek typically makes a distinction between them by employing *exomologēsis* primarily for the confession of sins and *homologia* primarily for the confession of faith and doctrine.[51] Within the total setting of *The Divine Liturgy According to Saint John Chrysostom,* both these meanings of "confessing" play a prominent part. In addition to the constant repetition throughout the liturgy of the petition "Lord, have mercy [*Kyrie eleēson*]"—which also appears (in Greek) at the beginning of the Western mass and then is repeated (in Latin) both in the Gloria in Excelsis and in the Agnus Dei but is not invoked in the same way nor nearly so often throughout—the prayer before Communion asks: "Have mercy upon me and forgive my transgressions both voluntary and involuntary, of word and of deed, committed in knowledge or in ignorance." That same prayer opens with words of "confession" in the other sense of the term, as the confession of a doctrinal faith both in the person of Christ and in the real presence: "I believe, O Lord, and I confess that thou are truly the Christ, the Son of the living God. . . . I believe also that this is truly thine own pure body, and

48. Harnack [1900] 1957a, 237–38.
49. P. Meyendorff 1984, 41.
50. See chapter 2 above, "The Creedal and Confessional Imperative."
51. *Jer II* 1.4. Lampe, 499–500, 957–58; Sophocles, 485–86, 806.

that this is truly thine own precious blood."[52] And earlier has come the confession of *The Niceno-Constantinopolitan Creed*, which, as is made clear by the formula "Let us love one another, that with one mind we may confess,"[53] presupposes the confession of sins, not only publicly through the *Liturgy*, but privately through an ongoing participation in the sacrament of confession.[54]

There is a somewhat similar, and mutually reinforcing, duality in the meaning of the term *orthodoxy* as it developed in Greek Christian usage and was translated into the Slavic languages after the mission of Cyril and Methodius in the ninth century. This goes back to a duality that is evident already in classical Greek. The noun *doxa* means "opinion," and the noun *orthotēs* means "correctness." Therefore Aristotle in his *Nicomachean Ethics*, without actually using the relatively rare term *orthodoxia*, can propound the definition: "Correctness of opinion is truth [*doxēs orthotēs alētheia*]."[55] But when the opinion of others about someone is favorable, *doxa* already in classical Greek has the meaning of "good reputation" or "honor," and therefore of "glory." In the New Testament this becomes the primary sense of the word.[56] It is a way of speaking about the "glory *of* God" and the derivative "glory" of the servants of God, leading to the "glory *to* God in the highest" of the Christmas angels[57]—and hence the Small and the Great "Doxology."[58] In Christian Greek, including the Greek of the *Liturgy*, *orthodoxia* and *orthodoxos* identify right belief and right teaching. The word *doxa* by itself, without the prefix *ortho-*, can still carry the meaning "belief" or "teaching" or "opinion," and in *The Confession of Dositheus and of the Synod of Jerusalem* it is used as a synonym for *hē pistis*, "the faith."[59] More usually, however, *doxa* means "glory," as in the frequently repeated Gloria Patri, "Glory [*Doxa*] to the Father and to

52. *Lit Chrys* 2.H.1.
53. *Lit Chrys* 2.D–E; see chapter 10.4 above, "Christian Love the Presupposition for Christian Confession."
54. *Mogila* 1.90; *Dosith* decr 15; *Russ Cat* 351–56.
55. Aristotle *Nicomachean Ethics* 6.9 (1142b11).
56. Bauer-Arndt-Gingrich, 203–4.
57. Lk 2.14.
58. Day, 73–74.
59. *Dosith* decr 9.

the Son and to the Holy Spirit."[60] In Church Slavonic, and then in the other Slavic languages, *doxa,* in this doxology and elsewhere, is translated with *slava,* and *Orthodoxia* becomes *Pravoslavie.* It means simultaneously the right way of believing or teaching and the right way of rendering glory to God, for ultimately the two are seen as identical.[61] The Sunday of Orthodoxy at the beginning of Great Lent came into the Eastern church calendar in 843 to celebrate the final victory of the icons over iconoclasm. It was eventually extended to apply to victory over all heresies past and present, thus to the vindication of *orthodoxia* both as right teaching and as right worship.[62]

It is this vindication of orthodoxy, together with the corresponding repudiation of heresy, that makes *The Divine Liturgy* not a text in which, as Harnack dismissed it, "doctrine as such is for the most part something unknown,"[63] but a "confession of faith" as we have been using that term throughout. This is true even though in its literary structure it does not adhere to the conventional format of the creed or confession, except, of course, for incorporating *The Niceno-Constantinopolitan Creed.*[64] This use of the creed in the liturgy went well beyond the Orthodox church of Byzantium. Through the mission of Cyril and Methodius and then in its translation by Ilarion, who was the first native to be named metropolitan of Kiev, it "was in use in *Rus*-Ukraine at the very beginnings of Christianity" there.[65] The confessional character of the Orthodox liturgy can be documented by a study of some of its doctrines, which may conveniently be reviewed in the order in which they became the subject matter for the seven ecumenical councils between 325 and 787.

The Doctrine of the Trinity (Nicaea I). Most Western orders of worship, Protestant as well as Roman Catholic, include the recitation of a creed that confesses the Trinity: in most Protestant orders, *The Apostles' Creed;* in the traditional Latin mass and its derivatives outside Roman Catholicism (chiefly Anglican and Lutheran), *The Niceno-*

60. Basil of Caesarea *On the Holy Spirit* (NPNF-II 8:2–50).
61. *Prav Slov* 1872–74.
62. *ODCC* 1199.
63. Harnack [1900] 1957a, 237–38.
64. *Lit Chrys* 2.E.
65. Labunka 1990, 23–24.

Constantinopolitan Creed; in some of them, on special occasions such as Trinity Sunday, *The Athanasian Creed.*[66] There are also other trinitarian embellishments, such as the Gloria Patri at the conclusion of a psalm[67] or, though more rarely, the addition of the words "in the name of the Father and of the Son and of the Holy Spirit" to the Aaronic benediction.[68] But even a superficial comparison of these liturgies with the Eastern Orthodox liturgy reveals the greater prominence accorded to the doctrine of the Trinity in Eastern formularies. In addition to the Sanctus, which they have in common with Western rites, these also contain the Trisagion: "Holy God, holy mighty, holy immortal, have mercy on us."[69] The conclusion to the Lord's Prayer, "For thine is the kingdom, and the power, and the glory, for ever,"[70] which in the Latin mass is spoken by the priest after the congregation and choir have prayed the petitions of the Our Father and which throughout Protestantism is an integral part of the prayer as recited by the congregation, is amplified in the Eastern Orthodox liturgy to read: "For thine is the kingdom, and the power, and the glory: *of the Father, and of the Son, and of the Holy Spirit,* now and ever and unto ages of ages. Amen."[71]

The Doctrine of the Holy Spirit (Constantinople I). The doctrine of the Holy Spirit, except for the observance of Pentecost, appears in most Western liturgies primarily in the context of the doctrine of the Trinity. But in *The Liturgy According to Saint John Chrysostom* the prayer for the Holy Spirit takes the special form, first of the invocation of the Spirit in the entrance prayer "O Heavenly King,"[72] and then of the Epiclesis in the eucharist.[73] According to Roman Catholic liturgical and eucharistic theology, especially as it was developed in medieval scholasticism and codified by the Council of Trent, the Words of Institution themselves effect the miraculous "change [*con-*

---

66. *BCP* (Blunt, 216–20).
67. *ODCC* 682.
68. Nm 6.24–26.
69. *Lit Chrys* I.C.2; Day, 292–94.
70. Mt 6.13 (AV); see chapter 13.5 above, "Prescribed Forms of Praying and of Confessing."
71. *Lit Chrys* 2.G.2; italics added.
72. *Lit Chrys* pr A.1; see chapter 6.4 above, "Councils and Confessions on Worship."
73. *ODCC* 551–52.

versio]"of the elements of bread and wine into the body and blood of Christ. But after its recitation of the Words of Institution, *The Liturgy According to Saint John Chrysostom* moves to a double Epiclesis: first, that the Holy Spirit, whom the Father sent down upon the apostles, might descend "upon us," the assembled congregation; but also, more specifically, that the "change [*metabolē*]" making "this bread the precious body of thy Christ" and making "that which is in this cup, the precious blood of thy Christ" might be effected "by thy Holy Spirit."[74] In spite of the language of Peter Mogila's *Orthodox Confession of the Catholic and Apostolic Eastern Church* about the change taking place "after" or "at [*meta*] these words" of the Epiclesis,[75] *The Confession of Metrophanes Critopoulos,* in opposition to Latin scholasticism, warns that "the manner in which they are changed is unknown to us and cannot be explained."[76]

    The Doctrine of the Theotokos and Ever-Virgin Mary (Ephesus). The polemical liturgical strictures of Protestant confessions upon the invocation of saints[77] are aimed above all against what are taken to be the idolatrous excesses of the cultus addressed in medieval Latin Christendom to the Virgin Mary, "Mariolatry" as Protestants have tended to call it.[78] A considerable part of that cultus, however, takes place outside the eucharistic liturgy, in nonliturgical devotions employing such prayers as the Ave Maria, the Stabat Mater, and the Salve Regina.[79] But the commemoration and celebration of Mary as the Mother of God or Theotokos occupies a prominent position in *The Divine Liturgy According to Saint John Chrysostom* from beginning to end. The last petition of the Great Litany at the opening of the liturgy affirms: "Commemorating our most holy, most pure, most blessed and glorious Lady Theotokos and Ever-Virgin Mary with all the saints, let us commend ourselves and each other, and all our life unto Christ our God."[80] The

74. *Lit Chrys* 2.F.5; Germanus of Constantinople *On the Divine Liturgy* 41 (P. Meyendorff 1984, 96).
75. *Mogila* 1.107; Day, 87.
76. *Metr Crit* 9.11. See Syndogmaticon 10.7.
77. See chapter 12.2 above, "Popular Religion, the Rule of Prayer, and Tradition," and Syndogmaticon 3.8.
78. *OED* 8–II:165; *ODCC* 1037.
79. *LTK* 7:49–50 (Emil J. Legeling).
80. *Lit Chrys* 1.A.2.

Little Litany repeats the same prayer, as, after the Great Entrance, does the Litany of Supplication.[81] The Intercession following the Epiclesis, offering "this reasonable worship for those who have fallen asleep in the faith," leads directly to its application to the chief among the departed (whose "falling asleep in the faith" or dormition is observed on 15 August, which in the West is the Feast of the Assumption),[82] "especially for our most holy, most pure, most blessed and glorious Lady Theotokos and Ever-Virgin Mary."[83]

The Doctrine of the Two Natures, Two Wills, and Two Activities in Christ (Chalcedon, Constantinople II, Constantinople III). As is evident from this apostrophe to Mary in the Hymn to the Theotokos, "Without defilement you gave birth to God the Word," the confession of the person of Christ in *The Liturgy of Chrysostom* is not confined to the liturgical celebration of the eternal being of the Son of God with the Father and the Holy Spirit in the Holy Trinity, of "Christ our God," as he is repeatedly identified.[84] For the Christ whom the liturgy celebrates is the

> Only-begotten Son and immortal Word of God,
> Who for our salvation didst will to be incarnate of
>   the Holy Theotokos and Ever-Virgin Mary,
> Who without change didst become man and wast
>   crucified,
> *Who art one of the Holy Trinity, glorified with the*
>   *Father and the Holy Spirit:*
> O Christ our God, *trampling down death by death,*
>   save us![85]

Without resorting to the language of technical christological dogma about "hypostasis" and "natures," that liturgical acclamation, composed by Emperor Justinian, who also composed the christological *Edict* of 551 (which does employ that language),[86] is nevertheless "a

81. *Lit Chrys* 1.A.4, 2.C.
82. See the texts collected in Daley 1998.
83. *Lit Chrys* 2.F.6.
84. *Lit Chrys* 1.A.2, 1.A.4, 2.C.
85. *Lit Chrys* 1.A.5; italics added.
86. *Edict.*

christological confession." [87] For the devotional and liturgical (and then conciliar and creedal) title "Theotokos" attributes birth from the Virgin Mary not simply to the human nature of Jesus the man, as the Nestorian title "Christokos" was accused of doing, but to the single and total person of the incarnate "God from God" confessed in *The Niceno-Constantinopolitan Creed*.[88] So also, this liturgical formula, rather than ascribing the death only to his human nature, ascribes crucifixion and death to the entire divine-human person of the One who is, paradoxically, still the second hypostasis of the Trinity and who remains one in glory with the Father and the Holy Spirit even as he tramples down death by his own death.

The Doctrine of Sacred Images (Nicaea II). Although we have been characterizing *The Divine Liturgy According to Saint John Chrysostom* here as the premiere Eastern Orthodox confession of the faith, it does differ from most other "confessions" in one decisive respect: the liturgy is intended not primarily to be read or even sung but to be celebrated in action as *leitourgia*.[89] Therefore its constant point of reference is the setting provided by the sacred space in which the celebration is being carried on, as defined by the iconostasis and the icons.[90] As the liturgy makes its progress through the festivals of the church year, the events in the life of Christ and the lives of the saints that it commemorates are being commemorated at the same time in sacred images, both those that are continually on view in the churches and those that are seasonal. John of Damascus gives a catalog of the themes of the icons: "his ineffable incarnation and descent into the flesh; his nativity from the Virgin; his baptism in the Jordan; his transfiguration on Mount Tabor; the passion and sufferings that have given us exemption from suffering; his miracles as signs of his divine nature and activity; the salvation-bearing burial of the Savior; his ascension into heaven." [91] This could just as easily be a recital of the Gospel events marked in the liturgy and in the lectionary for Sundays and feast days.

87. Kallis 1989, 57; Day, 200–201.
88. *N-CP* 2.
89. Lampe, 795–96.
90. *Metr Crit* 15.1–2; Day, 126–27; Syndogmaticon 8.10.
91. John of Damascus *Orations on the Holy Icons* 3.8 (*PG* 94:1328–29).

The Theotokos whom the liturgy honors in such language is the one who is seen facing her Son on the other side of the "royal doors" of the iconostasis and who is depicted with John the Baptist in the *Deēsis*.[92] Christ is, the liturgy declares quoting the Psalms, "wonderful in his saints,"[93] as they in turn are depicted in their own icons and commemorated on their own special days.[94] All of that, too, is the subject of the confession of faith articulated in the liturgy.

14.3. The Sacred Tradition of the Seven Ecumenical Councils

Drawing upon this liturgical confession of the faith of the church and shaping it in turn, the doctrinal decisions and formulations of the seven church councils between 325 and 787 stand as the formal deposit of normative dogma for Eastern Orthodox teaching.[95] "The West incessantly asks us for the symbolical books of Orthodoxy," the Bulgarian Orthodox New Testament scholar Nikolaj Nikaronovič Glubokovský once observed, with some annoyance. "We have no need of them. The faith of the seven first councils is sufficient for us."[96] In one sense, therefore, the sacred tradition of the seven ecumenical councils,[97] as it has been collected in Part One of *Creeds and Confessions of the Faith in the Christian Tradition*, is a legacy that Eastern Orthodoxy shares with Roman Catholicism as well as with those other Western confessions in which the validity of the ecumenical councils is acknowledged, albeit with varying degrees of authority being assigned to them.[98]

In another sense, however, the Eastern Orthodox view of the councils is peculiar to the East.[99] One reason for this is that no later actions of any church, neither those actions that lay claim to the title "ecumenical" in Western dogmatics and canon law nor even the actions

92. Pelikan 1990b, 121–26.
93. *Lit Chrys* 1.B; Ps 68.35 (LXX).
94. Onasch and Schnieper 1997, 184–215.
95. Bogolepov 1963.
96. ap. Scott 1928, 351.
97. See chapter 1.1 above, "Continuity versus Change in the Decrees of the Ecumenical Councils"; and chapter 13 above, "Rules of Faith in the Early Church."
98. See chapter 15.1 below, "The Western Reception of the Catholic Creedal and Conciliar Tradition"; and chapter 16.3 below, "Catholic Substance and Protestant Principle in Reformation Confessions." See also Syndogmaticon 9.8.
99. Paul R. Valliere in Nichols and Stavrou 1978, 183–201.

of the East itself since 787 at "provincial synods"[100] nor the Eastern
Orthodox "confessions" may be ranked on a level with the seven councils. Thus for example, the celebrated synod of Moscow in 1682 laid
down important decrees in the area of dealing with the conflict over
the Russian "schism [*raskol*]," but it is not regarded by anyone as standing alongside these ancient assemblies.[101] This has raised, especially
in a divided modern Christendom many of whose ancient capitals are
no longer in the hands of Orthodox rulers, the dilemma of whether
a similar gathering today would be, and should be called, "ecumenical or pan-Orthodox."[102] Primarily in the area of canon law, but also
in the area of dogmatic legislation, this dilemma had led, on the basis
of the legislation of the early centuries, to the concept of "the permanent synod [*synodos endēmousa*]," which exercises some, but not all,
of the judicial function of a council in the period after the last truly
"ecumenical council."[103]

Another reason for the distinctiveness of the Eastern view is
that the doctrinal legislation of the seven councils on each of the doctrines we have reviewed on the basis of *The Divine Liturgy According
to Saint John Chrysostom* has acquired a distinctively Eastern Orthodox interpretation, through the internal development of Orthodoxy
and through its conflicts with the West.

*The First Council of Nicaea (325); the First Council of Con-
stantinople (381).* With the First Council of Nicaea in 325 and the
First Council of Constantinople in 381 taken together, as for creedal
purposes they should be on account of *The Niceno-Constantinopolitan
Creed,* the authority of the ecumenical councils means for Eastern Orthodoxy that this creed as it stands is permanently binding. Initially
this implied primarily that no one was to teach in a way that went
against *The Niceno-Constantinopolitan Creed,* or to remove anything
from it, including the controversial term *homoousios,* which for many
still carried too many reminders of its heretical lineage.[104] But it was
the converse that came to figure more prominently in the East's con-

100. Afanas'ev 1931.
101. Vinogradský 1899, 1:38–78.
102. Kartašev 1932, 7–29.
103. Hajjar 1962, 130–36.
104. Prestige 1956, 197–218.

troversies with the West. It was wrong not only to go *against* the creed but to go *beyond* it, not only to remove anything from it but to add anything to it. More particularly, it was wrong for any province of the church, or for a single patriarchate, even the one that was *primus inter pares,* to arrogate to itself the sovereign right to alter the text of the creed or add to it. Only a genuinely ecumenical council would have such a right, and even it would be bound by precedent, as the re-iteration of the unchangeability of the councils and their creeds made plain.[105] Therefore the Western addition of the words "and from the Son [*ex Patre Filioque*]" to the article of the creed on the Holy Spirit was taken by the East as a usurpation of conciliar authority. There were also substantive dogmatic and metaphysical objections to this West-ern theologoumenon, which appeared to be positing a second origin or "source and ground of being [*pēgē kai archē, fons ac origo*]"[106] within the Trinity, namely, the Son in addition to the Father. This is a charge that Western confessions deny, for example in the assertion of the Sec-ond Council of Lyons in 1274 "that the Holy Spirit proceeds eternally from the Father and the Son, not as from two principles, but as from one principle; not by two spirations, but by a single spiration."[107] But the Eastern confessions insist that even if it were not doctrinally excep-tionable in itself, it does not belong in *The Niceno-Constantinopolitan Creed.* For example, the distinctively Eastern emphasis on "energies" or "activities" as well as "essence" and "hypostases" in the Godhead, as this comes to be fully stated only in the decisions of the Synods of Constantinople in 1341 and 1351 on the Hesychast controversy,[108] was never taken by any spokesman for the East as a justification for a re-vision and expansion of *The Niceno-Constantinopolitan Creed* to include something about the divine "energies." Indeed, in this case, even absent such a textual change, it was the West that could, and did, raise the accusation against the East of a substantive addition to the creed.[109]

   The Council of Ephesus (431). Throughout much of the history

---

105. See chapter 1.1 above, "Continuity versus Change in the Decrees of the Ecu-menical Councils."
106. *Mogila* 1.71.
107. *Lyons* 1.
108. *CP 1341; CP 1351.* See Syndogmaticon 1.9.
109. *DTC* 11:1777–1818 (Martin Jugie).

of the doctrine of Mary, the basic pattern has been a movement from East to West, even though Nestorius, the principal opponent of the title "Theotokos" for the Virgin, was bishop of Constantinople. The decree of the Council of Ephesus in 431, which hereticizes Nestorius, also makes "Theotokos" official, thereby confirming Eastern theology and devotion.[110] At the same time the Council of Ephesus stimulated a deepening of Marian theology and devotion also in the West, continuing the Western and Latin indigenization of Greek Mariology that had been associated especially with the name of Ambrose of Milan.[111] Augustine of Hippo, the most celebrated pupil of Ambrose, died in the year preceding the Council of Ephesus. The nearest his teachings against Pelagianism ever came to achieving official approbation by an ecumenical council was the action at Ephesus condemning his opponent and the partisan of Pelagius, Celestius, though without specifying whether it was for his teachings on sin and grace.[112] But the necessity of harmonizing Augustine's doctrine of original sin, as he formulated it in opposition to Pelagianism, with the high Mariology represented by the title "Theotokos"—and articulated in the liturgical celebration of her as "most holy, most pure [*panagias, achrantou*]"[113]—was responsible, at just this time, for giving Western Mariology a life and a development of its own, which would eventually carry it beyond the East, and beyond the ancient ecumenical councils.

Augustine himself recognized the problem. Having clinched a strong and seemingly all-inclusive argument for the universality of original sin, from which none of the saints of either the Old or the New Testament era was exempt, he immediately brought himself up short: "We must except the holy Virgin Mary, concerning whom I wish to raise no question when it touches the subject of sins, out of honor to the Lord; for from him we know what abundance of grace for overcoming sin in every particular [*ad vincendum omni ex parte peccatum*] was conferred upon her who had the merit to conceive and bear him who undoubtedly had no sin."[114] A thousand years after Augustine, the

110. *Eph 431* can 1.
111. Huhn 1954; see chapter 6.3 above, "The Place of Creed in Liturgy."
112. *Eph 431* anath.
113. *Lit Chrys* 1.A.2.
114. Augustine *On Nature and Grace* 36.42 (*NPNF*–I 5:135).

Council of Basel, the seventeenth ecumenical council by Western counting, attempted to legislate on that "exception" and to make the doctrine of the immaculate conception official. But by the time it did so, its legislation subordinating the authority of the pope to that of a council had made its later sessions unacceptable to subsequent canon law and dogma.[115] *The Canons and Decrees of the Council of Trent* are careful to explain "that it is not its intention to include in this decree, when it is dealing with original sin, the blessed and immaculate Virgin Mary, Mother of God."[116] As a result, the doctrine of the immaculate conception, though enjoying universal or nearly universal approval in the Roman Catholic Church, became official only with the bull *Ineffabilis Deus* of Pope Pius IX on 8 December 1854.[117] In spite of the effort of that bull to interpret this action as the logical consequence of the decree of the Council of Ephesus more than fourteen centuries earlier, it became in Eastern Orthodox eyes still another Western point of divergence from the sacred tradition of the seven ecumenical councils.

The Council of Chalcedon (451); the Second (553) and Third (680–81) Councils of Constantinople. In most historical accounts, including our own, pride of place among the sources on which *The Definition of Faith of the Council of Chalcedon* of 451 draws is usually given to *The Tome of Pope Leo I* of 449. For as "the pope of the council,"[118] he proposed in that document many of the specific formulations that not only carried the day at the fourth ecumenical council in 451, but became the basis for ongoing christological development—and for continuing controversy at the fifth and sixth ecumenical councils. But from 451 on, *The Definition of Faith of the Council of Chalcedon* remained substantially unchallenged in the West until after the Reformation, and it was chiefly the Greek East rather than the Latin West that was charged with defending its orthodoxy. That defense was addressed both to the "Nestorian" and to the "Monophysite" (as they were then called) churches of the Near East, to each of which Chalcedonianism appeared to have fallen into the error of the other. In that

115. *Chr Trad* 4:50.
116. *Trent* 5.1.6.
117. *Ineff.*
118. Hugo Rahner in Grillmeier-Bacht 1951–54, 1:323–39.

sense, the Orthodox East strove to represent itself, in response to these communions, which have now come to be called, respectively, "Oriental Orthodox" and "the Church of the East," as an evenhanded effort to preserve both the duality and the unity of Christ against those whom it believed to be overemphasizing either of these truths.[119] But in the light of subsequent history it must be agreed that also for East-West relations the most fateful of all the decrees at the two Councils of Constantinople in 553 and in 680/81 was the postmortem anathema pronounced by the latter upon "Honorius, who was at one time pope of Old Rome, because of what we found written by him to Sergius, where he in all respects followed the latter's view and confirmed his impious doctrine."[120]

The Second Council of Nicaea (787). Technically, the seventh ecumenical council occupies the same position in the canon law and the dogmatics of both Western and Eastern Christendom. But the decisions of that council meant incomparably more to the East than to the West, because what was at stake there was, as Karl Schwarzlose called it, the "distinctive identity and freedom" of the Eastern Orthodox Church.[121] Because of the special place of icons in the Eastern Orthodox liturgy, iconoclasm represented a serious doctrinal threat, just as Arianism and Nestorianism had, for the very reason that the liturgy, which includes the icons, is the confession of the faith.[122] The use of the christological argument in favor of the icons also makes their restoration by the seventh ecumenical council a necessary corollary, or an extension, of the dogmatic assertions promulgated by the preceding councils. Resting on a failure to translate correctly, and therefore to grasp, the distinction being made there between the "adoration [*latreia*]" proper to God alone and the "worship [*proskynēsis*]" appropriate also to the saints and the icons, *The Doctrinal Decrees of the Synod of Frankfort* in 794 condemn the Second Council of Nicaea and articulate a specifically Western effort to deal with the problem of

---

119. *Chr Trad* 2:37–61.
120. *CP III* anath; see chapter 12.2 above, "Popular Religion, the Rule of Prayer, and Tradition."
121. Schwarzlose [1890] 1970, ttl.
122. See chapter 14.2 above, "The Liturgy as the Church's Preeminent Confession of the Faith."

images.[123] But they also bring to light the growing differences between the two churches, jurisdictionally as well as liturgically and dogmatically.[124] Even in the East, as late as 867, *The Encyclical Letter of Photius* can speak of reports that "some churches [in Alexandria] . . . number ecumenical councils up to the sixth but do not know the seventh," although "what was ratified in it they hold with as much zeal and reverence as anything else." [125] When iconoclasm broke out again, it would be in the West, as part of the Protestant Reformation.[126]

14.4. The Eastern Confessions as Equal and Opposite Reactions

Not only is the term *symbolical books* an importation into Eastern Orthodoxy from the West, particularly from Reformation and post-Reformation Protestantism; but the confessions that have been compiled under such titles in various collections, including the present one, cannot be understood historically without attention to the confessional principle that dominated so much of Protestantism in the generations beginning with the Reformation.[127] These later Eastern confessions, therefore, were an illustration, in a rather unexpected venue, of the Newtonian teaching that "to every action there is an equal and opposite reaction."

One reason for the lack of Eastern confessional responses to the East-West schism was that Eastern Orthodoxy did not have at its disposal, for issuing statements of faith, instrumentalities that corresponded directly to those available to the medieval (and postmedieval) Roman Catholic West, the "ecumenical council" and the papal edict (encyclical, bull, epistle, constitution, decree, *motu proprio,* and so on). The reverential attitude toward the seven councils has as its corollary the unwillingness of Eastern churches—although they have the technical right to do so, in doctrine and canon law—to lay claim to the honorific title of "ecumenical council" for any of the later *Decrees of*

123. Hefele-Leclerq, 3–II:1045–60, 1240–46.
124. Potz 1971, 34–40.
125. *Phot* 40.
126. Wandel 1995.
127. See chapter 16.2 below, "Lutheran, Reformed, Roman Catholic, and Radical 'Confessionalisms.'"

the Synod of Constantinople that we have included here, not to mention others that we have not included.[128] For, official and valid though they certainly are, and deserving of obedience (as well as of inclusion in such a collection as that of Karmirēs), these assemblies are not labeled as ecumenical councils. The Western Church, meanwhile, has gone on assigning that title to fourteen councils that have been held in the West—and, more important, also *by* the West—since 787.[129] Similar limitations apply also to a modern confessional statement like *The Response of Orthodox Patriarchs to Pope Pius IX* of May 1848, which bears the signatures of Ecumenical Patriarch Anthimus of Constantinople, Patriarch Hierotheus of Alexandria, Patriarch Methodius of Antioch, and Patriarch Cyril of Jerusalem.[130]

Several of the earlier Eastern Orthodox formularies we have included were written by patriarchs of Constantinople: *The Encyclical Letter of Photius* (867); *The Edict of Michael Cerularius and of the Synod of Constantinople* (1054); *The Confession of Faith by Gennadius II, Patriarch of Constantinople* (1455–56); and *The Reply of Ecumenical Patriarch Jeremias II of Constantinople to the Augsburg Confession* (1576). Coming as they did from the ecumenical patriarch of New Rome, they carry all the authority attaching to that patriarchal see in Eastern eyes. But that is by no means the Eastern equivalent of the authority appertaining in Western doctrine and law to the bishop and patriarch of Old Rome. Three of these four Eastern patriarchal formularies (those of Photius, Michael Cerularius, and Jeremias II) were composed as reactions to the Christian West, whether Roman Catholic or Protestant, the other one (that of Gennadius II) as a response to Islam. But with the confession that was chronologically the fourth of these, *The Reply of Ecumenical Patriarch Jeremias II of Constantinople to the Augsburg Confession* near the end of the sixteenth century, it becomes even more appropriate to speak about an equal and opposite reaction, even about a point-by-point refutation of *The Augsburg Confession*.

The next four confessions of Eastern provenance were all writ-

128. See "Abbreviations for Creeds and Confessions" above.
129. See chapter 15.1 below, "The Western Reception of the Catholic Creedal and Conciliar Tradition."
130. *Resp Pius IX* con.

ten during the seventeenth century, all bore the title *Confession* [*Homologia*], and constitute by sheer page count the bulk of the texts in Part Two of *Creeds and Confessions of Faith in the Christian Tradition*. They were directly shaped by Western confessions coming out of the Protestant Reformation. Listing them chronologically, these four are: *The Confession of Faith by Metrophanes Critopoulos* (1625); *The Eastern Confession of the Christian Faith by Cyril Lucar* (1629); *The Orthodox Confession of the Catholic and Apostolic Eastern Church by Peter Mogila* (1638); and *The Confession of Dositheus and of the Synod of Jerusalem* (1672). The leading scholar of Eastern Orthodox statements of faith has trenchantly compared these four seventeenth-century confessions this way:

> The *Confession* of Metrophanes Critopoulos is the most original, independent, and the most free from heterodox influence, of the four Confessions of faith produced in the seventeenth century by Orthodox writers, Critopoulos, Cyril Lucar, Peter Mogila, and Dositheus of Jerusalem. From the point of view of academic theology it holds first place among the other confessions of the time, surpassing them and other Orthodox symbolical books in general, just as from an ecclesiastical point of view it is surpassed by the confessions of Mogila and Dositheus.[131]

This flatly chronological listing of them is, of course, marred by a glaring flaw. *The Eastern Confession of the Christian Faith by Cyril Lucar*, in spite of the eminence of its authorship by the ecumenical patriarch, turned out to be a reaction to Protestant confessions that may have been "equal" — but that was in fact not nearly "opposite" enough.[132] Rejected though it was doctrinally, however, it belongs here historically, on the same grounds that compel the inclusion of other creeds and confessions that were eventually rejected as "heterodox."[133] Therefore both *The Orthodox Confession of the Catholic and Apostolic Eastern*

131. Karmirēs 1949, 73, as translated in Davey 1987, 187.
132. Hadjiantoniou 1961.
133. *Sirm 359; Ecth.*

Church by Peter Mogila and *The Confession of Dositheus and of the Synod of Jerusalem,* and at least by a preemptive strike or perhaps by more direct anticipation even *The Confession of Faith by Metrophanes Critopoulos,*[134] should be interpreted as "opposite" reactions both to Ecumenical Patriarch Cyril Lucar and to the Protestantism that was seen as having affected (or infected) his *Eastern Confession of the Christian Faith,* with its view of authority based on, as Papadopoulos says, "the Holy Scripture without the tradition."[135] As Georgi notes, for example, *The Confession of Dositheus and of the Synod of Jerusalem* follows the outline of Cyril Lucar's *Eastern Confession of the Christian Faith* article by article and question by question.[136]

"Opposite" to Western confessions, both Roman Catholic and Protestant, these three confessions expressly are in their doctrine. This becomes evident in their repeated polemics against what Nectarius, patriarch of Jerusalem, in his foreword to *The Orthodox Confession of the Catholic and Apostolic Eastern Church by Peter Mogila,* calls "certain novel opinions of sectaries entirely contrary to the genuine and ancient doctrine of their forefathers [*neōterismois tisi tōn heterodoxountōn, apadousi pantēi tou orthou kai archaiou sphōn dogmatos*]."[137] Historically, for example, Eastern Orthodox writers had formulated their polemic against predestinarianism in response to what they took to be the determinism and fatalism of the Muslim emphasis on the all-pervading will of God.[138] But now it is clearly the Calvinist doctrines of predestination and reprobation that call forth a new and even more vigorous defense:[139] "of eternal punishment, cruelty, pitilessness, and inhumanity, we never say that the author is God."[140] Such polemics, however, must not be permitted to obscure the remarkable extent to which not only the confession of Cyril Lucar that was rejected, but

134. On his contacts with representatives of the West, especially with Protestants, see Karmirēs 1937, 72–160.
135. Papadopoulos 1939, 104.
136. Georgi 1940, 38.
137. *Mogila* pr.
138. Hildebrand Beck 1937.
139. *Metr Crit* 4.
140. *Dosith* decr 3.

also the three seventeenth-century Eastern Orthodox confessions that were accepted, are "equal" to their Western counterparts in other important respects. Although *The Confession of Metrophanes Critopoulos*, for example, states its purpose to be "that I may accurately present to you this Confession of the Eastern Church without any additions or omissions,"[141] it can be argued that the very concept of a "confession," at any rate in this form, would not have arisen spontaneously in an Orthodox setting, but only as a reaction to the West and under Western influence.

Like the concept of a "confession," the format and the method, too, show how much of a reaction to the West the Orthodox confessions of the seventeenth century are. The catechism was a venerable and ancient tool for the instruction of the young, also in the East, where it attained a "confessional" status of sorts with *The Christian Catechism of the Orthodox Catholic Greco-Russian Church* of 1839, by Metropolitan Philaret Drozdov of Moscow. But the use of a question-and-answer method in *The Orthodox Confession of the Catholic and Apostolic Eastern Church by Peter Mogila*, who also wrote a large and a small catechism and organized his confession as a catechism, is reminiscent as well as of Protestant catechetical confessions.[142] The opening question of *The Orthodox Confession,* "What does it behoove a catholic and orthodox Christian to believe and do, that he may have eternal life?"[143] almost seems to echo in Greek the second question of *The Heidelberg Catechism,* "How many things must you know that you may live and die in the blessedness of this comfort?"[144] *The Confession of Dositheus and of the Synod of Jerusalem* also presents questions, which constitute its second part and are reminiscent of this catechetical method of some Protestant confessions. Moreover, it follows the precedent of most of the standard Reformation confessions during the century between *The Augsburg Confession* of 1530 and *The Westminster Confession of Faith* of 1647, with their series of separate doctrinal articles, by affirming, in a

141. *Metr Crit* pr 3.
142. Žukovský 1997, 156, charts the genealogy of the confession and catechisms.
143. *Mogila* 1.1.
144. *Heid* 2.

series of eighteen "decrees [*horoi*]" of the Synod of Jerusalem of 1672, the principal doctrines of Eastern Orthodoxy. As its second article, for example, it presents the relation of Scripture and tradition,[145] as a counterpoise to the widespread practice of the Protestant confessions, which define the authority of *sola Scriptura* at or near the beginning of their declarations of doctrine as a foundation for all the other doctrines.[146]

Not only in their format and method, either of catechetical questions and answers or of discrete articles each devoted to a controverted doctrine, but sometimes also in their doctrinal terminology, these Eastern Orthodox confessions show an unmistakably Westernizing tendency. Probably the most striking example of such a tendency — apart, of course, from the not only Westernizing but Calvinizing slant pervading *The Eastern Confession of the Christian Faith by Cyril Lucar* — is eucharistic vocabulary. As has been noted earlier in this chapter, *The Divine Liturgy According to Saint John Chrysostom* uses the verb "to change [*metabolein*]" in speaking about the eucharist, but it says nothing to specify the detailed metaphysics of the "changing."[147] But *The Orthodox Confession of the Catholic and Apostolic Eastern Church by Peter Mogila*,[148] and then *The Confession of Dositheus and of the Synod of Jerusalem*,[149] identify this "change" more specifically as "transubstantiation [*metousiōsis*]." *The Eastern Confession of the Christian Faith by Cyril Lucar* rejects this term as "arbitrarily invented [*epheuretheisa eikēi*]."[150] John Meyendorff has said that *The Confession of Dositheus* "is the most important and also, fortunately, the less Latin manifestation of this reaction, where 'the errors of Luther and Calvin' were unmistakably condemned";[151] elsewhere he has called it "the most important Orthodox dogmatic text of this period."[152] For *The Confes-*

---

145. *Dosith* decr 2.
146. See chapter 5.2 above, "Scripture in the Creeds and Confessions," and Syndogmaticon 8.11.
147. *Lit Chrys* 2.F.5.
148. *Mogila* 1.107.
149. *Dosith* decr 16.
150. *Lucar* 17.
151. J. Meyendorff 1966, 136.
152. J. Meyendorff 1996, 86.

sion of Dositheus and of the Synod of Jerusalem sets this terminology of *metousiōsis* into sharp contrast with Protestant eucharistic teachings: the Reformed parallelism between the presence in the eucharist and the "presence" in baptism, as that parallel is drawn in order to reject any presence brought about by a "substantial [*wesentlich*]" eucharistic change;[153] and the theory of "impanation [*enartismos*]," which (although repudiated by the Lutherans themselves) it identifies as Lutheran.[154] In spite of this explicit polemic against both the Reformed and the Lutheran doctrines about the eucharistic presence, there is no direct indication of the medieval scholastic, and therefore Western and Roman Catholic, origin of the Greek word *metousiōsis,* apart from the use of the technical scholastic term *transsubstantiatio* in the Latin versions of both confessions to "translate" it—although in fact, of course, the Greek is a translation from the Latin. A synod of Constantinople later in the century equates the scholastic term *metousiōsis* with the liturgical term *metabolē.*[155]

Nevertheless, when they are read as they themselves specify that they should be read, as a defense of the authority of the ecumenical councils[156] and as a reinforcement of the authority of the liturgy,[157] these modern Eastern Orthodox confessions may be seen as having performed an important function historically and as continuing to perform it now. John Meyendorff has acknowledged that they "played a most important part in helping to strengthen the Orthodox position, regardless of their Latinizing tendencies."[158] Or, as Mastrantonis puts it, they "occupy a secondary place. . . . They are not to be considered on the same level as the decrees or symbols, or the dogmatical utterances known as *horoi* [definitions] of the seven Ecumenical Synods. . . . The symbolic books of the Eastern Orthodox Church should not be equated in validity to the Roman symbolic books (especially to the Council of Trent), nor to the Lutheran symbolic books (such as the

153. *Heid* 78.
154. *Dosith* decr 16.
155. *CP 1691.*
156. *Dosith* decr 12.
157. *Mogila* 1.87.
158. J. Meyendorff 1996, 87.

Lutheran *Book of Concord*)."[159] But they do make possible an inter-confessional comparison of doctrine that would be difficult without them, and they do help to clarify various doctrinal emphases in the liturgy, and even in the decrees of the councils, that could otherwise remain quite obscure.

159. Mastrantonis, xvii–xviii.

CHAPTER FIFTEEN

Professions of Faith
in the Medieval West

A LIST OF THE MOST important texts of Christian thought and doctrine in the nine centuries between *The Consolation of Philosophy* and
The Imitation of Christ, regardless of who might have compiled the list,
would probably not include any creeds or confessions of faith at all.
But it probably would have to include one or more (or most likely all)
of these four texts: the *Cur deus homo* of Anselm of Canterbury, the
Sentences of Peter Lombard, the *Summa Theologica* of Thomas Aquinas,
and *The Divine Comedy* of Dante Alighieri. All of these were master-
pieces of theological speculation, systematization, or prosody rather
than confessions of faith in the precise sense of the word. And yet in
books about religious and intellectual history, the period of the Latin
Middle Ages in the West is the one to which, more often than to any
other, historians, even those who diverge widely in their personal philosophies or theologies, attach the name "*the* age of faith,"[1] with the
word *faith* being used here in the objective sense of *fides quae creditur,*
"the faith which one believes," and not only in the subjective sense of
fides qua creditur, "the faith with which one believes."[2] Therefore it
might initially come as a surprise that this "age of faith" is not known
primarily for any of its professions of faith, as other periods of Christian history are. For example, the fourth century, also for the Latins,
is preeminently the age of *The Creed of Nicaea* of 325 and of *The
Niceno-Constantinopolitan Creed* of 381. The fifth century is identified
by *The Definition of Faith of the Council of Chalcedon* from the year 451,

1. *Chr Trad* 3:1–8.
2. See chapter 2.2 above, "Faith Defined."

which has been a major force in the theology of both East and West ever since. And from the sixteenth century, *The Augsburg Confession* of 1530, *The Heidelberg Catechism* of 1563, and *The Tridentine Profession of Faith* of 1564—listing them chronologically—still define much of what these churches (respectively, the Lutheran, the Reformed, and the Roman Catholic) believe, teach, and confess. But except perhaps for *The Lateran Creed* of 1215, no similar importance attaches to any medieval creed, confession of faith, or conciliar formulation of dogma. The place of the Western Middle Ages in the history of creeds and confessions of faith, consequently, must be sought by a somewhat different route.

15.1. The Western Reception of the Catholic Creedal and Conciliar Tradition

"If I were to sum up in two words what I believe is the essential message of medieval thought," the historian of medieval literature Ernst Robert Curtius once reflected, "I would say: It is the spirit in which it restated tradition; and this spirit is Faith and Joy."[3] When the particular part of that tradition being "restated" is the creedal and confessional one, the term for such an act of restating is "reception." As noted earlier, this has been defined by Yves Congar as "the process by means of which a church (body) truly takes over as its own a resolution that it did not originate as to its self, and acknowledges the measure it promulgates as a rule applicable to its own life. . . . It includes a degree of consent, and possibly of judgment, in which the life of a body is expressed which brings into play its own, original spiritual resources."[4] As applied to "resolutions" of this kind that have come from church councils, the term "reception" identifies an important element of the *a posteriori* process by which decisions made at a particular time and place have become "ecumenically" binding, often within a relatively short time.[5] But the concept of reception is no less applicable to the

3. Curtius 1953, 598.
4. Congar 1972, 45.
5. See chapter 9.2 above, "Reception of Creeds, Councils, and Confessions as Ratification."

longer-range transmission, translation, and transformation of classic Christian texts such as creeds.[6]

When we speak of the Western "reception" and "transformation" of the catholic creedal and conciliar tradition of the ancient church during the Middle Ages, however, it is essential to keep in mind that a substantial part of that tradition had in fact originated in the West. For it is an anachronism to read the division between East and West (to whichever century it may be assigned) back into the earliest centuries of the church. It is also anachronistic to proceed as though the distinction between East and West during the early centuries corresponded, as it eventually would during the first centuries of the Middle Ages, to the distinction between Greek and Latin. One of the first Christian texts addressed *to* the West was Paul's Epistle to the Romans, written in Greek. Moreover, one of the first Christian texts addressed *from* the West was Clement's *Epistle to the Corinthians,* or *The First Epistle of Clement,* written in Greek at the end of the first century by Clement of Rome, whom Irenaeus identifies as the fourth bishop of Rome, after Peter, Linus, and Anacletus.[7] It has been called by Johannes Quasten "the earliest piece of Christian literature outside the New Testament for which the name, position, and date of the author are historically attested."[8] When Clement appeals to the Corinthians, "Do we not have one God and one Christ and one Spirit of grace?"[9] it is, as Kelly has said, "not improbable that he has the interrogatory creed of baptism in mind,"[10] a creed that has not been preserved for us in its totality but that was simultaneously Western and Greek—and already existing around the end of the first century.[11]

Among such early creeds, the history of the relation between what eventually emerges—for the first time in complete form (though not quite in its present form), in the commentary of Rufinus of Aqui-

6. See chapter 11 above, "Transmission of Creeds and Confessions to Other Cultures."

7. Irenaeus *Against Heresies* 3.3.3 (*ANF* 1:416).

8. Quasten, 1:43.

9. Clement of Rome *Epistle to the Corinthians* 46.6 (*ANF* 1:38).

10. Kelly, 66.

11. See chapter 13.2 above, "The Kerygma and Baptismal Symbols."

leia around the year 400—as *The Apostles' Creed* and the text conventionally identified as *The Old Roman Creed* is a Western phenomenon. Therefore the medieval reception of *The Apostles' Creed* took place within the church of the West. For the history of *The Creed of Nicaea* of 325 and *The Niceno-Constantinopolitan Creed* of 381, both of which were geographically of Eastern provenance, the role of the West is more complicated. At the Council of Nicaea, Hosius (or Ossius) of Córdoba may have proposed the idea of a council to Emperor Constantine, probably presided over it, and (according to some) suggested the formula *homoousios tōi patri,* "consubstantial with the Father."[12] His participation shows that it is erroneous to conclude from the geographical location of the first ecumenical council, or from the exclusively Eastern provenance of the participants in the second ecumenical council, that they and their creeds are strictly Eastern. Therefore their medieval reception may in some sense be said to have taken place within the West, too, as well as from the East to the West.[13] That is much more definitely so in the case of the Council of Chalcedon. From the *Acts* of the council in 451 it is clear that a decisive contribution to the resolution of the doctrinal issue before it, and therefore to the eventual text of *The Definition of Faith of the Council of Chalcedon,* came from *The Tome of Pope Leo I* of 449. Though literally a Western statement of faith, this was not, as it turned out, a statement of the Western faith but of the catholic faith.[14]

It is, nevertheless, already in the Western reception of these conciliar creeds during the next century or two that something we could correctly call "a statement of the Western faith" begins to emerge, with the confession of Pope Gregory the Great.[15] He trenchantly formulates the catholic consensus shared by East and West when he draws the parallel: "We receive all the four councils of the holy universal church [Nicaea I, Constantinople I, Ephesus, and Chalcedon] as we do the four books of the holy Gospels."[16] But he gives that declaration the distinctively medieval Western interpretation of creedal and

12. *N* 2.
13. Ulrich 1994.
14. See chapter 7.3 above, "Creeds and Confessions as Instruments of Concord."
15. *Greg I.*
16. *Chr Trad* 1:335.

conciliar authority when he defines that "without the authority and the consent of the apostolic see [of Rome], none of the matters transacted [by a universal council] have any binding force."[17] There are several other defining characteristics that may be said to have made the Christian doctrinal theology of the Middle Ages "medieval," including the shift from baptism to the eucharist and the mass as the central sacramental paradigm of the faith, as well as its dependence on a knowledge of the Greek classics, and even of the Latin classics, that was derived from secondary Christian sources rather than from the primary texts themselves.[18] But in addition it may be said that what made its view of creeds, confessions, and conciliar statements of faith "medieval" was this definition by Gregory the Great. These authoritative formularies were asserted to have derived their authority from the authority of the apostolic Roman see, as that authority had been conferred upon it in the words of Christ to the apostle Peter, and through him to all his successors in perpetuity: "And I say also unto thee, that thou art Peter [*Petrus*], and upon this rock [*petra*] I will build my church, and the gates of hell shall not prevail against it. And I will give thee [*tibi*] the keys of the kingdom of heaven: and whatsoever thou shalt bind on earth shall be bound in heaven: and whatsoever thou shalt loose on earth shall be loosed in heaven."[19]

It was a direct implication of this doctrine of authority when, following the schism between East and West and continuing until the present, the fourteen Western general synods convoked by the see of Rome without the participation of the other patriarchates could nevertheless be identified and numbered as "ecumenical councils," bringing the total, with the Second Vatican Council of 1962–65, to twenty-one by the Western counting, but still only seven by the Eastern.[20] Eventually, and by the action of a council, it was deemed to be unnecessary (though still, of course, permissible) to convoke such an "ecumenical council." For *The Dogmatic Constitution on the Faith of the First Vatican Council* of 1869–70 declares:

17. *Chr Trad* 1:354.
18. *Chr Trad* 3:2–3.
19. Mt 16.18–19 (AV; Vulg).
20. See chapter 16.1 below, "The Proliferation of Confessions in the Age of the Reformation."

> We teach and define as a divinely revealed dogma that
> when the Roman pontiff speaks *ex cathedra,* that is,
> when, in the exercise of his office as shepherd and
> teacher of all Christians, in virtue of his supreme apos-
> tolic authority, he defines a doctrine concerning faith
> or morals to be held by the whole church, he possesses,
> by the divine assistance promised to him in blessed
> Peter, that infallibility which the divine Redeemer
> willed his church to enjoy in defining doctrine con-
> cerning faith or morals. Therefore, such definitions of
> the Roman pontiff are of themselves, and not by the
> consent of the church, irreformable.

That nineteenth-century Western formulation presents itself as retro-
active and as a doctrine that is consistent with "the constant custom
of the church . . . and the ecumenical councils, particularly those in
which East and West met in the union of faith and charity."[21]

Thus the creedal tradition that medieval Western thought "received" and "restated" was, in the first instance, the entire orthodox
and catholic heritage of the early church, which it shared with Eastern
Orthodoxy—at any rate to the extent that on both sides the barriers of
language and culture, or of reception and transmission, did not hinder
such sharing. But for the Christian thought of the medieval West, that
ancient orthodox and catholic heritage came to be represented in a special way by Augustine of Hippo, not only by his particular method of
reading the catholic heritage but by the terms, emphases, and modes of
thought that were special to him. Even after the crises of the sixteenth-
century Reformation, many of those Augustinian emphases and modes
of thought were to remain deeply implanted on both sides of the split
within the Western church. "Augustine is completely on our side" on
the doctrine of election and predestination, John Calvin felt entitled to
boast.[22] Therefore the continuities between medieval teachings and the
confessions of the Protestant Reformation proved to be more profound
than the polemics of the later defenders of either have usually acknowl-

21. *Vat I* 4.4.
22. *Chr Trad* 4:224–25.

edged. For the history of creeds and confessions as distinct from the history of doctrine or the history of theology, two central Augustinian doctrines above all were to have momentous implications: his doctrine of original sin and divine grace; and his doctrine of the Trinity.

Augustine's doctrine of sin and grace, formulated at greatest length in his controversy with Pelagius and the Pelagians, was built upon the catholic tradition he had received, especially from Cyprian of Carthage, and upon a particular reading of the Pauline epistles.[23] *The Niceno-Constantinopolitan Creed* in its Latin *Western Recension* affirms that the incarnation, suffering, death, and resurrection of Christ took place "for us humans and for our salvation [*propter nos homines et propter nostram salutem*]."[24] It also asserts: "We confess one baptism for the forgiving of sins [*in remissionem peccatorum*],"[25] which was beginning to mean primarily the baptism of infants. The juxtaposition of these two creedal statements led Augustine to the conclusion that infants, too, being included with the other humans who were saved by Christ, were baptized "for the forgiving of sins" even before they had had the opportunity to commit actual sins. Therefore they were sinful from conception and birth, and in need of divine grace. Augustine's doctrine of original sin was upheld against the Pelagian teaching by a series of local African synods, and eventually by the Second Synod of Orange in 529, as "the catholic faith."[26]

The doctrine of the Trinity set down in *The Niceno-Constantinopolitan Creed*, as he confessed it in his paraphrase and affirmation of it at the opening of his treatise *On the Trinity*,[27] was the most imposing piece of evidence in support of Augustine's claim that he stood in the direct succession of the catholic creedal and conciliar tradition. The creative speculative performance in the second half of that treatise, where Augustine probed the doctrine of the Trinity for its psychological and ultimately ontological implications and analogies,[28] must not be permitted to obscure the determination that he expressed throughout

23. *Chr Trad* 1:278–331.
24. *N-CP Occ* 5.
25. *N-CP Occ* 10.
26. *Orange* con.
27. Augustine *On the Trinity* 1.4.7 (*NPNF*-I 3:20).
28. Schmaus 1927; Schindler 1965; C. N. Cochrane 1944, 399–455.

to teach what the church taught, and to buttress it not only with literally hundreds of biblical proofs but with a "canonical rule" defining
the hermeneutical principles for a catholic and orthodox, that is to say,
a trinitarian, interpretation of Scripture.[29] That determination makes
it all the more ironic that it should have been specifically on the doctrine of the Trinity, and on the text of the only truly ecumenical creed,
that the medieval church of the West followed Augustine in a direction
that separated it from the Christian East.[30] The New Testament passages which said that "God has sent the Spirit of his Son,"[31] and that
called him "the Spirit of your Father,"[32] were evidence to Augustine
for "the procession of the Holy Spirit from both *apart from time.*"[33]
Or, as he put it elsewhere on the basis of the same New Testament evidence, "Why should we not believe that the Holy Spirit proceeds also
from the Son, since he is the Spirit of the Son as well?"[34] In Augustine's
paraphrase of *The Niceno-Constantinopolitan Creed* the Holy Spirit was
called "the Spirit of the Father and of the Son."[35]

Although the transmitted texts of Spanish synodal creeds from
the fifth and sixth centuries contain the Filioque, these are now usually taken to be later interpolations.[36] But the statement by a seventh-
century creed of the same provenance, that the Holy Spirit "is shown to
have proceeded at the same time from both [the Father and the Son],"
is apparently authentic.[37] At a local synod in Fréjus a century later, in
796 or 797, the text of the creed as confessed reads: "And the Holy
Spirit . . . proceeding, apart from time and without separation, from
the Father *and the Son.*"[38] It seems also to have been chanted that way
in the chapel of the emperor Charlemagne and to have been approved

29. Augustine *On the Trinity* 2.1.2 (NPNF–II 3:37–38); see chapter 5.1 above,
"Creeds in Scripture."
30. See Oberdorfer 2001; and chapter 7.4 above, "The Holy Spirit of Concord
and the Sacrament of Concord: Two Ironic Case Histories."
31. Gal 4.6.
32. Mt 10.20.
33. Augustine *On the Trinity* 15.26.45–47 (NPNF–I 3:223–25; italics added.
34. Augustine *Tractates on the Gospel of John* 99.7 (NPNF–I 7:383).
35. Augustine *On the Trinity* 1.4.7 (NPNF–I 3:20).
36. *Tol I* 5–6; *Tol III.*
37. *Tol XI.*
38. *Fréjus* 4.

at a synod he convoked in 809. But when Charlemagne petitioned Pope Leo III to make the formal addition of the Filioque to the creed, the pope demurred and would not take it upon himself to do so. He had *The Niceno-Constantinopolitan Creed* inscribed on two silver plates without the Filioque. A creed that he composed for himself, however, speaks of "the Holy Spirit, who proceeds equally from the Father and the Son. . . . In the Father there is eternity, in the Son equality, in the Holy Spirit the connection between eternity and equality." But he added the explanation: "We ourselves do not chant this, but we do speak it and by speaking teach it; yet we do not presume by our speaking and teaching to insert anything into the creed."[39] That distinction between "chanting" and "speaking" seems to mean that it was not part of the "rule of prayer" that was chanted in the liturgy, and therefore not really part of the "rule of faith" officially confessed by the universal church,[40] but a legitimate theologoumenon spoken and taught by Western theologians, including the pope. But in 1014, Pope Benedict VIII granted permission to Emperor Henry II to have *The Niceno-Constantinopolitan Creed* chanted with the insertion. And it was a mere four decades later, in 1054, that representatives of the East and the West exchanged writs of excommunication, with the Filioque cited by both sides as one of the principal grounds.[41]

This Augustinianism of the West was to achieve definitive creedal formulation in the Latin formulary that came to be labeled *The Athanasian Creed*.[42] Its language, "Now this is the catholic faith [*Fides autem catholica haec est*], that we worship one God in Trinity and Trinity in unity,"[43] echoes the words quoted earlier from Augustine's *On the Trinity*, "This is also my faith, since it is the catholic faith [*Haec et mea fides est quando haec est catholica fides*]."[44] And when it proceeds to confess, "The Holy Spirit is from the Father and the Son [*a Patre et Filio*], not made nor created nor begotten but pro-

39. *Leo III;* see Capelle 1954.
40. See chapter 6.2 above, *"Lex orandi lex credendi."*
41. *CP 1054* 4, 6.
42. Kelly 1964.
43. *Ath* 3.
44. Augustine *On the Trinity* 1.4.7 (*NPNF*–I 3:20).

ceeding,"[45] it is not expanding an earlier creed, as the addition of the words *ex Patre Filioque* to *The Niceno-Constantinopolitan Creed* does, but incorporating the Western doctrine as an original part of a Latin creed. This Latin creed, however, was attributed to the Greek church father Athanasius. In fact, some later Eastern confessions do treat it (in a Greek translation from the Latin) as though it were authentically Athanasian.[46] In these three Western creeds—*The Apostles' Creed, The Western Recension of the Niceno-Constantinopolitan Creed,* and *The Athanasian Creed*—the medieval church simultaneously affirmed its reception of the catholic creedal and confessional tradition and defined its own special identity in a form that was transmitted also to the churches of the Protestant Reformation. *The Profession of Faith by Valdes* uses these creeds to prove its orthodoxy.[47] In *The Thirty-Nine Articles of the Church of England* "the three creeds, Nicene Creed, Athanasius's Creed, and that which is commonly called the Apostles' Creed," are listed together.[48] And the Lutheran *Book of Concord* calls them "the three chief symbols or creeds of the Christian faith which are commonly used in the church."[49] Although neither *The Apostles' Creed* nor *The Athanasian Creed* has the standing in the East that it has in the West, even a twentieth-century Greek Orthodox textbook on comparative symbolics can speak of "the three so-called ecumenical symbols," and the most authoritative twentieth-century compilation of Eastern confessions can include all three (of course without the addition of the Filioque to *The Niceno-Constantinopolitan Creed*) under the heading "The Three Ancient Ecumenical Symbols."[50]

The hold of this creedal tradition on medieval thought can be gauged in a somewhat oblique manner from a text that might at first appear to be a rather unlikely source, *The Confession of Faith* composed by Peter Abelard as part of his final letter to Héloïse, or, as he called it, "the faith on which I rest, from which I draw my strength in hope."[51]

45. *Ath* 23.
46. *Metr Crit* 1.12; *Mogila* 1.10.
47. *Vald.*
48. *39 Art* 8.
49. *BLK* 21; *Form Conc Sol Dec* 12.37.
50. Androutsos 1930, 22–36; Karmirēs, 1:34–104.
51. *Petr Ab* 4.

He had been condemned in 1141 for several of his alleged doctrines.[52] But as Gilson has said, "All that should be said is here said. . . . Here he is, then, reciting his creed. It is the creed of all Christians. But being Abélard, he cannot recite it in the usual manner."[53]

15.2. The Confessionalization of Western Sacramental Doctrine

This process of reception assured to the creeds and the conciliar decrees of the first several centuries of Christian history a permanent place of authority in the catholic corpus of statements of faith during the Middle Ages, a place that they retained well beyond the medieval period.[54] But this did not mean that such authority was to be thought of as exclusive, as though only whatever had been defined there was normative, but whatever had not been defined was not and could not be normative. *The Athanasian Creed* specifies, "This is the catholic faith, that we worship one God in Trinity and Trinity in unity. . . . So one who desires to be saved should think thus of the Trinity. It is necessary, however, to eternal salvation that one should also faithfully believe in the incarnation of our Lord Jesus Christ,"[55] without listing other doctrines than the Trinity and the incarnation. But when it does this, no one would have been permitted to suppose that therefore *The Athanasian Creed* is saying that it does not matter what one believes or thinks about these other doctrines.[56] Pelagius, for example, seems to have argued that his acceptance of the Nicene trinitarian dogma made him orthodox. But Augustine vigorously refused to recognize him as such, on the grounds of his doctrines of sin and grace, not his doctrine of the Trinity.[57] The many verbal parallels between *The Athanasian Creed* and the works of Augustine, especially *On the Trinity*, indicate either that Augustine was quoting from it (or some predecessor) or, as seems more likely, that it may have arisen somewhere within the Augustinian tra-

52. *Sens.*
53. Gilson 1960, 108–9.
54. See chapter 16.3 below, "Catholic Substance and Protestant Principle in Reformation Confessions."
55. *Ath* 3, 28–29.
56. See chapter 3.3 above, "'Doctrines' and Doctrine."
57. Augustine *On the Proceedings of Pelagius* (*NPNF*-I 5:183–212).

dition during the following century or so. The anti-Pelagian polemic of Augustine against confining the content of orthodoxy to the dogmas of the Trinity and the incarnation makes clear that the authority of the ancient creeds was inclusive rather than exclusive and therefore that other doctrines, which could be seen as implied in them, could be expressly stated later. Among such other doctrines implicit in the early formularies, the doctrine of the sacraments occupied a special but rather unclear place within the creedal and confessional tradition. Such confessional polemics at the end of the medieval development as the statement of *The Thirty-Nine Articles of the Church of England* that "there are [only] two sacraments ordained of Christ our Lord in the Gospel, that is to say, baptism and the supper of the Lord,"[58] and the article of *The Apology of the Augsburg Confession* entitled "The Number and Use of the Sacraments," which teaches that "absolution may properly be called a sacrament of penitence"[59] alongside baptism and the eucharist but that other so-called sacraments may not, are able to take advantage of a significant lacuna in the early creedal tradition. The New Testament does not contain a discussion of sacraments as such—*de sacramentis in genere,* as it would later be labeled[60]—but chiefly individual references to various prescribed actions. These include references that could be applied to each of the seven such actions. Interestingly, that sacred number seven was retained even when there was variation in the list of the actions that qualified as sacraments.[61] The seven that were eventually to be given the name "sacrament" are: baptism, confirmation, the eucharist, penance, extreme unction, orders, and matrimony. But in the Gospels, Christ also appeared to have "instituted" other sacred acts, for example the washing of feet.[62] Yet this did not become a sacrament of the medieval church, although it did acquire that status later, in the liturgies and confessions of some groups of the Radical Reformation.[63] The New Testament does not relate these several "sacramental" actions to each other, except for such a symbolic relation

58. *39 Art* 26.
59. *Apol Aug* 12.41, 13.4.
60. *Trent* 7.1.
61. *Chr Trad* 3:209–10.
62. Jn 13.3–16.
63. *Cologne* 9; *Dordrecht* 11; *Menn Con* 13.

between baptism and eucharist as the connection between the cloud
by which the Israelites were "baptized into Moses" and the miraculous
food and drink of which they partook in the wilderness,[64] or the association between the blood and the water that flowed from the wounded
side of Christ on the cross.[65] The New Testament vocable *mystērion*,
moreover, which is the technical term in the Greek church fathers for
"sacrament,"[66] being used that way also in such Eastern Orthodox
confessions as *The Confession of Metrophanes Critopoulos*,[67] *The Orthodox Confession of the Catholic and Apostolic Eastern Church by Peter
Mogila*,[68] and *The Confession of Dositheus and of the Synod of Jerusalem*,[69] does not incontestably mean "sacrament" in any passage of the
New Testament. It does not have that specific meaning even in the title,
"stewards of the mysteries of God,"[70] which is quoted in various Roman Catholic, Eastern Orthodox, and Protestant confessions,[71] nor in
the description of matrimony as a *mystērion*,[72] which serves Orthodox
and Roman Catholic confessions as the proof text for the definition of
marriage as a sacrament.[73]

 The Niceno-Constantinopolitan Creed does include the clause,
"We confess one baptism for the forgiving of sins."[74] Arguing partly
on the basis of a parallel to this clause, Karl Holl took the phrase
"the forgiveness of sins" in *The Apostles' Creed*[75] also as a specific reference to baptism.[76] But a careful review of early creeds and confessions of faith, including the creedal and confessional decrees of the
councils, will produce little, if any, direct testimony to the sacraments
as such.[77] Even confessions of the sixteenth and seventeenth centuries

---

64. 1 Cor 10.1–4.
65. Jn 19.34; 1 Jn 5.6, 8.
66. Lampe, 891–93; Sophocles, 774.
67. *Metr Crit* 5.
68. *Mogila* 1.98.
69. *Dosith* decr 15.
70. 1 Cor 4.1.
71. *Trent* 21.2; *Mogila* 1.89, 1.109; *Helv II* 18.11.
72. Eph 5.32.
73. *Trent* 24; *Dosith* decr 15. See Syndogmaticon 10.15.
74. *N-CP* 10.
75. *Ap* 10.
76. Holl [1919] 1928, 121–22.
77. See chapter 6.2 above, *"Lex orandi lex credendi."*

that were framed as commentaries on these two early creeds were obliged to stretch a point in locating their discussions of the sacraments. *The Orthodox Confession of the Catholic and Apostolic Eastern Church by Peter Mogila* explains on the basis of this passage from *The Niceno-Constantinopolitan Creed* that "whereas we here have baptism, which is the first sacrament of the church, made mention of, this seems an appropriate place to discourse concerning the seven sacraments of the church";[78] *The Heidelberg Catechism* attaches its discussion of the two sacraments, "baptism and the holy supper," to the article of *The Apostles' Creed* on the Holy Spirit.[79] But when a controversy over the eucharistic presence finally broke out in the ninth century between the two Benedictine monks Ratramnus and Paschasius Radbertus, it revealed that in spite of the absence of any confession about the eucharist in the rule of faith, the rule of prayer had already begun to acquire one. That can be seen from the very way in which the question was put in the dispute, which asked whether the body on the altar was identical with the body born of Mary. The "body born of Mary" is the subject of the rule of faith, in the phraseology of *The Apostles' Creed*[80] and of *The Niceno-Constantinopolitan Creed*,[81] "born of the Virgin Mary." The "body on the altar," however, does not appear in the rule of faith but was the subject of the rule of prayer, in the evolving liturgy of the medieval mass and in the practices of eucharistic devotion.[82] Two centuries after Radbertus and Ratramnus, Berengar of Tours had contended for the position, which he subsequently retracted, "that the bread and the wine that are placed on the altar are, after the consecration, merely a sacrament and not the true body and the true blood of our Lord Jesus Christ."[83] At the Synod of Rome in 1059, he subscribed a profession of faith, composed by Cardinal Humbert of Silva Candida, recanting his earlier statement and affirming the real presence. Subsequently he reversed himself again, and then, at the Synod of Rome of 1079, accepted the doctrine of the real presence yet again:

78. *Mogila* 1.98.
79. *Heid* 68.
80. *Ap* 3.
81. *N-CP* 3.
82. *Chr Trad* 3:74–80.
83. ap. *Brngr 1059*.

I, Berengarius, in my heart believe and with my lips
confess that through the mystery of the sacred prayer
and the words of our Redeemer the bread and wine
which are placed on the altar are substantially changed
[*per mysterium sacrae orationis et verba nostri Redemp-*
toris substantialiter converti] into the true and proper
and living flesh and blood of Jesus Christ, our Lord,
and that after consecration it is the true body of Christ
which was born of the Virgin and which, offered for
the salvation of the world, was suspended on the cross,
and which sits at the right hand of the Father, and the
true blood of Christ, which was poured out from his
side not only through the sign and power of the sacrament, but in its property of nature and in truth of substance.[84]

Within Roman Catholicism this second *Confession* of Berengar provided both dogmatics and canon law with their most precise formulation to date of the doctrine of the real presence. But it would also
provide Protestant confessions of faith such as *The Second Helvetic*
Confession with a ready object for their criticism of the medieval Roman Catholic doctrine that the body of Christ was present in the eucharist *corporaliter vel essentialiter.*[85]

The Lateran Creed of 1215 confesses the dogma of transubstantiation, that the body and blood of Christ "are truly contained in
the sacrament of the altar under the forms of bread and wine, the bread
and wine having been changed in substance, by God's power, into his
body and blood."[86] But that did not end the controversy.[87] In many
Protestant confessions in the period of the Reformation and later, a
repudiation of this specific and technical Lateran doctrine of "transubstantiation" becomes a code word for what is actually a denial of the
doctrine of the real presence altogether and for the rejection of any
"change" of the elements of bread and wine into the true body and

84. *Brngr 1079.*
85. *Helv II 21.4.*
86. *Lat 1215 1.*
87. *Wyclif; Loll 4.*

blood of Christ. In some of these confessions, "transubstantiation" and "real presence" are simply equated as a "blasphemous opinion."[88] In response to them, *The Canons and Decrees of the Council of Trent* re-affirm this confession of *The Lateran Creed* in rather moderate language, referring to what "the holy catholic church has suitably and properly [*convenienter et proprie*] called transubstantiation."[89] This development suggests that there is a special sense in which the Middle Ages are a period in which "the orthodoxy of the body of the faithful" moved up to the official level of the church, by a kind of osmosis from "the rule of prayer" to "the rule of faith."[90] This is true even though the Middle Ages are usually, and with considerable justification, thought of as a time of doctrinal authoritarianism in which the clergy dominated the laity and the prelates dominated the clergy (and the tradition dominated the prelates). The codification of sacramental doctrine is the outstanding confessional achievement of that period, including, in the realm of practice, the administration of Holy Communion only under the form of the consecrated bread, at least partly because of the people's dread of spilling the true blood of Christ.[91]

A century after the Fourth Lateran Council in 1215, sacramental doctrine was further clarified—and more formally confessionalized—when the Council of Vienne of 1311–12 in its *Decree on the Foundation of the Catholic Faith* put itself on the side of the teaching not only that baptism grants the remission of guilt but also "that sanctifying grace and the virtues are conferred in baptism on both infants and adults."[92] It was, however, neither the Fourth Lateran Council nor the Council of Vienne but a later medieval council, the Council of Basel-Ferrara-Florence-Rome, at its eighth session, on 22 November 1439 in Florence, that produced, in its confessional systematization, the most comprehensive formal definition to date of the teachings of the Western church about all the sacraments.[93] It did so on the basis of Thomas

---

88. *Scot II; Heid* 80.
89. *Trent* 13.4.
90. See chapter 12 above, "The Orthodoxy of the Body of the Faithful"; and chapter 6 above, "The Rule of Prayer and the Rule of Faith."
91. Smend 1898.
92. *Vienne.*
93. On its importance, see Alberigo 1991.

Aquinas, by "reduc[ing] the truth about the sacraments of the church" to a "brief scheme," in its *Bull of Union with the Armenians*.[94] Itemizing the "seven sacraments of the New Law," this confession compactly identifies the distinctive gift of each: "By baptism we are reborn spiritually; by confirmation we grow in grace and are strengthened in faith. Once reborn and strengthened, we are nourished by the food of the divine eucharist. But if through sin we incur an illness of the soul, we are cured spiritually by penance. Spiritually also and bodily as suits the soul, by extreme unction. By orders the church is governed and spiritually multiplied; by matrimony it grows bodily."[95] *The Bull of Union with the Armenians* also makes official the scholastic specification of the three components without which a sacrament cannot be effected (or "confected"): "things as the matter, words as the form, and the person of the minister who confers the sacrament with the intention of doing what the church does." By means of the scholastic doctrine of the "indelible character" that is uniquely conferred on the recipient by baptism, confirmation, and ordination, it differentiates between these three sacraments, which cannot be repeated, and the other four, which can.[96]

"Holy baptism," the decree declares, "holds the first place among all the sacraments," because "through it we become members of Christ and of the body of the church." The sacrament of confirmation has as its effect "that a Christian should boldly confess the name of Christ, since the Holy Spirit is given in this sacrament for strengthening." In the sacrament of the eucharist, "the words of the Savior with which he effected this sacrament," when they are spoken over the elements by a priest, bring it about that "the substance of bread is changed into the body of Christ and the substance of wine into his blood," but in such a way "that the whole Christ is contained both under the form of bread and under the form of wine." The sacrament of penance consists of three steps, "contrition of heart," "oral confession," and "satisfaction for sins." Its "form" consists of "the words of absolution which the priest pronounces when he says: 'I absolve you.'" The fifth sacra-

94. *Flor Arm* 10.
95. *Flor Arm* 11.
96. *Flor Arm* 12–13.

ment is extreme unction, which "should not be given to the sick unless death is expected," and its effect is "to cure the mind and, in so far as it helps the soul, also the body." The sacrament of orders, or ordination, is conferred by a bishop, with the effect of "an increase of grace to make the person a suitable minister of Christ." The last and "seventh is the sacrament of matrimony, which is a sign of the union of Christ and the church," and its efficient cause is "usually mutual consent expressed in words" by the two spouses.

This summary was presented by the Council of Florence "for the easier instruction of the Armenians of today and in the future." The union with the Armenians came to naught, as did the entire reunion enterprise of the Council of Florence with the East, except for the attempts to revive it and continue it among the Slavs in the Union of Brest of 1595 and the Union of Užhorod of 1646.[97] But its formula did turn out to be much more useful for "the easier instruction" of Western Catholics, setting down more clearly and succinctly than any previous council had, before the Council of Trent did so in response to Protestant criticism,[98] the Western sacramental doctrine that had developed during the Middle Ages. Therefore it provided one of the most important of medieval contributions to the corpus of creeds and confessions of faith. At almost exactly the same time and also as a direct consequence of the Council of Basel-Ferrara-Florence, *The Confession of Faith of Mark of Ephesus* of 1439 provided a more definitive statement of Eastern teaching, too, on various controverted questions.[99]

15.3. Scholastic Theology as Reasoning on the Basis of the Creed

In addition to this movement of sacramental doctrine from the rule of prayer to the rule of faith, another confessional achievement of the Western Middle Ages consisted in a more profound and more definitive elaboration of both the concept and the content of "the faith" itself, by reasoning on the basis of the faith of the creeds. It was the whole deposit of creedal and conciliar doctrine that made medieval theology

97. Halecki 1958, 199–419; Lacko 1966.
98. *Trent* 7.1.
99. *Mark Eph.*

possible, but by a kind of reciprocity medieval theology added substantially to that deposit by articulating what the total intention of creedal and conciliar doctrine was taken to have been. Therefore the four virtuoso works of medieval Christian thought and doctrine listed at the beginning of this chapter—the *Cur deus homo* of Anselm of Canterbury, the *Sentences* of Peter Lombard, the *Summa Theologica* of Thomas Aquinas, and *The Divine Comedy* of Dante Alighieri—while certainly, as was said there, "not confessions of faith in the precise sense of the word," do all presuppose such creeds and confessions and would not have been possible without these confessions.

In its form of argumentation, Anselm's *Cur deus homo* is constructed as a speculative *Denkexperiment* rather than as an exposition of creedal or of biblical theology.[100] It claims to proceed "as though there were no Christ [*remoto Christo*]," analyzing by reason alone the human condition of sinfulness in relation to the justice and mercy of God. For God to carry out his mercy for the human race and yet not to do so at the cost of the moral order of the universe that is expressed in his justice or *rectitudo,* it is necessary to devise a means for "the redemption of mankind" that would have validity for individual human beings in satisfying the violated honor of God and would at the same time be of infinite worth. The agent of the redemption, therefore, needs to be completely human (for otherwise his act of satisfaction would not carry that validity) and completely divine (for otherwise it would be only finite in its value). This rational construct, though it is in a formal sense articulated *remoto Christo,* ends up prescribing a Redeemer who matches exactly the divine-human person of Jesus Christ as this had been defined by *The Niceno-Constantinopolitan Creed* and then especially by *The Definition of Faith of the Council of Chalcedon.* "The divine and human natures cannot be changed into each other, so that the divine becomes human or the human divine. Nor can they be so mingled that a third nature, neither fully divine nor fully human, is produced from the two," Anselm's *Cur deus homo* concludes.[101] That is what Chalcedon says when it speaks of "two natures

---

100. *Chr Trad* 3:129–43.
101. Anselm *Why God Became Man* 2.7 (tr. Eugene R. Fairweather); Syndogmaticon 3.10.

which undergo no confusion, no change, no division, no separation," and insists that "at no point was the difference between the natures taken away through the union," but "the property of both natures is preserved and comes together into a single person and a single subsistent being."[102] Thus, in the periodic sentence of George H. Williams,

> The theological pressures building up as a consequence of the millenary yet hitherto scarcely perceived displacement of theological interest—from the once-for-all Baptismal-Eucharistic experience of patristic Christianity with its stress on liberation from demons and the sacral enrollment of each Christian recruit under *Christus victor* to the scholastic interest in the penitential-Eucharistic experience of the repetitive restoration of justice and of progressive incorporation in the *Homo patiens* slain on the altar for the sins of the whole world—had finally, in Anselm, brought about a long-needed readjustment in the formulation of a doctrine of the atonement fully consonant with the matured sacramental system of the church.[103]

Thanks to this "matured sacramental system of the church," therefore, the creedal phrase about the purpose of the incarnation, "for us humans and for our salvation," which Bernard of Clairvaux used as a weapon against Abelard,[104] was now provided with a specificity that it does not have in any of the classic creeds. As articulated by Anselm, it becomes for the Western tradition the doctrine of the work of Christ corresponding to—and taken to be implicit in—the Chalcedonian and creedal doctrine of the person of Christ.

Peter Lombard's *Sentences* was the most widely used theological textbook of the Middle Ages, bringing together various (and varying) statements of the tradition on major questions.[105] It was expounded in literally thousands of commentaries, which used its ju-

---

102. *Chal* 18–21.
103. G. H. Williams 1960, 64.
104. *N-CP 5*; see chapter 10.3 above, "Orthodoxy and Asceticism."
105. *Chr Trad* 3:216–29.

dicious and balanced collection of passages to propose a harmonization of authorities.[106] The amazing diversity among the authors of such
commentaries (who included, among many others, Thomas Aquinas,
Bonaventure, Duns Scotus, William of Ockham, John Hus, and Martin
Luther) makes it possible to follow the career of a doctrine or a technical term through several centuries of medieval development. But the
underlying presupposition and the long-range purpose of the *Sentences*,
as well as of its commentators, was to discover the Catholic unity-in-
diversity as this is affirmed by the creeds and the councils. No Christian dogma manifests that unity-in-diversity more richly than does the
doctrine of the person of Christ, which, in one form or another, domi-
nates all seven of the councils of the undivided church.[107] The speculative elaborations of that doctrine in medieval theology are a documentation of pluralism and doctrinal development. But they are also
a testimony to the continuing authority and the persistent relevance of
the dogmatic decrees of those councils, and in a special sense of *The
Definition of Faith of the Council of Chalcedon*.[108] It is a curiosity to note
that it should have been Peter Lombard's version of the creedal doctrine of the person of Christ, in his teaching "that Christ according
to his humanity is nothing [*quod Christus secundum quod est homo non
est aliquid*]," that also became the most controversial of his theological
formulations, over which doctrinal conflict would continue to swirl.[109]

Building upon his own *Commentary on the Sentences* of Peter
Lombard as well as upon his other commentaries on Scripture and
on Aristotle, the *Summa Theologica* of Thomas Aquinas continues—
and, at any rate for its partisans in the thirteenth century and since,
climaxes—the medieval enterprise of "faith in search of understanding [*fides quaerens intellectum*]" (identifying it by Anselm's Augustinian
formula).[110] The *fides* in that formula is the *fides quae creditur*, the
faith that is believed, taught, and confessed by the tradition of the
church in its creeds, confessions, and conciliar and papal formulations.

106. Stegmüller 1947.
107. See chapter 1.4 above, "The Person of Christ as Exemplar of Continuity and
of Change."
108. Principe 1963–75.
109. Colish 1994, 1:427–38.
110. *Chr Trad* 3:255–67.

In the first question of the First Part of the *Summa Theologica,* therefore, Thomas defines it as the function of "sacred science" or theology "not [to] argue to establish its premises, which are the articles of faith [*articuli fidei*], but [to] advance from them to make something known." [111] Those "premises" or *articuli fidei* are, in the first instance, the teachings of the apostles that are set down in Scripture and summarized in the *symbolum apostolorum seu primum,* to whose authority Thomas then devotes the first question of the *Secunda Secundae,* the Second Part of the Second Part of the *Summa:*

> The church universal cannot err, because it is guided by the Holy Spirit, the Spirit of truth. . . . Now the creed is drawn up by virtue of the authority of the church universal. Nothing inappropriate, therefore, is contained in it. . . .
>
> No one can believe unless the truth he believes be set before him. Gathering together the truths of faith in one formulary, therefore, was necessary for a more ready presentation to all. . . . The name "symbol" derives from its being a gathering together of authentic teachings of faith.

"All the creeds," Thomas adds, "teach the same truth." [112] This is the truth and authority of the creeds on which he feels able to found his entire theological enterprise.

Dante's *Divine Comedy,* too, presupposes that authority, above all in its consideration of the church and of Christian doctrine. [113] Canto 24 of the *Paradiso,* depicting Dante the pilgrim in the role of a candidate being examined for an academic theological degree, albeit a celestial one, is the most direct consideration of the authority of faith in the *Comedy.* As Dante says there, "It is from the faith that we must reason, / deducing what we can from syllogisms." [114] Defining faith by a quotation from the New Testament, as "the substance of things to be

111. Thomas Aquinas *Summa Theologica* 1.1.8 (tr. Blackfriars).
112. Thomas Aquinas *Summa Theologica* 2a2ae.1.9 (tr. Blackfriars).
113. Pelikan 1990b, 78–100.
114. Dante *Paradiso* 24.76–77 (tr. Allen Mandelbaum).

hoped for, the evidence of things not seen,"[115] the pilgrim proceeds to identify its content by reciting a creed, or rather by composing one that is altogether his own and is nevertheless the faith of the catholic and orthodox church:

> I believe in one God—sole,
> eternal—He who, motionless, moves all
> the heavens with His love and love for Him. . . .
> And I believe in three Eternal Persons,
> and these I do believe to be of one essence,
> so single and threefold as to allow
> both *is* and *are*. Of this profound condition
> of God that I have touched on, Gospel
> teaching has often set the imprint on my mind.[116]

In response to this recital of the creed, "the apostolic light" encircles him three times: "the speech I spoke had brought him such delight."[117]

In one way or another, then, these four medieval classics not only reflect the creeds, confessions, and conciliar doctrines of their tradition but contribute to the shaping of later statements of faith. For example, *The Tridentine Profession of Faith* of 1564 is a medieval document both in its Latinity and in its doctrine.[118] Above all, the doctrine of atonement as satisfaction expounded in Anselm's *Cur deus homo* becomes, confessionally speaking, the most highly successful of all medieval doctrinal developments. For it retained a wide acceptance among Protestants during and long after the Reformation, even though they, of course, usually attributed it directly to the Bible rather than to Anselm of Canterbury.[119]

15.4. The Rise of Ecclesiological Confessions in the Later Middle Ages

This medieval reception of the ancient and ecumenical creeds had included the phrase "the holy catholic church" from *The Apostles'*

---

115. Heb 11.1.
116. Dante *Paradiso* 24.63–64, 130–32, 139–41; italics original in the translation.
117. Dante *Paradiso* 24.151–54.
118. *Trid Prof.*
119. See chapter 3.3 above, "'Doctrines' and Doctrine."

Creed[120] and its predecessors, where it sometimes read simply "the holy church,"[121] and the phrase "one holy catholic and apostolic church [*una sancta catholica et apostolica ecclesia*]" from the Latin of *The Western Recension* of *The Niceno-Constantinopolitan Creed* of 381.[122] It meant that anyone expounding either of these creeds was also obliged to address questions of ecclesiology. But the detailed definition of the doctrine of the church did not occupy a central position in the formulations of Christian doctrine and creed. The doctrine of the holiness of the church was at issue in the controversy between Augustine and the Donatists, who contended that the fall of the Catholic Church and its bishops from holiness had invalidated its sacraments. But the principal doctrinal points of concentration in those debates were the doctrines of baptism and holy orders.[123] Even in the disputes over church order between the Latin West and the Greek East and in the schism brought about by those disputes, attention to ecclesiological doctrine in the strict sense of the word is often secondary to the questions of jurisdiction and authority. The doctrine of the procession of the Holy Spirit, the Filioque, rather than the doctrine of the church, is seen as the primary dogmatic difference.[124] "In early scholasticism," as its leading historian has pointed out, "there is seldom a discussion of any question connected with the doctrine of the church."[125] Even to examine the doctrine of the church in high scholastic theology, it is necessary to probe for the ecclesiology that is at work as a presupposition in its treatment of other doctrines and in its handling of the patristic and conciliar "authorities" who comprise the tradition of the church, rather than to look for any *tractatus de ecclesia* as such.[126]

But in the later Middle Ages, the doctrine of the church, though it had never been absent, began to assume a more prominent

120. *Ap* 9.
121. *R*.
122. *N-CP Occ* 9.
123. See chapter 10.2 above, "Heresy and/or Schism," and Syndogmaticon 9.3.
124. See chapter 4.2 above, "Doctrines of Church Order East and West"; and chapter 7.4 above, "The Holy Spirit of Concord and the Sacrament of Concord: Two Ironic Case Histories."
125. Landgraf 1951, 1–I:30.
126. Chenu 1964, 126–39.

position in theological discussion, and eventually in the rise of specifically ecclesiological confessions.[127] The work that one scholar has called "the most ancient treatise on the church"[128] was *Christian Government [De regimine christiano]* by James of Viterbo, an Augustinian monk and archbishop of Naples, which was published in 1301 or 1302. That was also the date of the issuance of perhaps the best known of these specifically ecclesiological confessions, the bull *Unam Sanctam* of Pope Boniface VIII.[129] Already before Pope Boniface VIII, Pope Gregory VII and Pope Innocent III had issued declarations of faith that dealt with the church, especially with the authority of the papacy: *The Dictatus Papae of Pope Gregory VII* of 1075;[130] and *The Doctrinal Decrees of the Fourth Lateran Council* or *Lateran Creed* of 1215.[131] The decrees published by the so-called reform councils of the fifteenth century—Pisa (1409), Constance (1414–18), and Basel-Ferrara-Florence-Rome (1431–49)[132]—though they treat many other questions of faith, morals, and church order, may properly be said to concentrate on ecclesiology, especially the relative authority of council and pope.[133] That concentration remains audible also in the last category of texts in Part Three of *Creeds and Confessions of Faith in the Christian Tradition*, which we have called "Statements of Faith by Medieval Advocates of Reform and Confessions of Churches Founded by Forerunners of the Reformation," including the Waldensian and the Hussite confessions.[134]

Significantly, both the treatise of James of Viterbo on the church and the bull of Pope Boniface VIII on the church were evoked in considerable measure by the late medieval struggles between the church and the temporal powers.[135] If those struggles were to be some-

127. *Chr Trad* 4:69–126.
128. Arquillière 1926.
129. *Unam.*
130. *Dict Pap.*
131. *Lat 1215.*
132. *Flor.*
133. Bârlea 1989.
134. *Wald; Boh I; Boh II.*
135. See chapter 8.3 above, "Confessions and the Formation of Politics," and Syndogmaticon 7.3.

thing more than battles over turf and power—which, of course, they also were—it was obligatory for the spokesmen on both sides to clarify the definition of the nature of the church before they could specify the nature of its relation to the state. Did the final words of Christ to his disciples before his ascension, "All authority in heaven and on earth has been given to me. Go therefore, . . . teaching them to observe all that I have commanded you,"[136] vest this total authority of Christ in the apostles—and thus in their successors, the bishops, and above all in the successor of Peter, the pope of Rome—including the authority to teach and direct kings and emperors? Or did the words of Jesus to the representative of the Roman emperor, Pontius Pilate, "My kingship is not of this world" and "You would have no power over me unless it had been given you from above,"[137] imply, as Dante argued in *De Monarchia,* that the authority vested in the church and its functionaries pertained to opening and closing the gates of heaven, but not to directing the this-worldly institutions of state and society? Because one of the principal policy issues between the medieval church and the empire was the right of the temporal ruler to name bishops and to invest them with the symbols of the episcopal office (hence the term "investiture controversy"), both the defenders and the opponents of that right were obliged to address the doctrines of the episcopal office, of the priesthood, of the sacraments—and therefore eventually the entire doctrine of the church as such.

The new attention to the doctrine of the church in the later Middle Ages does seem to have some connection with a shift from canon law to dogmatic theology as the primary venue for treating the doctrine of the nature of the church. It is, however, dangerous to exaggerate the contrast, because there were in fact medieval theologians and prelates such as Ivo of Chartres who worked in both. The medieval science of canon law had proved itself indispensable, though also inadequate, as a methodology for coping with this doctrine. For many of the same ecclesiological issues, such as ordination and the sacraments, properly belonged to both.[138] So did the "heresy" of simony, the pur-

---

136. Mt 28.18–20.
137. Jn 18.36, 19.11.
138. See chapter 4 above, "Faith and Order."

chase of ecclesiastical office.[139] But as in the civil law (then and now) disputes over jurisprudence, when pressed to their root assumptions, become differences over the doctrines of political philosophy, so the ecclesiological debates of canon lawyers in the later Middle Ages were eventually compelled to probe the exegesis of crucial biblical texts, the phraseology of conciliar decrees about doctrine and not only of conciliar canons about discipline, and the presuppositions of church law that were embedded in church teaching.[140] An outstanding example of this pattern of transition is the doctrine of papal infallibility. It arose in the controversies of medieval canon law over papal jurisprudence, including the question of the right of one pope to contravene the decisions that an earlier pope had handed down.[141] But it eventually became the subject of one of the most momentous of all the modern statements of faith, with the issuance, on 18 July 1870, of *The Dogmatic Constitution on the Catholic Faith of the First Vatican Council.*[142]

As an issue both of canon law and of dogmatic theology, the crisis of authority in the church during the later Middle Ages demanded doctrinal, not only administrative, attention. The "Babylonian captivity" of the papacy in Avignon in the fourteenth century, followed as it was by the so-called Great Schism between one pope in Avignon and another in Rome, raised fundamental questions about the nature of the church and about the place of the papacy in the church. The doctrinal decrees of the reform councils of the first half of the fifteenth century sometimes seek to resolve the crisis of authority by subordinating the authority of the pope to that of a general council. Thus *The Decrees of the Council of Constance* declare: "that this synod, legitimately assembled in the Holy Spirit, constituting a general council, representing the Catholic Church militant, has power immediately from Christ, and that everyone of whatever state or dignity, *even papal,* is bound to obey it in those matters which pertain to the faith and the eradication of the said schism."[143] When the supporters of papal

---

139. *DTC* 14:2141–60 (A. Bride).
140. Tierney 1998.
141. Tierney 1972.
142. *Vat I.*
143. *Const* decr 4; italics added.

centralism reasserted the primacy of the pope over any council, it was urgent that a doctrinal justification be provided for both of the alternatives.[144] A special instance of the problem of authority, requiring a doctrinal answer and not only a liturgical or a juridical response, was the legitimacy of the medieval practice of withholding the chalice from the laity in the distribution of Holy Communion. Opposition to this practice on the basis of the command of Christ, "Drink of it all of you,"[145] became the identifying doctrine of the followers of John Hus,[146] and continued to be part of the Protestant agenda in the sixteenth century, especially around the time of the Council of Trent, as in two German confessions of 1551, while that council was continuing.[147] One party of the Hussites acquired the label "Utraquist" (from *sub utraque specie,* "under both forms," namely, the bread and the wine). Nothing short of a more comprehensive ecclesiology could meet these challenges.

At the same time that the Western church was desperately seeking a doctrinal (as well as an administrative and juridical) solution to its internal schism, the older and more intractable schism between East and West was also demanding attention. After the failure of thirteenth-century solutions—the creation of the Latin patriarchate of Constantinople in the wake of the Fourth Crusade of 1204, as well as the union attempts at the Council of Lyons in 1274[148]—there was new interest in a possible reunion between the Western church and (to use the present-day terminology) both the Oriental Orthodox Church of Armenia and the Eastern Orthodox Church of Constantinople. That interest led to *Laetentur coeli* and to *The Bull of Union with the Armenians* at the Council of Florence in 1439.[149] Issues of church discipline and of church jurisdiction (and, of course, the Filioque) were the subject of the negotiations at Florence. But each side, being faced by an opponent who also claimed to be professing the orthodox and catholic

---

144. *Chr Trad* 4:100–110.
145. Mt 26.27.
146. *Prague* 2.
147. *Sax; Wrt.*
148. *Lyons* 1.
149. *Flor Arm;* see chapter 15.2 above, "The Confessionalization of Western Sacramental Doctrine."

faith of the undivided church, was compelled to explain what divided them and what could unite them. And when the Union of Florence was eventually repudiated by the East, the decisive doctrinal question— above and beyond the political, cultural, and liturgical (and even military) questions that swayed the decisions—remained the doctrine of the church.[150] In the nineteenth and twentieth centuries, often called "the age of the doctrine of the church," creeds and confessions often made it the central, even the only, topic.

Once it had been placed on the confessional agenda in the later Middle Ages by these several developments, ecclesiology would grow in prominence, and even dominance. As part of that agenda, it became a standard article in one Reformation confession after another in the sixteenth century.[151] Even the concentration of so many of these Reformation confessions on the doctrine of the authority of Scripture may be seen as a continuation of this medieval ecclesiological concern.[152] For as the first article of the first such confession, *The Sixty-Seven Articles of Ulrich Zwingli* of 1523, asserts: "All who say that the gospel is nothing without the approbation of the church err and slander God."[153] The Lutheran *Augsburg Confession* of 1530 devotes two of its articles to ecclesiology,[154] in addition to the articles of its second part on abuses in the practical life of the church. In *The Thirty-Nine Articles of the Church of England,* too, the doctrine of the church is the subject of two distinct articles.[155] And the nature of the church, specifically its attribute of being "holy" according to both *The Niceno-Constantinopolitan Creed*[156] and *The Apostles' Creed,*[157] is, together with the doctrine of the Holy Spirit, a principal doctrinal foundation for the prominence of polity and church order in the con-

---

150. See chapter 9.2, "Reception of Creeds, Councils, and Confessions as Ratification."
151. See chapter 16.1 below, "The Proliferation of Confessions in the Age of the Reformation."
152. See chapter 5.2 above, "Scripture in the Creeds and Confessions."
153. *67 Art* 1.
154. *Aug* 7–8.
155. *39 Art* 19–20.
156. *N-CP* 9.
157. *Ap* 9.

fessions of the Reformed tradition,[158] and above all for the careful attention given to the understanding of Christian discipline in the Reformation confessions.[159]

158. See chapter 4.3, "Polity as Doctrine in the Reformed Confessions," and Syndogmaticon 9.7.
159. See chapter 10.1 above, "Doctrines of Christian Discipline in the Reformation Confessions," and Syndogmaticon 9.4.

CHAPTER SIXTEEN

Confessions of Faith
in the Reformation Era

WHEN DESCENDANTS OF THE Protestant Reformation use the word "creed," this is a designation for one or another of "the three creeds, Nicene Creed, Athanasius's Creed, and that which is commonly called the Apostles' Creed,"[1] which are listed in *The Thirty-Nine Articles of the Church of England* and in other confessions,[2] and which these churches share with Western Christendom generally. Most often, at least in common Protestant usage, "the Creed" has referred to the third of these, *The Apostles' Creed*, which *The Second Helvetic Confession* calls a "compendium" of Scripture.[3] But when Lutherans, Anglicans, or Presbyterians use the word "confession," or even "*the* confessions," that usually means the particular confession or confessions of their own church or branch of Protestantism. That is the meaning when *The Canons of the Synod of Dort* make a cross-reference to "the confessions of the Reformed churches," which readers are urged to consult,[4] or when the Congregationalist *Declaration of the Boston National Council* speaks of "the confessions and platforms which our synods of 1648 and 1680 set forth or reaffirmed."[5] Specifically in the case of Lutherans, Anglicans, and Presbyterians, "confession" refers to *The Augsburg Confession* of 1530 (and the entire *Book of Concord* of 1580) for Lutherans,[6] or to *The Thirty-Nine Articles of the Church of England* of 1571 for Anglicans (although this confession and its predecessors and suc-

---

1. *39 Art* 8.
2. *BLK* 21; *Form Conc Sol Dec* 12.37.
3. *Helv II* 17.17.
4. *Dort* con.
5. *Boston* pr.
6. Gassmann and Hendrix 1999.

cessors are ordinarily designated by Anglicans as "the Articles"[7] rather than as "the confession"), or to *The Westminster Confession of Faith* of 1647 for Presbyterians. All three of these "confessions" are products of the Reformation era. Sometimes, however, both groups of authoritative texts, the universal "creeds" of the early church and the particular "confessions" of the Reformation churches, can be referred to together by the ancient title "symbols."[8]

Necessary though it is, this distinction between "creeds" and "confessions of faith," which also appears in the discussions throughout this volume (and in the title of the set *Creeds and Confessions of Faith in the Christian Tradition*), is somewhat arbitrary and historically inconsistent. The ancient creeds, too, can sometimes be called "confessions [*confessiones*],"[9] although the Reformation confessions are not usually called "creeds."[10] In spite of some precedents in earlier formularies, most notably in such documents as *The Decree for the Armenians of the Council of Florence* of 22 November 1439,[11] it was with the Reformation of the sixteenth century that "confession of faith" as a theological and literary form distinct from "creed" came into its own and achieved dominance. So dominant did it in fact become that in the seventeenth century Eastern Orthodoxy would employ the title *Confession [Homologia]* for the several systematizations of its own doctrinal position over against both Roman Catholicism and the various subdivisions of Protestantism (most of which by then had themselves formulated their doctrinal positions in such "confessions"). The so-called *Eastern Confession of the Christian Faith by Cyril Lucar* of 1629 was repudiated by the Orthodox for the Protestantizing tendencies of its teaching on such questions as the authority of Scripture alone and the number of the sacraments, but not for its appropriation of the Protestant style of setting forth a series of articles on the major doctrines. *The Reply of Ecumenical Patriarch Jeremias II of Constantinople to the Augs-*

7. *OED* 1–I:470; *ODCC* 112.
8. *Form Conc Epit* 1.2–3.
9. *Form Conc Epit* pr 2.
10. One exception is Piepkorn 1993, 20.
11. See chapter 15.2 above, "The Confessionalization of Western Sacramental Doctrine."

burg Confession is divided into such articles, as a response to the articles of *The Augsburg Confession.*[12] *The Orthodox Confession of the Catholic and Apostolic Eastern Church by Peter Mogila*[13] of 1638 and *The Confession of Dositheus and of the Synod of Jerusalem* of 1672 also follow the system of questions and articles, as *The Confession of Metrophanes Critopoulos* of 1625 already does. All of these latter are Eastern Orthodox "confessions" that were, and are, more or less officially approved.[14]

Such comparisons suggest that in some respects it may be possible, with a due measure of qualification and nuance, to treat the sixteenth and seventeenth centuries in all the Christian denominations, even beyond Protestantism (to which the term is usually confined), as a distinct historical period called "the confessional age."[15] Vertical divisions do provide a natural taxonomy, and in some respects an unavoidable one, for presenting and studying confessions of faith, above all those from the period of the Reformation. These are the differences between Eastern Orthodoxy and Western Christianity, or between Roman Catholicism and Protestantism, or between Lutheranism, Calvinism, and Anglicanism, or between Magisterial Protestantism and Radical Protestantism. But there are also horizontal differences from one historical period to another. For in some decisive respects the era of Reformed Pietism bears greater similarities to the era of Lutheran Pietism than either of these does to the era of confessional scholasticism, which came before Pietism and after the Reformation in both Reformed and Lutheran churches. Such a schema of periodization does fit Roman Catholicism and Radical Protestantism less neatly than it does Calvinism and Lutheranism, and Eastern Orthodoxy less neatly still, for a variety of reasons. But at any rate for the history of confessions of faith during the age of the Reformation, there is enough coherence in it to justify a treatment here that considers together the confessions coming from the several Western denominations during the same period.

12. *Jer II* 1.
13. *Mogila.*
14. See chapter 14.4 above, "The Eastern Confessions as Equal and Opposite Reactions."
15. Reinhard 1977.

16.1. The Proliferation of Confessions
in the Age of the Reformation

The Reformed *Collectio Confessionum in Ecclesiis Reformatis Publicatarum* edited by H. A. Niemeyer and published in 1840; the Lutheran *Die Bekenntnisschriften der evangelisch-lutherischen Kirche* as prepared for the four-hundredth anniversary of *The Augsburg Confession* in 1930 and reissued with minor revisions several times since; and the Anglican *Documents of the English Reformation* edited by Gerald Bray in 1994[16] —the texts in these three standard nineteenth- and twentieth-century collections of Reformation confessions in their original languages add up, with few overlapping documents between the three volumes, to almost three thousand pages. The first and third of these, moreover, are also only selections. Likewise, the comparative page count of Part Four of *Creeds and Confessions of Faith in the Christian Tradition* (which takes up very nearly half of the total set), when set alongside any of the three preceding parts, or even alongside all of them together, is an indication of the quantum leap in the production of confessions of faith that took place during the sixteenth and seventeenth centuries. And what is collected there is only a fraction of the total number of Reformation confessions. For example, for the German territory of Franconia alone and only for the period leading up to *The Augsburg Confession* of 1530, Wilhelm Ferdinand Schmidt and Karl Schornbaum were able to compile five hundred pages of confessional texts.[17] As is evident from the collections of Ernst Gottfried Adolf Böckel and E. F. Karl Müller,[18] it is particularly for the Reformed churches that any collection of confessions must be only a selection. For the Dutch Reformation alone, and only for the sixteenth century, the detailed bibliography by Willem Heijting comes to two substantial volumes.[19] The importance of confessions for the age of the Reformation, and the importance of the age of the Reformation for confessions, may also be gauged from the prominence of references to Reformation confessions and of quotations from them in most of the chapters of the first three parts of this

16. See "Editions, Collections, and Reference Works" above.
17. Schmidt and Schornbaum, 157–655.
18. Böckel; Müller.
19. Heijting 1989.

historical introduction. The issue of confessional subscription, for example, has been formulated and debated on the basis of the authority of confessions coming out of the sixteenth and seventeenth centuries, even though the questions it raises are applicable to all creeds and confessions of faith from all centuries.[20] It has also been in the interpretation of these same Reformation confessions that the principles and methods for interpreting confessions generally have been worked out.[21]

As it must seem historically puzzling in many ways that there were so few creeds and confessions in the Orthodox East during the millennium preceding the appearance of the modern seventeenth-century texts bearing the title *Homologia*,[22] so also there does not appear to be any easy or obvious explanation for the opposite phenomenon here, the rise of confessions and then their proliferation just at the time of the Protestant Reformation.[23] Like the corollary phenomenon of the rise and proliferation of vernacular Bibles during the same period and under many of the same auspices in Germany, England, and elsewhere, it would not have been possible, or at any rate would not have been so successful, without the recent invention of printing in the fifteenth century. One need only imagine what a tedious and costly undertaking it would have been to produce by the copyist's hand the many sets that were circulated even of brief Reformation confessions,[24] not to speak of such compendious texts as *The Formula of Concord* in its *Solid Declaration* of 1577 or the entire *Book of Concord* of 1580 or *The Westminster Confession of Faith* of 1647 (also because the churches from which these confessions issued had meanwhile abolished the monastic communities on whose scriptoria such copying had depended in the Middle Ages). Both the confession as a printed book and the vernacular Bible as a printed book, moreover, were expressions of the fundamental Reformation conviction, as articulated by these confessions, that the correct interpretation of Scripture and the correct dec-

---

20. See chapter 9.4 above, "Confessional Subscription as Legal Compliance."
21. See chapter 9.5 above, "Rules of Confessional Hermeneutics."
22. See chapter 14.1 above, "The Ambivalence of the Orthodox Church Toward 'Symbolical Books.'"
23. Maurer 1939.
24. *Dordrecht* con.

laration of its doctrinal content are a right and a responsibility of the total church, of the laity as well as the clergy, not of the clergy or the theologians alone. The Bible has to speak *to* all the people, the confession has to speak *for* all the people.[25] As each major shift in what was taken to be the correct interpretation of Scripture led in turn to a new form for the correct declaration of its doctrinal content, the result would often be the formulation of a new confession, either within the same Reformation church or party or otherwise in a new movement or even a new church arising as a result of the controversy—a process that does not end in the period of the Reformation but continues into the modern era and spreads to all parts of the globe.[26]

One possible negative explanation for this growth of confessions is the corresponding decline, just as the crisis of authority represented by the Reformation was erupting, in any consensus about how to resolve theological debates and therefore in the credibility and standing of the institution of the church council, which in the classic period of Christian history had served as the primary agency for the church to affirm definitively what it believed, taught, and confessed. It had been such an agency preeminently between 325, the date of the First Council of Nicaea, and 787, the date of the Second Council of Nicaea. The doctrinal decrees of the first seven "ecumenical" councils remained the common foundation of church dogma for the Orthodox East and the Catholic West even after the two churches were separated by the schism. In a special way, the first four of those seven councils (Nicaea I in 325, Constantinople I in 381, Ephesus in 431, and Chalcedon in 451),[27] albeit with a considerable amount of picking and choosing by the various groups, were held in common by the Magisterial Protestant churches, not only with the Catholic West and the Orthodox East, but even with one another.[28] After the schism between East and West, the East did not—because of a complicated mixture of theological, canonical, and political reasons—summon a truly "ecumenical" council

25. See chapter 12.1 above, "What Did the Laity Believe, Teach, and Confess?"
26. See chapter 17.2 below, "Old and New Contexts of Christian Confessing."
27. *10 Art* 1.5; *Helv II* 11.18.
28. See chapter 16.3 below, "Catholic Substance and Protestant Principle in Reformation Confessions."

on its own to deal with issues of doctrine or discipline.[29] During the Western Middle Ages, however, the West felt free to do just that on its own, convoking several such councils and identifying them as "ecumenical." The most notable of these was the Fourth Lateran Council of 1215 under Pope Innocent III, at which several distinctively Western teachings, above all the doctrine of transubstantiation, achieved their binding form in what is sometimes termed *The Lateran Creed*.[30] The four (or five) reform councils assembled by the Western church during the single century from 1409 to 1512 were an attempt, seen as a last chance by some but by others as no more than a quixotic and desperate effort,[31] to employ the instrumentality of the council for the solution of a range of doctrinal and disciplinary problems within Western Christendom, as well as for the most recent and ultimately unsuccessful attempts, after the failure of such medieval gatherings as the Council of Lyons in 1274,[32] at healing the East-West schism: the Council of Pisa of 1409 (not usually counted as ecumenical, because it was not convoked by a pope); the Council of Constance of 1414–18 (the sixteenth); the Council of Basel of 1431–49; the Council of Florence of 1438–45 (the canonically valid and therefore legitimately "ecumenical" sessions of Basel-Ferrara-Florence-Rome now usually being counted in Roman Catholic canon law as a single ecumenical council, the seventeenth, and therefore being cited together in this work); and the Fifth Lateran Council of 1512–17 (the eighteenth).[33] The "ecumenical" standing of some of these fifteenth-century reform councils, or in some cases (Constance, Basel) of individual sessions of these councils, has continued to be a matter of debate in Western theology and canon law, chiefly because of their legislation on the relative authority of pope and council.[34]

Regardless of how they are counted, however, more church councils were held in the West during that one century before the Prot-

29. See Kartašev 1932, and chapter 14.3 above, "The Sacred Tradition of the Seven Ecumenical Councils."
30. *Lat 1215* 1; see chapter 15.2 above, "The Confessionalization of Western Sacramental Doctrine."
31. *Chr Trad* 4:69–126.
32. *Lyons.*
33. Tierney 1998.
34. Bogolepov 1963; Huizing and Walf 1983.

estant Reformation than ever since that time, even though the time span from the Reformation to the present is almost exactly the same as the period covered by all seven ecumenical councils between 325 and 787. The challenges of the Reformation had reawakened the hope among some Roman Catholics and even some Protestants that a truly universal council might be the forum for the adjudication of old and new doctrinal issues, as well as for the consideration of the new challenges being raised by Luther and the other Protestant Reformers.[35] In response to the condemnations of themselves and of their party by the pope, Reformation leaders repeatedly appealed from the actions of popes and bishops to such a council. Some of the early confessions, for example, Luther's *Smalcald Articles* of 1537, were part of that appellate process.[36] The repeated assertions by the decrees of such fifteenth-century reform councils as Constance and Basel that a council has ultimate authority even over the pope did little to commend the council to the papacy of the Reformation era as a mechanism for action or reform, and the project of another reform council moved from delays to fits and starts and back again. The opinions of theologians and churchmen in the sixteenth century, and of historians since the sixteenth century, vary greatly on the question of whether such a general council—if it had been called in timely fashion and if it had been permitted to become a forum for a candid and fraternal exercise of what an earlier ecumenical council had called "debate in common . . . when the disputed question is set out by each side in communal discussions . . . since everyone requires the assistance of his neighbor"[37]—might conceivably have reversed the schism (or schisms) of the Reformation before it was too late. The modest achievements of the Fifth Lateran Council of 1512–17 do not support an unequivocally affirmative answer to that question. But the Council of Trent did not meet for its first session until 13 December 1545, just two months before Martin Luther died. Another eighteen years and twenty-five sessions were required until it adjourned on 4 December 1563, with many important issues left unsolved or some even unaddressed. For these and other reasons, the church

35. Jedin 1957–61, 1.
36. *Smal Art* pr 1.
37. *CP II* decr.

council was not the principal venue for confessing what was believed and taught in the conflicts between Protestantism and Roman Catholicism, nor even in the continuing conflicts within Roman Catholicism. There was a hiatus of just over three centuries between the adjournment of the Council of Trent in 1563 and the assembling of the First Vatican Council in 1869—the very same centuries during which the various Protestant churches were composing so many confessions in separation from the rest of the church, and usually in separation from one another.

The Diet of Augsburg assembled by Emperor Charles V in June 1530 was the occasion for the presentation not only of the Lutheran confession that now bears that name, *The Augsburg Confession,* which was written by Philipp Melanchthon to summarize and vindicate the *magnus consensus* of "our churches"[38] and was presented to the diet and the emperor on 25 June, but also of the *Reckoning of the Faith* [*Fidei ratio*] of Ulrich Zwingli, which was presented to the diet and the emperor two weeks later, on 8 July, and of *The Tetrapolitan Confession,* which was written by Martin Bucer, Wolfgang Capito, and Caspar Hedio and presented to the diet and the emperor on 11 July. The nearly simultaneous presentation of these three confessions—Melanchthon's and Zwingli's opposed to each other above all on the doctrine of the eucharist, and Bucer's intended to mediate between them on this and other points—dramatizes a problem that has attended the confessions of Protestantism ever since the Reformation: polemically, they have been intended simultaneously as a united front against Roman Catholicism and as a definition against other forms of Protestantism. These two purposes have not necessarily coincided. Sometimes the interconfessionally Protestant (as with *The Wittenberg Concord* of 1536 and the *Variata* of *The Augsburg Confession* in 1540), sometimes the confessionally particularistic (as with *The Formula of Concord* in 1577 and *The Canons of the Synod of Dort* of 1618–19), predominated.

Another reason for the proliferation of confessions was, as has been noted earlier,[39] also one of the differences that set the Reformed or Calvinist churches of the Reformation apart from the Lutheran. Many

38. *Aug Lat* 1.1.
39. See chapter 8.2 above, "Civil Law on Adherence to Creeds."

of the Reformed confessions bear national titles: *The [First] Bohemian Confession* of 1535; *The First Helvetic Confession* of 1536; *The French Confession* of 1559; *The [First] Scots Confession* of 1560; *The Belgic Confession* of 1561; *The Second Helvetic Confession* of 1566; *The [Second] Bohemian Confession* of 1575; *The Second Scots Confession* of 1581 (also called *The King's Confession*). And although no one of these confessions by itself could match the sheer bulk of *The Book of Concord*, all of them put together could, and (depending on which other Reformed confessions are included) would certainly exceed it. In spite of their essential agreement with one another on most points, each was obliged, as a separate confession, to rehearse most of the cardinal doctrines of the Reformed faith and to respond to the opponents of that faith. As a result of this pluralism of Reformed confessions, incredible though this must seem, it was impossible, even in the nineteenth century, to find a copy of *The Westminster Confession of Faith* in Protestant and Reformed Germany, and the very existence of that confession was largely unknown; such is the report of a leading scholar and editor of the Reformed confessions.[40] Because, in the judgment of Wilhelm Niesel quoted earlier, "church order, too, bears a confessional character" for the Reformed churches and their confessions,[41] not only the differences over the sacraments within the Reformed family, between the Zwinglian and the Calvinist traditions, as reflected in the *Consensus Tigurinus* or *Zurich Agreement* of 1549,[42] but the continuing and intensifying differences over church order between episcopal, presbyterian, and congregationalist doctrines of polity would go on calling forth a series of new Reformed confessions throughout the Reformed communion, above all in the English-speaking world.[43]

16.2. Lutheran, Reformed, Roman Catholic, and Radical "Confessionalisms"

The term *confessional*, then, may serve as a designation for the entire era of the Reformation of the sixteenth and seventeenth centuries of

40. Müller, v.
41. Niesel, v.
42. *Tig* 7.
43. See chapter 4.3, "Polity as Doctrine in the Reformed Confessions."

Western Christian history. Even Eastern Orthodoxy during that same period could perhaps be included in the term, though with certain qualifications.[44] Nevertheless, each of the divided churches to emerge from the Reformation was "confessional" in its own special way.

What Claude Welch has said of the confessionalism of the nineteenth century was true already of the confessionalism of the sixteenth: "The paradigm . . . was without doubt the 'confessional' Lutheranism that appeared in Germany."[45] For, also in the era of the Reformation, "confessionalism" was probably emphasized by Lutheranism more persistently than it was by any other Protestant group; the nineteenth-century Lutheran champions of its "confessional principle"[46] and the nineteenth-century critics of the Lutheran "extreme of symbololatry and ultra-orthodoxy"[47] would agree on this, if not on other points. This was true of the requirement that ordinands and theological professors "subscribe" the confessions as a necessary condition of achieving and holding an official post.[48] Unlike Reformed ecclesiology, the Lutheran understanding of the church did not include discipline as a "mark" of the church.[49] Rather, *The Augsburg Confession* specified (in its Latin text): "For the true unity of the church it is enough to agree concerning the teaching of the gospel [*satis est consentire de doctrina evangelii*] and the administration of the sacraments."[50] The comparative indifference of Lutheranism to the issues of a normative church order and polity or of a fixed and prescribed liturgy, moreover, placed all of the weight on the confession of doctrine.[51] As early as *The Marburg Articles* of 1529 and *The Wittenberg Concord* of 1536, the irenic theology of many in the Reformed camp put Luther and his followers on the defensive.[52] That situation would continue in the

44. See chapter 14.1 above, "The Ambivalence of the Orthodox Church Toward 'Symbolical Books.'"
45. Welch 1972–85, 1:194.
46. Krauth [1899] 1963, 162–200.
47. Schaff, 1:222.
48. See chapter 9.4 above, "Confessional Subscription as Legal Compliance."
49. See chapter 10.1 above, "Doctrines of Christian Discipline in the Reformation Confessions."
50. *Aug Lat* 7.2.
51. See chapter 4.3 above, "Polity as Doctrine in the Reformed Confessions."
52. *Marburg* 15; *Witt Conc* 3.

Lutheranism of the nineteenth and twentieth centuries, both in Germany and in North America.[53] The unchallenged standing of *The Augsburg Confession* of 1530 as amplified in *The Book of Concord* of 1580 made insistence on creedal conformity more enforceable, as did the arrangement of church-state relations in the Lutheran states of Northern Europe.[54] Lutheran confessionalism eventuated in the acceptance and enforcement of a single standard of supreme confessional authority, *The Augsburg Confession* of 1530 and in most places the entire *Book of Concord* of 1580, of which *The Augsburg Confession* was the chief component. Although *The Formula of Concord* did not become normative church law in some nations, on the ground that it was a local, German confession, as well as on the grounds of its theological content,[55] *The Augsburg Confession* was the uniform standard from one nation to another. Additional statements did arise repeatedly in one or another nation to meet specific, and usually temporary, needs.

For the Reformed branch of Protestantism, however, "confessionalism" took the form of many confessions of faith, more or less equally authoritative, arising in many nations and cultures. To list only some of them from the first century of the history of Protestantism, and in chronological order: *The [First] Bohemian Confession* of 1535; *The First Helvetic Confession* of 1536; *The [First] Scots Confession* of 1560; *The Belgic Confession* of 1561; *The Heidelberg Catechism* of 1563, which is part of *The Church Order of the Palatinate* of that same year; *The Second Helvetic Confession* of 1566; *The Thirty-Nine Articles of the Church of England* of 1571; *The [Second] Bohemian Confession* of 1575; *The [Second] Scots Confession* of 1581; *The Irish Articles of Religion* of 1615. Only a few statements, notably *The Canons of the Synod of Dort,* acquired a transnational and even an international position, having been subscribed by delegates of the following churches, not alone from the Low Countries but also well beyond: "Great Britain, the Electoral Palatinate, Hessia, Switzerland, Wetteraw, the Republic and Church of Geneva, the Republic and Church of Bremen, the Republic and Church of Emden, the Duchy of Gelderland, and of Zutphen, South

53. See chapter 17.2 below, "Old and New Contexts of Christian Confessing."
54. See chapter 8.2 above, "Civil Law on Adherence to Creeds."
55. Spitz and Lohff 1977, 136–49.

Holland, North Holland, Zealand, the Province of Utrecht, Friesland, Transisalania, the State of Groningen, and Omland, Drent, and the French Churches."[56] Therefore *The Confession of the Waldenses* of 1655 could affirm "that we do agree in sound doctrine with all the Reformed Churches of France, Great Britain, the Low Countries, Germany, Switzerland, Bohemia, Poland, Hungary, and others, *as it is set forth by them in their confessions"*; these are, as Dowey puts it, "all first cousins, with strong family resemblances, but they cannot be mistaken for identical twins or triplets."[57]

Although it is not as common to speak about "Roman Catholic confessionalism" in the period of the Reformation, such a term comports well with the growing recognition of modern historiography that the traditional concept of "the Counter-Reformation" is too restrictive and negative a label for the development of Roman Catholicism during the sixteenth century, and that "the Catholic Reformation" is a more balanced and a more comprehensive designation, with important implications also for the question of periodization.[58] This is not, of course, to deny that there was a "Counter-Reformation" and that many of the changes within the Roman Catholicism of the sixteenth and seventeenth centuries make sense chiefly as a response and a reaction to the rise of Protestantism; these might include the vigorous efforts, political as well as liturgical and theological, to reclaim lost territories or to compensate for their loss by an expansion of foreign missions. But it is an oversimplification to assume that the reformatory impulse of the later Middle Ages, as expressed in the reform councils of the fifteenth century, was completely captured by the Protestant Reformation. Not only the continuing calls for reform by Erasmus and other humanists, but theology and churchmanship from Nicholas of Cusa to Girolamo Seripando (who died almost exactly a century apart) demonstrated the abiding power, also after the exit of the Protestants, of a deep-seated zeal for reformation and renewal.[59] "Roman Catholic confessionalism" is part of that phenomenon. In interpreting one section of

56. *Dort* con.
57. *Wald* 33; italics added. Dowey 1968, 176.
58. Jedin 1946, 39–49. But see also O'Malley 2000.
59. *Chr Trad* 4:248–74, 69–126, 274–303.

The Canons and Decrees of the Council of Trent after another, therefore, it is necessary to inquire both after the elements of continuity with late medieval reform movements and after the reactions to Protestant doctrine and practice that were at work. The decree of the council itself defines "the dual purpose on account of which the council was primarily brought together" as "the rooting out of heresy" externally and "the reform of conduct" internally.[60] That applies even to the issues that were the most central to the doctrinal controversy with Protestantism: the doctrine of the relation between the authority of Scripture and the authority of the church, as reflected also in the problem of the biblical canon;[61] and the doctrine of justification as this had been an issue between Thomists and Scotists.[62] Of course the Council of Trent was reacting to the teachings of the Protestant Reformers on these two issues, but it was also addressing—if not really settling—the persistent and long-deferred need to sort out and clarify the unresolved state of the patristic and medieval tradition.[63] Addressing that need to manage the tradition has always been, in a special way, the historic assignment of a confession of faith.

The validity of the unconventional term "Roman Catholic confessionalism" is vindicated even more directly by the appearance of a confessional text like *The Tridentine Profession of Faith* of 1564: "I, N., with firm faith believe and profess [*credo et profiteor*] each and every article contained in the symbol of faith which the Holy Roman Church uses."[64] "Symbol" in that declaration of believing, teaching, and confessing refers to *The Niceno-Constantinopolitan Creed* in its *Western Recension,* which is also affirmed in many Protestant confessions of the time.[65] But the confessional intent of *The Tridentine Profession of Faith* makes itself clear when it next affirms as a coordinate confession: "I most firmly accept and embrace the apostolic and ecclesiastical tradi-

---

60. *Trent* 3 decr.
61. Tavard 1959.
62. Rückert 1925, 134–43; Becker 1967.
63. Maichle 1929; see also chapter 5.3 above, "The Confessions and the Problem of the Canon."
64. *Trid Prof* 1.
65. See chapter 16.3 below, "Catholic Substance and Protestant Principle in Reformation Confessions."

tions, and all other observances and constitutions of the same church. I likewise accept Holy Scripture according to that sense which Holy Mother Church has held and does hold."[66] In addition to "each and every article contained in the symbol of faith," therefore, it enumerates the seven sacraments, original sin and justification, the sacrifice of the mass, purgatory, the intercession of the saints, and indulgences. All of these are seen as "the apostolic and ecclesiastical traditions, and all other observances and constitutions of the same church" (and, not incidentally, as doctrines not "contained in the symbol of faith" or confessed as such in *The Niceno-Constantinopolitan Creed*). In summary, one who subscribes the *Profession* "acknowledge[s] the holy, catholic, and apostolic Roman Church as the mother and teacher [*matrem et magistram*] of all the churches, and promise[s] and swear[s] true obedience" to the pope, as well as to the teachings of the ecumenical councils, especially the Council of Trent.[67] By promulgating such a confession after the relative paucity of confessions of faith in the medieval West, except for certain sacramental definitions,[68] the Catholic Reformation (or Counter-Reformation) did represent a "confessionalization" that was not confined, as the conventional usage might lead one to suppose, to the Reformed and Lutheran confessions, but spanned the ecclesiastical and doctrinal spectrum.[69]

Within that spectrum, even the adherents of the Radical Reformation had what the Mennonite scholar Howard John Loewen identifies as "the confessional period,"[70] just as the Baptist scholar William L. Lumpkin can speak of "the rising interest in confessionalism and in the Baptist view of the Church" during the twentieth century.[71] The Anabaptists joined in the universal sixteenth-century practice of "mak[ing] known, in points and articles," as *The Schleitheim Confession* of 1527 puts it,[72] what sets them apart from others, both from

66. *Trid Prof* 2.
67. *Trid Prof* 7–8.
68. See chapter 15.2 above, "The Confessionalization of Western Sacramental Doctrine."
69. Reinhard and Schilling 1995.
70. Loewen, 25.
71. Lumpkin, 5.
72. *Schleit* pr.

Roman Catholics and from other Protestants. That confession then presents the Mennonite positions on doctrines in controversy, including the sacraments, the ban, and the taking of oaths. Therefore even so untraditional and idiosyncratic a statement of faith as *Hans Denck's Confession Before the Council of Nuremberg* of 1525 is divided into separate articles, dealing in turn with faith, baptism, and the Lord's supper.[73] Indeed, as C. J. Dyck has described this ironic situation,

> It is generally true that the Anabaptists and later Mennonites have been and are non-creedal. Torture experienced because of doctrinal issues spelled out by representatives of the established churches, the stress of the learned clergy on doctrine at the expense of ethics, and particularly the desire to be biblical . . . led to clear antipathy to rational statements of faith. . . . So also spontaneity in worship eliminated the felt need for formal confessional recital.
>
> It is surprising, therefore, to find that the Anabaptists and especially the Dutch Mennonites wrote many confessions, . . . probably more than any of the other three Reformation traditions.[74]

The production of confessions by Mennonites, as well as by other Anabaptists, would continue well beyond the era of the Reformation into the late twentieth century.[75]

16.3. Catholic Substance and Protestant Principle in Reformation Confessions

In one way or another, almost every confession of the Protestant Reformation is shaped both by the polemical efforts of Roman Catholic or other Protestant opponents to tar it with the brush of past heresy and by its own inner dynamics, in response to both of which it is obliged to cope with the relation between the Catholic substance that it has inherited and the Protestant principle that it espouses. The Anglican-

73. *Denck* 1–3.
74. Foreword to Loewen, 16–17.
75. *Menn Con* (1963).

Lutheran *Wittenberg Articles* of 1536 go further than most of them when they open their first article, neither with the doctrine of one God as Trinity nor with the doctrine of the supreme and sole authority of Holy Scripture, which are the usual alternatives,[76] but with the declaration: "We confess simply and clearly, without any ambiguity, that we believe, hold, teach, and defend everything which is in the canon of the Bible and in the three creeds, i.e. the Apostles', Nicene, and Athanasian Creeds, in the same meaning which the creeds themselves intend and in which the approved holy fathers use and defend them." This oath of loyalty applies, moreover, to "the very form of words in those articles," which is to be "retained most precisely."[77] The Reformed *Second Helvetic Confession* of 1566, for all of its determined adherence to the sole authority of the Bible over all ecclesiastical traditions, including not only the councils but even the creeds, can nevertheless bracket Bible and creed by speaking of "the truth of God presented in the Scriptures and in the Apostles' Creed."[78]

For the epigram of Benjamin Breckenridge Warfield, author of scholarly studies of both Augustine and Calvin, that "the Reformation, inwardly considered, was just the ultimate triumph of Augustine's doctrine of grace over Augustine's doctrine of the church,"[79] does help to identify a stratification of the substance of the Catholic tradition that prevailed in the teachings of the Protestant Reformation and of its confessions. On portions of the Catholic substance such as the invocation of the saints, as the words quoted earlier from *The French Confession* of 1559 indicate,[80] it is a Protestant principle shared by the confessions of all the Reformers that "as Jesus Christ is our only advocate, and as he commands us to ask of the Father in his name, and as it is not lawful for us to pray except in accordance with the model God has taught us by his word, . . . all imaginations of men concerning the intercession of dead saints are an abuse and a device of Satan to lead men from the right way of worship,"[81] even though these "imagi-

76. See chapter 5.2 above, "Scripture in the Creeds and Confessions."
77. *Witt Art* 1.
78. *Helv II* 16.1.
79. Warfield 1956, 322.
80. See chapter 6 above, "The Rule of Prayer and the Rule of Faith."
81. *Gall* 24. See Syndogmaticon 3.8.

nations of men" are in fact the unanimous teaching of the Catholic substance shared by both East and West. Even the effort of *The Augsburg Confession* and other confessions to lay claim to the Catholic substance, by insisting that "our churches dissent from the church catholic in no article of faith but only omit some few abuses which are new and have been adopted by the fault of the times although contrary to the intent of the canons,"[82] proved to be ineffectual. When it comes to the doctrine of grace, however, as Warfield's words suggest, Luther and Calvin, and the confessions issued in their name, consistently pit Augustine's glorification of the free and sovereign grace of God against what they denounce as the Pelagian or Semi-Pelagian tendencies in late medieval scholasticism. For the Protestant principle of *sola gratia,* therefore, the claim to be Augustinian and in that sense truly Catholic can, and does, supply chapter and verse especially from Augustine's anti-Pelagian writings. The Calvinist doctrine of predestination as reprobation as well as election to salvation is anticipated in some of the later works of Augustine.[83] By contrast, the identification with Augustine, and thus with a version of "Catholic substance," is considerably less successful in the confessions' defense of the Protestant principle of *sola fide* in the doctrine of justification by faith alone.

Even on what Warfield called "Augustine's doctrine of the church" as distinct from "Augustine's doctrine of grace," moreover, the confessions of the Reformation do lay claim to being Augustinian, in the sense of not being Donatist.[84] Therefore it becomes a persistent refrain both of the Lutheran and of the Reformed confessions to dissociate the idea of "reform" as advocated by Luther, Zwingli, and Calvin from the Donatism of the earlier centuries, but likewise from the neo-Donatism consistently attributed, whether justly or not, to John Wycliffe and John Hus.[85] Already in *The Profession of Faith by Valdes,* known as a forerunner of the Reformation, the validity of the sacraments is affirmed "even though they be ministered by a sinful priest,"[86] a position that is reinforced in a confession by the fol-

82. *Aug Lat* 22 int.1.
83. *Chr Trad* 1:298–99; Syndogmaticon 3.2.
84. See chapter 10.2 above, "Heresy And/Or Schism," and Syndogmaticon 9.3.
85. Spinka 1966.
86. *Vald.*

lowers of Hus in the sixteenth century.[87] Sometimes without mentioning the Donatists but sometimes identifying them by name, Reformed
confessions frequently make a point of explaining that the well-known
emphasis on the necessity of discipline as a mark of the church, especially in the confessions of the Reformed churches by contrast with
the Lutheran confessions,[88] does not, in spite of superficial similarities,
mean that they have gone over to the Donatist view. *The Second Helvetic Confession* of 1566 follows its insistence, as quoted earlier, that
"discipline is an absolute necessity in the church" with this disavowal
in the very next paragraph: "We strongly detest the error of the Donatists."[89] Its predecessor of 1536, *The First Helvetic Confession,* identifies by name not the Donatists but the Anabaptists when it criticizes
"all those who separate and cut themselves off from the holy fellowship and society of the church,"[90] but clearly the Donatists (and neo-
Donatists) are included in the criticism. Even more clearly, the Swiss
Protestants were insisting that they themselves were not guilty of such
separatism. According to *The Thirty-Nine Articles of the Church of England,* because evil men ministering in the name of Christ "do minister by his commission and authority, we may use their ministry both
in hearing the word of God and in the receiving of the sacraments.
Neither is the effect of Christ's ordinance taken away by their wickedness, nor the grace of God's gifts diminished."[91] It is obvious that this
is intended to be a summary of the Augustinian case against Donatism,
as is true also of a similar passage in *The Irish Articles of Religion* of
1615.[92] Even in the context of "condemn[ing] the papal assemblies, as
the pure word of God is banished from them, their sacraments are corrupted, debased, falsified, or destroyed, and all superstitions and idolatries are in them," *The French Confession* of 1559 adds the Augustinian
proviso that "the efficacy of baptism does not depend upon the person
who administers it," not even, it would seem, when it is administered

87. *Boh I* 11.7.
88. See chapter 10.1 above, "Doctrines of Christian Discipline in the Reformation
Confessions," and Syndogmaticon 9.4.
89. *Helv II* 18.20–21.
90. *Helv I* 25.
91. *39 Art* 26.
92. *Irish* 70.

in those corrupted, superstitious, and idolatrous "papal assemblies."[93]
The neo-Donatism of the late Middle Ages and Reformation would
likewise appear to be the reason behind the formulation of *The Augsburg Confession*, which *The Confutation of the Augsburg Confession* of
the Roman Catholic opponents approves:[94] "Our churches condemn
the Donatists *and others like them* who have denied that the ministry of
evil men may be used in the church and who have thought the ministry
of evil men to be unprofitable and without effect."[95]

The relation of the "Protestant principle" to the dogma of the
Trinity as the central affirmation of the Catholic tradition, and therefore as the heart of "Catholic substance," evoked the assessment of
Edward Gibbon that "after a fair discussion we shall rather be sur-
prised by the timidity, than scandalized by the freedom, of our first
reformers."[96] That "surprise"—or stricture—applies in even greater
measure to the Reformation confessions than it does to the personal
writings of these "first reformers." The confessions and other writings of the Antitrinitarians and Socinians of the Reformation period
repeatedly charge that there is a blatant discrepancy between theory
and practice in the confessional stance of the Magisterial Reformation. In the words of *The Augsburg Confession,* it complains that on
many points the "teaching of Paul has been almost wholly smothered
by traditions,"[97] but at the same time it has no compunction about
affirming, as that same confession does, that the most massive tradition of them all, "the decree of the Nicene Synod concerning the
unity of the divine essence and concerning the three persons, is true
and should be believed without any doubting," complete with its entire
conceptual apparatus and traditional Latin terminology of one essence,
three persons, and all the rest.[98] This is, in the words of *The Marburg Articles,* bearing the signatures of Luther and his colleagues as
well as of Zwingli and his colleagues, what is "sung and read in the

93. *Gall* 28.
94. *Confut* 8.
95. *Aug Lat* 8.3; italics added.
96. Gibbon [1776–88] 1896–1900, 6:125 (ch 54).
97. *Aug Lat* 26.6.
98. *Aug Lat* 1.1.

Nicene Creed by the entire Christian church throughout the world." [99] Far from being a remnant of the Middle Ages or a mere political ploy, the trinitarianism of the mainline Protestant Reformers, whether Calvinist or Lutheran, is fundamental both to their theology and to their spirituality, as Thomas Torrance has shown.[100] So fundamental is it that, at least until the challenges of the Radical Reformation, it represents, within the circle of the Magisterial Reformation, what Alfred North Whitehead once called one of those "fundamental assumptions which all the variant systems . . . unconsciously presuppose. Such assumptions appear so obvious that people do not know what they are assuming because no other way of putting things has ever occurred to them." [101]

In fact, so wholeheartedly and uncritically did the Magisterial Reformers make the Western version of the Nicene trinitarian tradition their own that the Filioque passed over unscathed from the Latin theology of the Middle Ages to the confessions of the Protestant Reformation.[102] *The Belgic Confession* of 1561, which also argues for its list of the biblical canon by claiming that "the Holy Spirit testifies in our hearts that they are from God" and the Apocrypha are not,[103] argues for (among other trinitarian teachings) the Filioque by declaring: "*All these things* we know from the testimonies of Holy Scripture as well as from the effects of the persons [of the Trinity], *especially from those we feel within ourselves.*" [104] Within this Protestant trinitarianism, the Filioque seems to be largely taken for granted as a "fundamental assumption." This can be seen in the words of *The Augsburg Confession* about "the decree of the Nicene Synod," which, without mentioning the Filioque outright, are clearly referring not to *The Creed of Nicaea,* nor even to the original form of *The Niceno-Constantinopolitan*

99. *Marburg* 1.
100. Torrance, lxx–lxxii.
101. Whitehead [1925] 1952, 49.
102. See chapter 7.4 above, "The Holy Spirit of Concord and the Sacrament of Concord: Two Ironic Case Histories"; and chapter 15.1 above, "The Western Reception of the Catholic Creedal and Conciliar Tradition."
103. *Belg* 5; see chapter 5.3 above, "The Confessions and the Problem of the Canon."
104. *Belg* 9; italics added.

Creed, but to the *Western Recension* of *The Niceno-Constantinopolitan Creed* with the Filioque.[105] Teaching that "the Holy Spirit proceeds from him [the Son] as well as from the Father,"[106] *The Formula of Concord* reaffirms "the old, approved symbols, the Nicene and Athanasian Creeds," including the Filioque in both *The Niceno-Constantinopolitan Creed* and *The Athanasian Creed.*[107] So does *The Reaffirmed Consensus of the Truly Lutheran Faith* of 1655.[108] Both of these creeds in this form, together with *The Apostles' Creed,* lead the processions of creeds and confessions of faith in *The Book of Concord* of 1580, under the heading "The Three Chief Symbols or Creeds of the Christian Faith which Are Commonly Used in the Church."[109] Therefore in response to the presentation of the Lutheran theologians of Tübingen to the ecumenical patriarch of Constantinople, Jeremias II, with its appeal to the creed supposedly held in common with his church, his second *Reply,* sent in 1579, opens with a full-length disquisition "On the Procession of the Holy Spirit," impeaching, on the grounds of their adherence to the Filioque, any claim they make of being orthodox.[110]

According to article 8 of *The Belgic Confession,* the three persons of the one divine essence are "eternally distinct according to their incommunicable properties." It is the property of the Father in the Trinity to be "the cause, origin, and source of all things, visible as well as invisible," referring by that quotation from *The Niceno-Constantinopolitan Creed*[111] to the Father as the "origin [Greek *archē*, Latin *principium*]" of all creatures. It is the property of the Holy Spirit to be "the eternal power and might, proceeding from the Father *and the Son.*"[112] Taking the unusual step of setting aside an entire separate article for the doctrine of the Holy Spirit, *The Belgic Confession* subsequently goes well beyond that perfunctory recitation of the Filioque: "We believe and confess also that the Holy Spirit proceeds eternally from the Father

---

105. *Aug Lat* 1.1.
106. *Form Conc Sol Dec* 8.73.
107. *Form Conc Sol Dec* 12.37.
108. *Cons rep* 1.12.
109. *BLK* 21.
110. *Jer II* 2.1.1–42.
111. *N-CP* 1.
112. *Belg* 8; italics added.

and the Son—neither made, nor created, nor begotten, but only proceeding from the two of them"; and in support it cites the standard
Western proof texts for the Filioque.[113] *The French Confession* of two
years earlier similarly speaks of the Father as "first cause, principle, and
origin of all things," also referring to creatures, and of the Holy Spirit
as "his [the Father's] virtue, power, and efficacy," but nonetheless as
"proceeding eternally from them both."[114] *The Second Helvetic Confes-*
sion states that "the Holy Spirit truly proceeds from them both, and
the same from eternity and is to be worshiped with both [*cum utroque*
adorandus]."[115]

The British confessions of the Reformation, too, align themselves with the *Western Recension* and the Filioque. It is the teaching
of *The Thirty-Nine Articles of the Church of England*, both in the Latin
text of 1563 and in the English text of 1571, that "the Holy Ghost, proceeding from the Father and the Son, is of one substance, majesty, and
glory with the Father and the Son, very and eternal God."[116] That language is repeated verbatim in *The Irish Articles of Religion* of 1615,[117]
as it is again in *The Methodist Articles of Religion* of 1784/1804,[118] as
well as in *The Articles of Religion of the Reformed Episcopal Church in*
America of 1875.[119] In *The Westminster Confession of Faith* of 1647 the
distinction "in the unity of the Godhead" between the "three persons,
of one substance, power, and eternity" is said to be: "The Father is of
none, neither begotten, nor proceeding; the Son is eternally begotten
of the Father; the Holy Spirit eternally proceeding from the Father and
the Son."[120] Similarly, *The Westminster Larger Catechism* confesses: "It
is proper . . . to the Holy Spirit to proceed from the Father and the Son
from all eternity."[121] In *The Scots Confession* of 1560 there is no reference to the Filioque at all; it contains no separate article on the doc-

113. *Belg* 11.
114. *Gall* 6.
115. *Helv II* 3.3.
116. *39 Art* 5.
117. *Irish* 10.
118. *Meth Art* 4.
119. *Ref Ep* 4.
120. *West* 2.3.
121. *West Lg Cat* 10.

trine of the Trinity, and its article entitled "Faith in the Holy Ghost" confines itself to the statement that "we confess [the Holy Spirit] to be God, equal with the Father and with his Son."[122] But it is evident from such texts as *Craig's Catechism* of 1581 that the confessions of the Scottish Reformation, too, retain and affirm the Filioque.[123] So does the Brownist *True Confession* of 1596.[124] As part of the Western confessional heritage, the Filioque goes on appearing in later confessions, also in such confessions of the Third World as *The Declaration of the Faith and Articles of Religion of the Philippine Independent Church* of 1947, in the *Richmond Declaration of Faith* of the Quakers, and in the *Statement of Faith* of the Jehovah's Witnesses.[125] In this universal retention of the Filioque in the confessions of mainstream Protestantism, one exception deserves quoting in full, the confession of *The Easter Litany of the Moravian Church* of 1749: "I believe in the Holy Ghost, who *proceedeth* from the Father, and whom our Lord Jesus Christ *sent*, after he went away, that he should abide with us forever."[126] The Mennonite *Concept of Cologne* of 1591 reverts to the formula of the Council of Florence by its confession of the Holy Spirit as "proceeding from the Father through the Son [*van den Vader door den Sone*]."[127] But *The Mennonite Short Confession of Faith* of 1610 retains the traditional Western version, "proceeding from the Father and the Son."[128]

16.4. From Reformation Confessions to Confessional Scholasticism

Several of the major confessions of the Protestant Reformation, which are included in Part Four of *Creeds and Confessions of Faith in the Christian Tradition* under the heading "Confessions of Faith in the Reformation Era," came from the first generation of Protestant Reformers. Some of these Reformers—including Luther the Augustinian, Bucer the Dominican, Thomas Cranmer, and John Knox—had received a more

---

122. *Scot I* 12.
123. *Craig* 4.3.
124. *True Con* 2.
125. *Philip Ind* 1.3; *Richmond* 1; *Witness* 9.
126. *Morav* 3; italics added.
127. *Cologne* 3; *Flor Un.*
128. *Ries* 3.

or less thorough training in scholastic theology and then had gone on to reject it. Among the first-generation Reformers who composed confessions were: Ulrich Zwingli (*The Sixty-Seven Articles* of 1523 and *Reckoning of the Faith* [*Fidei ratio*] of 1530); Martin Luther (*Small Catechism* of 1529, *Large Catechism* of 1529, and *Smalcald Articles* of 1537); Philipp Melanchthon (*The Augsburg Confession* of 1530 and *The Apology of the Augsburg Confession* of 1531); Martin Bucer (*The Tetrapolitan Confession* of 1530 and *The Wittenberg Concord* of 1536); Thomas Cranmer (*The Ten Articles* of the Church of England of 1536); John Calvin (*The Geneva Catechism* of 1541/42); and John Knox (*The Scots Confession* of 1560).

But many more of the Protestant confessions came from the second, third, and subsequent generations. Those confessions, moreover, are not only more numerous but usually much longer, than the earlier texts had been. Nor is the difference a matter only of comparative length as such. For it was, paradoxically, the writers of confessions who had not been trained in medieval, Roman Catholic scholasticism who laid the foundations for a new, Protestant "confessional scholasticism." As Horatius Bonar put it, speaking about *The Westminster Confession of Faith* from the seventeenth century in a description that could as readily have been applied also to *The Canons of the Synod of Dort* from the same century or to *The Formula of Concord* from late in the preceding century,

> It may be questioned whether the Church gained anything by the exchange of the Reformation standards for those of the seventeenth century. The scholastic mould in which the latter are cast has somewhat trenched upon the ease and breadth which mark the former; and the skilful metaphysics employed at Westminster [or in *The Formula of Concord*] in giving lawyer-like precision to each statement, have imparted a local and temporary aspect to the new which did not belong to the more ancient standards.[129]

129. Quoted in Torrance, xvii.

Bonar's use of "scholastic," therefore, which commonly refers to Western Roman Catholic theology from the twelfth to the fourteenth century and to the revival of that theology in the modern era,[130] may also be applied to the Protestant "confessional scholasticism" of the sixteenth and seventeenth centuries, which manifested itself in both Lutheran and Reformed theology.

One presupposition for its rise, as it had been for the rise of medieval scholasticism, was the cultivation of Aristotelian philosophy, which, after its rejection by Luther and other Reformers, enjoyed a strong revival of interest during subsequent generations of Lutheran and Reformed theologians. It had been Melanchthon's ambition to prepare a new edition of Aristotle. Aristotelianism gave the Protestant dogmaticians of the seventeenth century a precision in their vocabulary and a capacity for making careful distinctions.[131] Partly as a consequence of this renewal of interest in the philosophy of Aristotle, another component of medieval scholasticism, the investigation of "natural theology," played a prominent part in this Protestant scholasticism, too. Therefore an exploration of what the unaided human reason could know about God, including the traditional proofs for the existence of God, became the prolegomenon to the systematic exposition of the revealed doctrines of Scripture.[132]

But as Etienne Gilson, widely regarded as the leading historian of medieval philosophy in his generation, nevertheless complained, "During the past hundred years the general tendency among historians of medieval thought seems to have been to imagine the middle ages as peopled by philosophers rather than theologians."[133] It is likewise more important to pay attention to another presupposition of both pre-Reformation and post-Reformation scholasticism, the availability of the doctrinal tradition in a codified form.[134] In the works of Thomas Aquinas and his contemporaries, that had meant above all the compilation of patristic doctrine that had been produced in the *Sentences*

130. *Chr Trad* 3:268–307.
131. Petersen [1921] 1964.
132. Troeltsch 1891, 194–206; Syndogmaticon 1.2.
133. Gilson [1951] 1957, 156.
134. Grabmann [1909] 1957, 2:359–407.

of Peter Lombard.[135] A three-step process of explaining the apparent contradictions within the tradition—raising objections, formulating a positive answer on the basis of tradition, and then responding to the objections and apparent contradictions—set the pattern for the scholastic method.[136] But for the Protestant scholastics like Johann Gerhard, whose *Confessio catholica* of 1634–37 and invention of the word *patrology* in 1653 showed him to be a scholar of the patristic tradition in his own right,[137] it was the ancient creeds as seen through the prism of the more recent confessions that supplied the codification of the tradition. This they did in a form that gave it a special Reformation flavor. For example, the tradition of the dogma of the person of Christ as represented by *The Definition of Faith of the Council of Chalcedon* was affirmed both by the Reformed confessions[138] and by the Lutheran confessions,[139] even as they disputed about its implication for eucharistic doctrine.[140] But the concentration in both confessional traditions on the work of Christ rather than primarily on the person of Christ[141] enabled seventeenth-century scholastic theologians to interpret *The Definition of Faith of the Council of Chalcedon* as a confirmation and a vindication of Reformation accents. In the celebrated formula of the first Protestant systematic theology, the *Loci communes* of Melanchthon first published in 1521, "to know Christ is to know the blessings he confers [*Hoc est enim Christum cognoscere, beneficia eius cognoscere*]."[142]

In spite of the continuing efforts throughout the sixteenth and seventeenth centuries to heal the separations in Western Christendom, above all the divisions between the several branches of Protestantism,[143] the "Confessions of Faith in the Reformation Era" that make up Part Four of *Creeds and Confessions of Faith in the Christian Tradition* had effectively made the separations permanent, at any rate until the nine-

135. Stegmüller 1947; see chapter 15.3 above, "Scholastic Theology as Reasoning on the Basis of the Creed."
136. Chenu 1964, 93–96.
137. Quasten, 1:1.
138. *West* 8.2; *Fid rat* 1; *Wald* 13.
139. *Form Conc Sol Dec* 8.18.
140. See chapter 12.1 above, "What Did the Laity Believe, Teach, and Confess?"
141. See chapter 3.3 above, "'Doctrines' and Doctrine."
142. *Chr Trad* 4:155–56.
143. McNeill 1964.

teenth and twentieth centuries, when new and more successful movements for reconciliation would lead to new confessional statements.[144]
Polemics continued back and forth, also after the various confessions
had been fixed. But the confessions, though they themselves became
the occasion for it, as with the exchange mentioned earlier between
the *Concordia discors* of Rudolf Hospinian and the *Concordia concors*
of Leonhard Hutter,[145] had meanwhile set the outcome of the controversies as a foundation on which a scholastic theology was able to
build. This included the standardization, at any rate within each of the
confessional groups, of a technical theological vocabulary, an indispensable component of any scholasticism. Prominent examples of this
were the terminology of "the theology of the covenant [*foedus*]" within
Reformed thought and of the christological "interchange of attributes
[*idiomatum communicatio*]" in Lutheran thought.[146] Similarly, as the
systematization of the fourfold sense of Scripture had helped to make
medieval scholasticism possible,[147] so also the confessions had worked
out the distinctive principles of biblical interpretation that had come
out of the exegetical work of the Reformation.[148] Therefore when, for
example, *The Second Helvetic Confession,* speaking in this case not for
its own Reformed tradition alone but for Protestant theology generally,
defines as "orthodox and genuine" only that interpretation "which is
gleaned from the Scriptures themselves," it specifies the constituent elements for such an interpretation: first, "the nature of the language in
which they were written"; second, "the circumstances in which they
were set down"; third, "like and unlike passages and many and clearer
passages"; fourth, "agree[ment] with the rule of faith and love"; and
fifth, compatibility with "the glory of God and man's salvation."[149]
Both in their exegetical writings on the books of Scripture and in the
interpretations of individual biblical passages that were a continuing
part of their works on dogmatics, the Protestant scholastics were able

144. See chapter 17.2 below, "Old and New Contexts of Christian Confessing."
145. See chapter 7 above, "Formulas of Concord—And of Discord."
146. *Chr Trad* 4:350–74.
147. Lubac 1998.
148. See chapter 5.4 above, "Confessional Rules of Biblical Hermeneutics," and
Syndogmaticon 8.15.
149. *Helv II* 2.1.

to capitalize on all of these accomplishments of "the confessional era." When the attacks of Pietism, of the Enlightenment, and of modern thought and Liberal theology challenged this confessional scholasticism, the confessions of the Reformation era often became the objects of the attack as well.

CHAPTER SEVENTEEN

Statements of Faith
in Modern Christianity

THE TITLE OF THIS CHAPTER may well seem to be an oxymoron, above all to anyone who equates modernity with religious skepticism and doctrinal relativism and who therefore feels that even if the time for faith as such may not have passed, the time for teaching Christian faith as authoritative dogma probably has, and the time for confessing it in a normative creedal formulary certainly has.[1] As noted earlier, one twentieth-century reference work of Liberal Protestant theology speaks for this modern view of creeds and confessions when, after positing the neutral and unobjectionable definition, "Historically considered, creeds are convenient summaries arising out of definite religious situations, designed to meet urgent contemporary needs, and serving as tests of orthodoxy," it proceeds, by means of a "therefore," to draw from that definition a conclusion diametrically opposed to the traditional one: "Therefore they are inadequate in new crises and unable to secure uniformity of belief."[2] In a time when faith itself has become problematical to so many serious and thoughtful seekers—for whom the confidence of the traditional confessional formula, "We believe, teach, and confess,"[3] has been replaced by the poignant cry of the anguished father in the Gospel story, "I believe; help my unbelief!"[4]—the role of the confession of faith cannot avoid being a problematic one. At most, it would seem to be the function of such a confession to acknowledge

1. As described in Baumer 1960.
2. Ferm 1945, 208 (Conrad Henry Moehlman).
3. See chapter 2 above, "The Creedal and Confessional Imperative."
4. Mk 9.24.

the reality of the secularization of society and to seek to define (or re-define) the Christian mission in response to it.[5]

Nevertheless, as becomes evident from even a preliminary examination of the dates cited for the texts listed under "Abbreviations for Creeds and Confessions" in the front matter of this work, or of the hundreds of pages of texts in "Statements of Faith in Modern Christianity," Part Five of *Creeds and Confessions of Faith in the Christian Tradition* (and as a further examination of the many other texts not included there would reinforce), there have been "statements of faith" aplenty in "modern Christianity." They continued to appear in almost every year from the end of the eighteenth century to the end of the twentieth, in many churches, including some that dissented fundamentally from the main body of the Christian tradition, already in the eighteen century[6] and then in the nineteenth[7] and twentieth,[8] in almost every part of the globe, and in many languages, some of these languages being quite novel as instruments for the formal confession of Christian doctrine. In fact, during the twentieth century the title "statement of faith" seems to have become preferable (at any rate in English translation) to either "creed" or "confession." To cite only some examples that are widely dispersed both theologically and geographically: *Statement of Faith of the American Baptist Association* of 1905;[9] *Brief Statement of the Doctrinal Position of the Evangelical Lutheran Synod of Missouri, Ohio, and Other States* of 1932;[10] *The Statement of Faith of the United Church of Christ* of 1959;[11] *Statement of Faith of the Church of Jesus Christ in Madagascar*, 1958/68;[12] *Statement of Faith of the United Church of Christ in the Philippines*, 1986 (1982);[13] *Common Statement of Faith* issued by the Commission on Faith and Order of the World Council of Churches, meeting at Bangalore, India, in 1978[14] — and even

---

5. *Camb Dec.*
6. *Shkr.*
7. *Winch* (1803); *LDS* (1842); *Salv Arm* (1878).
8. *Wash* (1935).
9. *Am Bap.*
10. *Br St Luth.*
11. *UCC.*
12. *Madag.*
13. *Philip UCC.*
14. *F&O Ban.*

such nontraditional confessions as the *Statement of Faith of the Jeho-vah's Witnesses* of 1918[15] and *Statement of Faith of Fundamental Truths of the Assemblies of God* in 1914.[16]

In some ways, moreover, both the new challenges and the new opportunities of Christian faith in the modern era since the opening of the nineteenth century, which has been identified as "the great century" of Christian missions,[17] have been responsible for unprecedented expansion and growth in previously non-Christian areas of Asia and, above all, of Sub-Saharan Africa, where new believers, and eventually new churches, have sought for their own ways of responding within their own culture and in their own language to the historic confessional imperative.[18] New movements dissenting from historic churches, including some very ancient ones, both in the East[19] and in the West,[20] have added to the list of confessions. It is these ambiguities as well as these challenges and opportunities that have helped to shape the history of Christian creeds and confessions of faith in the modern era.

17.1. The Discomfort with Creed Caused by the Consciousness of Modernity

Hinrich Stoevesandt has used the phrase "the discomfort with creed caused by the consciousness of modernity [*das durch jenes Gegenwarts-bewusstsein mitveranlasste Ungehagen am Symbolum*]" as the title for a book that describes the long-standing modern antipathy, outside and even inside the churches, to the very idea of a creed or confession[21]— as well as, of course, the antipathy to specific individual creeds, most vehemently to *The Athanasian Creed*.[22] In voicing that antipathy, many modern opponents of creedalism claimed to be carrying out, more consistently than the Protestant Reformers had been in a position to do, the full implications of the Reformation's attack on the authority

15. *Witness.*
16. *Assem.*
17. Latourette 1937–45, 4–6.
18. Rom 10.9–10; see chapter 11 above, "Transmission of Creeds and Confessions to Other Cultures."
19. *Arm Ev.*
20. *Pol Nat.*
21. Stoevesandt 1970, 12.
22. Compare *39 Art* 8 with *39 Art Am* 8.

of church and tradition. On the basis of a "domino theory" of religious authority, the Roman Catholic adversaries of the Reformation had warned already in the sixteenth century that an attack on the papacy would eventually lead to a repudiation of creedal orthodoxy itself. They had seized upon such obiter dicta as Luther's disparaging language about the term *homoousios* or Calvin's comment that it was better to sing *The Nicene Creed* than to speak it as evidence of the beginning of such a repudiation. In reply, the Magisterial Reformers, above all Luther, Calvin, and the spokesmen for Anglicanism, vigorously affirmed their loyalty to the orthodox dogmas of the Trinity and the person of Christ.[23] But during the eighteenth, nineteenth, and twentieth centuries, that Roman Catholic view of the Reformation achieved a vindication of sorts in Liberal Protestantism, for example in Adolf Harnack's description and critique of the vestigial remnants and "the Catholic elements retained by Luther" and the other Reformers.[24] Not only the retention of the Catholic creeds and dogmas by the confessions of the Magisterial Reformation,[25] but the addition of literally hundreds of Protestant creeds and confessions to them, was now seen as an indication that the Reformers themselves had not fully carried out the implications of their own position, which had finally become a possibility only with the modern era. The paradoxes in this situation will become evident to present-day readers when they note that it is the Protestant confessions of the Reformation era that repeatedly criticize Roman Catholicism (rather than the other way around, as later polemics might suggest) for allowing too much latitude to the ministry of women: "We teach that baptism should not be administered by women or midwives. For Paul deprived women of ecclesiastical duties, and baptism has to do with these."[26]

Without attempting to present here a capsule history of "the consciousness of modernity," or even of the development of critical theology in the modern period, it is possible to identify several of the movements of modern thought in which such a "discomfort with

---

23. *Chr Trad* 4:322–23.
24. Harnack [1893] 1961b, 7:230–66.
25. See chapter 16.3 above, "Catholic Substance and Protestant Principle in Reformation Confessions."
26. *Helv II* 20.6, citing 1 Tm 2.11–14, and *Scot I* 22, by contrast with *Lat 1215* 3.

creed," to the point of antipathy and hostility, has manifested itself, also among Christian theologians standing in various confessional traditions.[27] Claude Welch's comprehensive *Protestant Thought in the Nineteenth Century* may serve as a guide to those movements, although our account must confine itself, even more than his does, to "an interpretation of some central themes,"[28] which, while contradicting each other in many theological particulars, shared this "discomfort with creed."

"The eighteenth and nineteenth centuries" were marked, Welch observes, by "the antidogmatic, antienthusiastic temper of an age tired and disgusted with religious controversies."[29] The rationalism of the Enlightenment was "antidogmatic," and therefore it was anticreedal and anticonfessional. In the celebrated definition by Immanuel Kant, the "Enlightenment is man's exodus from his self-imposed tutelage," a tutelage that had expressed itself "in indecision and lack of courage to use the mind without the guidance of another." Or, in Paul Tillich's definition, the Enlightenment was "the revolution of man's autonomous potentialities over against the heteronomous powers which were no longer convincing." For many disciples of the Enlightenment, including its theological disciples, creeds and confessions were among the most obvious examples of such a "self-imposed tutelage." The rejection of creeds and confessions as "heteronomous powers" and as "no longer convincing," together with a "disgust with religious controversies," was a no less obvious example of such a "revolution." For "it's plain from Church History," the Deist Matthew Tindal wrote in 1730, "that Creeds were the spiritual Arms, with which contending Parties combated each other; and that those who were the Majority invented such unscriptural Terms, as they thought their adversaries wou'd most scruple, in Order to the stripping them of their Preferments." An Enlightenment thinker like Thomas Jefferson, nominal Anglican though he remained at least officially, strove to go back behind the creeds, and even behind the canonical Gospels as they had been transmitted by an

27. *Chr Trad* 5:29–32, 122–28, 269–72; the sources for many of the quotations not identified in footnotes here are given in the marginal notes there.
28. Welch 1972–85, 1:293.
29. Welch 1972–85, 1:31.

orthodox and creedal Christendom, to find the authentic figure of the human Jesus as the teacher of a rational and universal faith, to set him free from creed and dogma, and to see genuine—and therefore non-creedal and nondogmatic—religion and morality as embodied in him.

Although "the nineteenth century was in many respects a very Christian century," Lionel Trilling observed in 1950, "it is probably true that when the dogmatic principle in religion is slighted, religion goes along for a while on generalized emotion and ethical intention—'morality touched by emotion'—and then loses the force of its impulse, even the essence of its being."[30] For those thinkers who strove to retain some form of the Christian belief in Christ and in the Bible, therefore, the substitute for creeds and confessions in much of the Protestant theology of the eighteenth and nineteenth centuries was one or another configuration of what might be called a new trinity, which Welch identifies as "faith, history, and ethics in balance."[31] All three of these, as well as the relation of each to dogma and creed, had been important components in the tradition of creedal and confessional orthodoxy, too.[32] But now each of them acquired a new significance, and the "balance" of which Welch speaks was at the same time a fundamental and critical reconsideration of that tradition as a whole. There remained great variation in the radicality, as well as in the public acknowledgment, both of the rejection and of the alternatives.

An emphasis on authentic *faith*, which implied a subordination of the objective *fides quae creditur*, "the faith which one believes," of ecclesiastical doctrine, dogma, and creed to the subjective *fides qua creditur*, "the faith by which one believes," of personal feeling and experience,[33] had already been a pronounced tendency in the distinctive emphasis of Reformed and Lutheran Pietism on the Continent and of Methodism in England. In practice, however, both of these movements employed it to vindicate many traditional beliefs, if not always the formal authority of the creeds and confessions in which those be-

---

30. Trilling [1950] 2000, 180.
31. Welch 1972–85, 2:1–30.
32. On "faith," see chapter 2 above, "The Creedal and Confessional Imperative"; on "history," chapter 1.4 above, "The Person of Christ as Exemplar of Continuity and of Change"; and on "ethics," chapter 10 above, "Deeds, Not Creeds?"
33. See chapter 2.2 above, "Faith Defined," also Syndogmaticon 1.1, 1.6.

liefs had been definitively set down, as later confessions would make clear.[34] John Wesley, although he himself strove in his "theology of the heart" to remain orthodox and faithful to Anglicanism's "three creeds,"[35] insisted that "a man may assent to three or three-and-twenty creeds . . . and yet have no Christian faith at all." But when this emphasis on experience and feeling was defined by its outstanding expositor, Friedrich Schleiermacher, in his systematic theology, *The Christian Faith*, as "the feeling of absolute dependence," this eventually took the place not only of the traditional proofs for the existence of God, but of dogma, creed, and confession. Therefore, as Welch summarizes Schleiermacher's view, "every doctrinal form is bound to a particular time and no claim can be made for its permanent validity."[36] That applied also to the creeds and confessions of the churches—to all of them. This view of doctrinal forms brought on what Welch calls "the neglect by theologians (especially Schleiermacher) of the ancient dogmas" and creeds.[37] In Schleiermacher's *Christian Faith*, moreover, "the confessional writings of the Protestant church [*die evangelischen Bekenntnisschriften*]," Reformed and Lutheran confessions taken together, were to be cited in support of doctrinal propositions. In the tradition of the Prussian Union, the differences between the two sets of Reformation confessions on such doctrines as the eucharist were subordinated to those teachings that they held in common—and all of these in turn to experiential faith. For although all doctrinal propositions could be interpreted either as "descriptions of conditions of human life" or as "concepts of divine attributes" or as "statements about the way the world is constituted," it was in fact the first of these three forms of expression that recast and eventually replaced the conventional language of the creeds and confessions, including the creeds and confessions of the Protestant Reformation, both Reformed and Lutheran. Toward these creeds and confessions he felt himself bound only according to what he took to be their "meaning and spirit," rather than according to the letter of the doctrines they professed.[38] Probably the most notori-

34. *Morav.*
35. *39 Art 8.*
36. Welch 1972–85, 1:72.
37. Welch 1972–85, 1:100.
38. Hirsch 1960, 5:157–58.

ous instance of this treatment of creedal doctrine was the way Schleier-macher marginalized the dogma of the Trinity, literally relegating it to an appendix in *The Christian Faith.*

History, the second member of the triad, likewise led to the undermining of creedal and confessional authority. The question on all sides was: "Is historical research . . . a help to faith? And can any security for faith be found in history?"[39] It was a question that applied with special force to the historic creeds and confessions, which served as the outstanding illustrations of the correctness of Gotthold Ephraim Lessing's axiom that "contingent historical truths can never serve as proof for necessary truths of reason." Matthew Tindal found that "the imposers of creeds, canons, and constitutions" were "the common plagues of mankind." Although there were some efforts to argue "that the New Testament fully supports an Athanasian rather than a Socinian or an Arian Christology, provided we do not allow criticism to become our master,"[40] such efforts were seen as incompatible with the growing historical recognition that the attempt of the Reformation confessions and their later interpreters "to show continuity between the ancient church and the Reformation while distinguishing Protestant from Roman Catholic understandings" was misguided and doomed to fail.[41] Frederick Denison Maurice's *Subscription No Bondage* of 1835 argued "that the requirement at Oxford [of subscription to *The Thirty-Nine Articles of the Church of England*] was not actually a test of one's own religious convictions, but a statement of the basis on which instruction in the university was to be given."[42] But such an argument could be dismissed by both the left and the right as evasion and sophistry; and the accusation of "deviation from the standards of the Westminster Confession"[43] and other Reformation confessions, an accusation directed against the historical-critical study of Scripture, was ultimately ineffective. For the method of historical-critical study was applied not only to the Bible (where it was more readily accepted

39. Welch 1972–85, 2:146.
40. Welch 1972–85, 2:151.
41. Welch 1972–85, 2:15.
42. Welch 1972–85, 1:245; see also chapter 9.4 above, "Confessional Subscription as Legal Compliance."
43. Welch 1972–85, 2:166.

for the Old Testament than for the New) but, in keeping with the Protestant subordination of tradition to Scripture, with still greater freedom to creeds and confessions of faith, even to those that were the most ancient or the most ecumenical and authoritative.[44]

Increasingly, as it was being carried on by such Liberal scholars as Harnack, this historical-critical method was documenting a two-stage historical process: "the recasting of the baptismal confession into a rule of faith," which foliated into many creeds and conciliar confessions of faith in the first several centuries of the history of the church; and then in turn the development by which "the rule of faith was transformed into a compendium of Greek philosophical systems" climaxing in the Eastern and Western forms of scholasticism—two steps that had brought the orthodox creeds of the church a long distance away from the original and true gospel of Jesus.[45] The historical-critical examination of creedal development, above all of *The Definition of Faith of the Council of Chalcedon,* led Albert Schweitzer to the conclusion that "its doctrine of the two natures dissolved the unity of the Person, and thereby cut off the last possibility of a return to the historical Jesus. . . . He was still, like Lazarus of old, bound hand and foot with grave-clothes—the grave-clothes of the dogma of the Dual Nature."[46] In his *Quest of the Historical Jesus,* Schweitzer proceeded to document the historical process by which, beginning with Hermann Samuel Reimarus, an emancipation from that "dogma of the Dual Nature" had led the biblical scholarship of the eighteenth and nineteenth centuries to a series of reconstructions of "the historical Jesus," free of creedal or confessional restraint.

An apt illustration both of the impact and of the problem of such historical-critical study of the creeds and confessions was the "battle over *The Apostles' Creed* [*Apostolikumstreit*]," which Harnack precipitated, almost inadvertently, in 1892. When a Protestant pastor administered baptism to a child without using *The Apostles' Creed,* a storm of controversy broke out, and some of the participants in the

44. See chapter 17.3 below, "The Flowering of Creedal and Confessional Scholarship in the Modern Era."
45. Welch 1972–85, 2:179.
46. Schweitzer [1906] 1961, 3.

controversy appealed to Harnack as an eminent historical authority
for his expert opinion. He replied that "the acknowledgment of *The
Apostles' Creed* just as it reads is not the criterion of Christian and
theological maturity; on the contrary, a mature Christian, who is well
informed about the understanding of the gospel and about the history
of the church, must take offense at several of the statements in *The
Apostles' Creed*." Above all he singled out the article of the creed "con-
ceived by the Holy Spirit, born of the Virgin Mary"[47] as one that many
modern Protestants could no longer find acceptable and that it was
therefore dishonest to enforce as a compulsory belief for clergy or laity.
But at the same time he affirmed "the high value and great repository of
truth" in this creed, though only if it was properly, that is, historically
and critically, understood. The reaction in the German Protestant press
and in the churches, including the Roman Catholic Church, was partly
a continuation of the earlier protests that Harnack had evoked by his
historical research into the origins of dogma and by his critique of the
place of dogma and creed in the church. But it was also a symptom
of the far broader sense of unease over the entire problem of doctrinal
and creedal authority within modern Protestantism.[48]

The third member of the triad of "faith, history, and ethics in
balance," Christian *ethics*, had long been seen as existing in potential
tension with creed and dogma,[49] but that tension, too, acquired new
force in the nineteenth century. Sometimes the orthodox Protestant attempt "to relate the classical terms *persona* and *hypostasis* (both in the
christological and trinitarian usages) to modern conceptions of personhood centering in self-consciousness"[50] could be used to support
the interest in the ethical dimension. But in opposition to any such attempt, the most far-reaching espousal of a new understanding of Christian ethics, which "in the late nineteenth century seemed to be sweeping everything before it," came from an outlook that thought of itself
as "freed from dogma considered as unchangeable formulas for belief
. . . or the trinitarian dialectic of the Athanasian Creed."[51] The need

47. *Ap* 3.
48. Zahn-Harnack 1951, 144–60.
49. See chapter 10 above, "Deeds, Not Creeds?"
50. Welch 1972–85, 1:279.
51. Welch 1972–85, 2:229.

to discover (or, as they saw it, to recover after centuries of orthodox neglect) the social character of the Christian ethic and to carry it out in political and social action would march under the banner of "the social gospel." [52] This even produced a "social creed" of its own, first for the Methodist Church and then for the Federal Council of Churches in the United States and then for the Methodist Church in Brazil. [53] It evoked from Walter Rauschenbusch, in his *Christianity and the Social Crisis* of 1907, which "became one of the most influential religious books of the century," [54] the question that formed the title of one of his chapters: "Why Has Christianity Never Undertaken the Work of Social Reconstruction?" [55] In addition to sacramentalism, which promoted a mystical inwardness instead of social reconstruction, and asceticism, which urged a flight from the world and society, a chief culprit in the social apathy of the church, according to Rauschenbusch, was dogma, as it had been formulated by creeds such as *The Athanasian Creed,* with its "subtle definitions on the relation between the persons of the trinity" and "comparatively fruitless speculation." [56]

One direct consequence of this change was—somewhat incongruously, in view of the new emphasis of the social gospel on the corporate dimension of Christianity—the radical individualization of "confession of faith" as a personal religious act, the phenomenon that Welch calls "the Socratic turn to the self." [57] The English poet John Milton had already been its spokesman when, in his posthumously published *Christian Doctrine,* he stated his intention "to puzzle out a creed for myself by my own exertions," because he had "decided not to depend upon the belief or judgment of others in religious questions." But the creed that Milton had "puzzled out" by his own exertions turned out to be a "neo-Arian" departure from traditional Nicene and Chalcedonian orthodoxy both on the Trinity and on the person of Christ. [58] It is symptomatic of this new creedal freedom and confes-

52. Hopkins 1940; Handy 1966.
53. *Soc Meth; Soc Ch; Meth Braz.*
54. *ODCC* 1368.
55. Rauschenbusch 1907, 143–210.
56. Rauschenbusch 1907, 178–79.
57. Welch 1972–85, 1:126.
58. See also chapter 3.1, above, "The Teaching of the Church."

sional individualism that in some Protestant divinity schools, even if they are still affiliated with a church body, a course is offered, often for entering seminarians, with the assignment to each class member of producing a "credo," not of what the church has believed, taught, and confessed in its historic creeds and confessions of faith, but of what that particular seminarian *really* believes now—which might possibly correspond to some existing creedal and confessional affirmation but certainly does not need to.

17.2. Old and New Contexts of Christian Confessing

When, as part of its program of *aggiornamento, The Declaration on the Church's Relation to Non-Christian Religions* of the Second Vatican Council of the Roman Catholic Church at its seventh session, on 28 October 1965, opens with the phrase "*Nostra aetate,* In our age,"[59] from which that conciliar decree takes its title, it is expressing the recognition that in the modern era changing times are bringing unique challenges but also unprecedented opportunities to the confessional task of the church. Already its first decree, *The Constitution on the Sacred Liturgy,* entitled *Sacrosanctum concilium,* referring to "those structures which are subject to change" as distinguished from the fixed components of the liturgy and the unchangeable truths of Scripture and tradition, speaks of the obligation "to adapt" them "so as better to meet the needs of our time [*nostrae aetatis necessitates*]."[60] And *Gaudium et spes,* its *Pastoral Constitution on the Church in the World of Today,* calls upon the church to discern "the signs of the times" and devotes its introduction to "the condition of humanity in today's world."[61] A century earlier, the confession of the Roman Catholic faith in *The Syllabus of Errors of Pope Pius IX* of 1864 also looks for the signs of its times and locates itself historically in its age, though chiefly in an adversarial posture, when it condemns eighty of "the principal errors *of our time.*"[62] In the period of the Reformation, *The Canons and Decrees of the Council of Trent* speak of the church's right and duty to take

59. *Vat II* 7.5.1.
60. *Vat II* 3.1.
61. *Vat II* 9.4.4–10.
62. *Syl;* italics added. Also *Munif* 2.

account of "changing affairs, times, and places" in its practical life,[63] just as *The Augsburg Confession* singles out "the fault of the times" as the culprit in various abuses.[64]

Many other churches have recognized the challenges and opportunities of the modern era, and the imperative to deal with them has been articulated in many other modern statements of faith, including in a special way those that have emanated from Evangelical and "free churches."[65] In 1951, Indonesian Protestants produced their *Confession of Faith of the Protestant Christian Batak Church (H.K.B.P.)*, in which, while according due recognition to the confessions of the past, they nevertheless stated their view that "the church, in opposing heresies which arise, continuously requires *new confessions*. . . . Because of the pressures upon our church, our thinking must be aroused *at the present time* to confront the doctrines and religions around us."[66] As becomes clear from the subtitle, "Direction of Endeavor for Chinese Christianity in the Construction of New China," *The Christian Manifesto* of the China Three-Self Patriotic Movement issued in 1950, recognizes the new situation of the church in a "new China" dominated by Marxism-Leninism.[67] Though not a "confessional church" in the usual sense in spite of their creedal affirmations in the seventeenth[68] and nineteenth[69] centuries, the Society of Friends (Quakers) responded to the twentieth century by issuing *Essential Truths* in 1900 and 1930.[70] And a definition of this time as "the atomic age" raised for European Protestants after the Second World War the question of whether and how "the confession of Christ" could be possible now.[71]

The new contexts of Christian confessing "*nostra aetate*, in our age," were the consequence of forces both inside and outside the life and faith of the institutional churches, forces that were sometimes hostile and sometimes friendly to creeds. One of the most drastic changes,

63. *Trent* 21.1.2 decr.
64. *Aug Lat* 22 int 1.
65. *Sav* pr; *Laus Cov* pr; *Camb Dec* pr; Küppers, Hauptmann, and Baser 1964.
66. *Bat* pr; italics added.
67. *Chin Man* 1; see also *PRCC* 3.D–E.
68. *Friends I* (1673); *Friends II* (1675).
69. *Richmond* (1887).
70. *Ess.*
71. Wolf 1959.

with far-reaching implications for the authority of creeds, was the gradual shift from establishment to disestablishment of the church in relation to the state, as well as in relation to the university, to science,
and to culture generally. The implications of disestablishment became
visible, for example, when the Free Church of Geneva in 1848 issued
its elaboration of *The Apostles' Creed* as a confession but in 1883 abolished its authority, replacing it with the original text of *The Apostles'
Creed* plus an appendix.[72] For even beyond all of the intellectual, scientific, and religious objections to the traditional functions of creeds
and confessions of faith, the political revolutions of the modern era
have also made the confessional and creedal tradition, including especially the alliance of that tradition with the political establishment,
the object of attack. As part of his attack, Matthew Tindal singled
out "this imposing temper of the ecclesiastics." It was, he said, "plain
from history that the ambitious, domineering part of the clergy, the
imposers of creeds, canons, and constitutions, have proved to be the
common plagues of mankind."[73] The role of the emperor Constantine
at the First Council of Nicaea in 325, which legislated the dogma of
the Trinity, followed a half-century later by the adoption of the Nicene
trinitarian creed as part of the law of the Roman empire under Emperor
Theodosius I,[74] had made the empire and its successors, in Tindal's
phrase, "the imposer of creeds" for more than a millennium. Even the
political and religious upheavals of the Protestant Reformation did not,
at least initially, shake the hegemony of *The Niceno-Constantinopolitan
Creed* as a political force, and in some respects they even strengthened it.[75] Although the criticism of creeds and confessions was already
going on while that hegemony was still at least formally being acknowledged, the steady erosion of the religious and intellectual authority of creeds and confessions and the gradual political disestablishment of the churches reinforced each other throughout the eighteenth,
nineteenth, and twentieth centuries.

72. *PRE* 6:253–54 (Ch. Correvon).
73. *Chr Trad* 5:31.
74. *Theodosian Code* 16.1.2; see chapter 8.2 above, "Civil Law on Adherence to
Creeds."
75. See chapter 8 above, "The Formation of Confessions and the Politics of Religion."

Although the cultural and intellectual disestablishment of Christendom may have been less directly caught up in the power struggles of the time than was the political disestablishment, its effects on the context of Christian confessing were in some respects even more destructive, at least initially. The same critical-historical method that was used to investigate Homer or the Nordic sagas was applied to biblical, creedal, and confessional texts, showing them to have been fundamentally conditioned by the cosmological presuppositions of their own time, presuppositions, moreover, that the modern age did not and could not share.[76] The undermining, both by this historical-critical study and by the advances of science, of the credibility of biblical miracle stories, from the creation narrative in Genesis to the virgin birth of Christ and the resurrection of Christ in the Gospels to the eschatology of the Apocalypse—the same four events of the biblical narrative whose recitation, phrase by phrase, constitutes the core both of *The Niceno-Constantinopolitan Creed* and of *The Apostles' Creed*[77]—put the church of the eighteenth and nineteenth centuries on the defensive against the dominant zeitgeist of the culture.[78] Therefore it called forth reformulations of the Christian confession. Some of these sought for compromise, adjustment, or evasion in relation to Darwinian evolution and the new cosmologies.[79] Others strove to affirm the inspiration of the Bible and the truth of the creeds as unequivocally as had the confessional scholasticism of the seventeenth century.[80]

At the same time, political and cultural disestablishment seemed to some to provide a liberating opportunity for the churches to reaffirm their confession without the burden of having to act as apologists for an established order of society that had in various ways, both obvious and subtle, distorted the Christian gospel by adopting it. For confession and creed did not necessarily depend on the state and its laws for enforcement, as the experience of the churches in the United

76. Frei 1974.
77. N-CP 1–7; *Ap* 1–7.
78. *Syl* 7; *Bat* 4.
79. *Chr Trad* 5:238–41; also Syndogmaticon 1.10, 1.12.
80. See chapter 5.4 above, "Confessional Rules of Biblical Hermeneutics"; and chapter 16.4 above, "From Reformation Confessions to Confessional Scholasticism."

States proved. In spite of all the dire predictions of the eighteenth century, Christian faith and life, and even Christian creedal confession, had managed to thrive under political disestablishment. Therefore it is historically essential to pay equal attention to the continuing tenacity of those whom Welch describes as "traditionalists . . . for whom . . . the gospel portrait was essentially unquestioned as a basis for Christological dogma,"[81] and hence to the continuing context that this tradition went on providing for the formulation of creeds and confessions, also in response to the new contexts that were being forced on the churches by the modern age. The dynamic of this interrelation between the old and the new contexts of Christian confessing makes itself evident in most of the texts in any collection of modern confessions such as Part Five of *Creeds and Confessions of Faith in the Christian Tradition,* "Statements of Faith in Modern Christianity," under the headings "The Nineteenth Century: Putting Confessionalism and Denominationalism to the Test" and "The Twentieth Century: Globalization of Churches and Confessions."

Among the specific new contexts of confessing within the churches in the nineteenth and twentieth centuries, Geoffrey Wainwright has enumerated the "various 'movements' that had affected wide areas of Christendom over confessional boundaries: the biblical theology movement, the liturgical movement, the ecumenical movement in its more technical sense, the movement to discover our common patristic roots and even to recover the controversial figures of later history in their originality and authenticity." "These movements," he concludes, "have provided us with a common language and with a greater possibility of substantive understanding and agreement."[82] Each has also provided all the churches with new ways of looking at, and even of formulating, creeds and confessions of faith.

Christian creeds and confessions, as well as Christian theology generally, had, of course, always striven to be *biblical.*[83] In that sense, therefore, it may seem tautological or even arrogant to use the term "biblical theology" for a twentieth-century development. Nevertheless

81. Welch 1972–85, 2:146n.
82. Wainwright 1986, 13.
83. See chapter 5 above, "Scripture, Tradition, and Creed."

something new had definitely happened. With some anticipations in the eighteenth and nineteenth centuries, the phenomenon of the new biblical theology in the twentieth century was made possible in part by the revived interest in the vocabulary of the Bible, fostered by the new methods of biblical philology.[84] Biblical theology was an effort to replace the old and supposedly static categories of the creeds and of dogmatics, which were regarded as having been unduly shaped both by Greek philosophical presuppositions and by confessional polemics, with themes that were more dynamic and that corresponded more closely to the biblical "history of salvation [*Heilsgeschichte*]" — which was itself one such theme. The move to biblical theology had a mixed effect on the history of creeds and confessions, whatever it may have meant for the reinterpretation of the tasks both of systematic theology and of biblical exegesis.[85] For on one hand it reinforced the biblical foundations of the traditional doctrines that had been confessed in the creeds and in that sense contributed, at least indirectly, to the vindication of the creeds. But by sometimes exaggerating the contrast between the New Testament and the beginnings of the catholic Christianity that expressed itself in the creeds and eventually in the councils, it did not always lead directly to a rehabilitation of the historic creeds as such. There was, nevertheless, a difference also in newer creeds and confessions as a direct consequence of the new attention to biblical theology. Perhaps nowhere does that change become more evident than in a comparison between the decrees of the First Vatican Council of 1869–70 and those of the Second Vatican Council of 1962–65 — in their doctrinal emphasis, but even in their documentation and method of theological argumentation and proof. In the century between those two councils had come not only biblical theology as a whole, which was initially a largely Protestant phenomenon, but specifically the fundamental reappraisal of how the church should interpret Scripture that had been formulated in *Divino afflante Spiritu,* the encyclical issued by Pope Pius XII on 30 September 1943.[86]

Another striking difference of the Second Vatican Council from

84. *ABD* 6:483–505 (Henning Graf Reventlow).
85. *ABD* 1:1203–6 (John H. Leith). See, for only one example, *Leuen* 5.
86. Denzinger 3825–31.

the First was the prominence of the *liturgy* in its decrees. This applies in a special way, of course, to the *Constitution on the Sacred Liturgy* itself, which, as the first decree of the council, set the tone for all that was to follow.[87] This constitution declares the liturgy, rather than any other dimension of the life and teaching of the church, to be "*the chief means* through which believers are expressing in their lives and demonstrating to others the mystery which is Christ, and the sort of entity the true church really is."[88] That emphasis remained in force when the council, at its fifth session, came to define the nature of the church in *Lumen gentium, The Dogmatic Constitution on the Church.* While reaffirming the "doctrine of the institution, the perpetuity, the force and the nature of the sacred primacy of the Roman pontiff and of his infallible magisterium,"[89] as these were affirmed by the Council of Trent and the First Vatican Council, this constitution concentrates on the church's worship of God and its service to the world rather than on its juridical or even its dogmatic authority. In these and other ways, this Western council was also striving to find a closer affinity with the Christian East, where what the church believes, teaches, and confesses is articulated primarily in the liturgy rather than in the comprehensive confession of the doctrines of the faith, as it is in Reformation Protestantism.[90] There was an analogous development in the Anglican communion, as the historic tension between *The Thirty-Nine Articles of the Church of England* and *The Book of Common Prayer* was increasingly resolved in favor of the latter.[91] But the confessional impact of the liturgical movement extended far beyond these communions, manifesting itself as well in many of the churches that had traditionally eschewed "formalism" and "ritualism" in their worship, and necessitating new attention also to the creeds, notably *The Niceno-Constantinopolitan Creed* for both the Eastern and the Western tradition and *The Apostles' Creed* for the West, as these creeds were imbedded

87. *Vat II* 3.1.
88. *Vat II* 3.1.2; italics added.
89. *Vat II* 5.1.18.
90. See chapter 14.1 above, "The Ambivalence of the Orthodox Church Toward 'Symbolical Books'"; and chapter 14.2 above, "The Liturgy as the Church's Preeminent Confession of the Faith."
91. See chapter 6.2 above, "*Lex orandi lex credendi.*"

in the liturgies of the churches.[92] But as the Anglican example showed in a heightened form, this change could come at the cost of the specific confessions of the individual churches, in the case of Anglicanism *The Thirty-Nine Articles of the Church of England*.

Beginning as it did within Protestantism (including Anglicanism), *the ecumenical movement,* by bringing together representatives of many confessional traditions, also could have the effect of relativizing the authority of their particular confessions.[93] When the Congregationalist *Declaration of the Oberlin National Council* of 1871 declares, "We especially desire, in prosecuting the common work of evangelizing our own land and the world, to observe the common and sacred law, that in the wide field of the world's evangelization, we do our work in friendly cooperation with all those who love and serve our common Lord,"[94] that is based on the distressing spectacle of denominational competition in evangelism and the mission field. Many declarations of fellowship, concordats, mergers, and reunifications across historic confessional divisions took place during the nineteenth and especially the twentieth century.[95] These entailed, sometimes by what they said but perhaps more often by what they left unsaid, the demotion of the traditional confessions of the individual churches to a second-class status or their relegation to history.[96] But when ecumenism began to include not only various Protestant bodies but participants from Eastern Orthodoxy and eventually from Roman Catholicism, the authority of the church and of its traditions and creeds in those communions made the question of confessions more insistent, sometimes therefore reinforcing confessional identity even where it had not been dominant, or had been in decline, previously.[97] For in this ecumenical atmosphere, although it may seem paradoxical to some, members of the several confessional families, for example the Reformed, also found a new relation within their tradition.[98]

92. See chapter 6.3 above, "The Place of Creed in Liturgy."
93. See chapter 4 above, "Faith and Order."
94. *Oberlin 5.*
95. Ehrenstrom and Gassmann 1979.
96. *Ev All con; Leuen* 37, 27–28.
97. Békés and Meyer 1982.
98. *Un Pres; Ref All.*

17.3. The Flowering of Creedal and Confessional
Scholarship in the Modern Era

In its Decree on Ecumenism, the Second Vatican Council urged that "theology . . . *especially of an historical nature* must be taught with a due regard for the ecumenical point of view."[99] But according to an authoritative Roman Catholic theological dictionary, Roman Catholic "theology stagnates during the eighteenth century: development is almost exclusively confined to the historical disciplines (Church history)."[100] Similarly "in the history of Protestant theology," as Karl Barth once commented somewhat ruefully, "the nineteenth century brought with it the none too dignified sight of a general flight, of those heads that were wisest, into the study of history."[101] Although he himself was the leading exception to this pattern of the eighteenth, nineteenth, and twentieth centuries—while at the same time, in his monograph of 1931 on Anselm of Canterbury and above all in the history of Protestant theology during the nineteenth century of 1947 from which that quotation comes, making brilliant contributions to historical theology—he was speaking about some of his most eminent teachers, principally Adolf Harnack.[102] As Page Smith has said, describing a general cultural phenomenon of this era, "tradition had lost its authority," and "history was pressed into service."[103] For just as the decline of belief in the inerrancy of the Bible was, somewhat paradoxically, accompanied by a phenomenal growth in the scholarly study of the Bible, so the nineteenth and twentieth centuries in Protestant theology, for all their antipathy to creeds and confessions—or perhaps even because of it—were at the same time the golden age of a creedal and confessional research that had to be taken no less seriously by those for whom creeds, confessions, and church councils had retained their authority. Therefore *The Fourteen Theses* coming out of the first conference at Bonn between Old Catholic, Eastern Orthodox, and Anglican theologians in 1874 specify that authoritative tradition "is partly

99. *Vat II* 5.3.10; italics added.
100. Rahner-Vorgrimler 459.
101. Barth 1959, 311.
102. See Zahn-Harnack 1951, 412–18.
103. Smith 1964, 55.

to be found in the consensus of the great ecclesiastical bodies standing in historical continuity with the primitive church," an exercise in dogma, but also that it is "partly to be gathered by scientific method from the written documents of all centuries," an exercise in scholarship.[104] As another Roman Catholic reference book acknowledged in 1998, therefore, it was not with Roman Catholic or Eastern Orthodox or confessional Protestant traditionalists but with "Harnack and Kattenbusch that the study of confessions of faith arose at the end of the nineteenth century,"[105] in a way and to a degree that had never been true of more "creedal" and "confessional" ages. It was at that time that two massive editions of the Latin and the Greek church fathers by learned academies—the *Corpus Scriptorum Ecclesiasticorum Latinorum,* begun in 1866, and *Die griechischen christlichen Schriftsteller der ersten drei Jahrhunderte,* begun in 1897—made available, often for the first time, early Christian texts that were critically edited and philologically sound. On that basis it became possible to separate later accretions from original readings, and thus to document, with meticulous attention to detail, the history of the words and phrases that eventually came together into creeds. The monumental works on the text and history of *The Apostles' Creed* by Carl Paul Caspari, published between 1866 and 1879, and by Ferdinand Kattenbusch, which came out between 1894 and 1900, laid foundations and provided resources on which every subsequent study of that history, including the present one, has had to rely, and they virtually created a new field of scholarship. In the English-speaking world, such works as James Franklin Bethune-Baker's *Meaning of Homoousios in the "Constantinopolitan" Creed* of 1901 and A. C. McGiffert's *Apostles' Creed: Its Origin, Its Purpose, and Its Historical Interpretation* of 1902, and two generations later J. N. D. Kelly's *Early Christian Creeds* originally published in 1950 and *The Athanasian Creed* of 1964 made major contributions to this new field.

During the same period, partly as an effort to continue this research on early creeds into the Reformation era, and partly as a counterbalance to it, scholarly editions and works on other confessions of faith, including above all the Protestant confessions of the six-

104. *Bonn I* 9.1.
105. Lacoste, 248.

teenth and seventeenth centuries, also flourished. A catalog of only some of these will illustrate how many of the critical editions of individual confessions and how many of the collections of confessions on which any scholarship in the field must still draw are the products of the nineteenth and twentieth centuries in many churches and many countries (listed in chronological order of their first editions): J. C. W. Augusti, *Corpus Librorum Symbolicorum qui in Ecclesia Reformatorum auctoritatem publicam obtinuerunt* (1827); H. A. Niemeyer, *Collectio Confessionum in Ecclesiis Reformatis Publicatarum* (1840); E. J. Kimmel, *Libri symbolici ecclesiae orientalis* (1843; *Appendix,* 1850); E. L. T. Henke, *Theologorum Saxonicorum consensus repetitus fidei vere Lutheranae* (1846); E. G. A. Böckel, *Die Bekenntnisschriften der evangelisch-reformirten Kirche* (1847); Heinrich Joseph Denzinger, *Enchiridion Symbolorum et Definitionum* (1854, with dozens of editions since); Edward Bean Underhill, *Confessions of Faith and Other Public Documents Illustrative of the History of the Baptist Churches of England in the Seventeenth Century* (1854); Wilhelm Gass, *Symbolik der griechischen Kirche* (1872); Philip Schaff, *Bibliotheca Symbolica Ecclesiae Universalis: The Creeds of Christendom* (1877); Williston Walker, *The Creeds and Platforms of Congregationalism* (1893); and J. J. Overbeck, *The Orthodox Confession of the Catholic and Apostolic Eastern Church of Peter Mogila* (1898).

This development was continued and expanded in the twentieth century: Karl E. F. Müller, *Die Bekenntnisschriften der reformierten Kirche* (1903); Jon Michalcescu, *Thēsauros tēs Orthodoxias: Die Bekenntnisse und die wichtigsten Glaubenszeugnisse der griechisch-orientalischen Kirche* (1904); W. J. McGlothlin, *Baptist Confessions of Faith* (1910); Eduard Schwartz, *Acta Conciliorum Oecumenicorum* (1914); G. Friedrich Bente, *Concordia Triglotta* (1921); Antoine Malvy and Marcel Viller, *La confession orthodoxe de Pierre Moghila* (1927); Caius Fabricius, *Corpus Confessionum* (1928–43); *Die Bekenntnisschriften der evangelisch-lutherischen Kirche* (1930); W. F. Schmidt and K. Schornbaum, *Die fränkischen Bekenntnisse: Eine Vorstufe der Augsburgischen Konfession* (1930); J. Michael Reu, *The Augsburg Confession: A Collection of Sources with an Historical Introduction* (1930); Wilhelm Niesel, *Bekenntnisschriften und Kirchenordnungen der nach Gottes Wort reformierten Kirche* (1938); Ioannēs Karmirēs, *Ta dogmatika kai symbolika mnēmeia tēs orthodoxou katholikēs ekklēsias* [The dogmatic and symbolic monuments of the Orthodox Catholic Church] (1952); Thomas F. Torrance, *The School of Faith: The Catechisms of the Reformed Church* (1959); Theodore G. Tappert et al., *The Book of Concord: The Confessions of the Evangelical Lutheran Church* (1959); William L. Lumpkin, *Baptist Confessions of Faith* (1959); Joseph Alberigo, *Conciliorum Oecumenicorum Decreta* (1962); Brian A. Gerrish, *The Faith of Christendom* (1963); John H. Leith, *Creeds of the Churches: A Reader in Christian Doctrine from the Bible to the Present* (1963); Arthur C. Cochrane, *Reformed Confessions of the Sixteenth Century* (1966); George Mastrantonis, *Augsburg and Constantinople: The Correspondence Between the Tübingen Theologians and Patriarch Jeremiah II of Constantinople on the Augsburg Confession* (1982); Howard John Loewen, *One Lord, One Church, One Hope, and One God: Mennonite Confessions of Faith* (1985); Irvin B. Horst, *Mennonite Confession of Faith Adopted April 21st, 1632, at Dordrecht, The Netherlands* (1988); Norman P. Tanner et al., *Decrees of the Ecumenical Councils* (1990); Mark Noll, *Confessions and Catechisms of the Reformation* (1991); Gerald Bray, *Documents of the English Reformation* (1994); Romeo Fabbri, *Confessioni di fede delle chiese cristiane* (1996); and Robert Kolb and Timothy Wengert, *The Book of Concord: The Confessions of the Evangelical Lutheran Church* (2000).

    Creeds and Confessions of Faith in the Christian Tradition seeks to continue that scholarly editorial tradition into the twenty-first century.

17.4. In Light of Their History, Do Creeds Have a Future as Well as a Past?

When the review of the history of creeds and confessions of faith that has occupied the preceding four chapters is confronted with the unique predicament of creedal Christianity in the modern age as this is being examined in the present chapter, the question becomes urgent: In light of their history, do creeds and confessions of faith have a future as well as a past? This question is, of course, bound up with the broader question of "the future of belief" itself[106]—bound up with it, but not iden-

---

106. Dewart 1966.

tical to it. There have certainly been many individual Christians, and even some entire Christian communities and churches—to cite modern examples, the Church of the Brethren, and the Disciples of Christ or "Christians," in the spirit of Thomas and Alexander Campbell[107]—who did not originally respond to the imperative to "confess with your lips and believe in your heart"[108] by composing a fixed creed or confession at all, until they were compelled to do something of the sort in the twentieth century.[109] Instead, they took as literally and permanently true the promise of Christ in the Gospel: "When they deliver you up, do not be anxious how you are to speak or what you are to say; for what you are to say will be given to you *in that hour;* for it is not you who speak, but the Spirit of your Father speaking through you,"[110] a promise that even so creedal and catholic a theologian as Augustine recommended as more important than any intellectual and scholarly preparation.[111] Nevertheless, just as the response to that imperative by the vast majority of churches through the centuries has taken the form of a confession or creed, so the future of creeds is of fundamental importance for the future of belief and for the future of the churches as well, even of churches that might not be thought of as "confessional" in the usual sense. Thus Williston Walker summarizes the experience of American Congregationalism in the nineteenth century, leading up to *The "Commission" Creed* of 1883:

> The free system of Congregationalism allows every church to formulate its own creed; but this confession is coming more and more to be employed as a local statement of faith, especially by newly formed churches. . . . Though imposed by no authority and accepted only in so far as it is its own commendation, it gives the Congregational body what no other considerable denomination of Christians in America pos-

107. *Dec Addr.*
108. Rom 10.9.
109. See *Design* of 1968 from the Disciples of Christ.
110. Mt 10.19–20; italics added.
111. Augustine *On Christian Doctrine* 4.15.32 (*NPNF*-I 2:585).

sesses,—a widely recognized creed, written in the language and expressing the thought of living men.[112]

Therefore Walker concludes his collection of *Creeds and Platforms of Congregationalism* with this statement of faith.

Without minimizing in any way the likelihood that changes in worldview during the twenty-first and twenty-second centuries will be even more drastic than those of the nineteenth and twentieth have been—in Robert Frost's striking metaphor, a hundred-yard dash followed by a pole vault—it is appropriate to be reminded by history that there has in fact been a vast diversity of worldviews, as well as of creedal forms and confessional genres, during the two millennia of Christian history. On first glance, the seventeenth-century *Westminster Confession of Faith* and the twentieth-century *Masai Creed,* when set alongside each other, may not seem even to belong to the same species, and the cultures in which they arose are poles apart.[113] And yet the continuity between them is all the more substantial because of that great diversity. For the history of conflict, compromise, and accommodation of Christian thought and teaching in relation to shifting worldviews suggests the following paradoxical generalization: there has never been any picture of the world, whether scientific or philosophical or even "mythological," with which the confession of the Christian faith has been entirely compatible, although undoubtedly it has found a better fit with some than with others; but there has also never been any picture of the world within which the confession of the faith has proved to be altogether impossible.[114] It does not appear unwarranted to propose that this paradox will continue to apply to the confessions and creeds of the future, if any.

Even those who have little or no use for creeds and confessions of faith are usually prepared to concede, often even with considerable enthusiasm, that the moral example and the ethical teachings of Jesus have some sort of permanent, even transcendent, value. In the words quoted earlier from Roden Noël, "What if men take to fol-

112. Walker, 582.
113. *West; Masai.*
114. *Laus Cov* 10.

lowing where He leads, / Weary of mumbling Athanasian creeds?"[115] The motto of Charles M. Sheldon's immensely influential novel, *In His Steps,* of 1897, "What would Jesus do?" is a populist expression of the same elevation of deeds over creeds, which has, in one form of another, asserted itself repeatedly, especially in the modern period. It is undeniable that there is an initial attractiveness and a haunting charm to the eloquent words of Albert Schweitzer as he concluded his account of the process by which, in the modern period, the orthodox confessional dogma about the person of Christ had steadily lost its credibility:

> We can find no designation which expresses what He is for us. He comes to us as One unknown, without a name, as of old, by the lake-side, He came to those men who knew Him not. He speaks to us the same word: "Follow thou me!" and sets us to the tasks which He has to fulfil for our time. He commands. And to those who obey Him, whether they be wise or simple, He will reveal Himself in the toils, the conflicts, the sufferings which they shall pass through in His fellowship, and, as an ineffable mystery, they shall learn in their own experience Who He is.[116]

Schweitzer himself obeyed this command "Follow thou me," which is enunciated repeatedly in the Gospel of Matthew,[117] by giving up positions of great cultural and academic prestige and devoting himself to a life of service as a medical missionary in French Equatorial Africa. But in twentieth-century Africa, as in first-century Judaea and fourth-century Asia Minor and sixteenth-century Europe, the full measure of obedience to that command could not stop short of facing another challenge, likewise enunciated in the Gospel of Matthew, "Who do you say that I am?" and of dealing with the answer of the apostle Peter to that question, "You are the Christ, the Son of the living God"[118]— which was a confession and a creed, and as such an indispensable com-

---

115. Roden Noël "The Red Flag."
116. Schweitzer [1906] 1961, 403.
117. Mt 4.19, 8.29, 9.19, 19.21 (AV).
118. Mt 16.15–16.

ponent of obedience to the command and imperative of Jesus Christ.[119] In the future, too, the command must lead to the question, and the question must lead to some sort of answer.

In the European Protestant theology that had, during the nineteenth and twentieth centuries, produced Albert Schweitzer and the many other critics of orthodox Christology whose "discomfort with creed" we have been summarizing in this chapter, the cultural and political crisis of the first half of the twentieth century answered the question "Do creeds and confessions have a future as well as a past?" in another and an even more dramatic way. The attempt by the ideology of National Socialism to fill the vacuum created by the decline of creedalism seemed, on the face of it, to provide the "German Christians" with the opportunity for a new and "postconfessional" alternative that would be relevant to a new era. But in *The Barmen Declaration* of 1934, which was a confession of faith, the signatories spoke out against "the errors of the 'German Christians' of the present Reich Church government which are devastating the church," and resolved to "confess the following evangelical truths," one of which was: "We reject the false doctrine, as though the church were permitted to abandon the forms of its message and order to its own pleasure or to changes in prevailing ideological and political convictions [*ihrem Belieben oder dem Wechsel der jeweils herrschenden weltanschaulichen und politischen Überzeugungen*]."[120] It would be foolish to imagine that the Christian faith will never be subjected to such pressures and temptations again, or that when it is, it will not be obliged yet again to "confess evangelical truths" and its "message" in some similar fashion.

At Barmen, this obligation to reject the "false doctrine" of National Socialism and of the German Christians was addressed by German Protestants—Lutheran, Reformed, and United—all of whom stood in one or another confessional tradition and who were therefore accustomed to the use of a creedal statement to combat heresy, even though for some of them the historic confessions had lost some of their authority.[121] But history suggests that such an obligation may also

---

119. See chapter 2 above, "The Creedal and Confessional Imperative."
120. *Barm* pr, 3.
121. For an overview of confessional authority in these churches, see Urban 1972.

evoke confessional statements from those who had resisted the idea. Even the Presbyterian critics of extreme confessionalism and defenders of revivalism were obliged, in the Cumberland Presbyterian *Confession of Faith* of 1814/88 and then in *The Auburn Declaration* of 1837, to employ the formal instrumentality of a confession of faith to make their point. Another instance was the issuance of new "confessions [*homologiai*]" by Eastern Orthodoxy during the sixteenth and seventeenth centuries, which are described in an earlier chapter[122] and are collected in various editions and in "Affirmations of Faith in Eastern Orthodoxy," Part Two of *Creeds and Confessions of Faith in the Christian Tradition*. The statement quoted earlier from Nikolaj Nikaronovič Glubokovský, "The West incessantly asks us for the symbolical books of Orthodoxy. We have no need of them. The faith of the seven first councils is sufficient for us," expressed the characteristic and historic Eastern view of confessions.[123] But such an answer was in fact rather disingenuous, because Eastern Orthodoxy had indeed found a "need for them" as a response to the direct, and above all the indirect, threat that had come from the Protestant confessionalisms of the Reformation and immediately post-Reformation periods, both Lutheran and Reformed, as well as from the Roman Catholic confessionalism of the Council of Florence and the Council of Trent: the translation of *The Augsburg Confession* into Greek and the confessional texts sent as epistles to the patriarch of Constantinople by Lutheranism;[124] *The Eastern Confession of the Christian Faith by Cyril Lucar* of 1629,[125] which was perceived as Calvinism disguised in Greek Orthodox raiment; and the "Latinism" and scholasticism that dominated much of Eastern Orthodox teaching in the theological academies, also in the Russian empire. In a series of confessional documents, therefore, the East was compelled, at least for a while, to adopt the format of the Reformation confessions as an expression for the systematic statement of Orthodox doctrine. In the future, too, the adherents of beliefs that Christians will again find it

122. See chapter 14.4 above, "The Eastern Confessions as Equal and Opposite Reactions."
123. See chapter 14.3 above, "The Sacred Tradition of the Seven Ecumenical Councils."
124. *Jer II I; Jer II 2–3.*
125. *Lucar.*

necessary to condemn will compose creeds and confessions of some kind, requiring a condign rejoinder, if perhaps a reluctant one.

The ecumenical movement of the nineteenth and twentieth centuries produced its own version of that thesis. The unofficial practice by individual Christians and entire church bodies of ignoring denominational borders, to the point of condoning and encouraging eucharistic intercommunion in spite of fundamental doctrinal differences even about the eucharist, has often been seen as synonymous with confessional indifference: indifference not simply to this or that specific confession of the past but to the very notion of a binding and separating confessional definition. Repeatedly, however, when the time has come to make such practices of fellowship official and to justify them both within and beyond the new fellowship, the justification has perforce taken the form of a confessional statement.[126] An ecumenism based on ignoring or forgetting the historic creeds and confessions of faith may well be condemned to repeat the process that had originally produced them. Thus the successive revisions of the formula for reunion and common declaration of the Church of South India in the first half of the twentieth century[127] were made necessary in part by the continuing authority of the mother churches from which the missions had originally come and to which the uniting churches had to give an account. But an even more pressing demand was the need of these uniting churches to give an account to their own membership and to one another of the principles underlying their unification.[128] Whatever new initiatives may arise in the continuing and increasingly urgent quest for Christian unity, it is inherently difficult to imagine their being able to dispense with the confessional statement, even if it is only a statement of why earlier confessional statements are thought no longer to be normative.

The history of creeds and confessions of faith likewise documents the complexity of their relation to personal faith—or, to invoke the distinction explained earlier, of the relation between *fides*

126. *Un Pres* 30.
127. *CSI 1929; CSI 1947.*
128. See chapter 4.4 above, "Faith and Order in the Ecumenical Confessional Dialogue."

quae creditur, "the faith which one believes," and *fides qua creditur,*
"the faith with which one believes."[129] After affirming concerning *The
Niceno-Constantinopolitan Creed,* "This is also my faith, because this
is the catholic faith,"[130] Augustine proceeded to show how completely
it had become *his* faith by articulating a speculative and yet deeply
existential theory of the trinitarian structure of the human soul. Similarly, commenting on the first article of *The Apostles' Creed,* "I believe in God, the Father almighty, maker of heaven and earth," which
raises all the questions about the doctrine of *creatio ex nihilo* that had
dogged theology in the age of medieval scholasticism and the additional questions that would dog theology in the age of modern evo-
lutionism, Luther trumped them all by affirming that the creed was
speaking here and now about him, Martin Luther, the offspring of the
natural sexual union of his parents: "I believe that God has created me
and all that exists."[131] And in his "Legend of the Grand Inquisitor"
F. M. Dostoevsky brought a prelate of the church, who turned out to
be an atheist with a correct and orthodox creed, into confrontation
with the living presence of the One whom that creed confessed.[132]

Perhaps an analogy may be helpful. When compact disks are
stacked on the shelves of a record store or a living room, there is nothing so static as CDs. In that form they can be shipped and stored, preserved inert literally for centuries, handed down from parents to children and grandchildren without ever being played or heard. They are
a commodity, listed in a catalog to be bought and sold. Yet it is their
very "inertness" and static quality, their continuity, that enables them,
at a moment's notice, to become suddenly dynamic in the sound of a
Beethoven quartet or Mozart's *Magic Flute*—or, for that matter, the
Symbolum Nicaenum of Johann Sebastian Bach's Mass in B Minor. Historically, that is precisely what creeds and confessions of faith have
repeatedly done through the centuries.

And they can go on doing it.

129. See chapter 2.2 above, "Faith Defined," and Syndogmaticon 1.1, 1.6.
130. Augustine *On the Trinity* 1.4.7 (*NPNF*–II 3:20).
131. *Luth Sm Cat* 2.1–2.
132. F. M. Dostoevsky *The Brothers Karamazov,* book 5, ch 5.

V. Bibliography

Abraham, Gerald, ed. 1968. *The Age of Humanism, 1540–1630.* Volume 4 of *New Oxford History of Music.* London: Oxford University Press.

Afanas'ev, Nikolaj. 1931. *Provincial'nija sobranija rimskoj imperii i vselenskie sobory* [Provincial gatherings of the Roman Empire and the ecumenical councils]. Belgrade: Zapiski Russkago Otdělný ottisk.

Ahlers, Rolf. 1986. *The Barmen Theological Declaration of 1934: The Archeology of a Confessional Text.* Lewiston, N.Y.: Edwin Mellen Press.

Ainslie, James L. 1940. *The Doctrines of Ministerial Order in the Reformed Churches of the Sixteenth and Seventeenth Centuries.* Edinburgh: T. and T. Clark.

Alberigo, Giuseppe, ed. 1991. *Christian Unity: The Council of Ferrara-Florence, 1438/39–1989.* Leuven: Leuven University Press.

Allen, Reginald E., ed. and tr. 1984–87. *The Dialogues of Plato.* New Haven and London: Yale University Press.

Andersen, Niels Knud. 1954. *Confessio Hafniensis: Den københavnske Bekendelse af 1530* [Confessio Hafniensis: The Copenhagen Confession of 1530]. Copenhagen: G. E. C. Gads Forlag.

Anderson, David, tr. 1980. *On the Holy Spirit,* by Saint Basil the Great. Crestwood, N.Y.: Saint Vladimir's Seminary Press.

Androutsos, Chrēstos. 1930. *Symbolikē ex epopseōs Orthodoxou* [Symbolics from an Orthodox perspective]. 2d ed. Athens: Typois I. Λ. Aleuropoulou.

———. 1956. *Dogmatikē tēs Orthodoxou Anatolikēs Ekklēsias* [Dogmatics of the Eastern Orthodox Church]. 2d ed. Athens: Ekdotikos Oikos "Astēr."

Arens, Edmund. 1989. *Bezeugen und Bekennen: Elementare Handlungen des Glaubens.* Düsseldorf: Patmos.

Arquillière, Henri Xavier. 1926. *Le plus ancien traite de l'Eglise: Jacques de Viterbe "De regimine christiano" (1301–1302). Etude des sources et édition critique.* Paris: G. Beauchesne.

Arrupe, Pedro. 1979–86. *Selected Letters and Addresses.* 5 vols. Edited by Jerome Aixala. Saint Louis, Mo.: Institute of Jesuit Sources.

Aulén, Gustaf. 1969. *Christus Victor: An Historical Study of the Three Main Types of the Idea of the Atonement.* Translated by A. G. Hebert. Foreword by Jaroslav Pelikan. London: S.P.C.K.

Bârlea, Octavian. 1989. *Die Konzile des 13.–15. Jahrhunderts und die ökumenische Frage.* Wiesbaden: Harrassowitz.

Barth, Karl. 1935. *Das Bekenntnis der Reformation und unser Bekennen.* Munich: Christian Kaiser Verlag.

———. 1959. *Protestant Thought from Rousseau to Ritschl.* Translated by Brian

Cozens. Introduction by Jaroslav Pelikan. New York: Harper and Brothers.

————. 1964. *The Heidelberg Catechism for Today*. Translated by Shirley C. Guthrie, Jr. Richmond, Va.: John Knox Press.

Bauer, Walter. 1971. *Orthodoxy and Heresy in Earliest Christianity*. Translated by the Philadelphia Seminar on Christian Origins. Edited by Robert A. Kraft and Gerhard Krodel. Philadelphia: Fortress Press.

Baumer, Franklin Le Van. 1960. *Religion and the Rise of Scepticism*. New York: Harcourt, Brace and World.

Baur, Ferdinand Christian. [1852] 1962. *Die Epochen der kirchlichen Geschichtschreibung*. Reprint ed. Hildesheim: Georg Olms Verlagsbuchhandlung.

Beck, Hildebrand. 1937. *Vorsehung und Vorherbestimmung in der theologischen Literatur der Byzantiner*. Rome: Pontificale Institutum Orientalium Studiorum.

Becker, Karl Josef. 1967. *Die Rechtfertigungslehre nach Domingo de Soto: Das Denken eines Konzilstellnehmers vor, in und nach Trient*. Rome: Gregorian University.

Békés, Gerard J., and Harding Meyer, eds. 1982. *Confessio fidei: International Ecumenical Colloquium, Rome, 3–8 November 1980*. Rome: Pontificio Ateneo S. Anselmo.

Benz, Ernst. 1952. *Die Ostkirche im Lichte der protestantischen Geschichtschreibung von der Reformation bis zur Gegenwart*. Freiburg: K. Alber.

Besançon, Alain. 2000. *The Forbidden Image: An Intellectual History of Iconoclasm*. Translated by Jane Marie Todd. Chicago: University of Chicago Press.

Bethune-Baker, James Franklin. 1901. *The Meaning of Homoousios in the "Constantinopolitan" Creed*. Cambridge: Cambridge University Press.

Beyer, Ulrich. 1965. *Abendmahl und Messe: Sinn und Recht der 80. Frage des Heidelberger Katechismus*. Neukirchen-Vluyn: Neukirchener Verlag des Erziehungsvereins.

Boelens, Wim L. 1964. *Die Arnoldshainer Abendmahlsthesen: Die Suche nach einem Abendmahlskonsens in der Evangelischen Kirche in Deutschland, 1947–1957, und eine Würdigung aus katholischer Sicht*. Assen: Van Gorcum.

Boespflug, François, and Nicolas Lossky, eds. 1987. *Nicée II, 787–1987: Douze siècles d'images religieuses*. Paris: Editions du Cerf.

Bogolepov, Aleksandr Aleksandrovich. 1963. "Which Councils Are Recognized as Ecumenical?" *Saint Vladimir's Seminary Quarterly* 7–2:54–72.

Bornkamm, Günther. 1939. "Das Wort Jesu vom Bekennen." *Pastoraltheologie* 34:108–18.

Boyd, William Kenneth. 1905. *The Ecclesiastical Edicts of the Theodosian Code*. New York: Columbia University Press.

Bradow, Charles King. 1960. "The Career and Confession of Cyril Loukaris: The Greek Orthodox Church and Its Relations with Western Christians

(1543–1638).” Ph.D. diss., Ohio State University. Ann Arbor, Mich.: University Microfilms.

Bretschneider, Karl Gottlieb. 1841. *Die Unzulässigkeit des Symbolzwangs in der evangelischen Kirche, aus den symbolischen Büchern selbst und deren Beschaffenheit nachgewiesen für alle Freunde der Wahrheit.* Leipzig: F. C. W. Vogel.

Brilioth, Yngve. 1933. *The Anglican Revival: Studies in the Oxford Movement.* 2d ed. London: Longmans, Green.

Brown, Peter. 2000. *Augustine of Hippo: A Biography.* New ed. with Epilogue. Berkeley: University of California Press.

Burgsmüller, Alfred, and Rudolf Weth, eds. 1983. *Die Barmer Theologische Erklärung: Einführung und Dokumentation.* Foreword by Eduard Lohse. Neukirchen-Vluyn: Neukirchener Verlag des Erziehungsvereins.

Butler, Charles. 1816. *An Historical and Literary Account of the Formularies, Confessions of Faith, or Symbolical Books of the Roman Catholic, Greek, and Principal Protestant Churches.* London: A. J. Valpy.

Campenhausen, Hans Freiherr von. 1969. *Ecclesiastical Authority and Spiritual Power in the Church of the First Three Centuries.* Translated by J. A. Baker. Stanford, Calif.: Stanford University Press.

————. 1972. “Das Bekenntnis im Urchristentum.” *Zeitschrift für die neutestamentliche Wissenschaft und die Kunde der Alten Kirche* 63:210–53.

Capelle, Bernard. 1954. “Le Pape Léon III et la ‘Filioque.’” In *1054–1954, L’Eglise et les Eglises: Neuf siècles de douloureuse séparation entre l’Orient et l’Occident,* 1:309–22. Belgium: Editions de Chevetogne.

————. 1955–67. *Travaux liturgiques de doctrine et d’histoire.* 3 vols. Louvain: Centre liturgique, Abbaye du Mont César.

Carrington, Philip. 1940. *The Primitive Christian Catechism: A Study in the Epistles.* Cambridge: Cambridge University Press.

Caspar, Erich. 1926. *Die älteste römische Bischofsliste: Kritische Studien zum Formproblem des eusebianischen Kanons sowie zur Geschichte der ältesten Bischofslisten und ihrer Entstehung aus apostolischen Sukzessionsreihen.* Berlin: Deutsche Verlagsgesellschaft für Politik und Geschichte.

Cavadini, John C. 1993. *The Last Christology of the West: Adoptionism in Spain and Gaul, 785–820.* Philadelphia: University of Pennsylvania Press.

Chadwick, Henry, ed. and tr. 1953. *Contra Celsum,* by Origen. Cambridge: Cambridge University Press.

————. 1992. *Boethius: The Consolations of Music, Logic, Theology, and Philosophy.* Oxford: Clarendon Paperbacks.

Chenu, Marie-Dominique. 1964. *Toward Understanding Saint Thomas.* Translated by A.-M. Landry and D. Hughes. Chicago: Henry Regnery.

Chomjakov, Aleksej Stepanovič. [1907] 1995. *Sočinenija bogoslovskie* [Theological works]. Reprint ed. Saint Petersburg: Nauka.

Cochrane, Arthur C. 1962. *The Church’s Confession Under Hitler.* Philadelphia: Westminster Press.

Cochrane, Charles Norris. 1944. *Christianity and Classical Culture: A Study of*

Thought and Action from Augustus to Augustine. London: Oxford University Press.

Coenen, Lothar. 1963. *Handbuch zum Heidelberger Katechismus*. Neukirchen-Vluyn: Neukirchener Verlag des Erziehungsvereins.

Colish, Marcia L. 1994. *Peter Lombard*. 2 vols. Leiden: E. J. Brill.

———. 1997. *Medieval Foundations of the Western Intellectual Tradition, 400–1400*. New Haven and London: Yale University Press.

Congar, Yves. 1972. "Reception as an Ecclesiological Reality." In Giuseppe Alberigo and Anton Weiler, eds., *Election and Consensus in the Church*, 43–68. New York: Herder and Herder.

Creighton, Mandell. 1901–2. "Introductory Note." In *The Cambridge Modern History*, 1:1–6. Cambridge: Cambridge University Press.

Cullmann, Oscar. 1949. *The Earliest Christian Confessions*. Translated by J. K. S. Reid. London: Lutterworth Press.

Curtius, Ernst Robert. 1953. *European Literature and the Latin Middle Ages*. Translated by Willard R. Trask. Princeton, N.J.: Princeton University Press.

Daley, Brian E., ed. and tr. 1998. *On the Dormition of Mary: Early Patristic Homilies*. Crestwood, N.Y.: Saint Vladimir's Seminary Press.

Daniel, Evan. 1901. *The Prayer-Book: Its History, Language, and Contents*. London: W. Gardner, Darton.

Daniélou, Jean. 1955. *Origen*. Translated by Walter Mitchell. New York: Sheed and Ward.

———. 1960. *From Shadows to Reality: Studies in the Biblical Typology of the Fathers*. Translated by Wulstan Hibberd. Westminster, Md.: Newman Press.

Davey, Colin. 1987. *Pioneer for Unity: Metrophanes Kritopoulos (1589–1639) and Relations Between the Orthodox, Roman Catholic and Reformed Churches*. London: British Council of Churches.

David, Zdeněk V. 1999. "Utraquists, Lutherans, and the Bohemian Confession of 1575." *Church History* 68:294–336.

De Jong, Peter Ymen, ed. 1968. *Crisis in the Reformed Churches: Essays in Commemoration of the Great Synod of Dort, 1618–1619*. Grand Rapids, Mich.: Reformed Fellowship.

DeSimone, Russell J. 1970. *The Treatise of Novatian, the Roman Presbyter, on the Trinity: A Study of the Text and the Doctrine*. Rome: Institutum Patristicum Augustinianum.

Devadutt, V. E. 1949. "What Is an Indigenous Theology? (with Special Reference to India)." *ER* 2-I:40–51.

Dewart, Leslie. 1966. *The Future of Belief: Theism in a World Come of Age*. New York: Herder and Herder.

Diekamp, Franz. 1899. *Die origenistischen Streitigkeiten im sechsten Jahrhundert und das fünfte allgemeine Concil*. Münster: Aschendorff.

Dietrich, Donald J. 1988. *Catholic Citizens in the Third Reich: Psycho-Social Principles and Moral Reasoning*. New Brunswick, N.J.: Transaction Books.

Dingel, Irene. 1996. *Concordia controversa: Die öffentlichen Diskussionen um das lutherische Konkordienwerk am Ende des 16. Jahrhunderts.* Gütersloh: Gütersloher Verlagshaus.

Dobschütz, Ernst von. 1932. *Das Apostolicum in biblisch-theologischer Beleuchtung.* Giessen: Adolf Töpelmann.

Donovan, Vincent J. 1982. *Christianity Rediscovered.* 2d ed. Maryknoll, N.Y.: Orbis Books.

Dowey, Edward A., Jr. 1952. *The Knowledge of God in Calvin's Theology.* New York: Columbia University Press.

———. 1968. *A Commentary on the Confession of 1967 and an Introduction to "The Book of Confessions."* Philadelphia: Westminster Press.

Draper, Jonathan, ed. 1988. *Communion and Episcopacy: Essays to Mark the Centenary of the Chicago-Lambeth Quadrilateral.* Oxford: Ripon College Cuddesdon.

Driscoll, Jeremy. 1991. *The "Ad Monachos" of Evagrius Ponticus: Its Structure and a Select Commentary.* Rome: Benedictina Edizioni Abbazia S. Paolo.

Driscoll, Michael S. 1999. *Alcuin et la pénitence à l'époque carolingienne.* Münster: Aschendorff.

Duval, André. 1985. *Des sacrements au Concile de Trente.* Paris: Editions du Cerf.

Dvornik, Francis. 1948. *The Photian Schism, History and Legend.* Cambridge: Cambridge University Press.

———. 1958. *The Idea of Apostolicity and the Legend of the Apostle Andrew.* Cambridge, Mass.: Harvard University Press.

———. 1970. *Byzantine Missions Among the Slavs: SS. Constantine-Cyril and Methodius.* New Brunswick, N.J.: Rutgers University Press.

Ehrenström, Nils, and Günther Gassmann. 1979. *Confessions in Dialogue: Survey of Bilateral Conversations Among World Confessional Families.* 4th ed. Geneva: World Council of Churches.

Elert, Werner. 1957. *Der Ausgang der altkirchlichen Christologie: Eine Untersuchung über Theodor von Pharan und seine Zeit als Einführung in die alte Dogmengeschichte.* Edited by Wilhelm Maurer and Elisabeth Bergsträsser. Berlin: Lutherisches Verlagshaus.

———. 1962. *The Structure of Lutheranism.* Translated by Walter A. Hansen. Foreword by Jaroslav Pelikan. Saint Louis, Mo.: Concordia.

———. 1966. *Eucharist and Church Fellowship in the First Four Centuries.* Translated by Norman E. Nagel. Saint Louis, Mo.: Concordia.

Ericksen, Robert P. 1985. *Theologians Under Hitler: Gerhard Kittel, Paul Althaus, and Emanuel Hirsch.* New Haven and London: Yale University Press.

———, and Susannah Heschel, eds. 1999. *Betrayal: German Churches and the Holocaust.* Minneapolis, Minn.: Fortress Press.

Eschmann, Ignatius Theodore. 1997. *The Ethics of Saint Thomas Aquinas: Two Courses.* Edited by Edward A. Synan. Toronto: Pontifical Institute of Mediaeval Studies.

Eynde, Damien van den. 1933. *Les normes de l'enseignement chrétien dans la littérature patristique des trois premiers siècles.* Paris: Gabalda et Fils.

Feige, Gerhard. 1991. *Die Lehre Markells von Ankyra in der Darstellung seiner Gegner.* Leipzig: Benno.

Feine, Paul. 1925. *Die Gestalt des apostolischen Glaubensbekenntnisses in der Zeit des Neuen Testaments.* Leipzig: Dörffling und Franke.

Ferm, Vergilius Ture Anselm, ed. 1945. *An Encyclopedia of Religion.* New York: Philosophical Library.

Flesseman-Van Leer, Ellen. 1954. *Tradition and Scripture in the Early Church.* Assen: Van Gorcum.

Fletcher, Richard. 1997. *The Barbarian Conversion: From Paganism to Christianity.* New York: Henry Holt.

Florovsky, Georges V. 1972–89. *Collected Works.* 14 vols. Belmont, Mass.: Nordland.

Forbes, Alexander Penrose. 1890. *An Explanation of the Thirty-Nine Articles.* 6th ed. London: Parker.

Frei, Hans W. 1974. *The Eclipse of Biblical Narrative: A Study in Eighteenth- and Nineteenth-Century Hermeneutics.* New Haven and London: Yale University Press.

Freitag, Josef. 1991. *Sacramentum ordinis auf dem Konzil von Trient: Ausgeblendeter Dissens und erreichter Konsens.* Innsbruck: Tyrolia-Verlag.

Frend, W. H. C. 1952. *The Donatist Church: A Movement of Protest in Roman North Africa.* Oxford: Clarendon Press.

Frye, Northrop. 1982. *Great Code: The Bible and Literature.* New York: Harcourt Brace Jovanovich.

Fyzee, Asaf Ali Asghar, ed. 1942. *A Shi'ite Creed.* London: Oxford University Press.

Garet, Ronald R. 1985. "Comparative Normative Hermeneutics: Scripture, Literature, Constitution." *Southern California Law Review* 58:35–134.

Gassmann, Günther. 1979. *Konzeptionen der Einheit in der Bewegung für Glauben und Kirchenverfassung, 1910–1937.* Göttingen: Vandenhoeck und Ruprecht.

———, ed. 1993. *Documentary History of Faith and Order, 1963–1993.* Geneva: WCC Publications.

———, and Scott H. Hendrix. 1999. *Fortress Introduction to the Lutheran Confessions.* Minneapolis, Minn.: Fortress Press.

Geanakoplos, Deno John. 1966. "The Council of Florence (1438–39) and the Problem of Union Between the Byzantine and Latin Churches." In *Byzantine East and Latin West: Two Worlds of Christendom in Middle Ages and Renaissance; Studies in Ecclesiastical and Cultural History,* 84–109. New York: Harper Torchbooks.

Geary, Patrick. 1990. *Furta Sacra: Thefts of Relics in the Central Middle Ages.* Revised ed. Princeton, N.J.: Princeton University Press.

Geiselmann, Josef Rupert. 1966. *The Meaning of Tradition.* Translated by W. J. O'Hara. New York: Herder and Herder.

Gensichen, Hans-Werner. 1967. *We Condemn: How Luther and Sixteenth-Cen-*

tury Lutheranism Condemned False Doctrine. Translated by Herbert J. A.
Bouman. Saint Louis, Mo.: Concordia.

Georgi, Curt Robert Armin. 1940. *Die Confessio Dosithei (Jerusalem, 1672):
Geschichte, Inhalt und Bedeutung.* Munich: Ernst Reinhardt.

Giakalis, Ambrosios. 1994. *Images of the Divine: The Theology of Icons at
the Seventh Ecumenical Council.* Foreword by Henry Chadwick. Leiden:
E. J. Brill.

Gibbon, Edward. [1776–88] 1896–1900. *The History of the Decline and Fall
of the Roman Empire.* Edited by J. B. Bury. 7 vols. London: Methuen.

Gill, Joseph. 1965. *Personalities of the Council of Florence, and Other Essays.*
New York: Barnes and Noble.

———. 1982. *The Council of Florence.* Revised ed. New York: AMS Press.

Gilson, Etienne. [1951] 1957. "Historical Research and the Future of Scholasticism." In *A Gilson Reader,* 156–67. Edited with an Introduction by
Anton C. Pegis. Garden City, N.Y.: Hanover House.

———. 1960. *Heloise and Abelard.* Translated by L. K. Shook. Ann Arbor:
University of Michigan Press.

Glendon, Mary Ann. 2001. *A World Made New: Eleanor Roosevelt and the
Universal Declaration of Human Rights.* New York: Random House.

Gollwitzer, Helmut. 1962. "Die Bedeutung des Bekenntnisses für die Kirche."
In Helmut Gollwitzer and Hellmut Traub, eds., *Hören und Handeln:
Festschrift für Ernst Wolf zum 60. Geburtstag,* 153–90. Munich: Chris-
tian Kaiser Verlag.

Golubev, Stefan Timofeevič. 1883–98. *Kievský Mitropolit' Petr' Mogila i jego
spodvižniki* [The Metropolitan of Kiev Peter Mogila and his associates].
2 vols. Kiev: H. I. Korcak-Novický.

Grabmann, Martin. [1909] 1957. *Die Geschichte der scholastischen Methode.*
2 vols. Reprint ed. Graz: Akademische Druck- und Verlagsgesellschaft.

Graus, František. [1969] 1971. "The Crisis of the Middle Ages and the Hussites." Translated by James J. Heaney. In Steven E. Ozment, ed., *The Reformation in Medieval Perspective,* 76–103. Chicago: Quadrangle Books.

Greenslade, S. L. 1953. *Schism in the Early Church.* New York: Harper and
Brothers.

Gregorios, Paulos, William H. Lazareth, and Nikos A. Nissiotis, eds. 1981.
*Does Chalcedon Divide or Unite? Towards Convergence in Orthodox
Christology.* Geneva: World Council of Churches.

Grillmeier, Aloys. 1970. "Konzil und Rezeption." *Theologie und Philosophie*
45:321–52.

———, and Heinrich Bacht, eds. 1951–54. *Daz Konzil von Chalkedon: Geschichte und Gegenwart.* 3 vols. Würzburg: Echter Verlag.

Gutteridge, Richard. 1976. *Open Thy Mouth for the Dumb! The German Evangelical Church and the Jews, 1879–1950.* Oxford: Blackwell.

Hadjiantoniou, Georgios A. 1961. *Protestant Patriarch: The Life of Cyril Lu-
caris, 1572–1638, Patriarch of Constantinople.* Richmond, Va.: John
Knox Press.

Hague, Dyson. 1893. *The Protestantism of the Prayer Book*. 3d ed. London: Church Association.

Hajjar, Joseph N. 1962. *Le synode permanent (Synodos endēmousa) dans l'Eglise byzantine des origines au XIe siècle*. Rome: Pontificale Institutum Orientalium Studiorum.

Halecki, Oskar. 1958. *From Florence to Brest (1439-1596)*. Rome: Sacrum Poloniae Millennium.

Hall, David W., ed. 1995. *The Practice of Confessional Subscription*. Lanham, Md.: University Press of America.

Hamilton, Ian W. F. 1990. *The Erosion of Calvinist Orthodoxy: Seceders and Subscription in Scottish Presbyterianism*. Edinburgh: Rutherford House.

Hansen, Bent Smidt. 1986. "Indigenization of Worship: A Concern Among South Indian Christians." In Asko Parpola and Bent Smidt Hansen, eds., *South Asian Religion and Society*, 236-62. London: Curzon Press.

Harnack, Adolf. [1900] 1957a. *What Is Christianity?* Translated by Thomas Bailey Saunders. Reprint ed. Introduction by Rudolf Bultmann. New York: Harper Torchbooks.

———. [1889-91] 1957b. *Outlines of the History of Dogma*. Translated by Edwin Knox Mitchell. Reprint ed. Introduction by Philip Rieff. Boston: Starr King Press.

———. [1924] 1960. *Marcion: Das Evangelium vom fremden Gott. Eine Monographie zur Geschichte der Grundlegung der katholischen Kirche*. 2d ed. Reprint ed. Leipzig: J. C. Hinrichs.

———. [1908] 1961a. *The Mission and Expansion of Christianity in the First Three Centuries*. Translated by James Moffatt. Reprint ed. Introduction by Jaroslav Pelikan. New York: Harper Torchbooks.

———. [1893] 1961b. *History of Dogma*. Translated from the third German edition by Neil Buchanan. 7 vols. Reprint ed. New York: Dover.

Hauck, Albert. 1907. "Die Rezeption und die Umbildung der allgemeinen Synoden im Mittelalter." *Historische Vierteljahrschrift* 10:465-82.

Haugh, Richard. 1975. *Photius and the Carolingians: The Trinitarian Controversy*. Belmont, Mass.: Nordland.

Hazeltine, Harold Dexter. 1926. "Roman and Canon Law in the Middle Ages." *Cambridge Medieval History*, 5:697-764. Cambridge: Cambridge University Press.

Heijting, Willem. 1989. *De catechismi en confessies in de Nederlandse reformatie tot 1585* [The catechisms and confessions in the Dutch Reformation to 1585]. 2 vols. Nieuwkoop: De Graaf.

Heim, S. Mark, ed. 1991. *Faith to Creed: Ecumenical Perspectives on the Affirmation of the Apostolic Faith in the Fourth Century*. Commission on Faith and Order of the National Council of Churches of Christ in the U.S.A. Grand Rapids, Mich.: William B. Eerdmans.

Higham, Florence May Greir Evans. 1962. *Catholic and Reformed: A Study of the Anglican Church, 1559-1662*. London: S.P.C.K.

Hildebrandt, Walter, and Rudolf Zimmermann. 1938. *Bedeutung und Geschichte des zweiten Helvetischen Bekenntnisses*. Zurich: Zwingli-Verlag.

Hillman, Eugene. 1993. *Toward an African Christianity: Inculturation Applied.* New York: Paulist Press.

Hirsch, Emanuel. 1960. *Geschichte der neuern evangelischen Theologie im Zusammenhang mit den allgemeinen Bewegungen des europäischen Denkens.* 5 vols. Gütersloh: C. Bertelsmann Verlag.

Hodgson, Peter C. 1966. *The Formation of Historical Theology: A Study of Ferdinand Christian Baur.* New York: Harper and Row.

Hofmann, Rudolph. 1857. *Symbolik oder systematische Darstellung des symbolischen Lehrbegriffs der verschiedenen christlichen Kirchen und namhaften Sekten.* Leipzig: Friedrich Voigt.

Holl, Karl. [1919] 1928. "Zur Auslegung des 2. Artikels des sog. apostolischen Glaubensbekenntnisses." In *Gesammelte Aufsätze zur Kirchengeschichte,* 2:115–28. Tübingen: J. C. B. Mohr (Paul Siebeck).

Horn, Stephan Otto. 1982. *Petrou Kathedra: Der Bischof von Rom und die Synoden von Ephesus (449) und Chalcedon.* Paderborn: Verlag Bonifatius-Druckerei.

Huhn, Joseph. 1954. *Das Geheimnis der Jungfrau-Mutter Maria nach dem Kirchenvater Ambrosius.* Würzburg: Echter Verlag.

Huizing, Petrus, and Knut Walf. 1983. *The Ecumenical Council: Its Significance in the Constitution of the Church.* Edinburgh: T. and T. Clark.

Hutchison, William R. 1987. *Errand to the World: American Protestant Thought and Foreign Missions.* Chicago: University of Chicago Press.

Jay, Eric George, tr. 1954. *Origen's Treatise on Prayer.* London: S.P.C.K.

Jedin, Hubert. 1946. *Katholische Reformation oder Gegenreformation? Ein Versuch zur Klärung der Begriffe nebst einer Jubiläumsbetrachtung über das Trienter Konzil.* Lucerne: Josef Stocker.

———. 1957–61. *A History of the Council of Trent.* Translated by Ernest Graf. Saint Louis, Mo.: Herder.

Jenny-Kappers, Theodora. 1986. *Muttergöttin und Gottesmutter in Ephesos: Von Artemis zu Maria.* Zurich: Daimon.

Jobert, Ambroise. 1974. *De Luther à Mohila: La Pologne dans la crise de la Chrétienté, 1517–1648.* Paris: Institut d'études slaves.

Jones, Arnold Hugh Martin. 1966. *Were Ancient Heresies Disguised Social Movements?* Philadelphia: Fortress Press.

Jugie, Martin. 1944. *La mort et l'assomption de la Sainte Vierge: Etude historico-doctrinale.* Rome: Studi e Testi.

Julian, John. [1907] 1957. *A Dictionary of Hymnology, Setting Forth the Origin and History of Christian Hymns of All Ages and Nations.* Reprint ed. 2 vols. New York: Dover.

Jüngel, Eberhard. 1968. "Bekennen und Bekenntnis." In Siegfried Herrmann and Oskar Söhngen, eds., *Theologie in Geschichte und Kunst: Walter Elliger zum 65. Geburtstag,* 94–105. Witten: Luther Verlag.

Jürgens, Heiko. 1972. *Pompa diaboli: Die lateinischen Kirchenväter und das antike Theater.* Stuttgart: W. Kohlhammer.

Kallis, Anastasios, ed. 1989. *Liturgie: Die Göttliche Liturgie der Orthodoxen*

Kirche Deutsch—Griechisch—Kirchenslawisch. Mainz: Matthias-Grüne-wald-Verlag.

Kamen, Henry Arthur Francis. 1998. *The Spanish Inquisition: A Historical Revision*. New Haven and London: Yale University Press.

Kannengiesser, Charles. 1970. "La date de l'Apologie d'Athanase 'Contre les païens' et 'Sur l'incarnation du Verbe.'" *Recherches de Science Religieuse* 58:383–428.

Karmirēs, Iōannēs N., ed. 1937. *Mētrophanēs ho Kritopoulos kai hē anekdotos allēgographia autou*. Athens: Praskeua Leōnē.

Kartašev, Anton Vladimirovič. 1932. *Na put'ach k vselenskomu soboru* [On the way to an ecumenical council]. Paris: YMCA Press.

———. 1963. *Vselenskie sobory* [The ecumenical councils]. Paris: Izdanie Oso-bago komiteta pod predsědatel'stvom episkopa Sil'vestra.

Kellner, Menachem Marc. 1986. *Dogma in Medieval Jewish Thought: From Maimonides to Abravanel*. New York: Oxford University Press.

Kelly, John Norman Davidson. 1958. *Early Christian Doctrines*. New York: Harper and Brothers.

———. 1964. *The Athanasian Creed*. The Paddock Lectures for 1962–63. New York: Harper and Row.

Ker, Ian Turnbull, and Alan G. Hill, eds. 1990. *Newman After a Hundred Years*. Oxford: Clarendon Press.

Kilmartin, Edward J. 1998. *The Eucharist in the West: History and Theology*. Edited by Robert J. Daly. Collegeville, Minn.: Liturgical Press.

Kinzig, Wolfram, Christoph Markschies, and Markus Vinzent. 1999. *Tauffragen und Bekenntnis: Studien zur sogenannten "Traditio apostolica," zu den "Interrogationes de fide" und zum "Römischen Glaubensbekenntnis."* Berlin: Walter de Gruyter, 1999.

Koch, Ernst. 1968. *Die Theologie der Confessio Helvetica Posterior*. Neukirchen-Vluyn: Neukirchener Verlag des Erziehungsvereins.

Krajčar, Joannes, ed. 1976. *Acta Slavica Concilii Florentini: Narrationes et Documenta*. Rome: Pontificium Institutum Orientaliorum Studiorum.

Krämer, Werner. 1980. *Konsens und Rezeption: Verfassungsprinzipien der Kirche im Basler Konziliarismus*. Münster: Aschendorff.

Krauth, Charles Porterfield. [1899] 1963. *The Conservative Reformation and Its Theology*. Reprint ed. Minneapolis, Minn.: Augsburg.

Kropatschek, Friedrich Wilhelm. 1904. *Das Schriftprinzip der lutherischen Kirche: Geschichtliche und dogmatische Untersuchungen*. Vol. 1 (all published). Leipzig: A. Deichertsche Verlagsbuchhandlung Nachfolger.

Kuitert, Harminus Martinus. 1986. *Everything Is Politics but Politics Is Not Everything: A Theological Perspective on Faith and Politics*. Translated by John Bowden. Grand Rapids, Mich.: William B. Eerdmans.

Küppers, Werner, Peter Hauptmann, and Friedrich Baser. 1964. *Symbolik der kleineren Kirchen, Freikirchen und Sekten des Westens*. Stuttgart: A. Hiersemann.

Kuttner, Stephan G. 1960. *Harmony from Dissonance: An Interpretation of Medieval Canon Law*. Latrobe, Pa.: Archabbey Press.

Labunka, Miroslav. 1990. *Mitropolit Ilarion i joho pisannja* [Metropolitan Ilarion and his writings]. Rome: Ukrainian Catholic University.

Lacko, Michael. 1966. *The Union of Užhorod*. Cleveland, Ohio: Slovak Institute.

Landgraf, Artur Michael. 1952–56. *Dogmengeschichte der Frühscholastik*. 4 vols. Regensburg: Verlag Friedrich Pustet.

Laqueur, Walter, and Barry Rubin, eds. 1989. *The Human Rights Reader*. Revised ed. New York: Meridian Books.

Latourette, Kenneth Scott. 1937–45. *A History of the Expansion of Christianity*. 7 vols. New York: Harper and Brothers.

Lebedev, Aleksei Petrovič. 1904. *Vselenskie sobori IV i V věkov* [The ecumenical councils of the fourth and fifth centuries]. 3d ed. Saint Petersburg: I. L. Tusov.

Lehmann, Karl, and Wolfhart Pannenberg, eds. 1982. *Glaubensbekenntnis und Kirchengemeinschaft: Das Modell des Konzils von Konstantinopel (381)*. Göttingen: Vandenhoeck und Ruprecht.

Lerch, David. 1950. *Isaaks Opferung christlich gedeutet*. Tübingen: J. C. B. Mohr (Paul Siebeck).

Lewis, Bernard. 1997. *The Future of the Middle East*. London: Phoenix.

Lewy, Guenter. 1964. *The Catholic Church and Nazi Germany*. New York: McGraw-Hill.

L'Huillier, Peter. 1996. *The Church of the Ancient Councils: The Disciplinary Work of the First Four Ecumenical Councils*. Crestwood, N.Y.: Saint Vladimir's Seminary Press.

Lietzmann, Hans. 1966. *Symbolstudien I–XIV*. Darmstadt: Wissenschaftliche Buchgesellschaft.

Lindbeck, George A. 1984. *The Nature of Doctrine: Religion and Theology in a Postliberal Age*. Philadelphia: Westminster Press.

Link, Hans-Georg. 1998. *Bekennen und Bekenntnis*. Göttingen: Vandenhoeck und Ruprecht.

Littell, Franklin H. 1958. *The Anabaptist View of the Church: A Study in the Origins of Sectarian Protestantism*. 2d ed. Boston: Starr King Press.

Lubac, Henri de. 1998. *Medieval Exegesis*. Translated by Mark Sebanc. Grand Rapids, Mich.: William B. Eerdmans.

McCambley, Casimir, tr. 1987. *Commentary on the Song of Songs*, by Gregory of Nyssa. Preface by Panagiotes Chrestou. Brookline, Mass.: Hellenic College Press.

Macholz, Waldemar Karl Ludwig. 1902. *Spuren binitarischer Denkweise im Abendlande seit Tertullian*. Jena: A. Kämpfe.

McInerny, Ralph. 1997. *Ethica Thomistica: The Moral Philosophy of Thomas Aquinas*. Revised ed. Washington, D.C.: Catholic University of America Press.

McNeill, John Thomas. 1964. *Unitive Protestantism: The Ecumenical Spirit and Its Persistent Expression*. Revised ed. Richmond, Va.: John Knox Press.

———, ed. 1960. John Calvin. *Institutes of the Christian Religion*. Translated by Ford Lewis Battles. 2 vols. Philadelphia: Westminster Press.

————, Matthew Spinka, and Harold Rideout Willoughby, eds. 1939. *Environmental Factors in Christian History*. Chicago: University of Chicago Press.

Maichle, Albert. 1929. *Der Kanon der biblischen Bücher und das Konzil von Trient*. Freiburg: Herder.

Mananzan, Mary John. 1974. *The "Language Game" of Confessing One's Belief: A Wittgensteinian-Austinian Approach to the Linguistic Analysis of Creedal Statements*. Tübingen: M. Niemeyer.

Margerie, Bernard de. 1982. *The Christian Trinity in History*. Translated by Edmund J. Fortman. Foreword by Jaroslav Pelikan. Still River, Mass.: Saint Bede's Publications.

Marx, Hans Jürgen. 1977. *Filioque und Verbot eines anderen Glaubens auf dem Florentinum: Zum Pluralismus in dogmatischen Formeln*. Cologne: Steyler Verlag.

Maurer, Wilhelm. 1939. *Bekenntnis und Sakrament: Ein Beitrag zur Entstehung der christlichen Konfessionen*. Berlin: Töpelmann.

Maxwell, John Francis. 1975. *Slavery and the Catholic Church: The History of Catholic Teaching Concerning the Moral Legitimacy of the Institution of Slavery*. Foreword by Lord Wilberforce. Chichester: Anti-Slavery Society for the Protection of Human Rights.

May, Gerhard. 1994. *Creatio ex nihilo: The Doctrine of "Creation out of Nothing" in Early Christian Thought*. Translated by A. S. Worrall. Edinburgh: T. and T. Clark.

Mayer, Frederick Emanuel. 1954. *The Religious Bodies of America*. Saint Louis, Mo.: Concordia.

Mehl, Roger. 1971. "La place de la confession de foi dans l'élaboration dogmatique." *Foi et Vie* 70:214–25.

Metz, Wulf. 1970. *Necessitas satisfactionis? Eine systematische Studie zu den Fragen 12–18 des Heidelberger Katechismus und zur Theologie des Zacharias Ursinus*. Zurich: Zwingli-Verlag.

Meyendorff, John. 1966. *Orthodoxy and Catholicity*. New York: Sheed and Ward.

————. 1982. *The Byzantine Legacy in the Orthodox Church*. Crestwood, N.Y.: Saint Vladimir's Seminary Press.

————. 1989. *Imperial Unity and Christian Divisions: The Church, 450–680 A.D.* Crestwood, N.Y.: Saint Vladimir's Seminary Press.

————. 1996. *The Orthodox Church: Its Past and Its Role in the World Today*. Crestwood, N.Y.: Saint Vladimir's Seminary Press.

Meyendorff, Paul, ed. and tr. 1984. *Saint Germanus of Constantinople on the Divine Liturgy*. Crestwood, N.Y.: Saint Vladimir's Seminary Press.

Middleton, Robert Dudley. 1950. *Newman at Oxford: His Religious Development*. London: Oxford University Press.

————. 1951. "Tract Ninety." *Journal of Ecclesiastical History* 2:81–101.

Möhler, Johann Adam. [1832] 1958. *Symbolik, oder Darstellung der dogmatischen Gegensätze der Katholiken und Protestanten nach ihren öffentlichen*

Bekenntnisschriften. Edited by Josef Rupert Geiselmann. 2 vols. Darmstadt: Wissenschaftliche Buchgesellschaft.

Morison, Stanley. 1949. *English Prayer Books: An Introduction to the Literature of Christian Public Worship*. 3d ed. Cambridge: Cambridge University Press.

Mungello, David E., ed. 1994. *The Chinese Rites Controversy: Its History and Meaning*. Nettetal: Steyer Verlag.

Murray, John Courtney. 1964. *The Problem of God Yesterday and Today*. New Haven: Yale University Press.

Neufeld, Vernon Harry. 1963. *The Earliest Christian Confessions*. Grand Rapids, Mich.: William B. Eerdmans.

The New Jerusalem Bible. 1985. Garden City, N.Y.: Doubleday.

Newman, John Henry. [1859] 1901. "The Orthodoxy of the Body of the Faithful During the Supremacy of Arianism." In *The Arians of the Fourth Century*, 445–68. 4th ed. London: Longmans, Green.

———. [1841] 1964. "Tract Ninety: Remarks on Certain Passages in the Thirty-Nine Articles." In Eugene Rathbone Fairweather, ed., *The Oxford Movement*, 148–56. "A Library of Protestant Thought." New York: Oxford University Press.

———. [1864] 1967. *Apologia pro Vita Sua: Being a History of His Religious Opinions*. Edited by Martin J. Svaglic. Oxford: Clarendon Press.

———. [1845] 1974. *An Essay on the Development of Christian Doctrine*. 1st ed. Edited by James Munro Cameron. New York: Pelican Books.

Nichols, Robert L., and Theofanis George Stavrou, eds. 1978. *Russian Orthodoxy Under the Old Regime*. Minneapolis: University of Minnesota Press.

Niebuhr, H. Richard. 1951. *Christ and Culture*. New York: Harper and Brothers.

Nortier, C. W. 1941. *De belijdenis der jonge kerken* [The confession of the young churches]. The Hague: Boekencentrum.

Oberdorfer, Bernd. 2001. *Filioque: Geschichte und Theologie eines ökumenischen Problems*. Göttingen: Vandenhoeck und Ruprecht.

Oberman, Heiko Augustinus. 1963. *The Harvest of Medieval Theology: Gabriel Biel and Late Medieval Nominalism*. Cambridge, Mass.: Harvard University Press.

O'Gara, Margaret. 1988. *Triumph in Defeat: Infallibility, Vatican I, and the French Minority Bishops*. Washington, D.C.: Catholic University of America Press.

O'Malley, John W. 1979. *Praise and Blame in Renaissance Rome: Rhetoric, Doctrine, and Reform in the Sacred Orators of the Papal Court*. Durham, N.C.: Duke University Press.

———. 1993. *Religious Culture in the Sixteenth Century: Preaching, Rhetoric, Spirituality, and Reform*. Aldershot: Variorum Reprints.

———. 2000. *Trent and All That: Renaming Catholicism in the Early Modern Era*. Cambridge, Mass.: Harvard University Press.

Onasch, Konrad, and Annemarie Schnieper. 1997. *Icons: The Fascination and the Reality*. Translated by Daniel C. Conklin. New York: Riverside Book.

Oort, Johannes van, and Johannes Roldanus, eds. 1997. *Chalkedon: Geschichte und Aktualität: Studien zur Rezeption der christologischen Formel von Chalkedon*. Leuven: Peeters.

Ostrogorsky, George. 1969. *History of the Byzantine State*. Translated by Joan Hussey. Foreword by Peter Charanis. Revised ed. New Brunswick, N.J.: Rutgers University Press.

Ostroumoff, Ivan N. 1971. *The History of the Council of Florence*. Translated by Basil Popoff. Boston: Holy Transfiguration Monastery.

Papadopoulos, Chrysostomos. 1939. *Kyrillos Loukaris*. Edited by Grēgorios Papamichaël. 2d ed. Athens: Phoinikos.

Pauck, Wilhelm. 1961. *The Heritage of the Reformation*. 2d ed. Glencoe, Ill.: Free Press.

Pelikan, Jaroslav. 1971. *Historical Theology: Continuity and Change in Christian Doctrine*. Washington, D.C.: Corpus Books.

———. 1980. "The Two Sees of Peter: Reflections on the Pace of Normative Self-Definition East and West." In E. P. Sanders, ed., *The Shaping of Christianity in the Second and Third Centuries,* vol. 1 of *Jewish and Christian Self-Definition,* 57–73. Philadelphia: Fortress Press.

———. 1986. *The Mystery of Continuity: Time and History, Memory and Eternity in the Thought of Saint Augustine*. Charlottesville: University Press of Virginia.

———. 1990a. *Imago Dei: The Byzantine Apologia for Icons*. The Andrew W. Mellon Lectures at the National Gallery of Art. Princeton, N.J.: Princeton University Press.

———. 1990b. *Eternal Feminines: Three Theological Allegories in Dante's "Paradiso."* New Brunswick, N.J.: Rutgers University Press.

———. 1993. *Christianity and Classical Culture: The Metamorphosis of Natural Theology in the Christian Encounter with Hellenism*. New Haven and London: Yale University Press.

Person, Ralph E. 1978. *The Mode of Theological Decision-Making at the Early Ecumenical Councils: An Inquiry into the Function of Scripture and Tradition at the Councils of Nicaea and Ephesus*. Basel: F. Reinhardt.

Petersen, Peter. [1921] 1964. *Geschichte der aristotelischen Philosophie im protestantischen Deutschland*. Reprint ed. Stuttgart: Frommann.

Peterson, Erik. [1935] 1951. "Der Monotheismus als politisches Problem." *Theologische Traktate,* 45–147. Munich: Kösel Verlag.

Pharantos, Mega L. 1969. *Hē theologia Gennadiou tou Scholariou* [The theology of Gennadius Scholarius]. Athens: University of Athens.

Piepkorn, Arthur Carl. 1993. *The Church: Selected Writings of Arthur Carl Piepkorn*. Edited by Michael P. Plekon and William S. Wiecher. Afterword by Richard John Neuhaus. Delhi, N.Y.: ALPB Books.

Pokrovský, Aleksandr Ivanovič. 1914. *Sobori drevnej cerkvi: Epochi pervych' trech' věkov* [The councils of the ancient church of the era of the first three centuries]. Sergiev Posad: Tipografija I. I. Ivanova.

Popivchak, Ronald Peter. 1975. "Peter Mohila, Metropolitan of Kiev (1633–47): Translation and Evaluation of His 'Orthodox Confession of Faith'

(1640)." S.T.D. thesis, Catholic University of America. Ann Arbor, Mich.: University Microfilms.

Pospishil, Victor J. 1996. *Eastern Catholic Church Law.* 2d ed. Staten Island, N.Y.: Saint Maron Publications.

Potz, Richard. 1971. *Patriarch und Synode in Konstantinopel: Das Verfassungs-recht des ökumenischen Patriarchates.* Vienna: Herder.

Prestige, George Leonard. 1956. *God in Patristic Thought.* 2d ed. London: S.P.C.K.

Principe, Walter Henry. 1963–75. *The Theology of the Hypostatic Union in the Early Thirteenth Century.* 4 vols. Toronto: Pontifical Institute of Mediaeval Studies.

Proksch, Otto. 1936. *Das Bekenntnis im Alten Testament.* Leipzig: A. Deichert.

Prokurat, Michael, Alexander Golitzin, and Michael D. Peterson. 1996. *Historical Dictionary of the Orthodox Church.* Lanham, Md.: Scarecrow Press.

Rakove, Jack N. 1996. *Original Meanings: Politics and Ideas in the Making of the Constitution.* New York: Alfred A. Knopf.

Rauschenbusch, Walter. 1907. *Christianity and the Social Crisis.* Reprint ed. New York: Macmillan.

Reese, Hans-Jörg. 1974. *Bekenntnis und Bekennen: Vom 19. Jahrhundert zum Kirchenkampf der nationalsozialistischen Zeit.* Göttingen: Vandenhoeck und Ruprecht.

Reinhard, Wolfgang. 1977. "Gegenreformation als Modernisierung? Prolegomena zu einer Theorie des konfessionellen Zeitalters." *Archiv für Reformationsgeschichte* 68:226–52.

———, and Heinz Schilling, eds. 1995. *Die katholische Konfessionalisierung.* Gütersloh: Gütersloher Verlagshaus.

Ritschl, Otto. 1908–27. *Dogmengeschichte des Protestantismus.* 4 vols. Leipzig: J. C. Hinrichs (vols. 1, 2); Göttingen: Vandenhoeck und Ruprecht (vols. 3, 4).

Rogers, Jack Bartlett. 1985. *Presbyterian Creeds: A Guide to the "Book of Confessions."* Foreword by Charles A. Hammond. Philadelphia: Westminster Press.

Rovira Belloso, Josep Maria. 1979. *Trento: Una interpretación teológica.* Barcelona: Colectánea San Paciano.

Rückert, Hanns. 1925. *Die Rechtfertigungslehre auf dem Tridentinischen Konzil.* Bonn: A. Marcus und E. Weber.

Rusch, William G., and Daniel F. Martensen, eds. 1989. *The Leuenberg Agreement and Lutheran-Reformed Relationships: Evaluations by North American and European Theologians.* Minneapolis, Minn.: Augsburg.

Sanders, James A. 1972. *Torah and Canon.* Philadelphia: Fortress Press.

Sanneh, Lamin O. 1983. *West African Christianity: The Religious Impact.* London: Allen and Unwin.

———. 1989. *Translating the Message: The Missionary Impact on Culture.* Maryknoll, N.Y.: Orbis Books.

―――. 1996. *Religion and the Variety of Culture: A Study in Origin and Practice*. Valley Forge, Pa.: Trinity Press International.

―――, and Grant Wacker. 1999. "Christianity Appropriated: Conversion and the Intercultural Process." *Church History* 68:954–61.

Schindler, Alfred. 1965. *Wort und Analogie in Augustins Trinitätslehre*. Tübingen: J. C. B. Mohr.

Schlink, Edmund. 1961. *Theology of the Lutheran Confessions*. Translated by Paul F. Koehneke and Herbert J. A. Bouman. Philadelphia: Muhlenberg Press.

Schmauck, Theodore Emmanuel. 1911. *The Confessional Principle and the Confessions of the Lutheran Church*. Philadelphia: General Council Publication Board.

Schmaus, Michael. 1927. *Die psychologische Trinitätslehre des heiligen Augustinus*. Münster: Aschendorff.

Schmidt, Martin. 1966. "Die Kirche von England als Gegenstand der Konfessionskunde." In Joachim Lell, ed., *Erneuerung der Einen Kirche: Arbeiten aus Kirchengeschichte und Konfessionskunde Heinrich Bornkamm zum 65. Geburtstag gewidmet*, 82–114. Göttingen: Vandenhoeck und Ruprecht.

Scholder, Klaus. 1988. *The Churches and the Third Reich*. Translated by John Bowden. Philadelphia: Fortress Press.

Schubert, Hans von. 1910. *Bekenntnisbildung und Religionspolitik 1529/30 (1524–1534)*. Gotha: Friedrich Andreas Perthes.

Schwarzlose, Karl. [1890] 1970. *Der Bilderstreit: Ein Kampf der griechischen Kirche um ihre Eigenart und um ihre Freiheit*. Reprint ed. Amsterdam: Rodopi.

Schweitzer, Albert. [1906] 1961. *The Quest of the Historical Jesus: A Critical Study of Its Progress from Reimarus to Wrede*. Translated by W. Montgomery. Reprint ed. New York: Macmillan.

Scott, S. Herbert. 1928. *The Eastern Churches and the Papacy*. London: Sheed and Ward.

Seeberg, Alfred. [1903] 1966. *Der Katechismus der Urchristenheit*. Reprint ed. Introduction by Ferdinand Hahn. Munich: Christian Kaiser Verlag.

Seibt, Klaus. 1994. *Die Theologie des Markell von Ankyra*. Berlin: Walter de Gruyter.

Sellers, Robert Victor. 1940. *Two Ancient Christologies: A Study in the Christological Thought of the Schools of Alexandria and Antioch in the Early History of Christian Doctrine*. London: S.P.C.K.

Semmelroth, Otto. 1963. *Mary, Archetype of the Church*. Translated by Maria von Eroes and John Devlin. Introduction by Jaroslav Pelikan. New York: Sheed and Ward.

Ševčenko, Ihor. 1955. "Intellectual Repercussions of the Council of Florence." *Church History* 24:291–323.

―――. [1984] 1992. "The Many Worlds of Peter Mohyla." *Byzantium and the Slavs*, 651–87. Cambridge, Mass.: Harvard Ukrainian Research Institute.

Simpson, Robert. 1965. *The Interpretation of Prayer in the Early Church.* Philadelphia: Westminster Press.

Skoglund, John E., and J. Robert Nelson. 1963. *Fifty Years of Faith and Order: An Interpretation of the Faith and Order Movement.* New York: Committee for the Interseminary Movement of the National Student Christian Federation.

Smend, Julius. 1898. *Kelchversagung und Kelchspendung im Abendland: Ein Beitrag zur Kultusgeschichte.* Göttingen: Vandenhoeck und Ruprecht.

Smith, Page. 1964. *The Historian and History.* New York: Alfred A. Knopf.

Spence, Jonathan D. 1984. *The Memory Palace of Matteo Ricci.* New York: Viking Penguin.

Spinka, Matthew. 1954. *Church in Communist Society: A Study in J. L. Hromádka's Theological Politics.* Foreword by Reinhold Niebuhr. Hartford, Conn.: Hartford Seminary Press.

———. 1966. *John Hus' Concept of the Church.* Princeton, N.J.: Princeton University Press.

Spitz, Lewis W., and Wenzel Lohff, eds. 1977. *Discord, Dialogue, and Concord: Studies in the Lutheran Reformation's Formula of Concord.* Philadelphia: Fortress Press.

Staedtke, Joachim, ed. 1966. *Glaube und Bekennen. 400 Jahre Confessio Helvetica Posterior: Beiträge zu ihrer Geschichte und Theologie.* Zurich: Zwingli-Verlag.

Standaert, Nicolas. 1994. *Inculturation: The Gospel and Cultures.* Translated by A. Bruggeman and R. Murray. Manila: Saint Paul Publications

Stegmüller, Friedrich, ed. 1947. *Repertorium commentariorum in sententias Petri Lombardi.* 2 vols. Würzburg: F. Schöningh.

Steiner, George. 1992. *After Babel: Aspects of Language and Translation.* 2d ed. New York: Oxford University Press.

Stendahl, Krister. 1976. *Paul Among Jews and Gentiles and Other Essays.* Philadelphia: Fortress Press.

Stoevesandt, Hinrich. 1970. *Die Bedeutung des Symbolums in Theologie und Kirche: Versuch einer dogmatisch-kritischen Ortsbestimmung aus evangelischer Sicht.* Munich: Christian Kaiser Verlag.

Sundkler, Bengt. 1954. *Church of South India: The Movement Towards Union, 1900–1947.* London: Lutterworth Press.

———. 1960. *The Christian Ministry in Africa.* Uppsala: Swedish Institute of Missionary Research.

Tappert, Theodore G. 1947. "The Symbols of the Church." In Edward C. Fendt, ed., *What Lutherans Are Thinking: Symposium on Lutheran Faith and Life,* 343–67. Columbus, Ohio: Wartburg Press.

Tavard, George H. 1959. *Holy Writ or Holy Church: The Crisis of the Protestant Reformation.* New York: Harper and Brothers.

Thomas, Louis. 1853. *La confession helvétique: Etudes historicodogmatiques sur le XVIe siècle.* Geneva: J. Kessmann.

Thompson, Bard, et al. 1963. *Essays on the Heidelberg Catechism.* Philadelphia: United Church Press.

Tierney, Brian. 1972. *Origins of Papal Infallibility, 1150–1350: A Study on the Concepts of Infallibility, Sovereignty, and Tradition in the Middle Ages.* Leiden: E. J. Brill.

———. 1998. *Foundations of the Conciliar Theory: The Contributions of the Medieval Canonists from Gratian to the Great Schism.* 2d ed. Leiden: E. J. Brill.

Treadgold, Warren. 1997. *A History of the Byzantine State and Society.* Stanford, Calif.: Stanford University Press.

Trilling, Lionel. [1950] 2000. "Wordsworth and the Rabbis." In Leon Wieseltier, ed., *The Moral Obligation to Be Intelligent: Selected Essays,* 188–202. New York: Farrar, Straus, Giroux.

Troeltsch, Ernst. 1891. *Vernunft und Offenbarung bei Johann Gerhard und Melanchthon: Untersuchung zur Geschichte der altprotestantischen Theologie.* Göttingen: Vandenhoeck und Ruprecht.

———. [1931] 1960. *The Social Teachings of the Christian Churches.* Translated by Olive Wyon. Reprint ed. Introduction by H. Richard Niebuhr. 2 vols. New York: Harper Torchbooks.

Tyrer, John Walton. 1917. *The Eucharistic Epiclesis.* London: Longmans, Green.

Ulrich, Jörg. 1994. *Die Anfänge der abendländischen Rezeption des Nizänums.* Berlin: Walter de Gruyter.

Urban, Hans Jörg. 1972. *Bekenntnis, Dogma, kirchliches Lehramt: Die Lehrautorität der Kirche in heutiger evangelischer Theologie.* Wiesbaden: F. Steiner.

Vasileiadēs, Nikolaos P. 1983. *Markos ho Eugenikos kai hē henōsis tōn ekklēsiōn* [Markos Eugenikos and the union of the churches]. 3d ed. Athens: Adelphotēs Theologōn "Ho Sōtēr."

Vauchez, André. 1993. *The Laity in the Middle Ages: Religious Beliefs and Devotional Practices.* Edited and introduced by Daniel E. Bornstein. Translated by Margery J. Schneider. Notre Dame, Ind.: University of Notre Dame Press.

Vinogradský, Nikolaj Fedorovič. 1899. *Cerkovný sobor v Moskvě 1682 goda* [The ecclesiastical synod in Moscow of the year 1682]. Smolensk: Ja. N. Podzemský.

Vischer, Lukas, ed. 1963. *A Documentary History of the Faith and Order Movement, 1927–1963.* Saint Louis, Mo.: Bethany Press.

———, ed. 1981. *Spirit of God, Spirit of Christ: Ecumenical Reflections on the Filioque Controversy.* London: S.P.C.K.

Vogt, Hermann-Josef. 1986. "Die Bibel auf dem Konzil von Ephesus." *Annuarium historiae conciliorum* 18:31–40.

———. 1993. "Unterschiedliches Konzilsverständnis der Cyrillianer und der Orientalen beim Konzil von Ephesus 431." *Logos: Festschrift für Luise Abramowski,* 429–51. Berlin: Walter de Gruyter.

Volf, Miroslav. 1998. *After Our Likeness: The Church as the Image of the Trinity.* Grand Rapids, Mich.: William B. Eerdmans.

Wainwright, Geoffrey. 1986. "The Lima Text in the History of Faith and Order." *Studia Liturgica* 16:6–21.

Walls, Andrew Finlay. 1996. *The Missionary Movement in Christian History: Studies in the Transmission of Faith*. Maryknoll, N.Y.: Orbis Books.

Walther, Carl Ferdinand Wilhelm. [1858] 1972. "The Kind of Confessional Subscription Required." In Theodore G. Tappert, ed., *Lutheran Confessional Theology in America, 1840–1880*, 56–77. "A Library of Protestant Thought." New York: Oxford University Press.

Wandel, Lee Palmer. 1995. *Voracious Idols and Violent Hands: Iconoclasm in Reformation Zurich, Strasbourg, and Basel*. Cambridge: Cambridge University Press.

Ward, Alfred Dudley. 1961. *The Social Creed of the Methodist Church: A Living Document*. Nashville, Tenn.: Abingdon Press.

Ware, Kallistos. 1997. *The Orthodox Church*. Revised ed. Harmondsworth: Penguin Books.

———. 2000. *The Inner Kingdom. Collected Works*, vol. 1. Crestwood, N.Y.: Saint Vladimir's Seminary Press.

Warfield, Benjamin Breckenridge. 1956. *Calvin and Augustine*. Edited by Samuel G. Craig. Philadelphia: Presbyterian and Reformed Publishing Company.

Watt, William Montgomery. 1994. *Islamic Creeds: A Selection*. Edinburgh: Edinburgh University Press.

Weber, Max. [1930] 1992. *The Protestant Ethic and the Spirit of Capitalism*. Translated by Talcott Parsons. Reprint ed. Introduction by Anthony Giddens. London: Routledge.

Weisheipl, James A. 1974. *Friar Thomas d'Aquino: His Life, Thought, and Work*. Garden City, N.Y.: Doubleday.

Welch, Claude. 1952. *In This Name: The Doctrine of the Trinity in Contemporary Theology*. New York: Charles Scribner's Sons.

———. 1972–85. *Protestant Thought in the Nineteenth Century*. 2 vols. New Haven and London: Yale University Press.

Wensinck, Arent Jan. 1932. *The Muslim Creed: Its Genesis and Historical Development*. Cambridge: Cambridge University Press.

Wenz, Gunther. 1996–98. *Theologie der Bekenntnisschriften der evangelisch-lutherischen Kirche: Eine historische und systematische Einführung in das Konkordienbuch*. 2 vols. Berlin: Walter de Gruyter.

Whitehead, Alfred North. [1925] 1952. *Science and the Modern World*. Lowell Lectures for 1925. Reprint ed. New York: New American Library.

———. [1933] 1942. *Adventures of Ideas*. Reprint ed. Harmondsworth: Pelican Books.

Wilckens, Ulrich. 1961. *Die Missionsrede der Apostelgeschichte*. Neukirchen-Vluyn: Verlag des Erziehungsvereins.

Wiles, Maurice F. 1968. "The Unassumed Is the Unhealed." *Religious Studies* 4:47–56.

Williams, Charles. [1939] 1956. *The Descent of the Dove: A History of the Holy*

Spirit in the Church. Introduction by W. H. Auden. Reprint ed. New York: Living Age Books.

Williams, George Huntston. 1951. "Christology and Church-State Relations in the Fourth Century." *Church History* 20–III:3–33; 20–IV:3–26.

———. 1960. *Anselm: Communion and Atonement*. Saint Louis, Mo.: Concordia.

Willis, Geoffrey Grimshaw. 1950. *Saint Augustine and the Donatist Controversy*. London: S. P. C. K.

Witte, John, Jr. 1997. *From Sacrament to Contract: Marriage, Religion, and Law in the Western Tradition*. Louisville, Ky.: Westminster John Knox Press.

Wolf, Ernst, ed. 1959. *Christusbekenntnis im Atomzeitalter?* Munich: Christian Kaiser Verlag.

Wolff, Christoph. 1983. *The New Grove Bach Family*. New York: W. W. Norton.

———. 1991. *Bach: Essays on His Life and Music*. Cambridge, Mass.: Harvard University Press.

Wright, John Robert, ed. 1988. *Quadrilateral at One Hundred: Essays on the Centenary of the Chicago-Lambeth Quadrilateral, 1886/88–1986/88*. Cincinnati, Ohio: Anglican Theological Review.

Zahn-Harnack, Agnes von. 1951. *Adolf von Harnack*. 2d ed. Berlin: Walter de Gruyter.

Zēsēs, Theodoros. 1980. *Gennadios B' Scholarios — Bios, syngrammata, didaskalia* [Gennadius II Scholarius — life, writings, doctrine]. Thessalonica: Patriarchikon Idryma Paterikōn Meletōn.

Zizioulas, John D. 1985. *Being as Communion: Studies in Personhood and the Church*. Crestwood, N.Y.: Saint Vladimir's Seminary Press.

Žukovský, Arkadij. 1997. *Petro Mohyla j pytannja ednosty cerkov* [Peter Mohyla and the problem of the unity of the churches]. Kiev: Mystectvo.

VI. Indexes to *Creeds and Confessions of Faith in the Christian Tradition*

In both "A Comparative Creedal Syndogmaticon, with Alphabetical Index" and the "Ecclesiastical Index: Churches, Heresies, Creeds, Confessions, Councils," the references to individual creeds and confessions are arranged in the order in which these appear in the five parts of *Creeds and Confessions of Faith in the Christian Tradition*, with a separate listing for each of the parts: the parts are indicated by Roman numerals; the individual creeds and confessions are identified by the sigla that are listed alphabetically in the "Abbreviations for Creeds and Confessions" in the front matter of this volume, with the versification (if any) that is marked in the texts. Therefore a reader who does not have access to the set of *Creeds and Confessions of Faith in the Christian Tradition* should find it possible to make use of the Comparative Creedal Syndogmaticon and the Ecclesiastical Index as guides to creeds and confessions in any of the other editions, collections, and translations that are identified under "Editions, Collections, and Reference Works," also in the front matter of this volume.

A Comparative Creedal Syndogmaticon, with Alphabetical Index

Although it is, lamentably, still true, as Robert L. Collison observed in his handbook of 1962, *Indexing Books: A Manual of Basic Principles,* that "few indexes make a conscientious attempt to index ideas," precisely that must be the chief business of an index to *Creeds and Confessions of Faith in the Christian Tradition.* The title "Syndogmaticon" is adapted from "Syntopicon," which was coined to identify the comprehensive index of "102 Great Ideas," constructed for *Great Books of the Western World* under the editorship of Mortimer J. Adler and published in 1952 by *Encyclopaedia Britannica.* But here it is "Syn*dogmati*con," because the "topics" with which this index deals are in fact the *dogmata* and doctrines of the Christian tradition as these appear in the various creeds and confessions of faith. The problem is that not every dogma appears in every creed or confession, and that even when they do appear, the doctrines do not always employ the same terminology or follow in the same sequence. Instead of a conventional index, therefore, what is needed here is a doctrinal roadmap, a Syndogmaticon, to serve not as a substitute for, but as a guide to, the close reading of the creedal and confessional texts themselves. This Comparative Creedal Syndogmaticon does not pretend to be a comprehensive concordance to all the topics and theological opinions that happen to have been touched on somewhere in the thousands of pages of creeds and confessions, especially in texts as bulky and discursive as *The Westminster Confession of Faith* or *The Solid Declaration* of *The Formula of Concord* or *The Doctrinal Decrees of the Second Vatican Council.* Nor does it aspire to be used as a miniature *summa theologica,* as may be possible for indexes that confine themselves to the more or less homogeneous confessions coming out of a single tradition, the most notable of these being the "Index Systematicus Rerum" to the Denzinger *Enchiridion.* The Syndogmaticon is "comparative": it does not itself work out a point-by-point comparison, as a textbook or course in Comparative Symbolics might; but, by locating where a particular doctrine is treated in a particular confession, it does make such comparison and contrast possible across the boundaries of confessions, denominations, and historical periods, documenting the sometimes surprising convergences as well as the striking divergences among them. And it is "creedal," both because the texts it indexes are all creeds and confessions of faith and because it is organized on the basis of the text of *The Niceno-Constantinopolitan Creed* of 381 (more commonly, though less precisely, known as *The Nicene Creed*). The Alphabetical Index serves, in turn, as an "index to the index."

In the roster of all the hundreds and even thousands of creeds and confessions of faith that have been composed over a span of two millennia, *The Niceno-Constantinopolitan Creed* must hold pride of place. It has a special standing *among* all the creeds and confessions of faith of Christian history as the only truly ecumenical creed, one that is shared by West and East: including under "West" not only Western Catholicism but much (though by no means all) of Western Protestantism; and including under "East" not only the Eastern Orthodox Church but the Oriental Orthodox Churches and the Assyrian Church of the East. Though often linked with *The Apostles' Creed* and *The Athanasian Creed* as one of "the three ecumenical creeds," particularly in the West, this creed also occupies an authoritative place that is distinctive *within* many of the subsequent confessions of those several traditions (see Index B, s.v. *Niceno-Constantinopolitan Creed*). Thus it represents an outstanding instance of what professional indexers refer to as a "controlled vocabulary": all, or virtually all, the authors of subsequent creeds and confessions for over sixteen centuries have known its text; most of them have ascribed greater or lesser authority to it; and many of them have prayed its words in their liturgies. Therefore it is uniquely suited to provide, phrase by phrase, the outline for this Comparative Creedal Syndogmaticon. Even what later generations have sometimes perceived to be its lacunae—its silence on the doctrines of election (3.2), justification (3.5), and atonement (4.1); its evident indifference to particular questions of ethics and society (7.3; 8.4); its failure to affirm the inspiration and inerrancy of Holy Scripture (8.14); its lack of specific prescriptions about polity, ministry, and church order (9.8); its reference only to baptism among the sacraments (10.2)—may serve to emphasize this unparalleled position of *The Niceno-Constantinopolitan Creed*. Explicating the text of an ancient creed phrase by phrase to present a summary of Christian doctrine follows ecumenical precedent across the confessions and across the centuries, for example: *The Catechetical Lectures* by Cyril of Jerusalem for the Greek church fathers; *A Commentary on the Apostles' Creed* by Rufinus of Aquileia for the Latin fathers; *The Heidelberg Catechism* for the Protestant Reformation; *The Orthodox Confession of the Catholic and Apostolic Eastern Church* by Peter Mogila for Eastern Orthodoxy; and the *Catechism of the Catholic Church* for Roman Catholicism.

Basically, the Syndogmaticon reproduces and follows the text of *The Niceno-Constantinopolitan Creed* just as Part One of *Creeds and Confessions of Faith in the Christian Tradition* has presented it, dividing it into the traditional twelve articles. But on account of their historical importance, the two most significant of the later divergences from that original text of the First Council of Constantinople in 381 have been added, in brackets: the substitution—or, if it was originally a baptismal creed, actually the restoration—in both Eastern and Western Christendom, of the singular "I believe" in place of the council's original plural "We believe" as the opening of article 1 (which carries through to the other plural verbs, in articles 11 and 12 of the creed); and, in article 8, the addition, by Western Christendom, of "and from the Son [*Filioque*]" to the original phrase about the Holy Spirit, "proceeding forth from the Father," as this *Western Recension* appears at the beginning of Part Three.

Because *The Niceno-Constantinopolitan Creed* serves as the outline of the Syndogmaticon, it would have been redundant to include its individual articles among the references; the same applies to the "creeds" in the Bible, which go on to serve as proof texts for other creeds. Certain other brief creedal formulas, too, especially from the early period and then the modern period, are indexed sometimes according to the individual doctrines in them when these are distinctive or unusually emphatic or prominent (which in the early period is usually the Trinity or the incarnation, and in the modern period often the church and the ministry) or sometimes (as in the case of most early creeds, or of the one-sentence *Doctrinal Basis* of the World Council of Churches of 1948 and other ecumenical affirmations) simply under "1.1. The Faith and Creed of the Church." This heading is therefore also the place to look for early references to such teachings as "6.1. The Ascension of Christ" and others that did not become controversial questions and therefore creedal and confessional issues until later. For similar reasons, as the cross-references and the Alphabetical Index indicate but cannot of course indicate exhaustively, it is always necessary to look up not only a specific doctrinal subject but others that are adjacent or closely related to it (for instance, not only 8.1 on the person of the Holy Spirit, but 1.8 on the Trinity); otherwise, it would be easy to miss what a particular creed or confession teaches on that subject, or even to draw the mistaken conclusion that it says nothing about it.

1. WE BELIEVE [I BELIEVE] IN ONE GOD THE FATHER ALL-POWERFUL, MAKER OF HEAVEN AND EARTH, AND OF ALL THINGS BOTH SEEN AND UNSEEN.

2. AND IN ONE LORD JESUS CHRIST, THE ONLY-BEGOTTEN SON OF GOD, BEGOTTEN FROM THE FATHER BEFORE ALL THE AGES, LIGHT FROM LIGHT, TRUE GOD FROM TRUE GOD, BEGOTTEN NOT MADE, CONSUBSTANTIAL WITH THE FATHER; THROUGH WHOM ALL THINGS CAME TO BE,

3. WHO FOR US HUMANS AND FOR OUR SALVATION CAME DOWN FROM THE HEAVENS AND BECAME INCARNATE FROM THE HOLY SPIRIT AND THE VIRGIN MARY, BECAME HUMAN

4. AND WAS CRUCIFIED ON OUR BEHALF UNDER PONTIUS PILATE; HE SUFFERED AND WAS BURIED

5. AND ROSE UP ON THE THIRD DAY IN ACCORDANCE WITH THE SCRIPTURES.

6. AND HE WENT UP INTO THE HEAVENS AND IS SEATED AT THE FATHER'S RIGHT HAND;

7. HE IS COMING AGAIN WITH GLORY TO JUDGE THE LIVING AND THE DEAD; HIS KINGDOM WILL HAVE NO END.

8. AND IN THE SPIRIT, THE HOLY, THE LORDLY AND LIFE-GIVING ONE, PROCEEDING FORTH FROM THE FATHER [AND THE SON], CO-WORSHIPED AND CO-GLORIFIED WITH FATHER AND SON, THE ONE WHO SPOKE THROUGH THE PROPHETS;

9. IN ONE, HOLY, CATHOLIC, AND APOSTOLIC CHURCH.

10. WE CONFESS [I CONFESS] ONE BAPTISM FOR THE FORGIVING OF SINS.

11. WE LOOK FORWARD [I LOOK FORWARD] TO A RESURRECTION OF THE DEAD

12. AND LIFE IN THE AGE TO COME.

1. WE BELIEVE

1.1 . The Faith and Creed of the Church: Believing "that"
[*fides quae creditur*]

I: *Ign; Just; Tert; Hipp; Orig; Dêr Bal; Novat; Greg Thaum; Cyr Jer; Ant 325; Ant 341; N*

II: *Jer II* 1.2; *Metr Crit* 1; *Mogila* 1.4–5; *Dosith* decr 9; *Vald*

III: *Ap* 1; *Ath* 1–2, 42; *No Afr; Patr; Fid cath; Lat 1215*

IV: *17 Art* 1; *Luth Sm Cat* 3.5; *Apol Aug* 4.337–38, 4.383; *Form Conc Epit* 3.6; *Heid* 22–24; *Denck* 1; *Ries* 19; *Witt Art* 4; *Trid Prof* 9

V: *Geloof* 20.5; *Dec Addr* 6–7; *Vat I* 3.3, can 3.2; *Sacr ant* 6; *Br St Luth* 20; *WCC; Un Ch Japan* 5; *Sri Lanka* 3; *Zambia* 1; *Un Ref Ch* 12; *Laus Cov* 1; *F&O Ban; Un Ch Can: Crd; Chile; BEC*

1.2. Knowledge of God and of the Will of God Through Creation,
History, Conscience, and Reason

II: *Gennad* 12.2, 4; *Metr Crit* 4.2–6; *Dosith* decr 14

III: *Tol XI* 9; *Petr Ab* 1

IV: *17 Art* 12; *Apol Aug* 18.9; *Form Conc Epit* 1.9; *Form Conc Sol Dec* 2.9; *Genv Cat* 113; *Helv II* 9.6, 12.1, 16.9; *Dort* 3/4.4; *West* 1.1, 16.7

V: *Gen Bap* 4–10, 28; *Sav* 1.1, 16.7; *Geloof* 1, 11.1; *Cumb Pres* 38, 67; *Syl* 3–6, 8–9, 15–16, 56; *Vat I* 3.2, 3.4, 3 can 2.1, can 3.1–3; *Com Cr* 4; *Richmond* 3; *Sacr ant* 2; *Pol Nat* 1; *Un Ch Can: Union* 2; *Un Pres* 2; *Barm* 1; *Munif* 12; *Vat II* 8.6, 9.3; *Menn Con* 2.1; *Pres USA* 9.13, 9.41–42; *Laus Cov* 9–10; *Toraja* 2.2, 7.4

1.3. The Revelation of Divine Mystery, Its Scope and Language
(*see also* 8.11–15)

I: *Alex; Eph 431 Form Un*

II: *CP 1351* 15; *Metr Crit* 1.3; *Mogila* 1.8–10

IV: *Gall* 2; *Scot I* 4; *Belg* 2; *West* 1.1

V: *London I* 1; *Sav* 1.1; *Friends I* 11; *Geloof* 2.1–2, 9.4, 17.5; *Aub* 1; *Syl* 5; *Vat I* 3.2, 3.4, 3 can 2.2–3, 3 can 4.1; *Com Cr* 4; *Lam* 20–26, 58–65; *Pol Nat* 1; *Assem* 13b; *Un Ch Can: Union* 2; *Un Pres* 2, 15; *Br St Luth* 14–16; *Madag* pr 3; *Vat II* 8.2–6; *Menn Con* 1.2, 2.1; *PRCC* 1a; *Toraja* pr, 1.1, 2.2, 7.4; *Bap Conf* 1; *Morav Am* 1, 3

1.4. The Rule of Faith; Authority of Creeds and Confessions (*see also* 8.11–12, 9.6, 9.8, Ecclesiastical Index)

I: *Iren; Tert; Tome* 1–2

II: *Phot* 8; *Dosith* decr 9; *Jer II* 1.1

III: *Boh I* 2

IV: *Apol Aug* 27.60; *Form Conc Epit* int; *Form Conc Sol Dec* int; *Irish* 1; *Witt Art* 1; *Trid Prof* 1

V: *Dec Addr* 3; *Def Plat* 1.1, 2 pr; *Adv* pr; *Lamb Quad* 2; *Utrecht* 1; *Lam* 62; *Assem* pr; *Afr Orth* 2; *So Bap* pr; *Un Ch Can: Union* pr; *Un Pres* pr; *F&O Laus* 4; *Chin Un* 3; *Ess* 14; *Meth Kor* pr; *Br St Luth* 29, 45–48; *Wash; CSI 1947* 1; *Philip Ind* 2.3, 2.21; *Bat* pr; *Un Ch Japan* 5; *Madag* pr 2; *Sri Lanka* 3; *CNI* 3; *Ghana* 3.3–4; *Zambia* 2; *Pres USA* 9.01–05; *Togo* pr; *Un Ref Ch* 18; *Leuen* 4, 12, 37; *RCA* 7; *Toraja* pr; *Bap Conf* pr; *Morav Am* 4; *Camb Dec* 1; *Ad tuendam* 1

1.5. The One Faith: Confession of Orthodox Doctrine and Anathema Against Heresy (*see also* Ecclesiastical Index)

I: *Iren; Tome* 14; *Edict* 2, 56, 62–63, 77–78, anath 1–13; *Chal* ecth; *CP II* 1, 7, 12, anath 11; *CP III* 10

II: *Phot* 1; *CP 1351* 7, 51; *Mark Eph* 5; *Mogila* 1.91

III: *Lat 649* 18–20; *Sens* 1–19

IV: *Aug* 21 con; *Smal Art* 3.3.40; *Form Conc Epit* 12; *Form Conc Sol Dec* int 14–20, 12; *67 Art* 5; *10 Art* 1; *Ries* 29; *Trent* 3

V: *Sav* pr; *Cum occas; Dec Addr* 7; *Ev All* con; *Resp Pius IX* 1–3, 21; *Syl* 15–18; *Vat I* 3.pr; *Lam* 7–8, 22–24, 26; *Naz* pr; *Sacr ant* 1, 5, 7; *Br St Luth* 28–29, 44; *Barm* pr; *Munif* 12, 36; *Bap Assoc* 20; *Bat* pr 4, 9.4; *Madag* 1, 4; *Vat II* 5.3.11, 5.3.24; *CNI* 4–5; *Leuen* 2, 20, 23, 26, 27; *PRCC* pr, 1b; *Chr Dec* 4–5; *Morav Am* 3–4; *Camb Dec* pr; *Ad tuendam; LuRC Just* 7, 42

[I BELIEVE]

1.6. Saving Faith: Believing "in" [*fides qua creditur*] (*see also* 3.5)

II: *Jer II* 1.4, 6; *Lucar* 9, 13; *Mogila* 1.1–3; *Dosith* decr 9

III: *Ap* 1; *Ath* 1–2, 42; *R* 1; *Orange* 5–6; *Lat 1215*

IV: *17 Art* 2; *Luth Sm Cat* 1.1; *Luth Lg Cat* 1.1–29; *Aug* 20.8–26; *Apol Aug* 4.48–121, 4.153, 12.45; *Form Conc Epit* 3.5–6; *Form Conc Sol Dec* 3.11–14, 4.35; *Tetrapol* 3; *Bas Bek* 9; *Helv I* 13; *Genv Con* 11; *Genv Cat* 111–14; *Belg* 23; *Heid* 21; *Helv II* 16.1–4; *Irish* 37; *Dort* 3/4.14; *West* 11.2, 14.1–

3, 18.2–4; *West Sh Cat* 86; *18 Diss* 1–3, 8; *Denck* 1; *Ries* 19, 20; *Marburg* 5; *Witt Art* 4; *Trent* 6 can 12–14

V: *London I* 22–24; *Camb Plat* 12.2–3; *Sav* 11.2, 14.1–3, 18.2–4; *Friends I* 12; *Morav* 1; *Geloof* 18, 20.3; *Meth Art* 9, 12; *Dec Addr* 8–9; *Cumb Pres* 45–47, 62–65; *New Hamp* 6, 8; *Aub* 11; *LDS* 4; *Abst Prin* 10; *Swed Bap* 6; *Vat I* 3.3, 3.4; *Bonn I* 5; *Salv Arm* 8–9; *Richmond* 6; *Sacr ant* 6; *So Bap* 8; *Un Ch Can: Union* 10; *Un Pres* 17, 19, 24; *Ess* 1–2; *Br St Luth* 9; *F&O Edin* 1.2; *Philip Ind* 2.1; *Bat* 7, 15; *Arn* 8a; *UCC* 1; *Vat II* 8.5, 9.9–10; *Menn Con* 6; *Un Ref Ch* 3; *PRCC* 1; *Toraja* 5.4; *BEM* 1.8–10; *Morav Am* 2; *Camb Dec* 4; *LuRC Just* 25–27

IN ONE GOD

1.7. The Monotheistic Faith and Its Confession (*see also* 1.8)

I: *Tert; Smyr*

II: *Gennad* 1

III: *Ath* 3, 6, 16; *Tol I* 1; *Tol XI* 7

IV: *Genv Con* 2; *Helv II* 3.1–2; *West* 2.1; *West Sh Cat* 5, 46–47; *Ries* 1; *Dordrecht* 1

V: *True Con* 1; *Sav* 2.1; *Friends I* 1; *Morav* 1; *Geloof* 4.1,5; *New Hamp* 2; *Winch* 2; *Arm Ev* 1; *Ev All* 3; *Abst Prin* 2; *Swed Bap* 2; *Free Meth* 1; *Vat I* 3.1, 3 can 1.1; *Adv* 1; *Salv Arm* 2; *Chr Sci* 2; *Com Cr* 1; *Richmond* 1; *Naz* 1; *Assem* 2; *So Bap* 2; *Un Ch Can: Union* 1; *Un Pres* 1; *Meth Kor* 1; *Br St Luth* 4; *Philip Ind* 1.1; *Madag* 1, 4; *Menn Con* 1.1; *Zambia* 1; *Un Ref Ch* 17.1; *Laus Cov* 1; *Toraja* 1.1; *Bap Conf* 2; *Philip UCC* 1

THE FATHER

1.8. The Trinity of Father, Son, and Holy Spirit (*see also* 1.9, 2.1, 8.1)

I: *Iren; Orig* 4; *Greg Thaum; Ar; Alex; Eus; Ant 341; Sard; Sirm; CP 360; Ulph; Epiph; Eun; Aug; Edict* 3, anath 1; *Ecth* 1; *N; CP I; CP II* anath 1, 10

II: *Lit Chrys; Phot* 8–23; *CP 1351* 9, 44; *Greg Palam* 1; *Gennad* 2–3; *Jer II* 1.1; *Metr Crit* 1; *Lucar* 1; *Mogila* 1.7–11; *Dosith* decr 1

III: *Ap; Ath; R; Tol I* 1–11, anath 2–4; *Fid cath; Tol III; Lat 649* 1; *Tol XI; Rom Syn* 1; *Fréjus* 1–5; *Sens* 1–2, 4, 14, 17; *Petr Ab* 2; *Lat 1215* 1; *Lyons; Flor Un; Flor Arm; Vald Boh I* 3

IV: *Aug* 1; *Apol Aug* 1; *Smal Art* 1.1–2; *Tetrapol* 2; *Fid rat* 1; *Bas Bek* 1; *Helv I* 6; *Genv Cat* 19–20; *Gall* 6; *Scot I* 1; *Belg* 8–9; *Heid* 25; *Helv II* 3.3–4;

39 Art 1; *Irish* 8–10; *West* 2.3; *West Sh Cat* 6; *Cologne* 1; *Ries* 2–3; *Dordrecht* 1; *Marburg* 1

V: *True Con* 2; *London I* 2, 27; *Sav* 2.3; *Friends I* 1; *Morav* 1; *Geloof* 4; *Meth Art* 1; *Winch* 2; *Cumb Pres* 7; *New Hamp* 2; *LDS* 1; *Arm Ev* 2; *Ev All* 3; *Resp Pius IX* 5; *Abst Prin* 3; *Swed Bap* 2; *Free Meth* 1, 4; *Salv Arm* 3; *Chr Sci* 2; *Com Cr* 1; *Richmond* 1; *Am Bap* 2; *Naz* 1–2; *Assem* 2, 13; *So Bap* 2; *Un Ch Can: Union* 1; *Un Pres* 1, 11–13; *Meth Kor* 1–3; *Br St Luth* 4; *CSI 1947* 1; *Philip Ind* 1.1; *Bap Assoc* 1; *Bat* 2; *Un Ch Japan* 2; *Madag* 1–3; *Menn Con* 1; *CNI* 1; *Ghana* 3.1; *Zambia* 1, 4; *Pres USA* 9.07; *Meth Braz* 2.1–3; *Un Ref Ch* 12, 17.1; *Laus Cov* 1; *RCA* pr; *Toraja* 1.1–6; *Bap Conf* 2; *Philip UCC* 1; *Morav Am* 1; *Com Dec* 2

ALL-POWERFUL

1.9. The Attributes, Hypostases, and "Energies" of God
(*see also* 3.9–10)

I: *Edict* 33–41

II: *CP 1341* 8–46; *CP 1351* 9–11, 17–22, 27, 29–30, 32–35, 38, 40; *Greg Palam* 7; *Mogila* 1.11–17

III: *Tol I* 10; *Lat 649* 1; *Boh I* 3

IV: *Aug* 1.2; *Form Conc Epit* 2.8, 8.7, 11.2–4; *Form Conc Sol Dec* 4.16, 11 4–7; *Fid Rat* 2; *Genv Cat* 9, 23–24, 271–74; *Gall* 1; *Scot I* 1; *Belg* 1; *Heid* 11; *Irish* 8; *Dort* 1.11; *West* 2.1–2; *West Sh Cat* 4; *Ries* 3

V: *True Con* 2; *London I* 2; *Gen Bap* 1; *Sav* 2.1–2; *Geloof* 1.1, 3.1; *Winch* 2; *Cumb Pres* 5–6; *Arm Ev* 1; *Resp Pius IX* 5; *Abst Prin* 3; *Syl* 1–2; *Free Meth* 1; *Vat I* 3.1, 3 can 1.3–5; *Adv* 1; *Richmond* 1; *Naz* 1; *Pol Nat* 1; *So Bap* 2; *Un Ch Can: Union* 1; *Un Pres* 1, 11; *Wash*; *Philip Ind* 1.1; *Bat* 1; *Madag* 1; *Menn Con* 1.1; *Pres USA* 9.15; *Meth Braz* 2.1; *Bap Conf* 2

MAKER OF HEAVEN AND EARTH AND OF ALL THINGS BOTH SEEN

1.10. God the Creator: Creation, Preservation, and Providence

I: *Ep Ap; Tert; Orig* 7; *Novat*

II: *CP 1351* 26; *Metr Crit* 2; *Lucar* 4–5; *Mogila* 1.18, 1.29–31; *Dosith* decr 5

III: *Ap* 1; *Tol I* 1, anath 1, 9, 14; *Lat 1215* 1

IV: *Luth Sm Cat* 2.2; *Luth Lg Cat* 2.9–24; *Bas Bek* 1, 3; *Genv Cat* 25–27;

Gall 7–8; *Belg* 12; *Heid* 26–28; *Helv II* 6, 7.1–2; *Irish* 18; *West* 4–5; *West Sh Cat* 9, 11–12; *Dordrecht* 1

   V: *Gen Bap* 2–3; *Sav* 4–5; *Geloof* 6.1; *Cumb Pres* 8–9, 10, 12–16; *Abst Prin* 4; *Syl* 1–2; *Vat I* 3.1, 3 can 1.1–5; *Salv Arm* 2; *Com Cr* 2; *Am Bap* pr, 3; *Sacr ant* 3; *So Bap* 11; *Un Ch Can: Union* 3–4; *Un Pres* 4–6; *Br St Luth* 5; *CSI 1947* 1; *Sheng Kung* 2; *Bap Assoc* 3; *Bat* 3A; *Madag* 1; *UCC* 2; *Masai* 1; *Menn Con* 1.2, 3.1–2; *Ref All* 1; *Pres USA* 9.16; *Design* 1.3; *Meth Braz* 2.1, 2.10; *Togo* 1; *PRCC* 1; *Hond* pr; *Pres So Afr* 1; *Toraja* 1.2–3, 7.1, 7.11; *Bap Conf* 2a; *Philip UCC* 1

1.11. God and the Powers of Evil (*see also* 1.14, 3.4, 4.1)

   I: *Orig* 6; *CP III* 4
   II: *Phot* 1; *CP 1054* 3; *CP 1351* 1; *Greg Palam* 5; *Jer II* 1.19; *Metr Crit* 2.4–5, 2.10; *Lucar* 4; *Mogila* 1.21; *Dosith* decr 3, 4, 5
   III: *Sens* 7, 16; *Lat 1215* 1
   IV: *Aug* 19; *Apol Aug* 19; *Form Conc Epit* 11.4; *Form Conc Sol Dec* 11.7; *Genv Cat* 28–29; *Gall* 8; *Belg* 13; *Helv II* 8.8–10; *Irish* 28; *Ries* 6; *Trent* 6 can 6
   V: *True Con* 4; *Geloof* 36.4; *Cumb Pres* 14–15; *Chr Sci* 3; *Un Pres* 4, 7; *Wash; Bap Assoc* 4; *Bat* 5; *Menn Con* 3.2; *Laus Cov* 12; *Toraja* 7.3; *Bap Conf* 3

1.12. Creation of the Human Race in the Image of God (*see also* 3.4)

   II: *Metr Crit* 2.6–8; *Mogila* 1.22–23
   III: *Orange* 8; *Lat 1215* 1; *Vienne* 2
   IV: *17 Art* 12; *Aug* 18; *Apol Aug* 2.18–22, 4.27, 18.4–8; *Form Conc Epit* 6.2; *Form Conc Sol Dec* 1.34–42, 2.1–90; *Bas Bek* 2; *Helv I* 7, 9; *Gall* 9; *Scot I* 2; *Belg* 14; *Heid* 6; *Helv II* 7.5–7, 9.1; *Irish* 21; *Dort* 3/4.1; *West* 4.2; *West Sh Cat* 10; *Ries* 4; *Dordrecht* 1
   V: *True Con* 4; *London I* 4; *Gen Bap* 11–13; *Sav* 4.2; *Geloof* 5.1–3, 7.1; *Cumb Pres* 11; *Aub* 4; *Abst Prin* 6; *Swed Bap* 3; *Vat I* 3.1; *Chr Sci* 2; *Com Cr* 3; *Richmond* 5; *So Bap* 3; *Un Pres* 4, 11; *Br St Luth* 6; *UCC* 2; *Masai* 1; *Vat II* 9.2–3; *Menn Con* 3.1–2; *Pres USA* 9.17; *Meth Braz* 2.6, 3.1; *PRCC* 2a; *Hond* 1; *Toraja* 3.1–4; *Bap Conf* 3; *Philip UCC* 2

1.13. Freedom of the Will and the Sovereignty of God (*see also* 3.2, 8.5)

   I: *Orig*
   II: *Jer II* 1.18; *Lucar* 14; *Mogila* 1.27; *Dosith* decr 3

III: *Orange; Sens* 5

IV: *Aug* 18; *Apol Aug* 18; *West* 9; *Ries* 5; *Trent* 6 can 2, 4, 5

V: *Cum occas* 3; *Sav* 9; *Geloof* 11; *Meth Art* 8; *Cumb Pres* 34–37; *Aub* 14, 16; *Free Meth* 8; *Naz* 7; *So Bap* 9; *F&O Edin* 1.3; *Bat* 3A; *Menn Con* 3.2, 4.1

AND UNSEEN

1.14. The Doctrine of Angels (*see also* 1.11)

II: *CP 1341* 20–21; *Metr Crit* 2.2; *Lucar* 4; *Mogila* 1.19–20; *Dosith* decr 4
III: *Tol I* 11
IV: *Apol Aug* 21.8; *Gall* 7; *Helv II* 7.3–4; *Irish* 20; *Menn Con* 20
V: *Geloof* 5.1; *Vat I* 3.1; *Afr Orth* 6; *Un Pres* 7; *Bat* 17; *Bap Conf* 3

2. AND IN ONE LORD JESUS CHRIST, THE ONLY-BEGOTTEN SON OF GOD, BEGOTTEN FROM THE FATHER BEFORE ALL THE AGES, LIGHT FROM LIGHT, TRUE GOD FROM TRUE GOD, BEGOTTEN NOT MADE, CONSUBSTANTIAL WITH THE FATHER; THROUGH WHOM ALL THINGS CAME TO BE

2.1. Jesus Christ as Lord: Titles, Offices, States, Deeds, and Teachings

I: *Arist; Ep Ap; Tert; Smyr; N; Chal* 9

II: *Greg Palam* 2; *Mogila* 1.34–36

III: *Ap* 2; *Ath* 22, 29–41; *R* 2; *Tol I* 12–13, anath 3; *Lat 649* 2; *Tol XI* 2; *Boh I* 6

IV: *Luth Lg Cat* 3.27–31; *Apol Aug* 4.69, 21.17–20; *Laus Art* 2; *Genv Cat* 30–47, 54; *Gall* 13; *Scot I* 7–8; *Belg* 10, 26; *Heid* 29–31, 33–34; *Helv II* 5, 11, 18.4; *39 Art* 18; *Irish* 31; *West* 8; *West Sh Cat* 21, 23–26; *Cologne* 2; *Ries* 9, 11, 12, 17; *Tig* 4

V: *True Con* 9–15; *London I* 9–20; *Gen Bap* 20–23; *Friends I* 4; *Sav* 8; *Morav* 2; *Geloof* 4.3, 12–16; *Meth Art* 2; *Shkr* 3; *Cumb Pres* 27; *Abst Prin* 7; *Syl* 7; *Free Meth* 2; *Vat I* 3.3, 3 can 3.4; *Richmond* 2; *Am Bap* 5; *Lam* 13–18, 27–38; *Naz* 2; *Pol Nat* 2–3; *Assem* 13e-j; *Witness* 7; *Afr Orth* 3; *So Bap* 8; *Un Ch Can: Union* 2, 7; *Un Pres* 12; *Chin Un* 1; *Meth Kor* 2; *Barm* 2; *F&O Edin* 2.1–2; *Wash; CSI 1947* 1; *Philip Ind* 1.2, 2.16; *Bap Assoc* 6; *Bat* 9; *Madag* 2; *Masai* 2; *Menn Con* 5; *CNI* 1; *Ghana* 3.1; *Zambia* 5; *Ref All* 2; *Pres USA*

9.08-11, 9.19; *Design* 1.1-2; *Meth Braz* 2.2; *Togo* 2; *Leuen* 21; *Laus Cov* 3; *PRCC* 1a; *Pres So Afr* 2; *Toraja* pr, 1.4, 2.1, 4.3; *Philip UCC* 1

3. WHO FOR US HUMANS AND FOR OUR SALVATION

3.1. The Divine Economy of Salvation

I: *Iren; Tert; Orig* 4; *Tome* 6
II: *Metr Crit* 3; *Lucar* 7
III: *Ath* 38; *Sens* 3; *Lat 1215* 2; *Unam* 8
IV: *Form Conc Epit* 11.17-19; *Form Conc Sol Dec* 11.28; *Sax Vis* 1.4.2; *Belg* 17; *West* 7; *Cologne* 4; *Dordrecht* 3; *Trent* 6.2
V: *True Con* 5-6; *London I* 5-6; *Sav* 7; *Friends I* 10; *Geloof* 10; *Shkr* 1; *Dec Addr* 8; *Cumb Pres* 22-25; *New Hamp* 4; *Assem* 4; *So Bap* 4; *Un Ch Can: Union* 3, 6; *Philip Ind* 2.1; *UCC* 3; *Masai* 1; *Vat II* 8.2-4, 8.14-16; *Menn Con* 1.2; *Pres USA* 9.18; *PRCC* 3b; *Chr Dec* 6

3.2. Election, Predestination, and Divine Foreknowledge

II: *Metr Crit* 4; *Lucar* 3; *Mogila* 1.25-26, 1.30; *Dosith* decr 3
IV: *Form Conc Epit* 11; *Form Conc Sol Dec* 11; *Sax Vis* 1.4, 2.4; *Fid rat* 3; *Bas Bek* 1; *Helv I* 10; *Gall* 12; *Scot I* 8; *Belg* 16; *Lamb Art* 1-4; *Helv II* 10; *39 Art* 17; *Remon* 1; *Irish* 11-17; *Dort* 1; *West* 3.1-8, 17.2; *West Sh Cat* 7; *Ries* 7; *Trent* 6.12, 6 can 15, 17
V: *True Con* 3; *London I* 3, 21; *Sav* 3.1-8, 17.2; *Morav* 1; *Geloof* 9; *New Hamp* 9; *Aub* 2; *Abst Prin* 5; *Swed Bap* 6; *So Bap* 9; *Un Pres* 10; *Afr Orth* 11; *Br St Luth* 35-40; *Munif* 40; *Un Ch Japan* 3; *Vat II* 5.1.2-3; *Menn Con* 6; *Leuen* 24-26

3.3. Plan of Salvation; Gospel and Law; Preaching and Evangelization
(*see also* 8.5, 10.1)

II: *Metr Crit* 3.3-4
III: *Prague* 1; *Boh I* 10
IV: *Apol Aug* 4.5-6, 36-39, 43, 12.53-58; *Smal Art* 3.2, 3.4; *Form Conc Epit* 5; *Form Conc Sol Dec* 4.17, 5.3, 5.20; *67 Art* 1-2; *Helv I* 12; *Genv Con* 6; *Heid* 19, 65; *Helv II* 13; *Dort* 3/4.6-8; *West* 7.5-6; *18 Diss* 12; *Ries* 10; *Dordrecht* 5; *Marburg* 8; *Tig* 1

V: *London I* 24–25; *Sav* 7.5, 20.1–4; *Shkr* 2; *Cumb Pres* 69; *New Hamp* 12; *Arm Ev* 12; *Swed Bap* 7; *Richmond* 5; *So Bap* 23; *Un Ch Can: Union* 14; *Un Pres* 9, 15, 25; *F&O Laus* 2; *Barm* 6; *Bat* 9.1; *UCC* 7; *Vat II* 5.1.16–17, 5.1.25, 5.1.35, 8.18–19; *Menn Con* 8.2, 9; *CNI* 1; *Pres USA* 9.06, 9.49; *Meth Braz* 6; *Leuen* 13; *Laus Cov* pr, 1, 4, 6–10; *Pres So Afr* 3; *Toraja* 1.1, 2.1, 6.3; *Bap Conf* 5; *Morav Am* pr, 7; *LuRC Just* 31–33

3.4. The Need for Salvation: Sin and the Fall (*see also* 1.11, 1.13)

II: *Jer II* 1.3; *Metr Crit* 2.9–12; *Lucar* 6; *Mogila* 1.24–25; *Dosith* decr 6, 14
III: *Orange* 1–2, 8, 15, 21–22, con; *Sens* 8–10, 19; *Boh I* 4
IV: *Luth Lg Cat* 2.28; *Aug* 2; *Apol Aug* 2.3–6, 4.169–71; *Smal Art* 3.1; *Form Conc Epit* 1; *Form Conc Sol Dec* 1; *Fid rat* 2, 4–5; *Bas Bek* 2; *Helv I* 7–8; *Genv Con* 4–5; *Genv Cat* 197, 214–16; *Gall* 9–11; *Scot I* 3; *Belg* 15; *Heid* 3–10; *Helv II* 8.1–5, 9.2–12; *39 Art* 9–10, 15–16; *Remon* 3; *Irish* 22–24, 27, 43–44; *Dort* 3/4; *West* 6; *West Sh Cat* 13–19, 82–84; *Ries* 4; *Dordrecht* 2; *Marburg* 4; *Witt Art* 2; *Trent* 5, 6.1, 6 can 27–29; *Trid Prof* 4
V: *True Con* 4–5; *London I* 4–5; *Gen Bap* 14–16; *Cum occas* 2; *Sav* 6; *Geloof* 8; *Meth Art* 7; *Dec Addr* 8; *Cumb Pres* 17–21, 36; *New Hamp* 3; *Aub* 1, 3–7, 9; *LDS* 2; *Ev All* 4; *Abst Prin* 6; *Swed Bap* 3; *Free Meth* 7; *Salv Arm* 5; *Com Cr* 3; *Richmond* 5; *Naz* 5; *Assem* 3; *Arm Ev* 4; *So Bap* 3; *Un Ch Can: Union* 5; *Un Pres* 8; *Ess* 3, 9; *Br St Luth* 7; *Bap Assoc* 5; *Bat* 5, 6, *Madag* 5; *Menn Con* 4.1–2, *Zambia* 5; *Pres USA* 9.12–14; *Togo* 2; *PRCC* 3a; *RCA* 2; *Toraja* 3.5–8, 7.2–3; *Bap Conf* 4; *Morav Am* 1

3.5. Salvation as Forgiveness, Adoption, Justification
(*see also* 1.6, 4.1, 8.2–3)

II: *Jer II* 1.4; *Metr Crit* 6.5; *Lucar* 9, 13; *Dosith* decr 13
III: *Ap* 10; *R* 10; *Boh I* 6
IV: *Luth Sm Cat* 3.16; *Luth Lg Cat* 3.85–98; *Aug* 4; *Apol Aug* 4; *Smal Art* 2.1.4, 3.13; *Form Conc Epit* 3; *Form Conc Sol Dec* 3; *Tetrapol* 3; *Genv Con* 7, 9; *Genv Cat* 101–5, 114–20, 280–86; *Gall* 18–20; *Belg* 22, 23; *Heid* 56, 59–64; *Lamb Art* 5–6; *Helv II* 15; *39 Art* 13; *Irish* 34–35; *West* 11; *West Sh Cat* 32–33; *Ries* 21; *Marburg* 7; *Witt Art* 4; *Tig* 3; *Trent* 6; *Trid Prof* 4
V: *London I* 28; *Sav* 11–12; *Friends I* 12; *Geloof* 20; *Meth Art* 9; *Shkr* 5; *Cumb Pres* 48–50; *New Hamp* 5; *Aub* 15; *Arm Ev* 7; *Ev All* 6; *Abst Prin* 11; *Free Meth* 9; *Vat I* 3.3; *Adv* 15; *Bonn I* 5; *Salv Arm* 8; *Chr Sci* 3; *Richmond* 6; *Naz* 9.9; *Assem* 4a; *Afr Orth* 11; *So Bap* 5; *Un Ch Can: Union* 11; *Un Pres* 19–20; *Ess* 2; *Meth Kor* 4; *Br St Luth* 9, 17–19; *F&O Edin* 1.2; *CSI 1947* 1; *Bap*

Assoc 10; *Bat* 7; *UCC* 8; *Masai* 3; *Leuen* 6–8, 10, 12; *PRCC* 3c; *Toraja* 4.7, 5.3–4; *Bap Conf* 5; *Camb Dec* 4; *LuRC Just*

CAME DOWN FROM THE HEAVENS AND BECAME INCARNATE

3.6. The Incarnation of the Son of God

I: *Tert; Tome* 7–10; *Edict* 4, anath 2; *Ecth* 2; *Eph 431* ecth; *Chal* 13–15; *CP II* anath 2

II: *Greg Palam* 2; *Gennad* 4–5; *Metr Crit* 3.4–5; *Mogila* 1.38

III: *Ap* 3; *Ath* 29–37; *R* 3; *Tol I* 12–19, anath 5; *Lat 649* 2; *Tol XI* 9–15; *Rom Syn* 2; *Fréjus* 6–8; *Sens* 3; *Petr Ab* 3; *Lat 1215* 2; *Vienne* 1; *Vald*

IV: *Aug* 3; *Apol Aug* 3; *Smal Art* 1.3–4; *Form Conc Epit* 8; *Form Conc Sol Dec* 8.6; *Tetrapol* 2; *Fid rat* 1; *Bas Bek* 4; *Helv I* 11; *Genv Cat* 50–53; *Gall* 14; *Scot I* 6; *Belg* 18; *Heid* 35; *Helv II* 11; *39 Art* 2; *Irish* 29; *West* 8.2–3; *Ries* 8; *Dordrecht* 4; *Marburg* 2

V: *Sav* 8.2–3; *Friends I* 5; *Morav* 2; *Geloof* 12; *Meth Art* 2; *Cumb Pres* 28; *Ev All* 5; *Free Meth* 2; *Adv* 2; *Richmond* 2; *Naz* 2; *Witness* 8; *So Bap* 4; *Un Pres* 12; *Br St Luth* 8; *CSI 1947* 1; *Philip Ind* 2.16; *Bat* 3B; *Masai* 2; *Vat II* 8.4; *Menn Con* 1.3, 5.1; *Meth Braz* 2.3; *Leuen* 9; *PRCC* 1b; *RCA* 3; *Hond* 1; *Toraja* 1.4, 4.1; *Bap Conf* 2b; *Chr Dec* 1

FROM THE HOLY SPIRIT AND THE VIRGIN MARY

3.7. Mary Virgin Mother and Theotokos; Other Titles and Privileges of Mary

I: *Ign; Ep Ap; Tert; Tome* 4; *Edict* anath 5; *Ecth* 3; *Eph 431*; *Chal*; *CP II* 11, anath 6; *Nic II*

II: *Lit Chrys* I.A.2, II.F.5; *Greg Palam* 6; *Metr Crit* 9.5, 17.7–9; *Mogila* 1.39–42; *Dosith* decr 1.6, 8, q 4; *Rom Syn* 2

III: *Ap* 3; *R* 3; *Tol I* 12; *Lat 649* 3; *Tol XI* 9, 13; *Boh I* 17

IV: *Apol Aug* 21.27–28; *Smal Art* 1.4; *Trent* 5.6, 6 can 23; *Form Conc Epit* 8.12; *Form Conc Sol Dec* 8.24; *Genv Cat* 49

V: *Ineff; Bonn I* 10; *Utrecht* 3; *Am Bap* 4; *Afr Orth* 6; *Philip Ind* 2.14; *Munif; Bap Assoc* 6; *Bat* 3B1; *Vat II* 5.1.52–69, 5.3.15; *Hond* 1; *Chr Dec* 3

3.8. The Saints: Veneration and Invocation

II: *Jer II* 1.15, 1.21; *Metr Crit* 17; *Dosith* decr 8

III: *Ap* 9; *Boh I* 17

IV: *Aug* 21; *Apol Aug* 21; *Smal Art* 2.2; *67 Art* 19–21; *Bern* 6; *Tetrapol* 11; *10 Art* 7–8; *Genv Con* 12; *Genv Cat* 238–39; *Gall* 24; *Belg* 26; *Helv II* 5.4–6; *West* 21.2, 26.1–3; *Witt Art* 16; *Trent* 25.2

V: *Sav* 22.2; *Meth Art* 14; *Arm Ev* 9; *Bonn I* 7; *Afr Orth* 6–7; *Philip Ind* 2.15; *Vat II* 5.1.50–51, 5.1.66–69, 5.3.15

BECAME HUMAN

3.9. Fully Divine Nature and Fully Human Nature (*see also* 1.8–9, 3.10)

I: *Ign; Tome* 5; *Edict* 5–7, 13–18, 23–32, anath 8; *Ecth* 3–4; *Eph 431* ecth; *Chal* 5–12, 16–20; *Nic II*

II: *CP 1351* 13; *Greg Palam* 2; *Gennad* 6–7; *Metr Crit* 3.6–7

III: *Ath* 30–37; *Tol I* 13–15; *Lat 649* 4–5; *Rom Syn* 3; *Sens* 4; *Lat 1215* 2

IV: *Form Conc Epit* 8.8; *Form Conc Sol Dec* 1.43–44; *Sax Vis* 1.2, 2.2; *Fid rat* 1; *Gall* 15; *Belg* 19; *Helv II* 11.6–10

V: *Meth Art* 2; *Cumb Pres* 29; *Arm Ev* 5; *Swed Bap* 4; *Free Meth* 2; *Com Cr* 6; *Naz* 2; *Assem* 13f–g; *Witness* 8; *Un Pres* 12; *Ess* 8; *Bat* 3B; *Menn Con* 1.3; *Leuen* 22; *Hond* 2; *Toraja* 4.2; *Bap Conf* 2b; *Chr Dec* 2–3; *Com Dec* 3

3.10. Hypostatic Union of Two Natures, with Two Wills and Two "Energies" (*see also* 1.9, 3.9)

I: *Edict* 8–12, 19–22, anath 4, 9; *Ecth* 4–6; *Eph 431* ecth; *Chal* 19–24; *CP II* anath 3–5, 7–9; *CP III* 7–9; *Nic II*

II: *CP 1351* 14

III: *Tol I* anath 13; *Lat 649* 6–16; *Rom Syn* 3; *Flor Arm* 7–9

IV: *Form Conc Epit* 3.3, 3.12–13, 8.1–18; *Form Conc Sol Dec* 8.31–87; *Sax Vis* 1.2, 2.2; *Fid rat* 1; *Gall* 15; *Belg* 19; *Helv II* 11.6–10

V: *Def Plat* 2.7; *Free Meth* 2; *Salv Arm* 4; *Naz* 2; *Un Pres* 12; *Leuen* 22

4. AND WAS CRUCIFIED ON OUR BEHALF UNDER PONTIUS PILATE

4.1. Reconciliation, Redemption, and Atonement

II: *Gennad 9; Mogila 1.50–51*

III: *Ath 38; Vienne 1; Boh I 6*

IV: *17 Art 9; Luth Sm Cat 2.4; Luth Lg Cat 2.31; Aug 3.3; Apol Aug 4.179, 24.22–24, 58–59; Smal Art 2.1; Form Conc Sol Dec 5.20–22; 67 Art 54; Bern 3; Fid rat 3 Helv I 11; Genv Cat 56–61, 71; Gall 17; Scot I 9; Heid 12–18, 37–39; Helv II 11.15; 39 Art 31; Remon 2; Irish 30; Dort 2; West 8.4–7; West Sh Cat 25; 18 Diss 9; Ries 13; Dordrecht 4; Marburg 3; Trent 22.2*

V: *True Con 14; London I 17–18; Gen Bap 17–19; Cum occas 5; Sav 8.4–7; Friends I 6, 10; Geloof 13, 15.2; Meth Art 2, 20; Cumb Pres 31–33; Aub 8, 10; LDS 3; Arm Ev 5; Swed Bap 4; Free Meth 2, 20; Adv 2; Salv Arm 6; Chr Sci 4; Com Cr 6; Richmond 2, 6; Utrecht 6; Am Bap 6; Lam 38; Naz 2, 6; Pol Nat 3; Assem 12; Un Ch Can: Union 7; Un Pres 9, 12, 14; F&O Laus 2; Ess 8–9; Br St Luth 4, 8, 18; F&O Edin 1.1; Bap Assoc 7; Bat 3B; Un Ch Japan 2; Arn 3d; Madag 5; UCC 5; Menn Con 5.2; Ref All 2; Pres USA 9.09; Meth Braz 2.4; Un Ref Ch 17.2; Leuen 9; PRCC 1b; RCA 4; Toraja 4.4–5; Bap Conf 2b; Camb Dec 2*

HE SUFFERED AND WAS BURIED

4.2. Events of the Passion: Transfiguration, Crucifixion, Death, and Descent into Hades

I: *Ign; Tert; Tome 12–13*

II: *CP 1341; CP 1351 46; Metr Crit 3.8–11; Mogila 1.43–49*

III: *Ap 4; Ath 38; R 4; Tol I 16, anath 6–7; Sens 18; Lat 1215 2*

IV: *Form Conc Epit 9; Form Conc Sol Dec 9; Genv Cat 55, 65–70; Heid 40–44; Helv II 11.10; 39 Art 3; West Sh Cat 2*

V: *Geloof 15.2; Cumb Pres 30; Free Meth 2; Chr Sci 5; Com Cr 6; Richmond 2; Naz 2; Un Pres 12; Masai 2; Hond 2; Toraja 4.5*

5. AND ROSE UP ON THE THIRD DAY IN ACCORDANCE WITH THE SCRIPTURES

5.1. The Resurrection of Christ (*see also* 11.4)

I: *Polyc; Tert; Tome* 11; *CP II* anath 12
II: *Metr Crit* 3.12; *Mogila* 1.52–53
III: *Ap* 5; *Ath* 38; *R* 5; *Tol I* 16–17
IV: *Aug* 3.4; *Lu Sm Cat* 2.4; *Lu Lg Cat* 2.31; *Tetrapol* 2; *Bas Bek* 4; *Helv I* 11; *Genv Cat* 73–74; *Scot I* 10; *Heid* 45; *Helv II* 11.11; *39 Art* 4; *West Sh Cat* 28; *Ries* 15
V: *Geloof* 15.3; *Meth Art* 3; *Free Meth* 3; *Chr Sci* 5; *Com Cr* 7; *Richmond* 2; *Am Bap* 7; *Lam* 36–37; *Naz* 2; *Witness* 10; *So Bap* 16; *Un Pres* 12; *Ess* 8; *Bap Assoc* 8; *Bat* 3B; *Madag* 7; *Masai* 2; *Pres USA* 9.26; *RCA* 4; *Hond* 3; *Toraja* 4.6; *Bap Conf* 2b; *Philip UCC* 6

6. AND HE WENT UP INTO THE HEAVENS AND IS SEATED AT THE FATHER'S RIGHT HAND

6.1. The Ascension of Christ into Heaven

II: *Gennad* 10; *Metr Crit* 3.13; *Lucar* 8; *Mogila* 1.55–56
III: *Ap* 6; *Ath* 39; *R* 6; *Tol I* 18; *Tol XI* 17
IV: *Form Conc Sol Dec* 7.93–103; *Genv Cat* 75–82; *Scot I* 11; *Heid* 46–51; *Helv II* 11.12; *39 Art* 4; *Ries* 16; *Tig* 25
V: *Meth Art* 3; *Com Cr* 7; *Richmond* 2; *Am Bap* 7; *Un Pres* 12; *Bap Assoc* 8; *Bat* 3B; *Masai* 2; *RCA* 5; *Toraja* 4.8–9; *Bap Conf* 2b

7. HE IS COMING AGAIN WITH GLORY TO JUDGE THE LIVING AND THE DEAD

7.1. The Second Coming of Christ to Judgment (*see also* 11–12)

I: *Tert*
II: *Gennad* 10; *Jer II* 1.17; *Mogila* 1.57–68
III: *Ap* 7; *Ath* 39–41; *R* 7; *Tol XI* 17; *Sens* 17; *Lat 1215* 2
IV: *Aug* 17; *Apol Aug* 17; *Bas Bek* 10; *Helv I* 11.5; *Genv Cat* 83–87; *Scot I* 11; *Heid* 52; *Helv II* 11.13; *Irish* 104; *West* 33.1; *Ries* 40
V: *Sav* 32.1; *Geloof* 33.3–4, 34.4; *Shkr* 3–4; *Cumb Pres* 114–15; *New*

Hamp 18; *Ev All* 8; *Abst Prin* 20; *Swed Bap* 12; *Free Meth* 14; *Adv* 17–18; *Com Cr* 12; *Richmond* 2; *Am Bap* 8; *Naz* 11.14; *Assem* 15; *Witness* 2; *Afr Orth* 13; *So Bap* 17; *Un Ch Can: Union* 19; *Un Pres* 12, 40; *Br St Luth* 42; *Bap Assoc* 22; *Bat* 3B, 18; *Madag* 7; *Masai* 2; *Menn Con* 20; *Leuen* 9; *Laus Cov* 15; *RCA* con; *Toraja* 4.8, 8.2–3; *Bap Conf* 9; *Philip UCC* 6

HIS KINGDOM WILL HAVE NO END

7.2. The Kingdom of Christ and of God

II: *Jer II* 1.5

III: *Tol XI* 18

IV: *Luth Sm Cat* 3.7–8; *Luth Lg Cat* 3.51–58; *Aug* 17.5; *Genv Cat* 37, 42, 268–70; *Heid* 123; *Helv II* 11.14; *Irish* 104; *West Sh Cat* 26, 102; *Ries* 14, 18; *Tig* 4

V: *True Con* 15–16; *London I* 19–20; *Geloof* 16; *Com Cr* 9, 12; *Lam* 52; *Assem* 15; *So Bap* 25; *Un Ch Can: Union* 20; *Un Pres* 12, 37–38, 40, 43–44; *Chin Un* 1; *Meth Kor* 7; *Br St Luth* 42; *Barm* 5; *F&O Edin* 9; *Vat II* 5.1.3–5, 5.1.9–10, 5.1.36; *Pres USA* 9.53–55; *Design* 1.8; *Meth Braz* 2.5; *Korea* pr; *Laus Cov* 15; *PRCC* 4; *Hond* 3; *Pres So Afr* 3; *Toraja* 4.3, 5.2, 6.6; *BEM* 1.7, 2.22; *Philip UCC* 5

7.3. The Kingdoms of This World: Civil Government and Civil Society; Church and State

I: *Edict* 1; *Ecth* con; *CP II* 2; *CP III* 1, 5

II: *CP 1351* con; *Jer II* 1.14, 1.16

III: *Dict Pap* 9, 12, 19, 27; *Unam* 4–6; *Loll* 6, 10; *Prague* 3; *Boh I* 16

IV: *17 Art* 3, 4, 14; *Luth Sm Cat* pr 13, 21–22; *Aug* 16, 28; *Apol Aug* 16; *67 Art* 35–43; *Tetrapol* 23; *Fid rat* 11; *Bas Bek* 8; *Helv I* 26; *Laus Art* 8; *10 Art* pr 1; *Genv Con* 20; *Gall* 39–40; *Scot I* 24; *Belg* 36; *Helv II* 30; *39 Art* 37; *Irish* 57–62; *West* 22–23; *Schleit* 4, 6, 7; *Cologne* 12; *Ries* 37–38; *Dordrecht* 13–15; *Marburg* 12; *Witt Art* 11

V: *True Con* 39–44; *London I* 48–53; *Camb Plat* 17; *Sav* 23–24; *Friends I* 21–22; *Geloof* 28–30; *Meth Art* 23–25; *Cumb Pres* 81–88; *New Hamp* 16; *Swed Bap* 11; *Free Meth* 23; *LDS* 10, 12; *Syl* 20, 23–32, 39–55, 75–77; *Richmond* 12, 14, 15; *Soc Meth*; *Soc Ch*; *So Bap* 18–19; *Un Pres* 31, 37–38; *Ess* 12–13; *Br St Luth* 34; *Barm* pr, 4–5; *Philip Ind* 2.19; *Chin Man*; *Sheng Kung* 2, 6; *Bat* 8.3, 12; *Vat II* 5.3.12, 9.3, 9.6–7, 9.11–15; *Menn Con* 9, 17–19; *Pres USA* 9.43–47; *Meth Braz* 3; *Korea* 2–3; *Laus Cov* 5, 13; *PRCC* 2b, 3e; *RCA* 10–12; *Pres So Afr* 2; *Toraja* 7.5–8; *Bap Conf* 7; *Morav Am* con

8. AND IN THE SPIRIT, THE HOLY, THE LORDLY

8.1. The Divine Person of the Holy Spirit (*see also* 1.8)

I: *Tert; CP I*

II: *CP 1341* 30–31; *Greg Palam* 3; *Mogila* 1.69–70

III: *Ap* 8; *Ath* 23; *R* 8; *Tol I* anath 4; *Tol XI* 3; *Sens* 1–2

IV: *Belg* 11; *Heid* 53; *39 Art* 5; *Cologne* 3

V: *Morav* 3; *Geloof* 4.4, 14.4; *Meth Art* 4; *Free Meth* 4; *Richmond* 3; *Naz* 3; *Pol Nat* 4; *Witness* 9; *Un Ch Can: Union* 8; *Un Pres* 13; *F&O Laus* 1; *Meth Kor* 3; *CSI 1947* 1; *Philip Ind* 1.3; *Bap Assoc* 9; *Madag* 3; *Menn Con* 1.4; *Meth Braz* 2.3; *Laus Cov* 14; *Toraja* 1.5, 4.9, 5.1–3; *Philip UCC* 1

AND LIFE-GIVING ONE

8.2. Life in the Spirit: Conversion, Regeneration, Sanctification, Restoration of the Divine Image, Participation in the Divine Nature

II: *CP 1341* 19, 35–38; *CP 1351* 36–37

III: *Orange* 4, 6

IV: *Luth Sm Cat* 2.6; *Luth Lg Cat* 2.35–45; *Apol Aug* 4.126; *Form Conc Sol Dec* 2.25–27, 3.19–23, 8.34; *Helv I* 11; *Genv Con* 8; *Genv Cat* 88–91; *Gall* 21; *Scot I* 12; *Belg* 24; *Dort* 3/4.11–13; *West* 10, 12–13, 26.3; *West Sh Cat* 29–39; *Denck* 3; *Ries* 19; *Marburg* 6

V: *Sav* 10, 13, 27.1; *Friends I* 1–2, 7–8; *Geloof* 19; *Cumb Pres* 51–54; *New Hamp* 7, 10; *Aub* 12; *Arm Ev* 6; *Ev All* 7; *Abst Prin* 8, 12; *Adv* 5, 14; *Salv Arm* 7, 10; *Richmond* 3, 6; *Naz* 9.10, 10.13; *Assem* 4b, 19; *So Bap* 7, 10; *Un Ch Can: Union* 8–9, 12; *Un Pres* 11, 13, 16, 21; *Br St Luth* 10–16; *F&O Edin* 1.2; *Bap Assoc* 11; *Bat* 3C; *Madag* 3; *UCC* 6; *Masai* 3; *Vat II* 5.1.4; *Menn Con* 6–7; *Zambia* 6; *Ref All* 3; *Pres USA* 9.20; *Design* 1.5; *Meth Braz* 2.3; *Leuen* 10; *RCA* 6–9; *Hond* 3; *Toraja* 5.1–3

8.3. The Gifts of the Holy Spirit; Divine Grace and Human Merit

II: *Metr Crit* 3.14; *Mogila* 1.73–81; *Dosith* decr 3

III: *Orange* 3, 5–7, 12, 18–21, con; *Sens* 5

IV: *Apol Aug* 4.17, 4.19–20, 4.288, 4.316, 4.356–77; *Form Conc Sol Dec* 2.25–27; *Genv Cat* 115; *Lamb Art* 7; *Helv II* 16.11; *Remon* 4; *Irish* 26; *West* 7.3–6; *West Sh Cat* 20; *18 Diss* 16; *Witt Art* 5; *Trent* 6.15–16

V: *Gen Bap* 25–26, 29–33; *Cum occas* 1–4; *Sav* 7.3–5; *Geloof* 17; *Cumb Pres* 39–40; *Aub* 13; *LDS* 4, 7; *Adv* 15–16; *Bonn I* 6; *Naz* 7; *Pol Nat* 5; *Assem* 6; *Un Pres* 13; *Moth Kor* 4; *F&O Edin* 1.1, 1.6; *Bat* 7; *Un Ch Japan* 3; *Vat II* 8.8; *Menn Con* 6–7; *Pres So Afr* 3; *BEM* 1.5, *Camb Dec* 3; *LuRC Just* 19–21, 25–27

8.4. Sanctification as a Life of Love, Christian Service, Virtue, and Good Works

II: *Jer II* 1.2, 1.5, 1.6, 1.20; *Lucar* 13; *Mogila* 1.3; *Dosith* decr 13
III: *Orange* 17; *Sens* 13; *Boh I* 7
IV: *Luth Sm Cat* 1, 9; *Luth Lg Cat* 1; *Aug* 20; *Apol Aug* 4.111–16, 4.122–58, 4.189–94, 20; *Form Conc Epit* 4; *Form Conc Sol Dec* 4; *67 Art* 22; *Tetrapol* 4–6; *10 Art* 3.8–10; *Genv Con* 10; *Genv Cat* 121–27; *Gall* 22; *Scot I* 13–14; *Belg* 24; *Heid* 86–91; *Helv II* 16; *Remon* 5; *Irish* 39–45, 63–67; *West* 16.1–6; *West Sh Cat* 39–84; *18 Diss* 4, 18; *Cologne* 13, 14, 16; *Ries* 22–23; *Dordrecht* 14; *Marburg* 10; *Witt Art* 4, 5; *Trent* 6.11, 6 can 18–21, 24–26, 31–32

V: *Gen Bap* 33–42; *Sav* 16; *Friends I* 13–14, 21; *Geloof* 20.6, 21.1–5, 22.4; *Meth Art* 10–11; *Winch* 3; *Cumb Pres* 55–59; *LDS* 13; *Arm Ev* 8; *Syl* 56–64; *Free Meth* 10–11, 13; *Chr Sci* 6; *Com Cr* 8; *Naz* 10.13; *Assem* 7; *So Bap* 21, 24; *Un Ch Can: Union* 12; *Un Pres* 44; *Br St Luth* 20; *F&O Edin* 2.8–10; *Philip Ind* 2.12; *Sheng Kung* 5; *Bat* 15; *Un Ch Japan* 3; *Masai* 3; *Vat II* 5.1.39–42; *Pres USA* 9.22–25; *Meth Braz* 9; *Leuen* 11; *PRCC* 1c; *RCA* 10–14; *Toraja* 5.5–6; *Bap Conf* 2c, 8; *Morav Am* 7–9; *LuRC Just* 37–39

8.5. Sanctification as Free Obedience to the Law of God
(*see also* 1.13, 3.3, 8.4)

II: *Metr Crit* 6; *Mogila* 1.86–95
III: *Orange* 13
IV: *17 Art* 2; *Luth Sm Cat* pr 17–18, 1; *Luth Lg Cat* 1; *Aug* 6; *Form Conc Epit* 6; *Form Conc Sol Dec* 6; *Genv Con* 3; *Genv Cat* 131–232; *Gall* 23; *Scot I* 15; *Heid* 92–115; *Helv II* 12; *Irish* 84; *West* 19–20; *Witt Art* 5
V: *London I* 29; *Gen Bap* 28; *Cum occas* 1; *Sav* 19, 21; *Meth Art* 6; *Cumb Pres* 37, 66–74; *New Hamp* 12; *Abst Prin* 18; *Adv* 11; *Un Ch Can: Union* 14; *Un Pres* 25; *Bat* 15

PROCEEDING FORTH FROM THE FATHER [AND THE SON]

8.6. The Procession of the Holy Spirit

I: *Tert*

II: *Phot* 8–23; *CP 1054* 3, 4; *Greg Palam* 3; *Mark Eph* 1–2, 6; *Metr Crit* 1.5–31; *Mogila* 1.71

III: *Ath* 23; *Tol XI* 3; *Fréjus* 4; *Lyons; Flor Un* 5–9; *Flor Arm* 6

IV: *Smal Art* 1.2; *Form Conc Sol Dec* 8.73; *Gall* 6; *Belg* 9, 11; *39 Art* 5; *Helv II* 3.3; *Irish* 10; *West* 2.3; *West Lg Cat* 10; *Cologne* 3; *Ries* 3

V: *True Con* 2; *Morav* 3; *Geloof* 4.4; *Meth Art* 4; *Free Meth* 4; *Resp Pius IX* 5–7; *Bonn I* pr; *Bonn II; Richmond* 1; *Witness* 9; *Afr Orth* 2, 5; *Un Ch Can: Union* 8; *Un Pres* 11, 13; *F&O Laus* 4.1; *Philip Ind* 1.3

CO-WORSHIPED AND CO-GLORIFIED WITH FATHER AND SON

8.7. Worship

II: *Lit Chrys; Phot* 5, 29–30; *Jer II* 1.13, 1.24, 1.26; *Metr Crit* 9.2–6, 14–16, 18, 22.1–2, 23.9; *Mogila* 1.87–88, 1.93; *Dosith* q 4

III: *Ath* 27; *Tol I* anath 17; *Flor Arm* 27; *Loll* 5; *Boh I* 18

IV: *Luth Lg Cat* 1.79–102; *Aug* 15, 21, 24, 26; *Apol Aug* 4.10–11, 4.155, 15, 24.27–33, 24.81–83, 27.55–56; *Form Conc Epit* 10, *Form Conc Sol Dec* 10; *67 Art* 24–26; *Fid rat* 9; *Tetrapol* 7–10, 21; *Bas Bek* 11; *Helv I* 23–24; *Laus Art* 10; *10 Art* 9; *Genv Con* 13, 17; *Gall* 33; *Genv Cat* 141–42, 163–65, 183; *Helv II* 17, 22, 24.1–7, 27.1–3; *Irish* 49–56, 77; *West* 21; *18 Diss* 4–7, 10; *Denck* 3; *Cologne* 9; *Dordrecht* 11; *Marburg* 13; *Witt Art* 10, 12; *Tig* 26; *Trent* 13.5

V: *True Con* 30–31, 33; *Camb Plat* 1.3; *Gen Bap* 21, 35, 46; *Sav* 22; *Friends I* 17, 20; *Geloof* 23.7; *Meth Art* 15, 22; *Dec Addr* 5, 12–13; *Cumb Pres* 72, 75–80; *New Hamp* 15; *LDS* 11; *Arm Fv* 1, 9; *Resp Pius IX* 5.12; *Def Plat* 1.1, 1.3, 2.1, 2.2, 2.4; *Abst Prin* 17; *Swed Bap* 9–10; *Syl* 78–79; *Free Meth* 15, 19, 21; *Adv* 12–13; *Bonn I* 4; *Com Cr* 11; *Richmond* 10, 16; *Assem* 13j; *Afr Orth* 12; *So Bap* 14; *Un Ch Can: Union* 15, 20; *Un Pres* 28–29; *Ess* 3–6, 11; *Br St Luth* 41; *F&O Edin* 7; *CSI 1947* 1, 5; *Philip Ind* 2.5, 2.8–11; *Munif* 15–20, 23; *Bat* 11, 13, 14, 16; *Arn* 3; *Vat II* 5.3.8, 5.3.23, 5.3.66–67; *Menn Con* 8.4–5, 13–14; *Sri Lanka* 4–5; *CNI* 3; *Ghana* 11; *Ref All* 4; *Pres USA* 9.50; *Meth Braz* 2.11; *Un Ref Ch* 17.1, 17.4; *RCA* 17; *Toraja* 1.2, 6.7; *Camb Dec* 5

8.8. Prayer

II: *CP 1341* 13; *Jer II* 1.13, 1.15; *Metr Crit* 21; *Mogila* 1.92
III: *Orange* 3, 11; *Loll* 7; *Boh I* 2
IV: *17 Art* 3; *Luth Sm Cat* 3, 7–8; *Luth Lg Cat* 3; *67 Art* 44–46; *Tetrapol* 7; *Genv Cat* 233–95; *Heid* 116–29; *Helv II* 23; *Irish* 47–48; *West* 21.3–6; *West Sh Cat* 98–107; *Witt Art* 5
V: *True Con* 45; *Sav* 22.3–6; *Cumb Pres* 76; *Richmond* 11; *Un Ch Can: Union* 13; *Un Pres* 27; *Meth Kor* 4; *Sheng Kung* con; *Vat II* 5.1.15, 5.3.8; *Zambia* 6; *Toraja* 5.4; *Bap Conf* 2a

8.9. Prayer for the Departed (*see also* 12.1)

II: *Lit Chrys* I.D.1; *Jer II* 1.15; *Metr Crit* 20
III: *Loll* 7
IV: *Apol Aug* 24.89–98
V: *Cumb Pres* 76; *Arm Ev* 9; *Bonn I* 13; *Afr Orth* 10; *Vat II* 5.1.50; *Toraja* 8.5

8.10. Images in the Church

I: *Nic II* ecth, anath 1–3
II: *Phot* 43; *Greg Palam* 4; *Metr Crit* 15; *Lucar* q 4; *Dosith* q 4
III: *Loll* 8, 12; *Boh I* 17
IV: *Bern* 8; *Tetrapol* 22; *Laus Art* 7; *10 Art* 6; *Genv Cat* 143–49; *Heid* 96–98; *Helv II* 4; *Irish* 53; *West Sh Cat* 49–52; *18 Diss* 7; *Witt Art* 17; *Trent* 25.2; *Trid Prof* 6
V: *Meth Art* 14; *Arm Ev* 9; *Afr Orth* 7; *Madag* 1

THE ONE WHO SPOKE THROUGH THE PROPHETS

8.11. The Authority of Scripture as the Word of God (*see also* 1.4, 8.12, 9.6, 9.8)

I: *Chal* 25
II: *Gennad* 12.1; *Jer II* 1 int; *Metr Crit* 7.6, 7.9; *Lucar* 2, q 1–2; *Mogila* 1.54, 1.72; *Dosith* decr 2, q 1–2
III: *Tol I* anath 8; *Prague* 1; *Boh I* 1
IV: *Form Conc Epit* int 3; *Form Conc Sol Dec* int 1–8; *Tetrapol* 1; *Helv I* 1,

5; *Genv Con* 1; *Genv Cat* 300–306; *Scot I* 5, 19; *Belg* 5; *Helv II* 1, 13.2; *39 Art* 6; *West* 1.4–6; *West Sh Cat* 3; *18 Diss* 8, 11–12

V: *True Con* 7–8; *London I* 7–8; *Gen Bap* 46; *Sav* 1.4–6; *Friends I* 3; *Geloof* 2, 14.3; *Meth Art* 5–6; *Winch* 1; *Dec Addr* 4; *Cumb Pres* 2, 68; *LDS* 8–9; *Arm Ev* 3; *Abst Prin* 1; *Swed Bap* 1; *Free Meth* 5–6; *Vat I* 3.pr; *Adv* 3, 6–7; *Bonn I* 2–3; *Salv Arm* 1; *Chr Sci* 1; *Com Cr* 5; *Lamb Quad* 1; *Richmond* 4; *Naz* 4; *Sacr ant* 3; *Afr Orth* 1; *So Bap* pr 4, 1; *Un Ch Can: Union* pr, 2; *Un Pres* 3, 26; *Chin Un* 2; *Meth Kor* 5; *Br St Luth* 2; *CSI 1947* 1; *Philip Ind* 2.2; *Munif* 12; *Bat* 4; *Un Ch Japan* 1; *Arn* 4; *Madag* pr 2, art 4; *Vat II* 8.7–10, 8.21–26; *Menn Con* pr, 2.1; *Sri Lanka* 3; *CNI* 2; *Ghana* 3.2; *Zambia* 2–3; *Pres USA* 9.27–28; *Design* 1.7; *Meth Braz* 1.1; *Un Ref Ch* 12; *Leuen* 4; *Laus Cov* 2; *RCA* 1; *Toraja* 2.3, 2.6; *Bap Conf* 1; *Philip UCC* 4; *Morav Am* 3; *Camb Dec* 1

8.12. The Authority of Church and Tradition
(*see also* 1.4, 8.11, 9.6, 9.8)

I: *Iren; CP II* 7; *Nic II*

II: *Phot* 5; *Jer II* 1.26; *Metr Crit* 7.5, 7.10, 14.1–4; *Dosith* decr 2, 12

III: *Rom Syn* 4; *Boh I* 15

IV: *Aug* 26, *Apol Aug* pr 11, 4.393, 15.1–4; *Smal Art* 3.15; *Form Conc Sol Dec* 2.52; *67 Art* 11, 16; *Bern* 2; *Tetrapol* 14; *Helv I* 3–4; *Gall* 5; *Belg* 7; *Helv II* 2.2, 2.5; *39 Art* 34; *Scot II*; *Irish* 6; *Trent* 4.1; *Trid Prof* 2

V: *Dec Addr* 11; *Resp Pius IX* 17; *Vat I* 3.2, 4.4; *Bonn I* 9.1; *Utrecht* 1; *Lam* 1–8; *Sacr ant* 10–11; *Afr Orth* 1; *F&O Laus* 3A; *Ess* 10; *CSI 1947* 1; *Munif* 12; *Vat II* 5.1.20–21, 8.7–10, 8.21, 9.1, 9.14; *Com Dec* 2; *Ad tuendam* 4

8.13. The Canon of Scripture

II: *Metr Crit* 7.6–8; *Lucar* q 3; *Dosith* q 3

III: *Tol I* anath 12

IV: *Gall* 3–4; *Belg* 4, 6; *Helv II* 1.9; *39 Art* 6; *Irish* 2–3; *West* 1.2–3; *Trent* 4.1

V: *Sav* 1.2–3; *Geloof* 2.3; *Meth Art* 5; *Cumb Pres* 1; *Free Meth* 5; *Vat I* 3.2, 3 can 2.4; *Bonn I* 1; *Vat II* 8.8; *Sri Lanka* 3.3; *RCA* 7; *Toraja* 2.3

8.14. The Inspiration and Inerrancy of Scripture

II: *Gennad* 12.2

IV: *Belg* 3; *West* 1.8

V: *Gen Bap* 46; *Sav* 1.8; *Geloof* 2.3–4; *Cumb Pres* 1; *New Hamp* 1; *Arm Ev*

3; *Ev All* 1; *Abst Prin* 1; *Syl* 7; *Vat I* 3.2; *Salv Arm* 1; *Am Bap* 1, 3; *Lam* 9–
19; *Naz* 4; *Assem* 1; *So Bap* 1; *Un Pres* 3, 13; *Ess* 7; *Br St Luth* 1, 3; *Bap Assoc*
2–3; *Un Ch Japan* 1; *Vat II* 5.3.21, 8.7–8, 8.11, 8.14, 8.20; *Menn Con* 2.1;
Pres USA 9.29; *Laus Cov* 2; *RCA* 6; *Toraja* 2.7; *Bap Conf* 1, 2c; *Philip UCC*
4; *Camb Dec* 1

8.15. Criteria of Scriptural Interpretation

I: *Orig* 8; *Tome* 1–2
II: *Dosith* decr 2
IV: *Apol Aug* 24.35; *Helv I* 2; *Scot I* 18; *Helv II* 2; *Irish* 5; *West* 1.7–10; *18
Diss* 8, 10; *Denck* 1; *Trent* 4.2; *Trid Prof* 2
V: *True Con* 34; *Sav* 1.7–10; *Cumb Pres* 3–4; *Ev All* 2; *Syl* 22; *Vat I* 3.2;
Richmond 4; *Lam* 1–8; *Sacr ant* 10; *Munif* 26; *Vat II* 8.10, 8.12; *Zambia* 9;
Pres USA 9.29–30; *Leuen* 39; *Toraja* 2.5

9. IN ONE

9.1. Unity, Union, and Reunion with the Church of Christ

II: *Metr Crit* 7.2; *Mogila* 1.82–83
III: *Unam* 2–3; *Flor Un*; *Flor Arm*; *Boh I* 8
IV: *Aug* 7.2–4; *Apol Aug* 7/8.30–46; *Bas Bek* 5; *Helv II* 17.2–4; *Dordrecht*
int
V: *Friends I* 9; *Geloof* 23.2; *Dec Addr* 1; *Vat I* 4 pr; *Lamb Quad* 4; *Pol Nat*
6, 9; *So Bap* 22; *Un Pres* 22, 32, 35; *F&O Laus* 1; *Br St Luth* 29; *Barm* pr;
F&O Edin 1 pr, 2.1–10; *CSI 1947* 7–8; *Philip Ind* 2.18; *Bat* 8D; *Madag* 6; *Sri
Lanka* 1, 11; *CNI* 4; *Ghana* 1; *Meth Braz* 1.4, 2.7; *Leuen* 1, 29–49; *Laus Cov*
7; *Balamand* 6–18; *Chr Dec* 8–10; *BEM* 1.15–16; *Morav Am* 5; *Com Dec* 5–6

9.2. Schism, Separation, and Division

II: *Phot*; *CP 1054*
III: *Flor Un*
IV: *Apol Aug* 23.59; *Helv I* 25; *Helv II* 17.10; *Schleit* 4
V: *True Con* 36; *London I* 46; *Camb Plat* 13.5, 14.9; *Dec Addr* 2, 10–11;
Resp Pius IX 9; *Syl* 18, 38; *F&O Laus* 1; *Br St Luth* 28; *F&O Edin* 2.3–5;
Bat 8.1; *Vat II* 5.1.15, 5.3.1, 5.3.3; *Pres USA* 9.34; *Morav Am* 5–6

HOLY

9.3. The Holiness of the Church and of the Means of Grace

II: *Jer II* 1.8
III: *Ap* 9; *R* 9; *Loll* 1; *Prague* 4; *Boh I* 11
IV: *Luth Lg Cat* 5.15–19; *Aug* 8; *Apol Aug* 7/8.47–50; *Genv Cat* 96, 99; *Gall* 28; *Helv II* 1.4, 18.21, 19.12; *39 Art* 26; *Irish* 70; *West* 27.3; *Witt Conc* 3; *Trent* 7 can 1.12
V: *Geloof* 23.3, 8; *Un Ch Can: Union* 18; *Sheng Kung* 4; *Bat* 8B; *Vat II* 5.1.8, 5.1.39–42

9.4. Church Discipline (*see also* 10.10)

III: *Boh I* 14
IV: *17 Art* 16; *Aug* 26.33–39; *Apol Aug* 15.45–48; *Smal Art* 3.7, 3.9; *Form Conc Epit* 4.17–18; *67 Art* 31–32; *Bas Bek* 7; *Genv Con* 19; *Belg* 29, 32; *Heid* 83–85; *Helv II* 18.15, 20; *39 Art* 33; *Irish* 73; *West* 30; *Schleit* 2; *Cologne* 7; *Ries* 35–36; *Dordrecht* 16–17
V: *True Con* 23–25; *London I* 42–43; *Camb Plat* 14; *Gen Bap* 55–56, 67–72; *Geloof* 27; *Bat* 8D, 9.4; *Vat II* 5.3.6; *Menn Con* 8.3

CATHOLIC

9.5. Catholicity of the Church

I: *Iren*
II: *Mogila* 1.84; *Dosith* decr 10
III: *Ap* 9
IV: *Genv Cat* 97; *Belg* 27; *Helv II* 17.2; *West* 25.1
V: *Camb Plat* 2.1; *Sav* 26.1–2; *Geloof* 23.4; *Un Pres* 32; *Sheng Kung* 4; *Madag* 6; *Vat II* 5.1.13; *Toraja* 6.13

AND APOSTOLIC

9.6. Apostolic Authority in the Church (*see also* 1.4, 8.11–12, 9.8)

II: *Jer II* 1.int
III: *Dict Pap; Sens* 12; *Unam* 3, 7–8; *Flor Un* 14–15
IV: *Helv I* 16; *Helv II* 17.6–8; *39 Art* 20; *Scot II; Irish* 79–80

V: *Gen Bap* 51; *Cumb Pres* 108–11; *LDS* 5; *Resp Pius IX* 11–14; *Ineff*; *Syl* 21–23, 33; *Vat I* 4.4; *Utrecht* 1–2, 4; *Lam* 55–56; *Sacr ant* 1; *Afr Orth* 3; *Br St Luth* 30; *Barm* 4; *Munif* 12; *Bat* 3B3, 8.2; *Vat II* 5.1.12, 5.1.25; *Pres USA* 9.10

9.7. Apostolic Church Order and Polity; Hierarchy (*see also* 10.12)

II: *Jer II* 1.14, 1.28; *Metr Crit* 11.5–7, 11.9, 23.7–8; *Mogila* 1.84–85; *Dosith* decr 10

III: *Dict Pap*; *Boh I* 9

IV: *17 Art* pr; *Aug* 5, 14, 28; *Apol Aug* 14, 28; *Helv I* 15, 17, 19; *Laus Art* 5; *Genv Cat* 307–8; *Gall* 25–26, 29–32; *Belg* 30–32; *Helv II* 18; *39 Art* 23; *Irish* 71; *Schleit* 5; *Cologne* 10–11; *Ries* 25–28; *Dordrecht* 9; *Witt Art* 9; *Trent* 23 can 7

V: *True Con* 19–27; *London I* 44–45; *Camb Plat* 1, 4, 6, 7, 8; *Sav con* 1–30; *Dec Addr* 3; *Cumb Pres* 108–9; *LDS* 6; *Resp Pius IX* 6; *Vat I* 4.1–3; *Bonn I* 9.2; *Lamb Quad* 4; *Un Ch Can: Union* 17–18, con; *Un Pres* 33; *F&O Laus* 5; *CSI 1947* 3–4, 6; *Philip Ind* 2.6; *Bat* 11; *Vat II* 5.1.10, 5.1.18–29; *Sri Lanka* 7; *Ghana* 5.2; *Pres USA* 9.38–40; *BEM* 3.34–38

9.8. Authority of Church Councils and Synods (*see also* 1.4, 8.11–12, 9.7, Index B)

I: *Eph 431* can 7; *CP II* 4, 5, con; *Nic II*

II: *Phot* 40–44; *Greg Palam* 6–7; *Mark Eph* 4; *Jer II* 1.int, 1.29; *Metr Crit* 15.4; *Mogila* 1.4–5; *Dosith* decr 12

III: *Lat 649* 17, 20; *Dict Pap* 4, 16, 25

IV: *Smal Art* pr 1, 10–13; *Scot I* 20; *Helv II* 2.4; *39 Art* 21; *Irish* 76; *West* 31; *18 Diss* pr; *Trid Prof* 8

V: *Camb Plat* 16; *Resp Pius IX* 3, 5; *Syl* 23, 35–36; *Vat I* 3 pr, 4.4; *Utrecht* 1, 5; *Lam* 31; *Afr Orth* 1; *Philip Ind* 2.17; *Vat II* 5.1.22, 5.1.25; *Camb Dec* pr, 1

CHURCH

9.9. Definition of the True Church

II: *Jer II* 1.7, 1.8; *Metr Crit* 7; *Lucar* 10–12; *Mogila* 1.82–96; *Dosith* decr 10–12

III: *Ap* 9; *Tol XI* 18; *Unam* 1; *Boh I* 8

IV: *Luth Sm Cat* 2.6; *Luth Lg Cat* 2.47–56; *Aug* 7; *Apol Aug* 7/8.5–29; *Smal Art* 3.12; *67 Art* 8; *Tetrapol* 15; *Fid rat* 6; *Bas Bek* 5; *Helv I* 14; *Laus Art* 3; *Genv Con* 18; *Genv Cat* 93–95; *Gall* 27; *Scot I* 5, 16, 18; *Belg* 27, 29; *Heid* 54–55; *Helv II* 17; *39 Art* 19; *Irish* 68–69; *West* 25–26; *Ries* 24; *Dordrecht* 8; *Trid Prof* 7

V: *True Con* 17–18; *Camb Plat* 2–3; *Sav* 26–27; *Friends I* 16; *Morav* 3–4; *Meth Art* 13; *Shkr* 3; *Dec Addr* 1; *Cumb Pres* 93–97; *New Hamp* 13; *Arm Ev* 11; *Abst Prin* 14; *Swed Bap* 9; *Syl* 19; *Free Meth* 16; *Vat I* 3.3; *Com Cr* 10; *Richmond* 2; *Am Bap* 10–12; *Lam* 52–57; *Pol Nat* 6–8; *Assem* 8; *Witness* 1; *So Bap* 12; *Un Ch Can: Union* 15; *Un Pres* 32; *F&O Laus* 3; *Meth Kor* 6; *Br St Luth* 24–30; *Barm* 3; *F&O Edin* 1.4; *CSI 1947* 4; *Philip Ind* 1.4; *Chin Man*; *Bap Assoc* 15–19; *Bat* 8D; *Un Ch Japan* 4; *Arn* 6–7; *UCC* 7; *Vat II* 5.1; *Menn Con* pr, 8.1; *Sri Lanka* 2; *Ghana* 2; *Zambia* 7; *Pres USA* 9.31–33; *Design* 2; *Togo* 4; *Un Ref Ch* 17.4; *Laus Cov* 6; *PRCC* 1c; *RCA* 15–19; *Toraja* 6; *Bap Conf* 6; *Philip UCC* 3

10. WE CONFESS ONE BAPTISM FOR THE FORGIVING OF SINS

10.1. Word, Sacraments, and Means of Grace

II: *Jer II* 1.7, 1.13; *Metr Crit* 5; *Lucar* 15; *Mogila* 1.97–101; *Dosith decr* 10, 15

III: *Flor Arm* 10–20; *Boh I* 11

IV: *Luth Sm Cat* 4.10; *Luth Lg Cat* 4.21–22, 5.10–14; *Aug* 7.2, 13.1–3; *Apol Aug* 13, 24.69; *67 Art* 14; *Tetrapol* 16; *Fid rat* 7, 10; *Helv I* 16, 19–20; *Laus Art* 4; *Genv Con* 14; *Genv Cat* 309–20; *Gall* 34; *Scot I* 21–22; *Belg* 33; *Heid* 65–68; *Helv II* 17.7, 19, 25; *39 Art* 25; *Irish* 85–88; *West* 21.5, 27; *West Sh Cat* 88–93; *Ries* 17, 30; *Witt Art* 8; *Tig* 2, 6–20; *Trent* 5.2.9–10, 7, 13.3; *Trid Prof* 3

V: *True Con* 35; *Gen Bap* 47–52; *Sav* 28; *Meth Art* 16; *Cumb Pres* 25, 40–41, 98; *Arm Ev* 11; *Syl* 65–66; *Free Meth* 17; *Bonn I* 8; *Com Cr* 11; *Lamb Quad* 3; *Richmond* 10; *Lam* 39–51; *Afr Orth* 8; *Un Ch Can: Union* 16; *Un Pres* 16, 26, 30; *F&O Laus* 6; *Br St Luth* 21–23; *F&O Edin* 1.5; *CSI 1947* 2; *Philip Ind* 2.4; *Bat* 8D, 9.2, 10; *Un Ch Japan* 4; *Arn* 2b; *UCC* 7; *Masai* 3; *Vat II* 5.1.11; *Sri Lanka* 5; *Ghana* 4; *Zambia* 6, 8; *Pres USA* 9.48–52; *Leuen* 13; *RCA* 15–16; *Toraja* 2.4–5, 6.8–11; *Morav Am* 1

10.2 Baptism

I: *Did; Just; Hipp*

II: *Jer II* 1.3, 1.7, 1.9; *Metr Crit* 5.2–3, 7.10, 8.2; *Lucar* 16; *Mogila* 1.102–4; *Dosith* decr 16

III: *Tol I* anath 18; *Orange* 8, 13; *Tol XI* 18; *Petr Ab* 3; *Lat 1215* 3; *Vienne* 3; *Flor Arm* 14; *Boh I* 12

IV: *17 Art* 5; *Luth Sm Cat* 4; *Luth Lg Cat* 4; *Aug* 9; *Apol Aug* 2.35–45, 9.1–3; *Smal Art* 3.5; *Sax Vis* 1.3, 2.3; *Tetrapol* 17; *Bas Bek* 5; *Helv I* 21; *10 Art* 2; *Genv Con* 15; *Genv Cat* 323–39; *Gall* 28, 35, 38; *Scot I* 21; *Belg* 34; *Heid* 69–74; *Helv II* 20; *39 Art* 27; *Irish* 89–91; *West* 28; *West Sh Cat* 94; *18 Diss* 8–9; *Denck* 2; *Schleit* 1; *Cologne* 5; *Ries* 31–32; *Dordrecht* 7; *Marburg* 9; *Witt Art* 3; *Trent* 7 can 1.9, 7 can 2.1–14

V: *London I* 39–41; *Camb Plat* 12.7; *Sav* 29; *Friends I* 18; *Morav* 4; *Geloof* 25; *Meth Art* 17; *Cumb Pres* 99–103; *New Hamp* 14; *LDS* 4; *Arm Ev* 11; *Ev All* 9; *Def Plat* 1.4, 2.5; *Abst Prin* 15; *Free Meth* 18; *Adv* 4; *Com Cr* 11; *Lamb Quad* 3; *Richmond* 8; *Lam* 42–43; *Naz* 13.18; *Assem* 11; *So Bap* 13; *Un Ch Can: Union* 16.1; *Un Pres* 30; *F&O Laus* 6; *Ess*; *Br St Luth* 21; *CSI 1947* 2; *Philip Ind* 2.4.2; *Bap Assoc* 12, 21; *Bat* 10A; *Masai* 3; *Vat II* 5.1.7, 5.1.40, 5.3.22; *Menn Con* 11; *Sri Lanka* 2, 5.1; *Pres USA* 9.36, 9.51; *Design* 1.4; *Un Ref Ch* 14; *Leuen* 14; *RCA* 18; *Toraja* 6.8–10; *Bap Conf* 6; *BEM* 1.1–23; *Chr Dec* 7; *LuRC Just* 28

10.3. The Mode and the Subject of Baptism

I: *Did; Hipp*

II: *Mogila* 1.103; *Dosith* decr 16

III: *Vienne* 3; *Boh I* 12

IV: *Luth Lg Cat* 4.47–86; *Apol Aug* 9.2–3; *Smal Art* 3.5.4; *Form Conc Epit* 11.6–8; *Form Conc Sol Dec* 12.11–13; *Sax Vis* 2.3.6; *Tetrapol* 17; *Fid rat* 7; *Bas Bek* 12; *10 Art* 2.2–4; *Genv Con* 15; *Genv Cat* 333–39; *Gall* 35; *Scot I* 23; *Belg* 34; *Heid* 74; *Helv II* 20.6; *39 Art* 27.2; *Irish* 90; *West* 28.3–4; *West Sh Cat* 95; *18 Diss* 8; *Ries* 31; *Marburg* 14; *Witt Conc* 4; *Witt Art* 3; *Trent* 5.4, 7 can 2.13–14

V: *True Con* 35; *London I* 39–41; *Sav* 29.3–4; *Gen Bap* 48; *Geloof* 25.2, 5–6; *Meth Art* 17; *Cumb Pres* 26, 102–3; *New Hamp* 14; *LDS* 4; *Resp Pius IX* 5.11; *Def Plat* 2.5–6; *Abst Prin* 15; *Swed Bap* 8; *Free Meth* 18; *Adv* 4; *Com Cr* 11; *Lam* 43; *Naz* 13.18; *Un Ch Can: Union* 16.1; *Un Pres* 30; *Bap Assoc* 12; *Bat* 10A; *Menn Con* 11; *Pres USA* 9.51; *Un Ref Ch* 14; *Leuen* 15–16, 18–20; *Toraja* 6.10; *Bap Conf* 6; *BEM* 1.11–12

10.4. Confirmation/Chrismation

II: *Phot* 6–7, 32; *Jer II* 1.3, 1.7; *Metr Crit* 8; *Mogila* 1.104–5
III: *Flor Arm* 15
IV: *Apol Aug* 13.6; *Genv Cat* pr; *Trent* 7 can 1.9, 7 can 3.1–3
V: *Lam* 44; *Philip Ind* 2.4.3; *Sri Lanka* 5.1; *BEM* 1.14; *Chr Dec* 7

10.5. The Eucharist/Lord's Supper

II: *Jer II* 1.7, 1.10, 1.13; *Metr Crit* 5.2-3, 9.1–13; *Lucar* 17; *Mogila* 1.106–7; *Dosith* decr 17
III: *Brngr 1059*; *Brngr 1079*; *Lat 1215* 3; *Flor Arm* 16; *Wyclif*; *Boh I* 13
IV: *Luth Sm Cat* 6; *Luth Lg Cat* 5; *Aug* 10; *Apol Aug* 10; *Smal Art* 3.6; *Form Conc Epit* 7; *Form Conc Sol Dec* 7; *Sax Vis* 1.1; *Tetrapol* 18; *Fid rat* 8; *Bas Bek* 6; *Helv I* 22; *10 Art* 4; *Genv Con* 16; *Genv Cat* 340–73; *Gall* 36; *Belg* 35; *Heid* 75–82; *Helv II* 21; *39 Art* 28; *Irish* 92–100; *West* 29; *West Sh Cat* 96–97; *Denck* 3; *Schleit* 3; *Cologne* 6; *Ries* 33–34; *Dordrecht* 10; *Marburg* 15; *Trent* 13
V: *True Con* 35; *Camb Plat* 12.7; *Sav* 30; *Friends I* 19; *Morav* 4; *Geloof* 26; *Meth Art* 18; *Cumb Pres* 104–7; *New Hamp* 14; *Arm Ev* 11; *Ev All* 9; *Abst Prin* 16; *Free Meth* 19; *Com Cr* 11; *Lamb Quad* 3; *Richmond* 9; *Lam* 45, 49; *Naz* 14.19; *Assem* 10; *So Bap* 13; *Un Ch Can: Union* 16 2; *Un Pres* 30; *F&O Laus* 6; *Br St Luth* 21; *CSI 1947* 2; *Philip Ind* 2.4.5, 2.5; *Bap Assoc* 13; *Bat* 10B; *Arn* 1–8; *Masai* 3; *Menn Con* 12; *Sri Lanka* 5.2; *Pres USA* 9.36; *Design* 1.6; *Un Ref Ch* 15; *RCA* 19; *Toraja* 6.9,11; *Bap Conf* 6; *BEM* 2.1–33

10.6. The Real Presence of the Body and Blood of Christ

II: *Dosith* decr 17
III: *Brngr 1059*; *Brngr 1079*; *Lat 1215* 3; *Boh I* 13
IV: *17 Art* 6; *Luth Sm Cat* 6.2; *Luth Lg Cat* 5.8–14; *Aug* 10; *Apol Aug* 10; *Form Conc Epit* 7.6–20; *Form Conc Sol Dec* 7.45–58; *Sax Vis* 1.1.1–6, 2.1.6; *Bern* 4; *Fid rat* 8; *Genv Cat* 354–55; *Gall* 37; *Belg* 35; *Helv II* 21.4, 10; *Irish* 94–96; *Marburg* 15; *Witt Conc* 1; *Witt Art* 6; *Tig* 21–22; *Trent* 13.1, 13 can 1, 3–4; *Trid Prof* 5
V: *Cumb Pres* 105; *Def Plat* 1.5, 2.9; *Utrecht* 6; *Afr Orth* 9; *F&O Laus* 6; *Bat* 10B; *Arn* 4; *Leuen* 19; *BEM* 2.14–15, 2.32

10.7. Change of the Eucharistic Elements into the
Body and Blood of Christ

II: *Lit Chrys* II.F.5; *Jer II* 1.10; *Metr Crit* 9.11; *Mogila* 1.107; *Dosith* decr 17

III: *Brngr 1059*; *Brngr 1079*; *Lat 1215* 3; *Flor Un* 10; *Flor Arm* 16; *Loll* 4

IV: *Smal Art* 3.6.5; *Form Conc Epit* 7.22; *Form Conc Sol Dec* 7.108; *Scot I* 21; *Helv II* 19.9–10; *39 Art* 28.2; *Irish* 93; *West* 29.6; *Marburg*; *Witt Conc* 2; *Tig* 24; *Trent* 13.4, 13 can 2; *Trid Prof* 5

V: *Sav* 30.6; *Meth Art* 18; *Cumb Pres* 105; *Free Meth* 19; *Afr Orth* 9; *Arn* 5a

10.8. The Lord's Supper as Memorial and Communion

II: *Jer II* 1.22; *Metr Crit* 9.9–10; *Mogila* 1.107; *Dosith* decr 17

III: *Prague* 2

IV: *Aug* 22; *Apol Aug* 22; *Smal Art* 3.6.2–4; *Form Conc Epit* 7.24; *Form Conc Sol Dec* 7.110; *Genv Cat* 351–52; *Helv II* 21.2, 12; *39 Art* 30; *Irish* 97; *West* 29.2, 4; *18 Diss* 6–7; *Denck* 3; *Marburg* 15; *Witt Art* 12–13; *Trent* 21.1–3, 21 can 1–3; *Trid Prof* 5

V: *Gen Bap* 53; *Sav* 30.2, 4; *Meth Art* 19; *Cumb Pres* 104–5; *Resp Pius IX* 5.12; *Def Plat* 2.8; *Abst Prin* 16; *Utrecht* 6; *Naz* 14.19; *So Bap* 13; *Un Ch Can: Union* 16.2; *Un Pres* 30; *Vat II* 5.1.26, 5.3.2; *Pres USA* 9.52; *Bap Conf* 6; *Chr Dec* 8; *BEM* 2.5–13, 2.19–22

10.9. The Sacrifice of the Mass

II: *Mogila* 1.107; *Dosith* decr 17

III: *Flor Un* 11

IV: *Aug* 24; *Apol Aug* 24.9–77; *Smal Art* 2.2; *Form Conc Epit* 7.23; *67 Art* 18; *Bern* 5; *Tetrapol* 19; *Genv Con* 16; *Genv Cat* 350; *Scot I* 22; *Heid* 80; *Helv II* 21.13; *Irish* 99–100; *West* 30.2; *18 Diss* 5; *Witt Art* 12; *Trent* 22.1–9, 22 can 1–9; *Trid Prof* 5

V: *Sav* 30.2; *Meth Art* 20; *Free Meth* 20; *Bonn I* 14; *Utrecht* 6; *Bat* 3B2, 10B; *Arn* 5b; *Vat II* 5.1.3; *Chr Dec* 7; *BEM* 2.8

10.10. Penance/Repentance: Contrition, Confession, Absolution, Satisfaction

II: *Jer II* 1.4, 5, 7, 11–12, 25; *Metr Crit* 5.2–3, 10.1–4; *Mogila* 1.90, 1.112–14

III: *Flor Arm* 17; *Loll* 9; *Boh I* 5, 14

IV: *17 Art* 2, 7–9; *Luth Sm Cat* 5; *Luth Lg Cat* 6; *Aug* 11, 12, 25; *Apol Aug* 4.258–68, 4.272–74, 11, 12.11–12, 12.13–17, 35–38, 41, 98–177; *Smal Art* 3.3.1–8, 3.3.15–18, 3.3.39–45; *Form Conc Sol Dec* 5.7; *10 Art* 3; *Tetrapol* 20; *Laus Art* 6; *Genv Cat* 128; *Helv II* 14; *Irish* 74; *West* 15; *West Sh Cat* 87; *Dordrecht* 6; *Marburg* 11; *Witt Conc* 4; *Witt Art* 4, 7; *Trent* 14.1.1–9, 14 can 1.1–15

V: *Camb Plat* 12.5–7; *Gen Bap* 44–45; *Sav* 15; *Geloof* 19.3, 27.2–10; *Meth Art* 12; *Cumb Pres* 42–44; *New Hamp* 8; *LDS* 4; *Def Plat* 1.2, 2.3; *Abst Prin* 9; *Swed Bap* 5; *Bonn I* 11–12; *Salv Arm* 7; *Lam* 43, 46–47; *Naz* 8; *So Bap* 8; *Un Ch Can: Union* 10; *Un Pres* 18; *Philip Ind* 2.4.4; *Camb Dec* 6

10.11. The Anointing of the Sick/Extreme Unction

II: *Jer II* 1.7; *Metr Crit* 13; *Mogila* 1.117–19
III: *Flor Arm* 18
IV: *Apol Aug* 13.6; *Trent* 14.2, 14 can 2.1–4
V: *Lam* 48; *Friends I* 19; *Philip Ind* 2.4.6

10.12. Holy Orders/Ordination; Ordained Ministry and Priesthood (*see also* 9.7)

II: *Jer II* 1.7, 1.14; *Metr Crit* 11; *Mogila* 1.89, 1.108–11
III: *Flor Arm* 19; *Loll* 2; *Boh I* 9
IV: *Apol Aug* 13.12, 24.52–55; *Smal Art* 3.10; *67 Art* 61–63; *Tetrapol* 13; *Genv Con* 20; *Helv II* 18.8, 18.10–11; *39 Art* 36; *18 Diss* 12; *Trent* 7 can 1.9, 23.1–4, 23 can 1–8
V: *True Con* 19–27; *London I* 44–45; *Camb Plat* 9; *Gen Bap* 58–67, 73; *Sav* con 15; *Friends I* 16; *Geloof* 24; *Ev All* 9; *Syl* 30–32; *Lam* 50; *Assem* 9; *So Bap* 12; *Un Ch Can: Union* 17; *Un Pres* 34; *F&O Laus* 5; *Ess* 11; *Br St Luth* 31–33; *CSI 1947* 3–4, 6; *Philip Ind* 2.4.7, 2.6; *Bat* 9; *Vat II* 5.1.18–29; *Menn Con* 10; *Sri Lanka* 1, 6–8; *Ghana* 5; *Pres USA* 9.38–40; *Design* 1.7; *Toraja* 6.12; *BEM* 3.7–25, 3.39–50

10.13. Clerical Celibacy

II: *Phot 5*, 31; *CP 1054* 3; *Jer II 1.23*; *Metr Crit* 11.6
III: *Loll 3*; *Prague 4*; *Boh I 9*, 19
IV: *Aug 23*; *Apol Aug 23*; *Smal Art 3.11*; *67 Art 28–30*; *Bern 9–10*; *Helv I 27*; *Helv II 29*; *39 Art 32*; *Irish 64*; *Witt Art 14*; *Trent 24.9*
V: *Meth Art 21*; *Philip Ind 2.7*; *Vat II 5.1.29*, 5.1.42

10.14. Asceticism and Monasticism

II: *Jer II 1.16*, 1.20, 1.27; *Metr Crit 19*
III: *Loll 11*
IV: *Aug 27*; *Apol Aug 27*; *Smal Art 3.14*; *Tetrapol 12*; *Helv II 18.7*; *Witt Art 15*
V: *Sav 23.6*; *Vat II 5.1.43–47*, 5.3.15

10.15. Matrimony; Christian Marriage and the Family

II: *Jer II 1.7*; *Metr Crit 12*; *Mogila 1.115–16*
III: *Tol I 16*; *Flor Arm 20*
IV: *Luth Lg Cat 1.200–221*; *Apol Aug 13.14–15*; *Helv I 27*; *Laus Art 9*; *Helv II 29.2–4*; *Irish 64*; *West 24*; *Cologne 8*; *Ries 39*; *Dordrecht 12*; *Trent 7.1.1–2*, 24 decr
V: *Sav 25*; *Geloof 31*; *Cumb Pres 89–92*; *Syl 65–74*; *Richmond 13*; *Lam 51*; *Un Pres 36*; *Philip Ind 2.4.8*; *Vat II 5.1.35*, 9.5; *Menn Con 16*; *Sri Lanka 9*; *Pres USA 9.47*; *RCA 13*; *Toraja 7.9*

11. WE LOOK FORWARD TO A RESURRECTION OF THE DEAD

11.1. The Eschatological Hope (*see also* 7.1)

II: *Mogila 1.120–24*
III: *R 11*
IV: *Ries 40*; *Dordrecht 18*; *Trent 6 can 26*
V: *Morav 5–6*; *LDS 10*; *Syl 17*; *Adv 8–10*; *Pol Nat 11–12*; *Assem 14*; *Witness 4*, 6; *Meth Kor 8*; *UCC 8*; *Masai 3*; *Vat II 5.1.48–51*, 5.1.68; *Menn Con 20*; *Un Ref Ch 17.5*; *RCA 21*; *Bap Conf 9*

11.2. Final Preservation and Perseverance

III: *Boh I* 20
IV: *Remon* 5; *Dort* 5; *West* 17, 18.2–3; *Trent* 6.13, 6 can 16, 22–23
V: *London I* 23, 26; *Gen Bap* 43; *Sav* 17; *Friends I* 15; *Geloof* 22; *Cumb Pres* 60–61; *New Hamp* 11; *Abst Prin* 13; *So Bap* 11; *Un Pres* 23–24; *Bap Assoc* 15; *LuRC Just* 34–36

11.3. Antichrist

II: *Metr Crit* pr 3, 10.4, 23.2–4
III: *Boh I* 8
IV: *Apol Aug* 7/8.4, 15.18–19, 23.25; *Smal Art* 2.4.10–11; *Irish* 80; *West* 25.6
V: *True Con* 28; *Sav* 26.4–5; *Shkr* 3–4; *Adv* 13; *Br St Luth* 43; *Laus Cov* 15

11.4. The General Resurrection (*see also* 5.1)

II: *Gennad* 11
III: *Ap* 11; *Tol I* 20, anath 10; *Tol XI* 17; *Petr Ab* 4; *Lat 1215* 2
IV: *Luth Lg Cat* 2.60; *Form Conc Sol Dec* 1.46–47; *Genv Cat* 106–10; *Belg* 37; *Heid* 57; *Helv II* 11.14; *West* 32.2–3; *Cologne* 15
V: *Sav* 31.2–3; *Friends I* 23; *Morav* 5–6; *Geloof* 33; *Cumb Pres* 112–13; *New Hamp* 18; *Arm Ev* 10; *Ev All* 8; *Abst Prin* 19; *Swed Bap* 12; *Adv* 21–22; *Salv Arm* 11; *Com Cr* 12; *Richmond* 7; *Am Bap* 7; *Naz* 12.15; *Assem* 14; *So Bap* 16; *Un Ch Can: Union* 19; *Un Pres* 41; *Bap Assoc* 23; *Madag* 7; *Menn Con* 20; *Toraja* 4.6, 8.4; *Bap Conf* 9

11.5. Immortality of the Soul

II: *Gennad* 11; *Mogila* 1.28
III: *Tol I* 21, anath 11
IV: *Scot I* 17; *West* 32.1
V: *Sav* 31.1; *Geloof* 5.1, 32.3; *Cumb Pres* 112; *Ev All* 8; *Adv* 19–20; *Salv Arm* 11; *Un Pres* 5; *Bat* 16; *Toraja* 3.4

12. AND LIFE IN THE AGE TO COME

12.1. Life Everlasting; Heaven, Hell, and Purgatory

I: *Orig* 5

II: *Jer II* 1.17; *Metr Crit* 20.4; *Lucar* 18; *Mogila* 1.60–68, 1.124–26; *Dosith* decr 18

III: *Ap* 12; *Ath* 41; *Sens* 15; *Lat 1215* 2; *Flor Un* 11–13

IV: *Smal Art* 2.2.12–15; *67 Art* 57–60; *Bern* 7; *Fid rat* 12; *10 Art* 10; *Genv Cat* 110; *Gall* 24; *Scot I* 17, 25; *Heid* 58; *Helv II* 26.4; *39 Art* 22; *Irish* 101–2; *West* 33.1–2; *18 Diss* 14; *Trent* 6 can 30, 25; *Trid Prof* 6

V: *Sav* 32.1–2; *Geloof* 35–36; *Meth Art* 14; *Winch* 2; *Cumb Pres* 113–15; *New Hamp* 17–18; *Arm Ev* 10; *Ev All* 8; *Abst Prin* 20; *Swed Bap* 12; *Syl* 17; *Free Meth* 14; *Adv* 23–25; *Salv Arm* 11; *Com Cr* 12; *Richmond* 7; *Am Bap* 9; *Naz* 12.16–17; *Pol Nat* 11–12; *Assem* 16–17; *So Bap* 15; *Un Ch Can: Union* 19; *Un Pres* 39, 42–43; *Meth Kor* 8; *Bap Assoc* 24–25; *Bat* 16, 18; *Menn Con* 20; *RCA* 20–21; *Toraja* 8.6–8; *Bap Conf* 9; *Philip UCC* 6; *Camb Dec* 6

Alphabetical Index to the Comparative Creedal Syndogmaticon

Ecclesiastical Index: Churches, Heresies, Creeds, Confessions, Councils

What is a "church" (or even "*the* church") in one creed or confession is, of course, often a "heresy" for another. "Heresies" here are only those that are explicitly named as such (under one or another label) in a confession. Likewise, "creeds," "confessions," and "councils" are those that are expressly cited or quoted by another creed, confession, or council. Confessional references that speak in the name of a separate church, rather than about it (or against it), appear here in *italicized ALL CAPS*.

Adoptionism (Artemon)
  IV: *Helv II* 1.8
Aetianism
  IV: *Helv II* 3.5
Agnoetes
  IV: *Form Conc Sol Dec* 8.75
Anabaptism. *See* Baptists / Anabaptists
Anglicanism
  IV: *LAMB ART; 39 ART; WITT ART*
  V: *BONN* 9b; *LAMB QUAD; Vat II* 5.3.13
Anthropomorphism
  IV: *Helv II* 3.5
Apollinarianism
  I: *Edict* anath 9, 10; *Ecth* 7, *CP II* anath 4, 11, 14; *CP III* 1
  IV: *Helv II* 11.5
Apology of the Augsburg Confession (1531)
  IV: *Form Conc Epit* int 4; *Form Conc Sol Dec* int 6, 1.8–14, 2.25, 2.31–32, 3.6, 3.42–43, 4.14, 4.21, 4.33, 5.15, 5.27, 7.11, 7.55, 11.38
  V: *Def Plat*
Apostles' Creed
  IV: *Luth Sm Cat* 2; *Luth Lg Cat* 2; *Aug* 3.6; *Apol Aug* 3.1; *Smal Art* 1.4; *Form Conc Epit* int 3; *Form Conc Sol Dec* int 4; *Tetrapol* 15; *Genv Cat* 15–130; *Gall* 5; *Heid* 22–59; *Helv II* 17.17; *39 Art* 8; *Irish* 7; *West Sh Cat* con; *Witt Art* 1
  V: *Def Plat; Lamb Quad* 2; *Lam* 62; *Afr Orth* 2; *F&O Laus* 4; *Chin Un* 3; *Sri Lanka* 3; *CNI* 3; *Togo* pr; *Un Ref Ch* 18; *Toraja* pr; *Morav Am* 4; *Ad tuendam* 1
Arianism
  I: *AR; Sard; ULPH; EUN; Edict* 53, 59, anath 10; *Ecth* 1, 7; *N* anath; *CP II* anath 11; *CP III* 1; *Nic II*

II: *Phot* 1; *CP 1054* 6; *CP 1351* 1, 38; *Greg Palam* 6

III: *Lat 649* 18

IV: *Aug* 1.5; *Form Conc Epit* 8.22; *Form Conc Sol Dec* 7.126; *Scot I* 6; *Belg* 9; *Helv II* 3.5, 11.3

V: *Resp Pius IX* 4, 5.4

Armenia, Church of

II: *Phot* 2

III: *FLOR ARM*

V: *COM DEC*

Arminianism

IV: *REMON; Dort*

Assemblies of God

V: *ASSEM*

Assyrian Church of the East

V: *CHR DEC*

Athanasian Creed

II: *Metr Crit* 1.12

III: *Flor Arm* 21–24

IV: *Smal Art* 1.4; *Form Conc Epit* int 3; *Form Conc Sol Dec* int 4, 12.37; *Gall* 5; *Helv II* 11.18; *39 Art* 8; *Irish* 7; *Witt Art* 1

V: *Afr Orth* 2; *Toraja* pr; *Morav Am* 4

Audianism

IV: *Apol Aug* 7/8.43

Augsburg Confession (1530)

III: *Wald* 33

IV: *Form Conc Epit* int 4; *Form Conc Sol Dec* pr 3–9, int 2, int 5, 2.29, 4.14, 4.21, 4.24, 7.9, 11.38

V: *Def Plat; Morav Am* 5

Baptists / Anabaptists

II: *Metr Crit* 9.9

IV: *Aug* 5.4, 9.3, 12.7, 16.3, 17.4; *Apol Aug* 4.66, 9.2–3; *Form Conc Epit* 12.2–19; *Form Conc Sol Dec* 4.27, 12.9–27; *Scot I* 23; *Belg* 34, 36; *Helv II* 20.6, 30.4; *39 Art* 38; *18 DISS; DENCK; SCHLEIT; COLOGNE; RIES; DORDRECHT*

V: *LONDON I; GEN BAP; GELOOF; NEW HAMP; ABST PRIN; SWED BAP; SO BAP; BAP ASSOC; BAP CONF; MENN CON*

Barlaamism

II: *CP 1341; CP 1351; Greg Palam* 7

Barmen Declaration (1934)

V: *Bat* pr; *Morav Am* 5

Batak Protestant Christian Church

V: *BAT*

Declaration and Address of Thomas Campbell (1809)
   V: *Un Ref Ch* 18
Dioscorus
   I: *Edict* 75; *Ecth* 7; *CP III* 1
   II: *Phot* 1, 2
   V: *Resp Pius IX* 11
Disciples of Christ
   V: *DEC ADDR; DESIGN*
Donatism
   II: *CP 1054* 6
   IV: *Aug* 8.3; *Apol Aug* 7/8.29, 49; *Helv II* 17.2, 18.21

Eastern Orthodox Church (after the East-West schism)
   II: *PHOT; CP 1054; CP 1341; CP 1351; GREG PALAM; GENNAD; JER II; METR CRIT; LUCAR; MOGILA; DOSITH*
   IV: *Apol Aug* 10.2, 24.6, 24.39, 24.93
   V: *RESP PIUS IX; BONN I; F&O Laus* 4.1
Ebionitism
   IV: *Helv II* 11.4
Encratites
   IV: *Apol Aug* 23.45; *Helv II* 24.8
Enthusiasm
   IV: *Form Conc Epit* 2.13; *Form Conc Sol Dec* 2.4, 2.80; *Gall* 38
   V: *Bat* pr
Ephesus, Council of (431)
   I: *Edict* 49, 55; *Ecth* 8; *Chal; CP II* 5, 8, 9, 10, 11, anath 13, 14; *Nic II*
   II: *Greg Palam* 6
   IV: *Form Conc Sol Dec* 8.76; *Helv II* 11.18
   V: *Resp Pius IX* 5.5, 13; *Lam* 31;
Eunomianism
   I: *Edict* anath 10; *Ecth* 7; *CP II* anath 11
   IV: *Aug* 1.5; *Helv II* 11.5
Eustathianism
   IV: *Helv II* 24.8
Eutychianism
   I: *Tome; Edict* 51, anath 9, 10; *Ecth* 7; *Chal; CP II* anath 4, 11; *CP III* 1; *Nic II*
   II: *Phot* 1, 2; *Greg Palam* 6
   IV: *Form Conc Epit* 8.21; *Scot I* 6; *Helv II* 11.7
Evagrius
   I: *CP III* 1
Evangelical Church of Germany
   V: *ARN; LEUEN*

Florence, Council of (1439): Council of Basel-Ferrara-Florence, Rome
(1431–35)
  IV: *Trent* 25.1
  V: *Vat I* 4.4; *Vat II* 5.1.51

Gangra, Synod of (ca. 345)
  II: *Phot* 31 *CP 1054* 3
Geneva Confession (1536)
  V: *Toraja* pr

Heidelberg Catechism (1563)
  V: *Morav Am* 5

Iconoclasm
  II: *Greg Palam* 6
Ineffabilis Deus (1854)
  V: *Utrecht* 3
Islam
  II: *Gennad; Metr Crit* pr 3, 10.4, 23.2–4
  IV: *17 Art* 14; *Aug* 1.5, 21.1; *Apol Aug* 4.229, 15.18, 27.27; *Belg* 9; *Helv II*
3.5, 11.10
  V: *Bat* pr

Jacobites
  II: *Phot* 2
  IV: *Helv II* 11.10
Jansenism
  V: *Cum occas* 1–5
Jehovah's Witnesses
  V: *WITNESS*
Jovinianism
  IV: *Helv II* 8.7
Judaism
  I: *CP III* 10
  IV: *Apol Aug* 7/8.43, 24.6; *Belg* 9; *Helv II* 3.5; *Helv II* 11.14, 24.2

Lateran, Fourth Council of (1215)
  IV: *Trent* 13.4, 14.5, 14 can 8
Latter-Day Saints, Church of (Mormons)
  V: *LDS*
Liturgy of Saint John Chrysostom
  V: *Resp Pius IX* 13

United Church of Christ in the United States (*see also* Congregationalism)
   V: *UCC*

Valentinianism
   I: *Ar*
   IV: *Aug* 1.5; *Helv II* 1.8, 11.4
Vatican, First Council of (1869–70)
   V: *Utrecht* 2; *Vat II* 5.1.18, 5.1.25, 8.1, 8.6
Vatican, Second Council of (1962–65)
   V: *LuRC Just* 36

Westminster Confession of Faith (1647)
   V: *Sav* pr; *Un Pres* pr; *Un Ref Ch* 18; *Toraja* pr
Westminster Larger Catechism (1648)
   V: *Un Pres* pr
Westminster Shorter Catechism (1648)
   V: *Un Pres* pr
Wittenberg Concord (1536)
   IV: *Form Conc Sol Dec* 7.12–16, 38
Wycliffitism
   IV: *Apol Aug* 7/8.29

Zurich Consensus [*Consensus Tigurinus*] (1549)
   IV: *Form Conc Sol Dec* 7.2

VII. Indexes to *Credo*

A. References to Scripture

B. Creedal and Confessional References

	182–83, 189–90,	art 1	42, 203n, 264, 342, 458n
	202, 219, 257, 258–	art 2	197, 294n, 362n
	60, 346,	art 3	48n, 82n
	374, 410–11,	art 4	283n
	416–17, 462	art 7	151, 199–200, 212
Epiph	189		
Ess	498	art 8	199–200, 205, 342–43,
Eun	59n, 373		
Eus	8		346n, 478,
Eut	202n		483n
Ev All	504n	art 11	199–200, 286n
		art 12	76, 241, 457n, 478
Fac	15		
F&O Ban	219, 487	42 Art	43–44, 177, 224
F&O Edin	93, 206		
F&O Laus	93, 322	Free-Will Bap	167
Fid cath	320	*Fréjus*	321n, 434
Fid rat	41, 82, 88,	*Friends I*	300n, 498n
	127, 164,	*Friends II*	241–42
	205n, 221,		
	242–43,	*Gall*	95–96, 228, 466
	272, 364,		
	400, 465,	pr	65, 221
	481, 483n	art 1	41, 131
Flor	14, 107, 209–	art 2	74n, 235
	10, 254n,	art 3	140–41
	259–60,	art 3–4	152
	348, 402,	art 6	479
	443–44,	art 9	235
	451, 454–	art 14	197
	55, 458, 463,	art 20	206n
	480n	art 24	160, 165, 473–74
Form Conc	186–87, 275,		
	344, 461,	art 28	475–76
	465, 468,	art 29	110
	481	art 32	100n
pr	4n, 61, 138,	art 33	186n, 302, 303
	141, 155,	art 37	211n, 212
	199, 266,	art 40	221, 241n
	355, 458n	*Gel*	50n, 396

C. Names of Persons

Oberman, Heiko A. (1930–2001), 292, 360
Optatus of Mileve (fl. 370), 103
Origen of Alexandria (c. 185–c. 245), 21, 67–68, 143, 169, 293
Overbeck, J. J., 507

Pantaenus of Alexandria († c. 190), 21
Paschasius Radbertus (c. 790–c. 860), 440
Pauck, Wilhelm (1901–81), 276, 318–19
Pelagius (fl. c. 400), 196–97, 294, 416, 437–38
Peter Lombard (c. 1100–1160), 427, 446–47, 482–83
Philo of Alexandria (c. 20 B.C.–c. A.D. 50), 374–75
Philostorgius (c. 368–c. 439), 319
Photius (patriarch of Constantinople, 858–c. 895), 209, 297. See also *Phot*
Piepkorn, Arthur Carl (1907–73), 275–76
Pilate, Pontius (governor of Galilee, 26–36), 222, 225
Pius IX (pope, 1846–78), 75–76, 84, 355, 417, 497. See also *Ineff; Syl; Vat I*
Pius X (pope, 1903–14), 268–69
Pius XII (pope, 1939–58), 315
Plato (427–347 B.C.), 88
Polycarp (c. 69–c. 155), 223
Prosper of Aquitaine (c. 390–c. 463), 166, 351

Quasten, Johannes (1900–1987), 25, 144, 290, 372, 389, 429

Ratramnus of Corbie (9th c.), 440
Rauschenbusch, Walter (1861–1918), 496

Reu, J. Michael (1869–1943), 507
Ricci, Matteo (1552–1610), 314–15
Ritschl, Otto (1860–1944), 91
Rousseau, Jean-Jacques (1712–78), 55
Rufinus of Aquileia (c. 345–411), 36, 69

Schaff, Philip (1819–93), x, 232, 467, 507
Schleiermacher, Friedrich Daniel Ernst (1768–1834), 115–16, 492–93
Schmidt, W. J., 507
Schornbaum, K., 507
Schubert, Hans von (1859–1931), 217
Schwartz, Eduard (1858–1940), 507
Schwarzlose, Karl (b. 1866), 400
Schweitzer, Albert (1875–1965), 494, 511
Seeberg, Alfred (1863–1915), 389
Seripando, Girolamo (1492/93–1563), 253
Servetus, Michael (c. 1511–53), 197, 227
Ševčenko, Ihor, 260
Sheldon, Charles Monroe (1857–1946), 511
Shepherd, Massey H., Jr. (b. 1913), 318
Smith, Page, 505
Stoevesandt, Hinrich, 488

Tanner, Norman P., 508
Tappert, Theodore G. (1904–73), 275, 508
Tertullian (c. 160–c. 225), 60, 191, 290, 395
Theodore Abu Qûrra (c. 750–820), 400–401
Theodore of Mopsuestia (c. 350–428), 15